Virtually all of contemporary macroeconomics is underpinned by a Phillips Curve of one variety or another; yet most of this literature displays a curious neglect of the theoretical dynamic stabilisation perspective provided by A. W. H. Phillips. This volume collects for the first time the major works of one of the great economists, integrating Phillips' empirical work with this theoretical contribution. In addition to twelve substantive chapters, twenty-nine economists including Lawrence Klein, James Meade, Thomas Sargent, Adrian Pagan, Peter Phillips, David Hendry, William Baumol, Richard Lipsey and Geoffrey Harcourt highlight and interpret Phillips' on-going influence. This volume also contains six of Phillips' previously unpublished essays, four of which were thought to have been lost. The fifth such essay (Phillips' second empirical Phillips Curve) was previously an informal working paper of which few copies circulated, and the sixth essay is a forerunner of the Lucas Critique written by Phillips shortly before his death.

ROBERT LEESON is Associate Professor at Murdoch University, Australia and was previously Bradley Fellow at the University of Western Ontario.

i

A.W.H. Phillips

A. W. H. Phillips: Collected Works in Contemporary Perspective

Edited by
Robert Leeson

CAMBRIDGE
UNIVERSITY PRESS

PUBLISHED BY THE PRESS SYNDICATE OF THE UNIVERSITY OF CAMBRIDGE
The Pitt Building, Trumpington Street, Cambridge CB2 1RP,
United Kingdom

CAMBRIDGE UNIVERSITY PRESS
The Edinburgh Building, Cambridge, CB2 2RU, UK http://www.cup.cam.ac.uk
40 West 20th Street, New York, NY 10011-4211, USA http://www.cup.org
10 Stamford Road, Oakleigh, Melbourne 3166, Australia

First published 2000

Printed in the United Kingdom at the University Press, Cambridge

Typeset in 10/12pt Times [KW]

A catalogue record for this book is available from the British Library

ISBN 0 521 57135 9 hardback

Contents

Contents

Part IV Econometrics

The Published Papers

The Walras-Bowley Paper

The Unpublished Papers

Contents

Contributors

ARTHUR BROWN, Emeritus Professor of Economics, University of Leeds

NICHOLAS BARR, Senior Lecturer in Economics, London School of Economics

WILLIAM J. BAUMOL, Professor of Economics and Director, C.V. Starr Center for Applied Economics, New York University
Senior Research Economist and Emeritus Professor of Economics, Princeton University

A.R. BERGSTROM, Emeritus Professor of Economics, University of Essex

HENRY PHELPS BROWN, Emeritus Professor of Economics, London School of Economics

PHILLIP CAGAN, Professor of Economics, Columbia University

ROBIN COURT, Professor of Economics, University of Auckland

GRAEME DORRANCE, Visiting Fellow, University of New South Wales

R.M. GOODWIN, Emeritus Reader, University of Cambridge
Emeritus Fellow, Peterhouse, University of Cambridge
Professor Emeritus, University of Sienna

LARS P. HANSEN, Professor of Economics, University of Chicago

G.C. HARCOURT, Emeritus Reader in the History of Economic Theory, University of Cambridge
Emeritus Fellow, Jesus College, University of Cambridge
Professor Emeritus of Economics, University of Adelaide

DAVID F. HENDRY, Leverhulme Personal Research Professor of Economics, University of Oxford
Fellow, Nuffield College, University of Oxford

CHARLES C. HOLT, Emeritus Professor of Management, Graduate School of Business, University of Texas at Austin

ELIZABETH JOHNSON, Co-Editor, The Collected Writings of John Maynard Keynes

L.R. KLEIN, Emeritus Benjamin Franklin Professor of Economics, University of Pennsylvania
Recipient of the Nobel Memorial Prize for Economic Science

ROBERT LEESON, Senior Lecturer in Economics, Murdoch University

RICHARD G. LIPSEY, Emeritus Professor of Economics, Simon Fraser University
Fellow, Canadian Institute for Advanced Research

JAMES MEADE, Emeritus Professor of Economics, University of Cambridge
Honorary Fellow, University of Cambridge
Recipient of the Nobel Memorial Prize for Economic Science

E. MIZON, Leverhulme Professor of Econometrics, Southampton University
Professor of Economics, European University Institute, Florence

WALTER NEWLYN, Professor of Economics (retired), University of Leeds

ADRIAN PAGAN, Professor of Economics, Australian National University

PETER C.B. PHILLIPS, Sterling Professor of Economics
Cowles Foundation for Research in Economics
Yale University

JOHN PITCHFORD, Emeritus Professor of Economics, Australian National University

M.H. QUENOUILLE, Professor of Statistics, London School of Economics

THOMAS J. SARGENT, Senior Fellow, Hoover Institution

ANN S. SCHWIER, Emerita Professor of Economics
Southern Illinois University at Edwardsville

FATEMEH SHADMAN-MEHTA, Research Officer, IRES, Université Catholique de Louvain

BRIAN SILVERSTONE, Senior Lecturer in Economics, University of Waikato

DORON SWADE, Assistant Director and Head of Collections, Science Museum, London

STEPHEN J. TURNOVSKY, Castor Professor of Economics, University of Washington

DAVID VINES, Fellow and Tutor in Economics, Balliol College, University of Oxford
Adjunct Professor of Economics, Australian National University
Research Fellow, Centre for Economic Policy Research, London

BASIL S. YAMEY, Emeritus Professor of Economics, London School of Economics

Foreword

Arthur Brown

Almost two generations of economists across the world have been familiar with the name Phillips from its attachment to the curve depicting a relation between the unemployment rate and wage inflation. A generation of economists in half a dozen universities also learned to associate that name with an hydraulic model that demonstrated with brilliant clarity the consequences of the interrelations set out in Keynesian economics. A smaller number of readers would probably be aware of a variety of articles on macroeconomic and econometric subjects under the same name. In this book, mainly through the efforts of Robert Leeson, all the published (and some hitherto unpublished) writings of Alban William Housego Phillips are assembled, along with a selection of the discussions which they provoked at the time of their publication or, in a few cases, more recently.

Any collection of a writer's works has something of the character of a memorial to him. The man to whom the present collection stands in this relation was a very remarkable person indeed, whose writings (and hydraulic model) by no means exhaust the reasons for which he should be remembered. Bill Phillips' career, not in the least an orthodox academic one, was a switchback of triumphs and disasters. Born in New Zealand in 1914, he left school without any immediate prospect of higher education and passed into a wandering life, in the course of which he qualified and worked as an engineer. In the war he proved himself a hero, both in action and as a prisoner of war of the Japanese. This fact has been brought to light by Robert Leeson – Phillips was reticent on such matters. He survived, was decorated, and, like many other ex-servicemen, received a chance of university education which he had not had previously. But in his undergraduate years at the London School of Economics (LSE) he achieved only a poor degree – partly perhaps because he had chosen a subject (Sociology) that did not really suit his abilities, more certainly because the strains of war had affected his ability to perform in written examinations.

xii

In the course of his studies, however, his curiosity about the working of a monetary economy had been stimulated. It is possible that the idea of clarifying this by means of an hydraulic model had been given to him by a diagram in Kenneth Boulding's textbook of economics, representing an imaginary model of this kind designed to elucidate equilibrium in the market for a commodity. However that may be, with the help and advice on Keynesian economics of his LSE contemporary and friend Walter Newlyn, he set to work to build a much more elaborate machine representing a whole economy, with foreign trade, a public sector and a central bank.

The success of the model, when it was demonstrated at the LSE, was spectacular. It persuaded James Meade and others that, despite his otherwise lowly academic qualifications, Phillips should be appointed to an assistant lectureship in the School. Once his foot was on the academic ladder, his rise was meteoric. He expounded the mathematics of the model (and variants on it) in an article published in *Economica* in August 1950 (chapter 10), and completed a doctoral thesis on 'Dynamic Models in Economics', the gist of which appeared in the *Economic Journal* in 1954 (chapter 16). In the same year he was promoted to a Readership and four years later attracted worldwide attention with his 'curve' (chapter 25). In 1958, too, he was appointed to the Tooke Chair. This was the peak of his fortunes as an economist. He continued to work mainly on problems of control and related problems of estimation. Then in 1967 he moved to the Australian National University (ANU) and turned his attention partly to Chinese studies – he had learnt Chinese from fellow prisoners of war. In 1969 he suffered a disabling stroke, and returned home to New Zealand. Six years after that, at the age of sixty, he was dead.

I cannot claim to have known Phillips as well as his LSE colleagues, for instance, did, but our acquaintance, which was connected with the hydraulic model and, more fleetingly, with the curve, made a deep impression on me. It began when, by arrangement with Walter Newlyn who had recently become a colleague of mine, I visited him in the Croydon garage where he and Newlyn were constructing the prototype model, which the University of Leeds subsequently acquired. I got to know him better as he, more than once, came to Leeds to service the model. The last such occasion was after his appointment to the Tooke Chair; he was not one to stand on his dignity! Before the publication of his famous 1958 article which launched the curve, knowing my earlier work on the same subject he invited me to discuss with him the results recorded therein. I think our discussion turned on the difference made by our having used slightly different time lags in our respective plottings of largely similar data. As always, it was a pleasure to talk with him.

It seems to have been the general experience of Bill Phillips – it was certainly mine – that to know him was to like him. He was friendly, practical, full of quiet enthusiasm for whatever ideas he was pursuing at the time, and without the slightest trace of self-importance or pomposity. He seemed to bring a breath of Antipodean fresh air with him. Primarily, he was a problem-solver. In keeping with his engineering background and talents, he wanted to know how systems worked, and how they could be made to work better. He had come relatively late to economics, and I do not think he was much interested in the scholarship of the subject – who had said what, and when. Perhaps that is one reason why, when he felt that he had delved as far as he could into the vein of ideas about macroeconomic stability that he had found so productive, he began to turn his attention to a subject at least partly outside general economics.

Other engineers have appeared upon the economic scene at various times and with various results. Dupuit and Fleeming Jenkin scored notable successes because the applied mathematics of engineering could be brought to bear productively on important economic problems once those problems had been rightly understood. Major Douglas fared less happily because, while he perceived that demand deficiency was connected with the circular flow of money, he misperceived the nature of that flow. Phillips listened to the economists, got the flow of money right, could solve the differential equations describing its changes, and also had the enterprise and the very considerable manual skill needed to turn his perceptions into hardware that didn't leak – or didn't leak too much. His curve was less clearly a product of his engineering background. It had its roots in a theoretical relation between the level of activity and price inflation postulated in his 1954 essay 'Stabilisation Policy in a Closed Economy' (chapter 16). The success of its final, empirical version owed much to its timeliness. In 1958 people had stopped worrying about a post-war depression (a second 1920–2, or even a second 1929–33) and had started worrying about a new sort of creeping inflation connected with high employment. Moreover, there was still a decade to go before expectations of continuing inflation became strong enough to blow the curve away very markedly to the north-east; it had time to establish itself as an apparently simple guide after its publication.

One might say that Phillips' spectacular success in economics was owed partly, like most spectacular successes, to elements of good fortune. He had luck (as I have just said) in the time of producing his curve. He was lucky in being able to bring to macroeconomic problems some highly relevant ideas developed in control engineering over the preceding generation. He was lucky in coming to the sympathetic attention of James Meade, who had started his textbook twenty years before with an exposition of the circular flow of money (including why Major Douglas had been wrong) to which the Phillips Machine provided a perfect concrete illustration. Meade had himself dealt in a famous article with the stability conditions of a Keynesian system, and was also no mean amateur producer of precision artefacts – from kites to cabinets.

But the element of good luck is not what one dwells on when thinking of the career of one who contended so valiantly with so much of the other sort of fortune. In Bill Phillips' case, the real good luck was with those of us who had the privilege of knowing him.

Preface

Virtually all of contemporary macroeconomics is underpinned by a Phillips Curve of one variety or another; yet most of this literature displays a curious neglect of the theoretical dynamic stabilisation perspective provided by A.W.H. 'Bill' Phillips. This volume of Phillips' complete published output integrates Phillips' empirical work with his theoretical contribution. In addition to these twelve chapters, twenty-nine of the world's leading authorities in their field have contributed thirty-two chapters (thirty of which have been specially commissioned) to highlight and interpret Phillips' on-going influence. This volume also contains six of Phillips' previously unpublished essays, plus a little-known book review. Four of these essays were thought to have been lost. A fifth essay (Phillips' second empirical Phillips curve) was previously an obscure working paper of which few copies circulated. The sixth essay is a forerunner of the Lucas Critique written by Phillips, in longhand, shortly before his death. It seems likely that nobody has ever seen this remarkable essay before.

Regrettably, we have, so far, been unable to locate four of Phillips' unpublished papers. The Final Report of the London School of Economics Project on Dynamic Process Analysis (dated 1963) listed as 'substantially completed' three essays by Phillips: 'Minimum Identification Conditions for the Derivation of Optimum Linear Decision Rules', 'Efficient Estimation of Multivariate Difference Equations with Serially Correlated Disturbances' and 'A General Method of Obtaining Optimal Linear Decision Rules for Multivariate Dynamic Systems'. Phillips presented a summary of these papers entitled 'Some Developments in Time Series Analysis' at the December 1962 meeting of the Econometric Society. Any information about these essays will be gratefully received. In the late 1960s, Phillips worked on stabilisation theory with Alfred Maizels of the United Nations Conference on Trade and Development. But we decided not to reprint his UNCTAD paper on 'Analysis of the Operation of a Buffer Stock for Cocoa' because it did not readily fit into the scheme of the volume. However, a copy of this paper will be supplied upon request.

Numerous people have generously assisted with this project. Valda Phillips preserved her husband's private papers (including the papers that are published here for the first time) for nearly two decades after his death in 1975. Susan Howson initially suggested these papers might still exist, and Robert Mundell suggested that Phillips' *Collected Works* should be available under a single cover. Brian Silverstone was extraordinarily generous in reading – and improving – every chapter and Nena Bierbaum provided excellent guidance as the volume editor. Rex Bergstrom, Jim Thomas and Robin Court assisted in the process of eliminating reproduction errors in Phillips' unpublished chapters. Between us we have attempted to produce an error-free volume. We have corrected some typographical errors in Phillips' original essays and we have provided some bibliographical information that Phillips' listed as 'forthcoming'. Judy Klein, Adrian Pagan, David Giles, Malcolm Rutherford and Jim Thomas assisted in the process of tracking down information about these 'forthcoming' essays. Since I was responsible for more of the word processing than I care to remember, any remaining errors (of which I hope there are none) are quite literally mine.

In addition to the people already mentioned, I am grateful to the following for encouragement and information: Chris Archibald, Nick Barr, A.R. Bergstrom, Horst Bierbaum, Mark Blaug, Conrad Blyth, W.D. Borrie, A.J. Brown, Ray Byron, Warren Cooper, Robin Court, Nerissa David, Megnad Desai, Graeme Dorrance, Sir Edward Dunlop, Jim Durbin, Milton Friedman, Charles Goodhart, Richard Goodwin, Bob Gregory, Herb Grubel, Rene Grypma, Geoff Harcourt, Thelma Hunter, Carol Ibbotsen-Somervell, A. Ikonnokov, Raja Junankar, Peter Kenyon, Alex Kerr, Kurt Klappholz, Lawrence Klein, David Laidler, Richard Lipsey, James Meade, Max Neutze, Henry Phelps Brown, Anna Phillips, Peter Phillips, John Pitchford, Steven Resnick, Ruth Richardson, Paul Samuelson, J.D. Sargan, Graeme Snooks, Robert Solow, Max Steuer, Herb Thompson, Sir Laurens van der Post, David Vines and Basil Yamey. Of these, Chris Archibald, Sir Edward Dunlop, J.D. Sargan, Sir Laurens van der Post, James Meade, Richard Goodwin and Henry Phelps Brown died before the project was completed (the last three contributed chapters to this volume). The chapters by James Meade and Richard Goodwin are, I believe, their final essays.

Robert Leeson

Part I
Bill Phillips: Some Memories and Reflections

1   A.W.H. Phillips: An Extraordinary Life

Robert Leeson   ß3)

ß2L

For the last forty years, applied macroeconomics, in so far as it connects the instruments of fiscal, monetary and incomes policies to the objectives of inflation, unemployment and economic growth, has, to a large extent, been a series of footnotes and extensions to the work of A.W.H. 'Bill' Phillips. He was one of the most remarkable economists of all time and was deprived of a Nobel Prize for Economic Science by his ill-health and premature death.

The extant details of Phillips' life are remarkable enough, and can be briefly summarised.[1] He was born on 18 November 1914, at Te Rehunga, near Dannevirke in Southern Hawke's Bay in the North Island of New Zealand. His family generated their own electricity, and this may have stimulated his early interest in 'things electric' and in making crystal radio sets. He attended the local primary school and then went on to Dannevirke High School, a daily journey involving a six mile bike ride, a forty-five minute walk, plus a train ride. Phillips acquired a discarded truck, rebuilt and repaired it, and drove it to school every day, until the school authorities intervened.

In December 1929, Phillips passed matriculation, having just turned fifteen. He was too young to go to university and he became an electrical engineering apprentice on the Tuai Hydroelectric Station, one of the first government electricity-generating stations. He supplemented his income by running a 'Talking Theatre' in Tuai and the back country, to which he travelled on a motorbike. In 1935, he succumbed to wanderlust and set off for Australia. During the next two years he 'carried his swag' (and his violin) across Australia, doing a variety of casual jobs, including shooting crocodiles. In July 1937, at age twenty-two, he left Australia for Britain (via China and Russia) on a Japanese boat. Just one day out at sea the Japanese declared war on China. He made his way to Russia, but was unable to obtain a job in mining because of the plentiful supply of political prisoners.

Phillips had been studying by correspondence for the examinations of the Institute of Electrical Engineers (IEE) whilst working in a gold mine in outback Australia. Shortly after his arrival in London, in November 1938, he became a graduate of the IEE.

After the war, Phillips attended the LSE, rising from student to full professor in less than a decade. He is widely regarded as being more responsible than any other person for the introduction of econometrics into the teaching of economics degrees (Gilbert 1989); he was also probably the only professor of economics who spent his Friday afternoons reading Chinese. In August 1967 he left the LSE and took up a chair at the ANU. When he suffered a stroke two years later, he and his family moved to Auckland, New Zealand, where he continued to work on his Chinese and Russian. He insisted on running a course on 'The Development of the Chinese Economy Since 1949' at the University of Auckland, although the medical advice was that it could kill him. He suffered a final stroke on 4 March 1975, the day after his first lecture of the academic year.

Phillips was universally admired by those who knew him: 'his pupils and colleagues in London, Canberra, and Auckland respected him for his integrity and competence, and loved him for his humanity and enthusiasm' (Blyth 1978, xvii); 'His early death was a sad blow for the science of economics in this part of the world' (correspondence from W.D. Borrie); 'We went out to a Chinese restaurant after his lecture (in Chicago in the early 1960s) and to our surprise Bill proceeded to chat up the waiters in what sounded to us like fluent Cantonese. He told us that he had learned the language as a prisoner of war. It is, I think, characteristic of him that he led us to believe that he had the leisure to learn a language during that terrible time' (correspondence from David Laidler).

Phillips was remarkable in a variety of other ways. Megnad Desai remembers complaining (*circa* 1965) in the corridor at LSE that the central heating in his office had failed:

Bill's office was near mine. He heard me and came to my office. He pulled out (much to my surprise) an electrician's screwdriver, opened up the thermostat in my office and fixed my heating.

Only scant details of Phillips' wartime experiences have, hitherto, survived. When the European war broke out, he joined the Royal Air Force, and after the Officer Training Course was posted to Kallang, Singapore. He was commissioned into the RAF on 1 August 1940 and was appointed Munitions Officer at Kallany Aerodrome, Singapore, where the 243 and 488 New Zealand (Fighter) Squadrons were stationed. The citation accompanying his Member of the British Empire (MBE) award stated that Phillips:

displayed outstanding ability, both academically and technically, and showed great energy in overcoming the initial difficulties experienced in operating Buffalo aircraft. Flying Officer Phillips introduced a number of necessary modifications which were accepted by the Air Ministry. It was due to his efforts and guidance that the fighter aircraft on the station were able to complete the maximum operations.[2]

He was evacuated from Singapore on the *Empire Star* and volunteered for further service in Java. He was eventually captured by the Japanese, and spent three and a half years in prisoner-of-war camps (in Bandoeng, Batavia and then back to Bandoeng).

We now know of Kondratiev's fate (Nove 1992), but until now we have been able to identify very little that relates to Phillips' wartime incarceration and the effect that this had on his decision to become an economist. The following words, which I came across whilst sitting on a beach near Perth, Australia, may shed some light on this, and provide an appropriate introduction to this volume of his *Collected Works*. They are taken from Laurens van der Post's autobiographical reflections on the three and a half years he spent in a Japanese prisoner-of-war camp, entitled *The Night of the New Moon* (1985). The book is organised around a secretly built and operated radio, which kept the prisoners in touch with the progress of the war, and *The Night* refers to 6 August 1945.

We created a vast prison organisation for the re-education of ourselves...imprisonment for our men was transformed from an arid waste of time and life, into one of the most meaningful experiences they had ever known...A group of gifted and gallant young officers made a radio...we appreciated its overwhelming necessity to us...it was a near miracle...The gifted young New Zealand officer – a radio expert in civilian life – who had been responsible for reducing the set to its final minute form, and had proved himself capable of operating it for some eighteen months without any loss of nerve and with a real, if strange, enjoyment which I could not share – had impressed upon me how little he needed either to make the [malfunctioning] set operative or to build a new one...The New Zealand officer, in the dark underneath his mosquito net, began to repair, or rather reshape our radio. It was difficult, delicate and slow work, and if I remember rightly it took three nights and three dawns to give him the necessary light before the work was finished. They were among the longest days I have ever known, because everything in the atmosphere around us told us that the climax was near...only an expert like the New Zealand officer who had made the radio could take part in the listening operation...The listening officer had made three tiny coils which he slipped somewhere into his set to enable him to have a choice of three stations: if I remember rightly Delhi in India, Perth in

Australia and San Francisco in America.

I felt a hand tugging at my feet...It was the New Zealand officer, who lost no time in whispering to me in a tone which carried much more than just the satisfaction at the excitement of success: 'It worked Colonel! It worked'...He had some trouble making contact but after a great deal of fiddling had picked up a news broadcast from Delhi. Unfortunately he had not come in right at the beginning but near enough to realise that something tremendous had happened. He wasn't quite certain what precisely it was, but in the course of the morning of the day which was now ended, something more like an act of God than of man had been inflicted on Japan at a place called Hiroshima.

This previously anonymous young New Zealand officer was, without any doubt, Bill Phillips:

Bill's widow...has confirmed that van der Post was a prisoner of war with Bill and that Bill did in fact make and use a radio with which he got in touch with London and heard the news about Hiroshima.[3]

There is additional supporting evidence. Phillips' sister has described how her brother's childhood was filled with radio-making and other technical activities (Ibbotson-Somervell 1994, 5). Information supplied by the New Zealand Ministry of Defence has revealed that Phillips' parents received a transcript of a short wave radio broadcast from their son in April 1943. *The War Diaries* of Sir Edward 'Weary' Dunlop (1990, 96, 57, 128) contains a reference to an education instructor, F/LT Phillips, and a sole New Zealand officer. The entry for 5 November 1942 reads:

We are definitely [leaving Bandoeng] tomorrow...Saw Laurens [van der Post] about my X [wireless] who advised me to try and take it. Finally after the conference with Phillips (expert)...decided to carry pieces and hope to reassemble it.

Sir Edward Dunlop has confirmed that these entries relate to Bill Phillips:

I was most impressed with his courage and personality. He was a most fascinating man with many facets, something of a knockabout tramp, gallant soldier and gifted academic. I owed a great deal to Bill Phillips, for advice upon the tricky business of reducing a six valve wireless set to what became a one valve tiny wonder embedded in the bottom of a coffee tin.[4]

Finally, and conclusively, Sir Laurens van der Post has confirmed that:

There is no doubt that the Phillips you have come across is the Phillips who served us so gallantly in prison, and who built and operated the only really secret radio that we had in prison...Phillips was one of the most singularly contained people I knew, quiet, true and without any trace of exhibitionism...He was also shy and sensitive...the gift of being himself without ostentation and 'come what may' is what matters and will always matter and ripple out over the waters of the future when all is gone and forgotten...I am so glad that you've identified him, and that

I can pass on to you now what is the best salute of which an old soldier is capable, to a very gallant and unusual human being.

Van der Post concluded that without the intelligence provided by Phillips' radio 'we could not have lived our life in prison in what, I believe, was the triumphant manner we did ... It was our only sure defence against slow demoralisation' (van der Post 1985, 48, 101–7; Ebury 1994, 485).[5] Phillips and van der Post had obtained the components for the radio by breaking into the camp commander's office and stealing parts from his radiogram! This was not the only contribution that Phillips made to the survival of the prisoners:

Phillips invented a kind of immersion heater for the various collections of prisoners to use secretly when the kitchens (such as they were) closed down for the night ... in a starving prison a hot cup of tea last thing at night came to mean a great deal to us. Thanks to Phillips' invention, the whole camp could have a secret cup of tea before creeping to bed on their wooden boards. The result was when some 2,000 cups were suddenly brewed that the lights of the camp dimmed alarmingly since the public supply of electricity in any case was feeble. The Japanese were mystified by this dimming of the lights every night at about 10.00 p.m.[6]

When Phillips arrived at the ANU in 1967 'he startled Alex Hunter who recognised him as the bloke operating the machine gun on the boat leaving Singapore' (correspondence from Ray Byron). Phillips' parents received a reassuring letter from their son dated 22 February 1942. They were notified in October 1942 that Phillips had been captured by the Japanese.

Van der Post had managed to avoid execution upon capture by requesting his would-be murderers (in eloquent Japanese) to 'pause an honourable moment gentlemen'. Van der Post had learnt Japanese as a result of befriending two Japanese visitors to South Africa who had been ejected from a 'white' hotel (Dunlop 1990, 43). The details of Phillips' capture were equally remarkable. He volunteered for further action in Java, and was shot down by Japanese aircraft. With two colleagues he found an abandoned bus, which they proceeded to make seaworthy in preparation for the voyage to Australia. The Japanese had ordered a total surrender and had threatened villagers with reprisals if they did not report the whereabouts of allied soldiers. As a consequence Phillips and his fellow would-be bus-sailors were betrayed and captured.[7]

Phillips had visited Hiroshima in 1937, and had been arrested there for taking photographs of some troops (Blyth 1978, xiv). According to van der Post (1985, 145) the nuclear explosion saved the lives of these prisoners of war:

General Penney has assured me that, among the staff records captured at [Field-Marshal] Terauchi's headquarters, evidence was found of plans to kill all prisoners and internees when the invasion of South-East Asia began in earnest.

Phillips and his fellow prisoners were forced to dig mass graves shortly before the Japanese surrender.[8,9] Two of their guards were subsequently executed as war criminals. For most of his three and a half years as a prisoner of war, Phillips lived under the constant threat of torture and execution:

A radio was found [by the Japanese] . . . and both the owners of the flasks and the officer in charge had been decapitated for what the Japanese regarded as one of the most serious crimes of which a prisoner could be culpable.[10]

On one occasion, during a blitz search of the camp, a Japanese sergeant-major rocked up and down on the hollowed-out wooden chair which housed the secret radio (van der Post 1985, 51–2, 14, 100). Sir Edward Dunlop has informed me that Phillips' task of providing the news was filled with the 'grave danger of torture . . . others I knew were sinfully beaten to death'.[11]

Phillips' colleagues were aware that he had been a prisoner of war and of some of the minor consequences of this episode, such as an aversion to rice and an almost complete inability to taste food: 'I can't use salt or pepper without thinking of Bill Phillips' (conversation with Max Steuer). Phillips (like D.H. Robertson,[12] but unlike Radford) never wrote, and his colleagues have confirmed that he rarely spoke, about his wartime experiences: 'although we were very close, he never spoke about it and I had the strong feeling he did not want to' (correspondence from Walter Newlyn).[13] Kurt Klappholz, who almost perished in Dachau, was at the LSE with Phillips for twenty years, but they never spoke about the war.[14] Valda Phillips believes that her husband was not aware of van der Post's book (a first edition was published in 1970, five years before Phillips' death), so we can only speculate about whether he would have sympathised with its conclusions (1985, 36, 154):

It was amazing how often and how many of my men would confess to me, after some Japanese excess worse than usual, that for the first time in their lives they had realised the truth, and the dynamic liberating power of the first of the crucifixion utterances: 'Forgive them for they know not what they do' . . . I thought that the only hope for the future lay in an all-embracing attitude of forgiveness of the people who had been our enemies. Forgiveness, my prison experience taught me, was not mere religious sentimentality, it was as fundamental a law of the human spirit as the law of gravity.[15]

Phillips had been a qualified electrical engineer before the war and may well have conducted engineering classes in the Bandoeng prisoner-of-war camp (Dunlop 1990, 67). Sir Laurens van der Post recalled in correspondence that Phillips was 'really and truly a scholar, and one of his great passions was to study Chinese, and talk to some of the remarkable Chinese we had in prison with us'. He and his fellow instructors built up an atmosphere:

with the spirit of a university...with young people constantly exchanging ideas on all sorts of subjects and vastly improving their knowledge of life and their understanding. It is most noticeable that the men who have really made their mark here are all those first in the field of intellect.

Dunlop's (1990, 128, xxii–xxiii) experiences of incarceration left him

deeply conscious of the Buddhist belief that all men are equal in the face of suffering and death...Most uplifting of all is the timeless, enduring, special brotherhood shared with all survivors of prison camp's...[I] commend their unquenchable spirit to their children, to their children's children, and to those yet unborn. 'In thy face I see the map of honour truth and loyalty'.

After the war Dunlop kept in his desk the Buddha's words from *The Dhammapada*: 'Never in this world can hatred be stilled by hatred; it will be stilled only by non-hatred. This is the Eternal Law' (Ebury 1994, 620). His *Diary* entry for 16 August 1945 reads: 'I have resolved to make the care and welfare...of these maimed and damaged men...a life long mission' (Dunlop 1990, 435). In view of Phillips' wartime experiences it is, perhaps, understandable, if surprising, that he subsequently decided to devote his life to the problems of the social sciences rather than to engineering. He was particularly concerned with the problems of macro-economic stabilisation, and of locating the level of aggregate demand that would be consistent with stable prices. Whilst this conclusion must, to a certain extent, remain speculative, 'it was "common knowledge" that Bill's interest in the social sciences grew out of his wartime experiences' (correspondence from David Laidler).[16]

His wartime incarceration may also explain some further aspects of Phillips' career. Of the 132,000 Anglo-Americans held in Japanese custody, 27 per cent died: 'The Japanese killed more British troops in prison camps than on the field of battle...its POW camps were run on the same economic principles as Nazi and Soviet slave-camps' (Johnson 1983, 427–8). Van der Post (1985, 37–8, 51, 109) stated that:

By the beginning of 1945 we were all physically dying men...There was not a person in my own prisoner-of-war camp in 1945 who was not suffering from deficiency diseases of some kind...the few survivors looked like pictures of the last inmates of Belsen on the day of liberation . . . all slowly dying from lack of food.

Phillips left his family at age twenty, to 'see the world'; he returned ten years later weighing only seven stone. In spite of the (presumably) irreversible damage caused by this malnourishment and maltreatment, in the decade and a half (1946–61) after enrolling at the LSE, Phillips completed an undergraduate degree in Sociology, a Ph.D. in Economics (for which he was awarded the Hutchinson Medal), and eleven published articles or chapters.

Economics was a compulsory subject in his Sociology degree, and he became interested in Keynesian theory. Walter Newlyn, a student one year senior to Phillips, informally taught him monetary theory, and Phillips' curiosity led him to think of the economic system as an engineering problem. This led Phillips to design what became known as the 'Phillips Machine', or Moniac, whilst still an undergraduate! His machine was built only three years after the Electronic Numerical Integrator and Computer (the ENIAC), the world's first electronic, large scale, general purpose digital computer, a 50 feet by 30 feet machine, which had taken three years to build at the Moore School of Electronic Engineering at the University of Pennsylvania. The Phillips Machine continues to be regarded as an extraordinary pioneering achievement, with versions on permanent display in the Science Museum in London, Cambridge University and at the New Zealand Institute of Economic Research in Wellington (see Part II).

Yet, following his inaugural professorial lecture (28 November 1961) Phillips' research output almost dried up entirely. Those closest to him were concerned that his teaching and administrative burdens were hindering his research: Harry Johnson noticed that he was 'leaving papers in his desk' rather than publishing them,[17] while Richard Lipsey attempted to persuade Phillips to take a research-only chair at the University of Essex. Kelvin Lancaster (1979, 634) suggested that Phillips:

became increasingly aware of the difficulties of estimating the relationships he considered necessary for policy design and of the fact that the necessary techniques were beyond his grasp. His intellectual integrity was such that he felt he could not continue to 'profess' in an area in which he had no further contribution to make.

It is possible that Phillips, like many other ex-prisoners of war, unknowingly began to experience a series of 'micro' strokes, before the onset of his major stroke in 1969.[18] Multi-infarct dementia severely interferes with concentration. Yet, this can only serve as a partial explanation because, during this period, the inventor of the Phillips Machine and the Phillips

Curve also developed the 'Phillips Critique' (chapters 49, 50, 51, 52), which was subsequently named after Robert Lucas. Equally, his energetic and inspirational leadership at LSE prompted Sir John Crawford, the Vice-Chancellor of the ANU, to offer him a chair in Canberra. An additional explanation has been offered by Bob Gregory:

Bill accepted [the chair] on the condition that he only work on Economics three days a week. The other two days would be spent on Chinese Studies. *He had lost interest in Economics.* [emphasis added]

What were the origins of this disenchantment with the subject to which he had devoted so much and which had 'repaid' him in the form of eponymous immortality? The following speculative explanation is ventured. Phillips, at this time, warned junior staff members, such as Bob Gregory, that macroeconomics had acquired an irresistible momentum of its own: 'He said his best work was largely ignored – his early control work – and his Phillips Curve work was just done in a weekend.'

Phillips' work on stabilisation policy had been concerned to put in place automatic procedures which would increase the capacity of the economy to return to the position of zero inflation (chapter 16). Like Keynes, Phillips perceived that this stabilisation exercise would facilitate the survival of democracy and of the free enterprise system (chapter 50, p. 468). With a stable price level, a stable level of aggregate employment, a fixed exchange rate, free convertibility and diminishing levels of tariff protection, the residual role for macroeconomic policy advisers was perhaps suitable only for 'humble, competent people on a level with dentists' (Keynes 1963 [1930], 373). Yet, as Peter Howitt (1990, 71) pointed out, macroeconomists increasingly came to be perceived as 'not humble or competent but a menace to society'. In July 1967, on the eve of his departure from the northern hemisphere (and also, in a sense, from macroeconomics), Phillips (chapter 50, p. 470) acknowledged that the 'rational process of decision making' with respect to these stabilisation objectives was likely to be subverted or thwarted by policymakers who were 'reluctant to engage in the intellectually difficult and politically hazardous task of actually specifying quantitative objectives and a criterion of performance'.

It is not surprising that Phillips felt increasingly alienated from the acrimonious *direction* that macroeconomic policy disputes were taking. Phillips had no tolerance for weak or faulty arguments but his leadership style did not involve confrontation and he was free of the taint of *argumentum ad hominen*: 'To be his Colleague was to be his Friend' (Phelps Brown, chapter 3). This was the leadership style which both Dunlop and van der Post found to be successful during their wartime incarceration.

We may reasonably conclude that it was, at least in part, his non-Manichean frame of mind which preserved Phillips from the lingering death that befell many of his fellow wartime internees.[19] It was this frame of mind which he brought to macroeconomics and which so much impressed his colleagues: 'Bill Phillips was, and indeed is, a hero to me' (correspondence from Chris Archibald).

During the 1960s the macroeconomic consensus was breaking down and 'popularised' versions of Phillips' empirical work became pivotal to the controversy between monetarists and Keynesians. Mark Blaug (1980, 221) described this as 'one of the most frustrating and irritating controversies in the entire history of economic thought, frequently resembling medieval disputations at their worst'. Phillips' disenchantment with macroeconomics is, at least, contemporaneous with, and may be a consequence of, the intensification of these disputes, which at times involved the Manichean 'fallacy of the two species' (Halle 1972, 125; McCloskey 1986, 183–5).[20] Phillips was a modest man, not given to complaining, and 'showed less interest in politics than virtually every other economist I have ever met' (correspondence from Jim Durbin).[21]

In spite of this, during the 1960s he became a 'household name' in policy circles. In April 1967, the Chancellor of the Exchequer, James Callaghan, invoked Phillips' name to justify the Budget projections (Wulwick 1989, 187). Ironically, Phillips (chapter 22, p. 208) had devoted his inaugural lecture to policy analysis and had warned that British growth rates, both of productivity and GNP, were relatively low. He also cautioned that:

The average rate of rise of the retail price index between 1948 and 1960 was 3.7 per cent per annum. There would be a fairly general agreement that this rate of inflation is undesirable. It has undoubtedly been a major cause of the general weakness of the balance of payments and the foreign reserves and if continued it would almost certainly make the present rate of exchange untenable.

During the 1960s this rate of inflation in Britain not only continued but accelerated, and in November 1967 Sterling was devalued. This was the year in which Phillips retreated to Canberra and to Chinese economic studies.[22] Less than two years later the full consequences of his wartime incarceration took their toll and his professional life was effectively over.

This almost suggests a fourth eponymous legacy to economics: the 'Phillips Law of Macroeconomic Controversy', which is not so much that 'bad macroeconomics drives out good', but that, just as the noise generated by inflation jams the signal emanating from the price system, so the vacuous noise from Manichean disputation drowns out the wisdom of those who have transcended animosity. Phillips experienced and witnessed unimaginable levels of evil and suffering during his period of incarceration, yet his colleagues detected in him only integrity, generosity and boundless intellectual energy: 'He was one of the few thoroughly good persons I have ever known and I benefited greatly from being close to him' (correspondence from Richard Lipsey).

The experience of war had a profound effect on an earlier generation of economists.[23] Harry Johnson (1960, 153) recounted that Pigou's experience of war

... sickened him. There can be no doubt that this experience was responsible for transforming the gay, joke-loving, sociable hospitable young bachelor of the Edwardian period into the eccentric recluse of more recent times. In the words of his colleague and life-long friend C.R. Fay, 'World War I was a shock to him, and he was never the same afterwards'.

Phillips died in March 1975, shortly after his sixtieth birthday. He had been mentioned for 'fearlessness' in the citation accompanying his MBE, but towards the end of his life he became haunted by irrational fears. A crippling stroke at age fifty-four left him chain smoking, mobile only with the assistance of a tripod, and in need of constant medical care and medication, which was provided by his devoted wife, Valda. Visiting friends, such as Paul Samuelson and Bob Gregory, were taken aback by his physical condition.

The War Diaries of Weary Dunlop (1990, 88, 95) contain a chilling indication of where Phillips may have acquired his intense tobacco addiction:

Slapping and beating up of our soldiers is now almost a daily affair ... In their impoverished state they cannot resist tobacco which they are allowed to keep after wholesale smacking. Today saw about one dozen lined up and struck a heavy slap in the face with a slab of wood ... one wonders if there will be any ear drums left intact.

Phillips carried permanently the legacy of his incarceration. It is highly probable that his addiction to untipped cigarettes was a significant contributing factor in his deteriorating health and diminished research output in the 1960s, in his major stroke in 1969, and, in the end, in his premature death. His wartime experiences, combined with a natural aversion to controversy in general, and political controversy in particular, may also partially explain one of the mysteries of contemporary macroeconomics: why Phillips remained silent, in print at least, while the curve, with which he was eponymously associated, was used, by others, to justify the policy of tolerating inflation in order to achieve permanently low levels of unemployment, which he had specifically cautioned against.[24,25]

On 25 April 1915, J.M. Keynes wrote to Duncan Grant:

Yesterday came news that two of our undergraduates were killed, both of whom I knew, though not very well, and was fond of. And to-day Rupert's death. In spite of all one has ever said I find myself crying for him. It is too horrible, a nightmare to be stopt [*sic*] anyhow. May no other generation live under the cloud we have to live under.[26]

One of Keynes' biographers concluded that *The Economic Consequences of the Peace* was 'a revolt of economics against politics' (Skidelsky 1983, 302, 399). I suspect that these sentiments may also have been a hidden sub-text in Phillips' work.

Notes

1 Phillips' parents, Harold Housego (from Wellington) and Edith (nee Webber) were dairy farmers at 'Jersey Meadows' (they bred Jersey cattle); Edith was also a school teacher. Both parents became devout Anglicans and donated some land for the construction of St Alban's Church. This became almost a family church, with Phillips' father acting as organist, lay preacher and Sunday School teacher (Sundays were strictly observed in the Phillips' household). Phillips was the first baby christened in St Alban's Church (his sister always referred to him as 'Alban'; his wife called him 'Will') (Ibbotsen-Somervell 1994).
2 *Auckland Weekly*, 13 May 1948.
3 Correspondence from Conrad Blyth
4 Sir Edward Dunlop also mentioned the possibility of a television mini-series of his book in which the 'radio expert' would presumably figure prominently. Sir Edward Dunlop died on 2 July 1993. Twenty thousand people lined the streets of Melbourne for the state funeral.
5 For the importance of the secret radio for the morale of prisoners of war, see Walley (1991, 22) in *We Flew, We Fell, We Survived: Stories of Survival*, part II, edited by Alex Kerr, the Foundation Professor of Economics at Murdoch University, and Dunlop (1990).
6 Correspondence from Van der Post.
7 Conversations with Richard Lipsey and Valda Phillips.
8 Conversation with Valda Phillips.
9 Dunlop's diary entry for 12 July 1945 (his thirty-eighth birthday) reads: 'I discern a mounting tension in the situation, with highly sinister overtones ... Z, one of the Korean guards ... was pessimistic as to any hope of our being recovered alive. Invasion, he felt, would be met by massacres and death marches. The wall and *bund* of our camp, with the built-in machine guns facing *inwards*, lend ready credibility' (1990, 432) [emphasis in text].
10 Van der Post described some of these physical brutalities: 'I would never have thought it possible that in our time there could still have been so many different ways of killing people ... the Kempetai, the all-powerful Japanese

military secret police, were such experts in all matters of torture that they invariably extracted any secret from the most determined people in their hands' (1985, 35, 36, 86; see also Johnson 1983, 427–8; Ebury 1994, 330).

11 See also Ebury (1994, 456).

12 D. H. Robertson had been awarded the Military Cross during the First World War, but never spoke about these experiences (Johnson and Johnson 1978 [1974], 136).

13 Chris Archibald is almost alone in having initiated a conversation about Phillips' POW experience. Phillips replied 'she wasn't so bad once you got used to her; and I got to work on my Chinese'. There is nothing exceptional about this tendency to make light of the unspeakable horrors of war, as evidence by the song sung by soldiers in the trenches of the first World War:

> And when they ask us,
> And they're surely going to ask us,
> We'll never tell them,
> No, we'll never tell them.
> 'We drank our pay
> In some café...

14 Kurt Klappholz's entire family perished in Dachau. He often refers to 'the blessing of hunger – it kept my mind off the poison of hatred'.

15 Van der Post (1985, 154, 138–40) continued: 'If one broke the law of gravity one broke one's neck; if one broke this law of forgiveness one inflicted a mortal wound on one's own spirit and became once again a member of the chain gang of mere cause and effect from which life has laboured so long and painfully to escape... Soon after dark, some thousands of men and hundreds of their fellows too weak to walk, many near dying and carried on stretchers, marched out of the prison for the last time, all of them on the first stage of their way to liberation and home... As I watched the long slow procession of men marching into the night, this feeling of music everywhere rose within my liberated sense, like a chorale at the end of a great symphony, asserting the triumph of creation over death. All that was good and true in the dark experiences behind me, combined with my memory of how those thousands of men, who had endured so much, never failed to respond to the worst with what was best in them, and all that happened to me, in some mysterious fashion seemed to have found again the abiding rhythm of the universe, and to be making such a harmony of the moment as I have never experienced... one of the greatest and most uncompromising manifestoes of life written in my generation, with the title Look! "We have come through"'. Dunlop (1990, 92) reflected upon the occasion when some Japanese guards attended a music concert performed by the prisoners: 'They listened with growing sadness, finally all bursting into tears and leaving. Perhaps the brooding bitterness results in their occasional outbursts of bloody murderousness, a sort of *Gotterdammerung*.'

16 Jim Durbin has emphasised 'Bill's true originality...surely no other engineer other than Bill would have become a sociology undergraduate at his age, however ghastly his experiences'. It may be relevant to note that Radford (1945, 190) concluded that the 'principal significance' of his classic essay on the 'Economic Organisation of a P.O.W. Camp' was 'sociological'.

17 Conversation with Herb Grubel.

18 Megnad Desai noted that Phillips' 'hands shook whenever he had to teach, be it to one student or to many', although this may be unconnected to his declining health.

19 Henry Kissinger concluded that the survivors of the Nazi death camps with which he had contact in 1945 'had learnt that looking back meant sorrow, that sorrow was weakness and weakness was synonymous with death' (cited by Isaacson 1992).

20 D.H. Robertson, who was also a war hero, 'was not cut out for the rough life of politicking behind the scenes or for public debate' (Johnson and Johnson 1978, 138). Phillips remained aloof from the 'heroic posturing' and 'demonising' that characterised some of this macroeconomic controversy. Perhaps Phillips has seen too many real wartime villains to pretend to see 'stage villains' among those who formed different judgements about economic policy: 'It is almost as if the villain without is a Siamese twin of all that is wrong within ourselves. The only sure way to rid life of villains, I believed, after years of thinking about it in prison, was to rid ourselves first of the villain within...' (van der Post 1985, 152–3). Perhaps Phillips had, like Dunlop, concluded that it was disharmony among the prisoners which caused the most unhappiness during his incarceration: 'I left this melancholy affair in almost the lowest frame of mind imaginable' (1990, 17, 19, 105, 108).

21 In 1962–3 the Phillips's lived next to the Boston airfields, close to MIT. The experience of the Cuban missile crisis and the Suez episode left Phillips despairing of politicians (conversation with Valda Phillips).

22 The Chinese and Pacific studies connections are intriguing. Did Phillips see similarities between the terrorism of the Cultural Revolution, which began in 1965, and the sadism of his wartime guards, particularly the Koreans? We know that Phillips learnt Chinese during his incarceration. Van der Post (1985, 38–9) commented upon the 'remarkable' Chinese in Java who, on the basis of a verbal promise of recompense from the post-war British government, smuggled gilders into the camp, which enabled the prisoners to supplement their diet with fresh fruit and cereals and thus reduce the mortality rate.

23 Keynes (1946, 172), in his last posthumously published article, deplored how much 'modernist stuff, gone wrong and turned sour and silly, is circulating'. Hutchison (1977), amongst others, reflected how different 'Keynesian economics' might have been had Keynes lived longer. Herb Grubel initiated a conversation with Phillips one Friday afternoon, about the Friedman–Phelps critique. Phillips invited Grubel to see him on Monday morning for a full discussion. Sadly, the meeting never took place, because on that Monday,

shortly after morning tea, Phillips collapsed in the Economic History office having suffered a massive stroke (correspondence from Graeme Snooks; conversation with Herb Grubel). For Phillips' discussion of inflationary expectations, see Cagan (chapter 4) and Phillips (chapter 16).

24 Richard Lipsey noted that 'Phillips himself was interested only in analysing the potentially destabilising effects of fine tuning' (1981, 557, n. 16); '...He had no tolerance for accepting inflation as a price of reducing unemployment' (correspondence). A.J. Brown (correspondence) has written that 'Bill's first love was certainly the conditions of stability of activity... In the 1950s there seemed to be a hope that "full" employment could be maintained if only the tendency to inflation that went with it could be controlled... If it was the experience of the war that turned him from engineering to the social sciences, I suspect that what worried him was unemployment and poverty rather than the price level – except in so far as the latter makes governments do silly things about the former.' James Meade stated that the interpretation contained in this chapter 'certainly chimes in with my opinion of Bill's work and character... I am quite certain that Bill was very conscious of the limitations to which you could reduce the level of unemployment without incurring a runaway inflation' (correspondence). For a discussion of these, and related matters, see Leeson (1999).

25 Richard Lipsey agrees with this assessment. 'It is indeed a mystery that he did not protest in print. Perhaps it's just that writing did not come easily to him. To someone so insightful, his total publication record was scant. He was a great talker and spent hours talking to students and colleagues when the rest of us were drafting our latest article. I, and many others, benefited greatly from this, but it left no "hard copy" record behind' (correspondence). Fisher (1978, 32) also commented on Phillips' 'silences'. Silence on controversial issues also appears to have come naturally to both Dunlop (1990, xxi) and van der Post (1985, 155): 'I have shrunk from publishing these diaries for over forty years. It seemed that they might add further suffering to those bereaved and add to controversy and hatred'; '[For twenty-five years] I preferred to remain silent because I was convinced that the inevitable use to which [my recollections] would be put in this literal and two-dimensionally minded age of ours, would work against the whole truth of war and the meaning and consequence it should have for the world.' Equally, Valda Phillips described her husband as someone who always lost interest in finished work. He was always busy – driven by the compulsive feeling that his time was limited – and his thoughts were always on the next project.

26 In 1914 Keynes received a cheerful letter from Freddie Hardman, an ex-student, who was serving on the Western Front. Keynes' reply was returned with the word 'killed' scrawled across it (Skidelsky 1983, 296).

2   The Versatile Genius

James Meade

(A.W.H. Phillips)   B31
B22

I would very much like to express my general feelings about Bill Phillips. He was a most remarkable man, extremely simple and straightforward. He was a real genius in that he always saw the main point at issue, spoke of it with the utmost directness and in the simplest possible language, and produced comments and suggestions about it which were somehow obvious when he expressed them but which everyone else had somehow or another overlooked or had muddled up by trying to be clever about them. I was, in theory, his supervisor for his Ph.D. but our meetings simply meant that I learnt from him an immense amount about things about which I knew nothing. On one occasion, after a general sophisticated discussion in the LSE senior common room, he said to me: 'You English puzzle me. In order to understand what you are saying, I have to listen between the lines.' You never had to 'listen between the lines' to Bill's commonsensical arguments.

One anecdote shows how directly he was prepared to tackle any problem. He stayed with us one summer in a cottage which contained a broken-down out-of-tune old piano. We moaned what a pity that it was so out of tune that we really could not use it. Bill went to his car, fetched his spanner and set to work tuning the piano. He never complained about a difficulty; he just worked out how to put it right and then proceeded to do so.

Just before his stroke, I received a letter from him asking whether there would be any chance of getting a position in Cambridge to work with Dick Stone and myself on dynamic macroeconomics again. It all came to nothing because very soon after he had his stroke. But he was a rolling stone intellectually. He must have decided that Chinese economics was not proceeding as he had hoped and that he might have another go at macroeconomic modelling instead. Years before he had certainly given it up because his early expectations about it had been disappointed by the difficulties which he finally encountered after making his path-breaking start. Perhaps he had some very simple but immensely promising new thoughts on the subject. It is tragic that we will never know.

I must end this on a personal note expressing how greatly I admired him and how fond I and my family were of him. He was an unaffected, undemonstrative, true and lovable friend as well as being an unaffected, undemonstrative, commonsensical and versatile genius.

3 To Be His Colleague Was To Be His Friend

Henry Phelps Brown

By the time I got to know Bill Phillips, I think he had put his experiences as a prisoner behind him. He had borne them with the toughness and sustained morale that I took to be typical of his countrymen. The only other particular that I remember him mentioning was that he set himself to learn Chinese with the aid of a Chinese fellow prisoner. Thus began an interest in China which was a factor in his decision to leave econometrics at the LSE for Chinese Studies at the ANU.

Bill did not talk readily about his prisoner-of-war experiences. I remember only once, walking with him in the garden of his house in Hampstead, when he was moved to speak of some recollections. One of these was of a Japanese sergeant, who was subject to fits of rage, and would beat the prisoners with an iron bar. One evening he gathered Bill with two or three other prisoners and took them down to his quarters, when he showed them photographs of his wife and children, and burst into tears.

I can well believe that his decision to give up engineering for sociology when he came back from the war was prompted by his observation of the spontaneous formation of social structures among the individuals who were thrown together in the prison camp. I also know that his employment, when he first came to London before the war, as a supervisor of a gang laying electrical cables, confronted his always active and inquiring mind with issues of industrial psychology.

In the 1950s, his thoughts were formed around the design of his hydraulic model. For the completion of this he needed to build in various dependable relations (such as the response of investment to a change in the rate of interest), which would provide an endogenous determination of the course of change of the whole economy dependent upon some initial stimulus. One such relation was between the level and direction of change of unemployment and the current change of wage rates (that is, the loop, later made more manageable by being simplified into a single curve). I have been told that it is this aspect of the curve, as supplying an equation essential to the completion of a macroeconomic dynamic system, that secured its instant seizure by Samuelson and Solow (1960), whose sponsorship brought it wide currency and acceptance.

Concern with the hydraulic model would have given it further significance in Phillips' own eyes. As an engineer concerned with the current problems of the British economy, he was looking for some economic counterpart to the control device by which a feedback from the output of a motor is used to check aberrations of that output. In this light he saw his curve not as providing the germ of an automatic control device – indeed not, for it indicates positive rather than the required negative feedback – but as showing the authorities the conditions under which, by using instruments at their disposal to vary the level of unemployment, they could control the rate of rise of money wages. Thus he thought that the authorities might well choose a 'compromise solution' with 'perhaps 2 per cent unemployment with about 1 per cent per year rises in prices'. I do not know how the term 'trade-off' has been used in the secondary literature, but to my mind it conveys precisely the possibility of obtaining a measure of price stability by paying a price in higher unemployment put so clearly by Phillips himself in the passage just quoted.

4   Phillips' Adaptive Expectations Formula

Phillip Cagan

When studying money demand in hyperinflations in 1951 with Milton Friedman, later published as the 'Monetary Dynamics of Hyperinflations' (Cagan 1956), I could not find a workable representation of the expected change in prices (the cost of holding money). Friedman happened to discuss the problem with Bill Phillips, who suggested relating the change in the expected rate to the difference between the actual and expected rates. When Friedman conveyed this suggestion to me, I converted the implied differential equation into an exponentially weighted average of past price changes and found it provided an empirically workable money demand equation. Phillips deserves credit for what later came to be called 'adaptive expectations'.

When rational expectations captured the attention of the profession in the 1960s (following Muth's famous article), adaptive expectations were largely abandoned. Years later, I became aware that data on forward exchange rates existed for the German hyperinflation and could be used as observed expectations of changes in exchange rates and as proxies for expectations of price inflation. These data provided an opportunity to test whether adaptive or rational expectations provided a better explanation of (at least the German) hyperinflation. The test appeared to validate Phillips' suggestion (Cagan 1991). This article explains why adaptive expectations can be viewed as 'rational' in those circumstances.

5   Economist – Washing Machine Fixer

Elizabeth Johnson

As I remember, Bill Phillips fixed my washing machine – at least, that became the family myth. My husband, Harry Johnson, brought him home to talk economics after a Cambridge dinner in hall and they walked in on my frustration with the washer. I met a slight-statured, quiet man who modestly asked if he could help. He tried something with a screwdriver which may have worked – or perhaps it didn't work – and went back to talking economics.

Phillips' visit to Cambridge was preceded by the rumour that he had started life as an engineer, intriguing information in those days of more stratified and static academic careers. And, of course, we had heard about his teaching machine that modelled a working economy in a Heath Robinson conglomeration of glass tubes through which flowed a stream of coloured water representing the national income. There was one of these machines at the LSE and soon to be one at Cambridge where Richard Stone had recently gathered a group working in applied economics. I suspect it may have been Stone's interest that prompted Phillips' visit to Cambridge; the economics faculty as a whole was not particularly observant of what went on in their subject elsewhere in the world.

The trouble with the Phillips Machine was its inflationary tendencies – the national income demonstrated a strong propensity to overflow. Perhaps as the youngest and most recently arrived member of the faculty, Harry was frequently called out to deal with a monetary crisis in the shape of a pink cascade pouring down the stairway from the Department of Applied Economics. My Cambridge memories are rosy-hued. Bill Phillips was so quiet and gentle – his machine so original and quirky. This is the stuff of which affectionate stories are made.

6 Playing Around with Some Data

Ann S. Schwier

This brief note had its genesis over thirty years ago when, along with my now deceased husband, I had the pleasure of meeting Bill Phillips at a conference in San Francisco in December of 1966. He had just given the Econometric Society's Walras–Bowley Lecture. For some reason or another he was standing all alone in the lobby of the hotel – casually watching the world go by would, I think, describe it fairly accurately. Anyway, I had the temerity to introduce myself. He was charming. We visited with him a total of six or eight hours on at least three different occasions – once in the lobby, once in his room, and once in ours. He was a most interesting person, and a very pleasant 'regular guy'. There was not the slightest hint of condescension. He chatted and joked as if we had been friends for years. A very impressive person, not just as an economist, but as a man.

Of course, I'm not reconstructing from thirty years ago without help. In 1979 I put down some of these thoughts as the preface to a paper on 'Mr Phillips and His Curve'. And that is jogging my memory now. In any event, most of the conversations were not about economics – we talked about children, his and ours, education, Australia, New Zealand, the American Midwest, all sorts of things. One point that was particularly interesting to me was that he seemed to be rather worried about raising his daughters in London – Australasia would be more to his liking, safer, less drugs, and so on.

My recollections of those parts of our conversations which did pertain to economics and particularly to the Phillips Curve come down to three propositions. Of course in the actuality these three items were all intermingled. Their separation here is strictly an artificial construct.

First of all, Phillips was never as impressed with or as taken with 'The Phillips Curve' as other people were. And do not forget that in the beginning it was not just 'other people'. It was *practically everybody*. He described it to us as a 'quick and dirty' job. He had been 'playing around' with some data, came up with a curve which he said was largely freehand drawn. He submitted it to *Economica* and then left for sabbatical in Australia. When he returned he was amazed to find there was a 'Phillips Curve'!

Secondly, his curve was definitely *not* structural. It was a prediction relation – a crude one but he thought it did the job. We specifically asked about this matter of being structural and Phillips gave us a very emphatic 'no'. Admittedly we should have pursued the subject further but that is hindsight. Anyone particularly interested in the topic should consult chapter 21.

Thirdly, in 1966 Phillips seemed – to our surprise then but not in 1979 – to be having misgivings about the Phillips Curve, to be holding it at arm's length so to speak. Apparently he had *at most* been only moderately interested in it in the first place. He was amazed at the speed with which it had been taken over and also at the uses to which it had been put, and he was not at all sure, by 1966, about the desirability of such uses.

7 The *Festschrift*

Brian Silverstone

On the afternoon of 18 November 1974, a small group of us joined Bill and Valda Phillips in their New Zealand home in Auckland for a joint celebration. It was the occasion of Bill's sixtieth birthday. It was also the occasion when a collection of essays by former colleagues and students – a *festschrift* – was presented to Professor Phillips.

The idea for a *festschrift* appears to have occurred to several New Zealand economists on both sides of the world. My involvement began in 1972 when I was a young staff member in the Economics Department at the University of Waikato. A colleague from the Politics Department told me that Professor Phillips was living in Auckland, having moved there from Australia following a serious stroke. My colleague had had a meeting with Professor Phillips to discuss Bill's then major interest, Chinese studies. By coincidence, I had just been given a set of issues of the *Economic Journal* covering the decade from 1950 to 1960. One article stood out for me as being truly special. It was Professor Phillips' 1954 paper 'Stabilisation Policy in a Closed Economy' (chapter 16). I asked the politics lecturer if he thought Professor Phillips would be willing to see me to talk about the stabilisation paper. He assured me that Bill would be only too willing and undertook to ask. The reply was positive.

Although I was aware of Professor Phillips' academic contributions, and brief biography from the expatriates section of *An Encyclopedia of New Zealand* (McLintock 1966), I knew nothing about his personality. Would he really be welcoming, pleasant and encouraging? After all, some famous people can be difficult. I need not have worried. I was welcomed warmly and we went in to his study. Numerous issues of *Econometrica* were open on his desk. Perhaps he was working on the unpublished 'Lucas Critique' essay, dated July 1972, that concludes this volume. Whatever the project, Professor Phillips obviously had no intention of letting his health interfere with his academic pursuits.

We discussed some of my interests and the contemporary relevance of his stabilisation paper in the context of the then fashionable work on optimal control theory. I can remember his eyes fixing intensely on me. This had the effect of making me do my best to talk sensibly as we discussed his work, economic issues generally, his students and his teaching duties at the University of Auckland. After morning tea and a two-hour meeting, Professor Phillips farewelled me generously, and offered to help me in any way he could.

It occurred to me, as I returned home, that New Zealand economists should honour Professor Phillips with a *festschrift* on the occasion of his sixtieth birthday in 1974. I put the idea to my colleague, Allan Catt. After some initial enquiries and discussion in New Zealand, we wrote to a sample of New Zealand-born economists resident overseas, namely, Rex Bergstrom, Malcolm Fisher, Warren Hogan, Ronald Meek, Colin Simkin and Stephen Turnovsky. They all replied enthusiastically and most said they could offer a contribution.

We intended originally that the tribute to Bill would come only from New Zealand economists wishing to honour their most distinguished member. It quickly became apparent from correspondence that many of Bill's former colleagues, who were not New Zealanders, would be very keen to contribute to a volume in his honour. We also learned that Rex Bergstrom and Maurice Peston had been exploring the possibility of collecting a volume of essays in Bill's honour although not on the occasion of his birthday. In the event, it was decided that the project should take an international flavour and be published under the auspices of the New Zealand Association of Economists.

I returned to the Phillips' home on two subsequent occasions, both in 1974. The first visit was to ask Bill if my listing of his publications was complete and to request a photo for the book. He scanned my list, confirmed the entries, and remarked – with his characteristic tendency to make understatements about himself – that his output was 'a bit thin'. We all know, of course, from this volume of Bill's collected work and from the history of our subject, that most of his contributions were classics. Indeed, in a review of the *festschrift* in *Economica*, Robert Solow (1979) remarked that Bill did not 'suffer from the logorrhea that appears to be the occupational disease of economists. It is absolutely charming to be reminded that Phillips published only twelve papers during his career.'

At this visit, I also obtained a copy of Bill's unpublished Econometric Society Walras–Bowley conference paper on the 'Estimation of Systems of Difference Equations with Moving Average Disturbances' (chapter 45). This paper had been referred to widely in the econometric literature, yet remained unpublished because Bill had planned to extend it. We wanted to include the paper in the *festschrift*.

The second visit was on Bill's sixtieth birthday, 18 November 1974. Bill and Valda Phillips had invited Conrad Blyth and Geoffrey Braae (from the University of Auckland) and me to afternoon tea. Following comments by Conrad, I had the honour of presenting the manuscript version of the *festschrift* to Professor Phillips on behalf of the contributors, his colleagues and friends and the New Zealand Association of Economists. He was moved greatly and expressed his heartfelt thanks with the comment that he had not really done very much, just 'put out a few hares for people to chase'.

Bill never saw the book version of his *festschrift*. Sadly, just a few weeks after this celebration, in early March 1975, he died. Subsequent editing (with Rex Bergstrom, Allan Catt and Maurice Peston) resulted in *Stability and Inflation: A Volume of Essays to Honour the Memory of A.W.H. Phillips* (Bergstrom, Catt, Peston and Silverstone 1978). It appeared three years later in March 1978 and comprised sixteen chapters in three sections: 'The Phillips Curve', 'Models of Inflation and Stabilisation Policies', and 'Econometric Methods for Dynamic Models'. An appendix contained two further chapters. The publishers, John Wiley, produced a complicated volume very attractively and it was well received by the contributors and reviewers.

I shudder now at my youthful boldness in literally turning up at the Phillips' home. On reflection, I am glad I did. My meetings with Professor Phillips have left a lasting impact on me, particularly the need to bring humility to our understanding of how the economy works and how it might work better. It was a pleasure subsequently to become a member of an enthusiastic project to honour a truly gifted scholar, a humanitarian and a very special New Zealander. An extract from the preface to *Stability and Inflation* reflects my memories and would, I am sure, meet with universal agreement:

New Zealanders are proud of Bill not only because of his achievements but because he was very much the kind of man they most admire. He was unpretentious and on the surface seemed to be an ordinary man, yet he led no ordinary life. He was a modest man, but his modesty was based on innate self-confidence. He achieved greatness but without flamboyance and his reputation rested on what he did, not on any gift for self-advertisement. He was an eclectic, skilled with his hands as well as his brain, enjoyed intellectual effort for its own sake and also enjoyed the finest in both Eastern and Western cultures. Finally, and most important, for it is in line with the New Zealand worship of improvisation, he was an innovator.

Part II
The Phillips Machine

8   The Origins of the Machine in a Personal Context

Walter Newlyn

331   £10

(A.w.H.Phillips)   B22

Starting with a brief account of my relationship with Bill Phillips, I propose to tell the story of the origins of the machine in which I was involved with him. We first met among a group of mature ex-service undergraduates at the LSE in 1946. My subject was Economics with subsidiary courses; Bill's was Sociology with Economics as one of the subsidiary courses. I was one year ahead of him in the three-year BA course. Within this group only the barest minimum was discussed about our war experience. Even when Bill and I had developed a close personal relationship, I learnt little about his very varied career except that he had trained as an electrical engineer in New Zealand and that he had been a prisoner of war in a Japanese camp. I shared various social activities with him and I recall that at one stage these were within a quartet with two members of the company of the musical show 'Bless the Bride'! He was also one of a small group of students (men and women) who walked the footpaths of Surrey at weekends. Bill was certainly no misogynist, nor was he a workaholic.

It gradually became clear that Bill was dissatisfied with Sociology and was becoming increasingly interested in macroeconomics. We had occasional problem-solving sessions, but it was after I had taken up an appointment to the staff of the Department of Economics at Leeds that the crucial exchange took place. Early in 1949, I visited LSE to discuss with Richard Sayers a chapter I was writing for one of his books, and I met Bill in the refectory. He lost no time in showing me a paper he had written in which he had been unable to interest any of the LSE staff whom he had approached. I am privileged to possess that paper which is in Bill's own typing, and is the only copy. It was given to me by Bill as a memento. Before taking the story further I will summarise the paper.

It is entitled 'Saving and Investment: Rate of Interest and Level of Income'. The first section deals with commodities, the title being

31

'Stocks and Flows of Commodities: Price'. It is concerned with the analysis of any market 'where stocks are held from investment or speculative motives'. Figure 1 in Bill's paper, which relates price to the quantity of stock, shows the effect of a change in demand on price with stocks fixed, at an instant in time. In his Figure 2, price is related to the rate of flow of the commodity per unit of time and shows the effect on prices when this rate of flow is increased. The conclusion is that:

the combination cannot be shown in a diagram since stocks and rates of flow are incommensurable, as, for example, distance and speed. The process can, however, be illustrated by a hydraulic analogy.

His Figure 3 shows Boulding's supply and demand hydraulic analogy (1948, p. 117) modified for the inclusion of stocks and the interconnections between stocks and flows linked mechanically. The effect of different elasticities is examined.

Section 2 is more appropriately set out verbatim.

2 Stocks and Flows of Money

The analogy is further developed in fig. 4 [shown here as figure 8.1], to illustrate monetary theory. In the lower ring is the national income flow, and in the upper the flows of savings and investment. The income flow Y divides into savings and consumption, while expenditures from consumption and investment generate income. M is the stock of money held from investment or speculative motives, i.e. that portion of their resources that investors hold in money rather than securities. Any difference between the rate of flow of savings and the rate of flow of investment is equal to the rate of change of the income flow (assuming that both the budget and overseas trade accounts are balanced), and is also equal to the rate of change of the stock of money M (assuming there is no expansion or contraction of credit by the monetary authorities and banks).

The partition between the money and securities tanks represents liquidity preference. A movement to the right (due to investors expecting that the rate of interest will rise and the price of securities fall) indicates a general desire by investors to hold a larger portion of their resources in the form of money. Since, at any moment, the stocks of both money and securities are fixed no change in the allocation of the total investment resources between them is possible, so that the rate of interest (the price of money) rises and the price of securities falls. (Securities could be subdivided according to degree of liquidity, each class having a different price and rate of interest. An increase in liquidity preference would then be indicated by a movement of the partitions concertina-fashion to the right.) i is the Keynesian interest rate. The side of the money tank curves outwards, since the elasticity of the liquidity preference curve becomes very great at low rates of interest.

The propensity to save is represented by the width of the gap between the two valves in the savings tube. The marginal propensity to save (or income elasticity of savings) is indicated by the position of the fulcrum A, decreasing as the fulcrum is

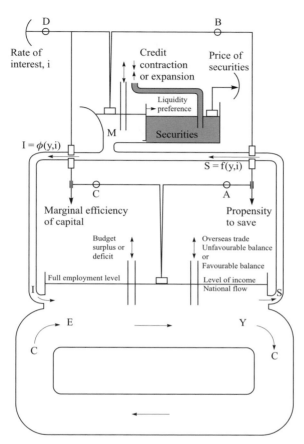

Figure 8.1

moved to the right, the interest elasticity of savings similarly decreasing as the fulcrum *B* is moved to the right.

The marginal efficiency of capital is represented by the position of the lower valve in the investment tube. The income elasticity of investment decreases as the fulcrum *C* is moved to the left, and the interest elasticity of investment decreases as the pivot *D* is moved to the left.

Section 3 is entitled 'The Rate of Interest and the Level of Income'. In this section three approaches to this relationship are examined. They were taken from the relatively recent literature (if allowance is made for the war years): Classical Theory, Loanable Fund Theory and Keynesian Theory (as in the *General Theory*). In each case, the hydraulic analogy is used to show and to solve their defects. The defect identified in the Classical Theory is its exclusive determination by flow. In the Loanable Funds Theory, the incompatibility of the stock and flow relationship (as in the Lerner (1938) diagram) is highlighted. In Keynesian Theory, liquidity preference is shown to be exclusively stock determined.

Combining the verbatim text in section 2 with the summarised text of section 3, it would not be unreasonable to conclude that the overall message was that the hydraulic analogy was necessary for combining stocks and flows. In view of the theme of this section, it is surprising that the IS/LM synthesis (Hicks 1937) was not scrutinised; perhaps the reference lists in Bill's subsidiary course did not include items in *Econometrica*.

But this is to disregard the significance of figure 8.1 (Bill's figure 4). In reading the paper, on the occasion described, I read no further than that. Indeed, the first time I read the paper in full was to write this chapter. Figure 8.1 clearly demonstrated an innovation. It showed a mechanical method, applicable to the use of the hydraulic analogy, of articulating, over time, the effects of changes in the relationships of a set of simultaneous equations. I was very excited about this. I said to Bill that it should be possible to construct a machine to reflect the articulation of the diagram as a teaching aid. I went on to ask whether, in view of his engineering skill, it would be possible for him to do it. He replied that he probably could. This led to my suggestion that Arthur Brown, then Head of Economics at Leeds, might be interested in financing the project from departmental funds.

It was clear that what could be done for the saving/investment sector could equally well be done for the government and external sectors. So, before confronting Arthur Brown, I drew the full economy version within the full economy frame of 'Injections and Leaks' shown in figure 8.2. Arthur responded enthusiastically and provided £100 for the costs of the project; quite a large sum in present prices.

During the Easter vacation, Bill spent a considerable amount of time solving the problems of converting a diagram into a physical form. An indication of the tasks which were involved in this can be deduced from the technical specification in chapter 10 (pp. 69–71). This undoubtedly detracted from work for his final examination at the end of the summer term. My part in this worried me very much when I learnt of his poor results; that I had no need to do so is demonstrated by his career – from assistant lecturer to professor in seven years.

The construction of the machine was carried out in the garage of friends of Bill's in Croydon during the summer of 1949. The photograph shows Bill (on left of picture) with myself and Mrs Phyllis

Langley, whose husband helped Bill with the construction. Both were invited by Bill to the famous first demonstration of the machine and he had them on the platform with him. This is typical of his kindness.

I was spending the vacation in London and this allowed me to be involved in the project. My job consisted of acting as craftman's mate – sanding and sticking pieces of perspex in place – and some economic input. One case in which an economic input from me was needed was the introduction of the Public Sector Borrowing Requirement; it was incorporated by linking the government's working balances to the money market. A hinged barrier in the centre opened and closed to reflect changes in the government deficit/surplus. The other case was that of the external balance. This was a closed book to Bill and, as one would expect, he wanted a full briefing on what lay behind the functions we proposed using to reflect the response of imports and exports to changes in the exchange rate which is determined by differences in the rates of change of imports and exports. I checked my file and found that I drew fifteen graphs to illustrate the multiplicity of the elasticities of domestic and foreign supply and demand which our values should have reflected. Only a computer could have solved the problem and our machine was to be a teaching aid in which plausible but changeable functions would be used to reflect the short-term results of exogenous changes imposed by those using the machine.

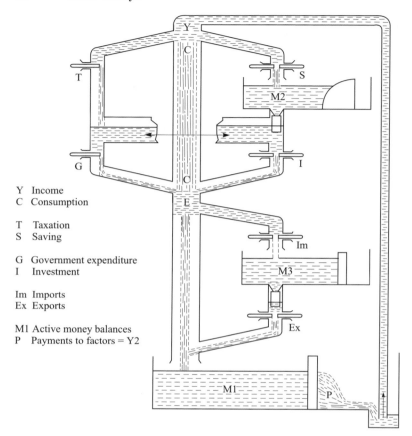

Y Income
C Consumption

T Taxation
S Saving

G Government expenditure
I Investment

Im Imports
Ex Exports

M1 Active money balances
P   Payments to factors = Y2

Figure 8.2 Full economy model outline

There is one case in which I failed to correct the design for the primary distribution of tax, consumption and saving flows from the income flow. They should have been located below the taxation flow to reflect post-tax decisions instead of a three-way distribution of income. It has to be assumed that rational expectation of post-tax income is reflected in the propensity to save, leaving consumption as the residue.

When the machine was finished, it was taken to the LSE and demonstrated at the celebrated Lionel Robbins seminar in November 1949. A photograph was taken during that event and reveals Bill's tendency to chain-smoking whenever he was working, thinking about a problem or declaiming (see chapter 11, p. 105). It was as a result of James Meade's enthusiastic response on this occasion that Bill was appointed an assistant lecturer to work on the Mark II version of the machine. It was this version which gained international success.

The Mark II version was certainly technically more efficient than the Mark I. The only economic difference, however, was the addition of an accelerator, the behaviour of which is described (prior to its construction) in chapter 10 (pp. 80–1). Its inclusion in the Mark II machines is the element which gave it the dynamic feature which stimulated the work of Richard Goodwin – a far cry from being a teaching aid! The prototype received a great deal of publicity while at the LSE: the visit of the Chancellor of the Exchequer, a drawing by Emett, and visitors from far and wide. It is not surprising that the origin of the machine was pervasively attributed to the LSE. On leaving the LSE, it went to Liverpool to be demonstrated to a conference of the Association of University Teachers of Economics, after which it went to the Department of Economics of the University of Leeds, where it belonged.

I demonstrated the machine at one of Arthur Brown's weekly seminars at which it was as highly acclaimed, as it had been in the Lionel Robbins seminar. Following a diversion from press attention, it was moved to a small, especially plumbed, teaching room, where it was used in small groups as a teaching aid for over two decades. In the 1980s it was still being shown on 'open days'; direction of responses was still clearly shown but with much less accuracy than its initial margin of error of ±4 per cent. Now it is a museum piece. A Mark III reconstruction of a Mark II by the Santory–Toyota Centre in 1989 went into the Science Museum on 23 March 1995 as the first simulator of the behaviour of an economy. The most recent developments include the restoration of the Cambridge Mark II, which was inaugurated on 15 December 1995.

I enjoyed working with Bill and appreciated the opportunity of observing the application of his skills. I was also fascinated by his 'propensity to improvise'. The two pumps were old air force stock and, for something to move the frame holding the graph on which income and interest changes were recorded, he used the inside of an old clockwork clock. I very much valued his friendship.

In chapter 10, Bill stresses the value of a visible presentation of the responses to macroeconomic changes in a hydraulic model. But he precedes his exposition of the characteristics of the prototype, described as the simple model, by the same general approach via the commodity market as in his paper discussed above. It is apparent from the generality of the subsequent presentation and from his title that his interest had already shifted to the area of his future work.

In my article on the prototype (Newlyn 1950), contemporary with Bill's, there is a major overlap with his (greatly superior) exposition of its characteristics, and my emphasis was on the teaching methods, drawing on experience, and therefore not relevant to the theme of this volume. However, in one sector devoted to discussion of the time-lag in the income generation process (much in vogue in the 1950s), I made a point about the time-lag in hydraulic models, the generality of which may justify its resurrection.

In the model, perforce, the time-lag is a function of the capacity of the 'active money balances' tank (see figure 8.2) which is adjustable within the structural limits. We have here a situation similar to that of the specification of the external effects. But that arose from the impossibility of calculating the results of a correct model: in the case of the time-lag, the model is not correct, being imposed by the hydraulic analogy as the frequency of the circulation of active balances. But, as in FM radio, it is the *modulation* of the frequency of carrier wavelengths, not the frequency of it, which generates the signal. It is the decisions to change the determinations of the rate of flow of money, with the capacity of the active balances tank fixed, which should determine the time-lag which will apply to any impulse.

My conclusion in Newlyn (1950) was that the accuracy was relatively unimportant compared with the real understanding of the relationships which the model so vividly illustrates. I would not wish to change that conclusion.

9   The Phillips Machine as a 'Progressive' Model   (A.W.H.Phillips)

David Vines

E10
322
831

Introduction

I would like to dedicate this chapter to James Meade.

On more than one occasion, James Meade described Bill Phillips to me as the 'nearest to a person of genius that I have known'.[1] This extraordinary volume is a consequence of the initial trust which Meade placed in Phillips. Amongst the LSE staff, it was Meade who initially encouraged Phillips, and it was Meade who offered Phillips the possibility of presenting his machine to Lionel Robbins' seminar. Meade then took a continuing interest in the machine, and also in Phillips' work on economic dynamics and control, to which the machine led.[2]

I had the honour to work with Meade on macroeconomic control questions for a period of ten years from the late 1970s. Meade regarded the work which we and a number of other colleagues did together during the 1980s as a continuation of the research which he had helped Phillips to begin. Meade introduced me to Phillips' work and told me stories about the man and his machine. He also understood the machine better than anybody else that I have met. Once in the late 1980s I had the privilege of watching the machine in operation with Meade, and asking him about it as the water was going round. It is a great sadness to me that I have not been able to discuss this paper with him.[3]

How should we now think of the Phillips Machine? The chapters in part II of this volume make it clear that it was an extraordinarily clever physical device. But these chapters do not address my question because they are quite consistent with a merely 'gee-whiz' evaluation of the machine as an historical curiosum: an analogue computer running on water, superseded by serious computer models; a model of a (perhaps outdated) Keynesian way of thinking about the economy, of no particular interest to students – or researchers – any longer. Instead, I believe that we should think of it as a truly 'progressive' economic model in the sense of Kuhn (1962) – a heuristic device that was of enormous value to

39

Phillips in his thinking about the economy and which can still give acute insights to us.

Two physical worldviews

Phillips' physical model of the economy is by no means the only remarkable physical worldview. There are two other noteworthy physical models: a model of the pre-Copernican universe, and Fultz's dish, developed to illustrate world weather. The reader uninterested in these analogies, and in my own early recollections of the machine, can skip this and the next section.

Astronomy: 1593

Recently I visited the science museum in Florence for the first time, and saw the great armillary sphere of Antonio Santucci. Santucci's sphere is the largest physical model of the pre-Copernican universe ever constructed. This 'Universal Machine of the World' is made of wood, richly painted and covered with pure gold leaves. Towering more than three meters high, it stands in the middle of the museum's main room, visible from the entrance hall, a brooding presence physically dominating the whole building. It was commissioned by Ferdinand I from his cosmographer, begun on 4 March 1588, and completed in May 1593:

... the Earth is at the centre of the sphere, in accordance with the Ptolomeic system ... Surrounding the earth are the seven spheres of the planets (the Moon, Mercury, Venus, the Sun, Mars, Jupiter and Saturn) and the sphere of the fixed stars, with a band representing the signs of the Zodiac. These eight mobile spheres are enclosed by a ninth, the so-called sphere of the 'Prime Mover'. This sphere supports the metal wire meridians and the polar caps, on the interior of which are painted the coats of arms of the Medici and the Lorraines ... Twenty four wooden circles branch out from the two caps and together form another fixed sphere.

Looking at this great, defunct, sphere the observer feels a mixture of awe and gladness. It is really skilfully constructed. But doing so makes you feel glad to belong to the epoch of history that has had a 'better', simpler, understanding of the heavens: the Copernican system.

Meteorology: late 1940s

David Fultz was a researcher at the University of Chicago in the early post-war years, at the same time as Phillips was building his machine.

Fultz sought an answer to the question: what factors are essential to generating the central features of world weather. This is a difficult question – there are irregular continents, large oceans with currents, and mountain ranges. It all looks very complex. Fultz, like Phillips, built a simple physical model to illuminate the central features of the problem.

Fultz took a dishpan filled with water, bent an electric heating element around the outside of the pan, and placed it on a slowly rotating turntable. He then dropped dye in the water in order to observe the movements of the water. This setup contained two physical analogies to two features of the global weather system: a temperature difference between the poles and the equator, and the Coriolis force that results from the earth's spin. Everything else was suppressed – no continents, no oceans, no mountain ranges. Yet the pan exhibited steady flows near the rim that correspond to the tropical trade winds, and great eddies that corresponded to the cyclonic storms of the temperate regions, and 'even a twisting ribbon of fast-flowing water that unmistakably corresponded to the only recently discovered jet stream. Fultz's dishpan, without a doubt showed the essential elements of actual weather' (Krugman 1995, 70–1; Lorenz 1993).

Relevance

Reading about Fultz's inspired dish we can immediately see how it might be a strong guide to intuition for meteorologists. The insight which it provokes works by analogy. Nobody would claim that the dish 'was the weather' or that it provided a substitute for a mathematical model of the weather. But the insight is nonetheless powerful: the dish helps an observer to see how such a mathematical model might be constructed. In this it is entirely different from the Ptolomeic system, which acted as a block to intuition. Only in a Copernican worldview is it easy to see how to construct Newton's laws. I believe that Phillips' Machine is like Fultz's dish.

The Phillips Machine and macroeconomic intuition: a personal recollection

I first heard about the Phillips Machine as a student at Melbourne University in the late 1960s. I had studied physics and mathematics in my first year. In my second year I began the study of macroeconomics and my teacher, Sam Soper, who had been at the LSE, drew the circular flow of income and pipes and tanks as a way of distinguishing between stocks (money, capital) and flows (income).

When we got to the part of the course in which Hicks' (1950) trade cycle model was presented, I went and looked at the Phillips Machine, and immediately saw the electrical analogy. I realised that, just as we could think of taps as regulators of water flows, and tanks as receptacles for stocks (that is, as integrators of the flows), we could also think of resistors as regulators of electrical flow, and capacitors as stock-integrators of the electrical flow. I knew from the theory part of my first year physics course that systems with resistors and capacitors could be represented as second-order differential equations with (possibly) complex roots, and so could have the capacity for cyclical behaviour. Indeed, during one of our practical classes, we had been made to produce such cycles using bits of wire, resistors and capacitors and cathode ray tube displays. Immediately, I got to work in my room with pictures of pipes and tanks, circuit diagrams of resistors and capacitors, and macroeconomic models in the form of second-order differential equations. Thus was my macroeconomic intuition born, and thus was it connected to formal theory. But it was not until the late 1980s that I saw the Phillips Machine working, and it was only when preparing to write this paper that I set out to try to really understand it.

1 The Phillips Machine as a guide to intuition

The only way to understand the significance of the Phillips Machine is to try to understand how it works. What follows is a detailed discussion of a few experiments on the machine. I would advise that this section is read in conjunction with chapter 10, especially section II and figure 10.2, and with reference to the operating manual which Phillips' prepared as a guide for users of his machine. This guide has the title 'National income monetary flow demonstrator', and is reprinted as an appendix to this chapter (henceforth 'Flow Demonstrator' or FD). Especially relevant are the sections headed 'Examples of the use of the machine' and figure 9.1.

The reader who does not have the inclination to work through my detailed description of each experiment is invited to turn to the end of each sub-section, where the insight provided by the experiment is described.

1.1 Money stocks, income flows and the rate of interest

This section considers:
(a) the operation of the Keynesian multiplier when the interest rate is kept constant;

(b) the operation of the multiplier when the money stock is held constant and the interest rate is allowed to vary; and
(c) the joint determination of the interest rate and the level of income following an increase in the quantity of money.

(a) The multiplier with a constant rate of interest

Consider an increase in investment in a closed economy with no government (as in the simplified version in figure 10.2 and section II.1 in chapter 10, and FD example 1). That is easily achieved in the full model depicted in figure 9.1 of FD by shutting off taxes (label 1), government expenditure (label 2), imports (label 6) and exports (label 7). (All references to labels which follow refer to this figure.)

We fix the interest rate by preventing the level in the surplus balances tank from falling (or rising). This is achieved by connecting that tank by means of a draining hose to a spare tank (see FD example 1 and label 12 in figure 9.1). That hose can be set up so as to replenish any loss of water from the surplus balances tank if its level has a tendency to fall (or to drain off water from the tank if its level has a tendency to rise).

We increase investment by shifting the investment function (label 5) so as to increase the flow of water through the investment expenditure pipe. The flow of total expenditure is thereby increased. In equilibrium the full effect of such an expenditure increase will – as we know from simple Keynesian economics – be 'multiplied' because the expenditure increase will increase income (round from the bottom left of the machine and up to the top), and that will raise consumption expenditure (label 3),[4] which further raises expenditure. Equilibrium is regained when the outflow of saving increases by the extent of the increase in investment.

But output only gradually follows any initial increase in expenditures, because of the lags in the circular flow of income between expenditure, output and income. In chapter 10 (p. 75), Phillips discusses these lags in detail. He opts to treat the lag as one between expenditure and income 'because an increase in expenditure and sales first leads to a reduction in stocks'. This rundown in stocks and its counterpart effect on production is not modelled. Instead it is assumed that the excess of receipts over income-outpayments is held by firms as working money balances, and that the rise in these money balances stimulates an increase in production in exactly the same manner as would the reduction in physical stocks. This is not entirely satisfactory, as Phillips concedes (p. 75), since there is no particular reason why these two lags of response should be the same.[5] The implementation of this lag on the machine is by means of the working balances or 'transactions' balances tank at the bottom on figure 9.1 (labelled M_1 in chapter 10, figure 10.2). The crucial thing about this tank is that the outflow from it (income, Y) is proportional to, and determined by, its height (the holdings of transactions balances, M_1).[6] Phillips describes this relationship as $M_1 = PY$ (where P is a parameter) in equation (2) (p. 77). But it is clear from the physical machine that causality in this process runs from M_1 to Y. I will comment on the significance of this fact below.

We are now in a position to discuss the operation of the dynamic process whereby, on the machine, income is driven to its equilibrium level. It is helpful to do this using figure 10.2 in chapter 10 and the algebra of that chapter (p. 77) in conjunction with each other. The excess of expenditure, E, over income, Y, is of course identically equal to the addition to transactions money balances, M_1. But by identity that is equal to the difference between investment and saving.[7] This gives equation (1), whose interpretation is that water accumulating in the bottom tank is equal to the difference between water being injected into the circular flow by investment and water withdrawn by saving. Investment is exogenous, as fixed at label 5. Saving is equal to σY (equation (3)), a residual after the operation of the function at label 3 relating consumption to income which has been described above.[8] To enable equations (1) to (3) to be turned into a differential equation for income Y, and to complete our understanding of the physical process of the machine, we must differentiate equation (2), which tells us that the rate of change of income is proportional to the rate of accumulation of water in the M_1 tank. Equation (4) immediately follows, showing that the rate of change of income is proportional to the gap between investment injections and saving leakages, where the speed of adjustment is lower, the larger is the ratio P of transactions balances to income. The solution to this system, equation (5), shows that income will gradually increase from zero, with no initial jump, finally asymptotically approaching its long-run value $Y = \Delta I / \sigma$. Equation (2) shows that, as a result of this process, M_1 balances will rise by P times the rise in Y.

A simulation on the machine shows exactly the time path just described for income and for transactions balances. On the settings of the model which I used, the process lasts for between two and four minutes, which, according to the parameterisation of the model, corresponds to between one and two years of real time (chapter 10, pp. 74–5).

At one level all this is now very well understood in macroeconomics. But the major additional benefit obtained from conducting this experiment on the machine is insight into the operation of stock-flow identities. In particular, the building up of transactions money holdings is made to obey stock-flow constraints in a significant manner. In standard macroeconomic treatments, the build up of transactions balances does not produce a lag of the kind which is central to the operation of the above process. If more transactions balances are needed, we would normally say, agents exchange securities for money. (In this experiment they would be able to do this at a completely fixed interest rate.) In the standard textbook version of the story, it is *not* the case that the process of the building up of the extra working balances, *by causing (output and) income to lag behind expenditure,* actually determine the dynamic process by which expenditure income and output adjust to aggregate demand. By contrast, in the machine this happens because income and output are explicitly tied to the level of $M1$ balances (see my comments on equation (2) above).

The ability of the machine to make this issue clear is extraordinary. This idea – that transactions holdings of money are an *impediment* to the circular flow of income – was one of Robertson's central messages.[9] This same idea was also at the centre of the real-balance-effect revolution described by Patinkin (1965), and crucial to Friedmanite monetarism (Friedman 1968, 1969, 1970), to the monetary approach to the balance of payments (Frenkel and Johnson 1976), to the macroeconomics of Godley and Cripps (1985), and to the cash-in-advance monetarism of Lucas and Stokey (1987). An understanding of the workings of the machine might have helped to smooth many of the controversies about those works.

(b) The multiplier with a constant quantity of money

Consider again an increase in investment, when the quantity of money is fixed (see chapter 10, section II.3, and FD example 2). We fix the quantity of money by disconnecting the surplus balances tank from the draining hose (see label 12) by means of a plug. Any excess of investment over saving will now cause the level in the surplus balances tank to fall, which is the machine's representation of a *rise* in the interest rate.[10]

We now increase investment by shifting open the valve on the left-hand side of the investment flow[11] but leaving the function on the right-hand side (label 5) in place, so that investment now depends on the interest rate. The flow of total expenditure is thereby increased. In equilibrium the full effect of such an expenditure increase will – as in the previous exercise – be 'multiplied'. But there will now be an offset to the multiplier. During the course of adjustment, investment will be greater than saving and surplus balances will be drained down (that is, the interest rate will have increased). This will depress investment through the function which relates investment to the interest rate (label 5), and it may also depress consumption (see label 4) and thereby increase saving. So the multiplier will be lower than in the previous constant-interest-rate case;

a fact that we are of course completely familiar with from IS-LM analysis.

As in the previous constant-interest-rate case, output will only gradually increase following the increase in investment, because the need to build up M_1 balances means that there is a lag in the circular flow of income. At first sight it might appear that the gradual draining away of surplus balances (because investment is greater than saving during the adjustment process) might introduce additional dynamic complications. But this is not so. With a constant money supply, all of any reduction in surplus balances caused by the excess of investment over saving flows down to the bottom of the machine and ends up as an increase in transactions balances. We shall see that tracking the dynamics caused by the gradual buildup of these transactions balances is sufficient to track the full dynamics of the system.

The operation of the dynamic process whereby, on the machine, income is driven to its equilibrium level can now be explained. It is helpful for this discussion to have figure 10.2 and the algebra in chapter 10 (pp. 79–80) to hand. The following additional equations must now be added to the system discussed in the previous section:

(1) any increase in M_1 balances must, as explained above, exactly match any rundown in M_2 balances (equation (7));
(2) the demand for surplus balances is a negative function of the rate of interest (which is captured by the sloping right-hand side of the surplus balances tank); and
(3) (as already discussed above) investment is a negative function of the interest rate (equation (9)) and saving may depend on the interest rate as well as on income (equation (10)).

A dynamic equation for income, equation (11), immediately follows, showing that the rate of change of income is proportional to the gap between injections and leakages, where this gap is now influenced by the dampening of investment injections and the increase in saving leakages caused by the rise in the interest rate. The solution to this system, equation (12), shows that income will gradually increase from zero, with no initial jump, finally asymptotically approaching its long-run value, $Y = \Delta I/[\sigma + (P/\lambda)(\eta - \xi)]$. The full multiplier is lower than in the constant-interest-rate case and the speed at which the full equilibrium value is approached is faster. It is also possible to write a dynamic equation for the interest rate, which gradually increases from zero, with no initial jump, asymptotically approaching a long-run value of $(P/\lambda)Y$.

We can see very clearly what has just been described in the workings of the machine. We can see vividly, during the adjustment process, the level of transactions balances tank rises as the level of surplus balances tank falls, and we can observe the impacts of the resulting interest rate changes on flows out of and into the circular flow. We can then verify the effects of these influences on the magnitude of the multiplier and the timing of the adjustment process.

At one level, all of this is very familiar from a dynamic IS-LM analysis. The economy is always on the LM curve, along which the rate of interest is determined so as to equate the demand for money to the fixed supply. But the economy only adjusts gradually towards the IS curve, along which saving equals investment. An outward shift in the IS curve thus leads to a *gradual* movement up along the LM curve to a new equilibrium with higher income and higher interest rates.

But by conducting this experiment on the machine, we obtain an additional insight into the operation of stock-flow identities. In particular, the running down of surplus balances is connected with the stock-flow identities of transactions balances in a significant manner. In standard macroeconomic treatments, the running down of speculative balances happens because, when more transactions balances are needed, agents exchange securities for money. The amount by which the interest rate will rise depends on the increase in the interest rate on securities which is necessary to induce, in aggregate, the holders of speculative balances to part with the extra cash needed for transactions purposes. But here we see very clearly (figure 10.2) that if injections are to increase ahead of leakages speculative balances *must* be run down. Investors issue securities (not modelled here) to get the money to pay for investment, the spending of that money adds to the circular flow of income and the rate of injection of this extra money is – must be – exactly equal to the rate at which extra money is trapped in transactions balances in the course of the circular income flow. Eventually income adjusts to a level at which it just equals expenditures and so no new money is being added to transactions balances; but at that point the circular flow must be such that saving withdrawals will just equal investment injections, and speculative balances will no longer be in the process of being run down.[12]

(c) The effect of an increase in the quantity of money

Consider now an exogenous increase in the quantity of money, after which the quantity of money is held fixed (see chapter 10, section II.5; and FD example 3). The relevant formal dynamic system is the same as that discussed in the previous section, and it produces the solutions for the interest rate and for the level of income shown in the equations in chapter 10 (pp. 82–3).

Phillips provides a full account of the dynamic process (pp. 81–2). The interest rate first falls, and then rises back part of the way during the process of adjustment as the level of income rises. I have simulated this process on the machine and can confirm that it is vividly portrayed.

Again, at one level all of this is very familiar from a dynamic IS-LM analysis. The economy is always on the LM curve, but adjusts only gradually towards the IS curve. Thus the outward shift in the LM curve leads to an initial drop in interest rates, and then a gradual movement along up the LM curve to a new equilibrium with higher income, and with interest rates higher than after the drop but lower than initially.

But at another level 'it is here that I have learned most from the Phillips Machine' (James Meade in a letter to Dennis Robertson, 7 November 1950), and we too can learn something that is not in a conventional IS-LM account. Meade continues[13] by describing how the observer can see: that

(1) the rate of interest is determined initially by the increased amount of 'idle' money relative to the liquidity preference function; that
(2) the fall in the rate of interest causes investment to rise (and possibly saving to fall); that
(3) equilibrium then begins to be restored by rising income bringing saving back into line with investment; but that
(4) the fall in surplus balances during the transition puts upward pressure on the rate of interest, with the consequence that the bringing of saving back into line with investment partly happens through interest rate effects: 'It is in demonstrating the interconnections here that I think the machine is most useful . . .'.

During the process of adjustment to the lower interest rate, investors issue securities (not modelled here) to get the money to pay for investment (and savers may supply less securities); the excess of investment over saving injects extra money into the circular flow of income at a rate which is exactly equal to the rate at which extra money is trapped in transactions balances in the course of the circular income flow. This injecting-and-trapping of money is *not* present in a conventional IS-LM treatment.

The insights provided in this way by the machine enable us to support Phillips' claim that the loanable funds theory and the liquidity preference theory of the interest rate 'are neither inconsistent with each other ... nor merely different ways of saying the same thing ... but complementary parts of a wider system' (chapter 10, p. 81), at least when the latter theory is presented in this 'injecting-and-trapping-manner'. Dennis Robertson appears to have been persuaded. In a letter to James Meade dated 27 August 1950 he wrote:

The account given... of [the] interaction between the effects [denoted by the parameters λ, η, and ξ] is, I think, consistent with that given... on p. 85 of my Essays... and also with Marshall's seminal account (M[oney] C[redit and] C[ommerce] p. 257) of the influence of an increase of gold supplies.

We can give three glosses on Phillips' remarks, in addition to his discussion (chapter 10, pp. 81–3). First, Robertsonian analysis *is* helpful in thinking about the process of transition to the new equilibrium. The draining away of speculative balances during the transition is indeed the consequence of an excess 'demand for loanable funds', and is jointly responsible for the determination of the rate of interest during the transition. Furthermore, if we were to add a 'finance motive' for holding money, then we would put a tank between the 'draining of loanable out of surplus balances' and injection of investment expenditure into the circular flow of income (chapter 10, pp. 85–6). That would create a lag between the draining of loanable funds and the resulting rise in transactions balances and associated rise in income. The consequence of this could be that, after an increase in investment, the interest rate might rise appreciably before much of an increase in income was observed, as Robertson warned repeatedly.[14]

Second, the full equilibrium of the process is – as already described – completely consistent with a fixed-price IS-LM analysis, and Robertsonian loanable funds analysis adds nothing to an understanding of that equilibrium (although it is clear that, in equilibrium, the demand from loanable funds will equal the supply, since the level of the surplus balances tank will not be changing). This is as we would expect from the summary by Patinkin (1965, chapter xv) of the loanable-funds versus liquidity-preference debate.

Third, the machine does not derive the flow of consumption from an underlying demand for a stock of wealth; nor does it derive the flow of investment from a demand for a stock of capital as in Tobin (1969, 1982) and Blinder and Solow (1973). But it does not seem – at least in principle – that it would be impossible to devise additions such as these to the machine. A full equilibrium of such a full stock-flow model would indeed require that the demand for loanable funds by investors (and the government) was consistent with the supply of them by savers.

One final observation to conclude this section. It is not true that 'everything is in the machine' in the way that used to be said that 'everything is in Marshall'. But there is in fact more in the machine on these subjects than is allowed in macroeconomic conventional wisdom. *And it is immensely visible.* It easily stimulates further thoughts and conjectures; and this is also true when considering other aspects of the machine.

1.2 Stocks, flows, lags, and economic cycles

Cycles are introduced into the machine by means of a lagged accelerator system for investment. A lagged accelerator adds two equations to the basic fixed-interest model of chapter 10 (described in section 1.1(a) above). These are shown in chapter 10 (pp. 80–1) as equation (13), which makes the desired level of induced investment a function of the rate of change of income; and equation (14), which makes the actual level of induced investment a lagged response to desired induced investment. The resulting full-system dynamic equation for output, equation (15), makes it clear that cycles occur if induced investment both responds strongly to output, and does so with a lag.[15]

The physical system for representing the lagged accelerator is very clever.

For a point of comparison I first describe the normal method of implementing a 'psychological' lag[16] in the level of a variable, which is explained (on the top of p. 85) in connection with the consumption function (see label 15). In that piece of apparatus, consumption is lifted up and down by electrodes immersed in a very small tank, connected by a hole to the quite small tank[17] which measures the circular flow of income. If the hole in the very small tank is large then the level in that tank will always equal that in the larger tank, and there will be no lag; however if the hole is small then the level in the very small tank will only gradually adjust to the level in the larger tank, thereby enabling consumption to be represented as a lagged function of income.

The device for representing induced investment is different. It is activated (label 14) by means of a:

narrow deep float with a small hole in the bottom, hanging from a spring, and connected by a bent lever to the investment valve. In equilibrium the level of water inside the float will be the same as that inside the M_1 tank, and the position of the valve is that of zero induced investment. If Y is decreasing, the level of M_1 will be falling and will be temporarily below the water level in the float, since the water level inside the float can leak out only slowly. Extra weight will be placed on the spring, which will extend, closing the investment valve a little [label 11], and so causing negative induced investment. Conversely, when Y is increasing induced investment will be positive, being always a lagged function of the rate of change of income (chapter 10, p. 76).

This ingenious arrangement indeed corresponds to the lagged accelerator process described in the previous paragraph and represented by equations (13) and (14). Recall that $M_1 = PY$, that is, that the level of the water in the M_1 tank is, by construction, exactly proportional to the level of income, with a constant of proportionality, P. Let x denote the level of

water in the narrow deep float, and let I denote actual induced investment, which corresponds to the extent of the movement of the lever
connected to the float. Now when $x = PY$ the spring is in balance with
the weight *of the float by itself*; and there is no additional gravitational
force exerted by the water. Induced investment is set at zero at this point.
But when, say, PY falls, the level of water in the tank falls below the level
of that in the float, which will exert downward pressure on the spring and
cause the float to sink in the tank, thereby pulling the lever, closing the
induced investment valve, and causing negative induced investment.
Thus

$$I = \varphi(PY - x), \tag{1}$$

where φ depends both on the resistance of the spring and on the relative
lengths of the two ends of the lever shown in label 11. If this is all there
was to things, then induced investment would simply be proportional to
income. But because of the hole in the bottom of this float, the level of
water in the float gradually adjusts to that in the tank enabling the
abnormal extension of the spring to disappear.
Therefore we may also write

$$dx/dt = \phi(PY - x), \tag{2}$$

where ϕ is larger the bigger the hole.

These two equations thus give a system in which induced investment is
equal φ/ϕ times the rate of change of the level of the water in the narrow
deep float, which in turn is just a lagged measure of income. Thus induced
investment is indeed a function of the rate of change of lagged income.
This corresponds to the idea in equations (13) and (14) that induced
investment has a lag in its response to the rate of change of income; it
simply puts the lag in a different place. If equations (1) and (2) above are
combined with Phillips' equations (1), (2), and (3) in a similar manner to
that described in chapter 10 (pp. 80–1), then the result is an equation for
Y of similar form to equation (15), whose solution may be oscillatory.

Clever though it is, the machine does not, in fact, correspond implicitly
to the capacitor-resistor system which I fiddled around with as an undergraduate. Although the ratio φ/ϕ captures the desired ratio of capital to
output (which is also represented by the coefficient β in equation (13) in
chapter 10), there is no tank (capacitor) to represent the actual capital
stock, and no hint of how a positive flow of investment-minus-
depreciation would be the device by which the actual capital stock was
adjusted to the desired capital stock. And of course, but more disturbing
still, there is no representation of how capital accumulation feeds into the
supply-side of the economy, as emphasised by Harrod (1939), by Hayek

(Hicks 1967, chapter 12), by the Solow–Swan growth model (Solow 1956) and by modern real business cycle theory (McCallum 1989).

Nevertheless we can make a plausible argument that working with his machine would have led Phillips to see the need for all of these things. And by 1961–2, in that remarkable and very early pair of essays (chapters 21 and 22), these things were there, along with a treatment of inflation.

2 The machine as a spur to new intuition

2.1 Control theory and economic policy in a closed economy

Nicholas Barr's essay (chapter 11) describes how Phillips began a Ph.D. in January 1950 under James Meade's supervision, at the same time as building his machine for the LSE. His thesis (1953) led to the justly famous 1954 essay on 'Stabilisation Policy in a Closed Economy' (chapter 16) in which the effects of feedback control policies on a dynamic economy are explored. I believe that the control questions which are addressed in section 1 of chapter 16 are *precisely* those which would have been presented themselves to the inventor of the machine. I thus think of the machine as the progenitor of those papers.

Indeed Phillips was already on to those questions in his 1950 description of the machine. He adds a government sector to the system by introducing a tax leakage, which is related to income (figure 9.1, label 1) and by introducing an expenditure injection (label 2).[18] In describing the function shown at label 2 he writes (chapter 10, p. 85):

Government expenditure, G, is controlled and measured by a valve which may also be operated as a function of income if it is desired to illustrate the stabilising effects of an automatic compensatory fiscal programme.

And at the very end of his description of the machine in the FD paper, Phillips explicitly discusses stabilisation policy, and suggests how the dynamic lags of the multiplier and the accelerator increase its difficulties.

There are two crucial things missing from the machine which prevent it actually simulating the system in section 1 of chapter 16. First, the feedback between income and government expenditure in the machine is only a 'proportional' connection, whereas the analysis in chapter 16 makes use of all of 'proportional, integral and derivative' (PID) control. Second, in the machine, government policy responds to the deviation of output from its desired value with no lag, whereas in chapter 16 there is such a lag. I believe that the machine would have made it plain as daylight that these two missing elements were needed for a full analysis. I also believe that the machine would have suggested how to introduce them algebraically into the mathematical models presented in chapter 10.

Chapter 16 begins with pure proportional control, so that the algebraic treatment initially follows the machine closely. The very first result proved (p. 139) is that with only proportional control, 'complete correction of an error is not achieved, since the correcting action continues only because the error exists'. But we can imagine how experimentation on the machine would have led Phillips immediately to this conclusion well ahead of any algebraic proof. We can see that such experimentation would have led him immediately to thinking about integral control as a means of getting rid of that steady state error. As chapter 16 (pp. 160–1) shows, having seen this, the extra step required in order to introduce integral control into the mathematical model is trivial.

The second result proved in chapter 16 is that proportional control can introduce a cycle into the system – possibly a severe one – if it is applied strongly, *but with a lag*. Again we can see how asking the obvious question when simulating with the machine – 'what if there was a policy response lag?'[19] – could have led to the intuitive discovery of this result, well ahead of any algebraic proof. And we can see too how that could, in turn, have led to the idea of introducing derivative control as a means of dampening the cycle.[20] Again, as chapter 16 (pp. 161–3) shows, having seen this, the extra step required in order to introduce derivative control into the mathematical model is also trivial.

The conclusion of chapter 16 is at one level negative. Badly formulated control policy, applied with a lag, can destabilise the economy. Friedman (1953b) said something similar at exactly the same time. Whereas Phillips' argument proceeds by means of deterministic differential equations, Friedman argued by means of variances. If economic activity is subject to exogenous stochastic shocks, then a government policy which introduces further shocks can end up increasing, rather than reducing, the variance of economic activity, unless the covariance between the government policy shocks and the exogenous shocks is sufficiently negative. Because of the lags in the formulation, implementation, and effect of policy, Friedman thought that this requirement was unlikely to be satisfied. The conclusions of Phillips' later essay on this subject (chapter 17, p. 180) were even more pessimistic:

[the problem of] economic stabilisation is, even in principle, a very intricate one, and . . . a much more thorough investigation of both theoretical principles and empirical relationships would be needed before detailed policy recommendations could be justified.

Nevertheless, Phillips' response to this problem was not that of Friedman (1953c, 1968) – to declare macroeconomic policy making too difficult, and worse still, too dangerous. Instead Phillips concluded chapter 17 on a doubly optimistic, if cautious, note. He calls for the use of multivariable control to regulate multiple objectives in an economy around a growing trend, in the face of multiple disturbances. He notes also that methods for doing this are 'becoming available'. He also calls for econometric estimation of the parameters of the econometric model necessary for the study of such regulation. His 1961–1962 essays were a remarkable response to his own call, as indeed was his estimation of the Phillips Curve. We would not have expected otherwise from the maker of the machine.

I like to think that Phillips would have approved of the project on which I worked during the 1980s, directed by James Meade. We carried out a detailed macroeconomic policy investigation, of as practical kind as possible, using control methods on an estimated model. The policy objectives – inflation and wealth accumulation – were different from the one – income – which Phillips originally used himself. And the introduction of forward-looking variables into the model, along with asset-price jump variables, added an extra degree of complexity. But the use of PID feedback rules from policy targets to the policy instruments was very much in the Phillips tradition.[21]

2.2 Full employment, inflation, and price flexibility

The treatment of prices in the Phillips Machine is unsatisfactory. Phillips acknowledged this, calling it 'rough and cumbersome' (chapter 10, p. 76) and, in a letter to Dennis Robertson dated 19 September 1950, 'clumsy'. I conjecture that the use of his machine might have led Phillips not only to a recognition of the real nature of the problem, but also to his formulation of the theoretical Phillips Curve (chapter 16, 1954) in response to this problem, well before the empirical Phillips Curve appeared (chapter 25, 1958). Finally, I wonder whether use of his machine might have suggested the remarkable demonstration in chapter 16 that too much price flexibility can be destabilising.

First, the treatment of prices in the machine is as follows. Income in the machine, Y, is argued to be in money units (not real units). But a relationship can be constructed between money income (on the horizontal axis, say) and real income (on the vertical axis), made non-linear and asymptoting towards the horizontal, in order to represent the fact that increases in money aggregate demand call forth less and less of an increase in real income as full employment is approached: 'Any relationship [in the machine] given in real units can then be converted into an equivalent relationship in money units, and the graph of the latter used on the machine.'

For this formulation to work, we require that there be a (static) relationship between the *level* of prices and the *level* of real output. But in the letter to Robertson dated 19 September 1950, Phillips suggests that he already did not really believe that such a relationship exists. Twice he talks about what happens 'when prices begin to rise' in the approach to full employment. This suggests a relationship between the *rate of change* of prices and the *level* of real output.

By 1954 this suggestion had blossomed into a fully fledged Phillips Curve (chapter 16, pp. 149–51).[22] But that is not all. First, there is a full technical discussion of how the price flexibility induced by such a Phillips Curve might help to regulate the economy around the full employment level of activity at which prices are not changing. Secondly, there is a formal proof of the idea presented by Keynes in chapter 20 of the *General Theory* that too much price flexibility can be destabilising, a proposition which has been formally – and as far as I can see – independently reproved by Tobin (1975) and Hahn and Solow (1995). Thirdly, there is a formal analysis of a system in which *both* price flexibility and macroeconomic policy together regulate the economy around the full employment level. This last exercise is especially remarkable in that Phillips takes the desired level of production to which the economy is to be regulated as 'that which would result in a constant level of product prices' (chapter 16, p. 150). He does not fall into the trap, which so many others did subsequently, of believing that the Phillips Curve would provide a stable menu of choice along which higher inflation could be traded for higher output. And, since he does not contemplate the possibility that policy makers might aim for a level of employment higher than the zero inflation level, his analysis would not have been vulnerable to the time-inconsistency critique of Barro and Gordon (1983a).[23]

It would be far fetched to argue that all of this would have been obvious on the machine. But I would argue that working on the machine might well have prompted all three of these pieces of analysis.

2.3 *Internal and external balance*

The final few paragraphs of chapter 10 discusses the conduct of macroeconomic policy in an open economy. James Meade (1951a) described this question extensively in *The Balance of Payments* and Trevor Swan (1968) immortalised the problems of finding policies for external and internal balance.[24] Three aspects of these problems are briefly mentioned in this section.

(a) The dynamics of policy adjustment

Just why the machine was a marvellous intuitive aid in helping to discuss these problems is made clear by section 7 of FD. Meade (1951a) and Swan (1968) present essentially static frameworks. The machine is dynamic; and there are many difficult dynamic problems in this area.

Section 7 of FD describes the potential for instability caused by the separately operated, and lagged, adjustment of fiscal and exchange rate policies in the pursuit of external and internal balance. LSE legend describes how generations of students were intuitively educated by Meade and Phillips in these matters. These issues were subsequently discussed semi-formally but verbally by Swan (1960) and the mathematics of an analogous assignment problem were studied by Mundell (1962). Vines, Maciejowski and Meade (1983) used multivariable versions of the feedback control techniques first introduced by Phillips (chapter 17) to discuss exactly this control problem on an empirical model.[25]

(b) The foreign exchange market and exchange rate determination

The formulation of the foreign exchange market in the machine is worthy of some comment. Imports (and exports) depend on domestic expenditures, not on income, as in many less carefully formulated models[26] (labels 6 and 7). Both imports and exports also depend on the exchange rate (labels 8 and 9). The exchange rate can be held fixed or allowed to float, alternatives which are analogous to the two treatments available for the rate of interest. In the former case, the system can describe the gradual dynamic operation of a gold standard system. In the latter case the exchange rate depends on foreign holdings of sterling balances, which are cumulated from the past excess of imports over exports, relative to the desire to hold these balances: as the balances rise the exchange rate is forced to depreciate. The balance of trade is not immediately self regulating, but correction takes place gradually alongside the building up and down of foreign holdings of sterling balances. This process introduces another dynamic lag into the operation of the macroeconomic system.

There are no capital flows in the above treatment.

But a moment's thought suggests that the machine could immediately be amended to describe the Mundell–Fleming model with perfect capital mobility. Fix the domestic money supply. Disconnect the exchange rate from the foreign sterling balances tank. Put electrodes in the surplus balances tank and connect them up to the exchange rate, making the exchange rate appreciate whenever there is any tendency for the domestic interest rate to rise and vice versa. Such a setup would ensure that any tendency of an increase in the demand for domestic output to raise the rate of interest would induce just that crowding out of net exports required to prevent this happening.

Simulating such a system would make it clear that a sustained increase in domestic aggregate demand (e.g., in investment) would cause a *gradual* – and completely predictable – appreciation of the exchange rate, because of the lagged operation of the multiplier. A moment's thought would then suggest that because of such a predictable gradual exchange rate appreciation, it would be unreasonable to suppose that the domestic interest rate stayed equal to the foreign interest rate. Such an exercise would quickly lead the experimenter on to a fixed-price version of the Dornbusch exchange rate model.

(c) International policy coordination

Nicholas Barr (chapter 11) describes how James Meade joined two machines together in the early 1950s in order to display in the LSE classroom the consequences of a lack of international policy coordination. It took thirty years after this for the theory of international macroeconomic policy coordination to emerge from the work of Hamada and others. Even now, the essential insights of that modern theory have become static ones – that if separate countries pursue separate domestic policy objectives in such a way as to impose externalities on each other, then the outcome will be globally inefficient. By contrast the policy coordination problems simulated in the LSE classroom on two machines were intrinsically dynamic ones. We can imagine that the machines illustrated very vividly the potentially destabilising effects of uncoordinated global economic policy.

Conclusion

The Phillips Machine is now nearly fifty years old. It is not state-of-the-art theoretically or mechanically. It cannot do microfoundations, or intertemporal optimisation, and it does not portray asset demand functions for wealth and capital. Nevertheless, the machine is not merely of historical interest.

First of all, the macroeconomics which the machine describes – 'hydraulic Keynesianism' – remains at the heart of modern extended dynamic macroeconomic models, even though these also have the extra modern features just mentioned. Looking at the machine can still give us heightened insight into the stock flow aspects of this hydraulic Keynesianism. Secondly, I have argued that working with the machine gave Phillips insights which led on to his extraordinarily powerful subsequent work. And finally I have shown how looking at the machine today can still enable us to visualise very vividly modern theoretical developments; for example in cycle theory, in dynamic control, in exchange rate economics and in international policy coordination.

The Phillips Machine is thus, I believe, a 'progressive' model, in the sense of Kuhn (1962); like Fultz's dish, and unlike Santucci's globe.

Appendix: National income monetary flow demonstrator

A.W.H. Phillips
This is the text of the operating manual which Phillips prepared as a guide for users of his machine, reprinted here without alteration.

Operational notes

    General notes
        To start the machine, first adjust the 'credit' and 'exchange rate' boxes (12 and 13, figure 9.1) to a suitable height at about the middle of their range, and see that the plugs are out. Then switch on the pumps and wait about a quarter of a minute before bringing national income into equilibrium somewhere near the centre of the income scale. Perhaps the easiest way to bring the machine into equilibrium is to set taxes equal to government expenditure, imports equal to exports, and investment to any desired figure, and then adjust the right-hand consumption valve until income remains steady at any desired value.

When first starting the machine always check the following two points:
1 See that the constant level floats in the investment expenditure tube and the exports tube are floating freely, and maintaining a constant level of water over their respective valves. If they are sticking, they can be lifted out with a piece of hooked wire, wiped clean and replaced, though it may be sufficient to tap the tube or move the float up and down a few times to remove any dirt that may be causing it to stick.
2 Check that the servo-motor mechanism on the boxes measuring income after taxes and domestic expenditure are operating correctly. The electrodes suspended in the small tubes at the side of the boxes (15 and 16) should always move to a position in which they are just dipping in the water in the tubes.

The readings on the various scales may be found not consistent with one another, and this is due in part to basic errors in the machine. No attempt has been made to achieve a high degree of accuracy. Occasional adjustment of the lengths of the cords may be necessary if the inconsistencies are to be kept to a minimum, and considerable errors may be introduced if any of the slots get blocked with dirt; but these points should be checked during regular maintenance of the machine.

In operating the machine, an appreciable error will be introduced if the flow through the taxation valve is greater than the sum of the flows through the government expenditure and the investment valves. In this case the excess will pass through the overflow tube into the spare tank at the back of the machine.

It should be remembered that the quantity of water in the system is controlled by both 'credit' and the 'exchange rate' control boxes (12 and 13) if the plugs are out. If the 'credit' plug is in while the 'exchange rate' plug is out, the quantity of water will be falling if there is a balance of payments deficit and rising if there is a balance of payments surplus and consequently income and the rate of interest will be moving in a way tending to restore balance of payments equilibrium.

Examples of the use of the machine

   1 Simple multiplier with constant rate of interest and constant prices, in a closed economy

(i) Take off all graphs, except the consumption function (3) and interest rate-investment function (5).

(ii) Shut off taxes, government expenditure, imports and exports, and set investment to any convenient value.

(iii) Switch on the pumps, and bring the machine into equilibrium with income at about the middle of the scale, by adjusting the right-hand consumption valve.

(iv) The rate of interest should be 'pegged' by setting the credit box (12) to any suitable height and taking the plug out of it.

(v) Switch on the recorders, and check that income and the rate of interest are remaining steady.

(vi) Increase or decrease investment expenditure (or consumption expenditure) by any convenient amount. Income will gradually rise or fall to a new equilibrium level determined by the usual multiplier formula. A number of different consumption functions are provided so that different values of the multiplier can be shown.

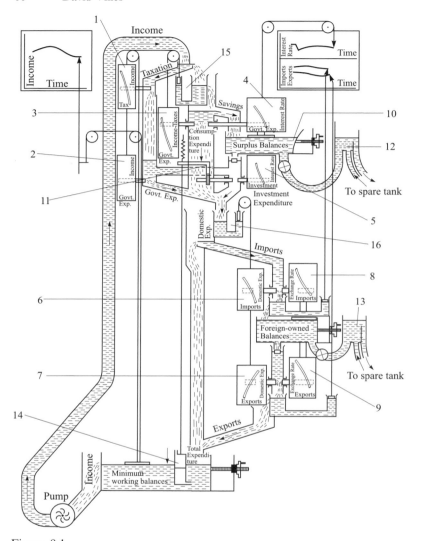

Figure 9.1

2 Simple multiplier with fixed quantity of money

Proceed as in the preceding example, but put the plugs in the credit box (12) and in the exchange rate box (13) before finally bringing the machine into equilibrium. Income will rise or fall by a multiple of the initial change of investment or consumption expenditure, while the rate of interest will move in the same direction as income. The extent to which the usual multiplier will be damped down by the changes induced in the rate of interest will depend on (i) the extent to which the rate of interest rises as money is drawn into transaction balances from idle hoards, i.e., the position of the liquidity preference function (10), and (ii) the extent to which a given change in the rate of interest directly changes investment and consumption expenditure, i.e., the shape of functions (4) and (5). (Any desired relationship between the rate of interest and saving can be obtained by inserting a graph relating the rate of interest to consumption expenditure (4), saving being the residual of income after the payment of taxes, less consumption expenditure.)

3 The rate of interest

A demonstration of the determination of the rate of interest can conveniently follow the preceding example. With the machine now in equilibrium and the quantity of money fixed, introduce a change in liquidity preference (10) by screwing the end of the top tank in or out. In the case of an increase in liquidity preference (movement of the end of the tank outwards), there will be an immediate rise in the rate of interest; but this will reduce investment and perhaps increase saving (if a negatively sloped function 4 has been attached), so that income will begin to fall. The excess of saving over investment leads to a gradual increase in surplus balances as money released from transaction balances is 'hoarded', so that in the absence of any further change in liquidity preference the rate of interest gradually falls back towards its original value.

How far the return will go depends on the relationship between income, on the one hand, and investment and saving, on the other. If they were unrelated the rate of interest would return completely to its original value. The stronger the relationship between income and saving, i.e., the greater the marginal propensity to save or the lower the marginal propensity to consume (function 3 on figure 9.1), the less will the rate of interest drift back towards its original value. The stronger the relationship between income and investment, i.e., the greater the marginal propensity to invest (which is not included on the machine) or the greater the acceleration coefficient (determined by the height of the lever 11, figure 9.1) the further will the rate of interest return. If changes in income affect investment more strongly than they affect saving, the rate of interest will temporarily return beyond its initial value.

4 Changes in the quantity of money

The effect of changes in the quantity of money on both the rate of interest and income, both immediately and after the full effects have worked themselves out, can be shown with the same setting of the

machine as in the preceding example. Instead of changing liquidity preference to initiate a disturbance, change the quantity of money by removing the plug from the credit box (12), raising or lowering the box to
increase or decrease the quantity of money in the system, and then replacing the plug and watching the effect on the income and the rate of interest
recorders. An increase in the quantity of money will be found to have the
same effect as a decrease in liquidity preference had in the preceding
example, and a decrease in the quantity of money will have the same
effect as an increase in liquidity preference.

5 More complex multipliers

The preceding demonstrations can be repeated with wider systems of relationships. Taxes and government expenditure can be included
by inserting an income-taxation graph (1) and either leaving government
expenditure independent or linking it in a desired way to income (2).

To introduce foreign trade with a fixed rate of exchange, 'peg' the rate
of exchange at any level by means of the exchange equalisation account
box (13) and insert graphs of the propensity to import (6) and the foreign
exchange elasticities (8) and (9). The investment multiplier then becomes

$$\frac{\Delta 1(1 - m)}{1 - c(1 - t)(1 - m)},$$

where m is the marginal propensity to import, t is the marginal 'propensity to tax', and c is the marginal propensity to consume, all in money
terms.

Again, if prices begin to rise at a certain income level, all these propensities change in value and the necessary adjustments to the curves can
be made either by hand or by using kinked curves. For instance, imports
can be made to rise more rapidly when prices begin to rise. It is also
possible to insert a relationship between domestic expenditure and
exports (7), kinked at about the full employment level of expenditure,
so that exports fall off as expenditure rises above this level.

With this number of relationships and assumptions concerning the
effects of price changes there is not much chance of getting very precise
numerical multiplier results on the machine. But since, under conditions
of rising prices there is not much chance of getting them in reality either,
this is not a very great disadvantage from the point of view of exposition.

6 The accelerator

Before connecting up the accelerator (level 11, figure 9.1), it is
advisable to bring the machine into equilibrium with income somewhere
near the centre of the scale, and with the left-hand investment valve in

such a position that it is free to move in either direction. The machine may be set up with either a fixed quantity of money or with a 'pegged' rate of interest, and as either a closed or an open economy.

The equilibrium should be maintained long enough for the water inside the container (14) hanging in the bottom tank to reach the same level as that in the tank itself. (After a little practice, it may be found quicker to adjust the level in the bottom tank to that in the inner container, rather than wait for the latter to become the same as the former.) The bent lever (11) operating the investment valve should then be connected to the cord from which the container is hanging, without disturbing the value of investment expenditure.

If any small change is then made in the system, investment expenditure will move as a lagged function of the rate of change of income. The form of the time path of income will depend on the values of four parameters, the values of acceleration coefficient, the lag in the accelerator, the expenditure–income lag, and the marginal 'leakages from the system'. For certain values of these parameters, income will move directly to the new equilibrium level given by the usual multiplier, but at a more rapid rate; for other values it will approach this point through a series of damped oscillations. With different values again, income may move in a series of increasing oscillations, or may diverge cumulatively without reaching any equilibrium.

To obtain oscillatory conditions on the machine, the bent lever (11) should be put at about the middle of its adjustment, to give moderate values of the acceleration coefficient, and the leakage adjustment screw in the container (14) should be unscrewed about one and a half to two turns from its fully closed position, which gives about a satisfactory accelerator lag. (Alteration of the leakage screw also alters the acceleration coefficient, for a given position of the lever.) With fairly large 'leakages', say a multiplier of about two, the oscillations will be heavily damped. With smaller leakages (i.e., larger values of the multiplier) the oscillations will be wider, while with still smaller leakages the system will become explosive, that is, the income reading will move right to the top or bottom of the scale and remain there.

To introduce the initial change into the system, any one of the valves on the machine should be moved about one quarter inch in either direction. If the initial movement is much smaller than this, the accelerator may be prevented by friction from coming into action, while, if it is much greater, the resulting swings in income may be very large.

7 Internal and external balance

Some of the problems involved in maintaining an economy in both internal balance (stable national income near the 'full employment' level), and in external balance (no surplus or deficit on the balance of payments) can be demonstrated on the machine. Since only balance of current trade is shown on the machine it must be assumed that there are no capital movements. The procedure is as follows:

(i)   Put functions 1, 3, 5, 6, 8, 9 and, if desired, 7 on the machine.

(ii) Peg the rate of interest by setting the credit box (12) at a suitable height.

(iii) Peg the rate of exchange at about the middle of the scale by adjusting the height of the exchange rate box (13). The plugs of both boxes should be out.

(iv) Disconnect the accelerator.

(v)   Choose a 'full employment' level of income, a suitable value being rather above half full scale, and bring the machine into equilibrium at this income, with a balanced budget and imports equal to exports. The right-hand consumption valve and left-hand investment valve can be adjusted to keep income steady under those conditions.

(vi) Switch on the recorders and check that income, imports, exports and the rate of interest are constant.

(vii) Introduce a change into the system, e.g., a fall in exports caused by a depression abroad or by a shift of overseas demand away from the home country's goods. Income will gradually fall by a multiple of the fall in exports. The rate at which foreign reserves are being lost will be shown by the gap between the imports and exports pens, and the quantity of reserves which have been lost, by the area between the graphs of imports and exports.

(viii) Apply a full employment policy by reducing taxes, increasing government expenditure, or expanding credit and so lowering the rate of interest, until full employment income or 'internal balance' is regained. It will be seen that the external deficit, which had fallen as income fell, is now greater than after the initial fall in exports.

(ix) To regain external balance, devalue the currency by raising the exchange equalisation box (13). Alternatively, put the plug in the box, so letting the rate of exchange depreciate on a free market. Imports and exports will then become equal.

(x)   The attainment of external balance will be seen to have upset the internal balance previously obtained by the full employment policy. Income will now be rising, and to stabilise it again the measures previously introduced to stimulate internal demand will have to be reversed.

The simultaneous attainment of internal and external balance can be made still more difficult by connecting up the accelerator. It is then a good exercise to detail one student to try to maintain internal balance by continuous adjustment of credit and annual adjustments of the budget, and another to try to maintain external balance by, say, annual adjustments of the rate of exchange. A change made by either will upset the attempts of the other unless their efforts are co-ordinated, and the dynamic lags of the multiplier and the accelerator will further increase their difficulties.

Notes

I am grateful to Bob Rowthorn for helpful discussions, to Steven Wright for helping me to simulate the machine, to Donald Moggridge for showing me letters about the machine between Phillips, Robertson, Meade and Newlyn, and to Robert Leeson and Geoff Harcourt for helpful comments on an earlier draft.

1 I did not ask Meade how this opinion connected with his view of Keynes, who inspired in him a mixture of awe, admiration and respect, and who he clearly thought of as a different sort of genius.
2 See the introductory notes to chapters 10, 16 and 17.
3 In particular, I would have liked to ask him more about the way in which work on the machine led to Phillips' work on stabilisation policy.
4 The device shown at labels 3 and 15 relates the level of consumption flow to the level of income flow. It does so by a clever piece of apparatus described in chapter 10 (pp. 83–5). A pair of water-sensitive electrodes are suspended in a little tank with a slit in its side, the *level* of water in which represents the (rate of) *flow* of income. (If the flow rate is higher, then the little tank will fill to a higher level before the flow rate out of it is equal to the flow rate in.) If the level of water rises then both of the electrodes are immersed in the water, and this switches on a motor which then raises the electrodes, and the thread connected to them, along with the water level; and vice versa if the water level falls. By contrast taxes (label 1) are related to income by a much simpler device: they are connected to a long wire down to a float in the level of working balances. At first sight that seems odd. But since (chapter 10, beginning of section II and notes 4 and 5) the model is set up so that there is exactly a one-to-one relationship between the *stock* level of those working balances and the *flow* level of income, this enables taxes to be made a function of income in a much simpler manner to that in which consumption is connected to disposable income. The reason that consumption is treated in a more complex way is that it depends on the flow of *post-tax income*, and there is no large tank the level of which is proportional to this flow. Similar electrode arrangements are necessary for the determination of imports as a function of domestic expenditure (label 6). By contrast it is possible to make the dependence of imports and exports (labels 8 and 9) on the exchange rate operate by means of a simple float mechanism without any electrodes, since the exchange rate itself is supposed to depend on the level of foreign-owned sterling balances in the tank below label 8.

5 Such an assumption amounts to assuming that the stock output ratio is equal to the time taken for money balances to circulate around the system. Empirical estimates of the latter time period are discussed in chapter 10 (pp. 77–5).

6 See chapter 10, note 5, and the insert to figure 10.2.

7 On the machine investment can be bigger than saving, and expenditure can be bigger than income, because of the way in which Phillips defines income. Income does *not* include receipts from those expenditures which are satisfied by producers by sales from stocks. (In national income accounts, of course, such receipts are treated as income.)

8 And after taxation, in a more general model with a government sector.

9 See his discussions with Keynes (XIII, 493 524; XIV, 86–100).

10 Notice that the interest rate graph at the top right-hand side of figure A is connected to a float in the surplus balances tank by means of an inverting mechanism: it registers a rise in the interest rate when the level of the water in the tank falls.

11 The accelerator (label 11) is of course disconnected, making this side free to move.

12 It is fascinating to realise that Phillips had not understood all this when writing his first document proposing the machine, in the paper to which Walter Newlyn refers in chapter 8. As a result, the idea for a machine depicted in Figure 10.1 in that chapter is flawed. The figure does not specify what happens to the money which is injected out of the M_2 tank and into the circular flow of income when investment increases: there is no transactions balances tank in which such money can build up. However without such a tank, there is no lag in the circular flow of income, and savings can never differ from investment. Keynesian macroeconomics becomes impossible. When first looking at this figure, I thought that 'any old lag' between expenditure and income would be good enough (for example, a lag between sales and output) and that one does not necessarily need an explicit transaction–balances tank. But that will not do the trick, because one still needs to know 'where the money goes'.

13 I paraphrase and reorder his letter slightly.

14 See the earlier reference in n. g above to Robertson's discussions with Keynes, and also the discussion in Kahn (1984).

15 'The relationship between income and induced investment must be lagged in some way if the system is to be oscillatory' (chapter 10, p. 80).

16 Phillips (p. 85) defines the kind of 'psychological' lag being described as one 'caused by inertia in the changing of habits'. He compares it with a 'structural' lag, like that associated with the withdrawal of money from the circular flow of income when M_1 balances are being built up. For a description of how the physical implementation of such a psychological lag differs from the physical implementation of a structural lag on the machine, see the next endnote.

17 This second 'quite small' tank is *large enough* to have a level which measures the flow of post-tax income. (Just like the M_1 tank there is a slit in its side so that outflow adjusts to inflow at a higher level when inflow is larger.) And it is

large relative to the very small tank. But it is *small enough* so that the withdrawal of income from the circular flow which happens when this tank fills up is, to a first approximation, negligible.

18 Phillips is careful [303] to ensure that an excess of government expenditure over taxation acts as a drain on surplus balances (as the government 'competes for loanable funds') and that the opposite happens if the government has a surplus of taxation over expenditure. This connection is effected by horizontal pipe running between the government expenditure function (label 2) and the investment function (label 5).

19 One could easily introduce a policy response lag here in the machine, in the same way that 'psychological' lags can be introduced elsewhere. See an earlier endnote.

20 Section 1.7 of chapter 16 provides evidence for this conjecture, as the effects of derivative control are there described as introducing into the system the same type of relationship as that postulated by the acceleration principle, but operating in reverse – in a stabilising rather than a destabilising direction. Phillips was familiar with the destabilising effects of the accelerator from the machine (see above). It would have required quite a small intuitive leap to imagine policy designed to operate like the accelerator, but in reverse.

21 See Weale *et al.* (1989). The penultimate chapters of that book provide a kind of 'practitioners guide' for actually doing control exercises, much in the spirit of Phillips (chapter 17).

22 The quotation by Leeson (1997, 166) of a 1993 letter from Friedman suggests that Phillips had already made the transition by 1952.

23 Leeson (1997) argues persuasively, with strong supporting evidence, that Phillips did not see his curve as providing a stable menu of choice along which higher inflation could be traded for lower unemployment. It is not possible to go on from this and argue, at least on the basis of chapter 16, that Phillips clearly saw that any attempt to exploit such a trade-off would lead to an acceleration of inflation. This is because, although in that chapter there is a clear understanding that inflationary expectations may be formed in an adaptive manner – with either regressive or extrapolative features – there is not the extra equation that would make current inflation the sum of an excess demand term and this inflationary expectation. The excess demand term is there, but no formal equation for the inflation expectation and therefore no formal treatment of its adaptation. Leeson has argued to me in discussion, and I think correctly, that Phillips was not interested in formal (and pathological) analysis of the policy outcomes which would result from attempting to exploit a Phillips Curve trade-off at non-trivial rates of inflation.

24 The original draft of the latter paper was written at the same time as Meade's work, and perhaps even before.

25 The final part of Vines, Maciejowski and Meade (1983), written by Maciejowski, provides an exceptionally clear account of the relevant methods.

26 Imports also depend on expenditures in Meade's (1951a) *Balance of Payments*.

10 Mechanical Models in Economic Dynamics

A.W. Phillips

E10
322
331

There has been an increasing use in economic theory of mathematical models, usually in the form of difference equations, sometimes of differential equations, for investigating the implications of systems of hypotheses. However, those students of economics who, like the present writer, are not expert mathematicians, often find some difficulty in handling these models effectively. This article describes an attempt to develop some mechanical models which may help non-mathematicians by enabling them to see the quantitative changes that occur in an interrelated system of variables following initial changes in one or more of them. One model has been made for the University of Leeds, a second and improved version is now being made for the London School of Economics.

I

Fundamentally, the problem is to design and build a machine the operations of which can be described by a particular system of equations which it may be found useful to set up as the hypotheses of a mathematical model, in other words, a calculating machine for solving differential equations. Since, however, the machines are intended for exposition rather than accurate calculation, a second requirement is that the whole of the operations should be clearly visible and comprehensible to an onlooker. For this reason hydraulic methods have been used in preference to electronic ones which may have given greater accuracy and flexibility, the machines being made of transparent plastic ('Perspex') tanks and tubes, through which is pumped coloured water. The accuracy obtained depends on the precision with which the machines are constructed, but there is no difficulty in keeping it within about ±4 per cent.

Both of the models mentioned above deal with macroeconomic theory in terms of money flows; but they are based on an analogy given by

Professor Boulding (1948, 117) to show how the production flow, consumption flow, stocks and price of a commodity may react on one another. Before describing them it will be convenient to show how Boulding's qualitative model can be developed to make the values of the variables and the relationships assumed to hold between them quantitatively precise and to enable shifts in these relationships to be introduced.

In the model shown diagrammatically in figure 10.1, the production flow of a commodity is represented by the flow of water into a tank. This flow is controlled by a valve, consisting of a flat plate sliding horizontally

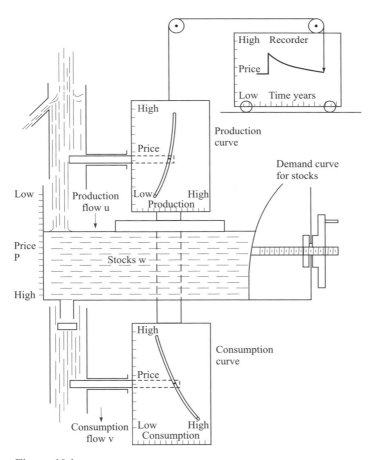

Figure 10.1

over a narrow parallel slot. The head of water over the valve is kept approximately constant by an overflow weir at a fixed height above it, so that the rate of flow of water through the valve is proportional to the length of slot uncovered, and can be measured by a linear scale attached to the valve. The production flow goes into the tank containing stocks, from which is drawn the consumption flow, controlled and measured by a second valve similar to the first. The small float in the consumption tube maintains a constant head of water over the valve, irrespective of the level of water in the tank and of the consumption flow.[1]

Price is assumed to be determined at any instant by the quantity of stocks, represented by the quantity of liquid in the tank, and the demand schedule for them, represented by the capacity of the tank at different levels, and is therefore shown inversely by the height of water in the tank. The tank is rectangular except for one end, the shape and position of which are derived from the demand curve for stocks so as to reproduce on the machine the relationship assumed or found to hold between stocks and price of the commodity. This end of the tank, though water-tight, slides freely when the hand-wheel is turned, enabling a shift in the demand curve for stocks to be introduced.

Attached to a float on the tank is a bar, free to move vertically between guides, and carrying two graphs, a production and a consumption curve, which move in front of their respective valves. Each graph is made by cutting a narrow slot in a thin sheet of plastic; a pin projecting from the end of the valve engages in this slot so that when the float moves the graph vertically, the graph moves the valve horizontally, opening or closing it according to the shape of the curve. The graphs are attached to the bar by spring clips and can be moved in any direction to enable shifts of the production and consumption functions to be introduced. Price can be read off a linear scale (the correct way up) marked along the ordinate of each graph, against a cursor line engraved along the side of the valve.

Given the dimensions of the tank and the valves, the choice of units for the scales determines a time constant for the model. This is perhaps most easily shown by an example. Assume that the price scale is so chosen that the required relationship between stocks and price of a commodity is reproduced on the model when one cubic inch of water is made equivalent to one hundred tons of the commodity. Assume also that the valves are so designed that for every inch of valve opening there is a flow of one hundred cubic inches of water per minute, equivalent to ten thousand tons of the commodity per minute of time on the model. If now scales marked ten thousand tons per year per inch of valve opening are chosen as being most suitable for the actual magnitudes of the production and consumption flows, a time constant has been fixed making one minute of time on the model equivalent to one year in reality. Having determined a time constant it is possible to record the path of the price change induced by a shift in one of the curves. The recorder consists of a clockwork mechanism, carrying a plate to which a chart can be attached, and moving towards the left along rails, at the rate of one inch per minute. With a time constant of one minute equalling one year, the abscissa of the chart can be marked off with a scale of one inch equal to one year. Against the chart rests a recorder pen connected to the graph bar by a thread so that it moves vertically with price, which may be marked along the ordinate of the chart. The pen then traces out a graph of price against time in years. Similar recorders could of course be fitted to the other variables.

It is easy to see from the diagram the results of a shift in one of the functions, from an equilibrium position. A spontaneous increase in consumption (shift of the consumption curve to the right) will result in a gradual decrease in stocks and rise in price. The price rise will induce a contraction of consumption and extension of production (movements along the curves) until a new equilibrium is established with higher values of consumption, production and price than at the previous equilibrium position. A spontaneous increase in production (shift of the production curve to the right) will induce a gradual change to a new equilibrium position, with higher values of production and consumption and a lower price than before the change. A spontaneous increase in the demand for stocks (a shift of the demand curve for stocks, or the end of the tank, to the right) will cause an immediate rise in price and production flow, and a fall in consumption flow. Production now being higher than consumption, stocks will gradually rise, inducing a gradual fall in price and production and a rise in consumption until production and consumption are equal again. If there has been no shift in the consumption and production curves this equality will only be reached when stocks have risen sufficiently to bring the price, and also the production and consumption flows, back to their original values. The shape of the graph of price against time drawn by the recorder will be something like that shown in figure 10.1.

This illustrates an interesting point. Although, on the assumptions of this model, it is correct to say that at every instant of time price is determined only by the quantity of stocks and the demand for them, yet it is also correct to say that the long-term trend of the price is completely unaffected by shifts in the demand curve for stocks, being determined only by the position of the production and consumption curves, that is, the 'flow' functions.

The hydraulic model will give solutions for non-linear systems as easily as for linear ones. It is not even necessary for the relationships to be in analytic form: so long as the curves can be drawn the machine will record the correct solutions, within the limits of its accuracy. In giving the equivalent mathematical model, however, the usual linearity assumption will be made, in view of the difficulty of working with non-linear differential or difference equations.

Let u be the production flow, v the consumption flow, w the stocks and p the price, all measured, for simplicity, from a base at which the system is in equilibrium. We have then, by definition, the identity

$$u - v = \frac{dw}{dt},$$

and three hypotheses,

$$u = lp$$

$$v = mp$$

and

$$w = np$$

where l, m and n are parameters.

If at time $t = 0$, from equilibrium, there is a spontaneous change, Δv, in consumption, then

$$\frac{dw}{dt} = u - (v + \Delta v) = (l - m)p - \Delta v.$$

Also

$$\frac{dp}{dw} = \frac{1}{n}.$$

Therefore

$$\frac{dp}{dt} = \frac{dp}{dw} \cdot \frac{dw}{dt} = \frac{l - m}{n} \cdot p - \frac{\Delta v}{n}$$

or

$$n\frac{dp}{dt} - (l - m)p + \Delta v = 0.$$

The solution of this equation,

$$p = \frac{\Delta v}{l - m}\left(1 - e^{\frac{l-m}{n}\cdot t}\right)$$

gives the path of the induced price change. The stability condition is that $\frac{l-m}{n} < 0$. If it is assumed that price falls as stocks increase, then $n < 0$ and the stability condition is that $1 - m > 0$ or that $l > m$. In this case the price converges exponentially towards the equilibrium value $\frac{\Delta v}{1-m}$ as $t \to \infty$. If $l < m$ the system is explosive.

For a spontaneous change, Δu, in the production flow the induced price change is

$$p = -\frac{\Delta u}{l - m}\left(1 - e^{\frac{l-m}{n} \cdot t}\right).$$

And for a spontaneous change in the demand for stocks, causing an immediate change in price of Δp, the path of the subsequent induced price change is

$$p = -\Delta p\left(1 - e^{\frac{l-m}{n} \cdot t}\right),$$

that is, the price returns to its original equilibrium value.

This simple model could be further developed, in particular by making a distinction between working and liquid stocks,[2] introducing lags into the production and consumption functions,[3] and linking the demand curve for liquid stocks to the rate of change of price through a co-efficient of expectations.[4] Each of these developments would result in an oscillatory system. They will not be considered further here, however; the simple model has been described to show the main principles of the mechanism, which will now be applied to macroeconomic models.

II

1 Description of a simple model

In the model shown in figure 10.2, an economy without foreign trade or government operations is assumed. These simplifying assumptions will be relaxed later. The water in the bottom tank, M_1, represents active or transactions money balances, defined as the minimum working balances needed to carry on a given level of economic activity, and assumed to be a function of income.[5] Income, Y, flows from M_1 through a slot, shown in the inset of figure 10.2. The slot is of such a shape that the rate of flow through it is proportional to the height of water in the tank;[6] the height can therefore be used to measure the income flow, on a linear scale. An electric pump carries the income flow to the top of the model, where it divides into savings, S, and consumption, C.[7]

Savings are controlled by two opposed valves, and measured by the opening between them, consumption being left as a residual. (In a later

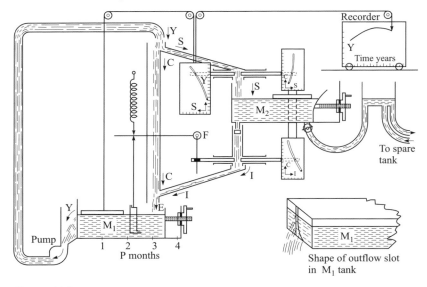

Recorder

Y
Time years

Y
S
C
Y
S
M₂
S
S

To spare
tank

F

C
I
I

Y
E
M₁
Pump
1   2   3   4
P months

M₁
Shape of outflow slot
in M₁ tank

Figure 10.2

model consumption is controlled and savings made the residual.)
Consumption expenditure flows directly back into M_1. Savings flow
into the tank containing idle or surplus balances, M_2, defined as all
money in excess of minimum working balances. Investment expenditure,
I, controlled and measured by two valves, is drawn from M_2 and, combining with consumption to form total expenditure, E, flows into M_1.

To allow for extension or contraction of the supply of money, water is
pumped from a separate tank (not shown in the diagram) into the small
box on the extreme right of the model, the overflow from the box returning to the tank. The box is connected by a flexible tube to the M_2 tank.
The height of the box can be varied to make the level of water in it higher
or lower than that in the M_2 tank, causing a flow to or from M_2 roughly
proportional to the difference between the two levels. A tap in the tube
can be closed when it is desired to operate with a constant quantity of
money.

The time taken for the active balances to circulate once round the
system, equal to M_1/Y, is the reciprocal of the income velocity of circulation of active balances and will be called the circulation period, P. The
actual length of the circulation period seems to be somewhere between
three and four months in England and the United States.[8] On the model,
if the adjustable end of the M_1 tank is vertical, P will be proportional to

the operative length of the tank irrespective of the value of Y, since both M_1 and Y are then proportional to the height of water in the tank. A linear scale may therefore be fitted along the tank, giving the circulating period in months. The position of this scale determines a time constant for the model. If, when the adjustable end of the tank is set at the mark three months on the scale, the time taken for the quantity of water in the tank to flow once round the circuit is half a minute, the time constant is two minutes on the model to one year in reality. A recorder may then be fitted to trace a chart of income against time in years.

When the system is in equilibrium $I = S$, $E = Y$, and the rate of change of M_1 and M_2 is zero. If, from this position there is an increase in investment and therefore in E, Y does not increase immediately by an equal amount, but only gradually as the excess of E over Y gradually increases M_1.

This lag between expenditure and income (and their real counterparts sales and output) occurs because an increase in expenditure and sales at first leads chiefly to a reduction in stocks, and must be transmitted through complex chains of intermediate transactions, some short, others very long, before it produces an equivalent increase in output and income.[9] In the model, there is no lag between income and expenditure, that is, no Robertsonian lag. If, however, we redefine Y to be identical with E, the inflow into M_1, and call the outflow from M_1 'disposable income', we no longer have a sales–output lag but have instead a distributed equivalent of the Robertsonian income–expenditure lag. The operation of the model is in no way affected by the choice between these sets of definitions, which lead to similar results providing the periods of the lags are the same. From empirical evidence[10] it seems that the income–expenditure lag is small in relation to the expenditure–income (or sales–output) lag, so the latter interpretation is used here.

There is, of course, no reason why a model including both lags should not be made. In the mechanical model this would require the inclusion of a small tank, the outflow from which would be proportional to the height of water in it, in the income flow. The inflow to this tank would be income, and the outflow would be the equivalent in continuous analysis terms of Robertsonian disposable income. Water in the first tank would represent business working balances and in the second would represent personal working balances. Business and personal savings would have to be treated separately, business savings being assumed to be a function of output (income), and personal savings a function of disposable income. It can be shown that a change in the system would then be made through a series of damped oscillations.[11]

The relationship between the variables can be seen from the diagram. The shape and position of the curved end of the M_2 tank are derived from the liquidity preference function, so that the height of the water in the M_2 tank measures (inversely) the rate of interest, i. The rate of interest operates the 'classical' savings curve and the marginal efficiency of capital curve to control savings and investment. Savings are also controlled through the left-hand valve by the propensity to save curve, which is operated by a float on the M_1 tank so that it moves vertically with income. A 'propensity to invest' curve could be used similarly to operate the left-hand valve controlling investment; but it has been thought preferable to introduce an accelerator relationship between income and investment.[12] The accelerator mechanism consists of a narrow, deep float with a small hole in the bottom, hanging from a spring, and connected by a bent lever to the investment valve. In equilibrium the level of water inside the float will be the same as that in the M_1 tank, and the position of the valve is that of zero induced investment. If Y is decreasing, the level of M_1 will be falling and will be temporarily below the level of water in the float, since the water inside the float can leak out only slowly. Extra weight will be placed on the spring, which will extend, closing the investment valve a little, and so causing negative induced investment. Conversely, when Y is increasing induced investment will be positive, being always a lagged function of the rate of change of income.

It will be noticed that in this model $S = f(Y) + \phi(i)$ and similarly for investment, though a better assumption would be that $S = \psi(Y, i)$. The latter assumption could be used if the two savings valves were replaced by a single spring-loaded one, bearing against a block with surface contours given by $S = \psi(Y, i)$, the block moving vertically with income and horizontally, at right angles to the valve movement, with the rate of interest.

In models of this type it is usual to assume either that the values are given in some kind of real units, or that they are in money units but that prices are constant. In the mechanical model we can, however, introduce prices indirectly into the system, though in a rough and cumbersome way, by making use of the fact that the machine will deal with non-linear relationships. The general price level is assumed to be a function of money income, Y. This function can be drawn on the side of the M_1 tank, with Y along the ordinate and the price level along the abscissa, the values being read off at the intersection of the curve and the level of the water. Another curve or real income against money income can also be drawn, derived from the price curve. Any relationship given in real units can then be converted into an equivalent relationship in money units, and the graph of the latter used on the machine.

2 *The multiplier with constant rate of interest*

In the mathematical treatment of the model the functions must be assumed to be linear and prices to be constant. If the rate of interest is held constant by appropriate variations in the supply of money, and the accelerator neglected so that investment is made an independent variable, we have the following identities by definition, the variables being measured, for simplicity, from a base at which the system is in equilibrium.

$$Y = C + S$$
$$E = C + I,$$

and

$$E - Y = \frac{dM_1}{dt}.$$

Therefore

$$I - S = \frac{dM_1}{dt}. \tag{1}$$

The hypotheses are

$$M_1 = PY, \text{ or } \frac{dM_1}{dt} = p\frac{dY}{dt}. \tag{2}$$

and

$$S = \sigma Y, \tag{3}$$

where σ is the marginal propensity to save.

If, from equilibrium at time $t = 0$, investment increases by ΔI, then, from equations (1), (2) and (3)

$$p\frac{dY}{dt} + \sigma Y - \Delta I = 0. \tag{4}$$

The solution is

$$Y_t = \frac{\Delta I}{\sigma}\left(1 - e^{-\frac{\sigma}{P} \cdot t}\right), \tag{5}$$

where t is time in years and P, the circulation period, is also given as a fraction of a year.

Also,

$$E_t = \frac{\Delta I}{\sigma}\left(1 - e^{-\frac{\sigma}{P} \cdot t}\right) + \Delta I e^{-\frac{\sigma}{P} \cdot t}. \tag{6}$$

Table 10.1

σ	L
0	P
0.2	$1.12P$
0.5	$1.39P$
0.8	$2.01P$
1.0	∞

Equations (5) and (6) give the same final value for the multiplier as is obtained in the usual period analysis, and the equilibrium values are approached along a similar path, though of course it is continuous instead of stepped. If the curves are drawn, however, it will be found that the process of adjustment in this model is slower than that obtained in a period analysis model in which the lag is made equal to the circulation period. This results from the form of distributed lag used here. This lag, L, may be defined as the time interval by which Y lags behind E, that is, the value of L which makes $Y_{t+L} = E_t$ for all values of t. For instance, if E increases by 100 units, it is the time which elapses before Y has also increased by 100 units. By substituting equations (5) and (6) in this expression, we obtain the relation[13]

$$L = P\left[-\frac{\log_e(I - \sigma)}{\sigma}\right].$$

Some values of L with different marginal propensities to save are worked out in the table 10.1.

The speed of the adjustment process is determined not by the circulating period alone, but by the distributed lag L, which is longer than the circulating period except when the marginal propensity to save is zero. Though both the continuous analysis and the period analysis are only crude approximations to reality, I think there is no doubt that the continuous analysis is more realistic than one in which adjustments are assumed to occur in steps at intervals of three or four months. If this is so, it must be concluded that the time taken for a multiplier process to work itself out is longer than that shown by a period analysis sequence in which the lag is made equal to the circulation period of active balances.

3 The multiplier with constant quantity of money

If the quantity of money is constant, the rate of interest being free to vary, we must make use of the part of the mechanical model which deals with the determination of the rate of interest. It is obvious from figure 10.2, that in this case the multiplier process following a spontaneous increase in investment ΔI will be to some extent checked if the transfer of money from M_2 to M_1 induces a rise in the rate of interest, since this will reduce the excess of investment over savings (unless the curves are such that a rise in the rate of interest decreases savings more than it does investment, which is highly improbable).

Measuring the variables again from a base at which the system is in equilibrium, and assuming linearity, we have another identity

$$M_2 = -M_1,\tag{7}$$

and two additional hypotheses,

$$M_2 = \lambda i\tag{8}$$

and

$$I - \eta i,\tag{9}$$

where λ is the liquidity preference function 'proper' (Keynes' L_2 function) and η is the marginal efficiency of capital function. Equation (3) must also be changed to

$$S = \sigma Y + \xi i,\tag{10}$$

where ξ is the slope of the interest–savings curve.

From (1), (9) and (10), and introducing the spontaneous change ΔI, we obtain

$$\frac{dM_1}{dt} = \Delta I + (\eta - \xi)i - \sigma Y,$$

and substituting (2), (7) and (8) in this and rearranging gives

$$p\frac{dY}{dt} + \left[\sigma + \frac{P}{\lambda}(\eta - \xi)\right]Y - \Delta I = 0.\tag{11}$$

The solution is:

$$Y_t = \frac{\Delta I}{\sigma + \frac{P}{\lambda}(\eta - \xi)}\left[1 - e^{-\left(\frac{\sigma}{p} + \frac{\eta - \xi}{\lambda}\right)t}\right]\tag{12}$$

which gives the path of the multiplier process.

P is always > 0, and since we may be confident that $\lambda < 0$, $\eta < 0$ and $\xi > \eta$, we know that $\eta - \xi/\lambda \geq 0$. Equation (12) therefore shows that when the quantity of money is constant the multiplier is smaller, and the process of adjustment more rapid, than when the rate of interest is constant. The stability condition, that $\sigma/P + \frac{\eta-\xi}{\lambda} > 0$, also shows that the system is more stable; a marginal propensity to consume of more than unity ($\sigma < 0$) does not necessarily make the system explosive. If the elasticity of the liquidity preference curve is infinite, $\frac{\eta-\xi}{\lambda} = 0$, and we have the Keynesian special case, in which equation (12) reduces to equation (5) to give the usual multiplier process and stability condition.

4 The accelerator

In this model the hypothesis is made that induced investment depends on the rate of change of income. It is not necessary to assume that all investment is induced investment, but as the equations will show only variations from an equilibrium position the constant part of investment need not appear. The relationship between income and induced investment must be lagged in some way if the system is to be oscillatory. We therefore set up the following hypotheses:

$$\bar{I} = \beta \frac{dY}{dt}, \tag{13}$$

where $\bar{I}$ is the value that induced investment would have if there were no lag, and β is the acceleration co-efficient, and

$$\gamma = \frac{dI}{dt} = \bar{I} - I, \tag{14}$$

where γ is a lag constant. In words, induced investment approaches the value it would have if there were no lag at a rate proportional to the difference between the actual and the unlagged values.

Referring to figure 10.2, for a given construction of float and valve mechanism, β will be increased if the bent lever is raised, by raising both the fulcrum F and the point of attachment to the cord carrying the float, since this will increase the valve movement for a given extension of the spring. The lag constant will be increased by decreasing the size of the leakage hole in the float. This will also alter β, however, so the position of the lever must be adjusted whenever the lag constant is changed, if β is to be kept constant.

If it is assumed again that the rate of interest is held constant, we obtain by combining equations (13) and (14)

$$\frac{dI}{dt} = \frac{\beta}{\gamma} \cdot \frac{dY}{dt} - \frac{I}{\gamma}.$$

Combining equations (1), (2) and (3) gives

$$I = P\frac{dY}{dt} + \sigma Y,$$

and, differentiating with respect to time

$$\frac{dI}{dt} = P\frac{d^2 Y}{dt^2} + \sigma\frac{dY}{dt}.$$

Substituting these expressions in the previous one, and rearranging, we obtain

$$\gamma P\frac{d^2 Y}{dt^2} + (\gamma\sigma + P - \beta)\frac{dY}{dt} + \sigma Y = 0 \tag{15}$$

for the homogeneous part of the accelerator-multiplier equation. The roots of the characteristic equation become complex when

$$(\gamma\sigma + P - \beta)^2 < 4\gamma P\sigma$$

and the system then becomes oscillatory.[14]

The accelerator will, of course, give different results if the rate of interest is allowed to vary; but there is not space to develop them here.

5. *The determination of the rate of interest*

Discussions about the rate of interest seem often to have suffered through lack of a suitable technique for showing the process of change through time of the inter-related factors. The model described here may help to make it clear that the liquidity preference and loanable funds theories are neither inconsistent with each other, as might be thought from some of the controversies between their exponents, nor merely different ways of saying the same thing, as is sometimes implied,[15] but are complementary parts of a wider system.

Referring to figure 10.2, we see that in the model the rate of interest is determined at any instant only by the supply of and demand for 'stocks' of idle balances. A decrease in liquidity preference 'proper', or an increase in M_2 if the liquidity preference curve is not infinitely elastic, will cause an immediate fall in the rate of interest. But if S and I are at all interest-elastic they will be changed both directly by the change in the rate of interest, and indirectly by the subsequent change in income, working through the propensity to save and the income–investment relation. Any difference between S and I causes a gradual change in M_2 and so reacts back on the rate of interest, so that the full effects of the change depend on the shapes of the 'flow' functions.

We may assume that owing to the initial fall in the rate of interest I will increase, while S may decrease and in any case will not increase as much as I. The resulting excess of I over S causes a gradual fall in M_2, so that the rate of interest tends to rise again; but it also causes a gradual rise in M_1 and Y. If, as Y increases, it induces a greater increase in S than in I, this tendency will be checked before the rate of interest has returned to its original value. If, however, owing to the effect of the accelerator, or to a spread of optimism leading to a shift in the schedule of the marginal efficiency of capital, the increase in Y causes a greater increase in I than in S, the process of expansion will go further, and the rate of interest may temporarily rise above its original value. On the other hand, the rise in Y may also cause a further decrease in liquidity preference, so checking the rise in the rate of interest and enabling the expansionary process to continue even longer.

Differences of opinion concerning the main determinants of the rate of interest, and the effects of a change in the rate of interest, thus depend on different assumptions made as to the shapes and stability of the relations involved, and it would seem more useful to attempt the difficult task of testing these relations empirically than to engage in arguments based on assumptions about them. However, one argument may be suggested here. If the liquidity preference curve is not infinitely elastic, and if a change in the rate of interest does not directly change savings in the same direction as, and by an equal or greater amount than, it changes investment, then the rate of interest has an equilibrating function in the system. Its effect is weaker and slower in action than was thought before the work of Keynes, and, moreover, in times of wide fluctuations in income it may be almost completely swamped by the effects of the accelerator and shifts in the liquidity preference and marginal efficiency of capital functions. But if sudden changes in the level of income are avoided by fiscal or other policies, the equilibrating influence of the rate of interest becomes relatively stronger, so that monetary policy becomes a necessary supplement to fiscal policy.

The paths followed by income and the rate of interest after initial changes in the system can be worked out mathematically. For instance, if from equilibrium at time $t = 0$, M_2 is increased by ΔM_2, the path of the change in the rate of interest (neglecting the accelerator) is given by

$$i_t = \Delta M_2 \left\{ \frac{1}{\lambda} - \frac{\eta - \xi}{\sigma P + \lambda(\eta - \xi)} \left[1 - e^{-\left(\frac{\sigma}{P} + \frac{\eta - \xi}{\lambda}\right)t} \right] \right\},$$

and the path of the change in income is given by

$$Y_t = \Delta M_2 \left\{ \frac{\eta - \xi}{\sigma\lambda + P(\eta - \xi)} \left[1 - e^{-\left(\frac{\sigma}{P} + \frac{\eta - \xi}{\lambda}\right)t} \right] \right\}.$$

The final effect on the rate of interest is therefore greater when $|\lambda|$ is small, $|\eta - \xi|$ is small and σ is large, while the final effect on income is greater when $|\lambda|$ is small, $|\eta - \xi|$ is large and σ is small. As in the case of the multiplier–accelerator process, such exercises have their uses, providing the limitations imposed by the assumptions are kept in mind.

Similar processes could be worked out on the mechanical model if the rate of interest were recorded. Non-linear relations could be used, and the effects of superposing shifts in different functions at different times could be observed, giving a sort of simplified picture of consecutive events in economic history.

III

So far we have assumed a closed economy with no government operations. In the model shown in figure 10.3, these assumptions are relaxed.[16] The income flow, after being pumped to the top of the model, divides into taxation, T, and income after taxation. The taxation flow is controlled and measured by a valve operated from the float on the M_1 tank through an income–taxation curve. Income after taxation flows into a small measuring box, the outflow slot of which is identical with that of the M_1 tank, so that the flow is measured by the height of liquid in the box, on the same scale as the measurement of income. The box is small so the error caused by water being trapped in it is negligible.[17] After flowing through the measuring box, income after taxation divides into consumption and savings, consumption being controlled by a propensity to consume curve and an interest-rate–consumption curve, savings being a residual.

The position of the consumption function is controlled by the level of water in the measuring box. As this box is too small for a float-operated control to work satisfactorily, it is necessary to use a small servo-motor mechanism. This consists of an electric motor driving the pulley over which the connecting thread passes. The speed and direction of the motor are controlled by two small electrodes partially immersed in the water. When the level rises, the motor turns the pulley in an anti-clockwise direction, lifting the electrodes and so maintaining their position relative to the water level. Conversely, when the level of the water falls, the motor turns the pulley in a clockwise direction. The operation is therefore similar to that which would occur if the electrodes were a float large enough to operate the consumption function directly.

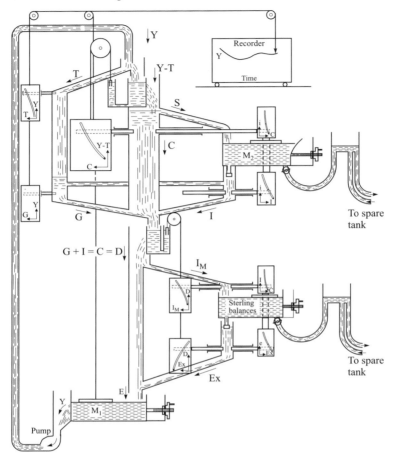

Figure 10.3

The servo-mechanism also makes it possible to lag consumption behind income after taxation. The electrodes are immersed in the water in a small tube connected to the measuring box, not in the box itself. The size of the hole connecting the tube to the box is adjustable, and when it is small the level in the tube lags behind that in the box, so that the consumption flow becomes a lagged function of income after taxation. A distinction may be made between this type of lag and that which occurs in, say, the Robertsonian model. In the latter, the lag occurs as a result of a time interval between income and expenditure. This might be called a 'structural' lag, and is represented in a continuous analysis by the time taken, after an increase in income, to build up working balances to a level commensurate with the higher expenditure. The type of lag just introduced acts in addition to the 'structural' lag; it might be called a 'psychological' lag, caused by inertia in the changing of habits.

Government expenditure, G, is controlled and measured by a valve, which may also be operated as a function of income if it is desired to illustrate the stabilising effects of an automatic compensatory fiscal programme. The level of water over this valve is kept constant by connecting it through the horizontal tube to the investment tube. This also causes any budget deficit to be met automatically by drawing from idle balances, M_2, and any budget surplus to contribute to investment expenditure, the drain on idle balances being diminished by an equivalent amount.

Consumption, investment, and government expenditure combine to form domestic expenditure, D. Expenditure abroad for imports, Im, is taken from domestic expenditure, and receipts from abroad for exports, Ex, are added to give total expenditure on the goods of the home country, E, which flows back to the M_1 tank. Domestic expenditure is measured by taking it through a small box similar to that described above, and a second servo-motor mechanism operates a propensity to import curve, making imports a function (lagged if desired) of domestic expenditure.[18]

Payments for imports flow into, and receipts from exports flow from, the small tank marked 'sterling balances', the water in which represents foreign holdings of the money of the home country.[19] The quantity of these balances together with the demand schedule for them, represented by the capacity of the tank at different levels, determine at any instant the rate of exchange, in the same way as in the case of price and of the rate of interest. This demand schedule might appropriately be called the sterling preference function.

The rate of exchange is thus represented by the level of liquid in the tank, and a float can be used to operate exchange-rate–imports and exchange-rate–exports graphs controlling imports and exports through the right-hand pair of valves. A small box, fed from a spare water tank and connected to the sterling balances tank by a flexible tube, can be used to represent the operations of an exchange equalisation account, putting funds on to, or taking them from, the foreign exchange market in order to control the rate of exchange. When the tap in the tube is turned off, a system with freely fluctuating exchange rates is represented.

National income is recorded as in the previous model, and in the version which is now being constructed small measuring boxes and floats are being inserted in the imports and exports flows, enabling imports and exports to be recorded on a single chart, so that the trade balance will be seen directly from the gap between them. Assuming there are no other items in the balance of payments, it will then be possible to demonstrate the operation of the gold standard by adjusting credit expansion or contraction to a multiple of the trade balance at any time.[20]

It seems possible that these small boxes, included in this model admittedly for a purely mechanical purpose, may have some economic significance. For instance, those in the imports and exports flows, which will contain a volume of water proportional to the arithmetic average of imports and exports, might be interpreted as containing working balances necessary for financing actual foreign trade transactions, the sterling balances tank containing balances surplus to those required for current transactions. Similarly a box inserted in the investment flow would contain what might be called investment working balances, a circulating fund covering the time interval between money being taken off the money market and its actual expenditure on investment goods. This would seem to be the equivalent of Keynes' 'Finance' balances. The additional relationships introduced into the system by such a division of working balances would considerably complicate the mathematical analysis in any particular case, though it can easily be shown that they would result in adjustments taking place through a series of oscillations.

It is possible to connect together two of the models shown in figure 10.3, to deal with the multiplier relationships between the incomes of two countries, or of one country and the rest of the world. To connect more than two would be difficult, since each country would have to have a propensity to import function for each other country. The easiest method of interconnection would be to assume a fixed rate of exchange, and run the imports flow of one model into the exports tube of the other. Another though rather more difficult way would be to use a servo-mechanism to operate the left-hand exports valve of each model, keeping exports always equal to imports on the other model multiplied by the rate of exchange, which could be held stable by the 'equalisation account' operations.

Notes

Economica, 18 (NS) (67),1950, pp. 283–305.

I wish to thank Mr W.T. Newlyn, in co-operation with whom the original model was made, for his valuable assistance in design and construction. An article by Mr Newlyn, based on his experience in using the model at the University of Leeds, will be published in the *Yorkshire Bulletin* in September, 1950. I also wish to thank Professor J.E. Meade, who suggested a number of improvements in the theoretical model and methods by which they might be included in the mechanical one. I am grateful to the London School of Economics for financial assistance which has enabled me to devote the last six months to developing the model. I am greatly indebted to Mr and Mrs R.W. Langley for their willing and generous help in the construction of the first machine.

1 The actual constant-level float mechanism used, though similar in principle, differs in construction from that shown.

2 See Keynes (1930, chapter 29), also Hicks (1950, pp. 47–55).

3 In the form appropriate to a continuous analysis, i.e., the actual value approaches the value that would obtain if there were no lag at a rate which is a function of the difference between the actual and the unlagged values.

4 As defined by Metzler (1941); but with slight changes to make the concept applicable to a continuous instead of a discontinuous model.

5 This hypothesis has been used in a mathematical model by Goodwin (1948, pp. 112–18). Expressed in a slightly different form, it is also made the basis of a model by Samuelson (1947, pp. 276–80).

6 The shape is given by the formula $W = c \cdot 1/\sqrt{b}$ where W is the width of the slot at any height b, and c is a constant depending on the viscosity of the liquid.

7 The pump motor is fed through two electrodes partially immersed in the water over the inflow to the pump, providing automatic speed regulation of the pump and keeping the level of water in the inflow tube constant. Since the quantity of water in the outflow tube is also constant, the flow into C and S at the top of the model always equals Y.

8 See Machlup (1939).

9 The sales–output lag used by Lundberg in his dynamic sequence analysis is in some ways more realistic than the one used here. He relates the length of this lag to the 'production-planning period', not to the circulation period of active balances, and also allows for attempts by producers to keep their stocks constant, or at a constant proportion of sales. Any change is then accompanied by a series of damped oscillations, as is shown by Metzler (1941). In the model described here the accelerator must be used to deal with the effects of changes in stocks, investment being interpreted to include expenditure by producers to maintain stocks. When total expenditure is rising and stocks are being depleted, there will be additional investment by producers attempting to maintain stocks, this additional induced investment being made a lagged function of the rate of change of income.

10 See Metzler (1948b).

11 For a geometrical treatment of a similar model on the assumption that the two lags are equal, see a forthcoming article by Ralph Turvey and Dr Hans Brems. For an account of how the macroeconomic concepts can be further broken down to give complex systems of lags and functions see Goodwin (1949).

12 The model built for the University of Leeds has a propensity to save and no accelerator.

13 I am indebted to W.T. Newlyn and J.D. Sargan, of Leeds University, for pointing out this relation.

14 The accelerator used here thus gives results identical with those obtained from a mathematical model by Goodwin (1948).
15 See Hicks (1946, pp. 153–62).
16 This model is basically similar to that built for the University of Leeds, but includes a number of improvements.
17 This box could be made larger, and the liquid in it interpreted as personal working balances, so introducing a Robertsonian lag into the model.
18 For the use of this relationship in the analysis of the multiplier effects of international trade, see Meade (1948; 1949).
19 There is probably some error involved in separating these balances from idle balances, since some part of them may be related to the rate of interest.
20 I am indebted to Professor J.E. Meade for suggesting this device, as well as a number of others described in this section.

11 The History of the Phillips Machine

(A.W.H. Phillips)

Nicholas Barr

B22
B31
£10

1 Introduction

When A.W.H. 'Bill' Phillips died in Auckland in March 1975 aged sixty he was mourned in a very personal way by many friends, who remembered a gentle, shy man with a wry sense of humour, and one who (in their eyes) was always absurdly modest about his major contributions to post-war economics.

He was best known to the world at large for the original exposition of what later became known as the 'Phillips Curve' (a name he would never have given it himself). The curve summarised the UK experience of the associated movements of the level of unemployment and the rate of wage inflation over the course of the business cycle. The relationship was seized on as showing the trade-off between unemployment and inflation faced by government policy. It was subsequently argued that the relationship was more complex than Phillips' formulation allowed, in that the trade-off disappeared if the Phillips Curve was extended to include certain types of expectations mechanism. In a sense, therefore, Phillips' work was an indirect progenitor of important later theoretical developments, in particular the systematic analysis of the role of expectations in macroeconomics.

To a smaller group of friends he was remembered also for the 'Phillips Machine', a hydraulic model of the UK economy about 7 feet high × 5 feet wide × 3 feet deep, in which the circular flow of income was represented by red water flowing round in clear plastic tubes. The machine was initially developed in 1949–50, and its heyday was the early 1950s.

This article is about the machine and its origins. It is in part a chapter in the biography of a remarkable man; in part a chapter in the history of economic thought; and in part a chapter in the life of the London School of Economics.

2 Bill Phillips

Pre-LSE days[1]

Bill Phillips was born on 18 November 1914, the son of a New Zealand dairy farmer. He left school at fifteen and was an apprentice engineer until 1935. Succumbing to a travel bug which he had resisted for some time, he then set off for Australia. After a number of casual jobs (which included running a cinema) he worked for six months in the outback as a maintenance shift electrician. Thereafter came a spell of hunting crocodiles, an electrician's job at a gold mine, and a job with the Brisbane Council Electric Department.

In early 1937 he decided to go to Britain via China and Russia and, after various complications (including the Japanese declaration of war on China), reached London via the Trans-Siberian railway in November 1937.

Before and during the journey to Britain he had been taking a correspondence course, and obtained his formal qualification as an electrical engineer in London in 1938. He had several jobs, including one with the County of London Electricity Supply Company, and also registered as a part-time student at the LSE in 1939–40.

When war came he joined the RAF, and in January 1941 was sent as an Armament Officer to Singapore. He worked in Burma and Singapore, which he left on the *Empire State* bound for Java in February 1942. The ship was attacked by enemy aircraft, whereupon

he obtained an unmounted machine gun, quickly improvised a successful mounting and operated the gun from the boat deck with outstanding courage for the whole period of the attack, which lasted for 3 1/2 hours. Even when the section of deck from which he was operating was hit by a bomb, Flying Officer Phillips continued to set a most valuable example of coolness, steadiness and fearlessness to all in his vicinity (citation accompanying his MBE, cited by Blyth 1975, 304–5).

In Java, he was eventually captured by the Japanese, and spent the rest of the war in a POW camp, where he learned Chinese and also some Russian from fellow prisoners, became interested in sociology, and developed a bad nicotine habit (anyone who remembers Bill sees him with an untipped cigarette in his hand).

At LSE 1946–50

Student days

Returning to England, Phillips registered for the B.Sc. (Econ) 1946–49, special subject sociology. '[H]e embarked on it partly as a result of being unsettled about his future at the end of the war and intended it merely as an adjunct to future engineering work' (letter from Valda Phillips, 7 April 1988). During the degree, however, he was deflected from sociology. In those days all B.Sc. (Econ.) students were required to do at least one paper in each of part I and part II of the degree in each of economics, government and history. Faced with compulsory economics, he developed a great interest in the subject and, like many of his generation, became very caught up by Keynesian theory.

Though he was fascinated by economics, the Keynesian model was hard going. He found help in two forms. First, he fell back on his engineering training: he saw that money stocks could be represented by tanks of water, and monetary flows by water circulating round plastic tubes. Second, his growing understanding of economics and increasing ability to translate economic concepts into hydraulic ones was fostered by his association with Walter Newlyn, an economics student one year ahead of him, who was shortly to take up a Lectureship at Leeds University (and who later became Professor of Development Economics there). It was from Newlyn, at least as much as from the Professors of Economics, that Phillips learned his monetary economics. Newlyn saw the rough early drawings of the machine, encouraged Phillips to build one, and was later instrumental in arranging for the Economics Department at Leeds to pay an advance of £100 for materials, thereby, as it subsequently turned out, commissioning the first machine (Newlyn 1950).

With hindsight it is clear that in the latter part of his student days, economics must have taken up almost all of Phillips' time. He ended up with a Pass degree in sociology, which subject he then practically abandoned.

After completing his degree in summer 1949, he received the Leeds advance of £100 (about £2,000 at 1998 prices), bought a number of perspex tubes and valves and:

found in Mr and Mrs Langley of Croydon a host and hostess who were ready to take him into their house and to turn their car out of their garage, in which improvised workshop Mr Phillips constructed the hydraulic model...(Meade 1951b)

The Robbins seminar

Having spent the summer and early autumn of 1949 working on the machine:

Mr Phillips had next to persuade the scientific world that it was a serious instrument. There are rumours of learned professors and dignitaries of the Royal Economic Society, as they walked from the entrance of the School, towards the lift, being interrupted by a wild man from New Zealand waving blue prints in one hand and queer shaped pieces of Perspex in the other. (Meade 1951b)

Reminiscing about this incident a year later in a letter to James Meade (28 September 1950) commenting on a draft of the article from which the previous paragraph was taken, Phillips wrote:

I particularly like your description of my approaching Professor Robbins at the lift. I should perhaps have apologised for my abruptness. Yet it was all intended for the good of the School. I had accepted an invitation by Professor Brown to go to Leeds the next day to discuss the model with him, and was making a desperate effort to give the School another opportunity to get in first.

Robbins asked James Meade (then Professor of Commerce at the School, and well-known as someone fascinated by things mechanical) to see this 'wild man' who had accosted him by the lift. Phillips met Meade for the first time in Meade's office in early autumn 1949, explained the idea of the machine and showed Meade the blueprints. Meade encouraged him to finish building the machine and, because he was impressed (and also to get Phillips out of his office), promised him the chance, if and when the machine was complete, to demonstrate it at Robbins' seminar.[2]

Robbins (1972) on his own admission was sceptical – 'all sorts of people had invented machines to demonstrate propositions which really didn't require machines to explain them'. Nevertheless, in fulfilment of Meade's promise, Phillips was invited to demonstrate his machine at Robbins' seminar on 29 November 1949.

Both Phillips and the machine acquitted themselves well. Everyone who mattered was there (some, according to Meade, having come mainly to laugh). They gazed in wonder at this large 'thing' in the middle of the room. Phillips, chain smoking, paced back and forth explaining it in a heavy New Zealand drawl, in the process giving one of the best lectures on Keynes and Robertson that anyone in the audience had heard. He then switched the machine on. And it worked! He really had created a machine which simplified the problems and arguments economists had been having for years.

Appointment as a temporary engineering consultant

That the machine made a deep impression is clear from a proposal by James Meade (30 November 1949) to his fellow Professors (W.T. Baxter, E.H. Phelps Brown, R.S. Edwards, F.A. Hayek, F.W. Paish, Sir Arnold Plant, L.C. Robbins and R.S. Sayers). The memorandum played a key part in the Phillips story, and is worth quoting at some length.

I was very much impressed yesterday by the demonstration which Mr A.W. Phillips gave in Professor Robbins' seminar of the hydraulic model... I thought that the machine (quite apart from its obvious qualities of great ingenuity and supreme craftsmanship) served a really useful role as a teaching device. It seemed to me, for example to show with great clarity the connection between the Keynesian and the Robertsonian ways of looking at the market...[3]

From conversation with Mr Phillips, I know that he is very anxious now to write a really scientific account of his model which will show exactly what it is demonstrating about the monetary circulation, and also to consider any modifications which might be made to it both from the point of view of economic analysis and also from the point of view of an instrument of teaching.

I would accordingly like to propose to the Director [Sir Alexander Carr-Saunders] that the School offer to Mr Phillips a Fellowship or Grant at an annual rate of, say £700 for a period of six to nine months for the purpose of writing up for us an account of his model which we could then publish in *Economica*...

Mr A.W. Phillips is a New Zealander, 35 years old, an electrical engineer by training and profession, who... took the B.Sc (Econ) in the summer of this year... specialising in Sociology. He obtained only a pass, but it is clear that in fact Mr Phillips spent most of his time here studying monetary theory – with, I venture to suggest, very considerable success. He studied here with a rehabilitation grant from the New Zealand government, and is under an obligation to return to New Zealand in a few weeks' time.[4] Indeed, I have already had to write to New Zealand House to obtain permission for Mr Phillips to stay as long as this in England to finish the proto-type of his machine. Mr Phillips thinks that we might be able to obtain a further extension of this time but we shall have to act quickly if we wish to keep Mr Phillips here.

The proposal was revised in the light of a number of potential problems pointed out by Sir Arnold Plant. The final form of Phillips' initial appointment was set out in a letter (7 December 1949) from Meade to his fellow Professors and to the Director.

I have been much impressed by Professor Sir Arnold Plant's minute of 2nd December. He mentions two difficulties in the way of my former proposal: first, that Phillips has only a Pass degree so that it is difficult to employ him academically at a high salary; and, second, that Phillips is trying to patent his machine,[5] so that we might be in danger of using the resources of the School to assist a private business enterprise.

To meet these points I revise my proposal as follows: that the School should ask Mr Phillips to build, or have built, for the School a new model of the machine, and that for this work we should pay Mr Phillips at the rate of £50 a month for a maximum of six months plus the cost of the materials and other proper expenses of construction, the total cost of the machine not to exceed £700. This would allow £300 for Mr Phillips' salary for six months plus £400 for the cost to him of getting the machine made...

This proposal should meet both of Professor Plant's points. We should be having a machine constructed in the best manner available to us; and we should be unconcerned with the formal academic record of the constructor or with the question of whether he tries to patent the machine or not...

I have discussed the matter with the Director who sees no objection to this proposal. It would presumably be necessary to have a small committee to watch the construction of the machine...

The New Zealand authorities agreed to extend Phillips' stay up to the end of 1950, though even before the extension came through, Phillips had already announced his decision in a letter to James Meade (11 December 1949): 'I definitely accept the proposal you outlined on Friday [that in the previous paragraph]. I would, if necessary, buy myself out of the bond to return immediately, rather than leave this job half done.'

The LSE machine

The deliberations of the overseeing committee (Professors Edwards, Meade and Phelps Brown) are summarised in a memo by Professor Edwards dated 20 January 1950. The proposal *ex ante* was to pay Phillips £300 (£6,000 at 1998 prices) for the period January–June 1950 to produce a more advanced machine with the assistance of Philip White of White-Ellerton Ltd, a small engineering firm in north London. White was to be paid £400 (£8,000 in 1998 terms) to cover the cost of materials and his own time; and the machine was to be delivered to the School by the end of June. Phillips was also to produce a written description of the machine.

Ex post the machine was not delivered until 13 October, mainly because Phillips and White over the course of the spring and summer were unable to resist a variety of ideas for improvement:

Phillips and White have thrown themselves without reserve into the development of the machine and into improving it...Probably if they had been somewhat more businesslike and had refused to be interested in fiddling about to find ways of improving it, we might have got a much less well developed machine by the contract date (letter from Meade to the Director, 7 November 1950).

Phillips and I demonstrated it to my seminar on Thursday; and it's a beauty (letter from Meade to Professors Edwards, Paish and Robbins, 16 October 1950).

A description of this machine both as a mechanical device and as an economic model is given in chapter 10, which, when it was first published in 1950, fulfilled his obligation to produce something in writing (see also Vines, chapter 9).[6]

Appointment as bona fide economist

The period August to December 1950 saw a confusing flurry of activity which, with hindsight, can be divided into two separate sets of events. First, by late summer 1950, James Meade was becoming uncomfortable about the amount of unpaid time Phillips had devoted to the machine:

> ...I feel that Phillips has made rather excessive financial sacrifices. Making the first machine which is now at Leeds University, he lived practically on air for six months while he could have been making a very good income as an engineer; his temporary employment by us was at a substantially lower rate than he could have got as an engineer; and again, from the end of June...he had to live on nothing (letter to the Director 7 November 1950).

Partly to compensate Phillips retrospectively, and partly because the arrangement would be genuinely useful to the Department, Meade therefore proposed to his fellow professors

> to pay Mr Phillips at the normal hourly rate for class work which, I understand, is £2.2.-. an hour, for his assistance in demonstrating the machine as and when required during the Michaelmas Term. I would propose a maximum of £100 for the total payment.

Those were unbureaucratic times. The proposal was dated 21 September 1950. Within a few days it had been approved by the professors and then by the director. Phillips' letter of acceptance to James Meade was dated 28 September.

This arrangement, however, was overtaken by the second set of events, which culminated in the offer of an assistant lectureship for the 1950–1 academic year. According to James Meade, some of the professors of economics had wanted to offer Phillips such an appointment in the immediate aftermath of his lecture and demonstration at the Robbins seminar the previous November. But the economists, having earlier criticised the sociologists for appointing people with what they (the economists) regarded as weak academic records, were hoist with their own petard. Phillips was therefore encouraged to embark immediately on a Ph.D. under Meade's supervision, and registered on a part-time basis in January 1950.

It was the reaction to Phillips' article in *Economica*, published in August 1950, which changed things. The paper was doubly original, in that it described the machine and was, in addition, the first application of dynamic control theory to macroeconomics. The story is taken up in a letter from Lionel Robbins to the Director dated 4 October 1950.[7]

Considering the burden of work ... we [the Professors of Economics] were of the opinion that an effort should be made to provide a further reinforcement here and now.

In this connection we discussed the name of Mr Phillips, the inventor of the hydraulic machine ... I ought to explain that at an earlier date we had considered the desirability of offering Mr Phillips an appointment. Some of us were in favour of doing so forthwith. Others felt that in view of Mr Phillips' poor performance in the final examination ... action should be suspended until he had demonstrated by some written contribution to the subject, that this poor performance was to be explained in terms of his somewhat lamentable experiences during the war when confined in a Japanese [POW] camp, he contracted so strong a habit of chain smoking that, without cigarettes in an examination room, he was completely at a loss after an hour. Mr Phillips has now published an article in *Economica* which, we are all convinced, at once puts him on the international map as an economist of profound grasp and originality. As a result of this article, enquiries have already begun to come in from the United States about the further manufacture of machines ... We do not know whether Mr Phillips could be induced to stay in this country by the offer which we should feel able to make. But it was our unanimous desire that Mr Phillips should be immediately offered an assistant lectureship at the top of the scale. We none of us feel that any further interview at our level is desirable since we all know Mr Phillips very well. If, therefore, you felt that this recommendation was acceptable, all that would be necessary would be for you yourself to see Mr Phillips, and if you were satisfied with him, make him an offer. We feel that this is a matter of some urgency because we know that Mr Phillips is in for a job in New Zealand and we suspect that there may be others coming along from the United States.

The chronology of events is thus:

August 1950	Paper in *Economica*.
4 October	Meeting of Professors of Economics recommends to the Director the appointment of Phillips as Assistant Lecturer.
Sometime between 5 and 10 October	Director saw Phillips.
12 October	Official letter offering appointment as from 16 October.
19 October	Letter of acceptance from Phillips.
23 October	Phillips took up duties.

Once the appointment had been confirmed, Meade proposed in a letter to the Director (7 November 1950) that to compensate Phillips for unpaid work over the summer, the appointment should be made retrospective by six–eight weeks.[8] In the same letter he raised the possibility of an ex gratia payment of up to £50 to Philip White. Thus the School got a machine that was more expensive, but also much better, than anticipated, and also an Assistant Lecturer in Economics with a Pass degree in Sociology.

The rest, as they say, is history. Phillips' Ph.D., *Dynamic Models in Economics*, was examined by Professor (later Sir) John Hicks on 10 December 1953, and the degree was awarded on 27 January 1954.[9] The New Zealand authorities waived the requirement of his rehabilitation grant that he return to New Zealand. He became Lecturer in Economics in 1951, Reader in 1954, and Tooke Professor of Economic Science and Statistics in 1958.

3 Other actors and later years

The machine

The success of the prototype machine together with the *Economica* paper in 1950 thus gave Phillips the possibility of an academic career. The initial opening was the reward for his ability and his tenacity working on the first machine in the garage in Croydon over the summer of 1949. Even so, little might have come of these efforts, apart possibly from a long-forgotten mechanical curiosity, had it not been for James Meade's enthusiastic support. Meade encouraged Phillips while the machine was being built; lobbied academic colleagues at LSE and elsewhere on Phillips' behalf; wrote to the New Zealand authorities supporting Phillips' request for an extension of his stay in Britain; and organised sufficient employment to keep body and soul together.

The relationship between the two of them, on the surface, appeared formal, as fitted the custom of the times. Phillips' letters always started 'Dear Professor Meade', Meade's letters began 'Dear Phillips'. In a rather English way, however, informality crept in between the lines. Phillips' letters were always handwritten, sometimes scrawled on rather tatty bits of paper with crossings out from time to time, and with occasional glimpses of what was obviously becoming a warm friendship. The texture of the relationship emerges in a letter of 6 September 1950, at a time when Phillips, his six months contract having expired at the end of June, was working unpaid with Philip White on the first LSE machine.

Dear Professor Meade,
Thanks for your note. I was sorry to hear of the tragic ending to the great kite enterprise, just when it was so near to success. I think even the fish must have felt a little sad about it. Better luck next year!

Thank you for writing to Auckland for me. I enclose a copy of my application...

Miss Bevan has typed out Professor Robertson's letter, and I enclose the original and two copies. I will let you have a copy of a reply in a few days, and also try to decide about difference and differential equations, though my knowledge of the former is, to put it mildly, rather sketchy.

The machine is going fairly well, it does at least look a little like a machine and if there are no unexpected snags should be ready by the end of the month. Production has also started on the next four, though an official order has been received only from Manchester. Cambridge have still not confirmed their order in writing, but I hope they will do so soon.

Professor Lerner was here the other day and was quite intrigued by the machine. He will try to arrange for Roosevelt College, Chicago, to order one as soon as he returns at the end of this month. The AEA [American Economic Association] Conference takes place in Chicago this year, and he would like to install a machine at his College for demonstrations. He has a new book in print in which he uses a lot of diagrams of water tanks and things; but it is based on definitional identities between S & I, and Y & E. He said he was rather puzzled by the fact that they could be different in our model; but I don't think he was really so puzzled as he professed. I find this rather amusing, since it was my dissatisfaction with his article using the S, I identity to 'prove' that the 'classical' theory was completely fallacious that started me off looking for a technique which would show the process more clearly than is possible with two-dimensional graphs.

I should be at White's place most of the time for the next few weeks, so come along at any time if you would like to see how things are going.

Yours sincerely,

A.W. Phillips.

It is a tribute to Meade that he took steps to make sure Phillips was not exploited, and a tribute to Phillips that at the time the letter was written he had no idea that within six weeks he would be offered an Assistant Lectureship.

As we saw earlier, other members of the teaching staff were involved to a lesser extent in the machine's early days, notably Robbins, and also Edwards and Phelps Brown who, with Meade, oversaw the building of the first LSE machine. Once the initial model was delivered, its presence was made known by a circular from James Meade dated 20 October 1950.

The Phillips-Hydraulic Machine is now installed, locked up in a cupboard, in Room 216. The key of the cupboard is being kept in the Porter's Lodge. The Porter's Lodge have instructions to give the key to all Professors and Readers in the [Economics and Statistics] departments, and to all other members of the teaching staff whose names are given to them. Would you let me know if you would like to have your name added to this list? It would be a wise precaution if, before using the machine, you would get Mr Phillips to show you how to operate it – and, incidentally, how to operate the cupboard!

To those who knew them later in their careers, the replies from a number of Young Turks were characteristic.

Could my name please be entered on the list of persons authorised to interfere with the employment engine? John [Jack] Wiseman

I should be grateful if my name might be added to the list of those who may obtain the key of the machine. H.C. Edey

Please add my name to the list of those entitled to the key of the machine cupboard. R. Turvey

Will you have my name put on the list of those able to use the key to the machine please? Alan Day

Work on the machine continued into the early 1950s and, as discussed later, a number were sold to other institutions both here and in the USA. But the advent of computers meant that the machine was not the success in purely commercial terms that Phillips, in its very early days, might have hoped. Colleagues continued enthusiastically to use the machine as a teaching device. But even the last generation of machines could be temperamental, and eventually Phillips tired of going to the rescue of colleagues whose classrooms were flooded with water and filled with giggling students. The LSE machines therefore stopped being used sometime during the later 1950s.[10]

Other interests

Phillips, in the meantime, had increasingly become caught up in other academic pursuits, among them a more general interest in the application of computers to economics. In that context he first met Richard Tizard, who in the early 1950s was in charge of the Automatic Control Group at the National Physical Laboratory (NPL), where he had developed a powerful electronic analogue computer. Phillips went to see Tizard, set up a macroeconomic model on the computer, and became very excited at the research prospects it opened up.

Around this time (the early 1950s), however, analogue computers began to be overtaken by digital ones (the difference is explained in n. 16). One of the first digital computers, the Auto Computing Engine (ACE) had been developed after the war at NPL by Alan Turing and others. The ACE never left the drawing board, but the prototype of a smaller version, the DEUCE, was built at NPL, and about six were subsequently produced by English Electric, one of which was installed in their Aldwych office.

A friendship between Phillips and Tizard grew up alongside what became a close working relationship. In consequence Tizard came to the LSE from 1956 to 1958 on a two-year Fellowship in Analytical Economics to work with Phillips and to use the Aldwych DEUCE, to which he was given access out of business hours.[11] Phillips' main interest at the time was the application of dynamic control theory to economic processes, and he and Tizard spent many evenings at each other's homes educating each other, Tizard learning about economics and Phillips developing a substantial expertise in control theory and digital computers.

This line of research (chapters 16 and 17), though highly innovative and, by most people's standards, very successful, was less fruitful than Phillips had hoped and, ever curious, he was moving into new fields, including the work which made his reputation internationally, as described earlier, on the Phillips Curve (chapter 25). He also developed an increasing interest in Chinese economic development.

In 1967 he moved to a chair in Economics at the Australian National University. The move was partly because he and his wife, Valda, wanted their daughters to grow up nearer their relatives; partly to further his Chinese studies; and partly because he was becoming restless and, after over twenty years there, increasingly unenthused about London (Yamey, chapter 35).

His years at ANU were active and fruitful, and included the foundation of a Centre for Contemporary Chinese Studies. In 1969 he suffered a major stroke and retired to Auckland, where for his last five years he continued to conduct a seminar in Chinese economic development.

4 The machine

Description

I shall describe the machine only in outline, since it is essentially so visual that attempts to explain it in writing almost inevitably become laborious. Readers seeking more detail are referred to Phillips (chapter 10), and Vines (chapter 9), or for detailed mechanical description to Moghadam (1988).

The machine as an economic device
A very simplified version of the machine is shown in figure 11.1. The circular flow of income leaves the transactions balances tank at the bottom, is pumped up the tube on the left, and then cascades down the central column. The government sector (top left) consists of taxes leaving

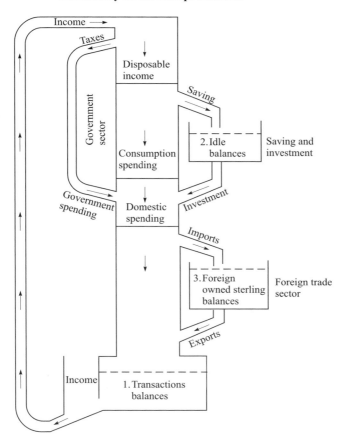

Figure 11.1 A simplified view of the Phillips machine

the circular flow and government spending entering. Saving (top right) leaves the circular flow, and investment adds to spending. The foreign trade sector (bottom right) consists of imports leaving the domestic spending cycle, and exports adding to it.

In terms of simple national income accounting, total income, Y, enters at the top; taxes are siphoned off leaving disposable (that is, after-tax) income; saving flows out of the central column, leaving consumption spending. To consumption, C, is added investment, I (flowing in from the right) and government spending, G (flowing in from the left) to give total domestic spending, from which imports, Q, are then deducted and exports, X, added. The machine thus shows visually the equilibrium condition

$$Y = C + I + G + (X - Q)$$

which should raise at least familiar echoes for those who once-upon-a-time did first year economics.[12]

The three tanks in figure 11.1, representing stocks of money, are crucial to understanding the machine. Transactions balances (tank 1) are used to finance expenditure: water flows from tank 1 through a slot into the adjacent box, the rate of flow being proportional to the height of water in the tank. Other things being equal, therefore, the higher the level of water in tank 1, the larger the income flow. Idle balances (tank 2) are broadly what Keynes called speculative balances; other things being equal, the higher the level of water in the tank, the lower is the interest rate. Foreign-owned sterling balances are contained in tank 3; the higher the level of water in the tank, the lower the foreign exchange value of sterling/the larger the UK balance of payments deficit.

Figure 11.2 shows the machine in somewhat more detail. The inflows and outflows are determined by a system of valves which open and close depending on the level of water in the three tanks, and on the flow of income. The connection is complicated in practice, but simple enough in principle. In some cases a float on top of one of the tanks is connected to the relevant valve via a cord and a pulley; as the level of water in the tank falls so does the float, exerting a downward pull on the cord. The downward pull, depending on the economic relationship involved, either opens or closes the valve. Thus if income goes down, consumption also goes down (that is, the consumption valve will partly close); if the interest rate goes down, investment will go up (that is, the investment valve will partly open). In other cases (for example, the effect of domestic expenditure on imports in figure 11.2) a similar effect is achieved by a small float connected to the relevant valve via a servo mechanism, which uses a small motor to amplify any downward or upward movement of the float.

The underlying economic model is as follows:

Saving, at a given level of taxation, is determined by the level of income (that is, the rate of flow of water into the top of the central column) and the interest rate (that is, the level of water in tank 2).

Consumption is what is left of disposable income after saving has taken place; consumption and saving are thus determined simultaneously by the level of income and the interest rate.

Investment is determined by the interest rate (tank 2) and the *rate of change* of income. (This so-called accelerator model of investment is amazingly cleverly done mechanically, but explanation would be laborious.)

Taxes and government spending are determined by the level of income.

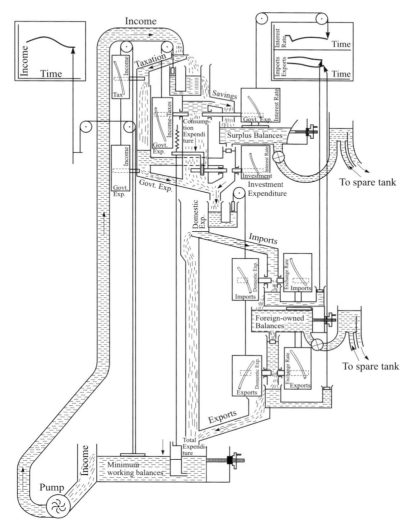

Figure 11.2 The Phillips Machine in more detail

Imports and exports are determined by domestic expenditure (via a servo mechanism – see figure 11.2) and by the exchange rate (tank 3).

In terms of economic theory the machine represents an open-economy IS-LM model.[13] The theoretical set up is very flexible. The operator can change the form of any of the relationships determining consumption, investment, etc. Depending on the exact way in which the monetary sector is set up, it is possible to have either a 'Keynesian' model, in which expansionary fiscal policy (e.g., higher government spending or lower taxation) is effective in increasing output and employment, or a 'Classical' model, in which fiscal policy has no effect on output. It is also possible for government to engage in deficit financing by tapping idle balances (tank 2) to increase its own spending, thus avoiding the need to increase taxes.

In addition, tanks 2 and 3 are connected to a spare tank (see figure 11.2). Opening the connection between tank 2 and the spare tank acts to keep the level of water in tank 2 constant (that is, the interest rate is fixed, and the money supply is free to vary); if the connection is closed, the money supply is fixed and the interest rate will vary. Similarly, opening the connection between tank 3 and the spare tank acts to keep the level of water in tank 3 constant, thereby fixing the exchange rate. It is thus possible to have different monetary regimes and either a fixed or a float-ing exchange rate.

We could therefore use the machine to examine the effect on income, the interest rate and the exchange rate of, say, a tax cut in a world of floating exchange rates, and with fixed UK money supply. The machine does not merely give a qualitative answer: it is calibrated to an accuracy of ±4 per cent; and the IS-LM model on which the machine is based has an explicit dynamic structure. In plain English, both the new level of income and the other variables, and the time path from the old level to the new level are accurate in terms of the underlying theoretical model. The time path of income, the interest rate, imports and exports is traced out by plotter pens (see figure 11.2), making it possible to analyse the quantitative effects of policy.

The machine mechanically

A photograph survives (see p. 105) showing Bill Phillips some time in 1950, cigarette in hand, with the machine, which visually has the magic of a Heath Robinson device at its finest, as red water flows through the complex system of tubes, valves and tanks. Whilst this adds to the enjoyment (without exception, the machine in action gives people pleasure), it should not be allowed to obscure the machine's originality,[14] all the more since the early models were built very much on the cheap, using war surplus items (the pumps on the original machine came from a Lancaster bomber).

It was the Heath Robinson aspect which attracted *Punch* (15 April 1953, p. 456; see p. 107 below).

[The machine] will tell at a glance the exact effect of a recession in sheet-music on, say, the Birmingham fancy-goods trade. It is held, virtually *incommunicado,* at the London School of Economics. But it should properly belong to the world ...

Our point could scarcely be made more aptly than on this post-Budget morning. To-day the whole of Britain is talking finance ... And the sad thing is that none of them really know what they are talking about – while all the time, tucked away in Houghton Street, W.C.2, is a creature capable of clarifying the whole situation before the man in the street could say John Maynard Keynes.

The machine is taller than the man in the street, and wider and heavier and much, much cleverer. It is also less reticent about its inner feelings, which are ...exposed in the frankest manner – a complex pattern of transparent tubes, of plungers, sluices, checks, balances, buttons, levers and pulleys, all combining to present an instantaneous picture of the nation's economy...Using coloured water for money (a convenience denied the man in the street) it reacts obediently to every morsel of economic information communicated to it.

...In our view there should be an installation in every town hall (or recreation ground, railway station or dog-track) in Britain...If the State will not step in...what of Commerce? Will not some public-spirited biscuit baron or marmalade mogul, now presenting winners of slogan competitions with the routine £5,000 house, television set and two seats for the Coronation, instead present their home town with one of these invaluable educational aids?...

Meanwhile, and in default of appropriate action by either State or Citizen, a simple model is under construction at this office from the data, necessarily incomplete, at our disposal [see figure 11.3].

The machine elsewhere.

The very first prototype (built in summer 1949 in the Langleys' garage in Croydon) was demonstrated at the Robbins seminar, and subsequently at the 1950 meeting of the Association of University Teachers of Economics. As discussed earlier, it then went to Leeds University where, at Walter Newlyn's instigation, Professor Arthur Brown, the head of the Economics Department, had used the departmental equipment budget to buy the machine for £100.[15] The second machine, built by Bill Phillips and Philip White in the spring and summer of 1950, was delivered to the School early in the Michaelmas term 1950. At least one more machine was supplied to the School by White-Ellerton in 1952 at a price of £450. Cambridge University also bought one (which still survives), and so did Oxford, Birmingham, Manchester and Melbourne (Blyth 1975, 305).

Amongst the many people excited by the machine was Abba Lerner, a member of the economics department at the School in the 1930s and, by the early 1950s, at Roosevelt College, Chicago. He had an animated correspondence with Meade and Phillips, and saw the first prototype on a visit to London in the summer of 1950. Lerner became Phillips' US agent, and it was through his efforts that machines were sold to Roosevelt College, Harvard, the Ford Motor Company and the Central Bank of Guatamala. The US machines were calibrated in dollars, and some additional development work went on in America in parallel to Phillips' own work.

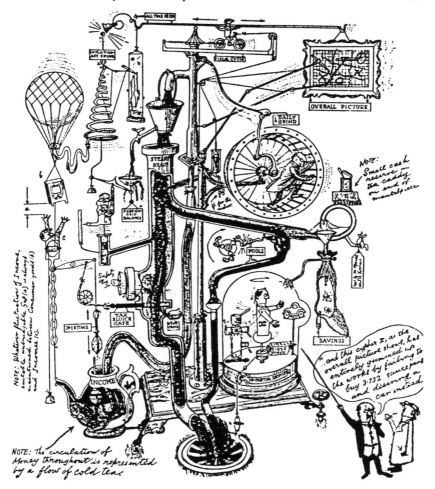

MACHINE DESIGNED TO SHOW THE WORKING OF THE ECONOMIC SYSTEM

Figure 11.3 The machine according to *Punch*

The machine was known in the USA as the 'Moniac', a coinage of Lerner 'to suggest money, the ENIAC [an early computer], and something maniacal' (*Fortune* March 1952, 101). The *Fortune* article described the machine briefly, together with a glossy colour picture. It also announced its availability for sale at a price of $4,300, that is, £1,536 at the then exchange rate (cf. White-Ellerton's price of £450).

5 The Machine's significance in the development of economic analysis

The machine contributed to the subject in at least four ways. First, 'it shows the continuous process of change through time of a multi-variable system, after a change in one or more of the variables' (Phillips in a letter to the New Zealand authorities, 10 December 1949). It was thus a dedicated analogue computer,[16] and as such one of the earliest uses, and certainly one of the most persuasive, of computers in economics.

Second, the machine resolved at least one major theoretical controversy, that between the Keynesian and Robertsonian schools of monetary theory. The debate was about the determination of interest rates. Keynes argued that the equilibrium interest rate is determined by liquidity preference, i.e., is that which induces people to hold exactly the available stock of money and the available supply of bonds. According to Robertson, the rate of interest is determined by the demand and supply of loanable funds, i.e., is that which equates the flow of saving with the flow of investment. The Phillips Machine showed clearly how in equilibrium both formulations are valid.[17] 'Keynes and Robertson need never have quarrelled if they had had the Phillips Machine before them' (Robbins 1972).

Third, the machine facilitated policy analysis in a number of ways. At Meade's request the School acquired another machine which was a mirror-image of the first. As he observed:

by far the most important, and from any point of view very exciting, thing which [Phillips] has done is to invent and construct a foreign exchange market. This has enabled us to link two machines together so that the exports of one control the imports of the other at a fixed or at a variable rate of exchange ... This, of course, is of very great importance for teaching in a country which ... is so dependent on its foreign trade position (letter from Meade to Andrew T. Court, 6 February 1953).

Thus the two machines formed a two-country world economy: it was possible to show the effect on the UK of, say, a budget deficit in the USA; and it was possible to show the effects of a trade war. The picture (p. 109) shows Meade lecturing with the two machines.

One of the uses to which Meade put the machines was to show the destabilising consequences of ill-considered policy intervention. He would make one student Chancellor of the Exchequer, with instructions to manipulate taxation and government spending so as to achieve a target level of national income; he would then make another student Governor of the Bank of England with instructions to use monetary policy to similar ends. Each student was instructed to ignore the other, to show how counter-cyclical fiscal and monetary policy, if uncoordinated, can

end up making matters worse. With the two machines connected, he would add the US Secretary of the Treasury and the Chairman of the Federal Reserve, and the four students, each acting independently of the others, would show how destabilising policy in one country can readily be transmitted to another and how, in the extreme, an inter-linked international economy can be even more unstable than a domestic economy. Richard Cooper subsequently US Assistant Secretary of the Treasury and Professor of Economics at Yale, said at the time that it was the Phillips Machine which first showed him how much one thing depended on another.

Finally, the machine was visual. It was therefore immensely useful as a teaching device though possibly, given its complexity, more useful for relatively advanced students. Though its calculating functions were fairly rapidly overtaken by digital computers, it still remains the only *visual* model of its type.

6 The Machine in recent years

From some time in the mid 1950s the LSE machines were used less and less, and eventually fell into disuse, though rumours still buzzed among students in the mid 1960s.[18]

Harry Johnson's initiative

By the early 1970s, Meade was in Cambridge, Phillips retired in Auckland, and LSE's two machines were gathering dust in a cellar. In autumn 1971, Harry Johnson, who had come across the machine in Cambridge in the early 1950s, set in hand a project for restoring at least one of the machines, and roped me in to give a hand. An American undergraduate volunteer, Joe Grundfest, spent most of the 1971 Christmas vacation cannibalising one of the machines to get the other one going.[19] Grundfest was immensely enthusiastic, and with an understanding of economics beyond his years and vacation work experience with swimming pool filtration systems, was ideally equipped for the task. He rapidly established himself as the resident expert on the machine, and his ingenuity and enthusiasm made it possible to demonstrate it to Harry Johnson's M.Sc. Group in the Lent term 1972, as described in the *LSE Magazine* at the time (Barr 1973).

It was clear, however, that the machine was in a very fragile state and really required resources of time and materials beyond those of a vacation project. Johnson therefore suggested a threefold arrangement: I was to track down White-Ellerton (who had moved from their former premises) to see if they could refurbish the machine; he would put up some money and persuade others to do likewise; and the LSE library would be asked to place the machine on permanent exhibition.

White-Ellerton was eventually found. I spoke to Philip White in early 1974. He remembered Bill Phillips with pleasure, and though he no longer had the drawings (they had been thrown out only a year earlier during a spring clean) remembered the construction so well that he felt that the lack of drawings would be no serious problem. Though a great deal of work would be involved, he would be happy to do it.

Nothing came of the venture for two reasons. Harry Johnson, having had a stroke, resigned in mid 1974 and returned to Chicago. His interest in the project continued but, inevitably given the distance, some of the urgency was lost. Second, and crucially, Philip White also had health problems and by mid 1975 felt that the task was too large for him to take on, much though he would have liked to have worked on the machine again.

Though the project was stalled, interest in the machine continued. The Museum of Science and Industry in Chicago, at Johnson's instigation, briefly entertained the idea of restoring it, and there were enquiries from the Science Museum in London, from the BBC (the machine made guest appearances on The Money Programme and on Panorama), and from Italian television.

The Imperial College initiative   ·

Partly as a result of this continuing interest, help was sought from Imperial College. Professor J.R.D. Francis of the Department of Civil Engineering looked over the machine (by then back in the basement and rather the worse for wear) in November 1977, expressed his willingness to help, and was guardedly optimistic about the possibility of overhauling it.

The School gave its permission for the machine to be moved to Imperial College and, after some delay over the organisation of transport, it was on the point of being moved when Professor Francis died. Appointing his successor took time, and was followed by increasing financial stringency, culminating in the major change in the overseas student fees regime in late 1979 after which Imperial College, like LSE, had to concentrate on putting its own financial house in order.

The STICERD initiative

The machine continued to gather dust over the 1980s, and though interest and enquiries continued, nothing much happened until spring 1987. Bill Brainard, Professor of Economics at Yale University, visiting the Suntory-Toyota International Centre for Economics and Related Disciplines (STICERD) at the School, asked after the machine, and one afternoon he, Tony Atkinson and I paid it a visit. Tony Atkinson, then chairman of STICERD, took up the running. At his request Bill Brainard and I gave a rough assessment of the necessary work, on the basis of which STICERD's Planning Sub-Committee authorised funding for the machine's restoration.

A post was advertised in May 1987. Remembering Joe Grundfest's success, given his 'double major' in economics and plumbing, I sought someone with a similar background, and appointed Reza Moghadam, who was just completing an M.Sc. in economics at the School, and whose first degree at Oxford was in mathematics and physics.

Moghadam started work in July 1987. The initial intention was that he would put together a set of detailed instructions as to the necessary work, the work itself to be done by an (unspecified) firm of engineers. Moghadam, however, showed great initiative in tackling the job; wanted to do the repair work himself; and brought in Colin Carter, an aeronautical engineer, to add depth of technical expertise.

The two of them worked through the summer; they stripped and cleaned many of the parts; made, or ordered from outside experts, parts to replace those which had broken; installed new pumps and servo mechanisms; and more or less remade the plotters from scratch. The task was largely one of painstaking mechanical detective work, greatly assisted by permission to inspect the Cambridge machine which, though not working, was much better preserved.

By mid October, after an injection of additional funding from STICERD, the machine, apart from a few small areas, was working well enough to be shown to a fascinated group of STICERD personnel, and to be filmed in action as part of a project on the life of Keynes. Valda Phillips attended the unveiling of the restored machine in 1989. James Meade gave an enthralling lecture and demonstration in 1990, and another in 1992 when the LSE machine was linked with one restored at Cambridge. Care and maintenance of the elderly, brittle material, however, turned out to be difficult. Both for that reason and to make it available to a wider public, the restored machine was transferred to the Science Museum in 1995. It is now on permanent display in the computing section.

The Phillips Machine, like some strange creature striding through the life of the School from 1949 onwards, has left footprints involving some of the LSE's greatest names: James Meade, Lionel Robbins, Abba Lerner, Bill Phillips himself, and in later years Harry Johnson and Tony Atkinson. The machine commemorates a remarkable man and exciting times in the School's history. Bill Phillips made major innovative contributions to economics, of which the machine was only the first, and he rose, seemingly effortlessly, from a Pass degree in Sociology to a Chair in Economics in nine short years. But he was remarkable also in human terms – adventurous, tenacious, insatiably curious, shy, and with a lovely sense of humour. He is one of those rare people memories of whom always bring a warm smile to those who knew him. As E.H. Phelps Brown wrote in the concluding words of Bill Phillips' obituary in *The Times* (6 March 1975):

His personality was as fresh and endearing as his mind was creative. The world of economics was enriched by his restless originality; to be his colleague was to be his friend.

Notes

Two people in particular have brought the Phillips machine project to life: Professor Tony Atkinson's enthusiastic support made the restoration project possible, Professor James Meade gave permission to consult and quote from his personal papers and both gave valuable comments on an early draft of this paper. I am very grateful also to Mrs. Valda Phillips for permission to quote from Professor Phillips' letters, to Dr G.E.A. Raspin, the Manuscript Librarian at the British Library of Political and Economic Science, for help with the archival material, and to Dr C. Bean, Professor Arthur Brown, Professor W.T. Newlyn, Dr M. Perlman, Mr R. Tizard and the LSE administration for factual information and help with earlier versions. None of them should be implicated in errors which remain. The cartoon in figure 11.3 and the extract on pp. 105–6 are reproduced with the kind permission of *Punch*. The restoration work described in this paper was financed by the Suntory-Toyota International Centre for Economics and Related Disciplines (STICERD), London School of Economics.

1 Most of the information on Bill Phillips' early years is taken from Blyth (1975), which is based on his biographical note for the *Festschrift* given to Bill Phillips on his sixtieth birthday. A draft of the biographical note was read and corrected by Bill Phillips.

2 Recollections of the seminar by Robbins (1972) and Meade (telephone conversation in January 1988), on which this and the following paragraphs are based, are vivid and in complete agreement.

3 See p. 108 below.

4 New Zealanders who had spent time in a POW camp were eligible for a Rehabilitation Grant from the New Zealand government to pay for their studies. A condition of the award was that recipients studying abroad thereafter returned to New Zealand.

5 In the event Phillips decided not to attempt to patent the machine.

6 Phillips' paper was written in early summer and published in August – in sharp contrast with today's publication lags.

7 The extract from Robbins' letter and the subsequent chronology of events come from the School's records.

8 This letter was put before the Appointments Committee on 6 December 1950. The next day the Director wrote to Phillips extending his original appointment as temporary engineering consultant from 1 July to 30 September 1950, and ante-dating his appointment as Assistant Lecturer to 1 October 1950.

9 The thesis was submitted after exactly four years, the minimum permissible for part-time registration, a fact which evoked a deep sigh from the current Dean of the Graduate School, beset by the problem of Ph.D. completion rates.

10 Those at the School between the late 1950s and mid 1960s might remember a 7 foot high shapeless bundle by the wall in room 237 (now called room A347) near the Robinson Room. The machine at Cambridge was in use for much longer. Tony Atkinson remembers attending a course 'The National Income Machine' in 1964/1965 taught on Saturdays by Richard Goodwin (see chapter 13).

11 Most of Tizard's work on the DEUCE was concerned with the development of a comprehensive set of statistical programmes for generating and testing sequences of random numbers for work by Professor Maurice Kendall and Alan Stuart (later Professor of Statistics at LSE). In a telephone conversation, Richard Tizard painted a riveting picture of a large room filled with a mass of valves and wires to which, on occasion, he had to take a soldering iron to repair a faulty connection. Today the equivalent of five million valves is contained in a microchip about the size of a postage stamp.

12 Readers wishing to refresh their theory by looking at a first year text should consult one of Begg, Fischer and Dornbusch (1997), Lipsey and Chrystal (1995), or Stiglitz (1993); for an intermediate (that is, second year) text see Dornbusch and Fischer (1994).

13 An open economy includes international trade; for details of the IS-LM model see any of the references mentioned in n.12.

14 A handwritten comment by Lionel Robbins in May 1978 on a rather facetious article about the machine reads: 'I can't help feeling that [the journalist] has no real conception of the pathbreaking significance of the Phillips invention.'

15 In the Department's account to the University of its expenditure, the machine appeared as 'calculator'.

16 A dedicated computer has only one use, for example, a computer which is set up *only* to be a word processor. An analogue computer performs its calculations by measuring the strength of an electric current or, in this case, the rate of flow of water, as opposed to a digital computer, which performs its calculations by manipulating binary digits.

17 In terms of the IS-LM model, Robertson argued that the interest rate is the outcome of equilibrium in the flow-of-funds market, which is the financial counterpart of saving and investment decisions; the equilibrium interest rate, according to Robertson, is thus a point on the IS curve. Keynes, in contrast, argued that the interest rate is the outcome of equilibrium in the money market, that is, a point on the LM curve. When the IS-LM model is in equilibrium, the interest rate is a point on both the IS *and* LM curves, that is, in equilibrium the Keynesian and Robertsonian formulations are consistent.

18 As a nervous undergraduate I was talking to Bill Phillips at a social gathering and told him of the rumours I had heard about a 'pink lemonade national income machine'. 'Yes', he said, 'I built it'. Given the education and enjoyment I have had from the machine since then, I am glad that the large hole in the ground for which I devoutly wished at the time did not materialise. It was typical of his modesty that none of us undergraduates knew anything about his life prior to the Phillips Curve.

19 The two machines were Meade's two-country world economy described earlier. The standard Phillips Machine is that illustrated in figures 11.1 and 11.2. Its companion in the two-country model was in all respects a mirror-image. When we inspected the machines in 1971, the latter was in better condition, and so the standard machine was cannibalised to restore it. As a historical accident, therefore, the restored machine is a mirror-image of all the other machines (and also a mirror-image of figures 11.1 and 11.2).

12   Early Reactions to Mark I and II

Graeme Dorrance

Richard Sayers was considered to be the most precise and most comprehensible lecturer at LSE. In the Spring of 1949 he received a letter that said in effect:

I have great difficulty in trying to understand your lectures. I know something about plumbing [a gross understatement], and have tried to sketch a hydraulic model similar to the one on page 117 of Boulding. I enclose a copy of my sketch. Could you please comment on it?

Sayers was meticulous in responding to any approach by a student. He asked me to see the author of the note. I met with Bill, discussed his model, suggested some changes in his flows, and arranged for him to meet with Ralph Turvey. By then, examinations were near and Bill had to spend the rest of the term working on his sociology.

At the end of term, two people, in particular, were enthusiastic regarding the design: Walter Newlyn and Bill's landlord (the Mr Langley, a former employee of the metropolitan Water Board with a well-equipped work shed in his garage, referred to in Bill's acknowledgement at the beginning of chapter 10). Walter Newlyn guaranteed an overdraft to allow Bill to purchase the components for his machine (Mark I). Mr and Mrs Langley offered him free room and board for the summer, one cinema visit with them and one packet of cigarettes per week (Bill must have had other resources to satisfy his nicotine needs).

Bill was on a post-war grant that required him to return to New Zealand as soon as his studies were finished. Hoping to extend his stay in England, he went to the LSE with a sketch in one hand and a pump made from surplus aircraft landing gear in the other. Fortunately, James Meade was the only staff member in the building during that vacation day. Meade, with his fascination in the structure of kites and similar apparatus, was immediately attracted to the design of the machine and

115

certified that Bill's stay in England was essential to the completion of his studies. Hence Mark I was completed.

In late 1949 or early 1950, Meade arranged for Bill's machine to be demonstrated to Lionel Robbins' graduate seminar, where it received an enthusiastic reception from the more perceptive members, and extreme scepticism from the less perceptive. At the time Alan Day and I shared a room along the hall from the seminar room. The machine was wheeled there for further demonstration. My research assistant learned to operate it and proceeded to demonstrate it to gaggles of goggle-eyed students.

The machine Mark I was a Heath Robinson contraption. Not the neat model shown in the simple sketches in figures 10.2 and 10.3 of chapter 10. Among other things, Bill had been unable to deal with the problem of inflation and had drilled a hole in one of the tubes through which water squirted whenever there was an inflation. Regularly, Alan and I returned to the room to find it a pool. We borrowed some towels from the refectory and wrung them out through the window. Fortunately, LSE was still the empire on which the concrete never set and there was only a builder's store pile beneath us. Hence, no one had the experience that Dr Johnson had approximately a hundred metres from where the School now stands when a woman heaved a bucket of slops outside her window.

In 1950, Bill was retained as a consultant by LSE and an engineering company was engaged to produce a much slicker and improved Mark II. Bill then proceeded to a Ph.D. in economics (his thesis was the origin of the Phillips Curve article), from which he progressed to the most prestigious chair at LSE and to be eligible for inclusion in Mark Blaug's list of *Great Economists Since Keynes* (1985).

Later, Meade combined two machines: one machine representing country A, with the other, (B), representing the rest of the world, or vice versa. In this structure, A's exports are B's imports and A's imports are B's exports. Hence the closed Keynesian economy becomes the open Harrodlian one. The demonstration of the machine to visitors to LSE aroused a diverse set of reactions. Dennis Robertson practically danced a jig, he was so fascinated by it. Abba Lerner immediately appointed himself as US agent for the sale of the machine, hoping to make an entrepreneurial income thereby. One dinner was reported to me where the Chancellor of the Exchequer and the Governor of the Bank of England were present. Afterwards the guests adjourned to the machine room and the Chancellor was given control of the fiscal levers and the Governor control of the monetary ones. I understand that this manipulation of the levers indicated why the UK economy was in the state it was. One surprising exception was Alvin Hansen who we took to see it, thinking that it would excite him. He glanced at it and quickly made it clear that he thought that it was an interesting toy.

Some of the dismissals of the machine resulted from a misunderstanding of its purpose. In 1950s, the superiority of digital apparatus over analog ones was not yet certain. Some onlookers made the mistake of thinking that it was a multiple regression calculator. It was designed as a teaching device to 'help non-mathematicians by enabling them to see the quantitative changes that occur in an inter-related system of variables following initial changes in one or more items'.

An error of ±4 per cent (chapter 10, p. 68) makes the device unusable for calculation. Now when any candidate has to qualify as a mathematician before acceptance as an economics student, there may be no need for a Phillips-type machine. One may wonder, however, if it would not be a good idea to make economists look at a machine, or sketches of one similar to Bill's, to comprehend the workings of their systems of equations.

With the unfortunate mathematisation of economics, lecturers are disdainful of considering the implications of their equations by demonstrations similar to those possible with a stock/flow machine, or sketches of ones comparable to the Phillips Machine. Hence, the 'new wave' following Samuelson's *Foundations* has resulted in little demand for the machine. Liverpool has one, as does Roosevelt University.

Lerner demonstrated it at the 1950 meeting of the American Economic Association before generally sceptical audiences. Only Andrew Court of General Motors and Jacques Polak of the IMF were enthusiastic. Lerner's demonstration model was shipped to General Motors in Detroit and Polak arranged for it to be delivered to the 1952 meeting of Central Bankers of the American Continents. Unfortunately the GM people did not screw the machine into its shipping container properly and I spent most of my time in Havana repairing and demonstrating the machine when I was not engaged in the discussions for which I had been sent by the IMF. I could find only one constant speed low voltage motor in Havana, and it could only be fitted in the machine so that it rotated in reverse direction to the original motor. Consequently all the positively sloped curves appeared as negatively sloped ones, and vice versa! As neither GM or the IMF were teaching institutions, neither bought a machine. One of Lerner's former students bought one for the Bank of Guatemala. When I was working in the Bank in 1955, I saw it being removed from the library. My mission chief insisted that I not interfere in the Bank's non-policy activities. Hence, I was not permitted to tell the movers to handle it gently after it had been screwed into position. Consequently I was able to hear its separate parts descend the stairway noisily.

13   A Superb Explanatory Device

R.M. Goodwin

It took a visionary man to design and construct this unique machine. The conception, elaboration and construction of the original model took place in the garage of a friend. It involved metal, liquid, plastic, electricity and glass. It could function linearly, but also could be used in an arbitrary non-linear way by cutting a narrow slot in a stiff plastic, placed visibly on the front of this diabolic machine.

In the Cambridge economics faculty there was (and still is) this remarkable contrivance. It was placed on one side of a lecture room in a large enclosure, facing many windows, thus allowing close observation while functioning.

The elaborate necessary machinery was all behind the large metal face of the machine, but the behaviour when in use took place in the front of the machine so that it was feasible for a moderate sized group to watch how a dynamic linear, or nonlinear, dynamic process slowly evolved with changing quantities and rates of flow. By comparison with present-day computers, it was large and cumbersome, but for communicating the dynamics of either linear or non-linear aggregative problems, it was a superb explanatory device. By linking up two machines, it was possible to introduce mutual controls, so that one had a very much wider set of varieties of interdependent behaviour.

Having successfully designed and built such a splendid machine, Bill Phillips should have become rich in consequence of its production and sale. But alas the electronic machines were visible on the horizon, so that not many were produced and sold. There were two at LSE in London. There may have been one or two more in the UK, and very few also in the USA.

After I ceased to use the machine for teaching in Cambridge, a younger member of the faculty began using it, which soon produced difficulties, as had often happened with me. But I could, and did once or twice, call Phillips to come and put things right. This ceased to be possible when he was no longer available, so that the machine sat quietly, and for me sadly, abandoned. Before its recent renovation it sat where it always was, like some ancient monument awaiting discovery.

For me it is an interesting and important ancient landmark in the gradual evolution of computers. It fully deserves its place in the Science Museum. It is a remarkable combination of electronic, liquid, plastic and manual control. It is an important example of a step in the evolution of all types of quantitative computer control, and deserves (as does its creator) a place in the history of quantitative computer control mechanisms.

14 The Phillips Machine and the History of Computing

Doron Swade   B22

B31

I first saw a working Phillips Machine at the LSE on 19 September 1991. The occasion was the formal handover of one of two restored LSE Phillips Machines to the New Zealand Institute of Economic Research (Stern 1992). James Meade and Walter Newlyn, figures inseparably linked with the history and folklore of the Phillips Machines, were present, as were Reza Moghadam and Colin Carter, who had played a major part in the restoration; Moghadam and Carter 1989). The machines were coupled together, and run. The uniting of the two machines, one a mirror image of the other, recreated demonstrations by James Meade in the 1950s of the interaction of two national economies. As before, much gurgling and sloshing ensued to the inevitable delight of the audience.

The sight of the Phillips Machines spurred an approach by the Science Museum in London to acquire the remaining LSE machine. Negotiations between the two institutions exposed a moral conflict. Some staff of the LSE were clearly attached to the machine. It was a memento of a member of their community for whom there is much personal affection. It was also the focus of institutional pride in one of its distinguished sons and there was an emotional reluctance to let go as though parting with the machine would be severing a link with a past. On the other hand, the small community of those familiar with Phillips and the history of his eponymous machine was dispersing and his surviving contemporaries were no longer in their prime. There was concern that the significance of the machine would fade with successive generations of staff and that custodial protection might consequently weaken. Professor Nick Stern, then Chairman of STICERD at the LSE, was acutely sensitive to these issues and had the difficult task of arbitrating the future of the prized device. Other factors had begun to weigh. The two restorers of the machine were pursuing careers elsewhere and would be unlikely to be in a position to provide the continuity of technical support necessary to maintain the increasingly frail device in working order. There was also concern for the gradual deterioration of the machine and the physical consequences of intermittent demonstration. Finally, there was Stern's genuine wish to make the machine more accessible to a wider public.

These considerations finally weighed in favour of transferring the machine to the Science Museum. The basis of the transfer was outright donation but with an undertaking to display the machine as a condition of acquisition. This was unusual. Until the Second World War, the Science Museum had no off-site storage and virtually all artefactual holdings were on public display. During the war objects were removed from the South Kensington site to secure storage outside London and this established the precedent for off-site holdings. It is now the case that as little as 5–10 per cent of object holdings are on public display at any time with the vast bulk of permanent holdings divided between large aircraft hangars outside London and a store three miles from South Kensington. The undertaking to display the machine was an acknowledgment of the concession the LSE had made in parting with the machine at all. The device was transported to the Science Museum on 21 June 1994 and placed on inventory. The short trip across London marked the LSE machine's formal passage into history.

The machine was drained, meticulously cleaned, and chemically stabilised. Over 200 hours of conservation work was expended on it to remove damaging residual deposits from the red ink used to color the water and from the salts added to the solution. Components were then treated to retard further deterioration (STICERD Bulletin 1995). The device had undergone the museological equivalent of embalming, and conservation concerns now militate against the machine being re-infused with its red life-blood to run again. It was placed on public display in the Computing Gallery at South Kensington on 22 March 1995, which, as it happened, was the United Nations World Day for Water. Alongside the exhibit is a short video programme showing the machine in operation using clips culled from a BBC TV *Newsnight* programme filmed at budget time in 1992. The video material is stored on a glass disc. While there is no substitute for a live machine with the attendant frisson of possible mishap, the glass disc may well serve as an archaeological record of the machine in operation.[1]

The Phillips Machine is a special-purpose hydromechanical analog system. It is special purpose in the sense that it implements a specific economic model. It is hydromechanical in that it uses liquid as a measure of economic resource, and mechanical coupling to provide internal feedback between parts of the system. Finally, it is analog in the sense that it works with continuously variable quantities as distinct from discrete or discontinuous quantities.

The history of economic modelling has not left a particularly rich trail of artefactual relics, and in the context of economic theory the Phillips Machine is an anomaly. A question for the historian is whether the machine is more or less anomalous in the larger context of the development of analog computing.

A central narrative in the history of analog machines features the transition, during the post-war years, from mechanical to electronic systems.[2] The differential analysers designed by Vannevar Bush at MIT in the 1930s and early 1940s are the most notable exemplars of the mechanical era. These vast machines were placed under increasing threat following the wartime impetus given to electronic techniques applied to analog simulation and digital computing. The computational elements of the Bush differential analysers were primarily mechanical disc-and-wheel integrators; the physical elements of the early electronic machines were vacuum tubes (or thermionic valves as they were known in the United Kingdom). In analog systems, vacuum-tube amplifiers were used as linear devices in various configurations to add, subtract, multiply and integrate and many computational units were interconnected to model complex systems. In digital systems, vacuum tubes were used in binary (two-state) switching circuits which formed the basis of digital computation and storage. The mature products of these mechanical and electronic technologies offered high levels of precision and varying degrees of speed and flexibility.

What is distinctive about well-engineered mechanical and electronic analog systems is the close correspondence between physical behaviour and mathematical description. The fairly rigorously deterministic behaviour of precisely machined mechanical assemblies, and of electronic systems based on high-gain feedback amplifiers, offered physically accurate realisations of the mathematical models that describe them.

Hydrodynamic systems, on the other hand, were comparatively inexact. Mathematical descriptions of turbulence and non-laminar flow were problematic, and the behaviour of liquids was both difficult to control and difficult to instrument. Apart from the incompleteness of mathematical descriptions, the behaviour of fluids did not offer the generality of electronic voltages or Newtonian mechanics as quantitative representational models. In short, hydrodynamics had little to offer general-purpose analog computing. In terms of its computational technology, the Phillips Machine therefore falls outside mainstream developments in analog computing: it is a special-purpose rather than general-purpose device, and the representational medium was not one that enjoyed general use.

In a wider context, the machine can be seen as part of the Cybernetics movement of the late 1940s and the heady promises brought by control engineering, and feed-back systems in particular, to an understanding of biological and social systems. However, these contextual considerations leave largely untouched the tantalising question as to why Phillips opted for plumbing and Perspex in preference to the emerging electronic technologies. Walter Newlyn collaborated in the design and assisted in the construction of the first prototype.[3] Newlyn recalls that during his visit to the LSE in early 1949 Phillips showed him some early diagrams and that discussions about specifications for a full machine took place during Easter 1949, with the first prototype being demonstrated in November of that year. So as far as the genesis of conception and design is concerned, the period of critical interest is the early part of 1949.

When pressed on the issue of whether Phillips had mentioned electronic alternatives during this period of early collaboration, Newlyn replied with some certainty that based on his exchanges with Phillips, he suspected that Phillips' knowledge of electronic computational techniques at that time 'was nil'.[4] In the first published description of the model, Phillips does refer to electronic methods. He states that 'hydraulic methods have been used in preference to electronic ones which might have given greater accuracy and flexibility' (chapter 10, p. 68). It is not clear whether Phillips had specific systems in mind (the Cambridge EDSAC, for example, a digital vacuum-tube computer built under Maurice Wilkes, and which came into service in June 1949 at the Mathematical Laboratory, Cambridge University) or whether the remark is simply an acknowledgment of the non-specific capabilities of a new but as yet unestablished technology. Newlyn is of the express view that whatever awareness Phillips demonstrates in this remark, such awareness postdates the development of the prototype.

When it comes to Phillips' knowledge of electronic analog computing, the margin for speculation is materially reduced by Phillips himself. In 1957 he expressed his indebtedness to Richard H. Tizard for suggesting to him 'the possibility of using electronic simulators for studying the problems of economic regulation' (chapter 17, note 2). If the date of the Phillips–Tizard meeting can be established, then the issue of precedence in Phillips' awareness of electronic analog techniques for modelling can be resolved. Tizard joined the National Physical Laboratory (NPL) in 1947 and later collaborated with Phillips in the use of NPL's electronic simulator for economic modelling (Yates 1997).[5] This collaboration resulted in Tizard's resignation in 1956 as Head of the Control Mechanisms and Electronics Division to take up a two-year Fellowship at the LSE to work with Phillips on applications of control theory to economics. Tizard clearly recalls Phillips' reaction to the possibilities presented by the simulator when Phillips first saw the NPL machine.

He is convinced from Phillips' reaction that Phillips had little relevant knowledge of electronic analog simulation prior to that meeting.[6] Tizard has been unable to establish the date of his first contact with Phillips but suggested it might have been 1952–1953. Nor is it clear how they learned of each others' work or which of the two initiated the first meeting.

The first mention of the electronic simulator appears in the NPL Annual Report covering the Laboratory's work during 1950 (1951, 46). Reference is made to the 'development of an accurate and flexible electronic simulator for studying the performance of closed loop control systems'. Reports for the years 1951, 1952 and 1953 record enhancements and expansion. It is not until 1954, however, that specific reference is made to the use of the simulator for 'an extensive study of economic systems, in conjunction with the London School of Economics' (1955, 24).[7] The indications are that the substantial work on the NPL simulator started during 1950 and that the work on economic modelling was undertaken as many as three years later. It follows that the Phillips–Tizard collaboration could not have influenced the conception and design of the 1949 prototype.[8]

The attempt to place the Phillips Machine in the context of the history of computing is premised on the notion that the machine is essentially a computational device. To categorise the machine by its computational capabilities alone is to miss its essential purpose. Phillips stated that his machine 'is intended for exposition rather than accurate calculation' and that 'the whole of the operations should be clearly visible and comprehensible to an onlooker' (chapter 10, p. 68). No contemporary electronic device, analog or digital, could have fulfilled this purpose. The digital computers of the time were fixed-installation systems that were physically vast and massively expensive;[9] the analog machines were slightly less so. Cost, size and lack of portability for teaching purposes were one set of prohibitive considerations. But more importantly, while contemporary electronic machines were equal to the computational demands of the Phillips' model, the problem for Phillips was not processing power but visual display.

Contemporary digital computers typically used punched paper tape for input and output. Results, punched automatically on paper tape, were printed off-line on electromechanical teleprinters. Neither tape nor tabulated results are remarkable for their visual immediacy. Direct visual output *was* achieved, using phosphor-screen oscilloscopes. On digital machines, these were not used to display output but to monitor internal states for engineering maintenance and fault-finding. On analog machines, oscilloscopes were used to monitor signal changes at specific points in the system including output waveforms. Pen-recorders were another method of capturing analog results. What these windows into the workings of the system could not provide was a visual representation of dynamic interactivity with the immediate intelligibility offered by the Phillips Machine. The inability of contemporary electronic systems to meet the demands of exposition deflates any residual urgency to establish the extent of Phillips' awareness or ignorance of alternatives to water, pumps and sluices.

It is the inseparable combination of computational capability and pedagogic transparency that dooms any attempt to understand the machine solely in terms of the history of computing technology. The Phillips Machine belongs more to the history of economic modelling or even to the history of classroom teaching aids than it does to the history of computing. It *is* an ingenious computational device. Moreover, it is an inspired piece of pedagogy.

Notes

1 The Cambridge machine has been restored to working order in the Department of Applied Economics. Brian Henry, who was an undergraduate at the LSE in 1959 and a student of Phillips, proposed to use the machine as originally intended – as a classroom teaching aid with live demonstrations.
2 See for example Small (1993).
3 Phillips explicitly acknowledges Newlyn's contribution in chapter 10 (endnote 1). See also 'A Back of the Garage Job' in which Newlyn (1992) recalls the early collaboration.
4 Personal communication, 23 February 1996.
5 I am indebted to David Yates, formerly of NPL, for biographical information on Richard Tizard and for his assistance with NPL sources.
6 Personal communication, 13 February 1996.
7 A fuller description of the simulator appears in *NPL News*, No. 61, 16 May 1955.
8 There is additional circumstantial evidence that the Tizard–Phillips meeting occurred later than July 1951. Tizard served on the Organising and Editorial Committee for a conference on Automatic Control held at Cranfield in July 1951 and actively participated in several discussions. A paper was presented by D.V. Blake of NPL and the NPL simulator was demonstrated. The Proceedings of the conference record a meeting on the 'Analysis of the Behaviour of Economic Systems' the purpose of which was to draw attention to the similarity of the problems confronting economists and engineers in the behaviour of economic and physical systems. The Proceedings contain no mention of Phillips' work. The omission supports the view that Tizard and Phillips had not yet met (see Tustin 1952). The loop with Tustin was evidently closed by 1954. In that year Phillips reviewed Tustin's book, *The Mechanisms of Economic Systems – An Approach to the Problems of Economic Stabilisation*

from the Point of View of Control-System Engineering in the *Economic Journal* (see chapter 18).

9 In the United States, the ENIAC (Electronic Numerical Integrator and Computer) which operated from 1945 to 1955 contained some 18,000 vacuum tube and 1,500 electromechanical relays. The cost of the machine is estimated at a little under $500,000.

10 For an exploration of the expository appeal of the Phillips machine, see Morgan and Boumans (1998).

Part III
Dynamic Stabilisation

Optimal Control

15   The Optimal Control Articles

Adrian Pagan   B22

B31

Chapters 16, 17, 18 and 19 summarise Bill Phillips' early thoughts on the problems of regulating an economy. There can be little doubt that the ideas were sourced from his background and interest in electrical engineering and were essentially a transcription of the methods of 'classical' control to the economic system. Concepts such as the multiplier, accelerator, real balance (Pigou) effects, etc. were used to describe the system in terms whereby the engineering concepts might be applied. These essays are still cited forty years after their publication. It is worth exploring why this is so, as few essays written in that era would have such longevity. To do so, it is useful to spell out what I perceive of as the innovations in the essays.

First, policy should not be thought of in a static but dynamic mode. This idea may seem trite but the accepted analysis of the time was largely one of comparative statics. 'Policy' consisted of shifting the aggregate demand curve up and down the '45° line'. The theoretical foundation of policy laid out in Tinbergen's (1952) classic work was also static. Where the past was recognised it was simply taken as predetermined. The objective of policy was either to manipulate instruments to hit a specified target value or to get as close as possible to this value in the event that some trade-off between targets was needed due to a lack of instruments. Thinking of policy in a dynamic way, with its attendant ideas that changes in policy now may have effects well into the future, and that the lags in a system will require policy to be initiated well before the data at which a target is to be achieved, represented a subtle but profound shift in attitudes. It is interesting to note that explicit recognition of the complexities raised by dynamics immediately brought the issue of expectations formation to the fore and chapter 16 therefore makes explicit allowances for the formation of expectations about inflation.

Secondly, policy is best thought of in terms of rules. It seems unlikely that Bill actually felt that policy was made that way. Certainly, any conversation I had with him showed that he was well aware of the mechanics of actual policy formulation, but for the purpose of analysis he clearly felt that the notion of rules was an extremely valuable one. Classical ideas from servomechanisms were brought into play, producing the categories of proportional, integral and derivative controls. He shows, via analogue simulation in chapter 17, that it is very likely that regulation of an economic system would demand all three types of control. Clearly, this makes regulation a difficult task.

Thirdly, it is very hard to assess the interaction of policy and system dynamics. To some extent the problem arose from his use of continuous time models, but even discrete time versions of the models would have been difficult to solve in those days. As the emphasis in these chapters is continually upon how the dynamics of the system are modified by the policy, it was always necessary to be able to compute the eigenvalues of a system with and without a control rule. Moreover, it would be desirable to be able to specify a policy that eliminated and did not induce cycles into a system. The ability to design rules that achieved a desired set of cyclical characteristics is referred to as 'pole assignment' and is a standard task with modern computational facilities, but a very much more challenging one in the limited computational environment of the 1950s.

Fourthly, some useful observations about the nature of policy were presented as a result of the simulations performed. For example, one of the conclusions of chapter 17 was that

. . . if there is a long delay before corrective action is taken or before it begins to have an appreciable effect it is better that the effect, when it does come, should be gradual rather than sudden. The worst possible condition for regulating purposes is one in which the adjustment of policy demand to a change in the error is delayed for a considerable time and then effected quickly and abruptly.

Such a prescription for caution was probably appreciated by policy-makers but was not one that had been given a formal defence before the articles being dealt with here appeared.

After these articles appeared, Bill seemed to follow control engineering in the direction of optimal rather than classical control. Certainly, by 1968, he seemed convinced that this approach was the superior one. One can appreciate the shift in attitude from the articles of the 1950s. Optimal control provided a method of implementing feedback rules that were relatively easy to compute, and which could be expected to have good system characteristics. Of course, the optimal rule might not eliminate cycles, but given it was specified in terms of achieving targets, there might not be any compelling reason to eliminate cycles. Unlike the Tinbergen approach, which also sets targets, the optimal control literature produced a sequence of policies that explicitly allowed for multi-period optimisation.

By the late 1960s and early 1970s the high point of the movement to optimal control was reached. Optimal control is a very powerful technique if the system is known, but knowledge of economic systems is much fuzzier. Moreover, the equations of the system might change in response to the policy rule, as emphasised by the rational expectations and 'Lucas critique' schools. Taken together, all of these phenomena have been very important in a decline of interest in optimal control work. This is not to say that there has been a decline of interest in the study of the impact of policy. Instead, we have seen a return to Phillips' original vision of studying the characteristics of feedback rules.[1] It is fascinating to speculate about what Bill's attitude to all these developments would have been.

There are other aspects of these chapters which are quite striking when one re-reads them. One is the emphasis upon the possible importance of non-linearities, a subject largely ignored in econometrics until recently. A second is the introduction of the term 'error correction'. Thirdly, in chapter 16 (pp. 151–6), one sees many of the elements found in macro-econometric models today, for example, the importance of the expectations generating mechanism and stock-flow interactions. Finally, and perhaps the most intriguing part of chapter 16, is the presentation in figure 16.11 of the Phillips Curve. What is particularly interesting here is the discussion surrounding it (p. 150). The statement:

Even with flexible factor prices, there will be some level of production and employment which, given the bargaining powers of the different groups in the economy, will just result in the average level of factor prices remaining constant...

sounds remarkably like the definition of a 'natural rate of unemployment' (NAIRU). Indeed, the explanation given of the mechanism is that prices and wages will adjust until the rate of return to entrepreneurs is restored to its original level (p. 150). Modern versions of the Phillips Curve have the rate of change of the real wage a function of the gap between the level of unemployment and the NAIRU. This viewpoint is certainly close to Phillips' description. In the curve that he presents, the rate of change of wages is proportional to the deviation of actual production from that level of output that results in zero product price inflation. Hence, the system presented in this chapter can be regarded as a remarkable foreshadowing of many of today's macroeconometric models.[2]

Notes

1 See, for example, McCallum (1988).
2 See, for example, McKibbin and Sachs (1991) and Powell and Murphy (1995).

16 Stabilisation Policy in a Closed Economy

A.W. Phillips

Recommendations for stabilising aggregate production and employment have usually been derived from the analysis of multiplier models, using the method of comparative statics. This type of analysis does not provide a very firm basis for policy recommendations, for two reasons. First, the time path of income, production and employment during the process of adjustment is not revealed. It is quite possible that certain types of policy may give rise to undesired fluctuations, or even cause a previously stable system to become unstable, although the final equilibrium position as shown by a static analysis appears to be quite satisfactory. Second, the effects of variations in prices and interest rates cannot be dealt with adequately with the simple multiplier models which usually form the basis of the analysis.

In section I of this chapter the usual assumption of constant prices and interest rates is retained, and a process analysis is used to illustrate some general principles of stabilisation policies. In section II these principles are used in developing and analysing a more general model, in which prices and interest rates are flexible.

I Some general principles of stabilisation

1 The model[1]

The model consists of only two relationships. On the supply side, it is assumed that the rate of flow of current production, measured in real units per year and identical with the flow of real income, is adjusted, after a time lag, to the rate of flow of aggregate demand, also measured in real units per year. On the demand side, it is assumed that aggregate demand varies with real income or production, without significant time lag.[2] The proportion by which any change in aggregate demand induced by a change in real income falls short of that change in income will be called

134

the marginal leakage from the system. In the simplest case of a closed economy with government ignored and with constant investment it is equal to the marginal propensity to save. In all the illustrations given below the marginal leakage is assumed to be 0.25.

The response of production to changes in demand is assumed to be gradual and continuous. For aggregative models this is more realistic than the usual assumption that production changes in sudden jumps. Even if each producer were to have a rigid production plan which he altered only at intervals of several months, the planning periods of the thousands of individual producers would overlap, and the response of aggregate production to a sudden change in aggregate demand would consequently be more nearly approximated by a continuously changing variable than by one changing only at discrete intervals of time. To obtain a model in which this continuous change is represented, a distributed time lag is introduced by the hypothesis that whenever the production flow is different from the flow of demand, the production flow will be changing in a direction which tends to eliminate the difference and at a rate proportional to the difference.

The implications of this hypothesis are illustrated in figure 16.1, which shows the change that would occur in production if, from an initial equilibrium position, demand were to fall by one unit at time zero and to remain constant thereafter, on the assumption that the rate of change of production, measured in units per year, is four times the difference between demand and production, both measured in units per year. The factor of proportionality, 4 in this case, is a measure of the speed of

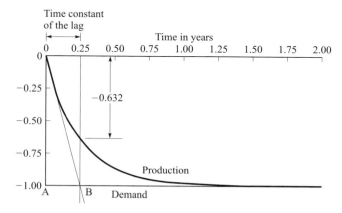

Figure 16.1 Single production lag

response of production to changes in demand, and is indicated in figure 16.1 by the slope of the line OB, drawn tangential to the production-response curve at O. Its reciprocal is a measure of the slowness of response, or time taken to adjust production to changes in demand, and is called the time constant of the production lag. In this case it is equal to three months or 0.25 of a year, and is indicated in figure 16.1 by the length of the line AB. The time constant may also be defined as the time that would be taken, after a sudden change in demand, for production to change by an amount equal to 0.632^3 of the full adjustment required for a new equilibrium, if demand were meanwhile to remain constant at its new value.

It is possible that a better representation of the real process of adjustment would be obtained by analysing the time lag into a number of separate components operating consecutively. For example, there may be a time lag in observing that an adjustment is necessary, another in making the decision to carry out the adjustment, and a third in actually making the adjustment. If two such lags are assumed, each with a time constant of $6\frac{1}{2}$ weeks so that the combined time constant is three months as in the previous example, the time path of the adjustment becomes that shown in curve (b) of figure 16.2, while if three consecutive lags are assumed, each with a time constant of $4\frac{1}{3}$ weeks, the time path becomes that shown in curve (c) of figure 16.2.[4] Although the slower adjustment obtained in the initial stages of the process with these multiple lags may be more realistic than that which results from the assumption of a single

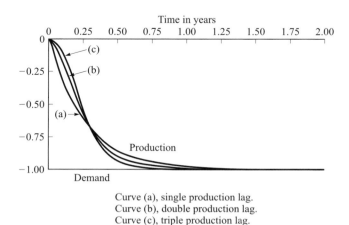

Curve (a), single production lag.
Curve (b), double production lag.
Curve (c), triple production lag.

Figure 16.2

lag, the single lag is retained in the following analysis in order to simplify the mathematics.[5] In all the illustrations given below, the time constant of this single production lag is assumed to be three months.

In the complete model demand does not remain constant during the process of adjustment, but itself responds to changes in real income and production. It is therefore necessary to distinguish between an initial or spontaneous change in demand, representing a disturbance or change in the relationships of the model, and the additional or induced changes in demand which result from the dependence of demand on production and in turn induce further changes in production by the familiar multiplier process. When these induced effects are taken into account the response of production, measured from an initial equilibrium value, to a sponta-neous fall in demand of one unit, occurring at time zero and continuing thereafter, is shown by curve (a) of figure 16.3. This is, of course, simply a continuous version of the ordinary multiplier process, the multiplier being the reciprocal of the marginal leakage, or 4.

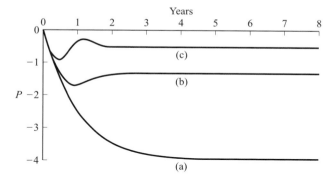

Curve (a), no stabilisation policy.
Curve (b), $f_p = 0.5$, $T = 6$ months.
Curve (c), $f_p = 2$, $T = 6$ months.

Figure 16.3 *Note*: The symbols used in figure 16.3–16.9 inclusive have the following meanings:
P Change in production (measured from initial equilibrium)
f_p Proportional correction factor
f_i Integral correction factor
f_d Derivative correction factor
T Time constant of the correction lag

2 The stabilisation problem

The adoption of a policy for stabilising production implies that there is some level of production which it is desired to maintain. The desired level may be that which, given the existing productive resources, would result in a certain level of employment, or it may be that which would result in a constant price index of consumers' goods, or the choice may be based on a number of other economic, political or social considerations. For the limited purpose of studying the principles of stabilisation in a closed economy, the choice of desired production may be considered as given. The difference between the actual production and desired production at any time will be called the error in production.

Stabilisation policy consists in detecting any error and taking correcting action, by altering government expenditure, taxation, or monetary and credit conditions, in order to change demand in a direction which tends to eliminate the error. The amount by which aggregate demand would be changed as a direct result of the stabilisation policy (i.e., excluding the further changes in demand which will be induced automatically through the operation of the multiplier process) if the policy were to operate without time lag will be called the potential policy demand, and the amount by which aggregate demand is in fact changed at any time as a direct result of the policy will be called the actual policy demand. Both may, of course, be either positive or negative.

The actual policy demand will usually be different from the potential policy demand, owing to the time required for observing changes in the error, adjusting the correcting action accordingly and for the changes in the correcting action to produce their full effects. A distributed time lag can again be introduced by the hypothesis that whenever such a difference exists the actual policy demand will be changing in a direction which tends to eliminate the difference and at a rate proportional to the difference. The time constant of this lag can then be defined in the same way as was done in the case of the production lag. The examples given below have been worked out for alternative correction lags with time constants of six months and six weeks respectively.

A number of different types of stabilisation policy will now be considered, corresponding to the different ways in which the correcting action taken may be related to the error in production.[6]

3 Proportional stabilisation policy

The simplest type of stabilisation policy is one in which the correcting action taken is such that the potential policy demand is made proportional in magnitude and opposite in sign[7] to the error in production. The ratio of the potential policy demand to the error, which is a measure of the strength of the stabilisation policy, will be called the proportional correction factor. As an example, a proportional correction factor of 0.5 would mean that if production was 2 per cent below the desired value the authorities concerned would attempt directly to stimulate demand by an amount equal to 1 per cent of production (excluding the further increase which would be induced through the multiplier effects), and as the error was gradually reduced as a result of this action they would decrease the potential policy demand proportionately.

To show the effect of such a policy, it will be assumed that from an equilibrium position with production at the desired value there occurs at time zero and continues thereafter a spontaneous fall in demand of one unit. The resulting time path of production, if the proportional correction factor is 0.5 and the correction lag has a time constant of six months, is shown by curve (b) of figure 16.3.

The marginal leakage is assumed, as before, to be 0.25 and the production lag to have a time constant of three months, so the effect of the stabilisation policy can be seen by comparing curve (b) with curve (a). Curve (c) of figure 16.3 shows the effect of a stronger policy with a proportional correction factor of 2, the time constant of the correction lag again being six months. In the examples illustrated in figure 16.4 the time constant of the correction lag has been reduced to six weeks, the proportional correction factor again being 0 for curve (a), 0.5 for curve (b) and 2 for curve (c).

Two defects of a proportional stabilisation policy are immediately apparent. First, complete correction of an error is not obtained, since the correcting action continues only because the error exists. If the spontaneous change in demand is denoted by δ, the error in the final equilibrium level of production by ε, the proportional correction factor by f_p and the marginal leakage by l, in the final equilibrium the sum of the spontaneous and the policy changes in demand will be $\delta - f_p\varepsilon$. The usual multiplier formula applies, so the total change in demand and production, including the change induced by the multiplier process, will be $\frac{\delta - f_p\varepsilon}{l}$. But the change in production is also the error, so that $\frac{\delta - f_p\varepsilon}{l}$, from which $\varepsilon = \frac{\delta}{l + f_p}$. When this type of policy is applied, therefore, the static multiplier becomes the reciprocal of the sum of the marginal leakage and the proportional correction factor, and a proportional correction factor of infinity would be required if the error were to be completely eliminated. The second defect of a proportional stabilisation policy is that it tends to cause a cyclical fluctuation in the time path of production, this fluctua-

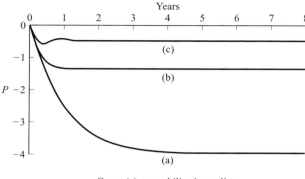

Curve (a), no stabilisation policy.
Curve (b), $f_p = 0.5$, $T = 6$ weeks.
Curve (c), $f_p = 2$, $T = 6$ weeks.

Figure 16.4

tion being the greater, the stronger the policy and the longer the time lag involved in applying it.

It may be noted that the proportional correction factor and the marginal propensity to save, or more generally any marginal leakage, have similar effects on the stability of the system. With a marginal propensity to save of zero, the simple multiplier system assumed so far would have no inherent regulation at all, i.e., no stable equilibrium position would exist. With a positive marginal propensity to save, the change in demand resulting from a given change in production would differ from what it would have been if the marginal propensity to save had been zero by an amount proportional in magnitude and opposite in sign to the change in production. The marginal propensity to save therefore acts as a regulating mechanism of the proportional type inherent in the economy.

4 Integral stabilisation policy

An integral stabilisation policy is one in which the potential policy demand at any time is made proportional in magnitude and opposite in sign to the cumulated error up to that time, i.e., to the time integral of the error instead of to the magnitude of the error. In terms of figures 16.3 and 16.4, with an integral stabilisation policy the potential policy demand at any time is made proportional to the area between the actual production curve and the desired production curve (or zero line) up to that time, whereas with a proportional stabilisation policy it is made proportional to the vertical distance between the two curves at that time. The ratio of the potential policy demand to the time integral of the error will be called the integral correction factor. If an error in production of 2 per cent were to occur and to persist for a year, then with an integral correction factor of 0.5 the potential policy demand would be increased steadily from zero at the beginning to 1 per cent of production at the end of the year. It is clear that with an integral stabilisation policy the final equilibrium position, if it exists, will be one in which the error is completely eliminated, since so long as even the smallest error persists the cumulated error or time integral of the error must be continuously increasing, and with it the magnitude of the correcting action, so that equilibrium is possible only when the error is zero.

It will be found, however, that in thus avoiding the first defect of a proportional correction policy, the second defect, the introduction of cyclical fluctuations, is greatly aggravated, and for this reason integral correction is rarely used alone in automatic control systems. There may, however, be a tendency for monetary authorities, when attempting to correct an 'error' in production, continuously to strengthen their correcting action the longer the error persists, in which case they would be applying an integral correction policy.[8] Also, it will be argued in section II of this article that flexible prices in an economy operate as an inherent regulating mechanism of the integral type. The integral relationship may therefore be of some importance in a number of economic adjustments.

Figures 16.5 and 16.6 show the effects of applying an integral stabilisation policy. The assumptions of the basic model and the type of disturbance are the same as in the previous examples. Curves (a) again show the response of production to unit spontaneous fall in demand when there is no stabilisation policy. In figure 16.5, curve (b) shows the effect of adopting a stabilisation policy with an integral correction factor of 0.5, and curve (c) the effect of a stronger policy with an integral correction factor of 2, the time constant of the correction lag being six months in each case. Curves (b) and (c) in figure 16.6 show how the response is modified when the time constant of the correction lag is reduced to six weeks, the integral correction factor again being 0.5 for curve (b) and 2 for curve (c).

It will be seen that even with a low value of the integral correction factor, cyclical fluctuations of considerable magnitude are caused by this type of policy, and also that the approach to the desired value of production is very slow. Moreover, any attempt to speed up the process by adopting a stronger policy is likely to do more harm than good by increasing the violence of the cyclical fluctuations, particularly when the time lag of the correcting action is long. With an integral correction

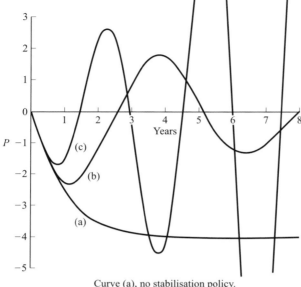

Curve (a), no stabilisation policy.
Curve (b), $f_i = 0.5$, $T = 6$ months.
Curve (c), $f_i = 2$, $T = 6$ months.

Figure 16.5

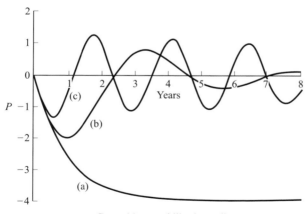

Curve (a), no stabilisation policy.
Curve (b), $f_i = 0.5$, $T = 6$ weeks.
Curve (c), $f_i = 2$, $T = 6$ weeks.

Figure 16.6

factor of 2 and a correction lag of six months, as illustrated in curve (c) of figure 16.3, the system has become dynamically unstable. In such a case the oscillations would increase in amplitude until limited by non-linearities in the system and would then persist within those limits so long as the policy was continued.

5 Proportional plus integral stabilisation policy

A combination of proportional and integral stabilisation policies gives much better results than either policy alone. This can be seen from figures 16.7 and 16.8, in which curves (a) again show the response of production to unit spontaneous fall in demand in the absence of stabilisation policy. Curve (b) of figure 16.7 shows how this response is modified if a stabilisation policy is adopted having a proportional correction factor of 0.5 plus an integral correction factor of 0.5, the time constant of the correction lag being six months. The proportional element in the policy helps to speed up correction and to limit the fluctuations caused by the integral policy, while the integral element provides the complete correction unobtainable with the proportional policy alone. Curve (c) of figure 16.7 shows the response when a stronger policy is adopted, keeping the same proportion between the two elements, both correction factors being raised to 2, while in curve (d) they are raised to 8, the correction lag remaining at six months in each case.

In the examples illustrated in figure 16.8 the time constant of the correction lag is reduced to six weeks. Curve (b) shows the response when both proportional and integral correction factors are 0.5. Comparing this with curve (b) of figure 16.7, it may appear paradoxical that with a shorter correction lag a longer time elapses before something near full correction is obtained. The reason for this is that the more rapid operation of the policy results in a smaller error in the early stages of the adjustment, so that the cumulated error which forms the basis of the integral element is reduced, so reducing the speed of the later states of the adjustment, which depend mainly on the integral element. The shorter the correction lag, therefore, the greater must be the integral correction factor if rapid correction is to be obtained. Conversely, of course, the longer the correction lag the smaller must be the integral correction factor if overshooting and fluctuations are to be avoided. A proportional correction factor of 0.5 plus an integral correction factor of 2 gives the response shown by curve (c) of figure 16.8, while for curve (d) the proportional and integral correction factors are 2 and 8, and for curve (e) 8 and 32 respectively.

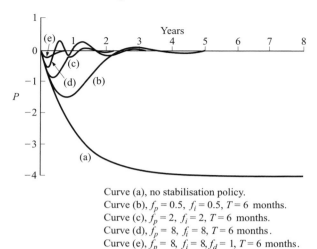

Curve (a), no stabilisation policy.
Curve (b), $f_p = 0.5$, $f_i = 0.5$, $T = 6$ months.
Curve (c), $f_p = 2$, $f_i = 2$, $T = 6$ months.
Curve (d), $f_p = 8$, $f_i = 8$, $T = 6$ months.
Curve (e), $f_p = 8$, $f_i = 8$, $f_d = 1$, $T = 6$ months.

Figure 16.7

The fluctuations in the responses shown in curves (b), (c) and (d) of figure 16.7 and in curves (c), (d) and (e) of figure 16.8 could be eliminated by a sufficient reduction in the integral correction factor in each case; but only at the cost of increasing both the maximum size of the error and the time taken to correct it. A better method is available which not only eliminates the fluctuations, but also reduces both the maximum size of the error and the time taken to obtain complete correction.

6 The addition of derivative correction

This method is to add to the potential policy demand, as determined by the proportional and integral relationships, a third element, proportional in magnitude and opposite in sign to the rate of change, or time derivative, of production. The effect of this is to make demand lower than it would otherwise have been whenever production is rising, and higher than it would otherwise have been whenever production is falling, so tending to check movements in either direction without affecting the final equilibrium position. The ratio of the magnitude of this element in the potential policy demand to the rate of change of production is called the derivative correction factor.

Curve (e) of figure 16.7 shows the response of production to a unit fall in demand when a proportional plus integral plus derivative stabilisation

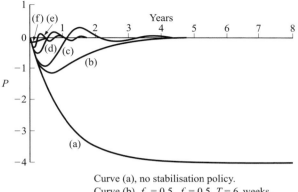

Curve (a), no stabilisation policy.
Curve (b), $f_p = 0.5$, $f_i = 0.5$, $T = 6$ weeks.
Curve (c), $f_p = 0.5$, $f_i = 2$, $T = 6$ weeks.
Curve (d), $f_p = 2$, $f_i = 8$, $T = 6$ weeks.
Curve (e), $f_p = 8$, $f_i = 32$, $T = 6$ weeks.
Curve (f), $f_p = 8$, $f_i = 32$, $f_d = 0.25$, $T = 6$ weeks.

Figure 16.8

policy is applied, the correction factors being 8, 8 and 1 respectively, with a correction lag of six months. This may be compared with curve (d) of figure 16.7, which shows the response when the derivative element of the policy is omitted, the other elements being unchanged. Similarly, the addition of a derivative element with a correction factor of 0.25 to a proportional plus integral policy with correction factors of 8 and 32 respectively and a correction lag of six weeks modifies the response from that shown by curve (e) of figure 16.8 to that shown by curve (f). It will be noticed that in order to maintain a suitable balance between the three elements in the policy when the length of the correction lag is reduced, it is necessary to reduce the derivative correction factor by about the same proportion as the time constant of the correction lag, whereas the integral correction factor had to be increased by about the same proportion.

The reader may have observed that the application of a derivative correction policy introduces into the system the same type of relationship as that postulated by the acceleration principle, but operating in the opposite direction, the additional policy demand being opposite in sign to the rate of change of production, whereas the additional investment demand resulting from the operation of the acceleration principle is of the same sign as the rate of change of production. This means that so far as its effect on system stability is concerned, the acceleration principle acts as a perverse or destabilising derivative correction element. The usefulness of the acceleration hypothesis has sometimes been questioned. But stated in the moderate form, that when production is rising entrepreneurs will want to invest at a greater rate, and after a time will in fact invest at a greater rate than they would have done if production had not been rising, and conversely in the case of falling production, there can hardly be any doubt that the principle is a valid one. It seems desirable, therefore, to investigate the effects of stabilisation policies when the basic multiplier model is modified by the inclusion of an acceleration relationship.

7 Stabilisation of a multiplier–accelerator model

We may define the term potential acceleration demand as the increase in investment demand that would occur as a direct result of rising production if the rise were to continue long enough for investment demand to become completely adjusted to it (and conversely in the case of falling production), and the term acceleration coefficient as the ratio between the potential acceleration demand and the rate of change of production which causes it.[9] Since investment demand will not respond instantaneously to alterations in the rate of change of production, a time lag may be introduced by the hypothesis that the actual acceleration demand tends continuously to approach the potential acceleration demand at a rate proportional to the difference between them. The time constant of this lag is defined in the same way as in the case of the production and correction lags.

Curve (a) of figure 16.9 (drawn with a different production scale from that used in figures 16.3–16.8 because of the greater fluctuations obtained) shows the response of production to unit spontaneous fall in demand when there is a marginal leakage of 0.25, a production lag with a time constant of three months, an acceleration coefficient of 0.6 and an acceleration lag with a time constant of one year, and when there is no stabilisation policy. With these values an explosive cycle is generated,[10] the fall in production in the first phase of the cycle being about 14 times as great as the spontaneous fall in demand. The cycle would eventually be limited by non-linearities in the system, and would then persist within those limits.

The application of a stabilisation policy having a proportional correction factor of 2 and a correction lag with a time constant of six months would change the response to that shown by curve (b) of figure 16.9, and the addition to this policy of an integral element with a correction factor of 2 would change the response to that

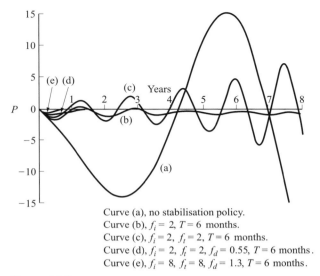

Curve (a), no stabilisation policy.
Curve (b), $f_i = 2$, $T = 6$ months.
Curve (c), $f_i = 2$, $f_t = 2$, $T = 6$ months.
Curve (d), $f_i = 2$, $f_t = 2$, $f_d = 0.55$, $T = 6$ months.
Curve (e), $f_i = 8$, $f_t = 8$, $f_d = 1.3$, $T = 6$ months.

Figure 16.9

shown by curve (c). As might be expected, the effect of the acceleration relationship has been to increase both the magnitude and the
duration of the fluctuations resulting from these policies. (These
responses may be compared with those shown by curve (c) of figure
16.3 and curve (c) of figure 16.7.)

To eliminate these fluctuations it would be necessary to add a derivative element to stabilisation policy. A derivative correction factor of 0.3
would be needed to offset the acceleration coefficient of 0.6 (the derivative correction factor need be only half the size of the acceleration coefficient in this case, since the length of the correction lag is only half that of
the acceleration lag), and an additional derivative correction factor of
0.25 would be needed to eliminate the fluctuations introduced by the
proportional and integral elements of the stabilisation policy. Adding
therefore a derivative element with a correction factor of 0.55 the
response shown by curve (d) of figure 16.9 is obtained. Finally, if the
stabilisation policy was strengthened by multiplying each correction factor (excepting that part of the derivative correction factor which was
needed to offset the acceleration coefficient) by four, the response
shown by curve (e) would be obtained.

These results appear to indicate that if any stabilisation policy[11] is to be
successful it must be made up of a suitable combination of proportional,

integral and derivative elements. A strong proportional element is needed as the main basis of the policy, sufficient integral correction should be added to obtain complete correction of an error within a reasonable time and an element of derivative correction is required to overcome the oscillatory tendencies which may be introduced by the other two elements of the policy. If the system itself has a considerable tendency to oscillate as a result of a perverse derivative relationship inherent in it in the form of the acceleration principle, the integral element in the policy should be made very weak or avoided entirely, unless it can be accompanied by sufficient derivative correction to offset the destabilising effects of the perverse derivative relationship.

8 Diagrammatic representation of the system

The system of relationships used in this section can be represented by a block diagram of the type frequently employed in the analysis of closed-loop systems. In figure 16.10 the lines represent variables and the squares represent relationships between variables, the particular relationship in each case being indicated by the symbol within the square. D indicates differentiation with respect to time, $\int$ indicates integration with respect to time and L indicates the operation of a distributed time lag in the adjustment of one variable to another. Brackets indicate multiplication by the parameter inside the brackets. The arrows show the direction of causation or the sequence of responses. Circles represent addition or subtraction according to the algebraic signs shown in each case.

The simple multiplier model is represented by the single closed loop at the bottom of the diagram. Production P is related to demand E through the operation of the production time lag L_p, and in turn influences demand through the marginal propensity to spend $(1 - l)$, l being the marginal leakage. The loop immediately above this represents the acceleration principle, which adds another component to demand equal to the rate of change of production dP/dt multiplied by the acceleration coefficient k and subject to the acceleration time lag L_a.

The three loops at the top of the diagram represent the three types of stabilisation policy. The error in production ε is obtained by subtracting the desired production P_d from the actual production. (In the illustrations given in this article all variables are measured as deviations from their values in an initial equilibrium position with production at the desired level. P_d is therefore zero and ε equals P.) The error, the integral of the error and the derivative of the error are multiplied by $-f_p$, $-f_i$, and $-f_d$ respectively, f_p being the proportional correction factor, f_i

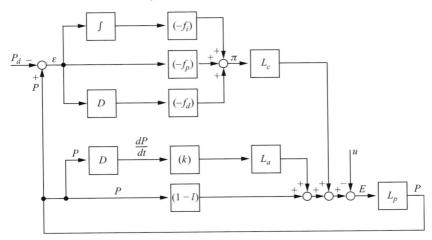

Figure 16.10

the integral correction factor and f_d the derivative correction factor. The potential policy demand π is the sum of these products, and subject to the operation of the correction time lag L_c determines the actual policy demand which is added to the other components of aggregate demand.

The variable u represents a disturbance to the system, assumed, throughout this article to take the form of a spontaneous fall in demand of one unit at time zero. Other forms of disturbance could, of course, be assumed and their effects investigated, and disturbances could be applied to other variables instead of, or in addition to, demand.

II A model with flexible prices

1 The relationship between prices and production

If changes in the quantity and productivity of the factors of production are ignored, the change in the average level of product prices which results from a given change in the aggregate level of production will be the sum of two components. First, if the prices of the services of the factors of production (which will be referred to for brevity as factor prices) are absolutely rigid, product prices, tending to move with marginal costs, will vary directly with the level of production. This component of the change in product prices is probably not very large, and will be neglected in the following analysis.

Second, if factor prices have some degree of flexibility, there will be changes in product prices resulting from the changes which take place in factor prices. Even with flexible factor prices, there will be some level of production and employment which, given the bargaining powers of the different groups in the economy, will just result in the average level of factor prices remaining constant, this level of production and employment being lower, the stronger and more aggressive the organisation of the factors of production. If aggregate real demand is high enough to make a higher level of production than this profitable, entrepreneurs will be more anxious to obtain (and to retain) the services of labour and other factors of production and so less inclined to resist demands for higher wages and other factor rewards. Factor prices will therefore rise. The level of demand being high, the rising costs will be passed on in the form of higher product prices. Factor and product prices will continue to rise in this way so long as the high level of demand and production is maintained, the rate at which they rise being greater, the higher the level of demand and production.

Conversely, if aggregate real demand is so low that production at the level which would result in constant factor prices is unprofitable, entrepreneurs will be more anxious to force down factor prices, while at the lower level of employment factors will be less able to press for higher rewards and more inclined to accept lower rewards. Factor prices will therefore gradually move downwards, and the level of demand being low, the falling costs will be reflected in falling product prices. Prices will continue to fall in this way so long as demand and production remain low, the rate of fall being greater, the lower the level of demand and production.

We may therefore postulate a relationship between the level of production and the rate of change of factor prices, which is probably of the form shown in figure 16.11, the fairly sharp bend in the curve where it passes through zero rate of change of prices being the result of the greater rigidity of factor prices in the downward than in the upward direction. The relationship between the level of production and the rate of change of product prices will be of a similar shape if productivity is constant. In spite of the marked curvature of the relationship, linearity may be assumed as an approximation for small changes in production. If the desired level of production is now taken to be that which would result in a constant level of product prices, we may say that the rate of change of product prices will be approximately proportional to the deviation of production from this level, i.e., to the error in production, this

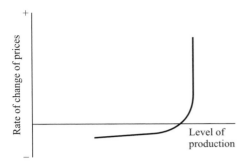

Figure 16.11

approximation being better, the smaller the fluctuations which occur in production.

2 Additional relationships when prices and interest rates are flexible

The model used in section I can now be extended by dropping the assumption of constant prices and interest rates. The complete model is shown diagrammatically in figure 16.12, which is the same as figure 16.10 excepting for the addition of the group of relationships in the centre of the diagram. Four additional sequences can be distinguished.

(i) A deviation of production from the desired level will be accompanied by a change in the number of transactions and so a change in the amount of money needed for conducting them, even if prices are rigid. If the quantity of money is less than perfectly elastic, this will cause interest rates, i, to change in the same direction[12] as the error in production. As a result of this change in interest rates there will be a potential change[13] in investment demand and production, in the opposite direction to the error in production and (assuming linearity throughout) proportional to the error. This sequence of responses is represented in figure 16.12 by the closed loop of relationships (a), $(-b)$, L_1, L_p, giving a potential feed-back of $-abP$ and so acting as a regulating mechanism of the proportional type.

(ii) If prices, p, are flexible, the error in production will also cause prices to change at a rate proportional to the error. The amount by which prices have changed at any given time, being identical with the time integral of their rate of change up to that time, will be proportional to the time integral of the error. This change in prices will cause a

further change in the amount of money needed for conducting transactions, in addition to that caused by the change in the number of
transactions conducted. There will therefore be an additional change
in interest rates[14] in the same direction as the error, causing a further
potential change in investment demand and production in the opposite direction to the error and proportional to the time integral of the
error. This sequence of responses thus operates as a regulating
mechanism of the integral type. The sequence is represented in figure
16.12 by the relationships (c), $\int$, (h), $(-b)$, L_1, L_P, which give a
potential feed-back of $-chb \int P$.

(iii) Professor Pigou (1943, 1947) has pointed out that even if the liquidity preference schedule was infinitely elastic at the prevailing level of

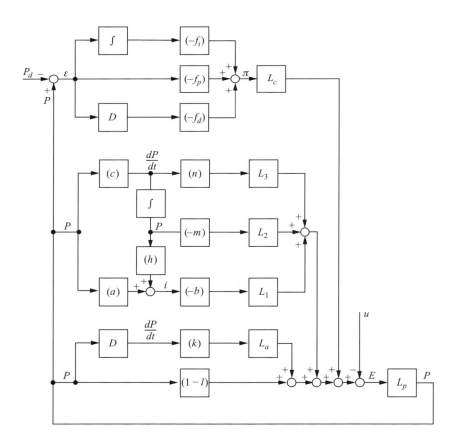

Figure 16.12

interest rates, so that interest rates failed to move with a change in production and prices, a change in the level of prices would still influence demand by changing the real value of money balances and so the amount of saving at given incomes and interest rates. This potential change in demand would be in the same direction as the change in the real value of money balances, and therefore in the opposite direction to the change in prices. For small changes it would be approximately proportional to the change in prices and therefore proportional to the time integral of the error in production. The Pigou effect is therefore equivalent to another integral regulating mechanism inherent in the economy. It is represented in figure 16.12 by the closed loop of relationships (c), $\int$, $(-m)$, L_2, L_P, giving a potential feed-back of $-cm \int P$.

(iv) Demand is also likely to be influenced by the rate at which prices are changing, or have been changing in the recent past, as distinct from the amount by which they have changed, this influence on demand being greater, the greater the rate of change of prices. Since the rate of change of prices in turn depends on the error in production, the potential change in demand and production resulting from these relationships will be approximately proportional to the error in production. This sequence of responses is represented in figure 16.12 by the relationships (c), (n), L_3, L_P, the potential feed-back therefore being cnP. The direction of this change in demand will depend on expectations about future price changes. If changing prices induce expectations of further changes in the same direction, as will probably be the case after fairly rapid and prolonged movements, demand will change in the same direction as the changing prices. That is, n will be positive, and there will be a positive feed-back tending to intensify the error, the response of demand to changing prices thus acting as a perverse or destabilising mechanism of the proportional type. If, on the other hand, there is confidence that any movement of prices away from the level ruling in the recent past will soon be reversed, demand is likely to change in the opposite direction to the changing prices. n will then be negative, and the response of demand to changing prices will act as a normal proportional regulating mechanism.

3 Inherent regulation of the system

Some examples will be given below to illustrate the stability of this system under different conditions of price flexibility and with different expectations concerning future price changes. As before, it will be assumed that the marginal leakage is 0.25 and that the time constant of the production lag is three months. The time constants of the lags L_1, L_2 and L_3 will be taken as six months. The acceleration relationship will be omitted (by putting $k = 0$) so that the effects of price flexibility can be seen by comparing the response of the system with that of the multiplier model.

In deciding upon suitable values for the remaining parameters it will be convenient to think of the units being such that in the initial equilibrium position production is 100 units per year, the price index also being 100. Changes can be expressed in either absolute or percentage terms with negligible error so long as prices and production do not move too far from their initial equilibrium values. The product of the parameters a and b will be given the value 0.2, which is equivalent to assuming that if production were to fall by 1 per cent or 1 unit, prices remaining constant, interest rates would fall sufficiently to stimulate investment demand by 0.2 of a unit. The product of the parameters h and b must be a little greater than this, since if the price level were to fall by 1 per cent, production remaining constant, there would be the same reduction in the demand for money for transactions purposes; but the real value of money balances would be slightly increased so that the fall in interest rates would be rather greater. The product hb will therefore be given the value 0.25. m will be taken as 0.05, equivalent to assuming that a 1 per cent fall in the price level would stimulate demand by 0.05 per cent through its effect in increasing the real value of money balances, if there was no change in interest rates.

The responses shown in figure 16.13 have been worked out on the assumption that n has the value 0.2. This means, for example, that if prices are falling at the rate of 1 per cent per year, demand will tend to be 0.2 of 1 per cent lower than it would have been if prices had been constant. Given these assumptions, curve (a) shows the response of production to unit fall in demand when there is zero price flexibility ($c = 0$). This response is similar to that of the multiplier model (curves (a) of figures 16.3–16.8); but the final error is less owing to the stabilising effects of the flexible interest rates.

Curve (b) shows the response when $c = 0.5$, that is, when for each 1 per cent error in production prices change at the rate of 0.5 per cent per year. The two integral regulating mechanisms now come into play, operating through interest rates and the Pigou effect respectively, so in the final equilibrium position the error is completely corrected. The total strength of the proportional regulating mechanisms is, however, reduced by the perverse effect of the response of demand to changing prices, with the

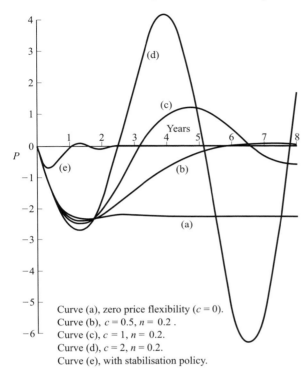

Curve (a), zero price flexibility ($c = 0$).
Curve (b), $c = 0.5$, $n = 0.2$.
Curve (c), $c = 1$, $n = 0.2$.
Curve (d), $c = 2$, $n = 0.2$.
Curve (e), with stabilisation policy.

Figure 16.13

result that the magnitude of the error in the early stages of the adjustment is slightly greater than in the case of zero price flexibility.

When $c = 1$ the response is that shown by curve (c) and when $c = 2$ it becomes that shown by curve (d). The strength of the integral regulating mechanisms increases with the increasing degree of price flexibility, while the total strength of the proportional regulating mechanisms decreases as demand responds perversely to the more rapid rate of change of prices, and both these effects tend to introduce fluctuations when price flexibility is increased beyond a certain point. When price expectations operate in this way, therefore, the system has fairly satisfactory self-regulating properties when prices are moderately flexible; but becomes unstable when there is a high degree of price flexibility.

If changing prices induce expectations of future changes in the reverse direction, n being given the value -0.2, the response of the system when there are different degrees of price flexibility is as shown in figure 16.14.

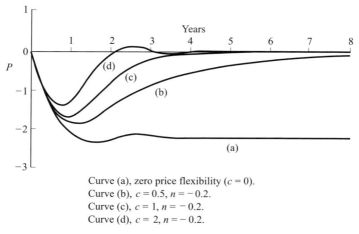

Curve (a), zero price flexibility ($c = 0$).
Curve (b), $c = 0.5$, $n = -0.2$.
Curve (c), $c = 1$, $n = -0.2$.
Curve (d), $c = 2$, $n = -0.2$.

Figure 16.14

Curves (a), (b), (c) and (d) have been worked out for values of c of 0, 0.5, 1 and 2 respectively, and so can be compared with the equivalent curves in figure 16.13. In this case the response of demand to changing prices provides a normal proportional regulating mechanism which increases in strength with the increasing degree of price flexibility. This increasing proportional regulation limits the fluctuations which would otherwise be introduced as a result of integral mechanisms, the strength of which also increases with increasing price flexibility, and at the same time increases the speed with which the error is corrected in the early stages of the adjustment. We may conclude that the self-regulating properties of the system will be considerably improved if there is confidence that any movement of prices away from the level ruling in the recent past will soon be reversed, and that if such confidence is sufficiently great the self-regulating properties will also be better, the higher the degree of price flexibility in the system.

4 Stabilisation of the system

If a stabilisation policy is applied to the system, the values of the correction factors required to produce any particular response will depend on the values of the parameters in the system. Examples of the values of correction factors which would result in the response shown by curve (e) of figure 16.13 if the time constant of the correction lag was six months are given in the following table.

Proposals have sometimes been made for improving the stability of the economic system by 'building in' additional regulating mechanisms. In the British Government's White Paper on Employment Policy[15] reference is made to a scheme for influencing consumption spending by varying the rates of social insurance contributions above or below the standard rates by amounts depending on the percentage by which the actual employment is above or below the average percentage over a period of years. On the basis of the figures given in the White Paper to illustrate how the scheme might operate, this would introduce a proportional regulating mechanism with a correction factor of about 0.2.[16] If schemes of this sort could be administered successfully they would undoubtedly improve the stability of the system considerably, and would probably be more effective than attempts to forecast conditions a year or more ahead and adjust an annual budget accordingly.

Monetary policy would be a more convenient instrument for stabilising an economy. Some may doubt whether it is a sufficiently powerful instrument; but if the right type of stabilisation policy is being applied continuously, comparatively small correcting forces are sufficient to hold the system near the desired position once that position has been attained. It is quite likely, therefore, that a monetary policy based on the principles of automatic regulating systems would be adequate to deal with all but the more severe disturbances to the economic system.

Mathematical appendix

1 Symbols used

P aggregate production, in units per year, measured from the initial equilibrium value.

E aggregate demand, in units per year, measured from the initial equilibrium value.

α the speed of response of production to changes in demand. The time constant of the production lag is $1/\alpha$ years.

D the differential operator d/dt.

t time in years.

l the marginal leakage.

u unit step function, equal to zero when $t \leq 0$ and to unity when $t > 0$.

β the speed of response of policy demand to changes in potential policy demand. The time constant of the correction lag is $1/\beta$ years.

f_p proportional correction factor.

Table 16.1

	Stabilisation policy required to produce the response shown by curve (e) of figure 16.13		
Response of unstabilised system	Proportional correction factor	Integral correction factor	Derivative correction factor
Curve (a), figure 16.13	1.8	2.0	0.2
Curve (b), figure 16.13	1.9	1.85	0.2
Curve (c), figure 16.13	2.0	1.7	0.2
Curve (d), figure 16.13	2.2	1.4	0.2
Curve (b), figure 16.14	1.7	1.85	0.2
Curve (c), figure 16.14	1.6	1.7	0.2
Curve (d), figure 16.14	1.4	1.4	0.2
Curve (a), figures 16.3–16.8	2.0	2.0	0.2
Curve (a), figure 16.9	2.0	2.0	0.5

f_i integral correction factor.
f_d derivative correction factor.
k acceleration coefficient.
κ speed of response of demand to changes in the rate of change of production. The time constant of the acceleration lag is $1/\kappa$ years.

If the rate of interest is denoted by i, the price level by p, and potential demand by E', the parameters of the price relationships shown in figure 16.12 are defined as

$$a = \frac{\partial i}{\partial P} \quad b = -\frac{\partial E'}{\partial i} \quad c = \frac{\partial\left(\frac{dp}{dt}\right)}{\partial P}$$

$$h = \frac{\partial i}{\partial p} \quad m = -\frac{\partial E'}{\partial p} \quad n = \frac{\partial E'}{\partial\left(\frac{dP}{dt}\right)}.$$

2 Distributed time lags

A single distributed time lag in the response of production to changes in demand is represented by the equation

$$DP = -\alpha(P - E) \tag{1}$$

from which

$$P = \frac{\alpha}{D + \alpha} E. \tag{2}$$

Similarly, the value of any variable which responds with a distributed time lag to changes in another is obtained by multiplying the value which that variable would have if there were no time lag by an operator of the form $\frac{\alpha}{D+\alpha}$, where $1/\alpha$ is the time constant of the lag. This rule will be used whenever a time lag is introduced.

If, from equilibrium, demand were to fall by one unit at time $t = 0$, we may substitute $E = -1$ when $t > 0$, giving

$$(D + \alpha)P = -\alpha \text{ when } t > 0 \tag{3}$$

with the initial condition

$$P = 0 \text{ when } t = 0 \tag{4}$$

since immediately after the change production will still be at its initial value.

The solution[17] of equations (3) and (4) is

$$P = -(1 - e^{-\alpha t})$$

which is plotted in figure 16.11 and curve (a) of figure 16.2 for $\alpha = 4$.

If there were two consecutive time lags in the response of production to demand, the time constant of each being $1/8$ year, equation (2) would become

$$P = \left(\frac{8}{D + 8}\right)^2 E. \tag{2a}$$

After the unit fall in demand, this gives

$$(D + 8)^2 P = -8^2 \text{ when } t > 0 \tag{3a}$$

with initial conditions

$$P = 0, \ DP = 0 \text{ when } t = 0. \tag{4a}$$

The solution is

$$P = -[1 - (1 + 8t)e^{-8t}]$$

which is plotted as curve (b) of figure 16.2.

With three consecutive time lags each having a time constant of $1/12$ year the equations for the response to unit fall in demand would be

$$(D + 12)^3 P = -12^3 \text{ when } t > 0 \tag{3b}$$

$$P = 0, \quad DP = 0, \quad D^2P = 0 \text{ when } t = 0. \tag{4b}$$

The solution is

$$P = -[1 - (1 + 12t + 72t^2)e^{-12t}]$$

which is plotted as curve (c) of figure 16.2.

3 The multiplier model

The response of demand to changes in production or real income is represented by the equation

$$E = (1 - l)P - u, \tag{5}$$

u being the spontaneous change in demand occurring at time $t = 0$. Substituting equation (5) in equation (1) and rearranging, we obtain

$$(D + \alpha l)P = -\alpha u. \tag{6}$$

After the initial change in demand this becomes

$$(D + \alpha l)P = -\alpha \text{ when } t > 0 \tag{7}$$

with the initial condition

$$P = 0 \text{ when } t = 0 \tag{8}$$

since immediately after the change production will still be at its initial equilibrium value.

The solution of equations (7) and (8) for $\alpha = 4$ and $l = 0.25$ is

$$P = -4(1 - e^{-t})$$

which is plotted as curves (a) of figures 16.3–16.9 inclusive.

4 Proportional stabilisation policy

The potential policy demand is $-f_p P$, giving an actual policy demand of $\frac{-\beta f_p}{D + \beta P}$.

Adding this to the demand shown in equation (5) we obtain

$$E(1 - l)P - \frac{\beta f_p}{D + \beta}P - u. \tag{5a}$$

Substituting this expression in equation (1) and rearranging gives

$$[D^2 + (\alpha l + \beta)D + \alpha\beta(l + f_p)]P = (-\alpha D - \alpha\beta)u. \tag{6a}$$

After the initial change in demand u equals unity and the derivatives of u are zero, so that

$$[D^2 + (\alpha l + \beta)D + \alpha\beta(l + f_p)]P = -\alpha\beta \text{ when } t > 0, \tag{7a}$$

the initial conditions being

$$P = 0, \ DP = -\alpha \text{ when } t = 0. \tag{8a}$$

The solutions of equations (7a) and (8a) for different values of f_p and β, α and l having the same values as before, are given in table 16.2.

5 Integral stabilisation policy

With an integral stabilisation policy the actual policy demand is $\frac{-\beta f_i}{D+\beta} \int P dt$. Adding this to equation (5), differentiating with respect to time, then substituting in equation (1) and rearranging the terms, we obtain

$$[D^3 = (\alpha l + \beta)D^2 + \alpha\beta lD + \alpha\beta f_i]P = (-\alpha D^2 - \alpha\beta D)u. \tag{6b}$$

After the initial change in demand this becomes

$$[D^3 + (\alpha l + \beta)D^2 + \alpha\beta lD + \alpha\beta f_i]P = 0 \text{ when } t > 0 \tag{7b}$$

with initial conditions[18]

$$P = 0, \ DP = -\alpha, \ D^2P = \alpha^2 l \text{ when } t = 0. \tag{8b}$$

The solutions of equations (7b) and (8b) for different values of f_i and β are given in table 16.3.

6 Proportional plus integral stabilisation policy

The actual policy demand in this case is $\frac{-\beta}{D+\beta}(f_p + f_i \int P dt)$.

Following the same procedure as in the previous example, we obtain the equations

$$[D^3 + (\alpha l + \beta)D^2 + \alpha\beta(l + f_p)D + \alpha\beta f_i]P = 0 \text{ when } t > 0 \tag{7c}$$

$$P = 0, \ DP = -\alpha, \ D^2P = \alpha^2 l \text{ when } t = 0. \tag{8c}$$

Solutions for different values of f_p, f_i and β are as shown in table 16.4.

7. Proportional plus integral plus derivative stabilisation policy

The actual policy demand becomes

$$-\frac{\beta}{D+\beta}(f_p P + f_i \int P dt + f_d DP).$$

Following the same procedure as before we obtain the equations

Table 16.2

f_p	β	P	Curve
0.5	2	$-1.33 - 1.69e^{-1.5t} \sin (111°t - 52°)$	Figure 16.3 (b)
2	2	$-0.44 - 0.95e^{-1.5t} \sin (227°t - 28°)$	Figure 16.3 (c)
0.5	8	$-1.33 - 1.69e^{-4.5t} \sin (111°t - 128°)$	Figure 16.4 (b)
2	8	$-0.44 - 0.52e^{-4.5t} \sin (412°t - 58°)$	Figure 16.4 (c)

Table 16.3

f_i	β	$P.$	Curve
0.5	2	$0.37e^{-2.80t} - 2.55e^{-0.10t} \sin (68.3°t + 8.3°)$	Figure 16.5 (b)
2	2	$0.33e^{-3.65t} - 1.34e^{0.33t} \sin (118°t + 14°)$	Figure 16.5 (c)
0.5	8	$0.02e^{-8.27t} - 2.88e^{0.37t} \sin (77.0°t + 0.34°)$	Figure 16.6 (b)
2	8	$0.04e^{-8.91t} - 1.35e^{-0.05t} \sin (154°t + 1.8°)$	Figure 16.6 (c)

Table 16.4

f_p	f_i	f_d	$P.$	Curve
0.5	0.5	2	$-1.33e^{-t} - 2.67e^{-t} \sin (99.4°t - 30°)$	Figure 16.7 (b)
2	2	2	$-0.27e^{-t} - 1.07e^{-t} \sin (221°t - 15°)$	Figure 16.7 (c)
8	8	2	$-0.06e^{-t} - 0.51e^{-t} \sin (455°t - 7°)$	Figure 16.7 (d)
0.5	0.5	8	$-3.11e^{-t} + (3.11 + 5.33t)e^{-4t}$	Figure 16.8 (b)
0.5	2	8	$-0.11e^{-6.86t} - 1.62e^{-1.07t} \sin (164°t - 4°)$	Figure 16.8 (c)
2	8	8	$-0.22e^{-4.93t} - 0.70e^{2.03t} \sin (396°t - 18°)$	Figure 16.8 (d)
8	32	8	$-0.06e^{-4.2t} - 0.27e^{-2.4t} \sin (880°t - 13°)$	Figure 16.8 (e)

$$[D^3 + (\alpha l + \beta + \alpha\beta f_d)D^2 + \alpha\beta(l + f_p)D + \alpha\beta f_i]P = 0 \text{ when } t > 0 \tag{7d}$$

$$P = 0, \quad DP = -\alpha, \quad D^2 P = \alpha^2(l + \beta f_d) \text{ when } t = 0. \tag{8d}$$

Solutions for various values of f_p, f_i, f_d and β are as shown in table 16.5.

Table 16.5

f_p	f_i	f_d	β	$P.$	Curve
8	8	1	2	$-0.08e^{-1.18t} - 0.68e^{-4.91t}\sin(315°t - 6°)$	Figure 16.7 (e)
8	32	0.25	8	$-0.07e^{-5.03t} - 0.31e^{-5.99t}\sin(741°t - 13°)$	Figure 16.8 (f)

8 The multiplier–accelerator model

The acceleration demand is $\frac{\kappa k}{D+\kappa}DP$. Adding this to the demand shown in equation (5) and following the usual procedure, the equations of the system are found to be

$$[D^2(\alpha l + \kappa - \alpha\kappa k)D + \alpha\kappa l]P = -\alpha\kappa \text{ when } t > 0 \tag{7e}$$

$$P = 0, \ DP = -\alpha \text{ when } t = 0. \tag{8e}$$

With $\alpha = 4$, $l = 0.25$, $\kappa = 1$ and $k = 0.6$ the solution, plotted as curve (a) of figure 16.9, is

$$P = -4.00 - 6.32e^{0.2t}\sin(56°t - 39°).$$

When a proportional stabilisation policy is applied the equations become

$$[D^3 + (\alpha l + \beta + \kappa - \alpha\kappa k)D^2 + (\alpha\beta l + \alpha\kappa l + \beta\kappa + \alpha\beta f_p$$
$$- \alpha\beta\kappa k)D + \alpha\beta\kappa(l + f_p)]P = -\alpha\beta\kappa \text{ when } t > 0 \tag{7f}$$

$$P = 0, \ DP = -\alpha, \ D^2P = \alpha^2(l - \kappa k) \text{ when } t = 0. \tag{8f}$$

With $f_p = 2$, $\beta = 2$ and the other parameters retaining their previous values the solution, plotted as curve (b) of figure 16.9, is

$$P = -0.44 - 0.025e^{-1.15t} - 1.10e^{-0.225t}\sin(227°t - 25°).$$

With a proportional plus integral stabilisation policy the equations of the system are

$$[D^4 + (\alpha l + \beta + \kappa + \alpha\kappa k)D^3 + (\alpha\beta l + \alpha\kappa l + \beta\kappa + \alpha\beta f_p$$
$$- \alpha\beta\kappa k)D^2 + (\alpha\beta\kappa l + \alpha\beta\kappa f_p + \alpha\beta f_i)D + \alpha\beta\kappa f_i]P = 0 \tag{7g}$$
$$\text{when } t > 0$$

$$\left. \begin{array}{l} P = 0, \ DP = -\alpha, \ D^2P = \alpha^2(l - \kappa k) \\ D^3P = \alpha^2(\beta f_p + \kappa^2 k) - \alpha^3(l - \kappa k)^2 \end{array} \right\} \text{ when } t = 0. \tag{8g}$$

With $f_i = 2$, the other parameters retaining their previous values, the solution, plotted as curve (c) of figure 16.9, is

$$P = -0.07e^{-1.43t} - 0.13e^{-0.69t} - 1.08e^{0.26t}\sin(231°t - 11°).$$

When a proportional plus integral plus derivative stabilisation policy is applied the equations become

$$[D^4 + (\alpha l + \beta + \kappa + \alpha\beta f_d - \alpha\kappa k)D^3 + (\alpha\beta l + \alpha\kappa l + \beta\kappa$$
$$+ \alpha\beta f_p + \alpha\beta\kappa f_d - \alpha\beta\kappa k)D^2 + (\alpha\beta\kappa l + \alpha\beta\kappa f_p + \alpha\beta f_i)D$$
$$+ \alpha\beta\kappa f_i]P = 0 \text{ when } t > 0 \qquad (7h)$$

$$\left.\begin{array}{l} P = 0, \ DP = -\alpha, \ D^2 P = \alpha^2(l + \beta f_d - \kappa k) \\ D^3 P = \alpha^2(\beta f_p + \kappa^2 k - \beta^2 f_d) - \alpha^3(l^2 - 2\kappa k l \\ \quad + \kappa^2 k^2 + 2\beta f_d l + \beta^2 f_d^2 - 2\beta\kappa f_d k) \end{array}\right\} \text{ when } t = 0.$$

$$(8h)$$

With $f_d = 0.55$, the other parameters retaining their previous values, the solution, plotted as curve (d) of figure 16.9, is

$$P = -0.11e^{-74t} + 0.07e^{-2.17t} - 1.40e^{-1.55t}\sin(158°t - 2°).$$

With $f_p = 8$, $f_i = 8$, $f_d = 1.3$ and the other parameters as before, the solution, plotted as curve (e) of figure 16.9, is

$$P = -0.02e^{-0.87t} - 0.04e^{-1.44t} - 0.73e^{-0.48t}\sin(300°t - 5°).$$

9 The model with flexible prices and interest rates

If the time constants of the lags L_1, L_2 and L_3 in figure 16.12 are assumed for simplicity to be the same as the time constant of the correction lag, the total demand resulting from the system (excluding the acceleration relationship) is

$$E = (1 - l)P - \frac{\beta}{D + \beta}[(ab - cn + f_p)P(cm + chb$$
$$+ f_i)\int P dt + f_d DP] - u.$$

Substituting this expression in equation (1) and carrying out the same operations as in previous examples, we obtain the following equations of the system

Table 16.6

c	n	$P.$	Curve
0	–	$-2.22 - 2.30e^{-1.5t}\sin(66.5°t - 75.5°)$	Figures 16.13 and 16.4(a)
0.5	0.2	$-0.38e^{-1.83t} - 8.00e^{-0.59t}\sin(32.0°t - 2.72°)$	Figure 16.13 (b)
1	0.2	$0.36e^{-2.59t} - 3.36e^{-0.21t}\sin(53.9°t + 6.1°)$	Figure 16.13 (c)
2	0.2	$0.39e^{-3.32t} - 2.25e^{0.16t}\sin(68.3°t + 10.0°)$	Figure 16.13 (d)
0.5	-0.2	$-2.46e^{-0.34t} - 2.7e^{-1.33t}\sin(75.2°t - 64.0°)$	Figure 16.14 (b)
1	-0.2	$-2.11e^{-0.66t} - 2.86e^{-1.17t}\sin(86.6°t - 47.6°)$	Figure 16.14 (c)
2	-0.2	$-1.05e^{-t} - 2.31e^{-t}\sin(112°t - 27.2°)$	Figure 16.14 (d)

$$[D^3 + (\alpha l + \beta + \alpha\beta f_d)D^2 + \alpha\beta(l + ab - cn + f_p)D$$
$$+ \alpha\beta(cm + chb + f_i)P = 0 \text{ when } t > 0, \tag{7i}$$

$$P = 0, \quad DP = -\alpha, \quad D^2P = \alpha^2(l + \beta f_d) \text{ when } t = 0. \tag{8i}$$

With $\alpha = 4$, $l = 0.25$, $\beta = 2$, $m = 0.05$, $ab = 0.2$, $hb = 0.25$ and f_p, f_i and f_d equal to zero, the solutions for various values of c and n are shown in table 16.6.

If for each set of values of c and n in the above table, f_p, f_i and f_d are given the corresponding values shown in table 16.1, the solution of the system becomes

$$P = 0.26e^{-1.14t} - 1.10e^{-1.73t}\sin(207°t - 13.6°)$$

which is plotted as curve (e) of figure 16.13.

Notes

Economic Journal, 64 (254), pp. 290–323).

This article is based on part of the material of a thesis submitted to the University of London for the degree of Ph.D. I am indebted to Mr A.C.L. Day, Mr A.D. Knox, Professor J.E. Meade, Mr W.T. Newlyn, Professor Lionel Robbins and Dr W.J.L. Ryan for helpful comments on an earlier draft.

1 A mathematical treatment of models used and of the stabilisation policies applied to them is given in the Mathematical appendix.
2 A demand lag could be introduced in addition to the production lag, but has been omitted to avoid complicating the mathematical treatment.
3 Or $1 - e^{-1}$, where e is the base of Napierian logarithms.

4 If the number of consecutive lags is increased indefinitely, the time constants of the separate lags being simultaneously reduced so that the combined time constant remains fixed, the time path approaches the limit of a step function, jumping form 0 to −1 after a period of time equal to the combined time constant. I am indebted to Mr J. Wise for providing me with a rigorous mathematical proof of this.

5 Since aggregate production includes services, the provision of which responds instantaneously to changes in the demand for them, the more rapid initial response obtained by assuming a single lag may in fact represent quite a good approximation to the real process of adjustment.

6 The following treatment is an application of the general principles of automatic regulating systems and closed-loop control systems, in the analysis of which notable advances have been made in recent years. Cf. Farrington (1951); and Brown and Campbell (1948). On the use of closed-loop control theory in economics, cf. Tustin (1954).

7 That is, the principle of 'negative feed-back' is used.

8 International adjustments are not dealt with in this article; but it may be worth noting here that a country which attempts to regulate its current balance of payments, whether by means of internal credit policy or quantitative import control, and in doing so responds mainly to the size of its foreign reserves (i.e., to the time integral of its current balance of payments) is applying an integral correction policy which is likely to cause cyclical fluctuations similar to those illustrated in figures 16.5 and 16.6. The short cycles which have occurred in the balances of payments of a number of countries since the war may be in part the result of such action.

9 Defined in this way, the acceleration coefficients is also the ratio of the change in the desired stock of capital to the change in the annual rate of production and real income, or what might be called the marginal desired capital–income ratio.

10 The system gives damped oscillations when the acceleration coefficient lies between 0 and 0.5, explosive oscillations when it lies between 0.5 and 1, and is explosive without oscillations when the acceleration coefficient is greater than 1. All these values would probably be raised if the production and acceleration lags were divided, as they no doubt should be, into a number of separate shorter lags (observation lags, decision lags, process lags, etc.), and if similar lags were introduced in the response of demand to changes in income.

11 The general principles of stabilisation have been illustrated here with particular reference to aggregate production in a closed economy, but they are of quite general applicability. They could equally well be used, for example, in investigating the stability of adjustments in international trade, or the problems involved in commodity price stabilisation schemes.

12 Provided that the liquidity preference schedule does not shift.

13 It will be remembered that by a potential change in any variable we mean the change that would take place if no time lag was involved.

14 The device of considering the quantity effects and price effects separately and then adding them can be justified as follows: Denoting interest rates, production and prices, measured from a zero base, by i_0, P_0 and p_0 respectively, and deviations from the initial equilibrium values by i, P and p, we have $i_0 = F(P_0, p_0)$.

Expanding this expression in a Taylor series and dropping all but the first two terms gives

$$\Delta i_0 = \frac{\partial i_0}{\partial P_0} \Delta P_0 + \frac{\partial i_0}{\partial p_0} \Delta p_0$$

or

$$i = \frac{\partial i}{\partial P} P + \frac{\partial i}{\partial p} p$$

as an approximation valid for small changes. For small changes $\partial i / \partial P$ and $\partial i / \partial p$ may also be considered constant, so we may write

$$i = aP + hp$$

which is the relationship shown in figure 16.12. Similar approximations are involved in considering the change in aggregate demand as the sum of a number of separate components.

15 Cmd. 6527, 1944, paragraphs 68–71 and appendix II.

16 Professor Meade has suggested a scheme, operating through special monthly taxes and credits related to the level of employment, which would have similar effects. With the scales of taxes and credits suggested by him the proportional correction factor would be about 0.4. The cumulative expansion and contraction of the quantity of money resulting from the proposed method of financing the scheme would also introduce an integral correction element. Professor Meade must have been aware that there would be some disadvantage in having too much integral correction, since he recommended that this effect should be partially offset through appropriate action by the central bank. Cf. Meade (1938).

17 For methods of solving ordinary linear differential equations with constant coefficients see Piaggio (1949, chapter 3). For equations of order higher than the second a considerable saving of labour is obtained by using the Laplace Transformation instead of the classical methods of solution. See Carslaw and Jaeger (1948), and Gardner and Barnes (1942).

18 The initial conditions are not intuitively obvious when the equations are of the third or higher order. The following rules, derived from Porter (1950, pp. 50–3) to which the reader is referred for their justification, lay down a simple procedure for finding the initial conditions of the system in these cases.

(i) Integrate the equation with respect to time between the limits: $t = -0$ and $t = +0$. Terms containing integrals of P and u between these limits are equal to zero and may be omitted.

(ii) Repeat the integrations until only the term in P remains. This gives the value of P when $t = 0$.

(iii) Substitute this value of P in the preceding equation, setting u equal to 1 and any derivatives of u equal to zero. This gives the value of DP when $t = 0$.
(iv) Repeat the substitution until all the initial conditions have been obtained.
Applying these rules to equation (7b) we obtain

1st integration $D^2P + (\alpha l + \beta)DP + \alpha\beta lP = -\alpha Du - \alpha\beta u$	(a)
2nd integration $DP + (\alpha l + \beta)P = -\alpha u$	(b)
3rd integration $P = 0$	(c)

Substituting equation (c) in (b) and setting u equal to unity

$$DP = -\alpha \tag{d}$$

Substituting (c) and (d) in (a) and setting u equal to unity and Du equal to zero

$$D^2P - \alpha(\alpha l + \beta) = -\alpha\beta$$

or $D^2P = \alpha^2 l$ (e)

Equations (c), (d) and (e) give the initial conditions of the system.

17   Stabilisation Policy and the Time-Forms of Lagged Responses

A.W. Phillips

E63

E32

E37

In an earlier article (chapter 16) I used a number of dynamic process models to illustrate the operation of certain types of stabilisation policy. In setting up the models I assumed that each lagged response was of the particular time-form known as an exponential lag. I pointed out (pp. 136–7) that other time-forms would probably give better representations of the real responses in an economic system, but did not introduce these more realistic lag forms into the models owing to the difficulty of solving the high-order differential equations to which they would have led.

Since then the National Physical Laboratory and Short Brothers and Harland, Ltd, have allowed me to use their electronic simulators, by means of which the time responses of quite complex systems with a variety of lag forms can be found very rapidly.[1] In addition, I have become more familiar with the frequency-response method of analysis based on the Nyquist stability criterion. This is a graphical method which not only enables considerable information to be obtained about the dynamic properties of a system without solving the differential equation of the system, but also gives valuable insight into the ways in which the dynamic properties would be altered if the relationships and lag forms in the system were modified or additional relationships included.[2]

A study, using frequency-response analysis and electronic simulators, of the properties of models in which the lags are given more realistic time-forms has shown that the problem of stabilisation is more complex than appeared to be the case when attention was confined to the simpler lag forms used in my earlier article. In this study a number of alternative models were first analysed by the frequency-response method, and the effects of variations in the lag forms and the values of the parameters on the stability of the models were investigated. Some of the models were then set up on the electronic simulators, disturbances were applied and the resulting time paths of the variables were found. In the present article

two of the models which were studied are described and their dynamic
properties illustrated by recordings from the electronic simulators.

1 A multiplier model with error correction

The first model is shown diagrammatically in figure 17.1, which is similar
to figure 16.10 of my earlier article (chapter 16, p. 149) except that the
accelerator relationship has been omitted. The lines in the diagram represent the variables of the system, measured as deviations from initial
equilibrium values. Relationships between variables are indicated by
the symbols in the squares, the arrows showing the causal direction of
the relationships. The lower closed loop in the diagram represents a
simple multiplier model. It is assumed that aggregate real income or
production, P, responds to changes in aggregate real demand, E, through
the lag relationship L_p. Changes in aggregate demand are analysed into
three components, E_Y, E_π and u. E_Y denotes those changes in demand
which are related to changes in income through the marginal propensity
to spend $1 - l$. We shall give l, the 'marginal leakage' from the circular
flow of income, the value 0.25, so that the multiplier is 4.0. E_π is the
policy demand, that is, it is the amount by which aggregate demand is
increased or decreased as a direct result of action taken by the regulating
authorities for the purpose of stabilising the system. All changes in aggregate demand caused by changes in factors other than income and stabilisation policy are included in the variable u.

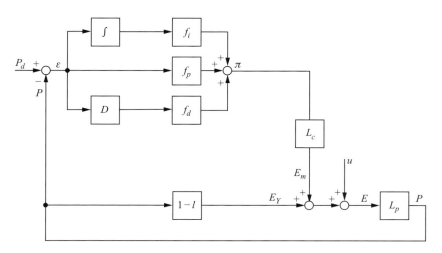

Figure 17.1

The relationships shown at the top of the diagram represent an error-correction type of stabilisation policy. The actual level of production is subtracted from the desired level of production, P_d, giving the error in production,[3] ε. It is assumed that the regulating authorities are able to make continuous adjustments in the strength of the correcting action they take but that there is a distributed time lag, L, between changes in the strength of the correcting action and the resulting changes in policy demand. The amount by which policy demand would be changed as a direct result of the policy measures if they operated without time lag will be called the potential policy demand, π, the amount by which it is in fact changed as a direct result of policy measures is the actual policy demand E_π.

The basic problem in stabilising production is to relate the actual policy demand to the error in production in such a way that errors caused by unpredicted disturbances are corrected as quickly and smoothly as possible.[4] For a given correction lag the problem reduces to that of finding the most suitable way of relating the potential policy demand to the error in production. In my earlier article (chapter 16) I argued that to obtain satisfactory regulation of a system it is usually necessary for the potential policy demand to be made the sum of three components, one component depending on the error itself, one depending on the time integral of the error and the third depending on the time derivative (or rate of change) of the error. That is, the relationship should be of the form $\pi = f_p \varepsilon + f_i \int \varepsilon \, dt + f_d \, d\varepsilon / dt$, where f_p, f_i and f_d are parameters which I called respectively the proportional, integral and derivative correction factors. This relationship is represented by the three loops at the top of figure 17.1, the symbol $\int$ indicating integration with respect to time and D indicating differentiation with respect to time.

We shall consider three different forms of the production lag L_p. These are illustrated by curves (a), (b) and (c) of figure 17.2, which show hypothetical time paths of the response of production to a unit step fall in demand occurring at time $t = 0$. With lag form (a) the rate of change of production at any time is proportional to the difference between demand and production at that time. We call this an exponential lag and define the time constant of the lag as the reciprocal of the factor of proportionality; for the response shown in curve (a) the time constant is 0.25 year. The exponential lag form is very convenient for mathematical treatment, but it implies a more rapid response in the early stages of an adjustment than is likely to be typical of economic behaviour. The time path of adjustment shown in curve (b) of figure 17.2 is probably more realistic.

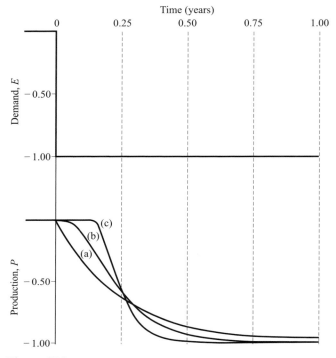

Figure 17.2

This time path is obtained if the lag is equivalent to three shorter exponential lags operating in sequence, the time constants of the individual lags being 0.0833 year, so that the total time constant of the composite lag is again 0.25 year. This triple exponential form of lag is probably a fairly good representation of many economic relationships. In some cases, however, we should expect that there would be no response at all until some considerable time after a change had occurred, the time path of the adjustment being somewhat like that shown in curve (c) of figure 17.2. We shall call an interval during which there is no response at all a time delay, to distinguish it from the exponential type of lag in which a continuous gradual adjustment takes place. The adjustment path in curve (c) results from a lag which is equivalent to a sequence consisting of a time delay of 0.125 year and three exponential lags each with a time constant of 0.0417 year, the total time constant of the composite lag again being 0.25 year.

The time forms which we shall use for the correction lag will be similar to those shown in figure 17.2, except that the time scale will be doubled. Thus lag form (a) for the correction lag will be a single exponential lag with a time constant of 0.50 year, lag form (b) will be a sequence of three exponential lags, each with a time constant of 0.167 year, and lag form (c) will be a sequence consisting of a time delay of 0.25 year and three exponential lags, each with a time constant of 0.0833 year.

Figures 17.3, 17.4 and 17.5 reproduce recordings from the electronic simulators showing the response of production to a unit step change in the variable u applied negatively at time $t = 0$, for different combinations of correction factors and lag forms. The responses shown in figure 17.3 are obtained when the proportional correction factor f_p is 0.5, the integral correction factor f_i is 0.5 and the derivative correction factor f_d is zero. When both the production and the correction lags are of form (a) the response is that shown in curve (a).[5] When the lags are changed to form (b), the rest of the system remaining the same, the response is that shown in curve (b). When the lags are of form (c) the response shown in curve (c) is obtained. In the case now being considered, with proportional and integral correction factors of 0.5, the 'overshoot' which occurs in the response when the lags are of form (b) or (c) can be eliminated by introducing a small amount of derivative correction. When the lags are of form (b) the overshoot is eliminated if the derivative correction factor is raised from zero to about 0.06; when they are of form (c) a derivative correction factor of about 0.09 is required to prevent overshoot in the response.

Curves (a), (b) and (c) of figure 17.4 show the responses obtained with lag forms (a), (b) and (c) respectively when both the proportional and the integral correction factors are 2.0 and the derivative correction factor is

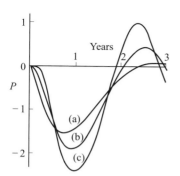

Figure 17.3

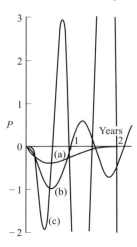

Figure 17.4

0.5. With the higher values of the proportional and integral correction factors the system has become less stable, and even when the lags are of form (a) some derivative correction is needed to prevent an oscillatory response. When the lags are of form (b) the system is on the verge of instability. Nor can the response be improved by adjustment of the derivative correction factor. Any appreciable increase or decrease in its value makes the system completely unstable. When the corrective action has some effect fairly quickly, as is the case when the lags are of form (a), the use of derivative correction is a powerful method of reducing or eliminating fluctuations. But when the corrective action does not have much effect until some considerable time after it is applied, as is the case when the lags are of form (b) and still more when they are of form (c), derivative correction is less effective in reducing oscillations, and indeed if used excessively it will introduce an additional cycle of high frequency. When the proportional and integral correction factors are 2.0 and the lags are of form (c) the system is unstable for all values of the derivative correction factor.

Curve (a) of figure 17.5 shows the response when both the proportional and integral correction factors are raised to 8.0 and the derivative correction factor is 1.0, the lags being of form (a)[6]. With lags of form (b) the response becomes that shown in curve (b). With lags of form (c) the system is so violently unstable that it proved impossible to obtain a satisfactory recording of the response given by the electronic simulator.

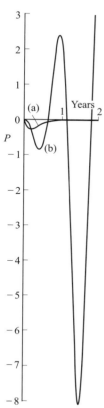

Figure 17.5

Adjustment of the derivative correction factor again fails to stabilise the system in this case when the lags are of form (b) or (c).

Figures 17.3, 17.4 and 17.5 show that a comparatively small change in the time forms of the lags may have a great effect on the stability of a closed-loop control system, especially if the values of the correction factors are high. It is in fact only in the simplest systems in which there are not more than two lags, each of single exponential form, that it is possible to give any value, no matter how large, to one correction factor and then to find values for the other correction factors such that the system is stable and non-oscillatory. Any system in which there is time delay or a sequence of more than two lags of single exponential form, or in which any lag is equivalent to a sequence which includes a time delay or more than two single exponential lags, as is the case with lags of form (b) or (c), will be stable and non-oscillatory only if the values of the correction factors are kept sufficiently low. This limitation of permissible values of the correction factors implies a corresponding limit to the speed with which it is possible to correct an error caused by a disturbance.

It is not possible to make any completely general statement about the effect on the response of a closed-loop system of an alteration to one part of the system unless the remainder of the system is fully specified. It will, however, be found that except in very special cases which are most unlikely to occur in practice a reduction in the length of the correction lag brought about by a reduction in the time scale, the form of the lag remaining unchanged, increases the maximum values of the correction factors that can be used without causing instability, and so permits a more rapid correction of errors. A similar effect is produced, again except in very special cases, if the form of the correction lag is altered from form (c) through form (b) to form (a). As can be seen from figure 17.2, this implies that the maximum values of the correction factors that can be used without causing instability are increased if the interval between the time when an error occurs and the time when the corrective action *begins* to take effect is reduced, even if the time required for the full effect of the corrective action to be obtained is simultaneously increased. Thus it is important, both for obtaining rapid correction and for avoiding instability, that the corrective action should be adjusted continuously and quickly to changes in the error and that it should have some initial effect quickly; whether its full effect is obtained quickly or slowly is comparatively unimportant.[7]

We have seen from figure 17.3 that a cycle with a period of about three years occurs if the lags in our system are of form (b) or (c) and if the proportional and integral correction factors are 0.5 (which may perhaps be about the order of magnitude of these correction factors that can be attained in actual economic regulation) unless a small amount of derivative correction is also applied. Since the basic multiplier model which has been used so far is non-oscillatory, this may properly be called a control cycle. A more adequate model of an economy might itself have cyclical properties, for example, inventory adjustments are likely to cause cycles with a period of three or four years. The question immediately arises whether the maximum values of the correction factors that can be used without causing instability are not further reduced when the system being controlled has oscillatory tendencies. This question is examined briefly in the next section.

2 An inventory model with error correction

A model with inventory adjustments is shown in figure 17.6. An 'inventory demand,' E_v, is now distinguished as an additional component of aggregate demand, total demand for purposes other than inventory adjustment being E_N. Thus $E = E_N + E_v$ and $E_N = E_Y + E_\pi + u$. We assume that any excess of the 'non-inventory demand' E_N over aggregate production P is met by drawing on inventories, and any excess of production over non-inventory demand is added to inventories. Then the rate of change of inventories, dV/dt, is equal to $P - E_N$. Integration of dV/dt with respect to time gives total inventories, V. Some part of the total inventories will be locked up in work in progress and essential stocks closely related to the level of production. These 'minimum working inventories', which we shall call V_1, are assumed to be a constant proportion, w, of production. We shall give w the value 0.2, that is, we shall assume that minimum working inventories are equal to one-fifth of a year's production. Inventories held in excess of minimum working inventories will be called V_2, so that $V_2 = V - V_1$.[8] From precautionary and speculative motives businesses will wish to hold some inventories in excess of minimum working inventories, but the amount they wish to hold, which we shall call V_{2d} or the desired value of V_2, will not always be equal to the amount they are holding. In this simplified model we shall assume that V_{2d} is a lagged function of non-inventory demand and we shall give the magnitude of this dependence, s, the value 0.125 and assume that the lag, L_s, is of form (b) with a time constant of 0.75 year. (In fact, of course, V_{2d} will also be influenced by other factors, in particular by interest rates and expected rates of change of prices.) Subtracting V_2 from V_{2d} gives the 'error in inventories', ε_v. We shall assume that the inventory demand E_v is a constant proportion, v, of the error in inventories and shall give v the value 2.0.

The only other change from the model shown in figure 17.1 is the addition of the demand lag, L_D, which, because of the fairly rapid adjustment of expenditure by wage-earners when their incomes change, we shall assume to be of form (a) with a time constant of 0.125 year. We shall, however, give the marginal leakage, l, the value 0.4 instead of its previous value 0.25. This reduces the multiplier from 4.0 to 2.5, which is probably a more realistic value, and makes the system more stable. We assume a correction lag of form (c) with a total time constant of 0.5 year and a production lag of form (b) with a total time constant of 0.25 year.

When all three correction factors are zero the response of production to a unit step change in the variable u, applied negatively at time $t = 0$, is the damped inventory cycle shown in curve (a) of figure 17.7. If derivative

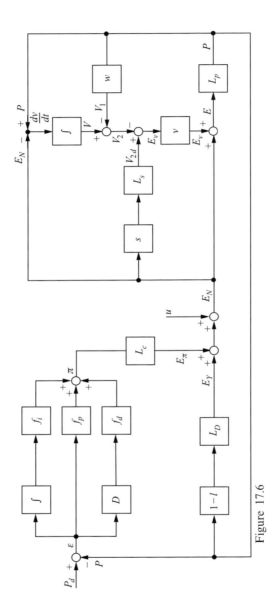

Figure 17.6

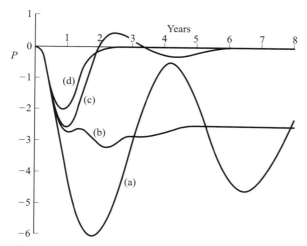

Figure 17.7

correction only is applied the equilibrium position of the system is unchanged, so the error in production persists. With low values of the derivative correction factor the fluctuations in the response are reduced, but with higher values another cycle appears within a period of just over one year, and if the derivative correction factor is raised above 0.38 this cycle becomes explosive. Curve (b) of figure 17.7 shows the response when the derivative correction factor is 0.25.

If proportional correction only is applied, the fluctuations in the response are slightly reduced when the value of the proportional correction factor is very low, but if it is raised above 0.1 the fluctuations become worse again and the system becomes unstable when the proportional correction factor is raised above about 0.28. If any integral correction at all is applied alone, the amplitudes of the fluctuations increase and the system becomes unstable if the integral correction factor is raised above about 0.08. Similarly, any combination of proportional and integral correction without the addition of derivative correction reduces the stability of the system and increases the magnitudes of the fluctuations unless the two correction factors have extremely low values, while if the values are extremely low the improvement in the response is negligible.

Even if derivative correction is included in the stabilisation policy, the speed with which an error can be corrected is rather limited. About the best response that can be obtained is that shown in curve (c) of figure 17.7. This response results when $f_p = 0.3$, $f_i = 0.4$ and $f_d = 0.2$. Higher values of the correction factors worsen the response by reducing the stability of the system. If the correction lag is changed from form (c) to form (b), the time constant remaining at 0.5 years, the correction factors can be increased a little. The best response is then that shown in curve (d) of figure 17.7, the correction factors being $f_p = 0.4$, $f_i = 0.5$ and $f_d = 0.3$.

If the correction lag is of form (b) with a total time constant of 0.25 year the best response is obtained when $f_p = 0.9$, $f_i = 0.9$ and $f_d = 0.25$. It is shown as curve (b) of figure 17.8. It is of interest to note that even with this correction lag the stabilisation policy is not satisfactory unless it includes an element of derivative correction. If $f_d = 0$ about the best response that can be obtained is that shown in curve (a) of figure 17.8, the proportional and integral correction factors being 0.4 and 0.1 respectively. With either higher or lower values of f_p and f_i the fluctuations are of greater amplitude.

3 Conclusions

Because of the simplified nature of the models considered in this chapter the results that have been obtained cannot be applied directly to the interpretation of actual economic situations. Indeed, one of the first lessons one learns from studying a variety of hypothetical models is that the problem of economic stabilisation is, even in principle, an extremely intricate one, and that a much more thorough investigation of both theoretical principles and empirical relationships would be needed before detailed policy recommendations could be justified. A few very elementary conclusions can, however, be drawn with some confidence.

The first is that the regulation of a system can be improved if the lengths of the time delays operating around the main control loop are

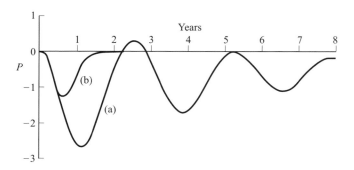

Figure 17.8

reduced. The distinction between delays and lags should here be noticed. What is of primary importance is that the correcting action should be adjusted continuously and with the minimum possible delay to changes in the error and that the adjustments should quickly produce some initial effect. It does not matter very much if it takes a long time for the policy changes to have their full effect. In fact, it can be shown that if there is a long delay before corrective action is taken or before it begins to have an appreciable effect it is better that the effect, when it does come, should be gradual rather than sudden. The worst possible condition for regulating purposes is one in which the adjustment of policy demand to a change in the error is delayed for a considerable time and then effected quickly and abruptly.

A second conclusion is that it is usually necessary to include an element of derivative correction in a stabilisation policy if regulation is to be satisfactory. In other words, the potential policy demand should be made to depend not only on the magnitude of the current error and on the sum of the past errors,[9] but also on the rate of change of the error, or when observations are at discrete intervals on the difference between the last two observed values of the error. The longer the time delays in the responses around the main control loop, the less effective is derivative correction in reducing fluctuations. Nevertheless, the longer the delays, the more desirable it is that some derivative correction be used, since the delays reduce the stability of the system and so make it more important that whatever stabilising effect can still be obtained by derivation correction should not be foregone.

A third conclusion is that if the lags in the real economic system are at all similar to those we have used in the models it is unlikely that the period needed to restore any desired equilibrium conditions after an economy has experienced a severe disturbance could be much less than two years, even assuming that the regulating authorities use the policy which is most appropriate to the real system of relationships existing in the economy. As these relationships are not known quantitively, it is unlikely that the policy applied will be the most appropriate one, it may well cause cyclical fluctuations rather than eliminate them.

It is true that many relationships inherent in the real economic system have been omitted from our models and that some of the omitted relationships seem intuitively to be of a stabilising type. But intuitions about dynamic processes may be dangerously misleading and need to be carefully tested. Most of the inherent relationships which at first sight would seem to have stabilising effects can be expressed in forms similar to the policy relationships in the models we have been using. If the lengths and forms of the time lags of these inherent relationships are also similar to those which we have assumed for the correction lag the effects of the inherent relationships will be similar to the effects of the policy relationships which we have already considered. The existence of inherent relationships which appear intuitively to be of a stabilising type may therefore reduce the amount of correction that needs to be applied deliberately by regulating authorities (particularly the proportional and integral elements of correction; it is difficult to think of any inherent relationship which is equivalent to the derivative element of a correction policy), but will not reduce the time required to restore equilibrium after a disturbance unless these relationships operate with shorter time lags and delays than we have been assuming. Nor do the additional inherent relationships make it more likely that cyclical fluctuations will be avoided. In fact, they make it less likely, since it becomes very difficult to judge what quantitative values should be given to the deliberate policy relationships when the system already contains numerous inherent relationships whose magnitudes and speeds of operation are unknown.

The main conclusion that must be drawn from this investigation is that much more research is needed in the general field of economic regulation. To throw light on the practical problems involved in regulating complex economic systems it is necessary to study the properties of more realistic models in which non-linear relationships, growth trends, multiple objectives and multiple disturbances are incorporated. The means for carrying out such studies are now becoming available and should be fully exploited. It is equally important that improved methods should be developed for estimating quantitatively the magnitudes and time-forms of economic relationships in order that the range of permissible hypothesis may be restricted more closely than is at present possible.

Notes

Economic Journal, 67, 1957, pp. 265–77.
    I wish to thank Professor R.G.D. Allen, Professor J.E. Meade, Professor Lionel Robbins and Mr R.H. Tizard for helpful comments on an earlier draft of this paper.

1 I am indebted to the Director of the National Physical Laboratory and to Short Brothers and Harland, Ltd., for permission to use the simulators. At the National Physical Laboratory, where most of the work was carried out, Mr D.V. Blake operated the simulator and gave invaluable help and advice. I benefited greatly from discussions with him and am most grateful to him for his willing co-operation. I also wish to thank Mr E. Lloyd Thomas, Mr R.J.A. Paul and Mr P.A.R. Wright of Short Brothers and Harland, Ltd., for their

assistance. The possibility of using electronic simulators for studying problems of economic regulation was suggested to me by Mr R.H. Tizard.

2 There is an extensive literature on the use of frequency-response methods in the analysis and synthesis of engineering systems. See, for example, James, Nichols and Phillips (1947), and Brown and Campbell (1948). For a brief description of the methods with some applications to economic problems see Tustin (1954), especially chapter III. See also Allen (1956), chapters 8 and 9.

3 The error is here defined to be $P_d - P$ rather than $P - P_d$ as in my earlier article. In the literature on regulating systems the error in a variable is usually defined as the desired value minus the actual value.

4 If reliable and frequent measurements of aggregate demand were available the potential policy demand could also be related to the error in demand. This would permit a more rapid correction of errors in production caused by shifts in aggregate demand.

5 This response was obtained mathematically in my earlier article and was shown as curve (b) of figure 16.7 chapter 16 (p. 144).

6 This response was also obtained mathematically in my earlier article and was shown as curve (c) of figure 16.7 (p. 144).

7 Justification of the above statements would require an extensive use of the frequency-response method of analysis and cannot be given here. The reader who wishes to acquire sufficient familiarity with the method to convince himself of their truth will find the necessary material in the works cited in n. 2.

8 It will be noticed that the distinction made here between V_1 and V_2 corresponds closely to the distinctions between working capital and liquid capital made by Keynes in chapters 28 and 29 of the *Treatise on Money*. It is also analogous to his later distinction between M_1 and M_2 in monetary theory.

9 The quantity to which integral correction is related is the integral, or sum, of all past errors. In practice a good approximation to integral correction would be obtained if the integral component of potential policy demand was made to depend on the sum of the errors over the past four of five years or on a weighted sum of these errors, the earlier errors being given less weight than the later one.

18   Arnold Tustin's *The Mechanism of Economic Systems*: A Review

A.W. Phillips

There are certain formal similarities between the problems of devising policies for economic stabilisation and those of designing automatic control systems in engineering. An automatic control system is made up of a number of interrelated components. The dynamic characteristics of each component can usually be described fairly accurately by a differential equation. The complete control system can therefore be represented by a system of equations or mathematical model. Methods have recently been developed by engineers for analysing the dynamic properties of quite complex models, and procedures have been evolved for finding ways in which a given system may be modified to reduce the fluctuations which occur when it is subjected to external disturbances. These methods and procedures can also be used for the analysis of dynamic process models in economics. There are several good books on the theory of closed-loop control systems, but they are written for engineers, and the technical language and examples used form an almost impenetrable barrier to those who have not had engineering training. Economists will therefore be grateful to Professor Tustin (1954), who is head of the Department of Electrical Engineering in the University of Birmingham, for writing a book on the subject which enables them to avoid these difficulties and for suggesting possible applications of the methods to the study of the problems of economic stabilisation.

The book commences with a brief description of the structure of systems of mutual interdependence, illustrated by some familiar economic models. Unfortunately, Professor Tustin has used his own private method of diagrammatic representation of these systems instead of the standard type of block diagram used in the engineering literature. The main principles of system analysis, presented in chapter III, involve the use of a graphical technique, the Nyquist diagram, for finding the frequency and damping of the free modes of oscillation of linear dynamic systems. Professor Tustin's exposition is admirably lucid and concise, and

184

can be followed by anyone with a moderate knowledge of mathematics and some familiarity with differential equations. Only one example is given (pp. 72–8) of the most important use of Nyquist diagrams, that is, as an aid in finding ways of modifying a system in order to improve its stability. This is not a deductive process; but an art requiring skill and judgment which can only be acquired by considerable practice in the use of this and other techniques. It would have been an advantage if more space had been devoted to this problem.

Although Nyquist diagrams enable one to gain valuable insight into the dynamic properties of fairly complex linear models, they cannot be used for analysing the more elaborate non-linear models that would be needed for an adequate representation of the economic system. Professor Tustin suggests that some further advance might be made by the construction of a special analogue machine for the study of more realistic models. Using a combination of econometric and trial-and-error methods, the system of relationships, forms of the time lags and values of parameters of the analogue might be adjusted to produce as good a 'fit' as possible to historical time series, and the resulting system used in making economic forecasts and formulating policies.

This would be a very ambitious project. Apart from the engineering problems involved, it would require a close co-ordination of theoretical, statistical and historical studies in economics, since it appears probable that different models could be fitted to the same empirical data if different judgments were made about the changes or disturbances which had occurred in the system. Partly for this reason, however, analogue machines may prove to be important instruments in economic research. It is possible, too, that existing types of electronic simulator may be more suitable for this purpose than Professor Tustin implies.

Professor Tustin's book contains material of fundamental importance for all who are engaged in either theoretical or empirical studies of dynamic processes in economics. It throws new light on the possibilities and the difficulties of quantitative research in this field.

Note
Economic Journal, 64, 1954, pp. 805–7.

19 Michel Kalecki's *Theory of Economic Dynamics: An Essay on Cyclical and Long-run Changes in the Capitalist Economy:* A Review

A.W. Phillips

This book consists of revised versions of Mr Kalecki's earlier works, *Essays in the Theory of Economic Fluctuations and Studies in Economic Dynamics*, which have been out of print for some time. The original papers have been rewritten and rearranged to lead up to a theory of cyclical fluctuations. Mr Kalecki first discusses the degree of monopoly and then postulates a number of relationships between income, profits, consumption and investment. Following the introduction of each relationship there is a regression analysis of relevant statistical data; but Mr Kalecki emphasises that the statistical analysis is intended to show the plausibility of the relation postulated rather to obtain the most likely value of the coefficients. The separation relationships are later combined in a dynamic model which exhibits cyclical fluctuations. Mr Kalecki favours the Frisch theory of dampened cycles continually excited by erratic shocks rather than the Hicks–Goodwin theory of limits cycles in a non-linear system, and has constructed some series to show that if the magnitude of the stocks are normally distributed fairly regular cycles are generated even when the system is rather heavily dampened. In the concluding chapters of the book a growth trend is added to the cyclical model and there is a brief and very formal treatment of the factors affecting long-run development.

Mr Kalecki does not claim that he has given anything approaching a complete explanation of cyclical changes, and one can of course devise many other systems equally consistent with the data and leading to similar fluctuations. Opinions will differ as to the explanatory value of this particular system. The argument given to support the assumption that investment decisions depend on the rate of change of profits and on the capital stock rather than on their levels seems rather weak. Interest rates are discussed but are considered to be of little or no importance, while no causal significance is attached to price movements. But whatever the limitations, Mr Kalecki's contributions have been of the greatest importance in the development of dynamic theories and methods of analysis and this new presentation of his ideas will repay careful study.

Note
Economica, 21 (NS) (84), 1954, p. 364.

Growth

20 The Growth Articles

A.R. Bergstrom

Chapter 21, first published in 1961, is one of the most important essays that Phillips ever wrote. It provided the first synthesis of real and monetary phenomena and cycles and growth in a dynamic disequilibrium macroeconomic model, together with a mathematical analysis of the steady state and stability properties of the model. It also provided the initial stimulus which led, via my own work, to the development of a series of continuous time macroeconometric models generating cyclical growth. During the last twenty years, such models have been estimated for most of the leading industrial countries of the world, and they share some of the basic features of the theoretical model developed in chapter 21. Moreover, they have been estimated by continuous time econometric methods whose development was stimulated by chapter 42 (1959).

At the time when Phillips wrote chapter 21, theoretical models of cyclical growth were rather mechanical, with cycles being generated by the multiplier–accelerator mechanism and growth introduced through exogenous trends in demand.[1] There was, clearly, a need for a more integrated model, which incorporated the price mechanism. Several leading economists, including Meade and Robertson had, for some time, been trying to persuade Phillips to introduce the price mechanism into his dynamic models. Chapter 21 was strongly influenced by the ideas of Meade, who had, himself, been working on this problem.

The model developed in chapter 21 is, essentially, a very simple one. It contains only five endogenous variables: output, consumption, capital, the interest rate and the price level, and one exogenous variable, the money supply, which is assumed to grow at a constant rate. A key role is played by the concept of 'normal capacity output', which is assumed to be proportional to the stock of capital. The ratio of actual output to normal capacity output is assumed to have a positive influence on both the proportional rate of increase in the stock of capital and the proportional rate of increase in the price level, the effect on the former variable occurring with a distributed time lag, through a differential equation.

The ratio of actual output to normal capacity output is also used in the stability analysis. Indeed, Phillips reduces the complete model to an approximate linear differential equation in this ratio, and from the coefficients of this equation derives the stability conditions in terms of the structural parameters of the model.

It is, perhaps, surprising in view of his earlier work on the relation between unemployment and the rate of increase in wage rates (chapter 25), that neither employment nor the wage rate are included as variables in the 1961 model. It is implicitly assumed, however, that the proportion of the labour force employed is closely related to the ratio of actual output to normal capacity output. The model must be regarded, therefore, as an approximation, whose accuracy depends on the closeness of the stock of capital to its steady state path relative to the labour supply. This raises the question of how, and under what conditions, capital and other variables are drawn towards their steady state paths by the price mechanism over a long period.

The first analysis of the stability of the neoclassical growth model was that of Solow (1956). Solow's analysis was greatly simplified, however, by assuming that employment follows an exogenous exponential growth path (which can be regarded as the full employment path), thus excluding the difficult problem of dealing with the effects of fluctuations in unemployment and the stability of these fluctuations. He essentially proved (under certain assumptions concerning the production function) that, if all prices adjust instantaneously and continuously to their full employment equilibrium levels, then the price mechanism ensures that output and capital converge to steady state exponential growth paths; that is, to the steady state neoclassical growth paths discovered independently by Solow (1956) and Swan (1956). Although this was an important step, there was clearly a need for a more general analysis which allowed both capital and employment to be out of equilibrium and prices to adjust gradually rather than instantaneously. Chapter 21 was a major step forward in this direction, although his model is, in some respects, a development of the model of Harrod (1948) rather than the neoclassical model.

Since reading Solow's 1956 article, I too had been thinking about the problem of introducing the price mechanism into a dynamic disequilibrium model which synthesised cycles and growth. Chapter 21 stimulated me into writing two articles on this subject (Bergstrom 1962, 1966b). The model developed in the second of these articles was more extensively discussed and analysed in chapters 5 and 6 of Bergstrom (1967). It provides a synthesis of neoclassical and Keynesian theory in a cyclical growth model. Its steady state and stability properties are analysed by methods which are easily applicable to much larger models and have been followed in most of the subsequent work on continuous time macro-econometric modelling.[2]

The model developed in my 1966 article also served as a prototype for the first continuous time macroeconometric model: the disequilibrium neoclassical growth model of the United Kingdom developed by Bergstrom and Wymer (1976). That model has in turn served as a prototype for continuous time macroeconometric models developed by other econometricians for many different countries, as well as for a recent second-order continuous time macroeconometric model of the United Kingdom.[3] Although not all of these macroeconometric models are neoclassical, they are all dynamic disequilibrium models which synthesise real and monetary phenomena and cycles and growth, as did Phillips' model in chapter 21. Moreover, it was his essay which provided the initial stimulus that led to their development.

Chapter 22 is much less technical. It is, in fact, Phillips' inaugural lecture given after he was appointed to the Tooke professorship at the LSE. It is, mainly, an exposition, for a general audience, of some of the implications of his own research and that of other economists working in the same fields.

The essay starts with a clear but non-mathematical explanation of certain basic principles concerning the behaviour of dynamic systems, the effect of feedbacks on the stability of such systems and the importance of time lags. This provides the basis for a discussion of the effects of policy feedbacks on fluctuations in employment and economic activity. Phillips had, of course, made pioneering contributions to this field of research in the early 1950s (see especially chapter 16). He concludes that, because of the long time lags with which interest rates affect investment, monetary policy can play only a minor role in reducing short period fluctuations and the main policy instrument for this purpose should be fiscal policy. This conclusion is strongly supported by recent research of Bergstrom, Nowman and Wandasiewicz (1994), in which optimal control theory is applied to the second-order continuous time model of the United Kingdom mentioned earlier. In this section of the essay, Phillips also makes a practical proposal for a stabilisation tax which, in the United Kingdom, would be implemented by adding or subtracting a varying percentage to the income tax computed from the PAYE tables.

The next section is concerned with the relation between unemployment and inflation, which is another subject to which Phillips had made an important and influential contribution (see chapter 25). It seems clear that, at this time, he believed, as did most economists, that there was a long-run trade-off between unemployment and inflation. I doubt if most economists still believe this. A more common belief, which I share, is that there is a non-accelerating inflation rate of unemployment which is compatible with various steady state rates of inflation. Various proposals which Phillips makes for shifting the long-run relation between unemployment and inflation could, however, be used to influence the non-accelerating inflation rate of unemployment.

In 1962, when Phillips first published chapter 22, it was frequently argued that using unemployment to check inflation would reduce the rate of growth of the economy. He discusses this argument, briefly, and concludes that the steady state rate of growth of the economy would not be significantly affected by a transition to a higher level of unemployment. The final section of the essay is devoted to a discussion of exchange rate policy. Here Phillips argues for some flexibility of exchange rates in order to allow countries a degree of independence in their choices of internal balance between unemployment and inflation.

Chapter 23 is a brief and previously unpublished essay, written as a basis for a seminar presentation. Like chapter 22, it is non-mathematical and is primarily concerned with policy issues. Indeed, it covers much the same ground as chapter 22 and contains similar policy recommendations, which are now related to the Australian economy.

In particular, Phillips again argues that taxation should be the principal policy instrument for controlling short-period fluctuations. He suggests, for this purpose, a percentage surcharge or rebate on personal income and payroll tax, adjustable at quarterly intervals. He also argues, as in the previous essay, for some flexibility of exchange rates in order to allow countries to pursue their independent policies relating to unemployment and inflation. Indeed, he proposes a rule which would allow a movement of the exchange rate of up to 2.5 per cent per annum in either direction.

Perhaps the most important change in economic thought, in relation to policy, during the thirty years since Phillips wrote these essays, is the wide acceptance by leading economists of the view that there is no long-run trade-off between unemployment and inflation. Indeed, it is conceivable that by the late 1960s Phillips himself no longer believed that there was such a trade-off. In any case, he never advocated policies that would increase the rate of inflation in order to reduce unemployment, but was interested in finding the level of unemployment that would be consistent with price stability (zero inflation). This goal of price stability is now back on the policy agenda. Moreover, some of the main policy issues with which Phillips was concerned, particularly the role of monetary and fiscal policy in economic stabilisation and the issue of fixed versus flexible exchange rates, are still being widely debated.

Notes

1 See, for example, Hicks (1950).
2 See Gandolfo (1981, chapter 2) for a clear and detailed exposition of this methodology.
3 See Bergstrom, Nowman and Wymer (1992) and the references therein.

21 A Simple Model of Employment, Money and Prices in a Growing Economy

A.W. Phillips

041
E24 E12
E32 E31

1 Introduction

The purpose of this article is to develop a simple aggregative model which may be used to study both the problem of reducing short-period fluctuations of an economy and the problem of attaining longer-term objectives relating to employment, the price level and growth. To do this the Keynesian model of employment, interest and money is extended in a number of ways. The concept of 'normal capacity output' is introduced, with the hypothesis that normal capacity output increases continuously as a result of investment in improving productive resources. Actual output is then expressed as a proportion of normal capacity output. The rate of change of the price level is assumed to depend on the ratio of actual output to normal capacity output and on the rate of change of productivity. The rate of interest is assumed to depend on the quantity of money, actual output and the price level. Investment demand is made a function of the ratio of actual output to normal capacity output, the expected rate of growth and the rate of interest.

By defining some variables in the model to be either logarithms or ratios of the usual economic variables, assuming continuously distributed time lags in the behaviour relations and making certain linear approximations, which should be satisfactory for moderate fluctuations in output and employment, the model can be written as a system of linear differential equations. The steady state solutions give the paths of the variables in conditions of steady or 'equilibrium' growth and in particular show the long-run relations between the rate of change of the quantity of money, the ratio of actual to normal capacity output, the rate of change of the price level and the rate of growth of normal capacity output. The transient solutions, which show deviations from, or short-period fluctuations about the 'growth equilibrium' paths, are used to investigate the stability of the system and the effect of a stabilisation policy.

195

2 Normal capacity output

By normal capacity output we shall mean the output that would be obtained if firms were operating with that percentage utilisation of available physical resources which they would consider to be the most satisfactory average percentage utilisation over a period of years. The concept of normal capacity output, like other aggregative concepts, is not precise. It is, however, indispensable in any discussion of unemployment and growth.

We should expect short-term fluctuations in the ratio of actual output to normal capacity output to be closely associated with fluctuations in the proportion of the labour force employed. A study of British data since 1948 (Paish 1962) shows that short-period fluctuations in the ratio of gross domestic product to a fitted exponential growth trend have been highly correlated with, but about five times as large as, the fluctuations in the proportion of the labour force employed. If we suppose that normal capacity output was approximately equal to the fitted growth trend this would mean that, over the range of unemployment experienced, fluctuations in the ratio of actual output to normal capacity output have also been about five times as large as the corresponding fluctuations in the proportion of the labour force employed.

3 The rate of economic growth

We shall mean by the rate of economic growth the proportional rate of change of normal capacity output. If Y_n is normal capacity output, considered a function of continuous time t, the rate of economic growth, denoted by y_n, is thus defined by

$$y_n = D Y_n / Y_n = D \log Y_n \tag{1}$$

where D is the differential operator d/dt.

We shall assume that the ratio of normal capacity output to the stock of capital is constant,[1] and write

$$Y_n = vK \tag{2}$$

where K is the stock of capital and v is the output–capital ratio.[2] Taking logarithms of (2), differentiating with respect to time and writing k for $D \log K$, the proportional rate of growth of the stock of capital, we obtain

$$y_n = k \tag{3}$$

4 The consumption function

Real consumption C is assumed to be a constant proportion $1 - s$ of actual real income or output Y, i.e.

$$C = (1 - s)Y \tag{4}$$

In section 10 below, this assumption will be modified by the introduction of a distributed time lag.

From (4) and the identity

$$Y = C + I \tag{5}$$

where I is real net investment we obtain

$$Y = I/s \tag{6}$$

By the meaning of net investment

$$I = DK \tag{7}$$

so that

$$I/K = DK/K = k \tag{8}$$

Denoting by x the ratio of actual output to normal capacity output, so that

$$x = Y/Y_n \tag{9}$$

we have from (2), (6) and (8)

$$x = DK/svK = k/sv \tag{10}$$

Also, from (10) and (3)

$$y_n = svx \tag{11}$$

5 The investment function

The investment function will be written as

$$\frac{1}{K} = \left(\frac{N\lambda}{D + N\lambda}\right)^N \{\alpha g + \gamma(x - 1) + \rho(c - r)\}. \tag{12}$$

Here, g denotes the proportional rate of growth expected by entrepreneurs, r is the rate of interest and c is a constant which may be interpreted as the marginal productivity of capital at normal capacity output.[3] α, γ, ρ and λ are positive constants and N is a positive integer. The term in the first bracket on the right-hand side of (12) is an operator representing a distributed time lag[4] in the response of I/K to changes in g, x and r. In the simplest case with $N = 1$, which we shall consider first, the operator represents an exponentially distributed time lag with a speed of response λ and a time-constant $1/\lambda$.

The parameter ρ indicates the influence on investment of the rate of interest and the productivity of capital. If the rate of interest were equal to the marginal productivity of capital at normal capacity output entrepreneurs might still proceed with investment, for two reasons. First, since actual output might not be equal to normal capacity output the quantity of capital existing at any time might not be exactly that desired for producing the actual level of output. It is assumed that an excess or deficiency of capital stock would lead to net investment (negative or positive) which would reduce the discrepancy at the proportional rate γ. Secondly, even if the quantity of capital were exactly that desired for the actual level of output, entrepreneurs might expect demand and output to increase through time and so invest at a rate which would maintain the desired relation between capital and expected output.[5] If entrepreneurs' expectations were held with certainty, α in (12) might be taken equal to unity, in practice we should expect it to lie between zero and unity.

Since the expected rate of change of output probably depends mainly on the past rates of change we shall assume that

$$g = \frac{\eta}{D + \eta} y \tag{13}$$

where

$$y = D \log Y \tag{14}$$

In (13), η is a measure of the speed with which expectations are adjusted to variations in the rate of change of actual output. In the limit as η tends to zero g becomes a constant. This will be considered as a special case of (13).

6 The model with constant rate of interest

Considering first the case with g constant and $N = 1$ we obtain from (8), (10), (11) and (12)

$$\{D + \lambda(1 - \gamma/sv)\}y_n = \lambda\{\alpha g - \gamma + \rho(c - r)\} \tag{15}$$

and

$$\{D + \lambda(1 - \gamma/sv)\}x = \lambda\{\alpha g - \gamma + \rho(c - r)\}/sv \tag{16}$$

The solutions of (15) and (16) for $t \geq 0$ are

$$y_n(t) = y_{ns} + \{y_n(0) - y_{ns}\} \exp\{-\lambda(1 - \gamma/sv)t\} \qquad (17)$$

and

$$x(t) = x_s + \{x(0) - x_s\} \exp\{-\lambda(1 - \gamma/sv)t\} \qquad (18)$$

where

$$y_{ns} = sv \frac{\alpha g - \gamma + \rho(c - r)}{sv - \gamma} \qquad (19)$$

and

$$x_s = \frac{\alpha g - \gamma + \rho(c - r)}{sv - \gamma} \qquad (20)$$

With these solutions for $y_n(t)$ and $x(t)$ and given initial conditions the solutions for $Y_n(t)$ and $Y(t)$ may be obtained from (1) and (9).

y_{ns} and x_s will be called the steady state solutions of (15) and (16) respectively. $y_n(t) - y_{ns}$ and $x(t) - x_s$ will be called the transient solutions. We also define a steady state solution $Y_{ns}(t)$ for normal capacity output by the equation $y_{ns} = D \log Y_{ns}(t)$ and a steady state solution $Y_s(t)$ for actual output by $Y_s(t) = x_s Y_{ns}(t)$, these equations being analogous to (1) and (9). The steady state solution for the proportional rate of change of actual output is then defined as $y_s = D \log Y_s(t)$, by analogy with (14).

With these definitions, y_{ns} is equivalent to Harrod's natural rate of growth, y_s is equivalent to his warranted rate of growth, while y is the proportional rate of change of actual output (Harrod 1948, chapter 3). From (19) and (20) we see that, with $r = c$ and $\alpha = 1$, when $g = sv$ we have $y_{ns} = sv$ and $x_s = l$, from which it follows that $y_s = sv$, which is the same as Harrod's solution for the warranted rate of growth.

From (17) and (18) we see that the system with a constant rate of interest will be stable only if $\gamma < sv$. With $\gamma > sv$ any deviation of actual output from its steady state or 'growth equilibrium' path will lead to further cumulative movement away from that path. As a numerical example put $s = 0.1$, $v = 0.25$ and define the unit of time as a year; for stability we require $\gamma < 0.025$, which means that the time-constant of the distributed time lag in the adjustment of the capital stock must be more than forty years. Such a long time lag seems most unlikely in practice; but if we use more likely values the model is extremely unstable.

If the assumption that $g = sv$ is replaced by (13) with $\eta > 0$, we find on solving the modified system that with $r = c$ and $\alpha = 1$ the steady state solutions are again $y_{ns} = y_s = sv$ and $x_s = 1$. The system is even more unstable than before. One of the stability conditions is that γ be less than $sv(1 - \alpha)$, which cannot be satisfied when $\alpha = 1$.

We proceed to extend the model by introducing money, a flexible price level and a flexible rate of interest, and to consider the stability of the extended system.

7 The rate of change of the price level

We shall mean by the price level, P, an index of the money prices of final output, and shall suppose that

$$p = \beta(x - 1) - y_n + \delta \tag{21}$$

where

$$p = D \log P \tag{22}$$

and β and δ are constants. The basic idea behind (21) is that the proportional rate of change, p, of the price level will be equal to the proportional rate of change of factor prices, which will be closely related to the ratio of actual to normal capacity output, minus the rate of change of productivity. If the labour force and the normal hours worked are constant, y_n may be taken as a measure of the rate of change of productivity. δ is then the rate at which factor prices would change if actual output were equal to normal capacity output. If the labour force or normal hours are changing at a constant proportionate rate, y_n needs to be adjusted by an additive constant which may be allowed for in the definition of δ.

Empirical studies suggest that in Britain, when unemployment varies within the range of about 1.5 per cent to 2.5 per cent, an increase of 0.1 per cent in unemployment is associated with a reduction in the rate of increase of wages of between 0.3 and 0.4 per cent per annum, and with a similar reduction in the rate of increase of the price level (Phillips, chapter 25; Dicks-Mireaux and Dow 1959; Klein and Ball 1959; Lipsey 1960; Lipsey and Steuer 1961; Routh 1959). Since variations in output as a percentage of trend were about five times as large as the variations in the percentage unemployment, the value of β, for this range of unemployment, is perhaps a little below unity. There is reason to believe that the relation between employment and wage changes is not linear and that at lower levels of unemployment a higher value of β would be appropriate while for variations between, say, 4 per cent and 5 per cent unemployment a suitable value of β might be as low as 0.1.

8 The rate of interest

We assume that the demand for money is a decreasing function of the rate of interest, that it has unit elasticity with respect to both real income and the price level and that the rate of interest is adjusted by the market without significant time lag to equate the quantity of money demanded to the existing stock of money, M. A simple interest function satisfying these assumptions is[6]

$$r = \kappa + \mu(\log Y + \log P - \log M) \tag{23}$$

As a flexible price level has been introduced into the model, the rate of interest r in the investment function (12) and in the interest function (23) will now be interpreted as the real rate of interest in Fisher's sense, i.e., as the money rate of interest minus the expected rate of change of the price level.

9 The model with money, interest and prices

In order to reduce the model with money, interest and prices to linear differential equations in x, y_n and p it is necessary to express $\log Y$, which occurs in (23), in terms of $\log Y_n$ and x. For this purpose we shall use the approximation

$$\log Y \cong \log Y_n + (Y - Y_n)/Y_n$$
$$= \log Y_n + x - 1 \tag{24}$$

The approximation is very good over the range of values of $(Y - Y_n)/Y_n$, say from -0.05 to 0.05, in which we are interested. Considering again the case with g constant and $N = 1$, we may reduce the model to a differential equation in x by substituting (23) in (16) and using (21), (22) and (24) to obtain

$$[D^2 + \lambda\{1 - (\gamma - \rho\mu)/sv\}D + \lambda\rho\mu\beta/sv]x = \lambda\rho\mu(m - \delta + \beta)/sv \tag{25}$$

where m has been written for $D \log M$, the proportional rate of change of the quantity of money. Differential equations in y_n and p are readily derived from (25) using (11) and (21). We assume that m is constant.

The steady state solutions (which may be obtained by putting D equal to zero and solving for x, y_n, and p) are

$$x_s = 1 + (m - \delta)/\beta \tag{26}$$

$$y_{ns} = svx_s \tag{27}$$

and

$$p_s = m - y_{ns} \tag{28}$$

If $m = \delta$ we see that $x_s = 1$, i.e., the normal capacity output is maintained so long as the economy remains on the 'growth equilibrium' path. y_{ns} and y_s are then equal to sv, i.e., the steady state rate of growth is again equal to the warranted rate of growth in Harrod's model, and $p_s = \delta - y_{ns}$. If $m = y_{ns}$ the price level is constant in conditions of steady growth. In this case we find from (26) and (27) that

$$x_s = (\beta - \delta)/(\beta - sv) \tag{29}$$

so that the maintenance of normal capacity output is consistent with a constant price level only if $\delta = sv$.

It may be noted that (28) is in accordance with an obvious extension of the classical quantity theory of money, applied to the growth equilibrium path of a steadily expanding economy. We may also solve the system for the steady state rate of interest, r_s , and we find that

$$r_s = c + (\alpha g - \gamma)/\rho + (\gamma - sv)(m - \delta + \beta)/\beta\rho \tag{30}$$

r_s is thus independent of the absolute quantity of money, again in accordance with classical theory. This agreement between the steady state solutions of the model and classical theory is, of course, the result of the assumption of unit elasticity of demand for money with respect to prices and real income and the assumption that the effects of technical change and of changes in the quantities of the factors of production are such that the output–capital ratio and the marginal productivity of capital remain constant through time. We note that if $m = \delta$, $\alpha = 1$ and $g = sv$, then $r_s = c$, i.e., the steady state rate of interest is equal to the marginal productivity of capital.

Remembering that all the parameters on the left-hand side of (25) are positive, we see that the condition for the stability of the system is that γ be less than $sv + \rho\mu$. $\rho\mu$ represents the strength of the influence on investment of changes in the quantity of money, so if monetary influences are sufficiently strong the system will be stable. If we put $s = 0.1$, $v = 0.25$, $\lambda = 1.0$ and $\gamma = 0.1$, so that the only parameters on the left-hand side of (25) which are not specified numerically are β and $\rho\mu$, the stability condition is that $\rho\mu$ be greater than 0.075. The area to the right of the vertical line a in figure 21.1 is therefore the stable region. From (25) we also find that the area above curve b of figure 21.1 is the region in which the system is oscillatory. If β and $\rho\mu$ correspond to a point in this region any deviation of output from its steady state path will lead to cyclical fluctuations about that path.

10 Lag distributions and stabilisation policy

The exponentially distributed time lag in the investment function obtained by taking $N = 1$ in (12) must be considered a very special case of a more general class of lag distributions. We probably approach nearer to reality by giving N higher (integral) values. The resulting lag distributions are of humped form, implying that the peak of the rate of response to a change is reached some time after the change has occurred. If the model used in section 9 is modified by taking $N = 2$ or $N = 3$ we obtain a much less comforting picture of the possible behaviour of economic systems.[7] When $N = 2$ and s, v, λ and γ have the same values as in the previous example, the stable region for the model becomes the area to the right of and below curve a in figure 21.2. When $N = 3$ it is reduced to the area below curve b in figure 21.2. In both cases the system is oscillatory over almost the entire stable region and also over the greater part of the unstable region.

The stability of the system can be improved by introducing what I have called elsewhere a derivative stabilisation policy (Phillips, chapters 16, 17 and 25). As an example, suppose there is a monetary authority which attempts to stabilise the system by relating the quantity of money to the rate of change of the ratio of actual output to normal capacity output, and assume that the relation it maintains is

$$\log M = \log M_s - \theta Dx \tag{31}$$

where M_s is the quantity of money that there would have been if there had not been a stabilisation policy. Then we find that with $\theta = 0.5$ and $N = 3$ the stable region of the model is the area to the right of curve c in figure 21.2.

The stability conditions are made rather more severe if the expected rate of growth g is defined by (13) instead of being a constant. With $\eta = 0.1$, $\alpha = 1.0$, $\theta = 0$ and $N = 3$ the stable region is the area enclosed by curve a in figure 21.3. If θ is changed to 0.5 the stable region becomes the area to the right of curve b in figure 21.3.

As a final example, we shall introduce a time lag into the consumption function, by replacing (4) by

$$\frac{C}{Y_n} = \left(\frac{3}{D+3}\right)^3 (1 - s)\frac{Y}{Y_n} \tag{32}$$

Using the same numerical values as in the last example, the stable region when $\theta = 0$ is the area to the right of curve a in figure 21.4. When $\theta = 0.5$ it is the area to the right of curve b in figure 21.4.

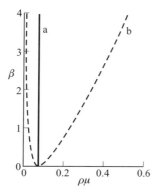

Figure 21.1

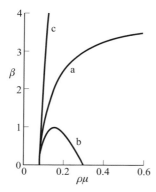

Figure 21.2

11 Concluding remarks

The model in this article has deliberately been kept as simple as is possible, given the aim of providing a synthesis of real and monetary quantities and of cycles and growth in a single system. A simple synthesis of this sort has, I think, some value both in teaching and in helping to organise one's thoughts on economic conditions and policies.

Since the behaviour of dynamic systems depends so much on the numerical values of the parameters in them a more direct application to economic affairs would need to be preceded by extensive work on empirical estimation, in the course of which the behaviour relations in the model would be modified and elaborated.[8]

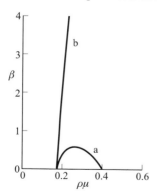

Figure 21.3

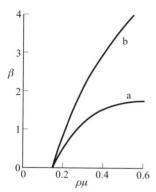

Figure 21.4

Notes

Economica, 28 (NS) (112), 1961, pp. 360–70.
1 Slow changes in this ratio would have little effect on the analysis of stability and short-period fluctuations.
2 A constant output–capital ratio is not inconsistent with diminishing returns to capital provided there is an appropriate rate of technical progress. Consider, for example, a Cobb–Douglas production function with neutral technical progress, which may be written $Y_n = AK^U L^Q e^{rt}$ where L is labour, r is the rate of technical progress and A, U and Q are constants. Taking logarithms of both sides of the equation, differentiating with respect to time and writing k for $D \log K$ and l for $D \log L$ we obtain $y_n = Uk + Ql + r$. If $r = (l - U)k - Ql$ we have $y_n = k$ and it follows that $Y_n = vK$, where v is a constant. For a more

general treatment of the production function in a model of equilibrium growth see Meade (1961). For a theoretical and empirical study of technical progress and the aggregate production function see Solow (1959).

3 The assumption of a constant marginal productivity of capital, like that of a constant output–capital ratio, is consistent with diminishing returns to capital provided technical progress is proceeding at the appropriate rate. See note 2.

4 For further explanation of this form of distributed time lag, see Phillips (chapters 16 and 17), Allen (1956) and Tustin (1954).

5 The need for this distinction between the 'forward-looking' and 'backward-looking' elements in investment decisions was suggested to me by Professor J.E. Meade who, in an unpublished paper, developed a model which has some similarities with the one described in this article.

6 This functional form is, of course, only suitable for a limited range of variation YP/M. r in (23) would become negative if this ratio were sufficiently small.

7 For another illustration of the effects on stability of these forms of lags see Phillips (chapter 17).

8 It seems to me that in considering methods of estimation of highly aggregated systems such as this it is important to take account of the fact that the adjustments in them are occurring almost continuously. This view of a system adjusting continuously in time immediately draws one's attention to the need for estimation procedures which are appropriate for systems with distributed time lags and autocorrelated disturbances. The advantages of a continuous treatment of time in estimation methods have been clearly stated by Koopmans (1950b). For an approach to time series estimation from this point of view see Phillips (chapter 42). Research on this matter has been proceeding at the London School of Economics with the help of a grant from the Ford Foundation.

22   Employment, Inflation and Growth

A.W. Phillips

1 Introduction

Since the end of the Second World War economic policy and controversy
in Britain have been directed to ways of attaining a number of related
objectives, prominent among which are the maintenance of a high and
stable level of employment, reasonable stability of the average level of
final product prices, a fairly rapid rate of economic growth, a satisfactory
balance of foreign trade and reasonable stability of foreign exchange
rates. It can hardly be claimed that there has been complete success in
the attainment of these objectives. It is true that employment has been
maintained at an extremely high level. The average level of unemployment since 1948 has been little more than 1.5 per cent of the work force.
This is probably a lower level of unemployment than that attained in any
single year in peace time during the previous century, except perhaps in
1872. Even in the boom years of the pre-war trade cycle the percentage of
trade unionists unemployed rarely fell below 2 per cent and over the fifty-
three years from 1861 to 1913 it averaged 4.5 per cent. The actions taken
to improve the stability of the system have also had some measure of
success. Before the First World War there was a fairly regular trade cycle
with an average period of about eight years, during which trade union
unemployment fluctuated between about 2 and 10 per cent. Since the
Second World War the cyclical movements in economic activity have
become more rapid, with a period of four or five years, but the fluctuations have been smaller. Unemployment, indeed, has only fluctuated
between about 1 per cent and 2.5 per cent, that is, over a range of
about 1.5 per cent, but the percentage fluctuations in gross national
product about the growth trend have been about five times as large as
this (Paish 1962), the range of the fluctuations as a percentage of the
trend being about 7 or 8 per cent. Between 1948 and 1960, gross national
product increased at an average rate of about 2.75 per cent per annum

and productivity per man hour at perhaps 1.75 per cent per annum. Though these rates of increase probably compare favourably with those in earlier periods of British history they are lower than those of a number of other industrial countries in the same period. The average rate of rise of the retail price index between 1948 and 1960 was 3.7 per cent per annum. There would be fairly general agreement that this rate of inflation is undesirable. It has undoubtedly been a major cause of the general weakness of the balance of payments and the foreign reserves, and if continued it would almost certainly make the present rate of exchange untenable.

It is my belief that one of the main reasons for the difficulties that have been experienced in devising and implementing appropriate economic policies is lack of adequate quantitative knowledge and understanding of how the economic system works. Of course, economists do understand, in a general sort of way, quite a lot about the working of the economic system and do now have a mass of quantitative information about important economic variables. But in order to bring this knowledge to bear on the problem of formulating and attaining a consistent set of policy objectives we require also knowledge of the quantitative relations between economic variables. In particular it is necessary to know what quantitative relations hold between those economic variables which are either the objectives of policy or the instruments through which we attempt to attain the objectives. For example, if some relation holds, in given institutional conditions and on average over a period of years, between the level of employment and the speed of inflation, failure to take account of it may lead to the adoption of inconsistent objectives and to a type of schizophrenic behaviour as attempts are made to attain these inconsistent aims. Knowledge of the relation would lead either to modification of the objectives to make them consistent or perhaps, since an economic relation is only the result of fairly regular patterns of human behaviour, to some modification of institutions or behaviour which would alter the relation so as to permit some more desirable combinations of consistent aims. Or again, if at a certain time unemployment is felt to be too high and short-term interest rates are lowered in order to raise the demand for goods and so for labour, how large will the effects be and when will they occur; will the higher demand also lead to an increase in fixed investment and if so how large an increase and after what interval of time; will wage rates and prices rise more rapidly as a result of the higher demand; if internal demand and prices rise will imports rise and exports fall, and if so when and by how much? If we are to assess the effects of our attempts to influence the course of economic affairs we need answers, numerical answers, to questions like these. If we do not have this knowledge the policy adjustments will almost certainly be inappropriate in magnitude or timing or both and may well cause, as I believe they have often caused in the past, unnecessary and harmful fluctuations in economic activity.

We may obtain tentative estimates of a quantitative relation in economics by making a preliminary subjective analysis of human motivation and behaviour and then carrying out a statistical analysis of relevant data from past records. We also need to investigate the degree of error that there may be in the estimate, the extent to which the relation in successive short time periods departs from its average over longer periods and whether there is any evidence that the average relation changes in any systematic way through time. On the basis of quantitative estimates of this sort it is possible to set up simplified models of the economic system and by studying the properties of different models with a variety of policy relationships we can form some judgement of the likely effects of alternative types of economic policy. The empirical study of economic relations and the quantitative investigation of the behaviour of models of economic processes are comparatively recent developments in our subject. The knowledge and understanding which have so far been gained are far from being adequate for a firm and detailed appraisal of economic policy. I think they do, however, make possible some attempt at clarification of the problems we face and justify some suggestions for methods of dealing with them.

2 Some general principles of fluctuations and stability

The first policy objective I should like to consider is that of maintaining a stable level of employment; but before proceeding to this it seems desirable to illustrate some general points about equilibrium, stability and fluctuations in the simplest possible way. Let me therefore consider a single commodity which is being continuously produced and consumed and which is traded on a perfectly competitive market. Assume that the rate of production is an increasing function of price, the rate of consumption is a decreasing function of price and that the rate of change of the price is proportional to the excess demand, that is, to the rate of consumption minus the rate of production. This is the simple text-book example of supply and demand in a single competitive market. It is frequently stated, and has indeed been stated with some emphasis by such eminent economists as Walras, Marshall and Wicksell, that such a system is necessarily stable, that is, that it always tends to an equilibrium in which the price is such that the rates of production and consumption are equal. The argument is usually very simple. Suppose the system is not in equilibrium; for example, suppose there is excess demand. Then the price will rise. This will increase production and reduce consumption and so reduce the excess demand. Since the price continues to rise so long as there is any excess demand and any rise in price reduces the excess demand the process will continue until the excess demand is eliminated. In brief; the existence of any discrepancy between production and consumption causes a movement in price which tends to correct the discrepancy. Therefore, the argument runs, the system is stable. This argument is, of course, fallacious except on the assumption that the complete response of the rates of production and consumption to any change in price occurs instantaneously. If there are any time lags in any of the responses the system will usually fluctuate. Whether the fluctuations will die away or whether they will increase in amplitude and tend to some regular and sustained limit cycle depends on the precise forms of the time lags, on the slopes of the supply and demand curves and on the speed at which the price changes when there is a given excess demand.

The competitive model which we have been considering, and other so-called 'self-equilibrating' models of economic processes are, in fact, examples of what are known in other fields of study as 'negative feed-back control systems'. In order to see intuitively why these systems are often oscillatory and may well be unstable (which means in practice that they tend to produce fairly large and regular cyclical movements) let us consider again the competitive market. Assume this time that some factor other than price causes small cyclical changes in production or consumption, so that excess demand is alternately positive and negative (see curve a of figure 22.1). We shall call this an exogenous movement of excess demand and see what further movements in excess demand would be induced by price changes which depended only on this exogenous movement. In other words we shall find what would usually be called the corrective movements in excess demand which result from the price changes caused by the exogenous movements in excess demand. Since we are assuming that the rate of change of price is proportional to the exogenous movements in excess demand, the rate of change of price would have the same time pattern as the exogenous movement. The price itself, however, would lag behind the rate of change of price by a quarter of a cycle (see curve b) since the price would be at its maximum when its rate of change was zero and changing from positive to negative, and would be at a minimum when its rate of change was zero and changing from negative to positive. If the complete response of production and consumption to any change in price was instantaneous, the excess demand induced by the movements of price would be at its minimum when price was at its maximum and vice versa (see curve c). Suppose,

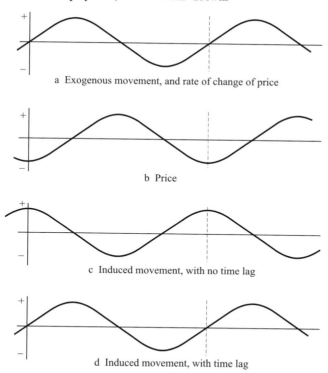

a Exogenous movement, and rate of change of price

b Price

c Induced movement, with no time lag

d Induced movement, with time lag

Figure 22.1

however, that production and consumption responded to changes in price with a time lag equal to one quarter of the period of the cycle. Then the excess demand induced by the price changes would be exactly in phase with the exogenous movements in excess demand (see curve d). Instead of tending to offset or correct the exogenous movement, the induced changes would tend to accentuate or amplify the fluctuations in excess demand caused by the exogenous movement. It is intuitively plausible, and can in fact be proved, that if, in this case, what are usually called the equilibrating or corrective forces are strong enough to make the amplitude of the induced movements in excess demand greater than the amplitude of the exogenous movements, the system will be unstable, that is, the fluctuations will increase and tend towards a regular and sustained limit cycle.

The exogenous movements or disturbances which affect economic activity are not usually, of course, of the simple type assumed in this example. They are more likely to be of a rather arbitrary or random pattern which can be described only in terms of a statistical or stochastic process. Such processes can, however, be analysed, by a method known as spectral density analysis, into cyclical components with periods ranging over the whole spectrum from zero to infinity. If disturbances of this sort operate on the model we have been considering, any cyclical component whose period is such that the time lag in the response of excess demand to price results in a lag in the neighbourhood of a quarter of the cyclical period will be amplified, while cyclical components whose periods are widely different from this will be reduced in amplitude. If the 'correcting forces' are sufficiently strong the cyclical components within a particular range of frequencies or periods will be amplified to such an extent that they will dominate the market movements, which will then exhibit large and somewhat irregular fluctuations, in which, however, cycles with this particular range of periodicities will predominate.

There are two more matters of some importance that I should like to refer to while dealing with the general principles of fluctuations and stability. The first concerns what I shall call the form or distribution of the time lags. Suppose the price in the commodity market we have been considering was constant for a long time and then suddenly rose and remained constant at the new level. The rate of production would eventually increase to some higher value, but there are any number of time paths that this increase might follow. For example, production might start to rise immediately and continue to rise at a gradually diminishing rate, or it might remain constant for a while and then increase gradually, or it might remain constant for a longer time and then increase very suddenly (see curves a and b and c in figure 22.2). Now it can be shown, but by methods which I shall not inflict on you here, that the

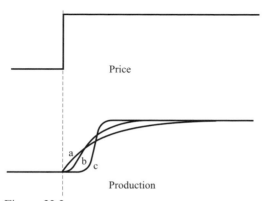

Figure 22.2

existence of a time lag of the first form in the corrective process is much less likely to cause fluctuations and instability than a lag of the second form, and a lag of the second form is less likely to cause these troubles than is the third form of lag. An important rule in devising a corrective system is therefore to get the corrective adjustment started immediately the discrepancy it is intended to correct begins to be observed. Provided a fair proportion of the effect of the corrective action is obtained fairly quickly it does not much matter if the remaining effects are delayed; but it does matter very much if the corrective action itself or all of its effects are delayed.

The second matter which I should like to deal with briefly is that of alternative types of corrective action. It is perhaps best introduced by asking what would happen if in the simple commodity model which we considered earlier it was the price rather than the rate of change of price which depended on the excess demand. We see from the curves that the price movements would occur a quarter of a cycle earlier as a result of this modification, and the induced movements in excess demand would no longer be in phase with the exogenous movements, so that the destabilising effects of the induced movements would be reduced or eliminated. Depending on the form of the time lag, it might or might not be possible to find a cycle of higher frequency, that is, of shorter period, for which the lag in the response of excess demand to price was half a cycle instead of a quarter cycle. If so, an exogenous movement of this higher frequency would lead to an induced movement in phase with the exogenous movement and if the amplitude of the induced movement was sufficiently large instability could still occur at the higher frequency. But since most forms of time lag are in effect weighted averages and tend to produce a low amplitude of response to high frequency cycles the likelihood of cyclical instability would be reduced. On the other hand this form of correction, which is called proportional control, could never ensure that production and consumption were brought into equality, since the price would be constant if excess demand were constant, even if it were not zero. However, a combination of proportional control and the type of correction used before, which is called integral control, overcomes this difficulty and gives better performance than integral control alone. We may go further in this direction and consider the effect of adding to the corrective action a component based on the rate of change of excess demand. Since the fluctuations in the rate of change of a cyclical variable lead the fluctuations in the variable itself by a quarter of a cycle, this component of corrective action, known as derivative control, has a somewhat similar effect to that which would be obtained by basing the corrective action on a forecast of excess demand. A derivative component of control is used in combination with proportional and integral components in most negative feedback control systems. By an appropriate combination of the three components it is usually possible to obtain very good regulating performance of a system, with corrective actions based only on the actual values of the variables and their rates of change in the immediate past, and without any recourse to predicted values or forecasts.

3 Fluctuations in employment and economic activity

I hope I have not bored you too much by this rather long and somewhat technical digression on the general principles of fluctuations and stability. But I think some understanding of these principles is helpful in a discussion of the stability of employment and economic activity. For the corrective adjustments which affect employment and activity in the whole economy, whether they be inherent in the working of the economy or applied as deliberate instruments of policy, are again examples of control by negative feedback. The use of forecasts in policy does not substantially affect this statement, since the forecasts are themselves largely based on observations of the economy and its movements in the recent past. Indeed, given the present state of the art of forecasting I believe that better results might be obtained by basing suitable corrective action directly on observations of the economy and its changes rather than on forecasts which are themselves largely derived, perhaps by dubious processes, from those observations.

Even if there were no special features which might accentuate disturbances and fluctuations in the economy as a whole, it could not be assumed that the existence of corrective adjustments, even quite powerful corrective adjustments, would stabilise an economy. If they operate with long time lags, and especially if there are long delays before they commence to operate, they will cause cyclical fluctuations, and the stronger the corrective forces the more violent will be the fluctuations. But there is fairly general agreement among economists that there are special features of an economic system, in particular the multiplier process and adjustments in inventories and capital equipment, which accentuate disturbances and tend to cause cyclical fluctuations. These features increase the need for deliberate stabilisation policies, but also make it more difficult to devise suitable policies.

The problem is best studied by investigating the properties of a variety of models in which use is made of the limited amount of quantitative knowledge at present available about economic relationships. The work involved in such investigations is greatly reduced and the range of possible models is widened by the use of modern electronic equipment. The results obtained in this way cannot, of course, be conclusive, but from the investigations I have done so far I have considerable confidence in two simple propositions. The first is that corrective action taken in an attempt to reduce the amplitude of the short cycle of four or five years which is typical of the post-war period is not likely to be successful unless it is based on recently observed rates of change of economic activity as well as on the level of activity. The other is that even if the corrective action is appropriate in this respect it will still be unsuccessful unless a fair proportion of its ultimate direct effect on demand, say about a quarter of it, occurs within three or four months of the occurrence of the error it is designed to correct, and at least one half of the full effect within about six months.

Let us examine some of the existing means of influencing demand in the light of these requirements. The response of investment to changes in monetary conditions and interest rates is almost certainly delayed and slow. There is probably a delay of some months before decisions to invest are significantly affected and with most types of investment there is probably a further long time lag between the decisions to invest and the actual production of capital goods. If this is so, fluctuations are likely to be intensified rather than reduced by attempts to correct them through operating on long-term interest rates and investment in fixed capital. This does not mean that interest rate policy is unimportant. I believe it has a vital role to play in the slower adjustments required as a result of changes in the desire to save or invest, and thus in influencing the average level of employment and the average rate of change of the price level over fairly long periods.

It is more difficult to judge the effect of operating on short-term credit and short interest rates. Adjustments in these can be made more quickly than in long rates, and to the extent that they affect the desire or ability to hold inventories they might have a significant effect on production within two or three months. But I think much more empirical work will be needed before one can judge with confidence the magnitude, speed and reliability of these effects. I suspect that if fairly large and rapid adjustments in short-term credit conditions were made in response to both the level and the rate of change of economic activity they would help to reduce the amplitude of the short cycle. But there is a difficulty in using adjustments of short-term credit and interest rates for this purpose. Short rates, and perhaps to a lesser extent credit, are closely related to bank rate, and the level of bank rate is often made to depend as much on the state of the foreign reserves as on the internal condition of the economy. To the extent that fluctuations in the foreign reserves are the result of fluctuations in the balance of trade they will tend to lag behind fluctuations in the balance of trade by a quarter of a cycle. Since the balance of trade moves fairly closely with internal activity, fluctuations in the reserves tend to lag behind internal activity, so that changes in bank rate tend to be too late for satisfactory correction of economic fluctuations.

My conclusion concerning monetary policy is thus similar to that of the Radcliffe Committee (1959, 183); 'monetary measures cannot alone be relied upon to keep in nice balance an economy subject to major strains from both without and within. Monetary measures can help, but that is all'. My reasons for this conclusion are perhaps a little different from those of the Committee. I think that changes in interest rates and credit conditions probably do have quite powerful effects on demand, but that their usefulness for correcting short-period fluctuations is seriously limited as a result of the long time lags in the response of investment to changes in interest rates, and in the case of credit as a result of the temptation or need to make the adjustments in response to the state of the foreign reserves rather than at the times appropriate to the correction of fluctuations in internal economic activity. Much more research will have to be done, however, before the last word is said on these matters, and I would heartily endorse the Committee's statement (1959, 336) that 'it is essential to have much greater and more systematic knowledge of the factors that make up the financial system and of their relative movements'.

Turning to fiscal methods of influencing demand, it is clear that adjustments through annual budgets do not meet the requirements I have stated for the correction of short-period cycles. Budget changes have probably played some part, together with monetary policy, in overcoming the more severe and longer cycles of pre-war days, though this may have come about as much through the confidence of business men that the budget could and would be used to avert a severe slump, with the consequent greater stability of their investment plans, as through the actual use of budget changes. The recent introduction of general adjustments of purchase tax as a regulating device is a more promising development. It suffers, however, from two defects; the rather arbitrary and limited range of goods affected, and the fact that when demand is high there might be expectations of an increase in purchase tax which would lead to a further increase in demand and when demand is low there might be expectations of a decrease in tax which would further diminish demand. Hire purchase controls suffer even more severely from these defects.

None of the fiscal instruments at present in use satisfies the conditions for a satisfactory means of correction. If the purchase tax were changed into a general sales tax and adjusted by small amounts at frequent intervals it would do the job. But a preferable alternative would be the introduction of adjustments of direct taxes. A fairly simple way of adjusting direct taxes would be to calculate every tax to be paid in exactly the same way as is now done and then to add or subtract a certain percentage to the calculated figure as a stabilisation adjustment. In the case of PAYE, which is calculated on the basis of income and allowances cumulated from the beginning of the tax year, the figure added or subtracted in each pay period as a stabilisation adjustment would be kept separate from the figure for the normal tax and would be neglected in forming the cumulated tax paid. The figure calculated for the normal tax in each pay period would thus not be affected by earlier stabilisation adjustments, and no change would be needed in existing PAYE tables or in the method of using them. The percentage to be added or subtracted could be changed if necessary at regular intervals; quarterly intervals might prove to be short enough, though changes at monthly intervals should be possible. In this case those PAYE taxes which are paid quarterly should be adjusted by the average of the percentages prevailing in the preceding three months. Similarly all annual assessments for direct tax should be calculated as at present and then the average of the percentage adjustments prevailing over the year applied to this figure. Sufficiently fine adjustment would probably be obtained if the changes in the percentage to be added or subtracted were made in steps of 2.5 per cent, that is, sixpence in the pound. The absolute value of the tax adjustment would of course be much larger for a person with a high income than for one with a low income. This has advantages from the point of view both of equity and of efficacy; the larger adjustment is needed to induce the person with the higher income to change his expenditure. There would no doubt be some administrative difficulties in introducing a scheme of this sort, but once it was in operation the additional work involved would not be very great. I believe that the choice lies between accepting the minor inconvenience of such a scheme and accepting the continuation of the fluctuations in employment and economic activity which we have experienced since the war.

4 Employment and inflation

I have so far been discussing fluctuations in employment and economic activity without any reference to the average level about which employment is fluctuating. Consideration of the average level of employment brings us to the question of the relations between employment, or unemployment, and inflation and the rate of growth. In the past few years a number of people have carried out empirical studies of the relation between unemployment, or some other index of the demand for labour, and the rate of change of wage rates or earnings. Somewhat different methods and hypotheses have been used by different people. In my own very crude attempt to study this relation (chapter 25) I assumed that changes in the cost of living only affect wage changes in years when prices are rising rapidly, usually as a result of rapidly rising import prices. Others have assumed that changes in the cost of living have a proportionate effect on wage rates in every year (Dicks-Mireaux and Dow 1959; Klein and Ball 1959; Lipsey 1960). For the post-war years this is probably nearer the truth than the assumption I used. But we must then recognise that changes in the cost of living are in turn mainly the result of earlier changes in wage rates and to a lesser extent of changes in import prices. If these two behaviour relations are fitted to empirical data we can proceed to eliminate price changes and obtain a single relation expressing wage changes in terms of unemployment and changes in import prices, or alternatively we may eliminate wage changes and express price changes in terms of unemployment and changes in import prices. These new relations are not, of course, behaviour relations, but they are valid relations for prediction purposes, and are indeed in the most useful form for prediction. The relation I obtained is best considered as a prediction relation of this sort. If the other studies are also interpreted in this way there is reasonable agreement on the results obtained. It seems that if the average level of unemployment were kept at a little less than 2.5 per cent the average rate of increase in wages over a period of years could be expected to be about 2 per cent per annum so that with the rate of increase of productivity experienced since the war the average level of prices would be almost constant. Also, in the range between 1.5 per cent and 2.5 per cent unemployment, for every 0.1 per cent that the average level of unemployment was reduced, wages and prices would rise at about 0.3 per cent per year faster. If it is true that such a relation holds we are faced with a difficult choice. Then we can only reduce inflation, for any given rate of increase of productivity, at the cost of higher unemployment. I think such a relation does hold now, and unless it can be changed we shall probably move towards a compromise solution with a rather higher average level of unemployment than in the past few years and a lower, though not zero, speed of inflation; perhaps about 2 per cent unemployment with about 1 per cent per year rise in prices.

To consider whether the relation can be modified we must know why it is that wages continue to rise while there is significant unemployment. A number of possible causes are often mentioned, in particular lack of mobility of labour and industry, resulting in uneven geographical and occupational distribution of unemployment, competitive bidding by employers for the most suitable labour and trade union pressure.

The mobility of labour and industry would be increased if geographical and occupational movements in relative wages were allowed to take place more freely. If wages in areas and occupations where unemployment is low or excess demand is high rise more than those where unemployment is high or excess demand is low, there will be a greater incentive for labour to move to the areas and occupations in which wages have risen most, and for industry to move to the areas where wages have risen least, and also for industry to adapt its production methods to use more labour in those occupations in which wages have risen least.

Competitive bidding up of wages in a particular occupation and area by employers can easily occur even when some labour in the same occupation and area is unemployed. The basic reason for this is the wide range of ability that exists among different individuals in the same occupation. Some people, even in a single narrow occupational classification, are worth to an employer considerably more than the average rate of pay in the occupation; others through individual defects of character, intelligence or physique, are worth less. A wide-awake employer will often find it profitable to pay 5 or 10 per cent above the average rate of wages for a particular class of labour in his locality. In this way he can choose the best men and may well finish up with employees whose productivity is 10 or 15 per cent above the average. If a large proportion of employers adopt this practice wages may be bid up quite rapidly even when there is a significant amount of unemployment. The best solution would seem to be to allow more flexibility in the wages paid to different individuals in the same occupation.

The fourth possible reason I mentioned for wage rates rising when there is significant unemployment was the power and pressure of trade unions. I have some doubts whether this has been an important factor, but if it has, and if the trade unions fully understand the results of their actions, it can only be countered at the cost of occasional major strikes. But have the results of an irresponsible use of their power been made clear to trade unions by governments? If it were widely and clearly understood among the members of trade unions that the full use of their power to force up money wages would only lead, at a given level of unemployment, to a faster rate of inflation and that the government would have no alternative but to check this higher rate of inflation, in part at least, by lowering demand and causing some increase in unemployment, it seems possible that the trade unions might see where their true interests lay.

I am not so naive as to expect that the suggestions I have made for trying to shift the relation between employment and the rate of rise of wage rates in a way which would make it possible to maintain a higher level of employment with any given speed of inflation are likely to meet with an enthusiastic response. They are all suggestions for more flexible arrangements which would allow freer play to the market forces of supply and demand. But for at least a century and a half before the Second World War wage-earners frequently had a pretty raw deal from the market forces of supply and demand, for in most of the years of the trade cycle, and especially in the catastrophic inter-war years, there was a deficiency of aggregate demand. The traditions built up over that period still persist and will continue to persist for some years yet. But in due course it may be realised that continuously rising standards of living come only from continuously rising productivity and that provided the Government is not prevented by inflation from maintaining a high aggregate level of demand for labour the market forces are no longer harmful but play a vital part in helping adaptation and progress.

5 Employment and growth

I have suggested that a slightly higher average level of unemployment than that which we have had in the last few years, perhaps a little over 2 per cent, may be accepted as a necessary condition for moderating the speed of inflation. One often hears heated arguments against checking inflation in this way, on the grounds that if the rate of growth of the economy were more rapid prices would not rise so fast, and that the rate of growth will be reduced by operating the economy at a slightly lower level of employment. It is true, of course, that a higher rate of growth with the same rate of change of wages would lead to a lower speed of inflation. It is also true that while unemployment was actually increasing, let us say from 1.5 per cent to 2 per cent, output would be rising less rapidly than it would have been if unemployment had been kept at 1.5 per cent. But the argument is often phrased as if the steady rate of growth of the economy with unemployment constant at 2 per cent would be less than the steady rate of growth with unemployment constant at 1.5 per cent. I doubt whether this is true.

During short-period cyclical fluctuations the variations in output as a percentage of the growth trend are about five times as large as the variations in the percentage unemployment. The difference is largely accounted for by variations in short-time and overtime; by some people, mainly married women, moving into and out of the labour force, and by 'hoarding' of labour during a recession which is expected to be short. If unemployment were to rise by 0.5 per cent and stay at the new level, the hoarding of labour and some of the initial change in short-time and overtime would be only temporary and when the adjustments were completed the percentage fall in output would be considerably less than five times the increase in the percentage unemployment. If account were taken of the value of leisure the fall in real income would be still smaller, since that part of the fall in output which was due to a reduction in overtime and movement of people out of the labour force would be partly compensated by the value to the people concerned of the extra leisure. If an increase of 0.5 per cent in unemployment caused a decrease of 1.5 per cent in output, with equal proportional decreases in investment and non-investment expenditures, investment would fall by 1.5 per cent of its own value, and assuming that the growth rate was proportional to investment the growth rate would also decrease by 1.5 per cent of its own value, for example, from 2.5 per cent to 2.4625 per cent; an extremely small decrease. If all the decrease in output resulted from a decrease in non-investment expenditure there would be no change in the rate of growth. The main conclusion from this is that the difference in the steady state rates of growth before and after the transition to the higher unemployment would be extremely small if the growth rates were proportional to investment. Other influences, such as possible extra incentive or compulsion to invest in cost-reducing equipment might easily outweigh any small difference due to the slight change in investment.

It is sometimes argued that the decrease in demand would slow down growth by reducing the desire of firms to invest; but this could always be remedied by reducing interest rates. Indeed since we are assuming that a government could hold unemployment at the new level, investment in the new steady state, as in the earlier one, would have to be brought into equality with savings. It is on the willingness to save, and the more general influences of educational improvement, research, and so on, that the rate of growth depends in present circumstances. I do not think that very small changes in aggregate demand and unemployment have much effect on these.

6 Rates of exchange

The final question I wish to discuss, very briefly, is that of rates of exchange. The other major trading countries have problems of employment, inflation and growth which are similar to those of Britain. The question arises whether all countries are likely to hold that balance of internal objectives which would be consistent with the maintenance of fixed exchange rates.

Professors Samuelson and Solow (1960) have considered the relation between unemployment and the rate of change of the consumer price index in the United States. Their tentative conclusion is that assuming continuation of the conditions of the post-war period the price index might be stable if unemployment were held at 5–6 per cent, and might rise at about 2 per cent per annum if unemployment were 4 per cent. Some estimates which I have made lead me to think that the situation in the United States is less favourable than this. I estimate that 7–8 per cent unemployment would be needed to maintain a stable price level, and that at 4 per cent unemployment the price level would rise at about 4 per cent per annum. Of course efforts to increase the rate of growth and to reduce structural unemployment may improve the relation between unemployment and price changes; but unless my estimates are badly out or considerable improvements are obtained it seems likely that if unemployment is reduced, as seems to be hoped, to 4 or 5 per cent, the United States may well have a rather faster rate of inflation than Britain would have with 2 per cent unemployment.

In Germany similar problems are beginning to appear. Unemployment has fallen steadily from about 10 per cent in 1950 to 1.2 per cent in 1960, and labour costs are now rising rapidly. The growth rate is still high but some special factors which contributed to it, such as reconstruction after the war and the currency difficulties, and availability of skilled labour from unemployed or from refugees, are passing. It may well be that in Germany too the problem of choosing between inflation and unemployment will become acute. These three countries, and others, may perhaps be prepared to adjust their own choices about internal balance in order to make them consistent with a regime of fixed exchanges. But I have some doubts whether they will be prepared to do so, or if they are whether they in fact know the quantitative workings of their own and other economies well enough to choose the appropriate objectives before gradual divergences in price levels have cumulated to such a degree that they impose a heavy strain on the international monetary system.

If this is so, it might be better to allow a limited flexibility into the exchange system, so that gradual drifts in relative prices, which would probably not be at a rate of more than 1 or at most 2 per cent per year, would not produce cumulative disequilibria in balances of trade which might eventually necessitate large and sudden movements of exchange rates and do serious damage to the international monetary system. A limited flexibility could be introduced by an agreement that the par value of any one currency, in terms of gold, could be changed at any time provided the total change in one direction in any period of twelve months did not exceed 1 per cent. There would, I think, be much more confidence that a country could in fact work within this rule than that it could for ever succeed in keeping the par value constant, so the fear, or hope, of a sudden large change in the rate, with the tremendous speculative movements it causes, would be greatly diminished. The maximum permissible rate of change of the par rate, 1 per cent per year, could easily be offset by short-term interest differentials, so it need not lead to any major transfers of capital. And this limited degree of exchange flexibility would allow each country time to find by trial and error that compromise between its internal objectives which was consistent with its exchange rate policy.

I said at the beginning of this lecture that I believed one of the main difficulties in devising and implementing appropriate economic policies is lack of quantitative knowledge and understanding of how the economic system works. By now I have no doubt amply demonstrated at any rate my own lack of knowledge and understanding, and it only remains to apologise to any of you who may have come here expecting clear and definite answers to the problems I have been discussing. I hope the next person to face the ordeal of giving an inaugural lecture on election to the Tooke Chair will be in a position to explain these matters more clearly.

Note

Economica, 29 (NS) (113), 1962, pp. 1–16.

Inaugural lecture given at the London School of Economics and Political Science on 28 November, 1961.

23   Economic Policy and Development

A.W. Phillips

It was with some misgivings that I accepted the invitation to talk at this seminar. For although I have now been in Australia for eight months I have not done the homework that would be needed to become familiar with the range of policy issues in the Australian setting. Moreover although the topic I have been given is economic policy *and* development, I have a feeling that you are mainly interested in economic policy *for* development, and I happen to hold the view that economists do not really know very much about economic development; ~~that their willingness to engage in debate and advocacy in this field reflects more a desire to do good and a yearning to play a role in public affairs rather than the usefulness of any expert knowledge they may have on the subject~~. Finally, I believe that the first priority for an academic economist should be to get on with the ~~difficult, painful and demanding~~ job of trying to find out more about how the economy works and that he should resist the temptation to divert his limited time and energy from this task to general debate on policy issues. However, I did accept your invitation and must do what I can, while you must endure the consequences.

Any discussion of economic policy and development in Australia cannot fail to take account of the monumental work of the Vernon Committee (Committee of Economic Inquiry 1965), and must indeed appear to be merely a matter of selection from the comprehensive report of that committee of what appear to be the major issues, and comment on the emphasis and conclusion given in the report.[1] I intend to proceed, as the committee did, by considering first the related group of policy objectives which involve short-term economic management, namely, full employment, price stability and the balance of payments, leaving until later the broader and longer-run objectives of development and growth. ~~There are two reasons for making this division. First, I believe that on questions of short-term economic management economists do now possess a body of expert knowledge of direct and immediate relevance to~~

~~policy decisions, while on matters of development and growth they can~~
~~speak only as laymen with little snippets of special knowledge which may~~
~~sometimes help, but have probably more often hindered, the formulation~~
~~of sensible policies. Secondly, my judgement is that the two sets of objec-~~
~~tives are or should be almost independent of each other, or at least should~~
~~be so if short-term economic management is properly conducted.~~

I shall take first the objective of full employment, without worrying about the precise definition of that term. It is now generally understood that in a free-enterprise economy there is a natural tendency to cyclical fluctuations in the aggregate level of demand and employment, as a result mainly of interaction over time between changes in the flows of consumption and production and changes in the actual and desired levels of stocks of inventories and capital equipment. These fluctuations can be, and since the war have been, moderated by deliberate government management of the level of aggregate demand, operated through adjustment in taxes, government spending and monetary policy. I share the view of the Vernon Committee that of these three policy instruments tax adjustment is the most suitable for short-term management of aggregate demand. Variations in government expenditure are too slow in operation to be an effective instrument for dealing with fluctuations, and also produce undesirable dislocation of spending programmes. While monetary policy may be able to give modest support in the control of fluctuations its main role should be to set the longer-term trend of availability and price of credit in order to obtain a balance of savings and investment demand, with given tax and spending policies.

Although government control of aggregate demand in all the major countries of the world has been successful in preventing major economic depressions since the war, there have still been minor economic fluctuations, typically with a periodicity of four to five years and with an amplitude from peak to trough of 8–10 per cent of the trend rate of gross national product, with associated changes in unemployment of about 2 per cent of the work force. While not catastrophic, these fluctuations still cause considerable hardship to individuals and complicate the process of making sound decisions in business and government. I agree with the Vernon Committee that there is a need for introducing more flexibility into fiscal policy by permitting a limited variation of tax rates within fiscal years, without the need for special legislation on each occasion. Careful quantitative examination of the problem of controlling economic fluctuations has made it quite clear that further significant reductions in the amplitude of the fluctuations can be obtained only by reducing the time interval between the occurrence of changes in economic conditions and the application of corrective action. The possibility of making limited changes in tax rates quarterly instead of annually would provide adequate means for obtaining a worthwhile improvement in performance. It can also be shown that with the possibility of more frequent adjustments, the actual magnitude of the adjustments, even when cumulated over annual periods, could be much smaller than would be required with annual adjustments. Although a rigorous proof of this proposition is not simple, it should be intuitively acceptable. If the driver of a car were permitted to move the steering wheel only at intervals of ten seconds, both the car and the steering wheel would swing about a lot more than if he were permitted to move the steering wheel at intervals of one second. The principle applies equally to the problem of controlling economic fluctuations.

It would, I think, be worth investigation whether this improvement could not be gained in Australia by the device of quarterly adjustment of a percentage surcharge or rebate on personal income tax and company payroll tax, the surcharge or rebate being applicable to all tax payments when they are made within the fiscal year, with the final annual settlement calculated using the average of the percentage surcharge or rebate over the four quarters. Probably a maximum surcharge or rebate of 5 per cent of the tax payable, with steps of 2.5 per cent, would serve the purpose. There may be some administrative difficulties in operating such a scheme but I do not think they would be insuperable. Of one thing I am quite certain, without this or some similar arrangements for small quarterly adjustments in tax payments there is no chance of getting any further significant reduction in the amplitude of fluctuations in economic activity and employment.

Let me turn now to the second objective in short-term economic management, price stability, and to simplify matters a little let us suppose for a moment that balance of payments considerations do not impose any constraints on policy. Now the rate of change of the average level of prices is influenced by a number of factors including the rates of change of external prices and internal productivity, the relative strengths of trade unions and employers organisations, the judgements of the Conciliation and Arbitration Commission, and the level of aggregate demand or employment. Of these factors the government has the power to control only the last, and since aggregate demand or employment is also one of the policy objectives there is clearly a likelihood of inconsistency or conflict between the objectives of full employment and price stability, with a resulting compromise in which neither objective is fully attained. This conflict of objectives could be avoided only if the government could control or influence one or more of the other factors affecting the rate of change of prices, and since external prices are beyond its control and there is no obvious way for it to induce a major increase in the rate of change of productivity the natural candidate is the complex of institutional arrangements consisting of trade unions, employers federations and the Arbitration Commission. And since the trade unions are not likely to cooperate in efforts to reduce the rate of increase of money wage rates unless firms are willing to act similarly with respect to prices, we end up among the thorny political problems of wage and price policies, which are engaging much of the time and energy of administrations throughout the world.

I do not know of any simple solutions in this field, which is so full of politics and passion. All I can do is make a few suggestions. First, it is desirable that ~~responsible~~ public discussion and debate should concentrate on the real problems rather than obscure them by running commentary on the current state of the continuous game of political football. Responsibility here lies with individuals and organisations, but also with the government, which should make a clear statement of the true situation with which it is faced; namely, that organised attempts to force up money wages and prices, ~~which in many cases largely leave the distribution of real income broadly unchanged,~~ accentuate the conflict between the objectives of full employment and price stability, and leave the government with no alternative but to operate the economy with a higher level of unemployment than would otherwise be possible, to the general detriment of the country and the people, and especially to the weaker and poorer members of the community.[2] Secondly, the welfare of the workers in Australia would be enhanced if the Conciliation and Arbitration Commission ceased altogether to make basic and general awards, and confined its activities to arbitration in cases of industrial dispute. ~~The general gain to the workers would be greatest if wage bargaining and arbitration were carried out separately for groups with similar skills and working under similar conditions.~~ For then organised upward pressure on money wages would be reduced and could be partially or completely replaced by the upward pull that would result from the government operating the economy with a higher level of aggregate demand and a lower level of unemployment. The general gain to the workers would be still greater if wage bargaining and arbitration were conducted separately for groups with similar skills and working under similar conditions, for this would further reduce the organised upward push and so permit a further increase in upward pull from operating the economy at a still higher level of demand and employment. Thirdly, to offset any effect these measures might have in reducing the relative bargaining power of organised labour, attention should be given to strengthening the legal and administrative sanctions against possible abuse of monopoly power and restrictive trade practices. Progress along the lines of these suggestions would not only reduce the conflict between the objectives of full employment and price stability, but would also improve the flexibility of the economy and so help to promote efficiency and higher real incomes.

I should like to move now to the third objective of economic management, the balance of payments. Balance of payments problems arise inevitably from an international system in which individual countries give first priority to their internal objectives of full employment and price stability. In other countries, as in Australia, there is not complete consistency between these objectives and political compromises are reached involving some degree of price inflation. These compromises will differ in different countries, and in one country at different times, so that differences in the rates of change of prices exist which, continued over a period of years, give rise to persistent balance of payments deficits in some countries and surpluses in others. This situation was foreseen when the International Monetary Fund was set up immediately after the war, and provision was made for adjustment of a country's exchange rates if there was a 'fundamental disequilibrium' in the balance of payments. Exchange rate movements of up to 10 per cent could be made without reference to the Fund, larger movements required approval of the Fund.

In practice, countries have been very reluctant to vary their exchange rates, and although quite a number of devaluations, and a few revaluations, have occurred, they have usually been delayed as long as possible, and have been preceded by emergency measures for protecting the balance of payments, such as import quotas, and tariff surcharges ~~and severe internal deflationary measures and export subsidies~~ as well as by intense speculative movements of funds which aggravate the difficulties. There are of course different and strongly held views about appropriate policy. My own view is that the appropriate method of dealing with persistent balance of payments difficulties is through variation of exchange rates, and that this should be the normal method, and not, as the Vernon Committee recommends, something to be used only as a last resort. Much of the opposition to exchange rate variation comes, I think, from understandable dislike of making a large and sudden change which has important effects throughout an economy and is liable to abuse by speculative movements of funds. I think that the best way of overcoming these difficulties is by replacing the rule of adhering to fixed rates of exchange, at a time when there is no clear case for a major variation, by the rule that the rate of exchange may be varied by an amount not exceeding plus or minus, say, 0.2 per cent per month, which would allow a maximum movement of about 2.5 per cent per year in either direction. This speed of movement would not be large enough to cause any major disturbance to an economy, or to cause large movements in speculative funds or large changes in the amount of foreign investment, particularly since it could, and probably would, be largely offset by relative interest and profit rates. It would, however, allow moderate differences in the rate of change of prices in different countries, and other factors affecting the balance of payments to be accommodated without giving rise to persistent balance of payments difficulties.

In my view the objective of economic development or growth is almost independent of the objectives of short-term economic management about which I have been speaking so far. There would be a relation between these sets of problems if it were true, as the Vernon Committee seemed inclined to believe, that the higher the level of demand at which an economy is operated the higher would be the rate of development or growth. It is no doubt true that if an economy is operated at a very low level of demand relative to capacity output, or with very high unemployment, the rate of growth of its full capacity will be lower than if demand were higher. But when an economy is operating at or near full employment the proposition that it would grow more rapidly if demand were held at a still higher level seems to me very doubtful. Indeed if demand is raised too far the rate of growth may be retarded rather than increased, as a result of general shortages and inefficient operation.

Notes

Handwritten and previously unpublished seminar presentation, April 1968. The crossings out in this chapter were made in the handwritten original. Phillips also wrote, in note form, a handwritten paper entitled 'Economic Policies and Development, and Comments on Trade and Protection Policy' which follows closely the content of this essay. Phillips organised his comments as a contribution to the debate about the Vernon Committee Report, published in 1965. The report discussed growth, wages, tariffs and the balance of payments in Australia. One of the members of the Committee was Sir John Crawford (1968), formerly Secretary of the Department of Trade, who as Vice Chancellor of the ANU was instrumental in persuading Phillips to migrate to Australia.

1 In 'Economic Policies and Development, and Comments on Trade and Protection Policy', Phillips noted that he differed from the Vernon Committee on the ground of 'basic methodology. Committee's method based on fairly long-term targets and projections, with policies based on forecast difficulties (e.g., balance of payments). I regard attachment to growth targets as harmful, and long-term projections as desirable exercises but treacherous

guides to policy. Since prediction is desirable but always faulty, I put emphasis on ~~(a) long-term sketches or 'forward looks', but without attempts to derive firm policy from the 'forward look';~~ (b) improvement of short-term methods of prediction; (c) clarification and improvement of instruments of short-term adjustment or economic management; (d) clarification of factors affecting longer-run development, which I believe to be largely independent of short-term objectives and management' (crossing out as in the handwritten original).

2 In 'Economic Policies and Development, and Comments on Trade and Protection Policy', Phillips added: 'Workers' real interests best served by preventing any <u>general</u> increase in money wages. <u>Explain.</u>'

The Empirical Phillips Curve

24   The Famous Phillips Curve Article

Richard G. Lipsey

Chapter 25, Phillips' essay on wages and unemployment was, for better or for worse both in its direct contributions and in the reactions that it provoked, one of the seminal articles of the last half of the twentieth century. Its theoretical origins lay in Phillips' work on stabilisation policy while its empirical origins lay in a casual comment by one of his colleagues on the LSE staff.

Phillips himself was one of the most remarkable persons I have ever met. He saw the economy as a dynamic system whose behaviour could not be understood using neoclassical static analysis – which, as someone who had been strongly influenced by Schumpeter in my student days, was a view that drew me to him. Although he had very little time for the comparative statics which was the stock in trade of conventional economists at the LSE in the 1950s and 1960s, he was always polite to us and never abrasive in any way. I believe he was proud of his varied career, his wartime accomplishments, his survival of a Japanese prisoner-of-war camp, his knowledge of languages, and his broad experiences of the world. But never did he show a suggestion of snobbery or condescension to we lesser mortals. He spoke with great authority and profoundly influenced many of us who came into close contact with him. As far as I knew, he had no strong political views. Certainly he never expressed opinions on the political matters that were constantly discussed in the LSE common room. His passion was for understanding the economy wherever that might lead him, and in that, he was in sympathy with those of us who were members of the LSE Staff Seminar on Methodology, Measurement and Testing in Economics (the M^2T seminar) which he did not regularly attend.

Theoretical roots

When Phillips began his work on stabilisation policy, the Keynesian models of the IS-LM variety that were taught in British universities were typically closed with a reverse L-shaped, upward-ratcheting, kinked, aggregate supply curve relating the price level to national income.[1] Below full-employment income (to use the terminology of the time), the price level was given at its historically determined value and all fluctuations in aggregate demand caused fluctuations in real national income. When aggregate demand exceeded full-employment income, the price level rose until the excess aggregate demand was removed. If aggregate demand then fell, real income would fall along the AS curve which, below full-employment income, was always horizontal at the current price level. In other words, the behaviour of the economy was dichotomised so that, below full-employment national income, fluctuations in aggregate demand caused real income to vary, while, at full-employment income, increases in aggregate demand caused the price level to rise, ratcheting up the horizontal portion of the kinked AS curve.

Behind this AS curve, lay a micro base of product and factor pricing. Product prices were determined by price setting, oligopolistic firms who met variations in aggregate demand with variations in quantity at all levels of output below capacity. Voluminous empirical evidence suggested that marginal cost curves were flat below capacity and that markups were fairly rigid, or at least not variable enough to cause major changes in the price level as output fluctuated below capacity. In the labour market, wages were assumed to be inflexible downwards, rising in the face of excess demand and staying constant in the face of excess supply. There were no strong theoretical underpinnings for this assumption about the behaviour of labour markets which was based mainly on the correct empirical observation that wages fell much more slowly in the face of excess supply than they rose in the face of excess demand.

At the time, this aggregate supply closure was understood to be unsatisfactory for at least two reasons (quite apart from the reason now commonly advanced, but seldom heard among my contemporaries, that it was a travesty of Keynes' own thinking on the subject). First, it was generally appreciated that the economy did not go sharply at one fixed level of national income from a state characterised by a stable price level and a variable real national income to a state characterised by a fixed real income and a variable price level. Second, although there was a large theoretical and empirical literature to buttress the assumptions about product pricing,[2] the assumption of fixed money wages seemed rather arbitrary.

Phillips found the kinked AS curve too restrictive for his models of stabilisation policy so he used a relation in which the rate of change of the price level was a non-linear function of the GNP gap, indicated by $Y - Y_t$. When there was zero excess aggregate demand, national income would be at its full-employment level and the price level would remain constant. As excess aggregate demand increased without limit, real national income would asymptotically approach its theoretical upper limit of a few percentage points above full-employment income while the rate of inflation would increase without limit. When excess aggregate supply developed, the price level would fall but, as excess supply increased and national income fell up to twenty or thirty percentage points below full-employment income, the rate of decrease of the price level would asymptotically approach a floor of some small negative value, say, −1 or −2 per cent.

This was a major improvement over the kinked AS curve. It allowed a continuous variation in the division of the effects of a change in aggregate demand between changing real national income and changing the price level. The higher the existing level of national income, the more the effects were on the price level and the less on real income.

This was all Phillips needed for his early models since his interest was in stabilisation policy. In his first essay on this subject (chapter 16), he was fairly optimistic about having an effective policy. In his second essay (chapter 17), however, he allowed for more complex and seemingly more realistic lags in response functions and became much more pessimistic about designing stabilisation policies that actually would stabilise. There is some debate as to how Phillips interpreted his models, but, as one of his junior colleagues, I took away from the second article a message of profound caution about the alleged beneficial effects of fine tuning. Long before I heard Milton Friedman on the subject, I was alerted by Phillips that some seemingly innocuous lags could render many 'stabilisation' policies counterproductive.

Empirical roots

I heard Phillips tell the following story of his development of the Phillips Curve many times. His colleague at the LSE, Professor Henry Phelps Brown, a great empirical economist in his time, suggested to Bill in the common room one Friday that he could illustrate his price–income curve by using historical data that had been gathered by Beveridge for unemployment and Phelps Brown and Hopkins for wage rates. It was accepted that the behaviour of the price level was largely driven by the behaviour of wages, both by cost–push advocates, of which Phelps Brown was one, and by demand–pull advocates. The latter used the Keynesian model in which markups were constant and excess aggregate demand first raised wages and the resulting cost increases were passed on into prices by oligopolistic price-setting firms. Phillips got the data and went home over the weekend to plot wage changes against unemployment. At first, the plots all looked a mess but then it occurred to him to do what others who had looked at the same data had not thought to do: he treated each cycle separately and joined up the points in chronological order. What then leapt to the eye were regular loops around what appeared to be a fairly stable average relation between money wage changes and unemployment. This subsequently led him to fit his famous curve and to interpret it as a stable relation around which the actual data fluctuated cyclically.

There has been some debate as to whether or not Henry Phelps Brown was the source of Phillips empirical excursion. Yet Phillips told the above story often in my hearing. I find it more plausible that Phelps Brown forgot making a casual comment than that Phillips forgot the source of a comment that had such momentous consequences for him. In any case, the identity of the person who gave Phillips the lead is unimportant, except as an historical curiosum. Certainly, whomever it was played no role in Phillips' subsequent development of his curve, which was done as a one-man operation. It is highly likely, however, that it was one of his LSE colleagues because this was not the sort of data that Phillips' own education or previous research would have been likely to have drawn to his attention.

The relation between the Phillips and the Lipsey pieces

Phillips wrote his article quite independently of our group of young Turks who, at the time, were worrying about the methodology of economics. We had formed the M^2T seminar and were trying to apply Popperian methodology to a subject that was then dominated, in the UK at least, by the Austrian–Robbinsian–Euclidean methodology in which theories were judged by the intuitive plausibility of their assumptions. According to this methodology, if the assumptions were plausible, the logical deductions based on them must be correct and, if the facts disagreed with the theory's predictions, the facts must be wrong. In this view, facts were used to illustrate, not to test theories. I have discussed these issues and our group's reaction to them in more detail elsewhere[3] but it should be clear that, as recent converts to the Popperian methodology, Phillips' Curve seemed an excellent test case. Indeed, if one reads the first few pages of Lipsey (1960) and Lipsey and Steuer (1961) one sees the strong influence of Popperian methodology.

We first became aware of Phillips' empirical work when we read it in manuscript, after Phillips had seen galley proofs from *Economica*. It was too late for any of our M^2T group to contribute to the original article, but Phillips did encourage the group in general, and me in particular, to study his relationship in more depth. Once we had all read Bill's article, we put it on the agenda for study in the M^2T group. For a year, I struggled to understand the Phillips Curve. Finally, I came up with the results, both empirical and theoretical, that are reported in my 1960 article.

The two essays by Phillips (chapter 25) and Lipsey (1960) really formed the unit that made the curve famous. Phillips discovered the relation and did a rudimentary empirical job on it, while I applied standard statistical procedures and tested a number of *ad hoc* hypotheses that Phillips had formulated. I also tried to give the curve a micro-theoretical explanation but was hampered by not having a good model of expectations. As a result, I related money wages to the price level by a catch-up rather than an expectations variable. Since the catch-up variable did not perform well, I dropped it and was left with a simple, stable Phillips Curve.

Acceptance

I suspect that my more orthodox statistical treatment of the curve did quite a bit to still some of the many early criticisms, helping the curve to gain acceptance within the profession.[4] There were, however, two more basic reasons for the wide degree of acceptance that the curve achieved. First, it was a distinct improvement on the old, kinked AS curve with its dichotomy between periods of stable prices and variable unemployment and stable unemployment and variable prices. Second, it allowed the profession to go beyond the *ad hoc* assumption of wage rigidity. The new curve related wage changes to aggregate demand and provided an empirical basis for a reaction of wages to excess supply (as proxied by the rate of unemployment) that was slow relative to their reaction to excess demand. The elimination of the aggregate supply curve, however, had momentous consequences in the long term.

Early reactions

Many early reactions to the curve were hostile, as shown by the list of articles published in the first two years after the original. British economists with left wing leanings were particularly critical. Richard Kahn was reputed to be giving a series of lectures at Cambridge attacking the curve on theoretical and empirical grounds.

I was surprised by his hostility – although Corry (1995) explains why I should not have been. But, at the time, I was interested in academic economics and did not take much interest in British economic performance or policy. (My interest in those subjects was first aroused by my experience with the reactions to the Phillips Curve and then developed through the 1960s.)

At the time, I identified two reasons for the hostility. The first was a feeling that such a relation made no theoretical sense and was merely a statistical artifact. Since the equivalent relation in price–income space had been around for a long time, playing, for example, an important part in Bent Hansen's *Theory of Inflation* (1951), I could not understand this line of objection. Leaving expectations aside by concentrating on the nineteenth century when the price level was relatively stable, there seemed to be very good precedent for assuming that the rate at which prices would change in the face of disequilibrium would be an increasing function of the magnitude of the disequilibrium.[5]

The second source of opposition seemed to be the old conflict between judging a theory on the standard grounds of its logical consistency and its empirical relevance and judging it for its policy implications. Many left-leaning economists were profoundly worried that the curve would provide strong support for those who would raise unemployment in order to suppress inflation. At the time, there was a great debate on the relative social values to be placed on unemployment and inflation, with the left tending to put a high value on avoiding unemployment and the right a high value on avoiding inflation. While the reverse L-shaped AS curve gave no trade-off, the Phillips Curve did. According to that curve, inflation could be reduced by raising unemployment, and the Phillips Curve suggested that rates of unemployment around 3 per cent would be sufficient to hold inflation at 1 per cent. This unemployment figure was high by post-war UK standards, but might be acceptable to right-leaning politicians. Hence there was great hostility to the suggestion of an effective trade-off involving levels of unemployment that would be acceptable to some policy makers.[6]

Early cost–push interpretations

From its inception, the Phillips Curve was often misinterpreted as a cost–push phenomenon. Of the many misinterpretations, my favourite is Meiselman's (1968, 745):

If it were not for the fact that many of these Phillips Curve studies are taken seriously, I would also be quite amused by their implied monetary theory. Because the price level measures the value of money, by tying the price level to the level of money wages, these models essentially present a labour theory of the value of money – one which contains neither a supply of nor a demand for money!

The most influential misinterpretation, however, must have been Samuelson's. In the 1961 edition of his world-famous text book, he introduced the curve and asserted that it depicted a cost–push phenomenon.

In fact, when embedded in an IS-LM structure, the curve had quite orthodox implications. It determined the rate at which wage costs, and hence the price level, changed in the face of macroeconomic disequilibrium. Given a fixed money supply, the rate of change of the price level then determined the rate at which the LM curve shifted – left in the face of excess aggregate demand and inflation and right in the face of excess supply and deflation. The curve thus accommodated a Keynesian demand–pull version of inflation in which full-cost prices marked up increases in wage costs which were, in turn, caused by excess demand in the labour market which, in its turn, was generated by firms attempting to raise output in the face of rising aggregate demand. The curve was also orthodox in denying money illusion in equilibrium. Given a constant money supply and no growth, the IS-LM model closed by the Phillips Curve provided unique equilibrium levels of real income and price level.[7]

Later interpretations

Over the subsequent years, many people have sought to infer what Phillips really had in mind in his curve. See for example several of the essays in Cross (1995), including Desai's contrast between what he believes Phillips actually meant and how he thinks Phillips was interpreted by myself, Samuelson and Solow (1960), and others.

My belief that I was reflecting Phillips' own interpretation of his curve is based on the following considerations. First, I was in close contact with Phillips during the year that I was working on my article. If he had thought my interpretation was at variance with his, I would have known it. Indeed, when I tried to work with a market-clearing interpretation in which each point on the curve was generated by the intersection of relevant demand and supply curves, Phillips told me forcibly that he thought I was on the wrong track because his curve was a disequilibrium phenomenon. Second, he constantly referred to Bent Hansen's *Theory of Inflation* as an antecedent of his work, and, in particular, to Hansen's reaction function which related excess demand to changes in the price level. Third, his abiding interest was in short-run stabilisation policy, as shown by his Ph.D. thesis (1953) and his first two major published articles (chapters 16 and 17). He saw his wage curve as an empirical underpinning of the curve he used to close his stabilisation models. The latter clearly was a disequilibrium reaction function relating excess aggregate demand or supply to the price level. Some authors, such as Desai (1995, 347), have accused others of judging Phillips' 1958 essay (chapter 25) without reading it. Be that as it may, those who interpret Phillips Curve on the basis of this article alone often fail to read the earlier two pieces on stabilisation policy, although all three articles need to be seen as a unit.

Some have interpreted his use of averages rather than the raw data as a desire to establish equilibrium, or at least long-term, relations rather than a dynamic reaction function. I asked Phillips many times why he had not used more conventional statistical methods for his original article. He had two answers. Early on, he said that, since the curve had a logarithmic form and since there are no logs of negative numbers, he was forced to use unconventional methods of first averaging the data into a few points and then fitting a curve to those points by eye. When he first said this to me, I accepted the challenge of finding a functional form that would take on the same shape as Phillips Curve but that could be treated by conventional statistical methods. I looked up my old statistics text, *Methods of Correlation Analysis* by Mordecai Ezekiel, and found several likely forms of which $Y = \alpha X^{-1} + bX^{-2}$ seemed the most promising. I tried fitting the curve

$$\dot{W} = a + bU^{-1} + cU^{-2}$$

to Phillips' data and found that it could track Phillips' own curve very well. I knew that the two unemployment variables would not seem significant separately because they must be closely related to each other, but my concerns were with finding a curve that could take on the same shape as Phillips' own curve, and with the resulting curve's *overall* fit.

Phillips' second response, which he used more often after my work was completed, was that he saw no half-way house between really crude eyeballing of data and what he regarded as a fully satisfactory econometric treatment, which would take him well beyond the conventional statistical methods which I had been taught.

Rejection of the naive version

Problems arose when the Phillips Curve was taken as showing a stable, long-term trade-off between unemployment and inflation. Ned Phelps led the theoretical criticism of the naive relation between unemployment and changes in money wages, which, when used at face value, suggested acute money illusion in the long run.

Since Phillips was mainly concerned with short-term stabilisation policy, it is not clear if he condoned the use of his curve as a long-term trade-off. But many others certainly did.[8] In any case, the theoretical objections to the long-term trade-off were strongly supported when stable empirical Phillips Curves came unstuck empirically in the 1970s in many countries.

Replacement by the expectations augmented curve

In a classic example of Popper's methodology, the failure of the naive curve resulted in the minimum amendment of the Keynesian macro model that was needed to accommodate the new observations. The IS-LM part of the model was compressed into an aggregate demand (AD) curve and two aggregate supply curves were reintroduced to complete the model. The short run aggregate supply (SRAS) curve was based on fixed input prices and was positively sloped in price level/real income space. The long-run aggregate supply (LRAS) curve was assumed (in simple cases at least) to be vertical at the unique point of macroeconomic equilibrium. To the best of my knowledge, Gordon (1978) was the first macro text to be organised around the natural rate hypothesis, while Lipsey and Steiner (1980) and Baumol and Blinder (1979) were the first two elementary text books to use aggregate demand–aggregate supply treatments.[9] In Lipsey and Steiner's version, the expectations-augmented Phillips Curve

$$\Delta W = F(U) + \Delta P^e$$

provided the explanation of how fast the SRAS curve shifted in the presence of macroeconomic disequilibrium. This model quickly found its way into many other text books.

The Keynesian AD–AS model closed by an expectations-augmented Phillips Curve is capable of explaining most of what we see better than the competing new classical model. The reintroduced SRAS curve allowed for cost–push through such forces as OPEC's massive increases in oil prices, and thus explained stagflation. The expectations-augmented Phillips Curve explained the speed of wage and price adjustment to macro disequilibrium. It also predicted accelerating inflation if the monetary authorities tried to hold unemployment below its natural rate.

When grafted on to Keynesian expenditure flow models, the expectations-augmented Phillips Curve performed satisfactorily by providing for a short-term trade-off and for the neutrality of money not only in the levels, as did the original Phillips Curve, but also in the rates of change. A stable level of unemployment below its natural rate could only be sustained by an ever-accelerating inflation. So the Keynesian model proved quite resilient. It was able to incorporate an expectations-augmented curve and, through it, to explain stagflation, which seemed utterly paradoxical when it broke out seriously in the mid 1970s, as well as the existence of an inflation–unemployment trade-off in the short term and its absence in the long term.[10]

A paradigm shift

Then, in a classic demonstration that, when broad paradigms are in conflict, economics is to a significant extent a political exercise rather than a science, the failure of the Phillips Curve became a reason for rejecting the whole Keynesian model and replacing it with a rational-expectations, new-classical, GE model which was unable to explain the stagflation that had undone the naive Phillips Curve.[11]

The victory of the new classical model had little to do with any empirical refutation of the Keynesian model (as amended to accommodate the new facts) in preference to a better, new classical explanation. The new-classical critics argued that the Keynesian model had no microeconomic underpinnings while their model did. This interesting claim turned out to mean that Keynesian macro relations could not be formally aggregated from the empirically based Keynesian underpinnings of oligopolistic, price-setting firms. Instead, the empirically unreal micro underpinnings of perfectly competitive firms could be used to make the desired aggregation formally.

I have pointed out elsewhere (Lipsey 1981), that there was a large body of evidence for the micro underpinnings of the Keynesian model based on factual observations of pricing behaviour of oligopolistic firms. The theoretical problem was that no one knew, and does not know today, how to aggregate this type of behaviour, which is observed in the real world, into consistent macro relations.[12] So, presented with empirical evidence that was theoretically messy to handle, many in the profession chose the logically consistent, new classical model whose relations could be aggregated from the empirically refuted micro model of pricing and employment under perfect competition.[13]

Conclusion

The expectations-augmented closure of the Keynesian model used the natural rate hypothesis with the location of the vertical long-run aggregate supply curve indicating the level of real income that corresponded to the natural rate. It is this natural rate hypothesis, embedded in both the new-classical models and those Keynesian models that are closed by the expectations-augmented Phillips Curve, that is the Achilles heel of both. As the essays in Cross (1995) amply demonstrate, and as many earlier critics such as Tobin (1980) and Lipsey (1978) predicted, the natural rate has defied attempts both to establish it in theoretical models that capture well-established features of the labour market and to find solid empirical support for its existence and stability.

Notes

1 As Bernard Corry (1995) has emphasised, this formulation bore little relation to Keynes' much more complex views on the behaviour of the general levels of prices and wages. It was, however, the formulation that had entered the formal models that built on Hicks's IS-LM interpretation of Keynes. Even in my time as a Ph.D. student at the LSE (1953–5), most of us got our Keynesian economics from text books and lectures and few of us opened the covers of the *General Theory*.

2 I have discussed this literature in several places; Lipsey (1981) provides the fullest discussion.

3 See the introductory essay for Lipsey (1997).

4 I reference and assess these early criticisms in a series of footnotes in Lipsey (1960).

5 In Lipsey (1974), I elaborated on the kind of micro process that I had in mind for driving the relation.

6 For myself, by the time I wrote the Phillips piece I strongly advocated putting up with significant amounts of inflation as the price of keeping unemployment low – thus illustrating that not everyone's economic analysis is determined by their value judgements.

7 I have developed these points in more detail in Lipsey (1978).

8 In Lipsey (1964) I drew a stable Phillips Curve and used policymakers' indifference curves to establish the optimal combination of unemployment and inflation.

9 Given publication lags, it is clear that these two treatments were written independently of each other.

10 For an empirically oriented treatment in this vein see Eckstein (1981); and for a more general discussion see Lipsey (1981).

11 In chapter 32 in this volume, Geoffrey Harcourt makes the same point, as does Corry (1995).

12 See Hahn (1995).

13 I have discussed the clash between the New Classical and Keynesian world in much more detail in Lipsey (2000).

25 The Relation Between Unemployment and the Rate of Change of Money Wage Rates in the United Kingdom, 1861–1957

A.W. Phillips

1 Hypothesis

When the demand for a commodity or service is high relatively to the supply of it we expect the price to rise, the rate of rise being greater the greater the excess demand. Conversely when the demand is low relatively to the supply we expect the price to fall, the rate of fall being greater the greater the deficiency of demand. It seems plausible that this principle should operate as one of the factors determining the rate of change of money wage rates, which are the price of labour services. When the demand for labour is high and there are very few unemployed we should expect employers to bid wage rates up quite rapidly, each firm and each industry being continually tempted to offer little above the prevailing rates to attract the most suitable labour from other firms and industries. On the other hand it appears that workers are reluctant to offer their services at less than the prevailing rates when the demand for labour is low and unemployment is high so that wage rates fall only very slowly. The relation between unemployment and the rate of change of wage rates is therefore likely to be highly non-linear.

It seems possible that a second factor influencing the rate of change of money wage rates might be the rate of change of the demand for labour, and so of unemployment. Thus in a year of rising business activity, with the demand for labour increasing and the percentage unemployment decreasing, employers will be bidding more vigorously for the services of labour than they would be in a year during which the average percentage unemployment was the same but the demand for labour was not increasing. Conversely in a year of falling business activity, with the demand for labour decreasing and the percentage unemployment increasing, employers will be less inclined to grant wage increases, and workers will be in a weaker position to press for them, than they would be in a

243

year during which the average percentage unemployment was the same but the demand for labour was not decreasing.

A third factor which may affect the rate of change of money wage rates is the rate of change of retail prices, operating through cost of living adjustments in wage rates. It will be argued here, however, that cost of living adjustments will have little or no effect on the rate of change of money wage rates except at times when retail prices are forced up by a very rapid rise in import prices (or, on rare occasions in the United Kingdom, in the prices of home-produced agricultural products). For suppose that productivity is increasing steadily at the rate of, say, 2 per cent per annum and that aggregate demand is increasing similarly so that unemployment is remaining constant at, say, 2 per cent. Assume that with this level of unemployment and without any cost of living adjustments wage rates rise by, say, 3 per cent per annum as the result of employers' competitive bidding for labour and that import prices and the prices of other factor services are also rising by 3 per cent per annum. Then retail prices will be rising on average at the rate of about 1 per cent per annum (the rate of change of factor costs minus the rate of change of productivity). Under these conditions the introduction of cost of living adjustments in wage rates will have no effect, for employers will merely be giving under the name of cost of living adjustments part of the wage increases which they would in any case have given as a result of their competitive bidding for labour.

Assuming that the value of imports is one fifth of national income, it is only at times when the annual rate of change of import prices exceeds the rate at which wage rates would rise as a result of competitive bidding by employers by more than five times the rate of increase of productivity that cost of living adjustments become an operative factor in increasing the rate of change of money wage rates. Thus in the example given above a rate of increase of import prices of more than 13 per cent per annum would more than offset the effects of rising productivity so that retail prices would rise by more than 3 per cent per annum. Cost of living adjustments would then lead to a greater increase in wage rates than would have occurred as a result of employers' demand for labour and this would cause a further increase in retail prices, the rapid rise in import prices thus initiating a wage–price spiral which would continue until the rate of increase of import prices dropped significantly below the critical value of about 13 per cent per annum.

The purpose of the present study is to see whether statistical evidence supports the hypothesis that the rate of change of money wage rates in the United Kingdom can be explained by the level of unemployment and the rate of change of unemployment, except in or immediately after those years in which there was a very rapid rise in import prices, and if so to form some quantitative estimate of the relation between unemployment and the rate of change of money wage rates. The periods 1861–1913, 1913–1948 and 1948–1957 will be considered separately.

2 1861–1913

Schlote's (1952, table 26) index of the average price of imports shows an increase of 12.5 per cent in import prices in 1862 as compared with the previous year, an increase of 7.6 per cent in 1900 and in 1910, and an increase of 7.0 per cent in 1872. In no other year between 1861 and 1913 was there an increase in import prices of as much as 5 per cent. If the hypothesis stated above is correct the rise in import prices in 1862 may just have been sufficient to start up a mild wage–price spiral, but in the remainder of the period changes in import prices will have had little or no effect on the rate of change of wage rates.

A scatter diagram of the rate of change of wage rates and the percentage unemployment for the years 1861–1913 is shown in figure 25.1. During this time there were 6.5 fairly regular trade cycles with an average period of about eight years. Scatter diagrams for the years of each trade cycle are shown in figures 25.2–25.8. Each dot in the diagrams represents a year, the average rate of change of money wage rates during the year being given by the scale on the vertical axis and the average unemployment during the year by the scale on the horizontal axis. The rate of

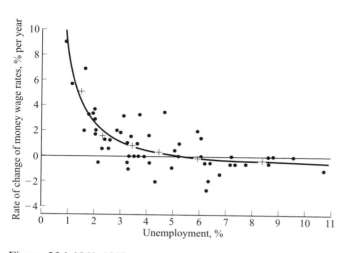

Figure 25.1 1861–1913

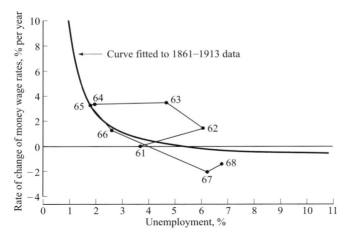

Figure 25.2 1861–1868

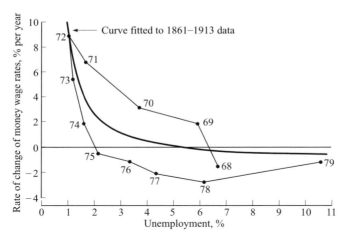

Figure 25.3 1868–1879

change of money wage rates was calculated from the index of hourly wage rates constructed by Phelps Brown and Sheila Hopkins (1950), by expressing the first central difference of the index for each year as a percentage of the index for the same year. Thus the rate of change for 1861 is taken to be half the difference between the index for 1862 and the index for 1860 expressed as a percentage of the index for 1861, and

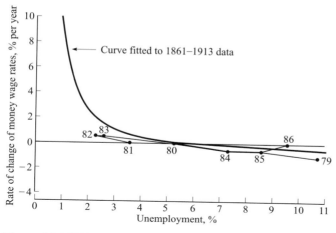

Figure 25.4 1879–1886

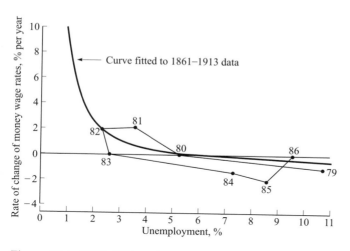

Figure 25.4a 1879–1886, using Bowley's wage index for the years 1881–1886

similarly for other years.[1] The percentage unemployment figures are those calculated by the Board of Trade and the Ministry of Labour[2] from trade union returns. The corresponding percentage employment figures are quoted in Beveridge, *Full Employment in a Free Society* (1944, table 22).

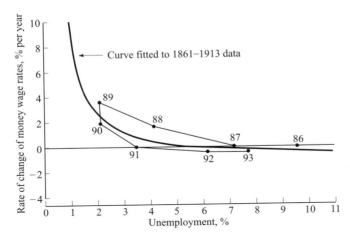

Figure 25.5 1886–1893

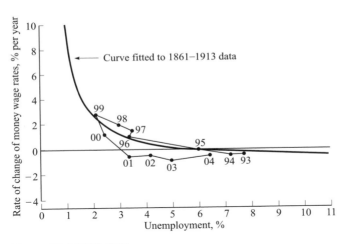

Figure 25.6 1893–1904

It will be seen from figures 25.2–25.8 that there is a clear tendency for the rate of change of money wage rates to be high when unemployment is low and to be low or negative when unemployment is high. There is also a clear tendency for the rate of change of money wage rates at any given level of unemployment to be above the average for that level of unemployment when unemployment is decreasing during the upswing of a

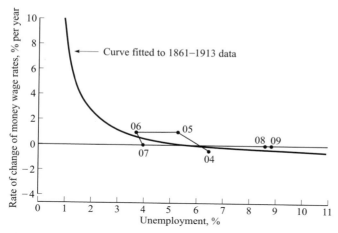

Figure 25.7 1904–1909

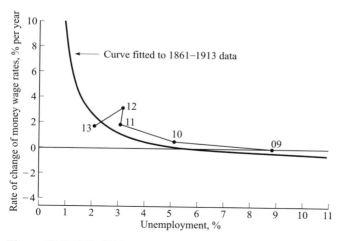

Figure 25.8 1909–1913

trade cycle and to be below the average for that level of unemployment when unemployment is increasing during the downswing of a trade cycle.

The crosses shown in figure 25.1 give the average values of the rate of change of money wage rates and of the percentage unemployment in those years in which unemployment lay between 0 and 2, 2 and 3, 3 and 4, 4 and 5, 5 and 7, and 7 and 11 per cent respectively (the upper bound being included in each interval). Since each interval includes years in which unemployment was increasing and years in which it was decreasing the effect of changing unemployment on the rate of change of wage rates tends to be cancelled out by this averaging, so that each cross gives an approximation to the rate of change of wages which would be associated with the indicated level of unemployment if unemployment were held constant at that level.

The curve shown in figure 25.1 (and repeated for comparison in later diagrams) was fitted to the crosses. The form of equation chosen was

$$y + a = bx^c$$

or

$$\log(y + a) = \log b + c \log x$$

where y is the rate of change of wage rates and x is the percentage unemployment. The constants b and c were estimated by least squares using the values of y and x corresponding to the crosses in the four intervals between 0 and 5 per cent unemployment, the constant a being chosen by trial and error to make the curve pass as close as possible to the remaining two crosses in the intervals between 5 and 11 per cent unemployment.[3] The equation of the fitted curve is

$$y + 0.900 = 9.638x^{-1.394}$$

or

$$\log(y + 0.900) = 0.984 - 1.394 \log x$$

Considering the wage changes in individual years in relation to the fitted curve, the wage increase in 1862 (see figure 25.2) is definitely larger than can be accounted for by the level of unemployment and the rate of change of unemployment, and the wage increase in 1863 is also larger than would be expected. It seems that the 12.5 per cent increase in import prices between 1861 and 1862 referred to above (and no doubt connected with the outbreak of the American Civil War) was in fact sufficient to have a real effect on wage rates by causing cost of living increases in wages which were greater than the increases which would have resulted from employers' demand for labour and that the consequent wage–price spiral continued into 1863. On the other hand, the increases in import prices of 7.6 per cent between 1899 and 1900 and again between 1909 and 1910 and the increase of 7.0 per cent between 1871 and 1872 do not seem to have had any noticeable effect on wage rates. This is consistent with the hypothesis stated above about the effect of rising import prices on wage rates.

Figure 25.3 and figures 25.5–25.8 show a very clear relation between the rate of change of wage rates and the level and rate of change of unemployment,[4] but the relation hardly appears at all in the cycle shown in figure 25.4. The wage index of Phelps Brown and Sheila Hopkins (1950, 264–5) from which the changes in wage rates were calculated was based on Wood's earlier index which shows the same stability during these years. From 1880 we have also Bowley's index of wage rates (1937, table vii, 30). If the rate of change of money wage rates for 1881 to 1886 is calculated from Bowley's index by the same method as was used before, the results shown in figure 25.4a are obtained, giving the typical relation between the rate of change of wage rates and the level and rate of change of unemployment. It seems possible that some peculiarity may have occurred in the construction of Wood's index for these years. Bowley's index for the remainder of the period up to 1913 gives results which are broadly similar to those shown in figures 25.5 to 25.8, but the pattern is rather less regular than that obtained with the index of Phelps Brown and Sheila Hopkins.

From figure 25.6 it can be seen that wage rates rose more slowly than usual in the upswing of business activity from 1893 to 1896 and then returned to their normal pattern of change; but with a temporary increase in unemployment during 1897. This suggests that there may have been exceptional resistance by employers to wage increases from 1894 to 1896, culminating in industrial strife in 1897. A glance at industrial history[5] confirms this suspicion. During the 1890s there was a rapid growth of employers' federations and from 1895 to 1897 there was resistance by the employers' federations to trade union demands for the introduction of an eight-hour working day, which would have involved a rise in hourly wage rates. This resulted in a strike by the Amalgamated Society of Engineers, countered by the Employers' Federation with a lock-out which lasted until January 1898.

From figure 25.8 it can be seen that the relation between wage changes and unemployment was again disturbed in 1912. From the monthly figures of percentage unemployment in trade unions[6] we find that unemployment rose from 2.8 per cent in February 1912 to 11.3 per cent in March, falling back to 3.6 per cent in April and 2.7 per cent in May, as the result of a general stoppage of work in coal mining. If an adjustment is made to eliminate the effect of the strike on unemployment the figure for the average percentage unemployment during 1912 would be reduced by about 0.8 per cent, restoring the typical pattern of the relation between the rate of change of wage rates and the level and rate of change of unemployment.

From a comparison of figures 25.2–25.8 it appears that the width of loops obtained in each trade cycle has tended to narrow, suggesting a reduction in the dependence of the rate of change of wage rates on the rate of change of unemployment. There seem to be two possible explanations of this. First, in the coal and steel industries before the First World War sliding scale adjustments were common, by which wage rates were linked to the prices of the products.[7] Given the tendency of product prices to rise with an increase in business activity and fall with a decrease in business activity, these agreements may have strengthened the relation between changes in wage rates and changes in unemployment in these industries. During the earlier years of the period these industries would have fairly large weights in the wage index, but with the greater coverage of the statistical material available in later years the weights of these industries in the index would be reduced. Second, it is possible that the decrease in the width of the loops resulted not so much from a reduction in the dependence of wage changes on changes in unemployment as from the introduction of a time lag in the response of wage changes to changes in the level of unemployment, caused by the extension of collective bargaining and particularly by the growth of arbitration and conciliation procedures. If such a time lag existed in the later years of the period the wage change in any year should be related, not to average unemployment during that year, but to the average unemployment lagged by, perhaps, several months. This would have the effect of moving each point in the diagrams horizontally part of the way towards the point of the preceding year and it can easily be seen that this would widen the loop in the diagrams. This fact makes it difficult to discriminate at all closely between the effect of time lags and the effect of dependence of wage changes on the rate of change of unemployment.

3 1913–1948

A scatter diagram of the rate of change of wage rates and percentage unemployment for the years 1913–1948 is shown in figure 25.9. From 1913 to 1920 the series used are a continuation of those used for the period 1861–1913. From 1921 to 1948 the Ministry of Labour's index of hourly wage rates at the end of December of each year[8] has been used, the percentage change in the index each year being taken as a measure of the average rate of change of wage rates during that year. The Ministry of Labour's figures for the percentage unemployment in the United Kingdom[9] have been used for the years 1921–1945. For the years 1946–1948 the unemployment figures were taken from the *Statistical Yearbooks* of the International Labour Organisation.

It will be seen from figure 25.9 that there was an increase in unemployment in 1914 (mainly due to a sharp rise in the three months following the commencement of the war). From 1915 to 1918 unemployment was low and wage rates rose rapidly. The cost of living was also rising rapidly and formal agreements for automatic cost of living adjustments in wage rates became widespread, but it is not clear whether the cost of living adjustments were a real factor in increasing wage rates or whether they merely replaced increases which would in any case have occurred as a result of the high demand for labour. Demobilisation brought increased unemployment in 1919 but wage rates continued to rise rapidly until 1920, probably as a result of the rapidly rising import prices, which reached their peak in 1920, and consequent cost of living adjustments in wage rates. There was then a sharp increase in unemployment from 2.6 per cent in 1920 to 17.0 per cent in 1921, accompanied by a fall of 22.2 per cent in wage rates in 1921. Part of the fall can be explained by the

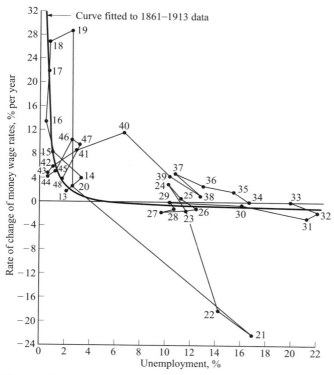

Figure 25.9 1913–1948

extremely rapid increase in unemployment, but a fall of 12.8 per cent in the cost of living, largely a result of falling import prices, was no doubt also a major factor. In 1922 unemployment was 14.3 per cent and wage rates fell by 19.1 per cent. Although unemployment was high in this year it was decreasing, and the major part of the large fall in wage rates must be explained by the fall of 17.5 per cent in the cost of living index between 1921 and 1922. After this experience trade unions became less enthusiastic about agreements for automatic cost of living adjustments and the number of these agreements declined.

From 1923 to 1929 there were only small changes in import prices and in the cost of living. In 1923 and 1924 unemployment was high but decreasing. Wage rates fell slightly in 1923 and rose by 3.1 per cent in 1924. It seems likely that if business activity had continued to improve after 1924 the changes in wage rates would have shown the usual pattern of the recovery phase of earlier trade cycles. However, the decision to check demand in an attempt to force the price level down in order to restore the gold standard at the pre-war parity of sterling prevented the recovery of business activity and unemployment remained fairly steady between 9.7 per cent and 12.5 per cent from 1925 to 1929. The average level of unemployment during these five years was 10.94 per cent and the average rate of change of wage rates was −0.60 per cent per year. The rate of change of wage rates calculated from the curve fitted to the 1861–1913 data for a level of unemployment of 10.94 per cent is −0.56 per cent per year, in close agreement with the average observed value. Thus the evidence does not support the view, which is sometimes expressed, that the policy of forcing the price level down failed because of increased resistance to downward movements of wage rates. The actual results obtained, given the levels of unemployment which were held, could have been predicted fairly accurately from a study of the pre-war data, if anyone had felt inclined to carry out the necessary analysis.

The relation between wage changes and unemployment during the 1929–1937 trade cycle follows the usual pattern of the cycles in the 1861–1913 period except for the higher level of unemployment throughout the cycle. The increases in wage rates in 1935, 1936 and 1937 are perhaps rather larger than would be expected to result from the rate of change of employment alone and part of the increases must probably be attributed to cost of living adjustments. The cost of living index rose 3.1 per cent in 1935, 3.0 per cent in 1936 and 5.2 per cent in 1937, the major part of the increase in each of these years being due to the rise in the food component of the index. Only in 1937 can the rise in food prices be fully accounted for by rising import prices; in 1935 and 1936 it seems likely that the policies introduced to raise prices of home-produced agricultural produce played a significant part in increasing food prices and so the cost of living index and wage rates. The extremely uneven geographical distribution of unemployment may also have been a factor tending to increase the rapidity of wage changes during the upswing of business activity between 1934 and 1937.

Increases in import prices probably contributed to the wage increases in 1940 and 1941. The points in figure 25.9 for the remaining war years show the effectiveness of the economic controls introduced. After an increase in unemployment in 1946 due to demobilisation and in 1947 due to the coal crisis, we return in 1948 almost exactly to the fitted relation between unemployment and wage changes.

4 1948–1957

A scatter diagram for the years 1948–1957 is shown in figure 25.10. The unemployment percentages shown are averages of the monthly unemployment percentages in Great Britain during the calendar years indicated, taken from the *Ministry of Labour Gazette*. The Ministry of Labour does not regularly publish figures of the percentage unemployment in the United Kingdom; but from data published in the *Statistical*

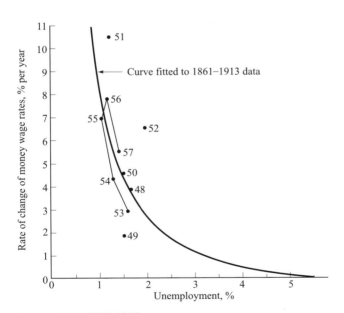

Figure 25.10 1948–1957

Yearbooks of the International Labour Organisation it appears that unemployment in the United Kingdom was fairly consistently about 0.1 per cent higher than that in Great Britain throughout this period. The wage index used was the index of weekly wage rates, published monthly in the *Ministry of Labour Gazette*, the percentage change during each calendar year being taken as a measure of the average rate of change of money wage rates during the year. The Ministry does not regularly publish an index of hourly wage rates;[10] but an index of normal weekly hours published in the *Ministry of Labour Gazette* of September 1957 shows a reduction of 0.2 per cent in 1948 and in 1949 and an average annual reduction of approximately 0.04 per cent from 1950 to 1957. The percentage changes in hourly rates would therefore be greater than the percentage changes in weekly rates by these amounts.

It will be argued later that a rapid rise in import prices during 1947 led to a sharp increase in retail prices in 1948 which tended to stimulate wage increases during 1948, but that this tendency was offset by the policy of wage restraint introduced by Sir Stafford Cripps in the spring of 1948; that wage increases during 1949 were exceptionally low as a result of the policy of wage restraint; that a rapid rise in import prices during 1950 and 1951 led to a rapid rise in retail prices during 1951 and 1952 which caused cost of living increases in wage rates in excess of the increases that would have occurred as a result of the demand for labour, but that there were no special factors of wage restraint or rapidly rising import prices to affect the wage increases in 1950 or in the five years from 1953 to 1957. It can be seen from figure 25.10 that the point for 1950 lies very close to the curve fitted to the 1861–1913 data and that the points for 1953 to 1957 lie on a narrow loop around this curve, the direction of the loop being the reverse of the direction of the loops shown in figures 25.2 to 25.8. A loop in this direction could result from a time lag in the adjustment of wage rates. If the rate of change of wage rates during each calendar year is related to unemployment lagged seven months, i.e., to the average of the monthly percentages of unemployment from June of the preceding year to May of that year, the scatter diagram shown in figure 25.11 is obtained. The loop has now disappeared and the points for the years 1950 and 1953 to 1957 lie closely along a smooth curve which coincides almost exactly with the curve fitted to the 1861–1913 data.

In table 25.1 below the percentage changes in money wage rates during the years 1948–1957 are shown in column (1). The figures in column (2) are the percentage changes in wage rates calculated from the curve fitted to the 1861–1913 data corresponding to the unemployment percentages shown in figure 25.11, i.e. the average percentages of unemployment lagged seven months. On the hypothesis that has been used in this

Table 25.1

	(1) Change in wage rates	(2) Demand pull	(3) Cost push	(4) Change in import prices
1947				20.1
1948	3.9	3.5	7.1	10.6
1949	1.9	4.1	2.9	4.1
1950	4.6	4.4	3.0	26.5
1951	10.5	5.2	9.0	23.3
1952	6.4	4.5	9.3	−11.7
1953	3.0	3.0	3.0	−4.8
1954	4.4	4.5	1.9	5.0
1955	6.9	6.8	4.6	1.9
1956	7.9	8.0	4.9	3.8
1957	5.4	5.2	3.8	−7.3

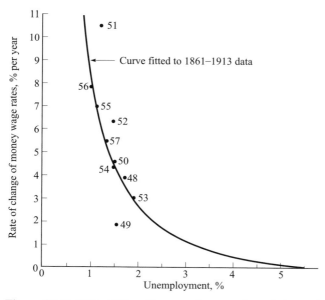

Figure 25.11 1948–1957, with unemployment lagged 7 months

paper, these figures represent the percentages by which wage rates would be expected to rise, given the level of employment for each year, as a result of employers' competitive bidding for labour, i.e. they represent the 'demand pull' element in wage adjustments. The relevant figure on the cost side in wage negotiations is the percentage increase shown by the retail price index in the month in which the negotiations are proceeding over the index of the corresponding month of the previous year. The average of these monthly percentages for each calendar year is an appropriate measure of the 'cost push' element in wage adjustments, and these averages[11] are given in column (3). The percentage change in the index of import prices[12] during each year is given in column (4).

From table 25.1 we see that in 1948 the cost push element was considerably greater than the demand pull element, as a result of the lagged effect on retail prices of the rapid rise in import prices during the previous year, and the change in wage rates was a little greater than could be accounted for by the demand pull element. It would probably have been considerably greater but for the co-operation of the trade unions in Sir Stafford Cripps' policy of wage restraint. In 1949 the cost element was less than the demand element and the actual change in wages rates was also much less, no doubt as a result of the policy of wage restraint which is generally acknowledged to have been effective in 1949. In 1950 the cost element was lower than the demand element and the actual wage change was approximately equal to the demand element.

Import prices rose very rapidly during 1950 and 1951 as a result of the devaluation of sterling in September 1949 and the outbreak of the Korean War in 1950. In consequence the retail price index rose rapidly during 1951 and 1952 so that the cost element in wage negotiations considerably exceeded the demand element. The actual wage increase in each year also considerably exceeded the demand element so that these two years provide a clear case of cost inflation.

In 1953 the cost element was equal to the demand element and in the years 1954 to 1957 it was well below the demand element. In each of these years the actual wage increase was almost exactly equal to the demand element. Thus in these five years, and also in 1950, there seems to have been pure demand inflation.

5 Conclusions

The statistical evidence in sections 2 to 4 above seems in general to support the hypothesis stated in section 1, that the rate of change of money wage rates can be explained by the level of unemployment and the rate of change of unemployment, except in or immediately after those years in which there is a sufficiently rapid rise in import prices to offset the tendency for increasing productivity to reduce the cost of living.

Ignoring years in which import prices rise rapidly enough to initiate a wage–price spiral, which seem to occur very rarely except as a result of war, and assuming an increase in productivity of 2 per cent per year, it seems from the relation fitted to the data that if aggregate demand were kept at a value which would maintain a stable level of product prices the associated level of unemployment would be a little under 2.5 per cent. If, as is sometimes recommended, demand were kept at a value which would maintain stable wage rates the associated level of unemployment would be about 5.5 per cent.

Because of the strong curvature of the fitted relation in the region of low percentage unemployment, there will be a lower average rate of increase of wage rates if unemployment is held constant at a given level than there will be if unemployment is allowed to fluctuate about that level.

These conclusions are of course tentative. There is need for much more detailed research into the relations between unemployment, wage rates, prices and productivity.

Notes

Economica, 25 (NS) (100), 1958, pp. 283–99.

This study is part of a wider research project financed by a grant from the Ford Foundation. The writer was assisted by Mrs Marjory Klonarides. Thanks are due to Professor E.H. Phelps Brown, Professor J.E. Meade and Dr R.G. Lipsey for comments on an earlier draft.

1 The index is apparently intended to measure the average of wage rates during each year. The first central difference is therefore the best simple approximation to the average absolute rate of change of wage rates during a year and the central difference expressed as a percentage of the index number is an appropriate measure of the average percentage rate of change of wage rates during the year.

2 Memoranda upon British and Foreign Trade and Industrial Conditions (Second Series) (Cd. 2337), B.P.P. 1905, Vol. 84; 21st Abstract of Labour Statistics, 1919–1933 (Cd. 4624), B.P.P. 1933–4, Vol. 26.

3 At first sight it might appear preferable to carry out a multiple regression of y on the variables x and dx/dt. However, owing to the particular form of the relation between y and x in the present case it is not easy to find a suitable linear multiple regression equation. An equation of the form $y + a = bx^c + k(1/x^m \cdot dx/dt)$ would probably be suitable. If so the procedure which has been adopted for estimating the relation that would hold between y and x if dx/dt were zero is satisfactory, since it can easily be shown that $1/x^m \cdot dx/dt$ is

uncorrelated with x or with any power of x provided that x is, as in this case, a trend-free variable.

4 Since the unemployment figures used are the averages of monthly percentages, the first central difference is again the best simple approximation to the average rate of change of unemployment during a year. It is obvious from an inspection of figures 25.3 and figures 25.5 to 25.8 that in each cycle there is a close relation between the deviations of the points from the fitted curve and the first central differences of the employment figures, though the magnitude of the relation does not seem to have remained constant over the whole period.

5 See Roberts (1958, chapter IV, especially 158–162).

6 *21st Abstract of Labour Statistics, 1919–1933.*

7 I am indebted to Professor Phelps Brown for pointing this out to me.

8 *Ministry of Labour Gazette*, April (1958, 133).

9 Ibid., January, 1940 and subsequent issues.

10 An index of hourly wage rates covering the years considered in this section is, however, given in the *Ministry of Labour Gazette* of April, 1958.

11 Calculated from the retail price index published in the *Monthly Digest of Statistics*. The figure for 1948 is the average of the last seven months of the year.

12 *Board of Trade Journal.*

26 Discussion of Dicks-Mireaux and Dow's The Determinants of Wage Inflation: United Kingdom, 1946–1956

A.W. Phillips

I have great pleasure in seconding the vote of thanks to the authors for this extremely interesting paper. One of the important policy problems of our time is that of maintaining a high level of economic activity and employment while avoiding a continual rise in prices. The results obtained in this paper provide valuable information on the possibilities of reconciling these objectives.

There are formidable difficulties in statistical analyses of this sort. A wide range of alternative hypotheses is possible and the series available for testing them are short. The hypotheses used in this paper seem very reasonable, though non-linear forms of the relationship might also have been considered.

The authors have chosen to work mainly with four-period moving averages of quarterly data. If there is anything in the notion of an 'annual wage round' a straightforward use of annual figures may have been more appropriate. It is of interest to see from table 5 that the estimates obtained using annual figures for the first quarter of each year are similar to those obtained using quarterly data, and the fit appears to be extremely good.

If we start with an error term which is a four-period moving average of independent errors of autoregressive transformation of the form $1 - \frac{3}{4}E^{-1}$ cannot reduce the autocorrelations for all lags to zero. The Durbin–Watson test applies only to the first autocorrelation coefficient whereas the validity of the significance test may therefore not be completely reliable. Autocorrelation of the error terms will also cause bias in the estimate of the causal relationship even though there is a distributed lag in the 'feed-back' relationship. Bias will only be avoided if there is a

261

delay or 'dead-time' in the feedback greater than the interval over which the error terms are autocorrelated. The case for believing that there is negligible bias must therefore rest on the argument implicit in para. 5.7, that the variance of the error term in the equation being estimated is small relative to the variance of the explanatory variables.

The introduction as an additional explanatory variable of a subjective judgement of the 'pushfulness' of trade unions is an interesting device. I personally would have put forward a somewhat different subjective judgement.

I feel that changes in the attitudes of trade unions have had little effect on the outcome of wage bargains except in the years 1948 and 1949 when the Cripps policy of wage restraint seems to have been effective. I believe also that in 1951, when prices were rising rapidly following the outbreak of the Korean war, trade unions recovered most of what they had lost during the period of wage restraints. I would therefore have made the variable negative in 1948 and 1949, positive in 1951 and zero in other years. From an inspection of figure 3 it appears that this would also have produced a better statistical fit than that obtained on the authors' hypothesis, since it would have raised the calculated wage change in 1951 and lowered it in 1955 and 1956.

The results obtained in this paper suggest that if the authors' index of excess demand were zero, which seems to correspond to an unemployment figure of a little under 2 per cent, and if price changes were zero, wage rates would rise at about 2.5 per cent per year. This rate of wage change would be consistent with zero price change if productivity per man-hour were rising at 2.5 per cent per year. It may be of interest to compare this result with one which I obtained on the hypothesis that the rate of change of wage rates depends only on the level of unemployment and the rate of change of unemployment, except in years of very rapid increase of import prices. This relation was estimated from data for the years 1861–1913, but also fits very well for the years 1953–1957. With unemployment constant at 2 per cent the rise in wage rates predicted from this relation is about 2.5 per cent per year. Assuming a rise in productivity of 2.5 per cent per year, this result would agree closely with the result given in the present paper. The relation I obtained is highly non-linear, but a linear approximation in the range between 1 per cent and 2 per cent per year unemployment gives a demand coefficient of about 4.25 as compared with the coefficient of about 3.5 obtained in the present study.

Note

Journal of the Royal Statistical Society, 123 (11), 1959, pp. 176–7.

27   The Melbourne Paper

John Pitchford

B22 B31
E12 E31 E24
(A.W.H.Phillips) (Australia)

Bill Phillips wrote chapter 27 in 1959 while visiting the University of
Melbourne, so it is convenient to refer to it as the 'Melbourne paper'.
As he related to Conrad Blyth (1978, xvi–xvii), he had then just finished
his 1958 'Phillips Curve' *Economica* article (chapter 25) which was

a rush job. I had to go off on sabbatical leave to Melbourne; but in that case it
was better for understanding to do it simply and not wait too long.

Blyth also explained that 'Bill himself was not very happy with the stable
wage assumption found in popular Keynesian models'. The simple
Phillips Curve concept was a first attempt to explain wage inflation and
adapt Keynesian models so that they could include the reality of rising
prices and wages. While the Melbourne paper was never formally published, it can be argued that it was a big advance on the original Phillips
Curve work. Had he gone on with it he might himself have modified the
simple Phillips Curve concept in ways which others were subsequently to
do. The paper is of considerable interest, but it should be said at the
outset that it was a working paper, and that Bill Phillips recognised it
to be unfinished. There were data problems, the regression results cited in
the endnotes do not include standard errors, R^2s or other statistics and
the theory was in need of tidying up.

In the 1950s, minimum (or award) wage rates and working conditions
were set by a centralised system based on an Arbitration Court, and
Australian labour unions were strong. One widely held view of inflation
was that it emanated largely from 'excessive' wage settlements interacting
with markup pricing. This theory gave little or no role to demand factors.
A more satisfactory approach recognised that at the very least demand
was important in 'over-award' wage payments and that monetary
restraint was a way to control excessive inflation. Nor was there then
much discussion of the way in which the fixed exchange rate (pegged to
sterling) would result in the import of foreign inflation and monetary

263

conditions. However, wage rates were tied to price movements through cost-of-living adjustments and it was recognised that movements in the prices of importables and exportables would therefore affect wages. Bill would have been made aware of these views in Melbourne, if he were not already familiar with them from his earlier stay in Australia.

The original Phillips Curve related the rate of change in money wages to the rate of unemployment.[1] In the Melbourne paper he combined this simple approach with the conventional Australian view of wage determination and inflation. This led to his relating *real* wage changes to unemployment and opening the economy to the influences of foreign inflation. He thereby started down a path which could have led him to a much more sophisticated and robust theory, though he never completed the journey.

Before substantiating these points, it is useful to look for reasons why the Melbourne paper was incomplete. At the time the Australian statistician supplied data on average hourly wage rates and average weekly wage and salary earnings. Figures for average hourly earnings were not available. Section 2 of the Melbourne paper on data contains estimates of hourly earning and devotes considerable space to discussing these estimates and their relation to other series. Yet when he comes to specify and estimate relationships he starts out explaining wage rates. At the end of section 3 on estimation he says

I should like to emphasise that much more statistical work of this sort remains to be done. In particular I intend to attempt a similar explanation of the rate of change of earnings...

Because of the lack of data on hourly earnings he was in a quandary familiar to students of Australian post-war inflation. Hourly earnings data were much more appropriate for his wage equation and his (implicit) price equation than rates. He had made estimates of hourly earnings by adjusting weekly earnings for movements in overtime, which in turn were proxied by movements in unemployment. But this meant that using unemployment as an explanator of the rate of change of his estimate of hourly earnings would be a dubious procedure. It is possible that this is why he never finished and published the paper.

The model he had in mind was set out verbally in section 3. The first relationship explains wage rate changes: 'the rate of change of wage rates depends directly on the demand for labour and the rates of change of consumers prices and export prices...'.

This could be written

$$\hat{W} = f(u) + \alpha \hat{I} + \beta \hat{P}_x \tag{1}$$

$$\hat{T} = a\hat{P}_N + b\hat{P}_M + c\hat{P}_X, \quad a + b + c = 1, \tag{2}$$

where

W = average wage rates,

u = the unemployment rate,

I = index of consumer prices,

P_i = price of non-traded goods, importables and exportables, as $i = N$, M, X, respectively,

$\hat{\ }$ = proportional rate of change of a variable,

f = the basic Phillips Curve function.

Equation (1) was an attempt to explain how the Arbitration system might determine wage rates. The authorities were supposed to set them partly by adjusting for movements in the 'cost-of-living' index I, the coefficient α probably being taken to be unity so that, other things being equal, real consumption wages would thus be preserved. In addition, the authorities were supposed to vary the real wage rate with the state of the labour market, represented by u. Equation (1) also allows for changes in the export price index to affect wage settings presumably because of some equity principle whereby the prosperity of 'agricultural-ists' would be shared with the 'industrial workers'.[2]

The second relationship was meant to explain price movements: 'the rate of change of consumers' prices depends directly on the rates of change of wages and of export and import prices...'

Consumers' prices, at least as I have represented them by the index in equation (2), are a composite of several categories of prices. Thus it is more satisfactory to have the above statement refer to non-traded goods prices. The hypothesis is then one of a fixed markup type and could be given the form

$$\hat{P}_N = p\hat{W} + q\hat{P}_X + r\hat{P}_M. \tag{3}$$

a, b, c, p, q, r are treated as constant parameters. Combining (1), (2), and (3) yields

$$\hat{W} = \left(\frac{f(u)}{1 - \alpha a p}\right) + \left(\frac{\alpha a q + \alpha c + \beta}{1 - \alpha a p}\right)\hat{P}_X + \left(\frac{\alpha a r + \alpha b}{1 - \alpha a p}\right)\hat{P}_M. \tag{4}$$

This is the (reduced form) equation that Bill Phillips seemed to be estimating.[3] As I understand it, the idea was that policy decisions and external shocks affect aggregate demand (and supply) for goods and services which is transmitted to labour demand and unemployment. P_X and P_M are exogenous if traded goods prices are determined in world markets and if the exchange rate is fixed. The first part of this rationale is an essentially Keynesian one, while the second part takes account of open economy influences in a regime of fixed exchange rates.

Leaving aside open economy questions, the big advance over the simple Phillips Curve is that, taking α to be unity, the change in real, not nominal, wages is related to unemployment. This was the first part of Friedman's (1968) subsequent contribution, the second part being that it was expected prices and so the expected real wage that he used.[4] Bill Phillips was part of the way there, but the paucity of data on earnings could well have discouraged him from going further.[5]

Taking another step, it is reasonable to assume that homogeneity would ensure that $p + q + r = 1$ in equation (3). That is, treating productivity growth as zero for simplicity, an equal proportional rise in wages and traded goods prices would result in the same proportional rise in non-traded goods prices. Neglecting the redistributive aspect of wage setting embodied in equation (1) (that is, taking β to be zero), it follows that the coefficients of export and import price change add to unity.

The model then yields several theoretical results which now would be taken as standard for open economy systems. For instance, if there were a uniform rate of inflation emanating from abroad, with a pegged exchange rate, the domestic money supply would be rising at that rate and so would all prices and wages when excess demand for labour was zero (unemployment at an equilibrium rate).[6] The rate of inflation of wages and non-traded goods prices could differ from this world inflation rate to the extent that there was excess demand for labour. So the effect of confronting conventional Australian views of inflation was to require Bill to open the economy and take account of traded goods price movements. The real wage was part of the story, but in its expected form would have to await Friedman in 1968.

Despite the fact that real rather than nominal wages are related to unemployment, there is still a long-run inflation/unemployment trade-off in the system. He deduced from his estimates that, assuming productivity growth of 2 per cent per year and constant traded goods prices, consumer prices would rise at about 1.5 per cent per year at the then unemployment rate of 1.7 per cent of the total work force. Attempts to reduce unemployment to much lower levels would lead to much higher inflation. 'Thus with unemployment at about 0.5 per cent we could expect wage and price changes of the order of 10 per cent per year' (p. 277). These were stable inflation rates. Unlike in Friedman and Phelps, there was no acceleration of inflation at low unemployment rates. An equilibrium (or natural) rate of unemployment would exist in this type of model where excess demand for labour is zero, but there is usually insufficient reliable data to establish the unemployment rate corresponding to this situation. It is expected inflation rates chasing actual inflation rates, combined with the monetary accommodation of inflation, which causes accelerating inflation.[7] Incidentally, the practice of the Arbitration system in Australia was that the 'cost-of-living' part of wage rate adjustment was based on *past* rather than expected increases in wages. It is not surprising that analysing Australian wage rate behaviour did not require Bill to think about expected price movements.

For Australia and many other countries, the experience of inflation before and after the first oil price shock of the 1970s was completely different. Indeed, analyses of inflation around the world based on data and experience before the mid 1970s were not satisfactory in explaining subsequent inflation. In one respect Bill's model would have coped quite well with this experience because it included traded goods prices. Consequently the 21 per cent and 36 per cent increases in export and import prices in Australia in 1974 would have helped to drive up the model's estimates of inflation for that time. Moreover, if the authorities had realised the extent to which inflation then was imported, and if they had taken note of Bill's results, they may have thought twice about the wisdom and value of their policy of severe monetary restraint. However, Australian inflation in the late 1970s and particularly the 1980s would have been difficult to explain without some concept of inflationary expectations.

To complete the system set out above it would have been necessary to give an account of the determinants of unemployment. In the Keynesian spirit in which Phillips worked this would require specifying the sources of various shocks to aggregate demand, including monetary and fiscal policy changes. In relation to monetary policy, the problem arises that the logic of what has been said about the nature of the model is that there would be no chance of autonomous monetary policy with pegged exchange rates.[8] In practice, however, monetary policy did seem to have some degree of influence on monetary conditions in Australia prior to the float in 1983 and empirical studies support this. But to incorporate such relationships into the model would have been a much larger task than Bill had set himself.

The ANU was fortunate to attract Bill Phillips to the second chair of Economics in the Research School of Social Sciences in 1967. He had taken the position on the understanding that his work would eventually involve the study of the Chinese economy. In the first several years of his appointment he successfully undertook the task of putting the department on a new track. Bill's unusual background enabled him to cut through the inhibitions that discourage conventional economists from trying out radically different approaches to the subject. Unfortunately

his illness deprived us of the benefit of his thoughtful, sensible and innovative approach to economics.

Notes

1 He considers the possibility of relating wage changes also to prices in chapter
  25, but rejected it in favour of their being affected only by large movements in
  import prices.
2 To appreciate this it should be recognised that agricultural products were a
  substantial part of exports in the 1950s.
3 One problem was that the wage variable in (3) should rightly be an earnings not
  a rates measure. Productivity should also enter (3), but he allowed for this by
  treating it as a constant.
4 Phelps (1967) also used price expectations, but in a priced not wage equation.
5 Notice that the framework (1), (2), (3) enables a simple resolution of the data
  problem. Eliminating the wage variable results in a reduced form relating the
  rate of change of the price index to unemployment and the rate of change of
  traded goods prices. This approach was taken in Pitchford (1968).
6 One challenge would have been to explain why the estimated coefficients of
  import and export price changes added to less than unity.
7 With the extreme form of rational expectations there is not even a short-run
  trade-off and so accelerating inflation at unemployment rates below the natural
  rate is not an issue.
8 In theory, a floating exchange rate system insulates the economy from the
  nominal effects of foreign price movements. In practice it is of interest to test
  whether and to what extent this works. It is clear that the model behind the
  Melbourne paper would need to be recast in order to investigate current
  Australian inflation issues.

28   Wage Changes and Unemployment in Australia, 1947–1958

A.W. Phillips

E24

J23 J31

J64

1 The problem

One of the main economic problems in Western countries today is whether it is possible to prevent continually rising prices of consumer goods while maintaining high levels of economic activity. The prices of final products will rise if the price of productive services rise more rapidly than their real productivity. On the basis of past experience we may expect technical advance to result in a rise in productivity of the order of 2 per cent per year. Thus the price of final goods will rise continuously if the prices of productive services rise on average by more than about 2 per cent per year. The main productive services in any economy are labour, land and capital, and of these labour is quantitatively the most important. It is fairly certain, also, that the owners of land and capital will succeed in keeping the prices of their services in step with those of labour. The problem therefore reduces to whether it is possible to prevent the money price of labour services, that is average money earnings per man-hour, from rising at more than about 2 per cent per year, while maintaining high levels of economic activity and employment. I wish to examine this question by considering Australian experience since 1947.

2 Data

The full line graphs in figure 28.1 show the rates of change, in per cent per year, of the index of nominal wages of adult males, the index of average weekly earnings in all industries and the 'C' series price index. In all cases the percentage changes were calculated quarterly, and the series were smoothed by applying a four-quarter moving average, to reduce seasonal and random fluctuations. The wage index is not very satisfactory for our purposes, since actual rates paid may be very different from award rates. There are also difficulties in using the earnings index, since it measures

269

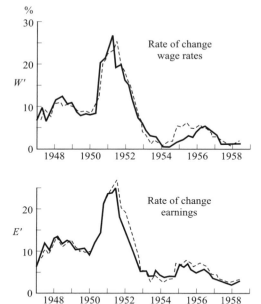

Figure 28.1

earnings per week and so changes with changes in the amount of overtime worked. The amount of overtime worked will change with changes in the level of economic activity, and these in turn will be associated with changes in the percentage of unemployment. I have therefore attempted to obtain a measure of the rate of change of earnings per hour by adjusting the index of weekly earnings by an amount depending on the percentage unemployment. The estimate of the rate of change of hourly earnings obtained in this way is shown in the dotted line on the earnings graph.[1] It is repeated, after subtracting 1.2 per cent throughout, superimposed on the rate of change of wages graph to facilitate comparison. It will be seen that hourly earnings have been rising on average at about 1.2 per cent per year faster than wage rates, but that the difference was less during the year following the sharp rise in the award rates in 1950, was again less during the recession in business activity in 1952–3, and was considerably greater during the period of fairly high demand in 1954 and 1955. The deviation between the two graphs in 1953 and in 1954–5 indicates that the rate of change of earnings varies with the level of demand for labour as a result of industrial bargaining, independently of changes in the arbitration award rates. On the other hand, the deviation between the graph in 1950–1 indicates that the large rise in the arbitration award in October 1950 initiated the increase in the rate of change of earnings in those years.

The estimated rate of change of hourly earnings is also repeated, after subtracting 2 per cent throughout, superimposed on the rate of change of prices graph. It will be seen that on average over the period 1947–58 hourly earnings rose more rapidly than the prices of consumers' goods, the difference being a little over 2 per cent per year. The difference was greater than this during the rapid rise in wage rates in 1950–1, as a result of a time lag in the adjustment of prices to rising costs. It was less than 2 per cent during the periods of fairly low demand in 1953 and in 1957–8, and greater than 2 per cent in the period of high demand in 1954–5. It seems that prices have tended to rise more rapidly than labour costs during times of low demand and less rapidly than labour costs during times of high demand. This may be partly a matter of a time lag in the adjustment of prices to costs, and partly the result of overhead costs being spread over a higher output when demand is higher than when it is low.

The main factors influencing the rates of change of wage rates and hourly earnings are probably the rate of change of prices of consumers' goods operating through cost of living adjustments, the demand for labour and the rates of change of export and import prices. The last two factors will operate chiefly through their effects on the price of consumers' goods, though very large rises in export prices are likely to have in addition a direct effect on wage rates and earnings since they alter the distribution of income in favour of agriculturalists and this tends to lead to higher arbitration court wage awards.

There is no direct measure available of the demand for labour. Two indirect indicators are unfilled vacancies and unemployed applicants registered with the Commonwealth Employment Service. I find that these two indicators are very closely correlated so that either one may be used alone. I have chosen to use the unemployment figure. The number of unemployed applicants as a percentage of the number of persons in civilian employment for the years 1947–58 is shown in the first graph[2] in figure 28.2. (It will be found that if the number of unemployed applicants is taken as a percentage of the estimated total work force, the percentage unemployment figure will be reduced to about three-quarters of the figure shown on the graph.) When the percentage unemployment is very high, it is likely to be a fairly good direct measure of the demand for labour. At low levels of unemployment, however, there may be considerable excess demand for labour, and quite large changes in the excess demand for labour will be associated with only small changes of the percentage unem-

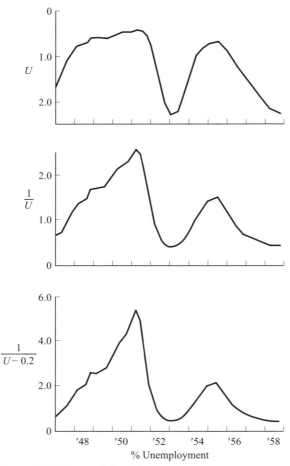

Figure 28.2 Demand for labour

ployed. To obtain an indicator of changes in demand for labour, therefore, it is necessary to accentuate changes in the percentage unemployed when unemployment is very low. This may be done by calculating the reciprocal of unemployment, or to accentuate the changes at low levels of unemployment still more, to take the reciprocal of unemployment after deducting a constant. Two transformations of this type are shown in the second and third graphs of figure 28.2. Another method of obtaining a similar effect is to calculate the reciprocal of the square, or some other power, of unemployment. I have used these methods in the later analysis.

The rates of change of export prices and import prices, also smoothed by a four-quarter moving average, are shown in the first two graphs of figure 28.3. In the third graph of figure 28.3 is shown the ratio of the export price index to the index of wage rates, both indexes being based on years 1936–9. It seemed that this ratio, which is a rough indicator of the relative prosperity of agriculturalists and industrial workers might also be a factor affecting arbitration court wage awards, but I have not in fact made use of it in a later analysis in this paper.

3 Statistical estimation

In attempting to estimate the quantitative effects of the various factors influencing the rates of change of wages and earnings, one difficulty immediately arises. Changes in wage rates are influenced by earlier changes in consumers' prices; but changes in consumers' prices are themselves largely determined by earlier changes in wage rates. With the short length of time-series available, it would be difficult to distinguish between the influence of prices on wages and the influence of wages on prices. It seems best, therefore, to eliminate the direct effect of consumers' prices altogether from the analysis. If the rate of change of wage rates depends directly on the demand for labour and on the rates of change of consumers' prices and export prices, while the rate of change of consumers' prices depends directly on the rates of change of wages and of export and import prices, then we may ignore consumers' prices completely and consider the rate of change of wages as determined directly, and also indirectly via cost of living adjustments, by the demand for labour and the rates of change of export and import prices.

By eliminating the direct effect of changes in consumers' prices in this way, we also obtain the advantage of explaining wage changes in terms only of export and import prices, which are largely independent of Australian policy, and the demand for labour, which, apart from minor fluctuations, can be controlled, and is continually being controlled, by Australian monetary and fiscal policy. This is particularly valuable

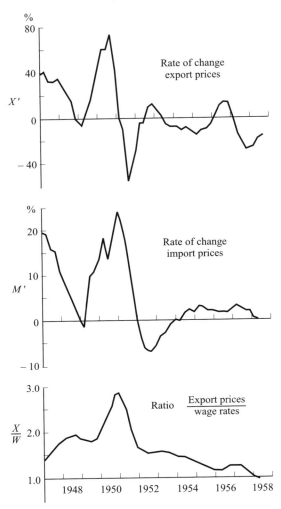

Figure 28.3

since one of the main purposes of this analysis is to consider what level of demand for labour the monetary and fiscal authorities should seek to maintain in their attempt to reconcile the two policy objectives of high levels of activity and stable prices.

As a first hypothesis I have tried to explain the observed rates of change of wage rates by the demand for labour, with a time lag of three-quarters of a year, the rate of change of export prices with an average of time lags one and two quarters, and the rate of change of import prices with a time lag of three quarters. On fitting these explanatory factors by the method of least squares to the actual rates of change of wages, we obtain the calculated rate of change of wages shown by the dotted line in the first graph of figure 28.4, compared with the actual rate of change of wages shown by the full line in the same graph.[3] It will be seen that the fit is fairly close excepting in the years 1957 and 1958.

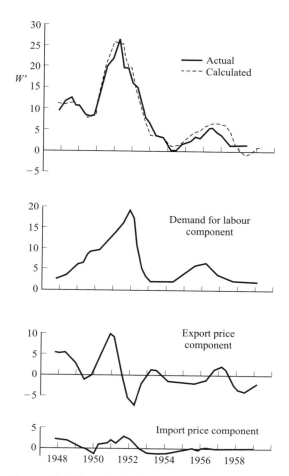

Figure 28.4 Hypothesis I

The separate influences of the demand for labour and the rates of change of export and import prices are shown in the other three graphs of figure 28.4. From these it is clear that the reason for the comparatively poor fit in 1957–8 is that too much weight has been given to changes in export prices in these years. It seems that the decisions of the Arbitration Court were strongly affected by the rapidly rising export prices immediately after the war and particularly by the spectacular rise which occurred in 1950, but that the smaller movements that have occurred since that time have had proportionally much less influence on wage changes. I have, therefore, tried a second hypothesis in which the effect of changing export prices is modified by accentuating very high rates of change and reducing the effects of lower and negative rates of change. In the second hypothesis I also slightly altered the time lags involved, by introducing distributed time lags, i.e., by assuming that the rate of change of wages depends on all earlier values of the explanatory factors, the weight attaching to them decreasing progressively for earlier periods. The fit obtained on the second hypothesis[4] is shown in the first graph of figure 28.5. It will be seen that it is considerably better than the previous one, though it still seems that rather too much weight is given to changes in export prices after 1951.

I should like to emphasise that much more statistical work of this sort remains to be done. In particular I intend to attempt a similar explanation of the rate of change of earnings instead of wages and to see the effect of differences in the assumptions made about time lags. I think, however, we may tentatively draw some conclusions from the work which has been done so far. For the policy problems which we wish to consider, it is of primary interest to find the effect on wage changes of the demand for labour, which is subject to Australian policy control, on the assumption that export and import prices are constant. Or rather, since we are interested here in long-run policy objectives, not in the short-run prediction of wage changes, we can assume that the fluctuations in export and import prices average out over a long period of years and can therefore be ignored in considering the level of demand for labour at which policy should be aimed. The relations, derived from the two statistical estimates, between the rate of change of wage rates and the level of unemployment assuming zero change in import and export prices, are shown in figure 28.6. It will be seen that the two estimates agree fairly closely and at the present level of unemployment of about 2.25 per cent of civilian employees, which is equivalent to about 1.7 per cent of the total work force, they indicate that, *on average over a period of years,* wage rates would rise at a little over 2 per cent per year. The estimate for the rate of change of hourly earnings would

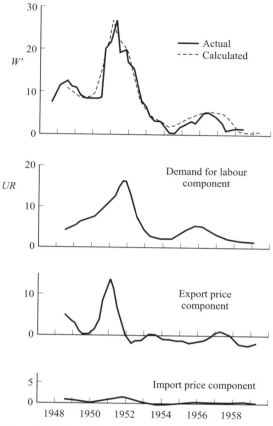

Figure 28.5 Hypothesis II

be about 1.2 per cent higher than this, say 3.5 per cent per year, and assuming a productivity increase of 2 per cent per year, this would mean that consumers' prices would rise about 1.5 per cent per year. The speed of inflation would increase if the demand for labour were held at a higher level, thus at 1 per cent unemployment wage rates would rise on average at about 4 per cent per year which would give about 3 per cent per year rise in consumers' prices. If demand were held at a level sufficient to reduce unemployment much below this level, the speed of inflation would be very greatly increased. Thus with unemployment at about 0.5 per cent we could expect wage and price changes of the order of 10 per cent per year.

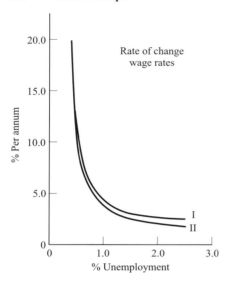

Figure 28.6 Rate of change

4 Policy implications

If the relationship which I have estimated is approximately the true one, it follows that the two main objectives of monetary and fiscal policy, namely full employment and stable prices, cannot be completely and simultaneously obtained without a change in the present attitudes to and methods of wage determination. Arguments for wage increases are usually put in terms of the need to increase money wages in order to increase real wages, or more strongly in terms of a conflict between labour and capital, an increase in money wages being needed to prevent capitalists from exploiting workers and grabbing too large a share of the national product. I think this line of argument is inappropriate under present conditions. I would question whether it is really in the interests of workers that the average level of hourly earnings should increase more rapidly than the average rate of increase of productivity, say about 2 per cent per year. The capitalist has control of the prices of the main products entering into consumption. The wage earner cannot prevent him from adjusting his prices in response to increasing costs. And if wages and prices rise together so that we have a steady inflation, it is not the capitalist who will lose by it. He owns real capital goods financed largely by borrowed money and so will usually gain relatively to workers as a result of inflation. The workers may gain temporarily from agriculturalists as a result of inflation since the prices of most agricultural commodities are determined in world markets, but if this process went very far it would have to be offset by a depreciation in the external value of the Australian pound which would restore the real incomes of agriculturalists. The group from which the workers can take real income by raising wages and prices is those living on fixed money incomes; mainly retired people, including workers.

The monetary and fiscal authorities may attempt to prevent the adjustment by capitalists of their prices to increasing costs when wage rates are rising rapidly by restricting the general demand for goods. I doubt whether such action would have much effect in squeezing profit margins on manufactured goods, but it would certainly have the effect of reducing the demand for labour and so increasing the level of unemployment. Is this really to the advantage of workers? I will go further. Is it really to the advantage of workers that the share of profits in the national product should be reduced? Technical innovation and capital expansion are financed mainly from profits and it is technical innovation and capital expansion which provide the continual increase in productivity which forms the only possible source of continuing increases in real wages.

It is not at all certain, however, that it is the attitude of workers and the power of trade unions that are mainly responsible for wage rates rising at an excessive rate when the demand for labour is high. It is quite possible that without any pressure from trade unions, the actual wage rates paid would rise under such conditions as a result of bidding for labour by employers. The fact that hourly earnings seem to have risen much more rapidly than award wage rates, particularly during the 1954–5 boom, would seem to indicate that employers were raising rates in the attempt to obtain suitable labour. This immediately raises the question of why employers may wish to raise wage rates in order to attract labour while there are still unemployed workers. Part of the answer clearly lies in the limited mobility of labour. The geographical and occupational distribution of labour may not be appropriate to the demand and cannot be quickly changed. It is likely that any measures that can be taken to increase the mobility and adaptability of labour would help to alleviate the problem of reconciling the objectives of high levels of employment and stable prices. I think that much more could be done by governments and other institutions. Assistance for technical training and retraining, the provision of more adequate housing facilities and granting of loans to assist in shifting one's place of residence are methods which come immediately to mind.

There is another factor, particularly strong in Australia, which seems to me to play a large part in increasing the speed at which wages rise, and so in increasing the level of unemployment which is compatible with stable prices. I refer to the practice of negotiating general wage changes covering workers in widely different groups of industries, occupations and areas. At any time there are some industries, occupations and areas which are developing rapidly and in which it is necessary to expand the labour force, and others which are developing less rapidly or are declining. The demand for labour in those which are expanding is likely to be dominant in determining general increases in wage rates. If those higher rates are automatically given also in the industries, occupations and areas where the demand for labour is not so high or is even declining, the average rate of increase of wages will clearly be higher than it would have been if the increase had been confined to the industries, occupations and areas in which the demand was high. Replacement of the practice of negotiating agreements covering wide groups of workers by a more flexible system of local negotiations would not only help to solve the problem of reconciling the objectives of full employment and stable prices, but would also lead to wage differentials more conducive to labour mobility and so would help to promote economic efficiency and economic progress.

Notes

This paper was written while I was Visiting Professor at the University of Melbourne. I wish to thank members of the Faculty of Economics and Commerce for suggestions and criticism.

1 The adjusted index E'' was calculated from the unadjusted index E' by the formula

$$E''_t = E'_t - 4.05 \frac{U_t + 1 - U_t - 1}{U_t},$$

where the subscript t denotes the time period and U is the percentage unemployment, as shown in figure 28.2. The coefficient 4.05 was obtained by minimising the sum of squares of $W'_t - E'$.

2 A four-quarter moving average has again been applied. Also the unemployment percentage for the third quarter of 1949 has been adjusted to eliminate the effect of the strike in the coal industry.

3 The regression equation is

$$W'_t = 1.463 \frac{1}{U^2_{t-3}} + 0.4145 \frac{1}{U^3_{t-3}} + 0.1498 \left\{ \frac{1}{2} \left(X'_{t-1} + X'_{t-2} \right) \right\}$$
$$+ 0.1337 M'_{t-3} + 2.110.$$

4 The regression equation is

$$W_t' = 0.570 W_{t-1}' + 0.932 \frac{1}{U_{t-2} - 0.26} + 0.0489 X_{t-1}''$$

$$+ 0.0222 M_{t-2}' + 0.295,$$

where $X_t'' = 50.0 \, (\exp 0.02 \, X_{t-1}')$.

A. W. H.

29 Phillips and Stabilisation Policy as a Threat to Stability

William J. Baumol   E31 E24 E63

B31 B22

Though we were both graduate students at the LSE, Bill Phillips arrived after I had left. Hence, I only met him after he had already joined the faculty. Even at our first meeting his delightful personality, kindliness and quick mind were all immediately evident. I can therefore say that I knew him, and that it is an enormous pleasure to be able to contribute to his *Collected Works*.

In chapter 16, a remarkable essay that emerged from his dissertation, Bill Phillips demonstrated that automatic stabilisation policies can exacerbate instability rather than contain it. Moreover, an adjustment of the parameters governing such a programme in the directions that common sense would suggest may well worsen the problem. The essay also offers an intuitive description of one process that can be taken to underlie the Phillips Curve. In addition, such a graph is drawn in the paper, though it is based neither on empirical data nor on any formal model. Nor does the discussion offer anything that can be used directly to meet the later monetarist challenge claiming to have demonstrated that in the long run the Phillips Curve must be vertical at 'the natural rate of unemployment'.

1 Those destabilising stabilisation policies

When, in 1960, I was writing my article, 'Pitfalls in Contracyclical Policies...', I was not aware that a paper demonstrating my main conclusions had already appeared in print six years earlier. The fault is only partly mine, for, with his usual modesty, Bill Phillips has eschewed melodramatics in describing these results. The paper, in fact, was devoted more to showing how a model of contracyclical programmes can be constructed. It can be considered primarily as a blueprint for the Phillips machine, using an engineer's control-theory approach to the matter. Yet, as a good essay should, the paper went well beyond mere description of a model and did draw out a number of important implications. The essay was written at a time when the monetarists were directing their artillery at those who advocated discretionary contracyclical programs and were suggesting that, if anything, policy designers should favour *automatic* measures, that is, built-in rules of monetary and budgetary behaviour that govern public sector intervention. At least the automatic measures avoid human delay, indecisiveness and inconsistent behaviour, as well as reducing the uncertainty that discretionary policy formulation imposes upon the economy. It was consequently not unimportant to explore any danger that the automatic measures may entail, and to this the essay makes an important contribution.

Before describing the model that led to the conclusions upon which I focus, let me first report those conclusions. In a series of graphs, the article shows the possible trajectories of national output in the wake of a shortfall of demand below the level of national output, with and without the imposition of various automatic contracyclical policies. Several of these graphs show that such programmes can impart cyclical behaviour to output, even where the time path would otherwise have been monotonic. Moreover, they show that the amplitude of the fluctuations can lead to troughs well below those that might otherwise have occurred, and may even yield explosive (unstable) oscillations whose amplitude grows without limit, or until (unspecified) non-linearities in the mechanism succeed in bounding the trajectory.

In Phillips' words (chapter 16, pp. 141–3), discussing his graph in which an automatic policy leads to unstable oscillation:

it will be seen that even with a low value of the [pertinent parameter], cyclical fluctuations of considerable magnitude are caused by this type of policy, and also that the approach to the desired value of production is very slow. Moreover, any attempt to speed up the process by adopting a stronger policy is likely to do more harm than good by increasing the violence of the cyclical fluctuations, particularly when the time lag of the correcting action is long. With [a fairly modest value of the correction parameter] and a correction lag of six months...the system [becomes] dynamically unstable. In such a case the oscillations would increase in amplitude until limited by non-linearities in the system and would then persist within these limits so long as the policy was continued.

The model that leads to these results and the type of correction policies considered are not too difficult to describe. Letting a subscript t represent the time derivative of a variable and changing Phillips' notation to symbols that are now more common, the fundamental equation is a distributed lag between national output, Y, and the incentive for adjustment constituted by the shortfall of quantity demanded, Q, below the level of Y

$$Y_t = a(Y - Q). \tag{1}$$

In the absence of intervention by the public sector, the quantity demanded is determined by output, so that

$$Q = (1 - s)Y + u, \tag{2}$$

where s is the marginal propensity to save, or some other leakage coefficient and u is the autonomous level of saving. The two general types of correction policies that are considered are described as a (lagged) 'proportional stabilisation policy', and an 'integral stabilisation policy', that is also lagged. The former is a correction of output demand proportionate to the (lagged) shortfall, contributing an addition to the rate of growth of demand equal to

$$Q_t^* = b(Y - Q). \tag{3}$$

In contrast, an integral stabilisation policy seeks to make up not only for the current shortfall, but for the *accumulated* deficiency of demand below output that has occurred over the entire pertinent period. This contributes an addition to demand growth given by

$$Q_t^{**} = k \int (Y - Q)dt. \tag{4}$$

If we differentiate (1) and (2) with respect to t, add (3) to the differentiated (2) and substitute this for Q_t in the differentiated (1) we end up with a second-order differential equation in Y alone (since the differentiation of (1) will have given us an equation for the second time derivative of Y). As is well known, the solution to such an equation can entail complex roots and so can provide an oscillatory trajectory. However, his unstable trajectory is derived by Phillips from his integral stabilisation policy equation (4), which itself must be differentiated with respect to t in order to rid it of the integral. Next, proceeding as before to add differentiated (4) into the differentiated demand equation (2) and substituting the result for Q_t in the differentiated basic relation (1) we again obtain a differential equation in Y, but this time of third order. It is that equation, when plotted, that yields the unstable trajectories in the graphs.

Phillips is able to show that the addition of an investment demand governed by the acceleration principle leads to similar conclusions. Moreover, because flexibility of input prices can increase the real money supply *cumulatively* when output exceeds the corresponding demand (the Pigou effect), this can raise the demand for output in the manner described by (4), also threatening instability in the manner just described.

2 Toward a theory of the Phillips Curve

It has been said that the Phillips Curve was an apparent empirical relationship with no theory upon which to base itself. However, in chapter 16, Phillips (pp. 150–1]) not only describes his curve, and draws it on an *a priori* basis, but he also offers us, in literary terms, a theory of its workings:

if factor prices have some degree of flexibility, there will be changes in product prices resulting from the changes which take place in factor prices. Even with flexible factor prices, there will be some level of production and employment which, given the bargaining powers of the different groups in the economy, will just result in the average level of factor prices remaining constant, this level of production and employment being lower, the stronger and more aggressive the organisation of the factors of production. If aggregate real demand is high enough to make a higher level of production than this profitable, entrepreneurs will be more anxious to obtain (and to retain) the services of labour and other factors of production and so less inclined to resist demands for higher wages and other factor rewards. Factor prices will therefore rise. The level of demand being high, the rising costs will be passed on in the form of higher product prices. Factor and product prices will continue to rise in this way so long as the high level of demand and production is maintained, the rate at which they rise being greater, the higher the level of demand and production.

Conversely, if aggregate real demand is so low that production at the level which would result in constant factor prices is unprofitable, entrepreneurs will be more anxious to force down factor prices, while at the lower level of employment factors will be less able to press for higher rewards and more inclined to accept lower rewards. Factors prices will therefore gradually move downwards, and the level of demand being low, the falling costs will be reflected in falling product prices. Prices will continue to fall in this way so long as demand and production remain low, the rate of fall being greater, the lower the level of demand and production.

We may therefore postulate a relationship between the level of production and the rate of change of factor prices, which is probably of the form shown in Figure 16.11, the fairly sharp bend in the curve where it passes through zero rate of change of prices being the result of the greater rigidity of factor prices in the downward than in the upward direction. The relationship between the level of production and the rate of change of product prices will be of a similar shape if productivity is constant. In spite of the marked curvature of the relationship, linearity may be assumed as an approximation for small changes in production. If the desired level of production is now taken to be that which would result in a constant level of product prices, we may say that the rate of change of product prices will be approximately proportional to the deviation of production from this level, i.e., to the error in production, this approximation being better, the smaller the fluctuations which occur in production.

This, then, is a literary version of a theory of the Phillips Curve. It is, unfortunately, one that may be vulnerable to the criticism of the monetarists, who note that if, in the wake of a policy-induced cut in unemployment, a rate of inflation higher than before persists for a period sufficiently long, then the higher wage demands generated by low unemployment and the weakened resistance of employers will take that enhanced inflation rate into account. The bargaining will result in a wage higher in expected *real* terms, after adjustment for the inflation generated by the previous bargaining process. Thus, the second-round wage negotiations will contribute to an inflation rate higher than the first, and a third and subsequent rounds will each produce still greater acceleration of inflation. Real-balance effects and other related influences will, as a result, gradually drain the demand for output and restore unemployment to its natural rate. On this argument, then, there is a non-trivial trade-off between inflation and unemployment – a substantive Phillips Curve – only in the short run.

In my essay for Bill Phillips' *festschrift*, I argued that a Phillips Curve, stable in the long run and entailing no money illusion, can be derived on other bases (Baumol 1978). I should now like to add one further argument to my earlier discussion. In my article, in deriving a stable long-run Phillips Curve, I constructed a model that employed the assumption $gp_c = gw_c$, where g is the growth-rate operator, so that gp_c represents the percentage rate of growth per period in the dynamic equilibrium price level. The other term represents the growth rate of equilibrium money wages. The equilibrium growth rate of wages is assumed to be an increasing function of x^*, the target percentage excess total demand for labour (presumably negative) aimed at by governmental fiscal and monetary policy. The assumption that in equilibrium wages and prices must grow at the same rate, however, seems to imply that in the long run government policy cannot change *real* wages. Therefore, the rate of growth of prices cannot be in a stable equilibrium when policy raises the demand for labour. For an upward shift in the demand curve for labour resulting from a governmentally induced increase in x^* must be presumed to raise the *real* wage demanded by workers, an aim pursued through an increase in money wages. If, in equilibrium, prices follow suit, then workers, disappointed in their first attempt to raise real wages, will subsequently demand an increase in nominal wages that more than compensates for the rise in price level, and so the acceleration of prices and wages must be under way.

However, I would now note that the pertinent changes must be studied by means of comparative dynamics, and must be taken to entail the substitution of a permanently higher value of x^* for an alternative x^* that is permanently lower. It seems clear that in the wake of such a substitution, real wages can well be increased. That is, the trajectory of money wages will shift upward under the higher x^* value, and may well do so by more than the trajectory of prices, even though both share the same permanent time derivatives, as they do when the x^* assumes its lower value. This can happen, if the rise in money wages at any given date is not matched by an equiproportionate rise in the prices of other inputs, thereby redistributing income in labour's favour. But even if there is no redistribution, the very increase in employment that government policy elicits must increase total output by virtue of the fact that idle hands have been put to work.

This has three consequences. Total output is now larger than before at any given moment of time, less of it need be devoted to the support of unemployed workers, and that net output must now be divided among a larger labour force – the three effects giving the new level of real wages. It should be obvious that the first two effects make for an increase in real wages while the third serves to reduce it. It is easy to prove for the case where labour is the only source of income that if returns to scale are not sharply diminishing, the net results will be a net increase in real wages. A few illustrative calculations suggest that the rise can be substantial. Hence, in a comparative dynamics experiment, a rise in net demand for labour induced by government policy may well increase real wages, perhaps even by more than the supply curve of labour calls for. Thus, though inflation will be raised, it need not be accelerated by a government attempt to stimulate employment, as is contended by proponents of the natural rate of unemployment hypothesis.

30 The Phillips Curve in Macroeconomics and Econometrics

L.R. Klein

B23 B22 E31 E24 B31 E63

Personal remembrances

Bill Phillips was a remarkable person, and in working up to the subject of the Phillips Curve, it may be useful for me to reminisce a bit about my memories of him. Our last encounter was in 1971, after he had returned to Auckland, smitten by a stroke. I was on a visit and asked if I could see Bill, when I was not fulfilling the separate purposes of my trip.

I drove to his home at an appropriate morning hour and passed him, on foot, making measured small steps, one at a time returning from his morning stroll. I waited at his doorstep and subsequently had a strained conversation in his home with the help of Mrs Phillips who acted somewhat as an interpreter. It was evident that the stroke had laid low the person that I remember from England of the mid 1950s, full of exuberance, fresh ideas and optimism about our subject. We had good opportunities then to discuss wages, inflation, unemployment and the many promising leads for econometric research, when he visited Oxford for a seminar at the Institute of Statistics.

I was able to tell him about an interesting and amusing incident concerning the hydraulic machine. Prior to my coming to Oxford, I had been at the University of Michigan, in Ann Arbor. One day, in 1952 or 1953, Abba Lerner came by to visit Kenneth Boulding. Abba told us (a group of young economists) why he was passing through – to deliver a working model of the Phillips Machine to General Motors, where Andrew Court was a chief economist. Abba was fascinated by the device, as was Kenneth Boulding, who had developed the 'bath-tub theorem' for pedagogical purposes in an elementary textbook. Abba, as sales agent in the US, was extremely proud to announce that the complicated device was shipped in a compact, unassembled package, and that he would put the working model together based on his logical analysis of the way it had looked in operation and the way the economy should function.

We economists were invited to General Motors headquarters in Detroit for a working demonstration. When the Ann Arbor group arrived, everything seemed to be in order, and Abba started the demonstration with flowing, coloured water. We noted that the flow eventually seemed to be slowing, in demonstration of a recessionary build-up. Andy Court insisted, loudly, that Abba should call in the FED, to ease monetary conditions, but Abba resisted, with a strong plea for patience.

The exchange between Abba and Andy became heated to the point at which Andy challenged Abba to a wager, in the neighbourhood of five or ten dollars. Abba took up the wager, assured that the hydraulic system would soon enter a recovery phase of the simulated business cycle, but after a few more minutes, without calling in the FED, the flow stopped completely, and it appeared that the Phillips Machine was totally drained. The economy had come to a complete halt. After some more minutes of detailed examination it was discovered that a valve had inadvertently been left open, sending all the water into a *foreign drain!* Abba lost the wager. The machine was later donated by General Motors to a local university for teaching purposes.

We spent the greater part of a day thinking about and analysing one simulation, but Bill Phillips was simply ahead of his time, before electronic circuits would be able to duplicate the painstaking movements through hydraulic circuits in microseconds rather than minutes or hours.

The Phillips Curve

Bill Phillips' career in econometrics spanned, for me at least, four major contributions
1. The hydraulic machine
2. Wage determination
3. Control theory
4. Time series analysis
Although I discussed all these issues with him and benefited greatly from his stimulating ideas, I feel closer to the discussions dealing with wage determination. As I have been dismantling my own library for use at the University of Pennsylvania, I ventured into the University Library stacks in order to re-examine his celebrated article of 1958 (chapter 25). I was struck by the fact that our library's bound volumes of *Economica* (volume 25) had a 'Xerox' copy of his article taped into the volume because some student was so eager to have a personal copy that the original printing was sliced away from the binding. The librarian had the good sense to provide a replacement for future generations of students who will surely want to ponder over this important contribution.

The importance of this article, and the very concept of the Phillips Curve, is that it provides an important link – for me, *the missing link* – in the chain of relationships that lead to determination of the absolute price level and inflation in the Keynesian system, indeed in a much wider class of macroeconomic models, known as the Keynesian–neoclassical synthesis.

In the period after the Second World War in Britain, and in other industrial countries, it was often remarked that the economy was on a 'labour standard', meaning that the agents of labour, the trade unions in most cases, had a great deal of influence on wage rates, and these, in turn, had strong effects on price levels and the rate of inflation. It was implied that the wage influence through trade union power supplanted monetary influence through central bank power. Eventually, these and other power sources played different roles of relative importance, but during the 1950s the role of labour was of extreme importance in Great Britain. The situation was not everywhere the same, and power has been shared. The world became more conservative, and gradually monetary authorities gained power, in a relative sense. Even in those countries where the head of the central bank is often said to be the second most powerful person in the nation – as is the case in the USA – both the central bank head and the central bank watchers in financial markets keep very close eyes on wage rates to see if the labour market, behaving along the lines described by Bill Phillips, will confirm, or deny, or partially obstruct the attainment of monetary policy targets.

While it is true that dedicated exponents of monetarism would like to get rid of the Phillips Curve, it persists as one of the most enduring macroeconometric relationships in industrial countries, operating according to the laws of markets, in this case the phases of labour markets. It can be ignored only at the peril of making incorrect policy assessments.

In judging the theoretical and analytical importance of the concept of the Phillips Curve, it is useful to consider Bill Phillips' carefully worded title and also his opening remarks in the 1958 article. In loose and very approximate reasoning, the Phillips Curve is said to provide a relationship between inflation and unemployment or inflation and output change. It is imperative, however, to distinguish between derived trade-off relationships and structural equations in a theory-based model.

It is clear that Bill Phillips looked upon the Phillips Curve as a structural relationship that shows how the labour market functions. He noted that the law of supply and demand states that excess supply is associated with price decreases, while excess demand is associated with price increases in the given market, the degree of decrease or increase being a function of the size of the supply–demand imbalance. The labour market, dealing with services of labour, should obey this law in the same way that goods markets try to clear, through price movement in the face of supply–demand imbalances.

Having this structural specification, he assembled data on wage rates, and their changes, and unemployment rates, and their changes, in the United Kingdom for historical time periods. Inflation and output changes are related to wage changes and unemployment rates, but they are definitely not identical. In the wake of the oil embargo in 1973–4, many economists cited strongly rising prices and rising unemployment or falling output as evidence that the Phillips Curve had broken down. The stagflation of that era did not contradict the Phillips Curve relation because structural models ought to have the property of generating a positive association between inflation and unemployment (negative with output change) under the impact of a supply-side shock – many kinds of supply-side shocks, not just energy price shocks.

A crucial factor standing between wage change and price change (inflation) is productivity, which reversed normal direction and took a turn for the worse after the first oil shock in 1973–4.

There are three other aspects of the Phillips Curve that need clarification:
  (i) shape of the relationship
 (ii) time span of the relationship
(iii) 'third' factors.

(i) In the original investigations, it was recognised that an inverse relationship existed between wage changes and unemployment, but it is usually the case in quantitative economics that we cannot always specify a unique parametric expression for empirical relationships or regularities. We usually choose a linear expression or some kind of logarithmic (or semi-logarithmic) transformation. In some cases other forms of non-linearity merit investigation. In the original article, Bill Phillips readily detected curvature in the relationship at either very low or very high rates of unemployment. A relationship between wage change and the reciprocal of the unemployment rate has frequently been used to show these extreme movements.

(ii) Market reactions are not instantaneous, especially in the presence of such institutional characteristics of labour markets as trade unions, wage tribunals, employer federations, labour laws, contract rules. These institutions and practices should naturally indicate that the time shape of market reaction should be built into a careful statistical specification of the Phillips Curve. Bill Phillips considered both the level and rate of change of unemployment as relevant variables. This is equivalent to using a one-period distributed lag. I would prefer to be more general and explore, depending on the economy being investigated, multi-period lag distributions.

In addition, theoretical economists argued about whether the curve had specific shapes in the short and the long run. Very short-run relationships matter a great deal to central bankers and other policy makers who are concerned about inflation. They must pay much attention to the Phillips Curve on a month-by-month basis, and for as long as prevailing labour contracts are in force – say one to three years. Strict monetarists, and some real business-cycle theorists, may be more concerned with the indefinitely long run. They claim or assert, without documentation, that the Phillips Curve is vertical in the long run.

Amendments that introduce more general lag distributions are 'friendly'; those that make the curve vertical are 'unfriendly'. They are made by economists who want to substitute their own brand of wage and price determination for those implied by Phillips Curve analysis. The original sample and historical analyses carried out by Bill Phillips indicate to me that he was giving a long-run interpretation to his findings. In contrast to the monetarists and other critics who would like to banish the influence of the Phillips Curve, he had some evidence. It is ironic that whenever monetarist thinkers point to the success of their policies, as in the heavy-handed tactics of the 1980s in Europe and North America, they have had to rely on labour market reactions, of a Phillips type, in order to realise their objective of inflation reduction. Presently they closely monitor wage developments for early warning signals about the way their efforts are going.

(iii) Economists generally try to avoid the complications of multivariate data-intensive analyses. In these respects, Phillips' original concept of a labour market adjustment relationship between excess supply or demand for workers and wage fluctuation has been ill-treated. It can be a 'friendly' amendment to look for various third factors that account for changes in the labour market environment in order to keep the basic relationship intact.

There have been significant demographic changes, such as the baby-boom, subsequent tendencies towards smaller families, single-parent families, female participation in the paid labour force, immigration waves. In addition to the strict demographic changes, there have been institutional changes such as the social welfare system to deal with family matters, unemployment compensation, and the decline of trade union power in the USA. These changes, both demographic and institutional, have given rise to a consideration of a more complicated specification for the wage equation in the last two or three decades. The basic underlying relationship between wage change and unemployment persists, but to get stable relationships that hold up well in a macroeconometric context, it is necessary to estimate wage equations with additional variables that were not considered in the original formulation.

The original title of chapter 25 specifies that the relationship is between *money* wage rates and unemployment. It is simply an extension of the concept to explore whether or not *real* wage rates should be considered instead of money wage rates and inflation rates should be considered simultaneously, as separate variables. In the original article there are explicit considerations of a price variable, but it was not proposed for the usual case; it was mainly considered in connection with unusual increases in import prices. Given the original interpretation of the curve, as a structural representation of bargaining in the labour market according to the laws of supply and demand, we should recognise that a cost-of-living-adjustment (COLA) has always been on the table since the Second World War. There are many reasons why market imperfections have kept wages and prices from moving in a strict proportional relationship; so an incomplete COLA is plausible. Also there is some time lag, and in recent years projections of prices (inflation expectations) have become relevant. This was not always so, and specific allowances have been made for exchange rate movements, tax changes, and other particular changes in price levels. It makes sense, therefore, for one to be open minded about the size of the price coefficient as well as the representation of expected inflation, but some amplification of the equation for COLA does not undermine Bill Phillips' concept of the relationship.

A by-product of the Phillips Curve is the calculation of the critical point, or region, at which wage increases accelerate when labour market conditions become tight, that is, move strongly toward excess demand for labour. Economists are presently preoccupied with calculation of the unemployment rate at full employment.

This policy application is very important and is an outgrowth of the original finding by Bill Phillips, but it is an extension that he did not deal with explicitly. The estimates of the so-called natural rate of unemployment and the interpretations of the Phillips Curve as a supply function fail to perceive the underlying meaning of the two-sided labour market adjustment process that was originally intended. It is not possible to determine the critical values of the unemployment rate at full employment without simultaneously embedding labour demand relationships, labour supply relationships, and labour market supply–demand bargaining relationships (the Phillips Curve) within a complete system, together with credible definitions of accelerating inflation and also full employment. This exercise has not been done properly, and we have many short-cut estimates of unemployment at full employment that lack credibility. Generally speaking, the estimates reflect economists' willingness to accept very high and changing rates of unemployment. I doubt that the author of the Phillips Curve had this development in mind in 1958.

The lasting role of the Phillips Curve in the history of economic thought

For the Keynesian theory of macroeconomics, and for the active role of government in stabilising the macroeconomy, the Phillips Curve serves as an important link in the determination of the absolute level of wages and prices. It does not fulfil this role alone, but as an important, indeed key, link in a system of relationships. For the policies that hold promise to lead to full employment without accelerating inflation it is an important ingredient in the use of incomes policy.

From the non-interventionist school, who attach extreme importance to orthodox monetary policy for controlling inflation, there have been derogatory commentaries about the Phillips Curve – its existence, particularly in the long run, its relevance, or its reliability. Yet, implicitly, I would claim that they rely on it. Those economies that have aimed for and achieved *zero* inflation through stringent monetary policy, Canada and, ironically New Zealand, have paid the price of high unemployment. Maybe the high unemployment will recede, but in the process of getting to zero inflation and in the period that has already elapsed since attaining that goal, a significant and predictable cost has been incurred, knowing what we do about the Phillips Curve.

In the implementation of monetary policy in the United States, the Federal Reserve authorities have admittedly focused on two key indicators, the potential growth rate and the unemployment rate at full employment (NAIRU, the non-accelerating-inflation-rate-of-unemployment). Apart from the particular values that have been estimated for these two concepts, it is important to note that versions of the Phillips Curve are used in a critical way. In this sense, chapter 25 has played a lasting role in policy setting, although it was not the original thought that its influence would be felt in this way.

Some thoughts about control theory and time series analysis

In this brief statement, I have referred to the ingenious research on the Phillips Machine and the Phillips Curve. I would like to close with some speculative thoughts about two other creative lines of research that Bill

Phillips initiated. They deal with control theory and time series analysis in econometrics.

Before he published the paper on the Phillips Curve in 1958, Bill Phillips wrote two stimulating articles on engineering techniques for stabilising an economy (chapters 16 and 17). These techniques attempted to make corrections for the level, the accumulation (integral) and the rate-of-change (derivative) of error in system performance. They were used to good advantage in a doctoral dissertation of Vijaya Duggal (1967)[1] that I supervised (in part) for Harvard. The applications were made to the Brookings Model of the US economy. Phillips' ideas proved to be extremely fruitful for early applications in econometrics. I wonder what Bill might have achieved for economics in the field of control theory had he lived a healthy existence into the era of the intensive research into this subject after the early 1970s when he was already ill.

Bill Phillips had many advanced ideas about time series analysis for econometrics and circulated important unpublished papers on this subject during the 1960s. During the previous decade, however, Maurice Kendall tried to marshal the econometric-statistics talent in London to provide a fresh approach to problems of economic prediction and policy analysis. Bill Phillips was involved in that collaboration. On the occasion of a visit to Oxford, Maurice Kendall told me that the main stumbling block for this effort was the extreme difficulty in assembling adequate data bases of informative statistics at high frequency – monthly or finer.

I appreciate the difficulties that they encountered, and I wonder what Bill Phillips might have achieved if he had had access, that we routinely possess now, to thousands of time series at a choice of high frequencies, especially in financial markets; powerful computers that are readily available; and versatile software that is able to handle many mathematical complications. My feeling is that he would have been able to go far towards Maurice Kendall's objectives and would have done insightful things in the field of optimal control.

We econometricians have much to be thankful about in drawing on Bill Phillips' accomplishments and would have had much more were it not for the comparative brevity of his life.

Note

1 Some main findings are reported in Duggal (1975).

31 Bill Phillips' Contribution to Dynamic Stabilisation Policy

Stephen J. Turnovsky

Bill Phillips made a fundamental contribution to dynamic stabilisation policy and to the application of control methods to this issue. His contribution is contained in chapters 16 and 17, a pair of essays originally published in the *Economic Journal*. These essays draw upon his background as an engineer and are the first papers to apply feedback control methods to the stabilisation of a macroeconomy. Today that is a burgeoning field, and despite certain challenges stemming from the subsequent development of rational expectations, the application of control methods is now an integral part of the analysis of dynamic economic systems. In fact the Society of Economic Dynamics and Control (now the Society of Economic Dynamics) and the *Journal of Economic Dynamics and Control*, originally developed in 1979 to foster the application of control methods to economics, are both now firmly established within the profession.[1]

Phillips' contribution, like many fundamental contributions, was a simple one. Previously, Samuelson (1939) and Hicks (1950) had shown how if one combines the multiplier in consumption with the accelerator in investment, one can derive a dynamic equation determining the evolution of national income (output). The precise nature of this dynamic relationship depends upon the types of lags one considered and many variants of such relationships are possible. The dynamics can be expressed in discrete time, as by Samuelson and Hicks, or in continuous time, as for example illustrated by R.G.D. Allen (1956) and used by Phillips himself. Phillips took these simple aggregate models and showed how if one introduces a government that, instead of remaining passive follows some active policy rule, then it will be able to influence the dynamic time path of the economy and thereby influence the welfare of the agents.

1 Phillips' policy rules

The basic ideas can be illustrated using the following simple model. Consider an economy in which the evolution of national income, $Y(t)$, is related to a policy variable, government expenditure say, $G(t)$, by the simple first-order linear differential equation

$$\dot{Y}(t) = aY(t) + bG(t), \tag{1}$$

where a, b are constants and the dot denotes a time derivative. This equation tells us how output changes over time given the current level of output and the current decisions of the government. If the policy variable remains constant at $G(t) = \bar{G}$ then output will converge to the stationary equilibrium level $\bar{Y} = b\bar{G}/(1 - a)$.

Within this simple framework, Phillips' important contribution was to treat government expenditure as a policy variable that is continuously adjusted to meet certain specified objectives. In his analysis he emphasised the lags associated with adjusting the policy instrument itself (policy lags), in addition to the lags inherent in the dynamics of the system (system lags). He assumed that the policy actually implemented at any point in time adjusts with an exponential lag to past policy decisions. Thus, if $G^d(t)$ is the desired value of the policy variable chosen at time t (the policy decision), the actual value of the policy variables, $G(t)$, is adjusted in accordance with

$$\dot{G}(t) = \beta(G^d(t) - G(t)) \quad \beta > 0.$$

The desired value of the policy variable, $G^d(t)$, is related according to some rule to the ultimate target objective, which he took to be the stabilisation of national income. Phillips considered three such policy rules, which he called: (i) proportional policy, (ii) integral policy and (iii) derivative policy. They all influenced the dynamics of the economy in different ways, having both desirable and undesirable effects on its evolution.

For our purposes we shall ignore the presence of policy lags, so that $G^d(t) \equiv G(t)$. The proportional policy is specified by

$$G(t) = -\gamma(Y - Y^*) \quad \gamma > 0, \tag{2a}$$

where Y^* is the target level of output. The parameter γ represents the intensity of the policy maker's response when output deviates from its target. For the specific example being considered, the assumption $\gamma > 0$ is natural, but in other applications a positive deviation in the target may call for a negative adjustment in the policy instrument. When combined with the basic dynamic equation (1), this leads to the autonomous differential equation

$$\dot{Y} = (a - b\gamma)Y + \gamma Y^*. \tag{3}$$

Two observations about this equation are worth noting. The first is that by appropriate choice of γ, the policy maker can always stabilise the system. Instability in an uncontrolled system can therefore be eliminated. Second, and less favourably, income in (3) converges to the steady state level $\bar{Y} = \gamma Y^*/(b\gamma - a)$, which in general does not coincide with the desired (target) level Y^*. This latter deficiency can be easily remedied, however, by modifying the rule (2a) to

$$G(t) - G^* = -\gamma(Y - Y^*) \tag{2a$'$}$$

and choosing $G^* = -(a/b)Y^*$, thereby ensuring that income converges to its target, Y^*.

The integral policy specifies policy in terms of the integral of past deviations in income from its target, rather than only the current deviation, namely

$$G(t) = -\gamma \int_0^t [Y(s) - Y^*]ds \quad \gamma > 0. \tag{2b}$$

Differentiating with respect to t enables the policy to be written in the equivalent form

$$\dot{G}(t) = -\gamma[Y(t) - Y^*]. \tag{2b$'$}$$

Expressed in this way, the rule asserts that the policy variable should be increased if output is above its target, and decreased otherwise. It is the form of policy adjustment rule specified by Mundell (1962) and others in their analysis of the assignment problem, relating the appropriate adjustment of policy instruments to targets.

Taken together, equations (1a) and (2b$'$) comprise a pair of dynamic equations in $Y(t)$ and $G(t)$. This yields two differences from the proportional rule. First, by appropriate choice of policy parameter, γ, convergence to the desired income target Y^*, is ensured. Second, with the dynamics being generated by a pair of first-order differential equations (making it equivalent to a second-order system), it becomes possible for the transitional adjustment to involve cyclical behaviour, so that the economy overshoots its target during the transition.

The third policy introduced by Phillips, the derivative policy, is of the form

$$G(t) = -\gamma \dot{Y}(t) \quad \gamma > 0.$$

In this case, the policy instrument responds to the rate of change of income, behaving like a 'negative accelerator'. For an appropriately chosen γ this can stabilise an otherwise unstable system, although it will not succeed in driving income to its target level.

Phillips also proposed combining these three policy rules, showing that this enables the various desirable features of the individual policies to be preserved. For example, the presence of the integral component ensures that income converges to its target, while at the same time undesired cyclical adjustments associated with this policy can be reduced with the simultaneous use of the proportional and derivative policies. Phillips' application of these rules was to fiscal policy, but they are equally applicable to problems of monetary stabilisation policy.[2] They also formed the basis for simulation studies of both monetary and fiscal policy in larger macro-models.[3]

2 Linear quadratic optimal stabilisation

The policy rules proposed by Phillips, while plausible, were arbitrary. Beginning in the 1960s, interest developed in the question of optimal stabilisation policy. The framework employed to address this issue was the linear-quadratic system.[4] In general, this can be outlined as follows. Consider an economy summarised by n state (target) variables, x, and m control (policy) variables, u. Without any loss of generality these can be assumed to be linked by the linear vector system

$$\dot{x} = Ax + Bu, \qquad (4a)$$

where A is an $n \times n$ matrix and B is an $n \times m$ matrix. Assume further that the objective is to minimise the quadratic cost function

$$\int_0^\infty [x'Mx + u'Nu]dt, \qquad (4b)$$

where M, N are positive definite matrices representing the costs of: (i) having the target variables deviate from their desired optimal values (taken to be zero); (ii) having the policy variables deviate from their corresponding optimal values. (Prime denotes vector transpose.) The optimal policy vector, $\hat{u}$, is a linear feedback rule of the form

$$\hat{u} = -N^{-1}B'Px, \qquad (5a)$$

where P is the unique positive semi-definite solution to the matrix equation

$$M + A'P + PA - PBN^{-1}B'P = 0. \qquad (5b)$$

The critical thing to note about this solution is that the optimal policy is a linear feedback control law, in which in general all of the control variables are linear functions of all of the current state variables. This can be characterised as being a kind of 'generalised proportional' policy of the type proposed by Phillips in chapter 16. Much of the interest in stabilisation policy was in stochastic systems, for which the optimal stabilisation policy is of the same general form (Turnovsky 1973).

Let us now consider some special cases. First, if the system is a purely scalar one, such as in equation (1) above, the optimal policy (5a) is correspondingly a purely proportional one, being of essentially the same form as originally proposed by Phillips. The only difference, and it is an important one, is that the policy variable is measured about its long-run desired equilibrium, which in the above formulation is normalised to zero. Turnovsky (1973) discusses the case of a multiplier-accelerator model in which investment occurs with an exponential lag and shows how the optimal policy in that case is a mixture of Phillips' proportional and integral policies. Furthermore, if the dynamics can be represented by a second-order differential equation (as can easily be done in some variants of the Samuelson–Hicks model of the business cycle), the optimal policy can be written as the sum of a purely proportional plus a derivative component (Turnovsky 1977). Other examples can also be found, but we have made the point that the form of policy rules proposed by Phillips in chapter 16 played a central role in the early applications of optimal control theory to stabilisation policy.

3 The challenge of rational expectations

The dynamic system considered by Phillips, as well as the early applications of dynamic control theory, are of the classical type in that all variables are assumed to evolve continuously from some given initial condition. In the jargon of modern macro-dynamics, all variables are 'sluggish'. This reflects the fact that economists were using the traditional techniques of differential equations as developed by applied mathematicians and engineers, which of course was consistent with Phillips' own background.

However, the development of rational expectations and its application to macro-dynamics in the 1970s introduced the notion that some economic variables, most notably financial variables, are forward looking. It is realistic to permit these variables to respond instantaneously to new information as it impinges on the economy, instead of assuming that they must evolve gradually from the past. They are said to be 'jump' variables. As Sargent and Wallace (1973) demonstrated, sensible economic behaviour of an economy represented by such a system requires the underlying differential equation to be inherently unstable, with the forward-looking variable (in their case the price level) jumping so as to ensure that the economy follows a bounded (stable) adjustment path. Most economic dynamic systems consist of a combination of sluggish variables, such as physical capital, which by their nature can be accumulated only gradually, and forward-looking jump variables, such as exchange rates, or financial variables, which are not so constrained. As a consequence, the standard dynamic macroeconomic system embodying rational expectations has a combination of stable and unstable dynamics, with the case of a unique convergent saddlepath arising when the number of unstable roots equals the number of jump variables.

This represents a fundamentally different approach to macroeconomic dynamics from the earlier literature. In addition, the introduction of rational expectations has had a profound effect on the application of control methods to stabilisation policy. Three issues are involved. The first arises from issues relating to the 'Lucas Critique' and 'Policy Neutrality'. As we have seen, the objective of stabilisation policy is to influence the time path of some target variable, say output. Lucas (1976) observed that for the authority to do so under the assumption that the coefficients describing the evolution of the target remain fixed and invariant with respect to its chosen policy is non-rational. In the dynamic system, (1), the structural parameters, a, b, will in general vary with the chosen policy parameter, γ. This dependence needs to be taken into account in determining the optimal stabilisation policy rule. But the matter of policy neutrality goes further. Sargent and Wallace (1976) argued that under rational expectations, only unanticipated policy changes can have real effects, so that any feedback policy rule, such as the Phillips' rules, will have no effect on output. In our example, the time path of output would become independent of the policy parameter γ. It turns out that the policy neutrality proposition, most damaging to the potential use of control theory as a tool of stabilisation policy, is not robust to model specification, and feedback rules may still indeed be highly effective in stabilising output.[5]

The second issue is the computation of optimal feedback rules in a situation in which some variables are free to jump instantaneously. The solution to this problem is straightforward. Currie and Levine (1985) have shown how in a system embodying rational expectations, one can partition the dynamic variables into predetermined (sluggish) variables and non-predetermined (jump) variables while taking account of the saddlepoint structure associated with the rational expectations equilibrium. For the usual quadratic loss function, the result is a linear feedback rule in which the control variables are expressed as linear functions of only the predetermined (state) variables. The comments we made in section 2 concerning the relationship of such rules to those proposed by Phillips continue to apply.

The third issue arising when the system contains forward-looking jump variables is the question of the 'time consistency' of optimal policy. This is the issue of whether or not a future policy decision that forms part of an optimal plan formulated at some initial date is still optimal when considered at some later date, even though no relevant information has changed in the meantime. If it is not, the optimal plan is said to be time inconsistent. This problem was first introduced by Kydland and Prescott (1977) who argued that the problem of time inconsistency has grave implications for the application of control theory methods to problems of economic stabilisation. In the abstract to their paper they write: 'We conclude that there is no way control theory can be made applicable to economic planning when expectations are rational.' In the conclusions they argue:

active stabilisation may very well be dangerous and it is best that it not be attempted. Reliance on policies such as a constant growth in the money supply and constant tax rates constitute a safer course of action.

The question of time consistency (or inconsistency) still remains, and attempts to resolve it have generated a lot of research. The pursuit of time inconsistent policies will eventually cause the government to lose credibility and issues such as commitment and reputational equilibria have been analysed by a number of authors.[6] One simple solution, very much within the spirit of the linear-quadratic framework, is the following. As noted, the attainment of a rational expectations equilibrium involves an initial jump in the forward-looking variable. These initial jumps impose real dislocational costs on the economy, and these should be taken into account in the design of the optimal policy system. Stemp and Turnovsky (1987) show that if these initial costs are large enough it may cease to be optimal for the policy maker to reoptimise along a transitional path. In other words, the costs imposed on the economy in revising an initial plan may be too high to make this an optimal thing to do. Instead, the policy maker sticks with the original policy, thereby rendering it time consistent.

In summary, the implementation of rational expectations presented a serious challenge to the use of control theory as an instrument of macroeconomic stabilisation policy. But it is fair to say that macroeconomists have accepted the challenge and that the methods of control theory are still being applied with success to dynamic macro-models involving rational expectations.

4 Simple versus complicated rules

Despite the fact that the generic form of the optimal policy rule is the generalised proportional policy as set out in (5), from a practical point of view the policy may turn out to be quite complicated to compute, especially for a large system. This leads to the question of the gains from applying optimal control over using some simple, but reasonable policy such as the three rules proposed by Phillips. This is an old question dating back to Friedman (1961) and early discussions of policy rules versus discretionary policy. Recent work by Feldstein and Stock (1993) has revisited this question in an analysis where the objective is to target nominal income. They reach the conclusion that there is little difference between a very simple adaptive rule and an optimal policy. If this kind of proposition is robust, then simple policy rules of the type originally proposed by Bill Phillips will continue to play an important role in the stabilisation of dynamic economic systems.

Notes

1 Recently, the creation of two other specific journals, *Macroeconomic Dynamics* and the *Review of Economic Dynamics* (the official journal of the renamed Society of Economic Dynamics), are further evidence of the growth of this field.
2 See, for example, Lovell and Prescott (1968).
3 See, for example, Cooper and Fischer (1974).
4 See, for example, Athans and Falb (1966).
5 See, for example, Turnovsky (1980).
6 See, for example, Barro and Gordon (1983b); and Backus and Driffill (1985).

32   A Left Keynesian View of the Phillips Curve Trade-Off

G.C. Harcourt

E12
E24
E31
E63

I

I only met Bill Phillips four times. The first time was in the mid 1950s when he was the selected 'heavy' of the host economics department (LSE) who spoke at the Cambridge–London–Oxford research students seminar. As far as I can remember he gave a paper on feedback mechanisms in Marshallian supply and demand analysis. It was refreshingly lacking in respect for Marshall in particular and economists in general. Not that he was a show-off, it was just that he said what he thought and backed up any critique with hard-headed analysis of the sort he was accustomed to use for engineering problems. That was one of his greatest strengths.

The second time was in Adelaide in the late 1950s where he gave a paper on an Australian Phillips Curve (chapter 28), having recently published *the* Phillips Curve itself (chapter 25). His paper was only a first draft but it was so criticised and dissected by Eric Russell in particular that it never saw the light of day in the public domain. In this instance his engineering background was a weakness, for he seemed inclined to take economic statistics as gospel, that is, that they actually meant something really *precise*. Eric, of course, knew the Australian statistics on wages, employment and prices intimately and was able to show that the data were so non-homogenous as to make completely unsound any attempt to fit a curve to them. Even if there were to be an underlying relationship to be teased out of the figures, they were just not in a form, and nor could they be put in one, to allow this procedure to occur. Moreover, Eric doubted that there *was* a stable relationship awaiting to be found. Bill Phillips took all this on board with good grace and, of course, while Eric's logic was remorseless and compelling, he was such a courteous and fine person that, as ever, as Al Watson once put it, his criticisms left no bruises.

I think I also saw Bill twice in Canberra when he was at the ANU, once before his dreadful stroke when he spoke enthusiastically about renewing his interest in China. The other time was after his stroke when he was very much knocked about. He told me about how he came to be captured by the Japanese during the Second World War. He was on a cliff and had to decide whether to jump and risk being killed either by the rocks or by drowning in the river below, or being captured on the top of the cliff. The moment of indecision led to the last occurring. He said that even the simple act of coming down stairs now brought the same feelings back to him. Bill was a most attractive, likeable and unassuming man and I found both Conrad Blyth's and Robert Leeson's obituary essays on him unbearably moving.

II

What though of a Left-Keynesian's view of the Phillips Curve trade-off itself? I have always regarded as an intellectual and political disaster the fact that the Phillips Curve trade-off came to be identified with Keynesianism, both as a view of how the world 'worked' and as a basis for policy. It was an intellectual disaster because there is no way that the Phillips Curve trade-off, as usually interpreted, may be found in either *The General Theory* or in Keynes' writings generally. Nor is it in anyway consistent with Keynes' views on the nature of economic theory or method, or on how economies work, or on how econometric work may or should be done. It was a political disaster because the stagflation episode allowed not only the Phillips Curve trade-off itself to be discredited but also Keynesianism itself. This was unjust and illogical, for no one who understood either Keynes or *The General Theory* – or the world and how it works – could have been surprised at the emergence of stagflation. But because the coupling was made, not least by Samuelson and Solow, this played into the hands of those who invented monetarism and its accompanying abhorrent anti-wage-earners, anti-the-poor and defenceless policies in so many countries. I cannot condemn too harshly those who did this – and those who allowed it to happen, or provided intellectual rationalisations for the policies, hired prize-fighters indeed.

III

Why cannot the Phillips Curve trade-off be found in *The General Theory*? First, because Keynes would have been horrified by the argument that a stable, dependable, *long-term* relationship between $\dot{p}$ (*or* $\dot{w}$) and u (and/or $\dot{u}$) could exist – horrified in the sense that it flew in the face of all his priors as to how the system worked. That is not to say that in a qualitative manner, what Arthur Brown has called an ordinal Phillips Curve relationship, may not sometimes be discerned in Keynes' understanding of the world in specific situations. He did expect, for example, that higher levels of activity would in general be associated with higher price levels and, near full employment, with higher money-wage levels. But to go further and postulate a stable dependable relationship between *rates* of change of p or w and levels of unemployment was alien to his thought forms. What would be the specific historical association between $\dot{p}$ (and $\dot{w}$) and $\dot{u}$ would depend very much on specific historical circumstances – whether the particular level of u was approached from above or below and how fast were the approaches involved. Such a situation-specific approach means that stable relationships with stable parameters can never be expected to be present.

IV

As to the stagflation episode, had Keynes' own aggregate demand and supply analysis from *The General Theory* not been largely driven out of the textbooks – perhaps it would be better to say that it never really got into them – any self-respecting student would have seen immediately that an imported cost shock, for example, an oil price rise, or an autonomous increase in money-wages, would have effects on the aggregate *supply* function which would tend, *ceteris paribus*, to raise the general price level and lower the level of activity and employment of the short period concerned. That this could set off further rises in prices and money-wages and further falls in activity and employment, emerge as distinct and plausible possibilities. The policy implication, therefore, was not to try to choose an *à la carte* mix of $\dot{p}$ and u by moving up or down a stable long-term relationship, but, rather, to try to devise a package deal of policies which included a permanent incomes policy consistent with the history, institutions and sociological characteristics of the society concerned. The object would be to bring the rate of change of money-wages and other incomes under some sort of control while preserving levels of *employment*, although, if necessary, at lower levels of real income, or increases of real income, if there had been a permanent worsening in, for example, the terms of trade.

In many countries the package deals of policies above were never adopted because of the identification of Keynesianism with the Phillips Curve trade-off and then the subsequent onslaught on it by the monetarists (and the new classical macroeconomists) who provided the intellectual ammunition for the implementation of what Tommy Balogh called 'the incomes policy of Karl Marx', that is, smash the wage-earners by creating unemployment through harsh prolonged monetary policy, and so change the balance of economic, social and political power as between labour and capital, both nationally and internationally. Of course, in the process these people forgot – most of them never knew it – an essential characteristic of capitalism, to wit, its inherent contradictions. By creating the conditions for a potential increase in the surplus of the system, that is to say, in the amounts potentially available for accumulation, they simultaneously destroyed the incentives and the abilities of the capitalists to turn what was potentially there into actuality, to realise the surplus. For the coarse and blunt instrument of monetary policy is a sure destroyer of those animal spirits on which, in the last analysis, the desire to accumulate depends. They were destroyed not only immediately but for such long periods as to ensure that much of the potential surplus remained unrealised.

Thus do the insights of Marx, who died in the year that Keynes was born, join up with those of his successor to illuminate the inequities of the conservative reaction to the bankruptcy of the Phillips Curve trade-off.

33 Interactions with a Fellow Research Engineer–Economist

Charles C. Holt

B31 E24

B22 E31

(A.W.H. Phillips) E63

Although born a world apart, Phillips' and my careers had striking parallels, warm interactions, and similar motivations. We both did research on electrical engineering, automatic control, computer simulation, economic stability, econometrics, and inflation–unemployment.

Control theory

We started corresponding in the summer of 1956 about bringing the tools of operations research and electrical engineering to bear on improving economic stability. Bill had already published several articles applying tools from electrical engineering to the stability of *single* loop economic models.

It was becoming clear, however, that economic stabilisation policy called for the analysis of economic systems incorporating multiple loops and multiple control variables. Fortunately operations research on industrial operations done at Carnegie Mellon University by a team composed of (in alphabetic order): Holt, Franco Modigliani, John F. Muth, and Herbert A. Simon, had shown that the optimal solution to that problem could be obtained under dynamic uncertainty (Holt *et al.* 1960). Where the criterion in a decision analysis could be adequately approximated with a quadratic function, and the dynamic system could be approximated by linear difference equations, the inversion of an infinite matrix would yield optimal linear decision rules. That model was discovered independently three times: by our operations research group, by economist Henri Theil, and by a group of process control engineers. Later it was adopted as the 'classic' model for engineering control.

I called this work to Bill's attention because of its relevance for his work on economic stability. He replied in a letter of October 1956 with the following brief report on his current work:

I am just now writing a short paper showing some results obtained by using frequency response analysis and electronic simulators for the study of aggregate control problems and will soon be using a simulator to investigate some more complex control problems. The analogue machines are, I think, essential if we are to go beyond linear models with a small number of relationships and deal with non-linear models with a fairly large number of relationships. It will be equally important, however, to develop more adequate methods of estimating quantitatively the relationships in real systems in order to restrict more closely than is presently possible the range of admissible hypotheses.

He also mentioned other researchers in the United Kingdom who were interested in these problems and with whom he was in active contact: R.G.D. Allen, M.G. Kendall, M.H. Quenouille, R.H. Tizard and Arnold Tustin.

Although he had not been following the latest work on decision theory used in operations research, he was applying frequency response analysis and had jumped ahead to use analogue computers which could handle multiple loop systems. He was also thinking about the statistical problems of estimating simultaneously the parameters of large systems, and the analogue simulation of large non-linear systems. Lacking the ability to make analytic solutions to large non-linear systems we could use computers to simulate them.

The Phillips Curve

Our exchange of research papers and our correspondence about research on economic stability led to my joining Bill at the LSE in September 1958 for a year and a half of research. Soon after my arrival, chapter 25 of this volume, on inflation and unemployment, appeared in *Economica*.

To Phillips' surprise the paper generated tremendous interest. Within months the trade-off between inflation and unemployment was being debated by parliament. Actually two decades earlier Tinbergen had used unemployment in a regression to explain wage changes. That seemed very reasonable at the time, hardly notable, but Phillips' long span of historical data and his dramatic, easily understood, graphs had a great impact on a large audience. Phillips viewed his relation in terms of the price adjustment relation in classical supply and demand analysis, but he had not really examined adjustment or expectational processes.

I think that he was a little embarrassed by the attention that the paper received, both because he was a genuinely modest chap, and perhaps because both the empirical econometric work and the theory were conspicuously sloppy. That was in notably sharp contrast to his mathematically rigorous research on control and advanced econometric estimation.

He talked very little about the paper which evidently was printed just as he had drafted it except for the addition of two sentences at the end: 'These conclusions are of course tentative. There is need for much more detailed research into the relations between unemployment, wage rates, prices, and productivity.' The need for research on adjustment processes was not even mentioned. Phillips' work in this paper had laid no basis for dealing with the coming challenge of the vertical Phillips Curve from a 'natural' rate of unemployment.

Examination of Phillips' Paper by the Staff Seminar on Methodology, Measurement and Testing

Phillips' paper on unemployment and inflation was, of course, of great interest to the LSE economics faculty and graduate students. The November and December 1958 meetings of the staff seminar were devoted to discussing Phillips' paper and presenting an 'investigation' by Dick Lipsey whose purpose was:

1 to try to quantify Phillips' results showing how much of the variance in wage rates he had actually explained,
2 to test a number of the subsidiary hypotheses that he throws out – i.e. to see if his own data bear them out, and
3 to test alternative hypotheses.

The initial discussion was followed by a written commentary on Phillips' paper by Chris Archibald. Both papers and their discussion, written up in four pages of who-said-what detail, were mimeographed and distributed. To my great surprise I recently discovered that my copy, even after four moves, was still in my research files.

Seminar participants had a great interest at the time in methodological rigour in testing theory, and Phillips' paper received thorough critical, but friendly, treatment. The mimeographed report on those sessions, shows not a single word from Bill although I assume he was there for at least some of these seminars. Interesting, I wonder how many economists are capable of sitting on their hands while their ox is being publicly gored – especially in the uniquely incisive style practiced by British academics.

Phillips viewed his inflation–unemployment relation in terms of classical supply and demand price adjustments, but had not examined specific adjustment processes, or the relation between unemployment and job vacancies. I studied these issues until I became convinced that the classical adjustment processes could not explain Phillips' relation, and that much more complex adjustment processes were involved. I resisted deeper involvement in research on labour–inflation issues at the time, because I had gone to London to work on economic stability with Phillips.

Phillips' research on economic stability

From working with Bill, I judged his greatest research interests at the time to be in the problems of economic stability, and in the advanced mathematical and statistical theories for dealing with them. He had mastered and was thoroughly comfortable with highly mathematical control theory far beyond the level of most economists. He was acutely aware of: (1) the risk that overly active feedback responses by government to economic fluctuations could make those fluctuations worse and the economy less stable; (2) determining the best response intensity requires making reasonably accurate estimates of economic dynamics; (3) government actions affect economic observations from which system parameters are estimated and (4), consequently, the effects of past government stabilisation policies must be unscrambled from system estimates.

He recognised that to deal with these problems economics would face formidable complex technical issues. In my view meeting this empirical-theoretical challenge would require a sizeable team effort. But at the time support for such an effort was not on the horizon in Britain, and, even if it were, Bill may not have been drawn to participate in such a team effort.

Perhaps it is not surprising that he lost much of his enthusiasm for this area of research a few years later as its profound difficulties became increasingly evident. He was fundamentally practical in his motivation, so simply writing academic papers would not satisfy him.

His family and mine became very close friends in London, so about five years later he and his family spent the summer with us at the University of Wisconsin. We had delightful times together swimming in Lake Mendota, etc. But I cannot now recall what his research interests were at the time – which tells me that they probably were unfocused.

Flow models of the labour market

Later in teaching a graduate course in macroeconomics at the University of Wisconsin, I felt it necessary to expose students to the Phillips Curve, even though the economics profession still did not really accept nor understand it – reminiscent of the slow acceptance of the Keynesian revolution. In preparing for class, I examined flow relationships from the labour market, and saw a way to derive the Phillips relation rigorously. A simple probabilistic search process of workers and jobs, declining wage aspirations for workers in response to unemployment duration, increasing wage offers in response to vacancy duration, and, of course, circular causation linking wage and price changes and expectations. When taken all together, these elements seemed to supply an economically meaningful explanation of the determinants of the Phillips relation.

These realistic adaptive dynamics reflected workers' personal experiences in receiving, or in not receiving, offers of jobs. Similarly they reflected experiences by employers in making offers to workers to fill particular vacancies, and having them accepted or rejected. The proposed theoretical relations seemed plausible in terms of: probability theory, which by then included formal search models; aspiration theory from psychology which was supported by experiments; and economic theory of motivations for various worker and employer decisions in labour and product markets.

A search of the labour literature ensued to test this theory. Descriptions of relationships and outcomes were found that seemed generally consistent with the mathematical relations that had been formulated, but very few quantitative measurements were found. Subsequent research by the author and others over the ensuing decade supported the above hypotheses about the determinants of the Phillips Curve and possible policy actions that could lower unemployment without increasing inflationary pressures (Holt and David 1966; Holt 1970; Holt, Smith and Vanski 1974).

Phillips' research contribution

Bill Phillips contributed significantly to the cutting edge of macroeconomics, but, as sketched above, his prime research focus was on technical areas that are extremely difficult, and are still neither fully understood nor appreciated by most economists. Evidence to support that statement can be offered by a relevant parallel. When the Federal Reserve Board had supported the building and operation of the best computerised econometric model of the US economy, and also had probably the best staff of economic control theorists in the country, the Board essentially ignored their quantitative policy recommendations on stabilisation actions, and continued to follow seat-of-the-pants policies. Recommendations based on control theory and econometric estimates were simply not valued nor understood enough to be used even though in this case they were readily available.

Recognition of Bill Phillips' contributions to macroeconomics certainly suffers from the same lack of understanding and appreciation. Phillips reduced the economic relevance of his research by carrying differential equations with continuous time from engineering into economics, where discrete time is dictated by data collection. That exacerbated the communication problem. His estimation paper (chapter 42) was first published in *Biometrica* – not exactly the ideal publication outlet for an econometrician.

Without question Phillips is best known, and for most economists exclusively known, for his paper on the inflation–unemployment relation. And without question that is his least solid piece of work although, as shown above, it triggered, almost by accident, important research on labour markets where quantitative and theoretical research had long been lagging.

How would Phillips have reacted to the rational expectations challenge?

With the perspective of hindsight, it is interesting to speculate on the role that Phillips might have played in the rational expectations debates – had not death intervened. He certainly would have played an active, perhaps critical, role in the debate. Some historical background on the issues involved may be helpful.

Henri Thiel was one of the developers of the linear decision rule analysis and first proved its stochastic optimality (certainty equivalence) for the static case. However, he had not recognised that it also was dynamically optimal until Herbert A. Simon, based on his research with the Carnegie Mellon research team, proved it to him. (See Holt *et al.*, 1960, chapter 6.)

Phillips had the necessary background to appreciate immediately the robust power of the quadratic-linear decision analysis. He was aware that it could simultaneously optimise stability by minimising the costs of fluctuations under dynamic uncertainty of large multi-loop multi-control variable systems whose parameter estimates and forecasts of exogenous variables meshed neatly with well-developed linear econometric methods (Holt *et al.* 1960; Holt 1962; Holt and Hay 1975; Holt and Lee 1978).

He immediately recognised the advance that the linear decision analysis offered over the servo stability approach which he had been using. He would certainly have appreciated the relevance of linear decision analysis for meeting the rational expectations challenge to the stabilisation efforts by governments. But he also would have been quick to point out the limitations of a linear model in a non-linear world.

John Muth (1961), another member of the Carnegie Mellon research team, wrote the paper that pioneered the rational expectations model and its theoretical assumptions. That paper was ignored by the economics profession for about a decade until Robert Lucas and others picked it up and developed rational expectations to a dominant, almost fad, position in the stability literature. Lucas received his Nobel prize for showing the implications of rational expectation assumptions for the ineffectiveness of government stabilisation policies.

Phillips would not have accepted for a minute the empirical validity of Muth's assumption that economic actors can foresee and adjust to the economic future including their roles and that of governments in producing that future. He almost surely would have strongly rejected Lucas' conclusions that government stabilisation actions would be unnecessary and ineffective.

Phillips would undoubtedly have advanced more realistic assumptions about the behaviour of economic actors. He might have anticipated some of the stabilisation developments of the 1990s. He would probably agree with Thomas J. Sargent (1993) and others in urging that rational expectations be replaced with a more adaptive and evolutionary approach to the formation of beliefs – much closer to Simon's bounded rationality.

Comparisons and contributions

When asked by the editor of this volume how Bill Phillips compared in style, brilliance, and contributions with outstanding economists that I have worked with or known well: Friedman, Modigliani, Miller, Markowitz, Muth, Samuelson and Simon, I would say that he was as brilliant as any of them. He was perhaps less driven to be productive than most of them. But he was more modest and self-effacing than any of them. In terms of integrity, and out-going helpfulness to other researchers, he was fully their match. In short, he was an economist of exceptional quality. He also made a great contribution to the quality of the economics program at the LSE which previously had offered no graduate courses in economics.

Bill Phillips excelled in combining theoretical power with practical common sense. He contributed to the understanding of the dynamic problems of economic stability and to developing tools for dealing with them. As important as his research contributions to economics were, as this volume makes clear, his personal contacts with other research economists made deep though informal contributions to their education, thinking, and individual productivities that will never be forgotten. To know Bill was to respect him, to value highly his contributions, and to love him. He will long be missed.

34 Does Modern Econometrics Replicate the Phillips Curve?

(UK)

Fatemeh Shadman-Mehta

E24
E31

CS2 N13

1 Introduction

It is probably fair to say that the analysis of the wage–price mechanism is one of the areas of applied macroeconomics that has received most attention. This is, of course, especially true ever since chapter 25 was first published in 1958. The 'Phillips Curve' became, at first, an essential, and then a controversial ingredient of macro-models of the economy. Over the years, numerous studies have been undertaken in different countries, to estimate and test many variants of the Phillips Curve.[1] Although there are some results with which most economists seem to agree, one is nevertheless left with the impression that the empirical evidence for or against the existence of a stable long-term relationship between the rate of change of wages (or of prices) and the rate of unemployment remains contradictory.

The last decade has seen much development in dynamic econometric modelling of economic time series. These developments, which have gone mainly ignored in most empirical studies of the wage–price mechanism, concern issues related to the exogeneity of variables, cointegration or the existence of a long-run relation between 'integrated' economic variables, and finally single equation versus system modelling. Much of the empirical evidence reviewed in Nickell (1990a) and in Bean (1994) is based on the estimation of conditional wage and price equations. If the regressor variables can legitimately be assumed to be weakly exogenous for the parameters of interest in the conditional model, then efficient estimation and testing may be conducted by analysing only the conditional model. On the other hand, ignoring the exogeneity status of a variable such as the unemployment rate can lead to invalid inference (Engle *et al.* 1983). Another common practice in the applied literature is to invert estimated wage and price equations to derive the so-called 'natural' rate of unemployment or the *NAIRU*. But such an inversion of conditional models

315

need not give estimated coefficients that are close to the parameters of the uninverted conditional model for the unemployment rate (Ericsson 1992; Shadman-Mehta 1996).

A further dimension needs to be borne in mind when dealing with integrated series that are expected to be cointegrated, such as wages, prices and productivity. Even the unemployment rate itself behaves at times as a unit root process. Granger (1981, 1986) and Engle and Granger (1987) have established the isomorphism between cointegration and error-correction models. It can therefore generally be expected that the parameters of interest in a conditional wage equation are linked with the parameters of the marginal distribution of the regressor variables, through the common cointegration vector(s), which would violate weak exogeneity.

These results underline the importance of employing a directed research strategy of modelling from the general to the specific. Apart from ensuring that the analysis begins from a congruent model of the data and avoiding the need to correct obvious shortcomings, such a strategy naturally widens the concept to define the optimal strategy as one that comprises an appropriate set of variables which ought to be modelled jointly. A system approach is preferable to single-equation modelling until weak exogeneity is ascertained (Banerjee *et al.* 1993).

The aim of this chapter is to use these important developments in econometric methodology to reevaluate the relationship between the unemployment rate and the rate of change of wages in the UK over the period 1860–1913. It seems a fitting tribute to A. W. Phillips' contribution to empirical economics, to apply econometric methods that were unavailable to him, to the same data set used in his study, to determine whether similar conclusions may be drawn.[2]

Section 2 briefly describes Phillips' data set and section 3 investigates the existence of long-run equilibrium relations between the basic variables in this data set, using the maximum likelihood method developed by Johansen (1988) and Johansen and Juselius (1990). A question of interest is whether the Phillips Curve, or a variant of it, is a long-run equilibrium relation in this approach which calculates LR tests obtained in a vector autoregressive framework, with a given lag structure. Section 4 models the unemployment rate equation with concluding remarks in section 5.

2 Data description

The basic variables used in this study are W, the index of average full-time weekly wage rates, P, the index of retail prices, U, the percentage unemployed of the working population, and Q, which is the measure of average labour productivity. Phillips did not publish the data he used to estimate his famous curve, no doubt because at the time of publication he did not expect the impact that his work was going to have. Lipsey (1960), who attempted soon after to interpret the relationship as a structural one, also failed to publish his data. The only available empirical evidence are the scatter diagrams and the 'crosses' provided in the various figures in chapter 25.[3] Other researchers have attempted to reconstruct the series by using Phillips' data sources.[4] The basic data set for $\dot{W}$, and $\dot{P}$, U and $\dot{U}$ used in this study[5] were reconstructed by A. Sleeman (1981) of Western Washington University,[6] for the years 1860 to 1957, and completed to 1979 by J.J. Thomas (1984). Using this data set, levels of W and P were calculated on the basis of $\dot{W}$, $\dot{P}$, and by reference to actual values available for later years. For observations between 1980 and 1990, actual values of W, P and U are used. Finally, the productivity variable Q, defined as output per worker, was also added to this basic data set. W, P and Q are expressed as indices, with 1985 as the base.[7]

The first step was to apply Phillips' own procedure to the data set, to ascertain that his results can be reproduced. This can be confirmed for the period 1861–1913 (there are some small discrepancies for the period 1920–1939 and 1947–1957). Figure 34.6, at the end of the paper, shows the scatter diagram of U and $\dot{W}$, for 1861–1913.[8]

Figure 34.1 (a, b, d and c clockwise) shows some of the features of these series during the period 1860–1913. Figure 34.1a graphs the logarithm of annual observations on W, the index for average full-time weekly wage rate (1985 = 1), and P, the index of retail prices (1985 = 1) in the UK. The evolution of the logarithm of their ratio, namely the index of real wages is also graphed for comparison. Let us denote these series by w_t, p_t and $(w - p)_t$. (The means and ranges of the variables have been adjusted to show maximum correlation.) For much of this period, prices were actually falling, beginning to rise from about 1896. Nominal wages, on the other hand, rose almost continually, with a sharp increase in the early 1870s, which was also accompanied by a rise in prices. But real wages nevertheless rose during this period.

Figure 34.1b graphs the first differences of these series. Compared to the levels, they are much more erratic, but as far as prices or wages are concerned, the growth rates still appear rather auto-correlated. Wages have had positive growth over most of the sample. The rate of inflation, on the other hand, fluctuated around zero much more frequently, starting an upward drift from the mid 1890s. The growth rate of real wages appears to be stationary, especially towards the end of the period. However, visual inspection alone does not establish the stationarity of a series. Formal tests are required to help clarify the issue.

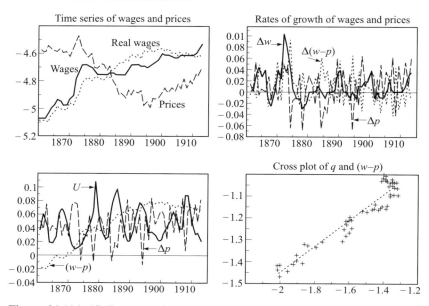

Figure 34.1(a)–(d) Features of the Phillips' data set (means and ranges adjusted)

Figure 34.1c graphs the evolution of the logarithm of real wages $(w - p)$, the unemployment rate U and the inflation rate Δp (means and ranges have once again been adjusted). The unemployment rate series appears stationary (with fluctuations around a positive value for U). The visual inspection of figure 34.1c shows no pairwise correlation between U_t and $(w - p)_t$. The inflation rate however moves closely with U and a negative correlation can be detected between them.

Finally, figure 34.1d shows a cross-plot of real wages against productivity. A regression line is also fitted to the sample. It shows clearly the co-movement of these series and points to the possibility of cointegration between them with a unitary coefficient.

3 Cointegration and long-run relations: 1863–1913

The general approach to the wage-setting equation in the literature today can be summarised by the following equation:

$$\Delta w = (p^e - p_{-1}) - \beta_1 U - \beta_2 (w - p)_{-1} + Z_w \Gamma + \varepsilon_w, \tag{1}$$

where Z_w is a host of variables believed to influence the mark-up over the reservation wage (for example, unemployment benefits, real interest rates, skill mismatch, productivity, tax wedge...). Written in this form, this equation allows the comparison of the case when $\beta_2 = 0$, which is interpreted as the traditional Phillips Curve relating the rate of change of wages to the unemployment rate, with the more general error-correction representation, first introduced by Sargan (1964), which allows the level of real wages to be related to the unemployment rate. As already mentioned, it is also generally the practice to derive the so-called 'natural' unemployment rate from the estimated wage equation as $Z_w\Gamma/\beta_1$ in this case.

In this chapter, the econometric analysis of the relation between the variables appearing in the above equation follows a general to specific modelling strategy, that is, beginning with the joint density of the observations. To investigate the existence of a long-run relation between the variables in the Phillips data set, use is made of the concept of cointegration which formalises such a property in statistical terms. A variable is integrated of order 1 ($I(1)$), if it requires differencing to make it stationary. A set of $I(1)$ time series is cointegrated if some linear combination of such (non-stationary) series is stationary. Thus, if the joint density of a vector process x_t with n variables, takes the form of a pth-order vector autoregression (VAR), we have

$$x_t = \sum_{i=1}^{p} \pi_i x_{t-i} + \varepsilon_t \qquad \varepsilon_t \sim IN(0, \Omega). \tag{2}$$

A constant term or dummies may also be added to (2). A simple re-parameterisation of (2) will lead to

$$\Delta x_t = \pi x_{t-1} + \sum_{i=1}^{p-1} \Gamma_i \Delta x_{t-i} + \varepsilon_t \tag{3}$$

with $\Gamma_i = -(\pi_{i+1} \ldots + \pi_p)$ and $\pi \equiv (\Sigma_{i=1}^{p} \pi_i) - I$. As shown by Engle and Granger (1987), π may be of reduced rank r, where $0 < r < n$. In this case the elements of x_t are $I(1)$, but there are r linear combinations of x_t which are stationary. The components of x_t are then said to be cointegrated and π can be written as the product of two full column rank ($n \times r$) matrices α and β, that is

$$\pi = \alpha\beta', \tag{4}$$

where β' is the matrix of cointegrating vectors, and α is the matrix of 'weighting elements' or speeds of adjustment. Using Granger's representation theorem (Granger 1983) as well as (4), equation (3) can be written in its error correction form

$$\Delta x_t = \alpha \beta' x_{t-1} + \sum_{i=1}^{p-1} \Gamma_i \Delta x_{t-i} + \varepsilon_t. \tag{5}$$

This study investigates cointegration in the VAR, involving the variables $(w - p_t, \Delta p_t, q_t, U_t)$ where lower case letters denote logarithms of the corresponding variables. This formulation imposes long-run price homogeneity, acceptable from the point of view of economic theory, but also allows the analysis of the role of inflation as a proxy for agents' price expectations. It is clear that a number of other variables are also likely to play a significant role in the determination of wages and prices. But this exercise is aimed at investigating the conclusions reached when applying new techniques to the same basic data used by Phillips. It would indeed be difficult to obtain reliable data for most other variables of interest, stretching back into the last century. The only additional variable used is productivity q, which is discussed by Phillips in chapter 25.

Since the degree of integration of a series is not an inherent property, and may change over different sample periods, it is important to base the analysis on a model which is $I(0)$ congruent and invariant, and not dependent on assumptions such as constancy of the order of integration. The starting point, therefore, will be the analysis of the system of the four stochastic variables $(w - p_t, \Delta p_t, q_t, U_t)$ with the aim of first arriving at such a model. Testing for cointegration will follow this initial stage.

A constant and a trend are included in the system. The inclusion of deterministic variables in the model calls for special attention. The constant cannot *a priori* be restricted to lie in the cointegration space, since we expect real wages and productivity to have an autonomous rate of growth, even though the unemployment rate should have no long-run autonomous growth, and therefore no separate intercept. The trend term, on the other hand, should be restricted to lie in the cointegration space only. If it were allowed to lie outside, it would create a quadratic trend in the levels of the variables. There is no evidence to suggest this might be a realistic representation.

3.1 The general system

The first step was an analysis of the lag structure of the VAR, starting with a maximal lag of 4. All selection criteria, as well as the F-tests of the validity of reducing the lag length, pointed to the choice of 2 as the appropriate lag length. In what follows, 2 is the maximum lag in the series, although higher-order lags were tried without the results changing significantly.

Table 34.1 reports some of the statistics that help evaluate the system. The standard deviations of the residuals provide a useful measure of the goodness of fit, because they are either in the same units as their corresponding dependent variable (for example, U), or are a proportion in the case of log models. They are also invariant under linear transformations of the variables. If the misspecification tests allow us to safely assume that the system errors are white noise, these standard deviations can act as the baseline innovation standard errors. The correlations between the residuals help guide the direction of modelling. In this case we observe a large negative correlation between the residuals of $(w - p)$ and Δp as well as correlations between residuals of q and $(w - p)$, and U and Δp of the order of 0.45.

Next we examine the reduction of the system to an appropriate lag length, as well as analyse its dynamics. The statistic $F_{s=i}$ tests the hypothesis of an i-period lag. As is clear from table 1(b), except the second lag on Δp and q, lags 1 and 2 of all variables are significantly different from 0. $|\lambda_{(\pi(1)-I)}|$'s are the moduli of the eigenvalues of the long-run matrix $\hat{P}_0 = \hat{\pi}(1) - I$, and the $|\lambda_{comp}|$'s those of its companion matrix. From the values of the $|\lambda_{(\pi(1)-I)}|$'s, it appears that the rank of $\hat{P}_0$ is less than 4, as at least one of them is quite small, but the rank is also greater than 0, with one eigenvalue having a modulus of 0.98. If so, then there is cointegration between the variables. As for the eigenvalues of the companion matrix, none is greater than one, which would imply an explosive system, and the number of roots close to one is less than 4, thus confirming that the system is indeed $I(1)$.

Other reported tests are tests of misspecification. A satisfactory model should have constant parameters (see figure 34.3) and residuals that are homoscedastic innovations. These tests can be performed both at the single equation level, and at the system level. $F_{ar}(\ )$ is the Lagrange-Multiplier test for auto-correlated residuals (here of the second order). $F_{arch}(\ )$ is the ARCH test for autoregressive conditional heteroscedasticity, or auto-correlated squared residuals (here of order (1) (Engle 1982). $F_{het}(\ )$ is the test of the null hypothesis of unconditional homoscedasticity, testing the significance of the regressors as well as their squares in the squares of the estimated residuals (White 1980). $\chi^2_{nd}(2)$ is a chi-square test for normality. The corresponding tests applied to the system are denoted by ^{v} (Doornik and Hendry 1994).

As suggested by table 34.1(c), most outcomes are satisfactory, except for some remaining auto-correlation in the errors of the inflation equation, and possibly non-normal errors in the unemployment equation, although the latter is probably not so important when testing for cointegration, given that the analysis by Cheung and Lai (1993) shows that

Table 34.1. *Goodness of fit and misspecification tests, 1863–1913*

(a) Residual correlations

	$w - p$	Δp	q	U
Δp	-0.84	.		.
q	0.42	-0.37	.	.
U	0.26	-0.45	0.23	.

(b) Dynamics

	$w - p$	Δp	q	U	
$F_{s=1}(4, 38)$	18.60^{**}	5.54^{**}	3.31^*	7.91^{**}	
$F_{s=2}(4, 38)$	2.87^*	0.72	1.84	5.77	
$\|\lambda_{\pi(1)-I)p}\|$	0.98	0.75	0.59	0.03	
$\|\lambda\|_{Comp}$	0.75	0.75	0.75	0.47	0.47 0.17 0.17 0.96

(c) Evaluation

Statistic	$w - p$	Δp	q	U	VAR
$\hat{\sigma}$	0.032	0.033	0.017	0.015	
$F_{ar}(2, 39)$	0.34	3.44^*	0.69	0.69	
$F_{arch}(1, 39)$	0.10	0.48	0.33	0.02	
$F_{het}(18, 22)$	0.78	0.85	0.90	0.55	
$\chi^2_{nd}(2)$	0.47	1.21	1.40	7.46^*	
$F^v_{ar}(32, 112)$					1.21
$F^v_{het}(180, 135)$					0.71
$\chi^{2v}_{nd}(8)$					12.27

Note: * and ** refer to significance at the 5 per cent and 1 per cent levels respectively.

Johansen's trace test is quite robust to both skewness and excess kurtosis in innovations.

Figures 34.2, 34.3 and 34.4 summarise more of the information about the estimated system. Figure 34.2 shows the fitted and actual values of the four variables, their cross-plots and their scaled residuals. One can detect clearly that there is a greater scatter for the equations relating to Δp and to U. Figure 34.3 shows graphically, diagnostic checking of parameter constancy, through recursive estimation of the system. One can notice from the one-step residuals $\pm 2\hat{\sigma}$, that all four equations can reasonably be assumed to have constant parameters, with one exceptional outlier for U. The individual equation break-point Chow (1960) F-tests are never larger than the corresponding 5 per cent critical value, and the system

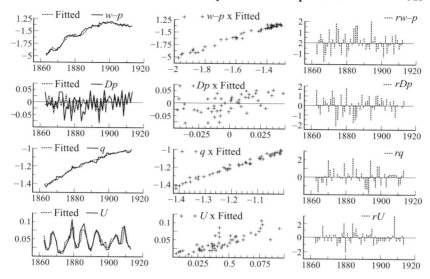

Figure 34.2 Actual and fitted values and scaled residuals, 1863–1913

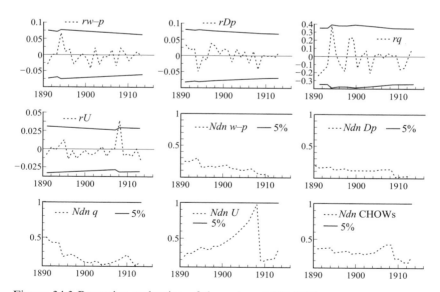

Figure 34.3 Recursive evaluation of the system, 1863–1913

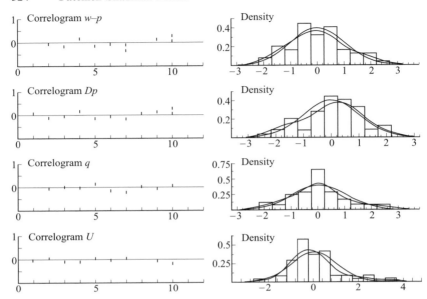

Figure 34.4 Graphical diagnostics, 1863–1913

break-point test values also remain insignificant throughout. None of these results changed substantially when a lag larger than two was adopted. Finally, figure 32.4 presents informal graphical representation of some of the tests reported in table 34.1(c). The correlogram shows no obvious dependence between successive residuals, and the histograms with non-parametric densities, and the cumulative distribution show no substantial departure from normality.

3.2 Cointegration analysis

The next step is to test for cointegration in the system. The trend is entered restricted to lie in the cointegration space, but the intercept is unrestricted.

Table 34.2 gives the eigenvalues (μ), the associated maximal eigenvalue statistic (Max), as well as the trace statistic (Tr). These are adjusted for degrees of freedom, by multiplying by $(T - nk)/T$, where T is the sample size, n is the number of variables in the VAR, and k is the lag length (Reimers 1992). The critical values are from Osterwald-Lenum (1992). At the 5 per cent significance level, we can clearly accept the hypothesis that there is one cointegrating vector or one stationary combination of the

Table 34.2. *Cointegration analysis, 1863–1913*

r	1	2	3	4
μ	0.52	0.34	0.21	0.12
Max	31.64*	18.22	10.4	5.5
Tr	65.76*	34.12	15.9	5.5

basic variables. Table 34.3 reports all eigenvectors of the system, the first row being the stationary component. The variables in the system have also been rearranged in the following order $(U, \Delta p, w - p, q)$, given that in fact it is more meaningful to normalise this vector by U. The loading factors α are also reported. Thus the cointegrating relation over this sample period suggests a definite negative effect from inflation on to the unemployment rate, with the real wage and productivity having very little effect.

The estimated long-run relationship between inflation and unemployment over the period 1863–1913[9] is: $U = -0.82\Delta p - 0.05(w - p) + 0.09q + 0.00004t$. The vector of adjustment coefficients with the rank of the Π matrix set to one shows that the main effect of this cointegrating vector is on U rather than on $\Delta(w - p)$ *or* $\Delta^2 p$. Figure 34.5 shows the estimated deviations from equilibrium for the cointegration vector, as well as the other components. It also portrays the behaviour of the eigenvalues, when estimated recursively. They all remain relatively stable over this period.

One important advantage of modelling a system is that it is possible to test the stationarity of individual series, having taken due account of the dynamics. Another important advantage of the Johansen maximum likelihood method is that it allows testing hypothesis about the long-run parameters, thus allowing them to be identified in a form that is interpretable by economic theory, as well as testing the weak exogeneity of various variables, at least for the long-run parameters. At this point therefore, we can test a number of interesting hypotheses. Starting with stationarity of the individual series, below are the list of hypotheses tested and their outcomes:

H_0^1: $(0,0,1,0,a) \in Sp(\beta) \equiv$ real wages stationary $\chi^2(3) = 30.78[0.00]^{**}$
H_0^2:$(0, 1, 0, 0, a) \in Sp(\beta) \equiv$ inflation rate stationary
$\quad \chi^2(3) = 20.11[0.00]^{**}$
H_0^3:$(0, 0, 0, 1, a) \in Sp(\beta) \equiv$ productivity stationary
$\quad \chi^2(3) = 30.68[0.00]^{**}$

Table 34.3. *Eigenvectors of the* Π *matrix and their loading factors*

Vector\Variable	U	Δp	$w - p$	q	t
β_1'	1.0	0.82	0.05	−0.09	−0.00004
v_2'	0.04	1.0	0.17	−0.33	0.0003
v_3'	0.80	−0.64	1.0	−3.95	0.02
v_4'	0.20	1.14	0.34	1.0	−0.004
$\hat{\alpha}$	1	2	3	4	
U	−0.79	0.27	0.001	−0.002	
Δp	−0.02	−1.10	0.035	0.033	
$w - p$	0.05	0.60	−0.071	−0.061	
q	0.10	0.15	0.107	−0.025	

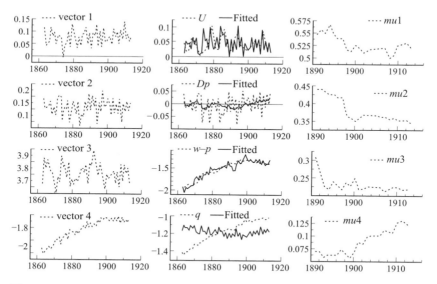

Figure 34.5 Cointegration vectors and recursive eigenvalues, 1863–1913
Note: The graphs in the centre refer to, for example in the case of U, a comparison between the actual value of U and that obtained from the first cointegration vector, that is $-0.82\Delta p - 0.05(w - p) + 0.09q + -0.0004t$

$H_0^4:(0, 0, 1, -1, a) \in Sp(\beta) \equiv$ wage share stationary
$\quad \chi^2(3) = 30.59[0.00]^{**}$
$H_0^5:(1, 0, 0, 0, a) \in Sp(\beta) \equiv$ unem. rate stationary $\chi^2(3) = 9.92[0.02]^*$
$H_0^6:(1, 0, 0, 0, 0) \in Sp(\beta) \equiv$ unem. rate stationary (no trend)
$\quad \chi^2(4) = 9.95[0.04]^*$
and as for cointegration, we get:
$\quad H_0^7:(1, a, 0, 0, 0) \in Sp(\beta) \qquad \chi^2(3) = 1.56[0.6680]$
$\quad H_0^8:(1, \alpha, 0, 0, 0) \in Sp(\beta) \qquad \chi^2(6) = 3.00[0.8088]$
and $\alpha = 0$ for $w - p, \Delta p, q$.

To summarise, the likelihood ratio tests indicate that none of the series: real wages ($w - p$), rate of inflation Δp, productivity q, or the wage share ($w - p - q$) are stationary over the period 1863–1913. For the unemployment rate, on the other hand, the hypothesis that it is stationary, even without a trend, is rejected at 5 per cent but cannot be rejected at the 1 per cent significance level. One might be tempted to conclude that U is a stationary variable. Finally, the hypothesis H_0^7, where the cointegrating vector simplifies to a relation between the rate of inflation and the unemployment rate, cannot be rejected. Given that Δp is not stationary (H_0^2), the latter result provides further evidence against the stationarity of U, since stationarity of U together with H_0^7 and H_0^8 implies stationarity of Δp.

Although the Johansen trace test indicates that in this period there is only one cointegration relation, the results obtained for the period 1868–1990 (Shadman-Mehta 1996), showed the presence of a second cointegration relation as well. A closer look at table 34.3 also suggests that the second vector has a substantial impact, especially on the rate of inflation. Setting the cointegration rank to 2, and imposing overidentification restrictions on the cointegration vectors yields the following result

$$H_0^9: \beta' = \begin{pmatrix} 1 & \beta_{21} & 0 & 0 & 0 \\ 0 & 1 & 0 & \beta_{42} & -0.009\beta_{42} \end{pmatrix} \in Sp(\beta)$$

$$\chi^2(4) = 4.095[0.39].$$

Note that the coefficient of trend in the second vector is restricted, such that the significant variable in this relation is the deviations of productivity from its long-run trend (the average value of Δq over this period is about 0.009, very close to the average rate of productivity growth between 1860 and 1990). Finally, the coefficient of q was restricted to the value of -0.1063, obtained in the large sample, with the following outcome

Table 34.4. *Model estimates (constrained FIML), 1863–1913*

ΔU_t	$=$	0.556 ΔU_{t-1}	-0.073 $\Delta^2 p_t$	-0.232 $\Delta(w-p)_{t-1}$
		(0.100)	(0.065)	(0.010)
		-0.327 Δq_{t-1}	-0.717 c^a_{1t-1}	$+0.005$
		(0.103)	(0.104)	(0.002)
$\Delta^2 p_t$	$=$	-0.421 $\Delta^2 p_t$	-0.351 ΔU_{t-1}	-0.853 c^a_{2t-1}
		(0.117)	(0.137)	(0.189)
$\Delta(w-p)_t$	$=$	0.456 $\Delta(w-p)_{t-1}$	$+0.407$ $\Delta^2 p_{t-1}$	$+0.271$ Δq_{t-1}
		(0.119)	(0.122)	(0.144)
		$+0.511$ c^a_{2t-1}		
		(0.189)		
Δq_t	$=$	-0.342 Δq_{t-1}	$+0.011$	
		(0.128)	(0.003)	

$$H_0^{10}:\beta' = \begin{pmatrix} 1 & \beta_{21} & 0 & 0 & 0 \\ 0 & 1 & 0 & -0.1063 & +.009^* & 0.1063 \end{pmatrix}$$

$$\in Sp(\beta)\chi^2(5) = 7.748[0.17]$$

The weak exogeneity of each variable may be considered next. This can be achieved by testing whether the adjustment coefficient or the α corresponding to each cointegration vector is zero in each equation. If no cointegration vector is present in the marginal distribution of a particular variable, this indicates that the variable may be treated as weakly exogenous, as far as the long-run parameters are concerned. In this case, sequential setting of various adjustment coefficients to zero leads to the conclusion that the hypothesis that the first vector appears only in the unemployment equation, whereas the second vector appears only in the inflation and the real wage equations cannot be rejected, with a test statistic $\chi^2(10) = 9.591[0.48]$.

4 Modelling the unemployment rate, 1863–1913

Given this outcome, the data can be mapped to $I(0)$ space by defining the error-correction mechanisms obtained under hypothesis H_0^{10}, that is

$$c_{1t} = U_t + 0.554\Delta p_t$$

$$c_{2t} = \Delta p_t - 0.1063(q_t - 0.0088t).$$

The mapped data will then define a new system with six variables (ΔU_t, $\Delta^2 p_t$, $\Delta(w-p)_t$, Δq_t, c_{1t}, c_{2t}) where both c_{1t} and c_{2t} are identities and the maximal lag is 1. The hypotheses tests in the previous section led to the conclusion that the variables ($\Delta^2 p_t$, $\Delta(w-p)_t$, Δq_t) may be treated as weakly exogenous for the unemployment rate, and one could at this stage proceed with estimating the conditional model for this variable. The following results are, however, based on continuing with the complete system.

The initial step is to reestimate the new $I(0)$ system and verify its stationarity with a cointegration analysis. The rank of the system is indeed confirmed as 4. Similarly, the error correction term c_{1t-1} is significant only in the equation for U, and c_{2t-1} is significant in the equations for $\Delta^2 p_t$ and $\Delta(w-p)_t$. Removing them, as well as all the other insignificant variables, leads to the model reported in table 34.4.[10]

Table 34.5 summarises tests of model evaluation and misspecification. The hypotheses of interest include auto-correlation F_{ar}, autoregressive conditional heteroscedasticity ($ARCH$) F_{arch}, the normality of the distribution of the residuals χ^2_{nd}, heteroscedasticity F_{het}, and functional form misspecification F^{mod}_{func}. The p-values for the model statistics are given inside brackets. The final statistic reported for the model is $\chi^2_{ov.ident}$, which tests the validity of the overidentifying restrictions.

The model misspecification tests are all insignificant (except for normality which is insignificant only at 1 per cent) thus confirming that the estimated model is a congruent model. Although real wages and productivity had no role to play in the long-run relationship, they both have a significant short-run effect on the unemployment rate over the period 1863–1913. The contemporaneous effect of the acceleration in the rate of inflation is not very significant, but the inclusion of this variable reduces residual correlations. As for the other variables, both the acceleration in the rate of inflation and the rate of growth of productivity exhibit negative auto-correlation. Similar results are obtained for the acceleration in inflation both in the full sample (1868–1990) estimates and in other studies (Shadman-Mehta 1996; Hendry and Doornik 1994).

There is no autonomous growth either in the acceleration in the inflation rate or in the rate of growth of real wages over this period. Table 34.6 gives the matrix of residual correlations for this system. The diagonal terms give residual standard deviations. The error covariances below the diagonal are those between the structural residuals, and those above the diagonal are the reduced form correlations.

The remaining high correlation of -0.83 between the residuals of the two equations for $\Delta^2 p_t$, and $\Delta(w-p)_t$, suggest that other important variables affecting both these variables over this period are missing

Table 34.5. *Model evaluation statistics, 1863–1913*

Statistic	$\Delta(w-p)$	$\Delta^2 p$	Δq	ΔU	Model
$\hat{\sigma}$	0.032	0.033	0.019	0.013	
$F_{ar}(2, 42)$	0.73	6.27**	3.24*	0.83	$F_{ar}^{mod}(32, 134) = 1.02[0.44]$
$F_{arch}(1, 42)$	0.01	0.60	0.50	0.04	
$F_{het}(12, 31)$	1.04	0.84	1.30	0.68	$F_{het}^{mod}(120, 208) = 1.04[0.40]$
$\chi^2_{nd}(2)$	1.43	3.22	1.85	7.76*	$\chi^2_{nd}(8) = 18.64[0.02]^*$
					$F_{func}^{mod} = 0.72[0.98]$
					$\chi^2_{ov.ident}(11) = 6.35[0.85]$

Table 34.6. *Residual correlations, 1863–1913*

	$\Delta(w-p)$	$\Delta^2 p$	Δq	ΔU
$\Delta(w-p)$	0.032	−0.84	0.42	0.26
$\Delta^2 p$	−0.83	0.033	−0.37	−0.45
Δq	0.42	−0.41	0.019	0.23
ΔU	0.10	−0.27	0.17	0.013

from the analysis. Nevertheless, the model in table 34.4 does offer an explanation of the data features.

Although doubts about the potential non-constancy of the parameters of econometric equations under changed states of nature have a long history, it is the critique voiced by Lucas (1976) about the use of econometric models in general, and of the Phillips Curve in particular, for policy analysis that seems to have marked the literature. But the critique should be viewed as a potential denial of the invariance of the parameters of interest to a particular set of interventions. Only then can its applicability be tested meaningfully, since refuting it in one instance cannot rule out the possibility that it might be confirmed in other instances. Engle and Hendry (1993) propose tests of superexogeneity based on checking whether the parameters of a conditional model are invariant to changes in the parameters of the marginal processes. If the determinants of the non-constancies of those processes are statistically insignificant when added to the conditional model, then superexogeneity cannot be refuted for that particular instance. Practically, this can be achieved by the inclusion of dummies. Here, the inclusion of an impulse dummy in the system for the year 1874 improves the general fit of the model in the sense that it removes all the remaining problems of auto-correlation in the residuals of $\Delta^2 p$ and Δq as well as lack of normality. This dummy variable turns out to be very significant in both the real wage equation and the equation for the acceleration in the rate of inflation. But it is insignificant in the unemployment rate equation, and this fact together with the weak exogeneity of these variables confirms their super exogeneity for the unemployment rate equation over this particular sample. Thus, if $\Delta^2 p$ had been a proxy for expectations, the parameters of the unemployment rate equation should have manifested changes when the expectations process changed during the sample. The evidence therefore favours agents using data-based expectations, which do not require further modelling.

5 Conclusions

Allowing for the fact that the relation derived here is expressed slightly differently, in terms of U rather than $\log U$ as Phillips had done, the results are remarkably close to his (see figures 34.6 and 34.7). In other words, if Phillips was conducting his analysis of the sample period 1863–1913, with the current developments in econometric theory, his overall conclusions would have been much the same. There existed indeed an apparent inverse relationship between the rate of inflation and the level of the unemployment rate.

However, the following remarks also result from such an analysis: firstly, the unemployment rate in the UK in that period was not an autonomous causal factor but an endogenous variable of the economy. Thus Phillips' views regarding the intervention of government through demand management in order to stabilise the inflation rate would probably have been different.

Secondly, the cointegration relation depicted in figure 34.7 does not equate equilibrium unemployment with zero inflation, as suggested in much of the discussions around the Phillips Curve. Equilibrium, in the sense that there is no tendency for the unemployment rate to change, is conceivable with both inflation and deflation. Thirdly, as far as inflation or the level of real wages are concerned, the level of the unemployment rate played no role in determining whether they remained stable or not. Their stability depended on discrepancies between the inflation rate and deviations of productivity from long-run trend.

Further results can be summarised as follows. There existed a constant econometric equation for this sample period, relating the change in the unemployment rate to the acceleration in inflation, the rate of growth of

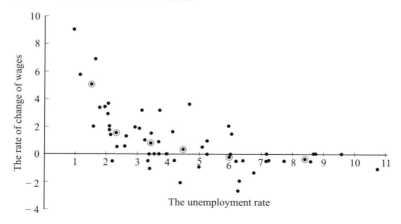

Figure 34.6 The Phillips Curve, 1861–1913
Note: The encircled points are Phillips' six average points.

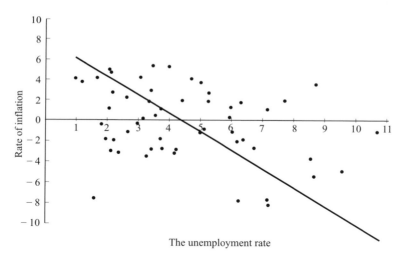

Figure 34.7 The cointegration relationship between the rate of inflation and the unemployment rate in the UK, 1863–1913

real wages, and that of productivity, even though some of these determinants themselves were subject to shifts. Although inflation, real wages and productivity are themselves endogenous variables, their marginal density contains no information of relevance to the long-run parameters of the unemployment rate equation. They can therefore be treated as weakly exogenous. Moreover, the irrelevance of the deterministic step dummy variable in this equation, despite its importance in both the equations for the rate of growth of real wages and the change in inflation, confirms superexogeneity of these variables. This result provides evidence against the applicability of the Lucas critique as far as the parameters of interest of the unemployment rate equation for this period are concerned, and highlights the importance of actually testing those aspects of the critique that are testable.

Somewhat different results are obtained when a similar analysis is conducted for the period 1868–1990 (Shadman-Mehta 1996). Two long-run relationships are once again depicted. One of these, which relates the rate of inflation to deviations of productivity from long-term trend, remains unchanged throughout the period. The second relationship relates real wages indexed on productivity to the level of unemployment and the rate of inflation, very much in line with present day theories of wage determination. There remains of course an inherent inverse relationship between the latter two variables. The existence of the link between the level of unemployment and the level of real wages in this sample reflects the changed nature of the labour market over the last part of this century-long data set. These long-run equilibrium relations are absent from both the productivity and the unemployment rate equations, suggesting not only that these variables are weakly exogenous for the long-run parameters of the real wage and inflation equations, but also that the determinants of the long-run levels of these variables are to be found outside the wage–price mechanism.

Notes

Financial support for this research from a grant 'Actions de Recherches Concertes' 93/98-162 of the Ministry of Scientific Research of the Belgian French Speaking Community is gratefully acknowledged. I am also grateful to Luc Bauwens, Neil Ericsson, David Hendry, Robert Leeson, Henri Sneessens, Jean-Pierre Urbain and Daniel Weiserbs for many helpful discussions. All numerical results in this paper were obtained using PC-FIML Version 8.0; cf. Doornik and Hendry (1994).

1 Nickell (1990a) and Bean (1994) provide excellent surveys of the applied research in this area over the last two decades.

2 A separate paper (Shadman-Mehta 1996, chapter 4) extends the analysis to the period 1860–1990.

3 The fact that Phillips' original data are now available, was brought to my attention after the completion of this study, by R. Leeson.

4 See among others, Gilbert (1976) and Wulwick (1989).

5 A dot over a variable signifies the first central difference of that variable, for example

$$\dot{W}_t = 50\left[\frac{W_{t+1} - W_{t-1}}{W_t}\right]$$

6 I am indebted to J.J. Thomas at the LSE for giving me this data set.

7 Full details on the various variables and their sources are given in Shadman-Mehta (1996).

8 A comparison with Phillips' original data (Leeson 1995) reveals that the reconstruction by Sleeman corresponds exactly to Phillips' for 1861–1913. Differences do exist, however, for later years.

9 Phillips estimated equation was: $\log(\dot{W} + 0.9) = 0.984 - 1.394 \log U$.

10 c^a_{1t-1} and c^a_{2t-1} are the two cointegration vectors adjusted for their sample means.

35 The Famous Phillips Curve Article: A Note on its Publication

Basil S. Yamey

Bill Phillips' article on the eponymous curve (chapter 25) was first published in 1958, the year in which he was appointed to a chair in economics at the LSE. This article ensured his reputation internationally, and marked the high point of his phenomenal progress at the School: obtaining the degree of B.Sc. (Econ.) in Sociology in 1949 (with a 'pass' grade), inventing the Phillips Machine, being awarded a doctorate in economics in 1954, and being appointed to a chair of economics in 1958; all within less than a decade. It is, incidentally, a reflection of the way things have changed that it is inconceivable that anyone could have had a similarly phenomenal academic career at the LSE forty years later: rules, regulations and more impersonal academic administration do not allow for such a special case as Bill undoubtedly was. A Bill Phillips today would not necessarily even be exposed to a single course in economics if he were to do the B.Sc. majoring in Sociology.

The Phillips Curve paper was submitted for publication in *Economica* in the second half of 1958. I was acting as editor of the journal. A digression on the editorial organisation of the journal is in order here.

Economica has always had an editorial board. At the time it was composed of all the professors of economics and professors in the neighbouring departments of accounting, economic history and statistics. One of the economics professors was designated 'acting editor'. He was responsible for the journal on the editorial side and also accountable to the School for the small office that looked after the commercial side and collaborated with the printers on the production of the journal. The acting editor was assisted by the 'assistant editor', whose main duties were to look after the book reviews section of the journal and to assist in the supervision of the office.

The adjective 'acting' in the title 'acting editor' did not have the more usual meaning of 'temporary', that is, acting as editor until a proper appointment had been made. I assume the adjective had been chosen

335

to indicate the collegial nature of the editing of the journal – the acting editor acted for and on behalf of the editorial board. In fact, the members of the editorial board, which ordinarily met three or four times a year, were much more a source of ideas and suggestions (for example, of books to be reviewed, of likely authors, and of books to be reprinted in the reprints series) than active participants in the selection of articles for publication and in the make-up of particular issues of the journal. Effectively, the acting editor edited and managed the journal.

At the time there was no formal routine system for the refereeing of papers submitted to the journal. In that respect *Economica* did not differ from other journals of economics published in the United Kingdom. The editor decided which papers to accept for publication, though he was free to consult individual colleagues and might seek the advice, if he thought it necessary, of economists outside the School. Formal refereeing was practised increasingly during the 1960s, and eventually became routine.

In the 1950s, the late Professor Richard Sayers was *Economica*'s acting editor. Sayers, however, had been appointed a member of the Radcliffe Committee on the monetary system, and was on leave of absence in 1958. I was the assistant editor, and the editorial board made me the acting 'acting editor'. (I became 'acting editor' in 1960, and, with a break in tradition, 'editor' a few years later.)

I do not recall whether Bill himself gave me a copy of his paper for editorial consideration. I think I was given a copy by Lionel Robbins or James Meade. Anyway, before the day was over the paper had been enthusiastically recommended to me by several members of the editorial board. I shared this enthusiasm after I had read the paper, and within a day of receiving it I accepted the paper for publication in *Economica* – a speed of decision impossible for any refereed journal today.

The planned make-up of the next issue was changed so as to include Bill's paper as the lead article. The indefatigable Betty Barron, who was the sole member of the *Economica* office, had the numerous diagrams redrawn, and arranged with the printers to supply proofs without delay. Perhaps the speed with which the entire process, from submission to page proofs, was carried out contributed to Bill's admission that there may have been 'an excessive haste to publish' (Blyth 1989). But the editorial decision to publish the paper was fully vindicated by its instant and striking success. One may compare its success (in terms of requests for permission to reproduce it) with that of another *Economica* article which achieved international recognition: Ronald Coase's 'The Nature of the Firm' was published in 1937, but made its impact only several decades later.

Bill concluded his article with this sentence: 'There is need for much more detailed research into the relations between unemployment, wage rates, prices and productivity'. As the publisher of Bill's article, *Economica* received for consideration many papers on various aspects of the Phillips Curve essay. I invariably showed the papers to Bill for his comments and advice (he had joined the editorial board in 1959 and was a member until he left London in 1967). He encouraged publication of most of the papers that were submitted, but always declined my invitation to write comments on the more substantial pieces or indeed to write a follow-up article to include his further reflections. He seemed to have lost interest in the subject soon after the paper was published. His fertile mind had moved on to other matters.[1]

In all, up to the end of 1970, *Economica* published a dozen papers on aspects of Bill's essay. The most substantial was Richard Lipsey's paper published in 1960, a contribution which caused Edmund Phelps (1989), in his *New Palgrave* entry on the Phillips Curve, to refer to it as the Phillips–Lipsey Curve. Phelps observed that 'statistical estimation of such Phillips–Lipsey equations rapidly developed from a cottage activity using electric calculators to a booming computerised industry'. In fact, *Economica* published only one such econometric contribution (Bhattia 1961).

Between 1971 and 1973, *Economica* published several short articles on earlier intimations of the Phillips Curve relationship in the economics literature. I imagine that this search for an earlier version of the curve that made him so well known would have appealed to Bill's sense of humour. He would have been amused to know that such luminaries as Irving Fisher (1926) and Jan Tinbergen (1939) were among his supposed precursors.

Bill and his family lived in Hampstead Garden Suburb, in North London, for several years before they moved to Australia. We were near-neighbours in this attractive suburb, to the north of Hampstead Heath and about six miles from the LSE. He and I frequently travelled together by tube to or from work. He smoked all the way in the usually congested carriages. (In those days London Underground allowed smoking in certain carriages.) He never spoke about his experiences during the war, nor about the famous curve or the machine. But we exchanged views on the passing academic scene and, not unkindly I hope, on the foibles of our colleagues. What I recall most clearly, however, were his complaints about living and working in London, with its congestion and long travelling distances. Travelling on the Northern Line – which popularly came to be known as the misery line – at or near rush hour was not a pleasant experience. But his increasing antipathy towards London went far beyond the disutility of commuting on an increasingly over-stretched railway system. It was not surprising to learn of his decision to return with his family to the wider and less-congested spaces of Australasia.

Notes

1 It is generally believed that Bill's work on what was to become the Phillips Curve represented his entry into a new field of enquiry. My colleague Roger Alford has told me, however, that Bill had told him that his interest in the relationship between unemployment and changes in wage rates had already developed when he was working on his macroeconomic machine. He had found it impossible to 'model' the Keynesian aggregate supply function in a way suitable for incorporation in the machine. He was looking for a more suitable – and in his view also more realistic – relationship.

Part IV
Econometrics

The Published Papers

36   The Bill Phillips Legacy of Continuous Time Modelling and Econometric Model Design

Peter C.B. Phillips

Bill Phillips' contributions to econometrics came at a time when the subject was almost exclusively concerned with applications that involved discrete time series data and models that were based on simultaneous equations. Not only was theoretical research in econometrics during the 1950s and 1960s, when Phillips did his work, dominated by the concerns of simultaneous equations systems, but empirical applications were also predominantly based on systems of this type. Since the available observations of economic variables were discrete time series data that were commonly measured at annual and quarterly intervals, it is logical that most econometric studies of the time were concerned with the development of statistical methods for simultaneous equations models that were fitted with discrete time series data.

One of Phillips' greatest contributions to econometrics is that he opened up a new field of research on continuous time econometric modelling and statistical inference. This field contrasted in important ways with the simultaneous equations paradigm that dominated the thinking of Phillips' contemporaries. In the first place, the probabilistic framework of continuous time stochastic models was necessarily more sophisticated than discrete time series in order to accommodate the function space realisations of random processes like Brownian motion. Secondly, the models themselves were formulated as recursive systems in terms of stochastic differential equations rather than as non-recursive systems like simultaneous equations. In consequence, the models were conceptually and causally quite different from simultaneous equations. These differences turn out to be pivotal in the construction of continuous systems of real-world economic processes, a fact that Phillips was acutely aware of in his own work. In several of the papers reprinted in this volume, Phillips remarks on these distinctions and points out their implications regarding matters of statistical estimation and identification. This is one of many examples in which Phillips' econometric work shows sensitivity to concerns of model design, as well as matters of statistical estimation and inference.

Mathematicians since Wiener (1923) had been interested in the development of the probability space underpinnings of these models. And some statisticians, notably Bartlett (1946, 1955) Grenander (1950) and Bartlett and Rajalakshman (1953), had written on issues of statistical estimation. But continuous time statistical models had been almost totally ignored by econometricians. The sole exception was a short paper by Koopmans (1950b) that provided some early arguments for the merits of modelling in continuous time.

In consequence, when Phillips commenced his research in the 1950s on continuous time econometrics, it was a brand new field and his work represented a bold new departure from the prevailing tradition of Cowles-Commission-style econometrics. It was a courageous move. For, while there was some interest in the United Kingdom, the new line of research that Phillips pioneered attracted only a small following and it was all but ignored by the large and growing community of econometricians in North America. In part, this is explained by the on-going preoccupation with implementing simultaneous equations methods. But, it is also fair to say that continuous time econometrics was a subject that seemed technically forbidding to researchers whose training was limited to discrete time series and this undoubtedly limited entry to the new field.

Phillips' work proceeded on two fronts. The first of these was the development of dynamic macroeconomic models in terms of systems of differential equations whose purpose was to explain business cycle behaviour and to study control mechanisms within such systems. The main papers that grew out of this work are reprinted in chapters 40 and 41. These papers not only added to economic knowledge concerning business cycles and economic policy, they also made important methodological contributions to the design of economic models. It is in the latter respect that they have had the most enduring influence. The models Phillips constructed had much in common with engineering models of physical systems. Most of the differential equations were formulated as adjustment mechanisms in which variables like aggregate consumption and investment adjusted in a continuous way toward steady state values of these variables that were formulated so that the system was balanced in equilibrium or along equilibrium growth paths. These trade cycle and cyclical growth models were the harbingers of a broad group of econometric models that have since come to be known as error-correction mechanisms. Discrete time analogues of these models later appeared in Sargan's (1964) celebrated study of wages and prices in the United Kingdom, and they were subsequently used in the frequently cited empirical consumption function study of Davidson, Hendry, Srba and Yeo (1978). With the recent advent of the field of unit root econometrics and cointegration, the original work of Phillips in formulating models as adjustment mechanisms about equilibrium values has taken on a new significance in terms of its empirical implications. The historical importance and relevance of his work to the subject of error-correction modelling has still to be widely recognised in the literature and is, unfortunately, not cited in any of the recent textbooks, handbooks or overviews of the subject, although the priority and significance of his work on this topic have been pointed out (Phillips and Loretan 1991).

One might speculate that it was the engineering discipline of formulating models that had well-defined steady state solutions and stable adjustment mechanisms about those solutions that guided Bill Phillips naturally to a class of model that was capable of dealing in a coherent way with both stationary and non-stationary time series. Interestingly, this discipline also seems to have steered Phillips away from mechanistic forms of univariate time series modelling like the methods of Box and Jenkins (1976) which later grew into prominence in statistics. On the contrary, the error-correction mechanisms that dominated the early models of Phillips were essentially multivariate in character. It is this class of model that has survived and prospered in econometrics and now forms an essential part of the toolbox of empirical researchers in macroeconomics.

The second front for Bill Phillips' research was the direct empirical task of constructing and estimating continuous time econometric systems with discrete data. In tackling this problem, Phillips wrote the first scientific paper to deal exclusively with the problem of estimating the parameters in systems of stochastic differential equations with discrete time series data. That paper was published in the statistical journal *Biometrika* in 1959 and is reprinted here as chapter 42. Since Phillips' original work, a very complete statistical methodology of continuous time econometrics has been developed covering methods of estimation, inference, forecasting, policy analysis and control, diagnostic testing and numerical computation. Many of the articles that are central to these developments are contained in the two volumes by Bergstrom (1976, 1990), and the methods are now discussed at an introductory level in some texts, like that of Gandolfo (1981).

All of this work on econometric model design and statistical estimation can rightfully be seen as research that is part of Bill Phillips' legacy to econometrics. While none of his models or his methods of statistical estimation are actually used in empirical econometric work today, Phillips was responsible for opening up an approach to modelling and an arena for research on continuous time econometrics that has proved to be of extraordinary consequence to present day research. Somewhat ironically, given the dominant preoccupation of his contemporaries in the 1950s and 1960s, Phillips' line of research has proved to be every bit as important to econometrics as the simultaneous equations model and it is potentially of much greater significance to modern time series econometric methods and applications. Moreover, in recent years, a much wider range of researchers have become interested in continuous time econometric systems and this has broadened the field in exciting new ways. There are several reasons for this widening of his legacy.

While it was macroeconomic applications of these methods that interested Bill Phillips, it is the large and growing subject area of finance that now offers fruitful applications of these methods and potential for a big empirical impact. In part, this is because data sources are much richer in finance than they are in macroeconomics, particularly so with regard to frequency of observation where we now have near continuous data recording of many financial variables like asset prices and exchange rates. In part too, financial econometric models have features that make them interesting potential candidates for continuous time econometric methodology. First, the economic theory models in finance on which they are based are most often themselves formulated in continuous time, prime examples being option price models in finance (for example, Merton 1990) and exchange rate target zone models in international finance (Krugman and Miller 1992). Also, many of these models involve non-linear rather than linear stochastic differential equations and offer an exciting area of development for researchers in continuous time econometrics, including methods of indirect inference (for example, Monfort 1996). Finally, stochastic calculus and the martingale structure of stochastic integrals have recently become firmly established as essential and revealing tools of analysis in models of asset pricing and exchange rate determination. In consequence, it has become natural to develop economic theory models in terms of stochastic differential equations (for example, Duffie 1988) and much more natural in turn to think of estimating such systems in empirical applications.

Knowing that stochastic differential equations generate data for which equispaced observations satisfy vector autoregressive moving average (VARMA) models in discrete time, Phillips recognised that the efficient estimation of continuous time models required algorithms for the estimation of VARMA models. Since none was available, Phillips devised one. His algorithm was presented in his Walras–Bowley lecture to the North American Meetings of the Econometric Society held in San Francisco in 1966. It was published posthumously in 1978 and is reprinted in chapter

45. Like his earlier paper in *Biometrika*, this paper broke new ground by being the first to tackle the general problem of estimating VARMA models and it predated the interest in these systems in the statistical literature of the 1970s and 1980s (Hannan and Dreistler 1988). Characteristically, the Phillips algorithm was one of creative improvisation. It used an iterated linearized least squares approach to overcome the central difficulty presented by the VARMA likelihood of being a very complicated rational function of the parameters. While the Phillips iteration is not used in VARMA estimation today, related recursive techniques (primarily those of Hannan and Rissanen (1982) and Hannan and Kavalieris (1984)) have indeed subsequently proved themselves to be a favoured practical method of estimating models with moving-average errors and of empirically determining the appropriate lag dimensions of these models. Interestingly, the latter problem is not addressed in Phillips' paper. One reason for this is that when the underlying system is a pth-order stochastic differential equation system the corresponding exact discrete model is a VARMA with known autoregressive order p and moving-average order of $p-1$. Thus, in this special case as Phillips was well aware, order estimation is unnecessary because the correct orders are determined by the original specification of the continuous time system. There is now a huge literature on the subject of VARMA modelling, and many aspects of it are reviewed by Hannan and Deistler (1988), although curiously they do not reference Phillips' paper. Phillips' work on this topic illustrates his capacity to take a neglected subject and make an important original contribution long before it evolves into a rich field of research.

A final fascinating example of Phillips' uncanny ability to home in early on subjects of great importance is given by Robin Court in his essay on the Lucas Critique introducing chapters 50, 51 and 52. Court reveals that the 1968 Phillips paper (chapter 50) demonstrates a fundamental lack of identifiability of econometric models in the presence of endogenous policy rules and that this lack of identifiability affects reduced forms. As Court's essay documents, this problem is closely related to the Lucas Critique that policy changes affect the structure of econometric models and thereby frustratingly discombobulate econometric evidence. One can carry Robin Court's interesting discussion a little further. The usual antidote to the Lucas Critique is to set up models in terms of so-called deep structural parameters (for example, the parameters of an economic agent's preferences) that are invariant to policy changes. However, Phillips' point that the effect of endogenous policy rules may be to lose the identifiability of the reduced form means that even deep structural parameters may be unrecoverable when the reduced-form coefficients are themselves unidentified. One can further speculate on the potential effects of unidentifiable reduced forms on the validity of econometric tests of the Lucas critique. To this extent at least, the 1968 Phillips paper (chapter 50) and his later unpublished work from 1972 (chapter 52) that is discussed by Court, may yet have an influence on subsequent research, irrespective of the historical issue of his work on this topic pre-dating that of Lucas (1976).

In conclusion, Bill Phillips' legacy to econometrics came primarily and most obviously from his direct scientific contributions to continuous time modelling and its associated statistical methods. However, his influence on the subject has been more pervasive than the immediate progeny of his scientific work on continuous time econometrics. Of great significance is his influence on matters of econometric model design, a subtle and vital subject on which there is no ultimate authority and on which there has been much debate and discussion in recent years. Phillips' work in the 1950s pointed a clear path to error correction mechanisms as a foundation for theoretical and empirical econometric models, a tradition that has been faithfully upheld in the continuous time literature ever since and that has recently gained strong support in discrete time series modelling. As discussed above, this approach is now very relevant to modern multivariate time series methods for modelling stationary and non-stationary processes. Moreover, Phillips' thinking on the effects of integrating endogenous policy into econometric analysis connects in surprisingly close ways with that of Lucas and seems to offer insights that are still worthy of exploration. Overall, his research is marked by a talent for creative thinking, improvisation and the courage to forge new ways forward rather than follow established scientific paradigms. And his papers demonstrate a concern for fundamentals and an ability to explain essentials in a simple and readable manner that makes for a wide readership. In all of this, Bill Phillips' work on econometrics continues to define its own unique paradigm and to be a fine example to the econometrics community.

37 The Published Papers

Peter C.B. Phillips

Nik

Chapters 40, 41, 42 and 43 comprise Bill Phillips' published works on the subject of formulating dynamic continuous time econometric models, estimating these models with discrete time series data, and using them in prediction and for economic policy. The papers represent a progressive series of attempts to tackle this subject and they show a growing recognition of its many different practical and conceptual aspects.

Chapter 42 on 'The Estimation of the Parameters in Systems of Stochastic Differential Equations' offers the most general treatment of the subject and it is the most cited of these papers. Historically, it is a landmark contribution, being the first paper in the literature of statistics and economics to deal exclusively with the problem of estimating continuous time systems with discrete observations. It is also the first paper in what has subsequently become a large econometric literature on this general subject. It can rightfully be thought of as the pioneering work in this research area.

The model formulated by Phillips in this paper is the linear system of lagged dependencies

$$y_i(t) = \sum_{j=1, j\neq i}^{n} \int_{-\infty}^{t} w_{ij}(t-s)y_j(s)ds + \sum_{j=1}^{n} \int_{-\infty}^{t} r_{ij}(t-s)\zeta_j(s)ds \qquad (1)$$

relating the observable variables $y_i(t)$ for $i = 1, \ldots, n$ and the unobservable disturbances $\zeta_i(t)$, all measured in continuous time. If the weighting functions $w_{ij}(\cdot)$ and $r_{ij}(\cdot)$ are restricted to the class of square integrable functions, whose Laplace transforms are proper rational functions, then (1) can be regarded as the solution of the stochastic differential equation system

$$F(D)y(t) = G(D)\zeta(T), \qquad (2)$$

where F and G are matrix polynomials in the stochastic differential operator $D = d/dt$, with the degree of G usually being lower than the degree of F.

As it stands, the system (2) is rather general and we can expect that many different models of economic behaviour can usefully be represented by such a system. Chapter 40, 'Some Notes on the Time-Forms of Reactions in Interdependent Dynamic Systems' discusses some explicit versions of this type of model, including the following consumption function which relates aggregate consumption, C, to past income, Y, according to the relation

$$C(t) = \int_0^l f(\tau) Y(t - \tau) d\tau + \kappa + \varepsilon(t). \tag{3}$$

Here, the time form of the response expires after a finite time period l, whereas in the general system (1) the initial conditions are effectively set in the infinite past. Much of chapter 40 (first published in 1956) is spent studying time forms of reactions of one economic variable to another in equations like (3) and interdependent systems involving several such stochastic integral equations.

In (3) the variables are quantified as instantaneous rates of consumption and instantaneous rates of income generation, whereas econometric measurements of them are time averages given by integrals over unit time periods such as $C_t = \int_{t-1}^t C(s) ds$, and $Y_t = \int_{t-1}^t Y(s) ds$. Such time averaging involves an information loss and hence discrete time dynamic relations between C_t and Y_{t-k}, for $k \geq 0$, will only approximately represent the true time form of the dynamic response in the original continuous time relation (3). Phillips studies this phenomena and illustrates how the original dynamic reaction function can be quite poorly represented in discrete time. Fifteen years later, Sims (1971a, 1971b) made precisely the same point and gave a formal mathematical analysis of discrete distributed lag approximations to continuously distributed lags. Curiously, Sims did not refer to Phillips' earlier 1956 contribution on this subject and must simply have been unaware of it.

In addition to studying the time forms of lagged responses, chapter 40 also makes some suggestions about econometric estimation of the discrete dynamic model approximation. This part of the paper has an interesting concluding section that surveys several practical possibilities which range from estimating unrestricted dynamic systems, through to estimating specific lag relationships (recognised by Phillips to be inevitably misspecified). An intriguing feature of this final section is the proposal by Phillips to use an analogue computing device (or 'simulator', as Phillips called it) to compute the integrated 'fitted' values of the dependent variable which could be compared with the observed discrete data on an oscilloscope. Phillips (chapter 40) goes on to propose

that the time-forms of the reaction functions set on the separate response simulators would be adjusted by a trial and error process to obtain the minimum integral of the square of the residual.

Interestingly, this proposal is very similar to modern methods of dealing with non-linear stochastic differential equations using the so-called method of indirect inference.[1]

In chapter 40, Phillips develops an estimation procedure for the general system of linear stochastic differential equations given in (2). His idea is to expand the Laplace transform of the auto-covariance matrix function of the system variates $y(t)$ in partial fractions and use sample auto-covariance matrices from discrete data to estimate the unknown elements in this expansion and recover the coefficients in the lag polynomials in (2) from this expansion.

Ingenious though this procedure was, it has several major shortcomings and appears never to have been applied in practice either by Phillips himself or anyone else, although the paper ends with a comment that simulation experiments were being conducted. One disadvantage is that the procedure makes no allowance for potential *a priori* restrictions on the parameters of the system (2). Conceivably, this difficulty could be dealt with by applying a generalised method of moment approach instead of Phillips' moment matching method. A more serious disadvantage is that the method does not take into account the aliasing problem in fitting continuous systems with discrete data, which was discussed later in papers by Telser (1967) and myself (Phillips 1973). Both of these points can be illustrated by reference to the special first-order differential equation case of (2) in which

$$F(D) = I - AD, \quad \text{and} \quad G(D) = I;$$

where the $n \times n$ matrix A has distinct eigenvalues in the left half plane, so the system is stationary. The method proposed by Phillips leads in this case to the estimate A^* satisfying

$$\exp(A^*) = C_1 C_0^{-1}, \tag{4}$$

where

$$C_1 = T^{-1} \sum_{t=1}^{T} y(t)y(t-1)', \quad C_0 = T^{-1} \sum_{t=1}^{T} y(t)y(t)'.$$

(In fact, somewhat earlier than Phillips, Quenouille (1957) had suggested this estimator for the first-order stochastic differential equation case.)

First, note that if there are restrictions on the coefficient matrix A, then the estimator A^* will not necessarily satisfy these restrictions. However, a GMM estimator could be designed to overcome this difficulty by writing down the moment matching equations, functionalising $A = A(\theta)$ in terms of the unrestricted parameters and then estimating θ by minimising an appropriately weighted quadratic form constructed from the differences $\exp(A(\theta)) - C_1 C_0^{-1}$. This type of GMM approach to the estimation of stochastic differential equations does not yet seem to have been tried, and may be useful here and in incomplete systems.

Second, the equation system (4) cannot be solved uniquely without imposing conditions on the imaginary parts of the complex eigenvalues of the matrix $B^* = C_1 C_0^{-1}$. This is because the matrix function $A^* = \log(B^*)$ is a multi-valued function when B^* has complex latent roots. This is the manifestation of the aliasing problem in econometric estimation of a continuous system coefficient matrix A with discrete data. If the latent roots of B^* are all real and positive then the problem does not arise, but complex roots can be expected in all but the smallest systems in practical applications. A final practical difficulty with this approach is that when negative real roots of B^* arise, the system does not admit a solution.

While all of these problems can potentially be overcome, the Phillips approach was never used. A short time after Phillips' work, Bergstrom (1966a) suggested a highly practical approach for econometric estimation that utilised standard simultaneous equations methodology. In 1972, I gave a non-linear regression approach that was based on the exact reduced-form model satisfied by the data in discrete time and this method yielded consistent and asymptotically efficient estimates of the parameters of first-order stochastic differential equations (Phillips 1972). These two methods and their various extensions have formed the basis of most empirical work in the field ever since.[2]

Chapters 42 and 43 are short studies that focus on certain issues of specification, prediction and regulation of continuous time econometric systems. The approach in both papers is to proceed by way of illustrative examples and no general treatment is attempted. The joint paper with Quenouille (chapter 43) discusses the specification of discrete time dynamic models – vector autoregressions (VARs) and structural VARs – and differential equations. Here, and in chapter 42, it is argued that recursive formulations provide more realistic models in continuous time than non-recursive systems basically because behavioural units like economic agents do not respond to change instantaneously. In terms of the formulation of systems like (1) and (3) this means that the response functions do not contain any delta function impulses, and then in (2) the numerator polynomials in the differential operator are of lower degree than the denominator polynomials. Such restrictions aid in the identification of these systems. To wit, in the authors' words in chapter 43 (although we may note that these ignore aliasing difficulties):

In both continuous and discrete systems the problem of identification will often be overcome if careful attention is given to the formulation of the basic model as a system of dynamic behaviour relationships.

Both these papers discuss the regulation of economic systems using feedback control mechanisms. Part of the discussion is conducted in terms of non-stochastic systems, but part also deals with stochastic optimum control in the sense of Wiener (1949), where the object is to minimise a certain mean squared error criterion function involving the variable that is the object of the stabilisation policy. Chapter 41, on 'Cybernetics and the Regulation of Economic Systems' makes the point particularly strongly that excessive feedback can easily be the cause of instability in economic systems, just as it is in mechanical systems. In stochastic systems 'the optimum strength of the stabilisation policy depends on the quantitative values of all the relationships in the system and also on the auto-correlation function of the disturbances'.

Phillips was cautious in drawing conclusions from the illustrative examples in these papers. He saw that they pointed out a clear need to know much more about the quantitative relations between economic variables before sensible and helpful economic policy could be formulated on a scientific econometric basis, a conclusion that was echoed years later by Christ (1975) in his empirical evaluation of the performance of econometric models of the USA.

Notes

Thanks go to the NSF for research support under Grant No. SES 94-22922.
1 See Monfort (1996).
2 See Bergstrom (1988) for an historical review.

38 The Influence of A.W. Phillips on Econometrics

David F. Hendry and Grayham E. Mizon

Introduction

It is a privilege to contribute to this volume of the *Collected Works* of A.W.H. 'Bill' Phillips. We both knew Bill as a teacher and later colleague, so we commence our chapter with some personal recollections of our first acquaintances. Then we turn to a consideration of the many ways in which Phillips influenced econometrics, focusing on three main aspects (control theory, moving-average errors in dynamic models, and exogeneity).[1]

Personal recollections

Initial contacts

GEM first became aware of Bill Phillips when he visited the Economists' Bookshop following an interview at the LSE for admission to the under-graduate B.Sc.(Econ) degree course. Having previously studied econom-ics from a single textbook in school, he was overwhelmed by the vast array of economics books, arranged not only alphabetically but by sub-discipline. Looking for an inexpensive and less daunting purchase, he came across a section containing very short pamphlets and published versions of public lectures. From this section, he found a copy of an inaugural lecture entitled 'Employment, Inflation and Growth' (chapter 22). The combination of subject matter and price attracted him, and so he was soon reading and learning from Bill Phillips. Topics covered in this lecture included discussion of the role of econometric models in economic policy analysis, emphasis on the value of feedback control mechanisms using proportional, derivative and integral controls in economic analysis, and interpretations and modifications to the Phillips Curve (chapter 25), which was to play an important role in macroeconomics during the 1960s and 1970s. During his subsequent studies at LSE, GEM began to realise

353

the importance of the material in this lecture. Also GEM has a vivid memory of listening (at the end of the first year of his studies when Phillips and Bergstrom ran a meeting describing the statistics and econometrics courses that were available to second- and third-year students) to two quietly spoken, neatly dressed, New Zealanders explain concisely the regulations concerning econometrics-based degrees, and describe without embellishment the content of the courses that they were to teach. They presented the case for following their courses in the way that they knew best, by their quiet enthusiasm. In the years that followed, GEM for one has rarely regretted following that path, and Pravin K. Trivedi (a contemporary of GEM as a student at the School) recently confirmed in personal conversation that Phillips' infectious enthusiasm for econometrics was also an important factor in his career choice.

In addition to having direct contact with Phillips in the econometrics courses, GEM's attention was drawn to his contributions to economics by reading R.D.G. Allen's *Mathematical Economics* (1963), a recommended text for mathematical economics courses at the time. Allen's discussion of the acceleration principle contained an exposition of material from chapter 16 of the present volume. The importance of dynamics in economic models was highlighted by Allen's discussion of the time form of lagged responses, which was based on chapter 17 of the present volume. Allen also provided an introduction to basic ideas in the theory of economic regulation, the use of control theory – including feedback control via proportional, derivative and integral control mechanisms – and the characterisation of economic systems in flow diagrams, which had their physical counterpart in the Phillips hydraulic machine. Indeed, Frank Paish's lectures, as a part of an applied economics course, were given in a room with the Phillips hydraulic model of the linkages of stocks and flows in the economy hidden under a dust cover. The implicit contrast between the application of control theory to dynamic economic systems patiently awaiting its time, and the less formal intuitive understanding of market interactions, which via a cylindrical slide rule was made more numerically concrete, was striking.

DFH first met Bill Phillips at the LSE in 1966, and had the stimulating experience of being taught by him as an M.Sc. student. The Phillips Curve was already a famous concept and chapter 24 was mandatory reading on the Quantitative Economics course, although jointly with Sargan (1964) (Denis ran that option!). DFH had also heard of the Phillips Machine, although had not witnessed it in action, so Phillips was a decidedly 'big name'.

Notwithstanding his fame, Phillips was a kindly and helpful person, if very private and shy. He was always encouraging one to persevere, despite all the obvious difficulties one could see. The warmth and sympathy that exuded from Phillips in his teaching relationship with students did not override the impression of a mysterious character. Whether the mystery resulted from his reaction to earlier episodes in his life (particularly being held as a prisoner of war by the Japanese) we can only conjecture. Max Steuer suggested to us that it was partly due to Phillips having come to social science through sociology – but never feeling at home there – so he was mainly self-taught in economics. His one real teacher was James Meade (who unfortunately died in 1995), who quickly recognised Phillips' unusual intelligence. This, combined with Phillips' creativity and his oblique view of economics, meant he was somewhat of an outsider. Nevertheless, Phillips played a key role in modernising the economics department at the LSE, winning the support of even Lionel Robbins to introduce mathematics and econometrics.

Phillips the teacher

His undergraduate lectures on 'Statistical Methods in Economics' were models of clarity, given by a person sympathetic to the problems experienced by students coming to econometrics for the first time. It was during these lectures that many LSE students gained an understanding of material in the early econometrics textbooks by Johnston and Goldberger, and acquired a better insight into the content of the previous lecture course given by Denis Sargan. As a teacher of graduate courses for the M.Sc. in Mathematical Economics and Econometrics, Phillips was equally brilliant. His lectures on optimal control of linear systems were masterly, and his contributions to the Quantitative Economics seminar always helpful and revealing. In that seminar, Bill and Denis would debate the merits of alternative modelling approaches, whether to use moving-average or autoregressive errors, and how effective economic policy could be. We listened in awe.[2] One of these seminars each year was concerned with the modelling of wages and prices. It was a rewarding experience for the participants to be guided through the existing literature and receive numerous suggestions for further research topics from Phillips and Sargan arguing about money-wage versus real-wage models, on which topic both had published seminal work.

Phillips the researcher

Coming from an electrical engineering background to economics, Phillips was in the forefront of the researchers seeking to develop formal models of the economic system. Bill Phillips and Karl Popper were greatly revered by their young and dynamic colleagues such as Richard Lipsey, Chris Archibald, Maurice Peston, Max Steuer and Ralph Turvey. There was a fervour for a scientific approach to economics, and clamour for increased and improved empirical studies of economic phenomena, exemplified and maintained by the regular meeting of the seminar entitled 'Methodology, Measurement and Testing'.

An invaluable and long-lasting illustration of the fact that research results do not always (perhaps rarely) come quickly or easily, was provided by the prolonged gestation period for the production and eventual publication of what was to become the 1966 Walras–Bowley lecture to the Econometric Society meeting in San Francisco (chapter 45). Early versions of the paper on the estimation of linear dynamic systems with vector moving-average errors were presented to the Econometrics Doctoral workshop run by Sargan and Phillips. An important feature of this research was the design of estimation methods that were feasible with the then available computing facilities. Had Phillips had access to the computing facilities available today, we can only speculate about his productivity.

The legacy of Phillips' contributions

Here, we are concerned with how Phillips' work influenced UK econometricians. We note five main topics:
1 the application of control methods to dynamic econometric models;
2 the estimation of dynamic equations with moving-average errors;
3 the formalisation of exogeneity;
4 the estimation of continuous time econometric systems; and
5 the modelling of wage and price inflation.
Within this already limited set, the first three topics will receive most attention.

A search of the Social Science Citation Index from 1981 to 1995 reveals that much of his work remains influential: there were approximately 270 citations, relating to all five topics listed above and involving a wide range of journals. Certainly, the modal cite was to the 'Phillips Curve', but 1–4 also appeared regularly.

Control methods

Because of his engineering background, and his influential papers on economic policy, Phillips had ensured that control theoretic ideas were taught at the School. His work showed that the variability of macroeconomies could be reduced by appropriately designed feedback stabilisers.

When Phillips left the School, DFH had to undertake some of his teaching, particularly the analysis and application of control methods to macroeconomic stabilisation.

This teaching was based on three components: the techniques for derivative, proportional and integral control servomechanisms which Phillips had helped to introduce to economics (chapters 16 and 40), the linear least-squares methods lucidly explained by Whittle (1963); and the linearquadratic model, optimising a quadratic function of departures from pre-specified target trajectories for a linear dynamic system over a finite future horizon.[3] The lecture notes for this part were 'inherited' from Phillips (indirectly), since few contemporaneous textbooks explained the main procedures involved in factorising lead-lag polynomials in time operators (usually the lag operator, denoted L). While such material is common now, we believe it was unusual in mid 1960s courses.

Consider, for example, the quadratic cost function $C_{(T)}$ which penalises the deviations of a variable x_t from a pre-specified target trajectory $\{x^*_{t+j}\}$ subject to costs of adjustment represented by changes $\Delta x_{t+j} = x_{t+j} - x_{t+j-1}$ over a T-period horizon

$$C_{(T)} = \sum_{j=0}^{T} C_t = \sum_{j=0}^{T} \frac{1}{2}\left[(x_{t+j} - x^*_{t+j})^2 + \alpha(\Delta x_{t+j})^2\right].$$

To minimise C_T at time $t+j$, differentiate with respect to x_{t+j}, noting that $\Delta x_{t+j+1} = x_{t+j+1} - x_{t+j}$, thereby depends on x_{t+j}, which yields (ignoring the end point for simplicity)

$$\frac{\partial C_{(T)}}{\partial x_{t+j}} = \frac{\partial C_{t+j}}{\partial x_{t+j}} + \frac{\partial C_{t+j+1}}{\partial x_{t+j}} = x_{t+j} - x^*_{t+j} + \alpha(\Delta x_{t+j}) - \alpha(\Delta x_{t+j+1})$$

so equating to zero for a minimum

$$x_{t+j} - x^*_{t+j} + \alpha\Delta x_{t+j} - \alpha\Delta x_{t+j+1} = 0.$$

This can be re-expressed as a polynomial involving leads and lags in L

$$x_{t+j} + \alpha x_{t+j} - \alpha L x_{t+j} - \alpha L^{-1} x_{t+j} + \alpha x_{t+j} = x^*_{t+j}$$

or (for $\alpha \neq 0$)

$$(L^{-1} - (2 + \alpha^{-1}) + L)x_{t+j} = (L^{-1} - \lambda_2)(1 - \lambda_1 L)x_{t+j} = -\frac{x^*_{t+j}}{\alpha}$$

The polynomial has roots λ_1 and λ_2 with a product of unity (so are inverses, λ_1 inside, λ_2 outside the unit circle) and a sum of $(2 + \alpha^{-1})$. Inverting the first factor expresses x_{t+j}, as a function of lagged x_{t+j}, and current and future values of the target x^*_{t+j}

$$(1 - \lambda_1 L)x_{t+j} = -(L^{-1} - \lambda_2)^{-1}\frac{x_{t+j}^*}{\alpha} = \lambda_1(1 - \lambda_1 L^{-1})^{-1}\frac{x_{t+j}^*}{\alpha}$$

since $(1/\lambda_2) = \lambda_1$. The last term can be expanded as a power series in L^{-1} as $\lambda_1 < 1$

$$(1 - \lambda_1 L)x_{t+j} = \frac{\lambda_1}{\alpha}[1 + \lambda_1 L^{-1} + \lambda_1^2 L^{-2} + \ldots]x_{t+j}^*$$

$$= \frac{\lambda_1}{\alpha}\sum_{k=0}^{\infty}\lambda_1^k x_{t+j+k}^*.$$

An operational procedure is obtained by replacing any unknown future targets by their expected values. However, the implication that all future values of the target needed to be known in advance, or correctly anticipated, persuaded DFH that the approach was not very relevant for empirical modelling, although the special case of a one-period horizon was used in Hendry and Anderson (1977).

That last formulation also contained the germ of the notion of an 'Error Correction Mechanism' (ECM) which was initially based on log-ratios of economic series that might nevertheless be 'equilibria'.[4] For example, UK building societies, which were non-profit organisations, were modelled as striving to maintain constant ratios of lending to borrowing, by adjusting lending margins and growth rates. With hindsight, the ECM was that ratio, and the derived model was one with derivative and proportional control, though that interpretation was not made at the time. Let

$$x_{t+j}^{**} = (1 - \lambda_1)\sum_{k=0}^{\infty}\lambda_1^k x_{t+j+k}^*$$

denote the 'ultimate' target (scaled so that the weights sum to unity),[5] then (other than the end point)

$$x_{t+j} = \lambda_1 x_{t+j-1} + \frac{\lambda_1}{\alpha(1 - \lambda_1)}x_{t+j}^{**}$$

so that

$$\Delta x_{t+j} = -(1 - \lambda_1)x_{t+j-1} + (1 - \lambda_1)x_{t+j}^{**} = -(1 - \lambda_1)[x_{t+j-1} - x_{t+j}^{**}] \tag{1}$$

noting that

$$\frac{1 - 2\lambda_1 + \lambda_1^2}{(1 - \lambda_1)} = (1 - \lambda_1) = \frac{\lambda_1}{\alpha(1 - \lambda_1)}.$$

Thus, once one knows where to look for the formulation, ECMs appear readily in transformations of the optimal control problem, although (1) is a restricted specification, involving only proportional control, and excluding derivative (Δx^{**}_{t+j}).

Nevertheless, having the latent idea helped when puzzling over anomalies in UK consumers' expenditure equations, as it led to noticing the 'DHSY' formulation (Davidson, Hendry, Srba and Yeo 1978). Although the model in Sargan (1964) was already an ECM, the idea of the class being a general one does not seem to have been perceived before DHSY.[6] Together with the realisation that it is not necessary to have stationary regressors and regressand in order to have a stationary error (Hendry and Mizon 1978), this follow up to Phillips' work helped to precipitate the notion of 'cointegration' (Granger 1981).

The interpretation of DHSY in terms of servo-mechanistic control was *post hoc*, as DFH did not see the connection initially. Worse still, he did not even think of using Phillips' famous work on policy control (chapters 16 and 40) as a basis for empirical specifications despite both knowing his work well, and having studied Sargan (1964) many times. It is surprising how hard it is to cross-link ideas, even such a simple step as using work on controlling dynamic equations when specifying empirical dynamic models. The notion of integral control referred to in Mizon and Hendry (1980) and used in Hendry and von Ungern-Sternberg (1981), however, was directly based on chapter 40 of this volume, once the connections had become clearer.

Since then, other researchers have pursued many related avenues. In particular, Salmon (1982) related the ECM idea to the general control theory literature to show the need for the three 'correctors' that Phillips had proposed (namely integral, derivative and proportional). Engle and Granger (1987) showed that cointegration and proportional ECM were equivalent, linking time series approaches more closely with econometric modelling. However, recent research on the impact of regime shifts on cointegrated processes has highlighted the need to distinguish equilibrium correction, which includes cointegration and operates successfully only within regimes, from error correction which stabilises even in the face of other non-stationarities.[7] The assumptions concerning the stationarity or otherwise of the entity to be controlled were rarely explicitly stated, although the notion of 'stabilisation' regularly occurred. This suggests, perhaps, a stationary state or a system centred around a steady state growth path, but also consistent with preventing an unstable system from diverging. When processes are highly nonstationary, even after differencing and cointegration, it is unclear how well servo-mechanisms will function, and more adaptive methods merit consideration. It is possible that integral control could correct for systematic deviations due to shifts in equilibria, but that idea is hard to reconcile with all variables having coherent numbers of unit roots (preferably none) without introducing multi-cointegration,[8] which recreates the regime-shift problem at a higher level.

Other solutions also merit consideration. For example, exponentially weighted moving averages are an error-correction model, adjusting more or less rapidly to wherever the target variable moves; in contrast, cointegrated relations converge on their means, which would be the incorrect target when the mean altered. In essence, either the dynamics must ensure correction, or the target implicit in the econometric model must move when the regime alters. This last result explains why models in differences are not as susceptible to certain forms of structural break as equilibrium correction systems.[9]

The introduction of moving-average models leads conveniently to the next topic.

Moving-average errors

Following his development of the theory for the maximum likelihood estimation of linear dynamic models with moving-average errors, Phillips (1966) was assisted in 1966–7 by Trivedi to write a computer program to implement the new method. Much of the difficulty lay in computing the estimator, which did not have an obvious non-iterative numerical solution. Phillips (1966) was concerned to make the approach operational. Although Phillips presented the Walras–Bowley lecture in 1966, he had lingering doubts about the identification of the autoregressive and moving-average parameters, and as a result publication did not come until 1978, with only a passing mention of identification issues. In fact, the reference to the empirical determination of the orders of the autoregressive and moving-average lag polynomials (chapter 45) suggests a simple-to-general procedure, no doubt to avoid the lack of identification when the orders are overspecified. Trivedi (1970), who was then one of Phillips' doctoral students, had also been studying inventory behaviour based on control-type models following Holt et al. (1960). Thus, the first two strands are more closely linked than might appear at first sight.

Considerable research had been undertaken on autoregressive errors.[10] Prior to the papers underlying the first edition in 1970 of Box and Jenkins (1976), less attention had been devoted to moving-average errors, although a member of the LSE Statistics Department, M. Quenouille (1957), had provided a detailed study of systems with moving-average errors. From the time of Slutsky's (1937) analysis, it was known that moving averages could induce cyclical behaviour similar to auto-regressions,[11] so they were a promising model for auto-correlated error processes. Consequently, Trivedi undertook a Monte Carlo study of that estimator for dynamic equations with moving-average errors.

DFH was simultaneously investigating the small-sample behaviour of estimators for models with autoregressive errors, following Sargan (1964), so he and Trivedi cooperated in a comparative study that estimated both types of assumed error process on data generated by both forms.[12] The outcome showed primarily that getting the correct order for the error auto-correlation was more important than getting the correct form; that estimators could often be quite badly biased in either approximation (even to the same form); and that multiple optima posed convergence problems. The first finding has since been reflected in the idea that (say) the Lagrange multiplier test for residual auto-correlation has the same power for the two local alternatives.[13] DFH and Trivedi also followed up the ideas prevalent at the time in LSE on more efficient methods of conducting Monte Carlo studies as in for example Sargan and Mikhail (1971).[14]

Since Phillips (1966), much other work has been done on moving-average estimation.[15]

Exogeneity

Chapter 40 focuses on the specification of dynamic models which would sustain least-squares estimation. The relevant notion, now known as 'strict exogeneity', is concerned with regressors being uncorrelated with errors in dynamic systems,[16] and was related to the approach in Wold (1949a), who was Peter Whittle's doctoral supervisor. When errors were potentially auto-correlated, a lack of feedback, or absence of Granger causality (Granger 1969), was needed to obtain consistent estimators.[17] That Phillips was aware of this is apparent from inspection of chapter 45 which contains a brief discussion of exogeneity conditions remarkably similar to those required for strong exogeneity.[18] Indeed, a feature of the equations considered in Phillips (1966) and chapter 43 was the inclusion of non-modelled variables, which helped in the identification of the auto-regressive and moving-average parameters, and also raised the issue of the validity of conditioning on the non-modelled or exogenous variables. Rather than following the standard simultaneous equations literature of the time and asserting that certain variables are exogenous, Phillips (chapter 45) considered the joint density for all variables conditional on initial conditions, which he noted could be factored into a conditional and marginal density. He stated explicitly that the marginal density for the exogenous variables did not involve the parameters of interest.

The work on weak exogeneity in Engle, Hendry and Richard (1983) originally failed to build on the essay that is reprinted in this volume as chapter 17. It was Christopher Sims who suggested a link. However, the motivation for the concepts was very different. Weak exogeneity did not specify the Granger-causality properties of variables, but focused on the situation when there was no loss of information in a conditional model about the parameters of interest. An example in Engle, Hendry and Richard (1983) showed that this could potentially occur even in the presence of autoregressive errors, and, conversely, weak exogeneity of a variable for a parameter of interest did not by itself justify least squares.

Taken together with the work noted above on controlling economic systems and moving-average errors, the important theme of dynamic model specification provides a common thread and remains a major preoccupation of econometricians seeking to understand time series data. That same theme encompasses the next topic, namely continuous time models.

Continuous time modelling

Another topic on which both Phillips (chapter 42) and Sargan (1974) made valuable and influential contributions was that of modelling continuous time processes. Indeed, in the Preface to *Continuous Time Econometric Modelling*, Bergstrom (1990) states that in writing chapters 1 and 3 of that book,[19] he was much influenced by Phillips' research. Further, although Cliff Wymer and Peter Phillips completed their doctoral theses on aspects of continuous time modelling under the supervision of Denis Sargan, Wymer, at least, had previously been jointly supervised by Bill Phillips. With the advent of considerable modelling of large samples of high-frequency financial data, results in these early contributions to continuous time modelling are seeing increasing application. Again, the subsequent literature is large.[20]

Modelling wage and price inflation

Following the seminal work in chapter 25 concerning the inverse relationship between wage inflation and the rate of unemployment, numerous LSE economists have written on the subject.[21] More generally, the Phillips Curve made it into the big time of economics textbooks during the 1960s and 1970s and, modified so as to incorporate inflation expectations, survived for much longer. As noted above, this contribution to both empirical economics and econometrics continues to be cited frequently for both aspects, despite the unconventional initial estimates based on fitting to averages designed to eliminate business-cycle effects.[22] One of the critics of the Phillips Curve, Milton Friedman (1977), was in turn criticised for an inappropriate use of phase averaging by Hendry and Ericsson (1991), and Campos, Ericsson and Hendry (1990).

A recent replication and evaluation of the Phillips Curve using the UK annual data over 1863–1913 by Shadman-Mehta (1996, and chapter 34 of this volume), employing all the modern techniques of multivariate cointegration analysis, recursive system maximum likelihood, and system diagnostic tests concluded that 'the results are remarkably close to his . . . if Phillips was conducting his analysis . . . with the current developments in econometric theory, his overall conclusions would have been much the same'. Her unique cointegrating vector involves only unemployment and nominal inflation, and does not depend on real wages or productivity. But that cointegrating relation influences unemployment rather than inflation, so the dynamic equation is the reverse of how Phillips wrote his model. Such ease of replication of results first established more than forty years ago, and satisfaction of rigorous testing, is impressive testimony to the quality of Phillips' empirical research. Over the whole period to 1990, however, Shadman-Mehta finds noticeably different results, suggesting a regime shift in the later part of the century that has been the subject of considerable controversy.

Conclusion

This section is not aptly titled, since as yet there is no conclusion to the legacy of Bill Phillips' contributions to econometrics. Later researchers were probably often unaware of the extent to which they were building on his contributions, or even how useful his ideas could be in related contexts. We hope this short retrospective has highlighted some of the developments in the main areas of his work.

Notes

Financial support from the UK Economic and Social Research Council under grant R000233447 is gratefully acknowledged. We thank Meghnad Desai, Robert Leeson, Mark Salmon, Max Steuer and Pravin Trivedi for helpful comments on an earlier draft, and Steven Cook for research assistance.
  1 For a recent brief history of the development of dynamic modelling at LSE, including Phillips' role in this, see Mizon (1995); also, Rex Bergstrom relates his work to that of Bill Phillips and notes the stimulus he received in P.C.B. Phillips (1993).

2 See Hendry and Wallis (1984) for an overview of Sargan's contribution – it was an exciting time to be at LSE.
3 See Holt *et al.* (1960)
4 See Hendry (1977).
5 See, for example, Nickell (1985).
6 See Hendry (1993) for a general discussion.
7 See Clements and Hendry (1995a, 1995b).
8 See Granger and Lee (1991).
9 See Clements and Hendry (1995a, 1995b).
10 See Cochrane and Orcutt (1949) for an early example.
11 See Yule (1927).
12 Later published as Hendry and Trivedi (1972).
13 See, for example, Godfrey and Wickens (1982).
14 See also Hammersley and Handscomb (1964).
15 See, inter alia, Aigner (1971); Anderson (1980); Box and Jenkins (1976); Davidson (1981); Harvey and Phillips (1979); Kang (1973); Nicholls *et al.* (1975); Osborn (1976, 1977); Pagan and Nichols (1976); Reinsel (1979); and Sargan and Bhargava (1983).
16 See, for example, Koopmans (1950c); Christ (1966); and Sims (1972).
17 See Geweke (1984).
18 See Engle, Hendry and Richard (1983).
19 Originally published as Bergstrom (1962), and Bergstrom, (1966a) respectively.
20 See Bergstrom (1984) for a bibliographic perspective.
21 Including Desai (1975, 1984); Lipsey (1960); Nickell (1984, 1990b); and Sargan (1964, 1980).
22 See, for example, Gilbert (1989).

39   An Appreciation of A.W. Phillips

Lars P. Hansen and Thomas J. Sargent   B22
B31

Introduction

A way to honour A.W.H. Phillips is to describe the continuing influence of one of his enduring contributions to economic dynamics, his remarkable essay (chapter 42) about how discrete time observations can be used to restrict a continuous time linear model. That chapter precisely described what later came to be known as the problem of 'aggregation over time', set forth a framework for studying it, and achieved useful characterisations of it. Chapter 42 partly shared the destiny of John F. Muth's (1960, 1961) papers about rational expectations. It took years for other economists to recognise how much more could be done with their ideas. In 1960, both Phillips and Muth were far ahead of most other economists in their understanding of the technicalities of time series analysis, and their appreciation of its potential applications to economic dynamics. Economists were not to take up the inquiry from the point left off by Phillips until the early 1970s, when Rex Bergstrom, Christopher Sims, Peter Phillips and others returned to the problem of aggregation over time.

Phillips' framework

Phillips assumed that observations on a vector of data are generated by a continuous time vector stochastic process with a rational spectral density matrix.[1] Continuous time processes with rational spectral densities form a natural environment for studying the effects of aggregation over time, for several interrelated reasons that Phillips described and exploited. In particular, a rational spectral density for the continuous time process implies that:

(a) The spectral density of the discrete time stochastic process implied by skip-sampling (that is, point-in-time sampling) the continuous time process is also rational.

365

(b) The auto-covariance function of the continuous time process is a positive semi-definite *function* defined on the real line that forms a weighted sum of exponentials, with decay parameters λ_i satisfying $|\lambda_i| < 1$.

(c) The auto-covariance sequence of the discrete time process is a positive semi-definite *sequence* defined on the integers, which can be expressed as a weighted sum of geometric functions, with decay factors $\alpha_1 = \exp(\lambda_i)$, where the λ_i's are the same as those in (b), with the *same* weights composing the continuous time auto-covariance function.

(d) The continuous time data can be represented as a system of linear differential equations driven by a continuous time vector 'white noise', itself physically 'unrealisable' as a stochastic process, but which is well defined via processes formed by convoluting it with functions in L^2.

(e) The discrete time data can be represented by a system of linear difference equations, driven by a discrete time vector white noise process.

(f) The continuous time differential equation can be solved to express the continuous time process as a convolution of a function in L^2 with the continuous time noise, i.e., as a continuous time distributed lag of the white noise.

(g) The difference equation for the discrete time data can be solved to express the data as a convolution of a sequence in l^2 with the discrete time white noise.

Chapter 42 describes some of the relationships among these various types of representations, and uses them to discuss how to infer, in so far as this is possible, the parameters of the continuous time process from skip-sampled discrete time data. Chapter 42 assumes that consistent estimates of the discrete auto-covariance function in (c) are available. Results (b) and (c) are the foundation of Phillips' approach, which intends properly to 'fill in' the missing elements of the continuous time auto-covariance function, in light of the restrictions imposed by (b) and (c). Though he does not complete the job of characterising its solution, he makes a great start. The formulas that Phillips develops for (b) and (c) prepare the way for a complete analysis of the identification or 'aliasing problem' involved in inferring a continuous time model from skip-sampled discrete data. The aliasing problem is that, in general, multiple continuous time models have the same discrete time auto-covariance function. The source of multiplicity is that for any integer k, $\alpha_i = \exp(\lambda_i \pm 2\pi i k)$ satisfies the formula linking the exponential factors in (b) and (c). That there are multiple sets of λ_i's that satisfy this equation for given discrete α_i's is the beginning of the aliasing problem. Peter Phillips (1972, 1973, 1974) and Hansen and Sargent (1983, 1991b) pursued this aspect of Phillips' work, and in a sense completed it.

Sims (1971a) and John Geweke (1978) took up another theme of chapter 42, the issue of whether and how closely discrete time distributed lags resemble continuous time distributed lags. Sims developed a powerful formula expressing the discrete time distributed lag in terms of a convolution of the underlying continuous time distributed lag with a particular function of the continuous time auto-covariance function of the regressors. Sims' formula can be interpreted as a sophisticated adaptation of Theil's omitted variable theorem, in which the 'particular function' just mentioned embodies the projection of the missing variables (in this case, a continuum of variables at the missing points between the sampling points) on the included variables (the point-in-time-sampled regressors).

Another matter taken up in recent work concerns inferring features of continuous time vector autoregressions, including innovation accountings, from their discrete time counterparts. This work is about comparing pairs of Phillips' representations, either (d) and (e), or (f) and (g). Hansen and Sargent (1991b) studied situations in which discrete time impulse response functions resemble the underlying continuous time impulse responses. Hansen and Sargent remained within Phillips' framework of a rational continuous time spectral density, and study the role of mean square continuity and differentiability of the vector stochastic process in yielding or breaking resemblance. The order of mean square differentiability for the vector process is inherited directly from the orders of the polynomials determining the rational spectral density matrix. Albert Marcet (1991) studied these questions in a framework that breaks with Phillips by dealing with continuous time processes without rational spectral densities. The assumption of a rational spectral density imposes continuity and higher-order differentiability on the kernel (that is, the continuous time distributed lag) in representation (f). Marcet kept the kernel in L^2, but let it be discontinuous. He showed how those discontinuities substantially complicate the problem of aggregation over time, and make it possible for the discrete time impulse response functions to badly misrepresent the continuous time representations.[2]

The problem of aggregation over time was at first taken up mainly by macroeconomists interested in the practical implementation of another line of work to which A.W. Phillips contributed: the quantitative analysis and design of macroeconomic and monetary policy. Because they wanted to inform monetary policy (which is executed hourly), economists at the Federal Reserve wanted to estimate weekly, daily, or even continuous time models, and approached the aliasing problem via the analysis of information processing for monetary control. Kareken, Muench and Wallace's (1973) work on timely use of information for controlling a Keynesian macroeconomic model attributed an intricate type of 'rational expectations' to the monetary authority, but none to the private agents in the economy. That same year, Wallace and others began building macro-economic models with private agents whose possession of rational expectations substantially, sometimes adversely, affected what the monetary authorities could achieve by way of stabilisation policy.

Rational expectations threw new light over wide areas of macroeconomics and econometrics, including the aggregation over time or aliasing problem. The assumption of rational expectations often provides enough identifying information to infer a unique continuous time model from discrete time data. Christiano (1984), Christiano and Eichenbaum (1987), Heaton (1993) and Hansen and Sargent (1991b) have exploited this route to identification, in the context of models with rational spectral densities. Interestingly, the rational expectations cross-equation restrictions can achieve identification without using the restriction to a rational spectral density matrix.[3]

A recent paper on aggregation over time for non-linear models is by Hansen and Scheinkman (1995). They use moment conditions for 'test functions' to identify non-linear continuous time Markov processes from discrete time data.[4] Their main examples are models specified as non-linear stochastic differential equations generalising (d) but within the confines of Markov theory. Operator counterparts to the issues raised by Phillips under (b) and (c) recur in Hansen and Scheinkman (1995).

Notes

1 For continuous time, a rational spectral density is one that can be expressed as a (matrix) *ratio* of two finite-order polynomials in angular frequency w, where for a matrix, 'division' means multiplying by its inverse.

2 Sims (1984) deduced a 'local martingale' characterisation for a class of continuous time processes, a result that he uses to interpret the good fits of random walk models for a variety of asset prices. Sims' continuous time processes are not martingales, but are 'locally unpredictable'.

3 Christiano contributed a vivid heuristic image of how the rational expectations cross-equation restrictions can resolve the aliasing problem. A manifestation of the aliasing problem familiar to movie-goers is the illusion that wheels appear to be moving backwards when they should be moving forward, and that occasionally when a vehicle speeds up, its wheels appear first to accelerate, then to move backwards. This illusion stems from the fact that the movie camera is skip-sampling a continuous process, leading the eye to solve the equation $\alpha_i = \exp(\lambda_i + 2\pi i k)$ for a *negative* value of α_i when the actual α_i is positive. If one focuses on the wheel alone, there is no way to determine from the skip-sampled camera shots whether or not the backward motion is an illusion. The motion of the vehicle relative to other objects (e.g., trees in the background) allows the viewer to determine the speed and direction of the vehicle, and so to

resolve the aliasing problem. The motion relative to other objects plays a role similar to one exploited by the econometrician in rational expectations models, who interprets discrete time observations on people's behaviour in terms of their forecasts of the underlying continuous time stochastic process.

4 See also Ait-Sahalia (1996).

40 Some Notes on the Estimation of Time-Forms of Reactions in Interdependent Dynamic Systems

A.W. Phillips

1 The need for quantitative knowledge of economic reactions

In dealing with questions of economic policy it is necessary to form some judgement about the magnitudes and time-forms of the responses of individuals or groups of individuals to changes in certain of the conditions confronting them. We may take as an example the problems facing a government which is pursuing a policy of keeping employment at the highest level consistent with the maintenance of free convertibility, at a fixed rate of exchange, between its own currency and that of another major country, it being the policy of the other country to keep its own employment at the highest level consistent with the maintenance of stable product prices.

Let us assume that some change, say an increase in the desire of home firms to invest in new capital equipment, leads to an increase in production and in the demand for factors of production, and that as a result factor prices begin to rise more rapidly than the secular rise in productivity, so that product prices rise. Because of the higher home demand and rising costs and prices, imports will gradually rise and exports decline, the consequent deficit in the balance of payments being met by drawing upon reserves of foreign currency. The government will take action to correct the adverse balance of payments by reducing home demand, either through a reduction in its own expenditure or, more likely, by increasing taxes, or reducing the quantity of money and raising interest rates, in order to induce private individuals and firms to reduce their expenditure. The degree to which a given policy measure will correct the adverse balance, and the speed with which it will do so, will depend on the magnitudes and the speeds of a long chain of reactions, or rather a complex network of interdependent reactions or responses. Examples of these are the response of investment demand to changes in the availability and price of credit and to changes in income, the response of production and income to changes in demand, the response of consumption to changes in income, the responses of prices of products and of factors of production to changes in the demand for them, the responses of consumption and investment demand to changes in the rate of change of prices, and the responses of imports and exports to changes in income and prices, both at home and abroad.

The extent to which it will be necessary to depress economic activity and employment during the correction process will depend on the magnitudes and speeds of these responses, on the size of the foreign reserves at the disposal of the government, and on the magnitude of the initial disturbance. Alternatively, if the reduction in economic activity and employment is to be kept within some limit which is considered tolerable, the size of the reserves that will be needed will depend on the magnitudes and speeds of the responses and on the magnitude of the initial disturbance. It is clear that some quantitative knowledge about the responses in the system is necessary both for rational discussion of the relative merits of alternative policies and for the satisfactory implementation of whatever policy is adopted.

There is another reason, less obvious but no less important, for wishing to obtain quantitative knowledge about the different responses. It can be shown that any interdependent dynamic system may have an inherent tendency to fluctuate when subjected to disturbances. Whether it will fluctuate, and the severity with which it will do so, will depend on the quantitative values of all the relationships in the system, including the policy relationships. Moreover, these dynamic properties of the system depend not only on the magnitudes and speeds of the responses, but also on their time-forms. A change in the time-form of a response, even with no change in the total time required for the response to be completed, may very significantly affect the stability of the system.[1]

There are, therefore, two questions to be asked when judging how effective a certain policy would be in attaining any given equilibrium objectives. First, what dynamic properties and cyclical tendencies will the system as a whole possess when the policy relationships under consideration themselves form part of the system? Second, when the system has these dynamic properties, will the equilibrium objectives be attained, given the size of the probable disturbances and the permissible limits to movements in employment, foreign reserves, etc. The answer to the first question is important, not only because the reduction of cyclical tendencies is itself a desirable objective, but also because the second question cannot be answered without knowing the answer to the first. And the first question cannot be answered without knowing the magnitudes and time-forms of the main relationships forming the system.

2 Theoretical specification of an interdependent system

In this chapter we shall be concerned with estimating the time-forms of structural or behaviour relationships. We shall consider a particular economic example, the dependence of aggregate consumption on the aggregate disposable income of consumers.

Theoretical considerations lead us to the hypothesis that the total quantity of consumers goods purchased per unit of time by all the consumers in a country depends on the total real incomes at their disposal per unit time and on a number of other factors, such as the value of their assets and the rate of change of the average level on product prices. If income changes, the other factors affecting consumption remaining constant, consumers will adjust their purchases of consumers goods. Each consumer affected by the change will take some time to adjust his expenditure, and the speed of adjustment will be different for different consumers. The adjustment in aggregate consumption resulting from a single change in aggregate disposable income will therefore be distributed through time. This is illustrated in figure 40.1. The step in the curve Y at time $t = 0$ represents a unit change in disposable income from a level to which consumption has become fully adjusted. We should expect the time-path of the resulting adjustment of consumption to be somewhat like that shown by curve C, consumption rising slowly for a while, then more rapidly, then more slowly again until at a certain time, say $t = l$, it has again become fully adjusted to the level of income. We shall call the time-path followed by C during this adjustment the direct response of C to a unit step in Y.

In order to obtain a general expression for the relationship between consumption, C, and disposable income, Y, when Y is free to vary continuously, we note that the hypothesis that consumers react to a single change in Y at time $t = 0$ by changing their purchases of consumers goods at different points of time in the interval between $t = 0$ and $t = l$ implies that the value of C at any time t depends on the values taken by Y at earlier points of time in the interval between t and $t - l$. We shall assume that the relationship is linear. Then if the magnitude of the dependence of C at the point of time t on Y at the point of time $t - \tau$ is denoted by $f(\tau)$, the hypothesis can be written in the form of an integral equation

$$C(t) = \int_0^l f(\tau) Y(t - \tau) d\tau + \kappa + \varepsilon(t), \tag{1}$$

in which κ is a constant and $\varepsilon(t)$, which we assume to have zero mean and constant variance, denotes all variations in consumption except those

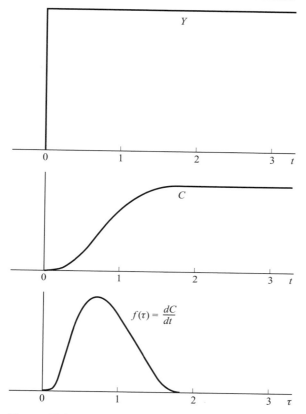

Figure 40.1

resulting from the direct reaction of consumption to changes in income. Following Koyck (1954, 9), we shall call $f(\tau)$ the time-shape, or time-form, of the reaction of C to Y, or the reaction function. Equation (1), and in general any equation expressing a hypothesis, derived from theoretical consideration of the behaviour units constituting the system, will be called a reaction equation.

If $f(\tau)$ is known, the time-path of the adjustment of C resulting from any specified changes in Y, assuming $\varepsilon(t)$ remains constant, can be found from (1). It will be useful to derive the direct response of C to a unit step change in Y, since this response is closely related to the reaction function $f(\tau)$ which it is desired to estimate. If Y remains constant, say at value Y' from a time before $-l$ until time 0, C will reach a constant value, say C', before time 0. Suppose now that the value of Y increases to $Y' + 1$ at time 0 and remains constant at that value until time l. From the principle of superposition in linear systems, the value of C at any time between 0 and l is obtained by adding to the value it would have had if Y had not changed (i.e., C') the effect of the unit increase in Y operating over the interval from 0 to t. That is, the direct response of C to a unit step in Y at $t = 0$ is given by

$$C(t) = \int_0^t f(\tau)d\tau + C', \quad (0 \le t \le l), \tag{2}$$

the integral term in (2) being obtained from that in (1) by setting $Y(t - \tau)$ equal to unity for $0 \le \tau \le t$.

Differentiating (2) with respect to time, we obtain

$$\frac{dC}{dt} = f(t), \quad (0 \le t \le l). \tag{3}$$

Thus setting τ equal to t, the reaction function $f(\tau)$ is given by the direct response of C to unit step in Y at $t = 0$. In figure 40.1, if curve C is the response of C to unit step in Y, the curve $f(\tau) = dC/dt$ is the reaction function. The dependence of consumption on any other factor affecting it can be analysed in a similar way. As we are assuming that the system is linear, the effects of changes in the different factors will be additive and can be allowed for explicitly by putting additional integral terms in (1).

The hypothesis that consumption decisions will be affected by changes in income gives the relationship between C and Y stated in (1). There will also be other relationships between C and Y resulting from other classes of decisions. For example, firms producing consumption goods will alter their output in response to changes in the quantity purchased from them per unit time, causing changes in the disposable income derived from the production of consumption goods. This reaction can be written as

$$X(t) = \int_0^m \phi(h)C(t - h)dh + \lambda + \xi(t), \tag{4}$$

where $X(t)$ is disposable income derived from the production of consumption goods, $\phi(h)$ is the magnitude of the dependence of X at time t on C at time $t - h$, or the time-form of the reaction of X to C, m is the interval over which the dependence exists, λ is a constant and $\xi(t)$ denotes all variations in X except those resulting from the reaction of X to C.

We should expect the time-form of the response of X to a unit step change in C, assuming that $\xi(t)$ remains constant, to be somewhat like that shown by curve X in figure 40.2. The increased purchases of consumption goods would be met for some time by drawing on stocks held by retailers, wholesalers and producers, causing little or no rise in dis-

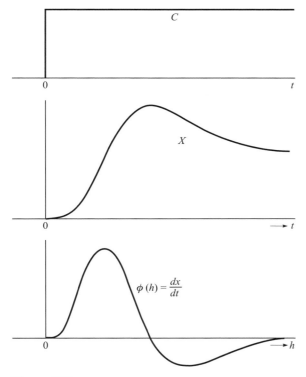

Figure 40.2

posable income. After a time, producers would increase output, some
more rapidly than others, causing a gradual rise in incomes derived
from the production of consumption goods. The desire to replenish
stocks, depleted as a result of the lag in the response of production,
would lead to a rise in production above the level required to meet the
new level of consumption, but as stocks were gradually built up production would fall back again to its new equilibrium level. The corresponding
reaction function, showing the time-form of the dependence of X on past
values of C, is given by the curve $\phi(h) = dX/dt$. The negative values of the
reaction function over part of its range are characteristic of relationships
in which stock and flow adjustments are combined.

   If now we denote disposable income derived from all sources other
than the production of consumption goods by $\zeta(t)$, so that
$Y(t) = X(t) + \zeta(t)$, we obtain from (4) a second relationship between Y
and C

$$Y(t) = \int_0^m \phi(h)C(t - h)dh + \lambda + \xi(t) + \zeta(t). \tag{5}$$

(1) and (5) are a pair of simultaneous integral equations forming an interdependent system.

3 Relationships between discrete series derived from a continuous process

The variables C, Y and ε in (1) are functions of continuous time, and we can think of them as flows per unit time. Our observations, however, are of the quantities resulting from cumulating the flows over discrete periods of time. If the length of the period is Δt, and if we number the period between $t = 0$ and $t = \Delta t$ period 0, that between $t = \Delta t$, and $t = 2\Delta t$ period 1, and so on, then the observed value of C in period n, which we shall denote by C_n, is given by $C_n = \int_{n\Delta t}^{(n+1)\Delta t} C(t)$ and the observed value of Y in period n is $Y_n = \int_{n\Delta t}^{(n+1)\Delta t} Y(t)dt$. Similarly we may define ε_n (which will not be observable) as the time integral, over the nth period, of $\varepsilon(t)$.

Because of the discrete nature of the empirical data, and also because statistical methods for analysing discrete series are more fully developed than those for analysing continuous processes, it has been customary in empirical work in economics to estimate relationships between the discrete observed series, and to use these estimates to make inferences about the relationships existing in the real continuous process. In order to investigate the validity of such inferences, let us suppose that one relationship in a real process is exactly described by (1), and to avoid estimation problems let us eliminate the stochastic element by supposing that $\varepsilon(t)$ remains constant, say at ε'. There is then a unique functional relationship between the continuous variables C and Y. There is not, however, any unique relationship between the observed series of C and Y, since the observed value of C for any period n depends not only on the observed values of Y for the periods n, $n - 1$, etc., but also on the values taken by Y within the periods. Only if Y has a definite intra-period time-form, the same for all periods, will there be a determinate relationship between the observed series.

To take a simple case, let us assume that $Y(t)$ changes only at the final instant of each period, so that $Y(t) = Y_n/\Delta t$ for $n\Delta t \leq t < (n + 1)\Delta t$. Since (1) is linear, the effects on C of the values taken by Y in each period are additive and so can be considered separately. Now the value of Y during period n can be analysed into the sum of two step functions, a step from 0 to $Y_n/\Delta t$ at time $n\Delta t$ and a step from $Y_n/\Delta t$ to 0 at time $(n + l)\Delta t$. If curve (a) in figure 40.3, which has the same form as curve C in figure

40.1, is the direct response of C to unit step in Y at time $n\Delta t$, and curve (b), obtained by shifting (a) one time period along the time axis, is the direct response to unit step in Y at $(n + l)\Delta t$, then the direct response of C to a step to $Y_n/\Delta t$ at time $n\Delta t$ followed by a step $-Y_n/\Delta t$ at time $(n + l)\Delta t$ is equal to the vertical distance between the (a) and (b) curves multiplied by $Y_n/\Delta t$. The amount of consumption during each of the periods $n, n + 1$, and $n + 2$ resulting from the income of period n is therefore the area between the (a) and (b) curves over each of these periods (equal to the rectangles A_0, A_1 and A_2) multiplied by $Y_n/\Delta t$.

By similar reasoning, the consumption of period n resulting from the income of period $n - 1$ is $\frac{Y_{n-1}}{\Delta t}$, A_1 and the consumption of period n resulting from the income of period $n - 2$ is $\frac{Y_{n-2}}{\Delta t}$, A_2. The total consumption in period n is the sum of that resulting from the income of each of the periods $n, n - 1$, and $n - 2$, together with an amount $(\kappa + \varepsilon')\Delta t$ resulting from the constant terms in (1). The relationship between the discrete series for C and Y is therefore

$$C_n = \frac{A_0}{\Delta t} Y_n + \frac{A_1}{\Delta t} Y_{n-1} + \frac{A_2}{\Delta t} Y_{n-2} + (\kappa + \varepsilon')\Delta t. \tag{6}$$

In figure 40.3 the period has been chosen equal to the unit of continuous time, so $\Delta t = 1$. In the lower part of the figure the coefficients of the Y's are drawn as a histogram on the same axes as the reaction function $f(\tau)$. It will be seen that the histogram is a very poor approximation to the reaction function.

From the construction of figure 40.3 it can be seen that the number of periods over which the discrete variables are related is always one more than the number of periods within which the continuous response is completed. It follows that the discrete variables must be related over at least two periods unless the reaction in the continuous system is instantaneous. This is obviously true, since if the reaction is not instantaneous the values taken by C in the early part of any period depend on the values taken by Y in the later part of the preceding period. Very often in econometric work the estimated magnitude of the relationship between two discrete variables in the same period has been interpreted as a measure of the relationship between the continuous variables. This procedure, which in the example we have been considering amounts to taking the estimated height of the rectangle A_0 as a measure of the height of the response curve (a), is clearly invalid unless the reaction is so rapid, relatively to the length of the observation period, that it can be considered almost instantaneous.

To allow for variations in the length of the period, we can write in place of (6) the more general equation

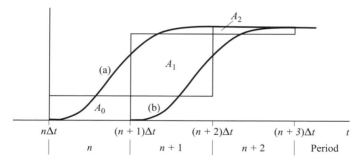

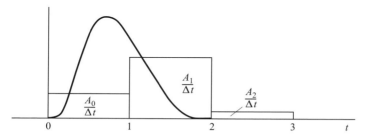

Figure 40.3

$$C_n = \alpha_0 Y_n + \alpha_1 Y_{n-1} + \ldots + \alpha_r Y_{n-r} + (\kappa + \varepsilon')\Delta t, \qquad (7)$$

in which the α's can be found graphically as before and r is the integer which satisfies the condition $\frac{l}{\Delta t} \leq r \leq \frac{l}{\Delta t} + 1$, so that C_n depends upon Y_{n-r} but not upon Y_{n-r-1}, Y_{n-r-2}, etc. In figure 40.4, the length of the period has been reduced to one fifth of that used in figure 40.3, and it will be seen that the histogram of the coefficients of the Y's is now a much better approximation to the reaction function. As the length of the observation period is reduced towards zero the relationship between the discrete variables tends to become independent of the intra-period time-form of the Y's and the histogram of the α's tends to the real reaction function $f(\tau)$.

Since we cannot in practice assume that the Y's will have any definite intra-period time-form, the α's in (7) will not be strictly determinate. In discussing estimation problems in the next section we shall assume that the observation period is sufficiently short for the α's to be fairly well determined, so that it will be possible to speak with some meaning, though not a precise one, about the consistency of estimates of their values.

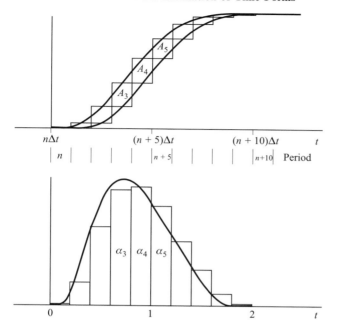

Figure 40.4

4 Estimation problems

When $\varepsilon(t)$ is free to vary (7) becomes

$$C_n = \alpha_0 Y_n + \alpha_1 Y_{n-1} + \ldots + \alpha_r Y_{n-r} + \kappa \Delta t + \varepsilon_n. \tag{8}$$

Equation (5) gives rise to a second relationship between the discrete variables which can be expressed approximately, for small Δt, by the equation

$$Y_n = \beta_0 C_n + \beta_1 C_{n-1} + \ldots + \beta_s C_{n-5} + \lambda \Delta t + \delta_n, \tag{9}$$

in which s is the integer which satisfies the condition

$$\frac{m}{\Delta t} \leq s < \frac{m}{\Delta t} + 1 \text{ and } \delta_n = \int_{n\Delta t}^{(n+1)\Delta t} (\xi + \zeta)dt.$$

We may consider the possibility of estimating the α's in (8) by fitting the estimating equation

$$\hat{C}_n = a_0 Y_n + a_1 Y_{n-1} + \ldots + a_R Y_{n-R} + K \tag{10}$$

to the observed series by the method of least squares. We shall call C_n the observed value of the dependent variable, $\hat{C}_n$ the fitted value of the dependent variable, and $C_n - \hat{C}_n$ the residual. The variables on the right-hand side of the estimating equation will be called the explanatory variables. All the factors to which C directly reacts in the real system will be called determining factors. Any determining factors not included among the explanatory variables will be called omitted factors. Variations in C caused by changes in the omitted factors will be called a disturbance. From standard regression theory, the values of the a's in (10) obtained by minimising the sum of the squares of the residuals will be consistent estimates of the α's in (8) (i.e., the values of the a's will tend to those of the α's as the size of the sample approaches infinity) provided the disturbance is not correlated with any of the explanatory variables.

If there is to be no correlation between the disturbance and the explanatory variables, the following conditions must be satisfied, except in special cases which are trivial:

Condition 1 R in (10) must be equal to or greater than r in (8). For if $R < r$, the determining variables $Y_{n-(R+1)}, Y_{n-(R+2)}, \ldots, Y_{n-r}$ have been omitted from the estimating equation and the disturbance is

$$\alpha_{R+1} Y_{n-(R+1)} + \alpha_{R+2} Y_{n-(R+2)} + \ldots + \alpha_r Y_{n-r} + \varepsilon_n.$$

By substituting (8) in (9) we see that the Y's are generated from the δ's and ε's by an autoregressive process and must therefore be autocorrelated, so the disturbance will in general be correlated with the explanatory variables $Y_n, Y_{n-1}, \ldots, Y_{n-R}$.

Condition 2 β_0 in (9) must be zero[2]. For if β_0 is not zero Y_n will depend on C_n and, from (8), C_n depends on ε_n, so that Y_n will depend on ε_n and so will be correlated with it. Now β_0 will be zero if the reaction of X to C is zero during an interval equal to one observation period, i.e., if the reaction function $\phi(h)$ in (4) and (5), shown graphically in figure 40.2, is zero for $0 \leq h < \Delta t$. It has been argued above that there will be some interval during which the reaction of X to a change in C will be zero or negligible, so with sufficiently short observation periods β_0 may be zero, and if the period is further reduced β_1, β_2, etc. may also become zero.

Condition 3 The disturbance must not be autocorrelated over intervals equal to or greater than the number of periods during which the reaction of X to a change in C is zero.[3] To prove this, suppose that conditions (1) and (2) are satisfied, so that the disturbance is ε_n and $\beta_0 = 0$, and solve (8) and (9) for Y_n. It will be found that the general solution can be written

$$Y_n = (B_1\varepsilon_{n-1} + B_2\varepsilon_{n-2} + \ldots) + (\delta_n + L_1\delta_{n-1} + L_2\delta_{n-2} + \ldots) + M,$$
$$(11)$$

where M is a function of the αs, βs, κ, λ and Δt, and so is a constant for given Δt, the expressions in the brackets are infinite series, and the B's and the L's are functions of the α's and β's. It can be shown that if $\beta_i = 0$ for all i from 1 to k, where k is any integer, then $B_i = 0$ for all i from 1 to k; and if $\beta_i \neq 0$ for $i = k + 1$, then $B_i \neq 0$ for $i > k + 1$. Multiplying (11) by ε_n and summing over all observations, we obtain

$$\Sigma\varepsilon_n Y_n = (B_1\Sigma\varepsilon_n\varepsilon_{n-1} + B_2\Sigma\varepsilon_n\varepsilon_{n-2} + \ldots)$$
$$+ (\Sigma\varepsilon_n\delta_n + L_1\Sigma\varepsilon_n\delta_{n-1} + L_2\Sigma\varepsilon_n\delta_{n-2} + \ldots) + M\Sigma\varepsilon_n.$$
$$(12)$$

There will be no correlation between ε_n and Y_n if, and only if, $\Sigma\varepsilon_n Y_n = 0$. If, $\beta_i = 0$ for all i from 1 to k, and if $\beta_i \neq 0$ for $i = k + 1, k + 2, \ldots, s$, then all the terms inside the first pair of brackets will be zero if, and only if, $\Sigma\varepsilon_n\varepsilon_{n-j} = 0$ for all $j > k$.

Condition 4 The ε's must be uncorrelated with δ's of the same and earlier periods. For if this is not so the terms inside the second pair of brackets in (12) will not all be zero.

If these four conditions were all satisfied ε_n would be uncorrelated with Y_n in an infinite sample since all the terms inside both pairs of brackets would vanish, and the last term also vanishes, since ε has zero mean. And by obtaining from (11) the equations for Y_{n-1}, Y_{n-2}, etc., multiplying through by ε_n and summing over all observations it is easily seen that under these conditions ε_n would also be uncorrelated with the other explanatory variables $Y_{n-1}, Y_{n-2}, \ldots, Y_{n-R}$.

However, conditions 3 and 4 cannot in fact be satisfied, since equations (8) and (9) represent only part of a much wider interdependent system, in which there are additional relationships involving reactions of C to changes in the explanatory variables, reactions of both C and the explanatory variables to changes in 'exogenous' factors, i.e., to factors which are themselves independent of the system, and reactions of the explanatory variables to changes in C.

As an example of the first class of reactions, which we shall call forward reactions since the causation runs from the explanatory variables to the dependent variable, we may suppose that changes in income give rise to changes in the value of assets owned by consumers, and that consumers react to changes in the value of their assets by changing their consumption expenditure. Then the variation in consumption resulting from these reactions is included in ε and so ε is dependent on the values taken by Y and δ in the same or earlier periods. In order to prevent correlation between the disturbance and the explanatory variables resulting from these and other sets of forward reactions it is necessary to include among the explanatory variables each factor to which C directly reacts and which itself reacts, directly or indirectly, to changes in any other explanatory variable, unless the variations in C caused by that factor can be estimated by methods independent of the time series data and eliminated from the observed series for C. And from the discussion of condition (1) above it is clear that for each factor included among the explanatory variables sufficient lagged values must be inserted to allow for all the periods over which the dependence of C on that factor exists in the real system.

If those factors to which C directly reacts, and which themselves react, directly or indirectly, to changes in Y, are omitted from the estimating equation, and if the conditions outlined in the next two paragraphs are satisfied, then we may obtain an estimate of the total reaction of C to Y, resulting from the combined effects of all the forward reactions. An estimate of the time-form of a total reaction may be useful for some purposes.

We may take seasonal influences, affecting both the explanatory and the dependent variables, as an example of the second class of reactions, which we shall call parallel reactions to exogenous factors. Again it is possible, in principle, to prevent correlation between the disturbance and the explanatory variables resulting from parallel reactions to exogenous factors, either by estimating separately the direct reaction of C to the relevant exogenous factors and eliminating the estimated variation from the observed series, or by including the relevant exogenous factors among the explanatory variables.

The third class of reactions will be called feedback reactions. As an example, we might expect changes in the sales of consumption goods to lead to changes in firms' investment in capital goods, and so to changes in incomes derived from the production of capital goods. By a similar argument to that used in discussing conditions 2 and 3 above it can be shown that these feedback reactions will cause correlation between the disturbance and the explanatory variables unless the observation period is sufficiently short to prevent any feedback within an observation period, through any of these reactions, from the dependent variable to any of the explanatory variables, and unless the disturbance is non-autocorrelated over all intervals equal to and greater than the number of periods during which there is zero feedback through any of these reactions. Therefore even if C is the only variable in the system which reacts directly to a particular exogenous factor, if the variations in C resulting directly from changes in that factor are autocorrelated over intervals longer than the interval during which there is zero feedback from C to any explanatory variable, either the variation caused by that factor must be estimated separately and eliminated from the observed series for C, or else that factor must be included among the explanatory variables, if correlation between the disturbance and the explanatory variables is to be avoided.

5 Brief survey of practical possibilities

The conditions outlined above for obtaining consistent estimates of the time-forms of reactions in interdependent systems are very stringent and it is clear that they cannot be completely satisfied in any economic investigation. It may, however, be worthwhile looking at the magnitude of the problem that would be involved if we were prepared to accept rough approximations to the real relationships.

The number of factors which directly influence any economic variable is usually large, but it might be possible to account for most of the variation in certain variables by including four or five determining factors in the estimating equation. To reduce to reasonable proportions the errors arising from feedback and from the use of discrete relationships it might be sufficient in some cases to have observations in quarterly periods, in other cases monthly or even weekly data might be required. We should expect responses in aggregative economic relationships to extend over a couple of years or more, so that at least ten or a dozen lagged values of each factor would be needed in the estimating equation, giving at least fifty explanatory variables. Difficult problems would arise in the elimination or fitting of seasonal variations and in dealing with trends. There would also be problems of multi-collinearity, since we can expect to find a high degree of correlation between explanatory variables. The computational work involved in fitting fifty or perhaps a hundred coefficients of an estimating equation would be very great, though it might be managed by using electronic digital computers. It might be possible to reduce the work, and also perhaps to obtain more efficient estimates, by fitting a few general time-forms of reactions instead of numerous coefficients, though there would be some statistical difficulties in doing this (Koyck 1954, 32–9).

One major difficulty is that both the dependent and the explanatory variables may be influenced by factors which give rise to large movements, but which cannot be treated quantitatively, though they may be quite comprehensible, and readily interpreted historically. To use qualitative judgement to allow as far as possible for such movements leaves the door wide open to the introduction of subjective bias, but failure to allow for them makes it certain that statistical inference will be invalid. The former course seems preferable.

It seems possible that an electronic analogue machine, or simulator, might be a useful device for making rapid approximate trials to see whether any clear relationships at all can be derived from given data, and if so for trying a number of alternative hypotheses in order to judge, in the light of relevant economic and historical considerations, which ones give the most convincing explanation of the phenomena being investigated. An electronic simulator consists of a number of units such as adding units, delay units, multipliers, integrators, differentiators, etc., which can be connected together in different ways to simulate responses of a wide variety of time-forms by variations in electrical voltages. The time required for a complete response can be varied, but it is usual to make it a fraction of a second and to repeat it several times a second so that it can be made to appear as a steady picture on an oscilloscope. The simulator operates with continuous time and it would be necessary to convert the observed series into continuous electrical voltages.

In using the simulator the series for say four or five explanatory factors would be represented by continuous voltages. The voltages would be applied to the inputs of separate response-simulators, and the outputs from them would be added electronically to give the 'fitted' values of the dependent variable, which would be shown on an oscilloscope together with the observed values. The voltage representing the 'fitted' values would be subtracted from that representing the observed values to give the 'residual' as a continuous voltage. This voltage would be squared and then integrated over time, and the integral would be shown on another oscilloscope. The time-forms of the reaction functions set on the separate response-simulators would be adjusted by a trial and error process to obtain the minimum integral of the square of the residual.

One advantage of an electronic simulator is that it can be used to simulate certain types of non-linear relationships.

Notes

Economica, 23 (NS) (90), 1956, pp. 99–113.
I am indebted to J. Durbin, F.G. Foster, M.G. Kendall, A. Stuart and R.H. Tizard for helpful discussion on some of the points dealt with in this paper.
1 For an example of this, see Phillips (chapter 17).
2 In Wold's terminology, the system is then recursive (Wold and Juréen 1953, 14).
3 J. Wise (1956) has shown that in a recursive system in which there is zero reaction of the explanatory variable to a change in the dependent variable for only one period, autocorrelation in the disturbance causes correlation between the disturbance and the explanatory variables.

41   Cybernetics and the Regulation of Economic Systems

A.W. Phillips

C 60

E 63

1 Introduction

One of the problems with which economists have been concerned throughout the last two centuries is the extent to which economic systems are inherently self-regulating. During the eighteenth and nineteenth centuries a body of theoretical analysis was built up which showed that, given a reasonable degree of competition, any changes or disturbances which upset equilibrium in any part of the economic system would set in motion 'forces tending to restore equilibrium'. It seems to have been widely believed that the existence of these inherent 'equilibrating forces' would be sufficient to ensure satisfactory regulation of the system. It is easily shown, however, that the concept of 'equilibrating forces' in economics is formally identical with the concept of 'negative feedback' in cybernetics and it is an elementary proposition in cybernetics that too much negative feedback causes instability. The forces which economists have called 'equilibrating' may therefore, if they are too strong, be dis-equilibrating and far from ensuring satisfactory regulation they may be the cause of unsatisfactory regulation.

In *The General Theory of Employment, Interest and Money*, Keynes (1936) attacked the argument that economic systems are inherently self-regulating, on the grounds that certain of the 'equilibrating forces', notably those acting through changes in interest rates, would under some conditions be very weak or even completely inoperative. He advocated the adoption of deliberate policies for regulating the level of demand with the object of improving aggregative stability. Today the governments of many countries are committed to the use of stabilisation policies of this sort. Thus if the aggregate demand for final products or for productive services falls below some level which is considered desirable, monetary and fiscal adjustments will be made which will tend to increase demand, while if aggregate demand rises above the value which is considered desirable adjustments will be made which tend to reduce demand.

385

These stabilisation policies introduce regulation through negative feed-back in the same way as do the inherent 'equilibrating forces' and if they are too strong they may similarly cause the system to become unstable.

The extent to which negative feedback can be increased without caus-ing instability depends on the quantitative values of all the relationships in the system. As we do not have adequate quantitative knowledge of economic relationships it is not possible to make a firm statement about the effectiveness of any suggested method of regulation of an actual economic system. It is, however, worthwhile to investigate a variety of hypothetical systems in order to gain insight into the nature of the prob-lems involved. In section 2 of this chapter a very simple hypothetical model is used to illustrate how instability may result from excessive negative feedback. In section 3 we deal with the problem of finding the optimum strength of stabilisation policy when the system is subjected to a specified stochastic disturbance, on the assumption that the objective is to minimise the mean square of the error in the variable which it is desired to stabilise. The optimum strength of the stabilisation policy is seen to depend on the quantitative values of all the relationships in the system and also on the auto-correlation function of the disturbances.

2 A simple model of economic regulation

Consider the system

$$\frac{dy}{dt} = \alpha(z - y) \tag{1}$$

$$z = x + v \tag{2}$$

$$x = cy + K + u \tag{3}$$

$$\frac{dv}{dt} = \beta(w - v) \tag{4}$$

$$\frac{dw}{dt} = b(y_d - y) \tag{5}$$

in which t is time, y is aggregate income or production per year, z is aggregate demand or sales per year, v is the actual policy demand result-ing from policy measures introduced by the government with the object of keeping y as nearly as possible at a constant desired value y_d, w is the 'potential policy demand', defined as the value which actual policy demand would have if it responded without time lag to changes in the policy measures, x is all demand except policy demand, u is a variable representing changes in x resulting from changes in factors other than income and α, c, K, β and b are constants.

Equation (1) states that production responds with a time lag to changes in demand, the speed of the response being indicated by the parameter α. The quantity $1/\alpha$ is a convenient index of the time required for the adjustment and is called the time constant of the lag. Assuming that this lag has a time constant of 0.25 year, so that $\alpha = 4$ we may write (1) as

$$y = \frac{4}{D+4} z,$$ (1a)

where D is the differential operator d/dt. The expression $4/D + 4$ may be considered as a 'transfer operator' representing a lag of exponential form in the response of y to changes in z (see chapters 16 and 17). More complex and realistic forms of lagged dependencies can be represented by transfer operators of the type $F_1(D)/F_2(D)$ in which F_1 and F_2 are polynomials in D, the degree of F_1 being lower than the degree of F_2. It will usually be found that a system becomes less stable if the lags in it are changed from exponential form to some more complex form (see chapter 17).

Equation (3) states that 'non-policy demand' depends on income and on other unspecified factors. We shall assume that the parameter c, the 'marginal propensity to spend out of income', has the value 0.75. It is also implicitly assumed that the time lag of this dependence is so short that it can be neglected.

Equation (4) states that the actual policy demand responds to changes in potential policy demand with a time lag of exponential form. Assuming that this lag has a time constant of 0.5 year (4) may be written

$$v = \frac{2}{D+2} w.$$ (4a)

Equation (5) describes a type of stabilisation policy in which the potential policy demand is gradually increased whenever income is below the desired level and gradually decreased whenever income is above the desired level, the rate of change of potential policy demand being made proportional to the 'error in income' $y_d - y$. Equation (5) may be written

$$w = \frac{b}{D}(y_d - y),$$ (5a)

from which it can be seen that this type of policy can alternatively be described as one in which the potential policy demand is made proportional to the time integral of the error in income. Other types of stabilisation policy are possible in which the potential policy demand is related to the magnitude and the rate of change of the error in income as well as to the time integral of the error (see chapters 16 and 17; and Allen 1956). The parameter b, which will be called the integral correction factor, indicates the 'strength' of the stabilisation policy.

If the variables z, x, v and w are eliminated by substitution among equations (1a), (2), (3), (4a) and (5a), and c is given the value 0.75 we obtain the differential equation

$$(D^3 + 3D^2 + 2D + 8b)y = 8by_d + 4D(D + 2)(K + u) \tag{6}$$

whose characteristic equation is

$$\lambda^3 + 3\lambda^2 + 2\lambda + 8b = 0 \tag{7}$$

It is easily verified that if $0 < b < 0.048$ all three roots of (7) are real and negative so that the system is stable and non-oscillatory, if $0.048 < b < 0.75$ one root of (7) is negative and the other two are complex with negative real parts so that the system is stable but oscillatory, while if $b > 0.75$ there are roots which are positive or have positive real parts so that the system is unstable; i.e., it is anti-damped or explosive. If $b < 0$ the system is unstable, since the term $8b$ in (7) is then negative. If $b = 0$, equation (6) reduces to

$$(D + 1)y = 4(K + u) \tag{8}$$

and the system is stable.

3 Optimum strength of a stabilisation policy

To find whether there is some 'optimum' value of b within the range $0 \leq b < 0.75$ it is necessary to define more precisely the object of the policy and the nature of the disturbances to the system. We shall consider the problem on the assumptions that the objective is to minimise the mean square of the error in income and that the disturbance is a stationary stochastic variable.[1]

Let ε be the error in income and $\bar{\varepsilon}^2$ be the mean square error. Then

$$\varepsilon = y_d - y \tag{9}$$

and $\bar{\varepsilon}^2$ is defined by

$$\bar{\varepsilon}^2 = E\{\varepsilon^2\} \tag{10}$$

where E indicates expected values. We shall first find an expression for $\bar{\varepsilon}^2$ which is valid when $0 < b < 0.75$ and later consider the case when $b = 0$. Substituting $y = y_d - \varepsilon$ in (6) we obtain

$$(D^3 + 3D^2 + 2D + 8b)\varepsilon = -4D(D + 2)u, \tag{11}$$

or

$$\varepsilon = F(D)u, \tag{12}$$

where

$$F(D) = \frac{-4D(D + 2)}{D^3 + 3D^2 + 2D + 8b}. \tag{13}$$

Suppose that u is a stationary stochastic variable. Without loss of generality we may assume that u has zero mean. Let the autocovariance function of u be $\phi_u(\tau)$, defined by

$$\phi 1_u(\tau) = E\{u(t)u(t + \tau)\}. \tag{14}$$

As a simple example we shall assume that the auto-covariance function is

$$\phi_u(\tau) = e^{-\rho|\tau|}. \tag{15}$$

Denote the spectral density of u, defined as the Fourier transform of the auto-covariance function, by $G_u(\omega)$. Then

$$\begin{aligned}
G_u(\omega) &= \frac{1}{\pi} \int_{-\infty}^{\infty} e^{-\rho|\tau|} e^{-i\omega\tau} d\tau \\
&= \frac{2}{\pi} \int_0^{\infty} e^{-\rho\tau} \cos \omega\tau d\tau.
\end{aligned} \tag{16}$$

Evaluation of the integral gives

$$G_u(\omega) = \frac{2\rho}{\pi(\rho^2 + \omega^2)}. \tag{17}$$

Since the system is stable for $0 \le b < 0.75$ the error is also a stationary stochastic variable. Let $G_\varepsilon(\omega)$ denote the spectral density of ε. Then it is known[2] that $G_\varepsilon(\omega)$ is related to $G_u(\omega)$ by the equation

$$G_\varepsilon(\omega) = F^*(i\omega)F(i\omega)G_u(\omega), \tag{18}$$

where $F(i\omega)$ is the frequency response function of the system, obtained from (13) by writing $i\omega$ in place of D, and $F^*(i\omega)$ is the complex conjugate of $F(i\omega)$. Further, the mean square error is given by

$$\bar{\varepsilon}^2 = \int_0^{\infty} G_\varepsilon(\omega)d\omega. \tag{19}$$

As it is difficult to evaluate the integral in (19) by ordinary methods, we proceed in the following way. Define the functions

$$H(i\omega) = \sqrt{\frac{2\rho}{\pi}} \cdot \frac{1}{\rho + i\omega} \qquad (20)$$

and

$$H^*(i\omega) = \sqrt{\frac{2\rho}{\pi}} \cdot \frac{1}{\rho - i\omega} . \qquad (21)$$

Then from (17), (20) and (21)

$$G_u(\omega) = H^*(i\omega)H(i\omega) \qquad (22)$$

and from (18) and (22)

$$G_\varepsilon(\omega) = F^*(i\omega)H^*(i\omega)F(i\omega)H(i\omega)$$
$$= \psi^*(i\omega)\psi(i\omega) \qquad (23)$$

where

$$\psi(i\omega) = F(i\omega)H(i\omega)$$

$$= \sqrt{\frac{2\rho}{\pi}} \frac{-4i\omega(i\omega + 2)}{(\rho + i\omega)\{(i\omega)^3 + 3(i\omega)^2 + 2i\omega + 8b\}}$$

$$= \sqrt{\frac{32}{\pi}} \frac{\omega^2 + 2i\omega}{\omega^4 - i(\rho + 3)\omega^3 - (3\rho + 2)\omega^2 + i(2\rho + 8b)\omega + 8\rho b} . \qquad (24)$$

and

$$\psi^*(i\omega) = \sqrt{\frac{32\rho}{\pi}} \frac{\omega^2 + 2i\omega}{\omega^4 + i(\rho + 3)\omega^3(3\rho + 2)\omega^2 - i(2\rho + 8b)\omega + 8\rho b} \qquad (25)$$

Introduce the functions

$$g(\omega) = (\omega^2 - 2i\omega)(\omega^2 + 2i\omega)$$
$$= \omega^4 + 4\omega^2 \qquad (26)$$

and

$$h(\omega) = \omega^4 - i(\rho + 3)\omega^3 - (3\rho + 2)\omega^2 + i(2\rho + 8b)\omega + 8\rho b. \qquad (27)$$

Then (23) can be written

$$G_\varepsilon(\omega) = \frac{32\rho}{\pi} \cdot \frac{g(\omega)}{h(\omega)h(-\omega)}, \tag{28}$$

so that from (19) and (28)

$$\bar{\varepsilon}^2 = \frac{32\rho}{\pi} \int_0^\infty \frac{g(\omega)}{h(\omega)h(-\omega)} d\omega. \tag{29}$$

Using the standard form given by Laning and Battin (1956, appendix E), for the solution of the integral in (29) we find that

$$\bar{\varepsilon}^2 = -16\rho i \frac{N}{\Delta}, \tag{30}$$

where Δ is the Hurwitz determinant of $h(\omega)$

$$\Delta = \begin{vmatrix} -i(\rho+3) & 1 & 0 & 0 \\ i(2\rho+8b) & -(3\rho+2) & -i(\rho+3) & 1 \\ 0 & 8\rho b & i(2\rho+8b) & -(3\rho+2) \\ 0 & 0 & 0 & 8\rho b \end{vmatrix} \tag{31}$$

and N is the determinant formed by replacing the first column in Δ by the coefficients of successive powers of ω^2 in $g(\omega)$,

$$N = \begin{vmatrix} 0 & 1 & 0 & 0 \\ 1 & -(3\rho+2) & -i(\rho+3) & 1 \\ 4 & 8\rho b & i(2\rho+8b) & -(3\rho+2) \\ 0 & 0 & 0 & 8\rho b \end{vmatrix}. \tag{32}$$

Evaluating the determinants and substituting the results in (30) we obtain finally

$$\bar{\varepsilon}^2 = \frac{16\rho(3\rho+6+4b)}{3\rho(\rho^2+3\rho+2) - 4(\rho^3+3\rho^2+2\rho-6)b - 32b^2}. \tag{33}$$

The values of $\sqrt{\bar{\varepsilon}^2}$ obtained from (33) for $0 < b < 0.75$ and for various values of ρ are shown in figure 41.1.

When $b = 0$ the system is described by equation (8). Substituting $y = y_d - \varepsilon$ into (8) we obtain

$$(D+1)\varepsilon = y_d - 4(K+u). \tag{34}$$

If we now introduce the new variable η defined by

$$\eta = \varepsilon - (y_d - 4K), \tag{35}$$

equation (34) can be written

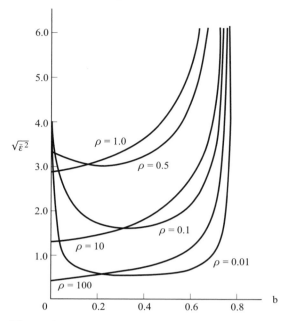

Figure 41.1

$$(D + 1)\eta = -4u. \tag{36}$$

η therefore has zero mean. From (36) and (17) its spectral density $G\eta(\omega)$ is seen to be

$$G_{\eta}(\omega) = \left(\frac{-4}{1 + i\omega}\right)\left(\frac{-4}{1 - i\omega}\right)\frac{2\rho}{\pi(\rho^2 + \omega^2)}$$
$$= \frac{32\rho}{\pi}\frac{1}{(1 + \omega^2)(\rho^2 + \omega^2)}. \tag{37}$$

The variance of η is therefore

$$\bar{\eta}^2 = \frac{32\rho}{\pi}\int_0^{\infty}\frac{d\omega}{(1 + \omega^2)(\rho^2 + \omega^2)}. \tag{38}$$

On evaluating the integral in (38) by expansion in partial fractions and straightforward integration, or by the method used above, we find that

$$\bar{\eta}^2 = \frac{16}{1 + \rho}. \tag{39}$$

It follows from (39) and (35) that when $b = 0$

$$\bar{\varepsilon}^2 = \frac{16}{1+\rho} + (y_d - 4K)^2. \tag{40}$$

From (33) we see that when b tends to zero through positive values, $\bar{\varepsilon}^2$ tends to the limit

$$\frac{\lim \bar{\varepsilon}^2}{b \to 0} = \frac{16}{1+\rho}. \tag{41}$$

The functions shown in figure 41.1 are therefore discontinuous at $b = 0$ unless $y_d = 4K$, i.e., unless the mean error is zero when no stabilisation policy is being used.

4 Conclusions

From the results obtained in section 3 we may conclude that the application of a very weak stabilisation policy of the integral type will reduce the mean square of the error in income in the system we have been considering, and may reduce it very substantially, if the mean of the error is not zero when no stabilisation policy is being used. A stronger stabilisation policy, with a value of b up to about 0.3, will further reduce the mean square error if ρ is small, i.e., if the disturbances to the system change only slowly; but will increase the mean square error if ρ is large, i.e., if the disturbances change rapidly. As b is increased above about 0.3 the mean square error increases, whatever the value of ρ, the increase in the mean square error becoming very great as b approaches the critical value of 0.75 at which point the system becomes unstable. The 'optimum' strength of stabilisation policy cannot be found unless the autocorrelation function of the disturbances is known, but the mean square error will not be very far from the minimum obtainable with this particular system if the value of b lies anywhere in the interval between, say, 0.1 and 0.3.

It can be shown that if the time lags in the model are given more realistic forms than the simple exponential form which we have used the system becomes less stable and the 'optimum' strength of the stabilisation policy is reduced (see chapter 17). On the other hand the regulation of the system can be improved by relating the policy demand to the magnitude and the rate of change of the error as well as to the time integral of the error (see chapters 16 and 17). For these reasons, and also because the basic model we have used is far too simplified to be an adequate representation of an economic system, the results we have obtained cannot be applied in any direct way in the formulation of economic policy. They do, however, show how the methods developed in cybernetics can be used to clarify some fundamental aspects of economic

regulation and to reveal a possible cause of instability of which economists have not been sufficiently aware.

Notes

Calviers de l'Institut de Science Economique Appliquée, Série N, 2, 1958, pp. 41–50.
1 The use of the mean square error criterion in the design of control systems was
   proposed by Wiener (1949) and is described in the texts by James, Nichols and
   Phillips (1947), Truxal (1955) and Laning and Battin (1956).
2 See James *et al.* (1947, pp. 288–90) and Laning and Battin (1956, pp. 196–7).

42 The Estimation of Parameters in Systems of Stochastic Differential Equations

C22

A. W. Phillips

1 Summary

In many fields of study there occur systems of lagged dependencies which can be described approximately by systems of linear stationary stochastic differential equations. In this paper we consider the estimation of parameters in such systems, using an approach similar to that of Bartlett (1946, 1955) and Quenouille (1957), and discuss conditions for identification of the separate behaviour relationships of a system. Little is known about the small sample properties of estimates in systems of this kind, but sampling experiments are being carried out and the results will be published later.

2 Systems of linear stochastic lagged dependencies

A system of linear stochastic lagged dependencies between n variables $x_i(t)$ which are functions of continuous time can be described by the system of convolution integrals

$$x_i(t) = \sum_{j \neq i} \int_0^\infty w_{ij}(h)x; (t - h)dh + \xi_i(t) \quad (i, j = 1, 2, \ldots, n), \quad (1)$$

in which each of the weighting functions $w_{ij}(h)$ specifies the magnitude of the dependence of the value taken by x_i at time t on the values taken by x_j at times $t - h$, and the $\xi_i(t)$ are stochastic disturbance terms. The Laplace transform of the weighting function of a lagged dependence is called the transfer function of the dependence. If all the transfer functions of the system (1) are rational functions, that is, if

$$\int_0^\infty e^{-sh}w_{ij}(h)dh = \frac{\beta_{ij}(s)}{\alpha_{ij}(s)}, \quad (2)$$

where $\beta_{ij}(s)$ and $\alpha_{ij}(s)$ are polynomials of finite degree in s, (1) can be written as the system of differential equations

$$x_i(t) = \sum_{j \neq i} \frac{\beta_{ij}(D)}{\alpha_{ij}(D)} x_j(t) + \xi_i(t) \quad (i, j = 1, 2, \ldots, n) \tag{3}$$

in which D is the differential operator d/dt. For the ith equation in (1) is then a particular integral of the ith equation in (3), and if the system is stable and the initial conditions are at $t = -\infty$ it is the general solution of the ith equation in (3).

Let $Q(D)$ be an $n \times n$ matrix whose elements $Q_{ij}(D)$ are given by

$$Q_{ij}(D) = \begin{cases} -\dfrac{\beta_{ij}(D)}{\alpha_{ij}(D)} & \text{if} \quad j \neq i, \\ 1 & \text{if} \quad j = i \end{cases} \tag{4}$$

and let $x(t)$ and $\xi(t)$ be column vectors with elements $x_i(t)$ and $\xi_i(t)$. Then (3) may be written

$$Q(D)x(t) = \xi(t). \tag{5}$$

In many fields of study a system like (3) may be used to represent the behaviour of a number of separate units which form an interdependent system. Thus the equations may represent the behaviour of units of physical equipment, as in control engineering, or of groups of persons or firms, as in economics, or of animals or organisms, as in ecological or biological studies. In describing real behaviour systems of this sort it is often reasonable to assume that the behaviour units cannot respond to change instantaneously. This is equivalent to the assumption that the weighting functions $w_{ij}(h)$ in (1) do not contain delta-function impulse terms,[1] which in turn implies that the numerator polynomial $\beta_{ij}(s)$ of each transfer function is of lower degree than the denominator polynomial $\alpha_{ij}(s)$. In this chapter we shall consider only systems in which the numerator of each transfer function is of lower degree than the denominator. It will be seen later that this restriction plays an important part in the identification of the separate behaviour equations of a system.

3 Specification of the stochastic disturbances $\xi(t)$

We shall consider only systems which are stable and in which the disturbances $\xi(t)$ are stationary stochastic variables whose covariance functions possess rational two-sided Laplace transforms. It will be convenient to assume that the disturbances $\xi(t)$ are generated from another set of stationary stochastic variables $\zeta_k(t)$ by the transformation

$$\xi_i(t) = \sum_{k=1}^{n} \int_0^\infty r_{ik}(h)\zeta_k(t-h)dh \quad (i = 1, 2, \ldots, n) \tag{6}$$

in which the functions $r_{ik}(h)$ have Laplace transforms $R_{ik}(s)$ of the form

$$R_{ik}(s) = \frac{\eta_{ik}(s)}{\gamma_{ik}(s)}, \tag{7}$$

where $\eta_{ik}(s)$ and $\gamma_{ik}(s)$ are polynomials in s, the degree of $\eta_{ik}(s)$ being lower than that of $\gamma_{ik}(s)$. Equations (6) can then be written as the set of differential equations

$$\xi(t) = R(D)\zeta(t), \tag{8}$$

where $R(D)$ is a matrix with elements $R_{ik}(D)$ and $\zeta(t)$ is a column vector with elements $\zeta_k(t)$. In order that the variables $\zeta(t)$ be stationary it is necessary that all the roots of the equations $\gamma_{ik}(s) = 0$ have negative real parts.

We define the following covariance functions

$$\left. \begin{aligned} \theta(\tau) &= E\{\xi(t)\xi'(t-\tau)\}, \\ \psi(\tau) &= E\{\zeta(t)\zeta'(t-\tau)\}, \\ \lambda(\tau) &= E\{\xi(t)\xi'(t-\tau)\} \end{aligned} \right\} \tag{9}$$

and denote their Laplace transforms by $\theta(s)$, $\Psi(s)$ and $\Lambda(s)$. Thus

$$\left. \begin{aligned} \theta(s) &= \int_{-\infty}^\infty e^{-s\tau}\theta(\tau)d\tau, \\ \Psi(s) &= \int_{-\infty}^\infty e^{-s\tau}\Psi(\tau)d\tau, \\ \Lambda(s) &= \int_{-\infty}^\infty e^{-s\tau}\lambda(\tau)d\tau. \end{aligned} \right\} \tag{10}$$

It will now be shown that $\theta(s)$ is given by

$$\theta(s) = R(s)\Psi(s)R'(-s). \tag{11}$$

The functions $r_{ik}(h)$ in (6) may be regarded as defined but zero for $h < 0$, and the lower limit of integration extended to $-\infty$. In matrix notation (6) then becomes

$$\xi(t) = \int_{-\infty}^\infty r(h)\zeta(t-h)dh, \tag{12}$$

$r(h)$ being the matrix with elements $r_{ik}(h)$. Post-multiplying (12) by $\xi'(t-\tau)$ and taking expectations we obtain using (9)

$$\partial(\tau) = \int_{-\infty}^\infty r(h)\lambda(\tau-h)dh. \tag{13}$$

Taking the Laplace transform of (13) and remembering that the transform of the convolution of two functions is the product of their transforms[2] we have

$$\theta(s) = R(s)\Lambda(s). \tag{14}$$

Also, post-multiplying (12) by $\zeta'(t + \tau)$ and taking expectations we find, using (9)

$$\lambda'(\tau) = \int_{-\infty}^{\infty} r(h)\Psi'(\tau + h)dh. \tag{15}$$

On making the substitution $h_1 = -h$ this becomes

$$\lambda'(\tau) = \int_{-\infty}^{\infty} r(-h_1)\Psi'(\tau - h_1)dh_1 \tag{16}$$

and it follows that

$$\Lambda'(s) = R(-s)\Psi'(s). \tag{17}$$

Substituting the transpose of (17) in (14) we obtain (11).

We now postulate that $\Psi(s)$ be identically the unit matrix

$$\Psi(s) = I. \tag{18}$$

Substitution of (18) in (11) then gives

$$\theta(s) = R(s)R'(-s). \tag{19}$$

Since the spectral density and cross-spectral density functions of a set of variables can be obtained from the two-sided Laplace transforms of their covariance functions by replacing the complex number s by the pure imaginary $i\omega$ (the Laplace transform then reducing to a Fourier transform), the spectral densities of the variables $\zeta(t)$ are constants for all frequencies ω and their cross-spectral densities are identically zero. The matrix $\Psi(\tau)$ of their covariance functions is diagonal, the leading elements being δ-function impulses. Since this implies that the variances are infinite, the variables $\zeta(t)$ are not physically realisable.[3] However, (6) remains a valid mathematical model for the generation of the physically realisable variables $\xi(t)$, whose spectral density and cross-spectral density functions, given by $\theta(i\omega)$, are proper rational functions of $i\omega$ as a result of the restriction that $\eta_{ik}(s)$ in (7) be of lower degree than $\gamma_{ik}(s)$.

4 Covariance functions of the system variables $x(t)$

Substituting (8) in (5) we have

$$Q(D)x(t) = R(D)\zeta(t). \tag{20}$$

Let $P(D)$ be a diagonal matrix whose ith leading element is the lowest common multiple of the denominators of the elements in the ith row of $Q(D)$ and in the ith row of $R(D)$, i.e., the lowest common multiple of the polynomials $\alpha_{ij}(D)$, $j \neq i$, in (4) and $\gamma_{ik}(D)$, $k = 1, 2, \ldots, n$ in (7), and let $F(D)$ and $G(D)$ be matrices defined by

$$F(D) = P(D)Q(D) \tag{21}$$

and

$$G(D) = P(D)R(D). \tag{22}$$

Then pre-multiplying (20) by $P(D)$ we obtain

$$F(D)x(t) = G(D)\zeta(t). \tag{23}$$

The elements of $F(D)$ and $G(D)$ are polynomials in D, the diagonal element in any row of $F(D)$ being of higher degree than the non-diagonal elements in the same row and also of higher degree than the elements in the same row of $G(D)$. Thus the determinant $|F(D)|$ cannot vanish identically, and we may write (23) as

$$x(t) = F^{-1}(D)G(D)\zeta(t). \tag{24}$$

Let $\phi(\tau)$ be the matrix of covariance functions of the system variables $x(t)$, so that

$$\phi(\tau) = E\{x(t)x'(t - \tau)\} \tag{25}$$

and let $\Phi(s)$ be the Laplace transform of $\phi(\tau)$. Then, by a similar argument to that used in section 3, we have

$$\Phi(s) = F^{-1}(s)(G)(s)\Psi(s)G'(-s)F'^{-1}(-s) \tag{26}$$

or, since $\Psi(s) = I$

$$\Phi(s) = F^{-1}(s)(G)(s)G'(-s)F'^{-1}(-s). \tag{27}$$

If we define the polynomial $p(s)$ by

$$p(s) = |F(s)|$$

$$= \prod_{r=1}^{m}(s - \lambda_r) \tag{28}$$

and write $F^a(s)$ for the adjoint of $F(s)$, (27) becomes

$$\Phi(s) = \frac{F^a(s)G(s)G'(-s)F'^a(-s)}{p(s)p(-s)}. \tag{29}$$

For simplicity we shall consider in this paper only cases in which the roots λ_r, $r = 1, 2, \ldots, m$, of the equation $p(s) = 0$ are all distinct, and shall also assume that $p(s)$ does not contain any factor which is common to all the elements of $F^a(s)$. Expanding the right-hand side of (29) in partial fractions we then obtain

$$\Phi(s) = \sum_{r=1}^{m} \frac{K_r}{s - \lambda_r} + \sum_{r=1}^{m} \frac{K_r'}{-s - \lambda_r}, \tag{30}$$

where

$$K_r = \left. \frac{(s - \lambda_r)F^a(s)G(s)G'(-s)F'^a(-s)}{p(s)p(-s)} \right|_{s=\lambda_r}. \tag{31}$$

For a simple root λ_r the matrix $F(\lambda_r)$ is necessarily simply degenerate. The adjoint matrix $F^a(\lambda_r)$ is of unit rank and can be written

$$F^a(\lambda_r) = k_r \kappa_r, \tag{32}$$

where k_r is a column vector which satisfies the equation

$$F(\lambda_r)k_r = 0 \tag{33}$$

and κ_r is a row vector which satisfies

$$\kappa_r F(\lambda_r) = 0.^4 \tag{34}$$

Let l_r be a row vector defined by

$$l_r = \left. \frac{(s - \lambda_r)\kappa_r G(s)G'(-s)F'^a(-s)}{p(s)p(-s)} \right|_{s=\lambda_r}. \tag{35}$$

Then substituting (32) in (31) and using (35) we have

$$K_r = k_r l_r. \tag{36}$$

Thus the matrix K_r is of unit rank, with columns proportional to the vector k_r. It follows from (36) and (33) that

$$F(\lambda_r)K_r = 0 \quad (r = 1, 2, \ldots, m) \tag{37}$$

a result which could also have been obtained by premultiplying (31) by $F(s)$ and putting $s = \lambda_r$.

The matrix $\phi(\tau)$ of the system covariance functions is obtained by taking the inverse transform of (30). Formally, (30) does not have a unique inverse. However, for a stationary system the roots λ_r are negative or have negative real parts and $\phi(\tau) \to 0$ as $\tau \to \pm\infty$. It can readily be verified that the only inverse which is consistent with these conditions is that obtained by taking the first sum in (30) to be the one-sided transform of $\phi(\tau)$ for $\tau \geq 0$ and the second sum to be the one-sided transform for $\tau < 0$. The inverse of the first sum in (30) then gives

$$\phi(\tau) = \sum_{r=1}^{m} K_r e^{\lambda_r \tau} \quad (\tau \geq 0) \tag{38}$$

while from the inverse of the second sum we see that $\phi(-\tau) = \phi'(\tau)$, a fact which is also obvious from (25).

5 Calculation of $\Phi(s)$ from given points on $\phi(\tau)$

Let ϕ_τ be the matrix of discrete functions consisting of points at unit intervals of τ on the continuous functions $\phi(\tau)$, that is, let

$$\phi_\tau = \phi(\tau) \text{ for } (\tau =, \ldots, -2, -1, 0, 1, 2, \ldots), \tag{39}$$

and let $M(z)$ be the one-sided generating function defined by

$$M(z) = \sum_{\tau=0}^{\infty} \varphi_\tau z^\tau. \tag{40}$$

Then from (38), (39) and (40) we find that

$$M(z) = \sum_{r=1}^{m} \frac{K_\tau}{1 - \mu_r z}, \tag{41}$$

where

$$\mu_r = e^{\lambda r}. \tag{42}$$

We define the polynomial

$$\Delta(z) = \prod_{r=1}^{m} (1 - \mu_r z), \tag{43}$$

and seek matrices $U(z)$ and $V(z)$, whose elements are polynomials in z, such that

$$M(z) = U^{-1}(z) V(z). \tag{44}$$

If (44) is to hold we require that

$$|U(z)| = \Delta(z) \tag{45}$$

and that

$$U(z) \sum_{r=1}^{m} \frac{K_r}{1 - \mu_r z} = V(z). \tag{46}$$

Multiplying (46) $1 - \mu_q z$ we obtain

$$U(z)\left\{K_q + (1 - \mu_q z)\sum_{r \neq q}\frac{K_r}{1 - \mu_r z}\right\} = (1 - \mu_q z)V(z) \qquad (47)$$

and on putting $z = 1/\mu_q$, $q = 1, 2, \ldots, m$, this gives

$$U\left(\frac{1}{\mu_q}\right)K_q = 0 \quad (1 = 1, 2, \ldots, m). \qquad (48)$$

Since K_q is of unit rank, (48) provides m scalar equations in the coefficients of the polynomials occurring in each row of $U(z)$. If $U(z)$ is given the form

$$U(z) = I + U_1 z + U_2 z^2 + \ldots + U_c z^c, \qquad (49)$$

where $U_1, U_2, \ldots, U_c$ are $n \times n$ matrices whose elements are constants, each row of $U(z)$ will contain cn coefficients of powers of z (excluding the constant terms, which are unity or zero). It can be shown that if c is given a suitable value and $cn - m$ coefficients in the row of $U(z)$ are put equal to zero, equations (48) suffice to determine the remaining m coefficients in each row of $U(z)$, provided the positions of the zeros are chosen in such a way that $|U(z)|$ is of degree m. It will always be possible to find positions for the zeros such that this condition is satisfied, and equation (45) will then also be satisfied. If m is an integral multiple of n it will usually, but not always, be possible to take c equal to m/n, in which case $cn - m = 0$ and none of the coefficients is put equal to zero.

When $U(z)$ has been determined $V(z)$ can be found from (46). It can be seen from (48) that $1 - \mu_r z$ is a factor of $U(z)K_r$ and it follows from this and (46) that the degree of $V(z)$ is at least one less than that of $U(z)$. Thus $V(z)$ is of the form

$$V(z) = V_0 + V_1 z + \ldots + V_{c-1} z^{c-1}, \qquad (50)$$

where $V_0, V_1, \ldots, V_{-1}$ are matrices whose elements are constants.

Pre-multiplying (44) by $U(z)$ and writing the matrices in expanded form, we have

$$(I + U_1 z + \ldots U_c z^c)(\phi_0 + \phi_1 z + \ldots) = V_0 + V_1 z + \ldots + V_{c-1} z^{c-1}. \qquad (51)$$

Equating the coefficients of $z^c, z^{c+1}, \ldots$, in (51) we obtain the difference equation

$$\phi_\tau + U_1 \phi_{\tau-1} + \ldots + U_c \phi_{\tau-c} = 0 \quad (\tau \geq c), \qquad (52)$$

from which the matrices $U_1, U_2, \ldots, U_c$ can be calculated if ϕ_τ is given for a sufficient number of values of τ. Equating the constant terms in (51) we have

$$V_0 = \phi_0 \tag{53}$$

and equating the coefficients of $z, z^2, \ldots, z^{c-1}$ we find

$$V_l = \phi_l + \sum_{k=1}^{l} U_k \phi_{l-k} \quad (l = 1, 2, \ldots, c - 1), \tag{54}$$

from which the matrices $V_0, V_1, \ldots, V_{c-1}$ can be calculated.

Thus given a sufficient number of points at equal intervals on the system covariance functions $\phi(\tau)$ it is possible to calculate $U(z)$ and $V(z)$. $M(z)$ is then given by (44), and can be expanded in partial fractions to give (41), from which the matrices K_r and the scalars μ_r are obtained immediately. The roots λ_r of the equation $p(s) = 0$ can then be calculated from

$$\lambda_r = \log \mu_r, \tag{55}$$

which follows from (42), and the matrix $\Phi(s)$ can then be found from the K_r and λ_r using (30).

6 Calculation of $Q(s)$ and $\theta(s)$ from $\Phi(s)$ when all equations are of the same order

Consider an n variable system defined by (20) or (23), in which all the scalar equations of $F(D)x(t) = G(D)\zeta(t)$ are of the same order u, and which cannot be reduced to an equivalent system in which any equation is of lower order. The elements on the leading diagonal of $F(s)$ are polynomials of degree u; but as a result of the restriction on the degree of the numerator terms of the transfer functions in the matrix $Q(s)$, discussed in section 2 above, the non-diagonal elements are of degree $u - 1$ at most. The coefficient of s^u in each of the diagonal elements of $F(s)$ can be taken as unity. There are u other coefficients of powers of s (including the constant term) in each of the diagonal elements and u coefficients in each of the non-diagonal elements. In calculating $F(s)$ from $\Phi(s)$, or equivalently from the K_r and λ_r, $r = 1, 2, \ldots, m$, there are therefore nu coefficients to be determined in each row of $F(s)$. Since $|F(s)|$ is of degree nu we have $m = nu$. We obtain from (37) a set of nu non-homogeneous equations in the coefficients of each row of $F(s)$. It can be shown that the equations in each set are linearly independent. Thus all the coefficients in $F(s)$ are uniquely determined.

Given $F(s)$ we can find $Q(s)$ from

$$Q(s) = P^{-1}(s)F(s),   \tag{56}$$

which follows from (21). It will be noticed that the elements of the diagonal matrix $P(s)$ are identical with the elements on the leading diagonal of $F(s)$. The numerator and denominator polynomials of the elements of $Q(s)$ as calculated from (56) may have common factors which can be cancelled.

Given $F(s)$ and the K_r and λ_r, $G(s)G'(-s)$ is readily obtained from the equation

$$G(s)G'(-s) = \sum_{r=1}^{m} \frac{F(s)K_r F'(-s)}{s - \lambda_r} + \sum_{r=1}^{m} \frac{F(s)K_r' F'(-s)}{-s - \lambda_r}   \tag{57}$$

which is derived from (27) and (30). Using (19) and (22) we then obtain

$$\theta(s) = P^{-1}(s)G(s)G'(-s)P^{-1}(-s).   \tag{58}$$

The numerator and denominator polynomials of the elements of $\theta(s)$ as calculated from (58) may also have common factors which can be cancelled.

7 Calculation of $Q(s)$ and $\theta(s)$ from $\Phi(s)$ when all the equations are not of the same order, but the disturbances are not cross-correlated

If all the equations in a system are not of the same order they cannot all be identified unless further restrictions are placed on the system. Consider a system $F(D)x(t) = G(D)\zeta(t)$ in which the equations are not all of the same order, and in which the arrangement of the equations is such that the first equation is of the lowest order and the order of each successive equation is at least as high as that of the one preceding it. If (27) is satisfied by the matrices $F(s)$ and $G(s)$ of this system it is also satisfied by $\mu F(s)$ and $\mu G(s)$ where μ is an arbitrary matrix of constants. We can add to any row of $F(s)$ a multiple of an earlier row corresponding to an equation of lower order without violating the condition that the non-diagonal elements in each row be of lower degree than the diagonal elements; but we cannot add a multiple of any succeeding row without violating this condition. As a result of this condition, therefore, μ is restricted to a triangular matrix with zeros above the leading diagonal. Given $\Phi(s)$ for this system, the first equation is therefore determinate (and so are any other equations of the same order as the first one) but the remaining equations of higher order than the first one are not identified without further restrictions on the system.

If it is known that the disturbances to the system are not cross-correlated, $G(s)G'(-s)$ must be diagonal. If $\mu F(s)$ and $\mu G(s)$ are to be admissible solutions, therefore, μ must satisfy the further restriction that the non-diagonal elements of $\mu G(s)G'(-s)\mu'$ be identically zero. Writing g_{ii} for the diagonal elements of $G(s)G'(-s)$ the first part of the array formed by the elements lying above the leading diagonal of the matrix product $\mu G(s)G'(-s)\mu'$ is found to be

$$
\begin{array}{lll}
\mu_{11}g_{11}\mu_{21} & \mu_{11}g_{11}\mu_{31} & \mu_{11}g_{11}\mu_{41} \\
& \mu_{21}g_{11}\mu_{31} + \mu_{22}g_{22}\mu_{32} & \mu_{21}g_{11}\mu_{41} + \mu_{22}g_{22}\mu_{42} \\
& & \mu_{31}g_{11}\mu_{41} + \mu_{32}g_{22}\mu_{42} + \mu_{33}g_{33}\mu_{43}
\end{array}
$$

Since u_{ii} cannot be made zero, we see from the first element in the array that if $g_{11} \neq 0$, μ_{21} must vanish. From the second row of the array we see that if $g_{11} \neq 0$ and $g_{22} \neq 0$, μ_{31} and μ_{32} must vanish. Similarly, from the third row, μ_{41}, μ_{42} and μ_{43} must vanish if g_{11}, g_{22} and g_{33} are non-zero. Continuing in this way it can be shown that all the elements μ_{ij}, $(i > j)$ must vanish if all the elements g_{ii}, $(i = 1, 2, \ldots, n-1)$ are non-zero. The matrix μ is then diagonal, and all the equations in the system are identified.

To calculate $F(s)$ for the system we have just been considering, given $\Phi(s)$ we first note that since the equations of lowest order are identified without restriction of the disturbance covariance functions, it will be possible to find coefficients in at least one of the rows of $F(s)$ which satisfy the appropriate set of scalar equations derived from (37) for all the values of r. The number of equations will be greater than the number of non-zero coefficients in this row, but they will form a consistent set with a sufficient number of independent equations to determine the non-zero coefficients. In the present case the first equation in the system is of lowest order, so the coefficients in the first row of $F(s)$ can be found in this way.

From (27) we have

$$F(s)\Phi(s)F'(-s) = G(s)G'(-s). \tag{59}$$

On the assumption that $G(s) G'(-s)$ is diagonal the first column of the matrix product in (59) yields the equations

$$\sum_{j=1}^{n}\sum_{q=1}^{n} F_{ij}(s)\Phi_{jq}(s)F_{1q}(-s) = 0 \quad (i = 2, 3, \ldots, n). \tag{60}$$

If we give $\Phi_{jq}(s)$ and $F_{1q}(-s)$ in (60) their known numerical values, multiply through by $p(s)p(-s)$ and equate the coefficients of each power of s we obtain for each value of i a constant set of linear equations in the coefficients of the polynomials in the ith row of $F(s)$, which can be solved for these coefficients. $Q(s)$ can then be calculated from $F(s)$, and $\theta(s)$ is given by

$$\theta(s) = Q(s)\Phi(s)Q'(-s). \tag{61}$$

8 Stochastic difference equation for discrete points on $x(t)$

Let $\Gamma(z)$ be the two-sided generating function of the discrete functions ϕ_τ, defined in (39), so, that

$$\Gamma(z) = \sum_{\tau=-\infty}^{\infty} \phi_\tau z^\tau. \tag{62}$$

Since $\phi_{-\tau} = \phi'_\tau$ we have from (40)

$$\Gamma(z) = M(z) + M'(z^{-1}) - \phi_0. \tag{63}$$

Substituting (44) in (63) we obtain

$$\Gamma(z) = U^{-1}(z)V(z) + V'(z^{-1})U'^{-1}(z^{-1}) - \phi_0 \tag{64}$$

or

$$U(z)\Gamma(z)U'(z^{-1}) = W(z)W'(z^{-1}), \tag{65}$$

where $W(z)$ is any matrix which satisfies the equation

$$W(z)W'(z^{-1}) = V(z)U'(z^{-1}) + U(z)V'(z^{-1}) - U(z)\phi_0 U'(z^{-1}). \tag{66}$$

It follows from (65) that $\Gamma(z)$ is also the generating function of the covariance functions of discrete variables x_t which are generated by the system of difference equations

$$U(E^{-1})x_t = W(E^{-1})\varepsilon_t \tag{67}$$

from stationary stochastic variables ε_t with covariance functions

$$E\{\varepsilon_\tau \varepsilon'_{t-\tau}\} = \begin{cases} I & \text{if} \quad \tau = 0 \\ 0 & \text{if} \quad \tau \neq 0 \end{cases} \tag{68}$$

(The symbol E^{-1} in (67) is the shift operator, defined by $E^{-h}y_t = y_{t-h}$.)

The discrete variables x_t in (67) may be identified with points at unit time intervals on the continuous variables $x(t)$ in (20), and it follows that the sampling properties of estimates of the continuous system (20) may be studied by considering the sampling properties of estimates of the discrete system (67). The work done by Bartlett (1946, 1955), Kendall (1945, 1946, 1949), Quenouille (1947, 1957), Whittle (1952, 1953a), Wold (1949b) and others on sampling properties and goodness-of-fit tests for autoregressive, moving average and mixed processes is therefore relevant to the estimation of parameters in systems of stochastic differential equations. Most of the theoretical results which have been obtained, however, are valid only for large samples. Some sampling experiments are being carried out on systems of the type considered in this chapter. The results will be published later.

Notes

Biometrika, 46 (1,2), 1959, pp. 67–76.

1 The δ-function or unit impulse function, $\delta(h)$ is defined by the equations

$$\delta(h) = \begin{cases} 0 & \text{if } h \neq 0 \\ \infty & \text{if } h = 0 \end{cases} \quad \text{and} \quad \int_{-\infty}^{\infty} \delta(h)dh = 1.$$

See James, Nichols and Phillips (1947) chapter 2, especially section 2.4. The Laplace transform of $\delta(h)$ is clearly unity. If $\beta_{ij}(s)$ were not of lower degree than $\alpha_{ij}(s)$ the partial fraction expansion of $\beta_{ij}(s)/\alpha_{ij}(s)$ would contain a constant term and so its inverse transform $w_{ij}(h)$ would contain a δ-function impulse term.

2 See Widder (1946, 258, theorem 16b). The conditions for the theorem are satisfied as a result of the stationarity of $\zeta(t)$ and the conditions that the roots of the equations $\gamma_{ik}(s) = 0$ have negative real parts.

3 In engineering literature the variables $\zeta(t)$ are called independent white noise sources. See Laning and Battin (1956, 136–44) and Miller (1956, 282–4).

4 See Frazer, Duncan and Collar (1950, 5.6).

43 Estimation, Regulation and Prediction in Interdependent Dynamic Systems

A.W. Phillips and M.H. Quenouille C6 1

Summary

The statistical analysis of interdependent dynamic systems has developed separately in different fields of study, particularly in control engineering and in economics. Control engineers have usually formulated their theories in terms of differential equations, giving careful attention to continuously distributed lagged dependencies and other forms of dynamic relationship. Economists have tended to formulate their theories in terms of difference equations, partly because some discrete adjustments do occur in economic systems but often for the less satisfactory reason that their observations are taken at discrete points of time or over discrete time intervals. Both continuous and discrete systems are considered in this chapter. In econometric work predictions are often made of the future values of certain variables in the economic systems, on the assumption that the system and the stochastic properties of the disturbances to it remain unchanged. In both control engineering and economics it is usually more useful to consider conditional predictions on various assumptions concerning the values of those variables which are subject to direct control, or predictions about the changes in the operating performance of the system which would result from a modification of its structure. Such predictions require knowledge of the structural equations and so raise the problems of estimation and identification. In both continuous and discrete systems the problem of identification will often be overcome if careful attention is given to the formulation of the basic model as a system of dynamic behaviour relationships.

The problem of optimising the performance of a system by suitable modification of its structure is illustrated with reference to a simple model of economic regulation.

1 Introduction

The theory and methods of analysing interdependent dynamic systems have, as with so many branches of statistics, developed simultaneously in different fields of application. Not least of these has been the field of engineering where for many years engineers have felt the problems associated with such systems and have tackled them in their own particular fashions. In the first instance, rule of thumb methods, frequency response analysis and electronic simulation have been used. More recently, however, it has been found necessary to consider theoretical aspects involving stochastic elements to a greater extent than previously.

The engineer has therefore become aware both of the extent to which theory developed in other fields may be of use in his own particular problems and of the extent to which his own previously developed theory might be applied in tackling problems of a different nature.

To illustrate a simple type of problem which occurs in engineering consider a steam turbine which is driving some mechanical load and whose speed is automatically regulated by a governor controlling the size of the opening of the steam valves. Owing to the inertia of the turbine rotor, its speed at any time t will depend on the valve opening at earlier times, as well as on the variations occurring in the load. Assuming that the dependence is linear and that the load variation can be considered as a stationary stochastic variable, the relationship can be written

$$x_1(t) = \int_0^\infty w_{12}(r)x_2(t-r)dr + \xi_1(t) \tag{1}$$

where x_1 is the speed of the turbine, x_2, is the size of the valve opening ξ_1 is the stochastic term representing the effect of load variation on speed, and $w_{12}(r)$ is the weighting function of the dependence. The governor of the turbine will be designed to alter the valve opening when there is a discrepancy between the actual speed and the desired constant speed. Inertia of moving parts will again prevent instantaneous adjustment and there will be small random variations in the operation of the governor. Assuming linearity and with a suitable choice of origin of the variables the response of the valve opening to changes in the speed of the turbine can be described by the equation

$$x_2(t) = \int_0^\infty w_{21}(r)x_1(t-r)dr + \xi_2(t) \tag{2}$$

The basic problem for the engineer is to design a control unit (here the governor). This is required to reproduce a weighting function $w_{21}(r)$ chosen with the object of minimising fluctuations in the controlled variable x_1. In doing this the engineer resorts primarily to theoretical analysis, but he has the further advantage of being able to experiment with different components having various weighting functions. This has reduced his need for estimation, while the major emphasis has been on regulation. The increasing demand for high performance systems, both for industrial and military purposes, has more recently led the engineer to develop the statistical analysis required for dealing with the problems. It is here that the economist has most to learn from the engineer.[1]

2 Forms of specification

Equations (1) and (2) are a mathematical description of a simple two-variable interdependent dynamic system. The generality of these equations may be convenient from a theoretical viewpoint, but in order to make any progress in actual problems it rapidly becomes necessary to consider weighting functions w_{ij} which can be specified by a finite number of parameters. This leads to the consideration of the particular types of specification:

(A) *Weighting functions* $w_{ij}(r)$ *which are assumed to be zero for* $r > r_0$. These will be called systems of finite moving averages. Although each variable is a simple moving average of the other variables in such systems, it will by itself follow an autoregressive scheme with moving-average residuals.

As a simple example, consider a discrete analogue of equations (1) and (2)

$$x_{1,t} = w_{12,0}x_{2,t} + w_{12,1}x_{2,t-1} + \xi_{1,t}$$
$$x_{2,t} = w_{21,0}x_{1,t} + w_{21,1}x_{t-1} + \xi_{2,t}. \tag{3}$$

(For these equations to be a realistic description of a real behaviour system (and for identification) at least one variable must be lagged relative to the other, i.e., either $w_{12,0}$, or $w_{21,0}$ must be zero. In Wold's terminology, this then represents a recursive system.)

The variable $x_{1,t}$ may then be considered as being generated by the autoregressive scheme

$$(1 - w_{12,0}w_{21,0})x_{1,t} = (w_{12,0}w_{21,1} + w_{21,0}w_{12,1})x_{1,t-1}$$
$$+ w_{12,1}w_{21,1}x_{1,t-2} \tag{4}$$
$$+ (w_{12,0}\xi_{2,t} + w_{12,1}\xi_{2,t-1} + \xi_{1,t})$$

(B) *Weighting functions* $w_{ij}(r)$ *which are assumed to be a linear combination of a finite number of damped exponentials, real or complex.* In this instance, equations of types (1) and (2) may be expressed as differential equations whose orders equal the number of exponential terms in each weighting function

$$x_{1(t)} = F_{12}(D)x_{2(t)} + \xi_{1(t)}$$
$$x_{2(t)} = F_{21}(D)x_{1(t)} + \xi_{2(t)}$$
(5)

Here D represents the differential operator and $F_{ij}(D) = \int_0^\infty e^{-rD} w_{ij}(r)dr$ is the Laplace transform of the weighting function. It will be the ratio of two polynomials in D, the numerator being of lower degree than the denominator.

These will be called systems of stochastic differential equations. They provide the equivalent system for continuous variables that the auto-regressive systems provide for variables observed at discrete intervals. There is, however, an important distinction which should be noted here.

A simple illustration of an autoregressive system would be

$$x_{1,t} = a_{11,1}x_{1,t-1} + a_{12,0}x_{2,t} + a_{12,1}x_{2,t-1} + \varepsilon_{1,t}$$
$$x_{2,t} = a_{22,1}x_{2,t-1} + a_{21,0}x_{1,t} + a_{21,1}x_{1,t-1} + \varepsilon_{2,t}$$
(6)

Any pair of first-order differential equations may be reduced to a pair of equations of the type (6) with identities connecting the parameters. The reverse is not however true to the existence of these identities. This leads to important differences between the two formulations both in estimation and regulation, but not prediction.

3 Prediction

Any linear combination of a set of equations of type (3), (5) or (6) gives the same solution and reduced form.

Since it is the reduced form which is usually obtained by the normal estimation procedure, this does not necessarily provide estimates of a unique set of structural equations. However, for prediction purposes, it is the reduced form of the equations which is employed, hence it is possible to make predictions, on the assumption of a stationary linear model, without specifying the exact form or characteristics of the model.

This does not, of course, affect the fact that different predictions may be obtained if the model is extended to include further variables. Such extensions may be possible where the stochastic element in the model is not fully random.

An illustration of a situation in which this would occur is provided by equation (4). Here the prediction of $x_{1,t}$ employing $x_{1,t-1}x_{1,t-2}, \ldots$ and model (4) would be different from the prediction employing $x_{1,t-1}$ and $x_{2,t-1}$ and model (3). The improvement in prediction in the latter instance arises, in effect, as a result of a more precise formulation of the nature of the residual in (4).

Although for the statistician once the model is given prediction presents no problem, for the economist there is the wider problem of predicting the likely results of policy decisions which will affect the structure of the model or the variables included in it. For example, a prediction may be made from reduced-form equations of future movements in business activity in the United States. Any such prediction will depend on the assumption that the basic structure of relationships and the stochastic properties of the disturbances remain constant. For those who are concerned with formulating economic policy, the assumption of stationarity made in such a prediction may not be appropriate; it is within their power to change some of the operative variables of the system or even to make a fundamental alteration in the structure of the system. For instance, in their control of the quantity of money and of interest rates, Central Banking authorities evolve systems of decision-making which become a part of the structural system.

These authorities, starting with preconceived notions about the structure of the system, will form predictions about the likely consequences of any proposed change and, in turn, will revise their notions in the light of the actual effects of the change. Thus an evolutionary or learning process becomes part of the system and this may proceed gradually or by major changes (such as that due to Keynes, which introduced new behavioural relationship into the structure of the system). In such circumstances, prediction clearly requires some knowledge of the structural equations rather than of the reduced form of the system, and so is more closely related to problems of estimation.

4 Estimation

Theoretically the problem of estimating efficiently the parameters of a given system of equations from a finite number of observations or length of series is purely that of applying known statistical techniques. In practice, some extra difficulty may, however, arise in that most statistical estimation procedures are large-sample techniques and in time-series analysis it is not easy to say what contributes a sufficiently large sample. Indeed, it is possible that any particular sample may be sufficiently large for the efficient estimation of some parameters or parts of the system, but may also be completely inadequate for the estimation of other parameters. In such circumstances, it sometimes becomes necessary to reject some of the estimates in favour of values known on *a priori* grounds to be more reasonable. Quenouille (1957, 72) gives an example where a difficulty of this type arises.

That the mathematics or computations involved in estimation may be unduly complicated is of less importance than the question of whether a unique set of estimates exists. This problem, which exists whatever the length of series available, is basically the problem of identification and will primarily concern us here.

The most general discrete formulation of a system of linear equations involving m variables each of which depends on values of all of the variables with lags of up to p time intervals employs $m\,(mp + m - 1)$ parameters. For example, for equations (6), $m = 2$, $p = 1$ and there are $2(2 + 2 - 1) = 6$ parameters.

Any estimation procedure will, however, estimate the parameters of the reduced form equations in which each variable is expressed in terms of earlier values of all the variables. This involves the estimation of $m^2 p$ coefficients and these will not suffice to estimate the larger number of parameters. In order to achieve this the values of $m(m - 1)$ parameters or functions of them must be known. For example, estimation of the parameters of equation (6) would involve estimating the manner in which x_1, t and x_2,t depend upon $x_{1,t-1}$ and $x_{2,t-1}$. Eliminating $x_{2,t}$ and $x_{1,t}$ from the right-hand sides of the equations gives

$$(1 - a_{12,0}a_{21,0})x_{1,t} = (a_{11,1} - a_{12,0}a_{22,1})x_{1,t-1} + (a_{12,1} - a_{12,0}a_{21,0})$$
$$x_{2,t-1} + \eta_{1,t}$$
$$(1 - a_{12,0}a_{21,0})x_{2,t} = (a_{22,1} - a_{21,0}a_{11,1})x_{1,t-1} + (a_{21,1} - a_{21,0}a_{21,1})$$
$$x_{2,t-1} + \eta_{2,t}.$$

(7)

i.e.,

$$x_{1t} = b_{11,1}x_{1,t-1} + b_{12,1}x_{2,t-1} + \xi_{1,t}$$
$$x_{2,t} = b_{22,1}x_{1,t-1} + b_{21,1}x_{2,t-1} + \xi_{2,t}$$

(8)

The four coefficients $b_{ij,1}$, which are estimated do not suffice to give the values of the $a_{ij,k}$. Two further restrictions are needed on the coefficient $a_{ij,k}$.

This problem formulated here in terms of discrete systems has its analogue in continuous systems. For instance as the continuous analogue of equations (6) we have

$$\dot{x}_1(t) = \alpha_{11,1}x_1(t) + \alpha_{12,0}\dot{x}_2(t) + \alpha_{12,1}x_2(t) + \varepsilon_1(t)$$
$$\dot{x}_2(t) = \alpha_{22,1}x_2(t) + \alpha_{21,0}\dot{x}_1(t) + \alpha_{21,1}x_1(t) + \varepsilon_2(t)$$

(9)

with a reduced form

$$\dot{x}_1(t) = \beta_{11,1}x_1(t) + \beta_{12,1}x_2(t) + \xi_1(t)$$
$$\dot{x}_2(t) = \beta_{22,1}x_1(t) + \beta_{21,1}x_2(t) + \xi_2(t)$$

(10)

Again the $\beta_{ij,1}$ may be estimated, but two further restrictions are required if the $\alpha_{ij,k}$, are to be found.

It is interesting to note that practical reasons have been advanced for preferring formulations of types (8) and (10) to those of types (6) and (9). Equations (8) are an example of a recursive system which Wold and Jureen (1953) have advanced as a more satisfactory model of a real system than (6). Similarly, Phillips (chapter 42) has argued that (10) is a more realistic model for continuous systems than (9). Choice of either model (8) or model (10) allows the parameters to be estimated directly since in effect $m(m - 1)$ coefficients of the formulations (6) and (9) are set equal to zero. Thus it would appear that in many circumstances careful attention to the formulation of the model will overcome the problem of identification.

5 Regulation

By regulation of a system we mean modification of its structure, either by the introduction of new relationships or by changing the parameters in existing relationships, with the object of improving the performance of the system. In the engineering example given in section 1 the design of the control unit involves choosing suitable parameters of the weighting function $w_{21}(r)$ in equation (2) or of its Laplace Transform $F_{21}(D)$ in equation (5). In this and many other cases the objective is the minimisation of the variance of one or more of the variables in the system.

As an example of the problem of regulation of economic systems, consider the following simple discrete model

$$y_t = ay_{t-1} + (1 - a)z_t$$

(11)

$$z_t = cy_{t-1} + \zeta_t$$

(12)

in which y_t is aggregate income or production in period t, z_t is aggregate demand or sales in period t, ζ_t is a stationary stochastic variable representing changes in demand resulting from factors other than income, and a and c are constants which satisfy the inequalities $0 \le a < 1$ and $0 \le c < 1$. We choose origins and units of measurement such that all the variables have zero mean and ζt has unit variance. Equation (11) states that income responds with a distributed time lag to changes in demand, while (12) states that demand in any period depends on income of the previous period.

Now suppose that a Government wishes to introduce a policy for stabilising or regulating income. One possible way of doing this would be to introduce a 'policy demand', x_t , proportional to the difference between a constant desired level of income and the actual income of the last period, a positive value of x_t corresponding to a budget deficit and a negative value to a budget surplus. For simplicity, suppose that the desired level of income coincides with the mean income in the unregulated system. With this policy, equation (12) is modified to

$$z_t = cy_{t-1} + x_t + \zeta_t \tag{13}$$

and another equation

$$x_t = -by_{t-1} \tag{14}$$

is added to the system, the parameter b in (14) indicating the strength of the stabilisation policy.

Eliminating x_t and z_t from (11), (13) and (14) we obtain

$$y_t = a + (1 - a)(c - b)y_{t-1} + (1 - a)\zeta_t. \tag{15}$$

If t is not autocorrelated the variance of y_t is given by

$$\text{var.}y = \frac{(1 - a)^2}{1 - \{a + (1 - a)(c - b)\}^2} . \tag{16}$$

This clearly is a minimum with respect to b when

$$a + (1 - a)(c - b) = 0 \tag{17}$$

i.e., when

$$b = \frac{a}{1 - a} + c. \tag{18}$$

For given values of a and c this indicates an optimum value for b.

For example, suppose in a real system $a = 0.5$ and $c = 0.75$, the optimum value of b is then 1.75. Curve (i) of figure 43.1 gives the variance of y_t as a function of b for these values of a and c. The variance is 1.067

when $b = 0$, falls to a minimum of 0.25 when $b = 1.75$, then rises with a further increase in b and tends to infinity as b tends to 3.75.

The optimum value of b in fact depends not only on the parameters a and c, but also on the autocorrelation function of ζ_t. For example, suppose now that ζ_t has the autocovariance function

$$E\{\zeta_t\zeta_{t-a}\} = \lambda^{|a|}. \tag{19}$$

Then it can be shown that the variance of y_t becomes

$$\text{var. } y = \frac{(1-a)^2(1+\lambda k)}{(1-k^2)(1-\lambda k)}, \tag{20}$$

where

$$k = a + (1-a)(c-b). \tag{21}$$

In the limit as λ tends to zero, (20) and (21) reduce to (16). If $\lambda = 0.75$ and a and c retain their previous numerical values, we find that

$$\text{var. } y = \frac{0.25(1+0.75k)}{(1-k^2)(1-0.75k)}, \tag{22}$$

where

$$k = 0.875 - 0.5b, \tag{23}$$

equations (22) and (23) being valid provided $-0.25 < b < 3.75$. Minimising the variance of y with respect to b using (22) and (23) we find that the optimum value of b is now 2.953, the minimum variance of y being 0.150. The variance of y as a function of b when $\lambda = 0.75$ is shown in curve (ii) of figure 43.1. It is interesting to note that in this example, although the optimum value of b is considerably affected by changes in λ, the effectiveness of the stabilisation policy, as indicated by the variance of y, is insensitive to moderate inaccuracies in the estimation of λ and of the optimum value of b.

Procedures for determining the optimum values of parameters for regulating continuous systems when the structural equations and the covariance functions of the disturbances are known are given by Laning and Battin (1956). For an example of their application to the regulation of a simple continuous economic model see Phillips (chapter 41).

When the system being analysed is more complex, it becomes difficult to obtain numerical solutions to the minimising equations. Methods for overcoming these difficulties by electronic simulation are described by Laning and Battin (1956). An alternative approach in which electronic

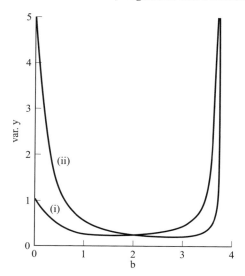

Figure 43.1

simulation is used to study the regulation of a fairly complex continuous economic model, is discussed by Phillips (chapter 17).

Notes

Bulletin de l'Institute de Statistique, Tome 37(2), 1960, pp. 335–43.
1 For a comprehensive survey of these developments see Laning and Battin (1956).
2 Indeed where the observations are taken at discrete intervals the efficient estimation procedure is to estimate the $b_{ij,1}$ of (8) and to transform these to give the $\beta_{ij,1}$ of (10). See, for example, Quenouille (1957, p. 80).

The Walras–Bowley Paper

44   The Walras–Bowley Paper

Adrian Pagan

In 1966, Bill Phillips delivered chapter 45 as the Walras–Bowley Lecture at the North American Meeting of the Econometric Society in San Francisco. The paper set out the maximum likelihood estimation of parameters of a system of simultaneous equations when there are lagged endogenous variables and moving average (MA) errors. At that point in time, what work there was on estimating equations with MA errors was largely restricted to a single equation, so that a paper purporting to describe how to produce estimators within a simultaneous equations context was very advanced. One can see how advanced by noting that the first paper to appear in the statistics literature on estimating systems of ARMA equations in the time domain was Wilson (1973), although Hannan (1970) had proposed frequency domain estimators. To this day the paper is probably the clearest analysis of how to construct a full information estimator of the parameters of simultaneous equation models with moving average errors.

A number of interesting questions arise over the origins and fate of the paper. There were, I think, two reasons why Bill was interested in this problem. Both of these reasons are consistent with lectures he delivered at the ANU in 1969. First, there was the fact that rational approximations to dynamic systems, of the sort in Jorgenson (1966), ended up inducing moving average errors into the specifications to be estimated. Griliches' (1967) survey reflects this concern very well. Of course the Koyck lag was the simplest type of rational lag and it had long been recognised that the standard transformation employed to estimate such a model actually induced an MA(1) error, which was conveniently ignored by most of those using the transformation.

Secondly, the discretisations employed in converting a continuous time model into discrete time could induce moving average errors. As well as these issues, which were important to econometricians, Bill may also have been influenced by the fact that his colleague Jim Durbin (1959) had

420

worked on the problem of estimating a single ARMA equation but not via maximum likelihood. The problem was one of interest in the control literature, and Bill may also have been influenced by developments in that area.

What was the reception to the paper? Bill once told me that, after he gave it, a number of people came up and mentioned Box and Jenkins' (1970) work to him. He had not been aware of their work when writing the paper, but admitted that his single equation estimator was very close to theirs. The essence of both approaches was to recognise that, once one conditions upon the unknown initial errors, the estimation of ARMA or ARMAX models just became a problem in non-linear least squares. Box and Jenkins were probably clearer about this fact, but anyone familiar with the Gauss–Newton algorithm for solving non-linear least-squares problems could see that this was what Bill was doing. It might have been useful if he had spelt this out more clearly, because one would then realise that the particular algorithm Bill had chosen, Gauss–Newton, could be replaced by others (for example, Powell's).

It is worth noting another distinction between Box–Jenkins' and Phillips' proposals. Bill treated the unknown initial errors as parameters to be estimated along with the other parameters of the model, whereas Box and Jenkins estimated them by a 'backcasting' method that was similar to an E-M algorithm for missing observations. Of course, Box and Jenkins' initial work was not as broad as Phillips', in that they did not consider systems of equations. However, their extensive use of data to illustrate the methods may have made their treatment more accessible.

Why wasn't the paper published? As the Walras–Bowley lecture on a topic of importance to econometricians, it is unlikely that it would not receive automatic publication in *Econometrica*. Obviously the move to the ANU and the decision to proceed with Chinese studies cannot have been a spur to him to prepare it for publication. But my own recollection, as well as those of others at the ANU at the time, was that the primary reason resided in his dissatisfaction with the section of the paper on identification of the parameters. Tellingly, this section was omitted when a version of the paper was printed in Bergstrom *et al.* (1978). It was well known around the ANU that Bill and Ted Hannan had been involved in vigorous controversy over whether Bill had properly addressed the identifiability of parameters. Hannan's papers (1969, 1971) were almost certainly a response to this debate.

I know that Bill was concerned by this problem. After his stroke, he once asked me whether I would look at the issue and become a co-author of the paper. I do not think I refused directly, but certainly did by default, as I felt that it was really his paper and that I did not really understand the debate over identification. After Preston's (1978) paper appeared, I think I finally realised why I, and Bill, had found the question so difficult. Like most econometricians, we were used to thinking of identification as whether there were unique parameter values for a given set of structural equations, whereas the concept of identification propounded by Hannan was whether one could discriminate between different structures, that is, models. Within the Cowles Commission framework, where a structure comes from theory, it was only the uniqueness of numerical values of the parameters in a given structure that mattered. But once a theory was no longer part of the picture, one quite rightly was interested in whether one could reduce the numbers of structures by appeal to the data.

The saga of the paper shows a number of characteristics about Bill's work. Firstly, that he was rarely satisfied with partial solutions. Finding a single equation estimator was not enough when economists were interested in systems. Secondly, the intellectual integrity displayed in his response to the controversy with Ted Hannan was wholly consistent with the man. Most of us would have been more than happy to send such a paper off to *Econometrica* and to see it published. But that was not Bill's style. If he thought that there was any chance of a defect in the paper, he would never succumb to such a temptation. Thirty years after it first appeared, it is a pleasure to see it included as part of this volume.

45 Estimation of Systems of Difference Equations with Moving Average Disturbances

A.W. Phillips

CS1

1 Introduction

C61

A method is developed for estimating the parameters in models of the form

$$\Gamma y_t = \sum_{\tau=1}^{c} \Gamma_\tau y_{t-\tau} + \sum_{\tau=0}^{a} A_\tau z_{t-\tau} + u_t, \qquad (1)$$

where u_t is a vector of disturbances which have the moving average representation

$$u_t = \sum_{\tau=0}^{m} M_\tau \varepsilon_{t-\tau} M_0 = I, \qquad (2)$$

ε_t being a Gaussian stationary stochastic process which is not serially correlated. In section 2 we consider the single equation case, in which the variables and parameters in equations (1) and (2) are scalars. The general case of a system of equations is treated in section 3. It will be noted that in the special case with $m = 0$ the system reduces to the usual simultaneous equation model. Some applications are considered in section 4.

The method of estimation is based on maximisation of the likelihood of the observations for the time periods $t = 1, 2, \ldots, T$, the values of all variables for $t \leq 0$ being taken as fixed. Since the derivatives of the likelihood function are non-linear in the parameters an iterative procedure is adopted, which may be described as repeated application of linearised least squares. Under mild regularity conditions the successive estimates converge to the maximum likelihood estimates.

A method is given for obtaining first estimates which are consistent and of order $T^{-1/2}$ in probability. Using these as starting values, the first iteration gives second estimates which differ from the maximum likelihood estimates by terms of order T^{-1} in probability. In the usual case the

423

maximum likelihood estimates are of order $T^{-1/2}$ in probability, and the second estimates are then asymptotically efficient.

2 A single equation with moving average disturbances

The single-equation model

Consider the model

$$y_t = \sum_{\tau=1}^{c} \gamma_\tau y_{t-\tau} + \sum_{\tau=0}^{a} \alpha_\tau z_{t-\tau} + u_t \quad (t = 1, 2, \ldots, T), \tag{3}$$

where y_t and z_t are observed time series and u_t is an unobservable series of disturbances. For the purpose of estimating the parameters γ_τ and α_τ we assume that the observed series y_t and z_t are realisations from stochastic processes $\{y_t\}$ and $\{z_t\}$ that the series u_t is the corresponding realisation from a Gaussian stationary stochastic process $\{u_t\}$ with zero mean and finite variance. We shall specify that $E(u_t u_{t-r}) = 0$ for $|r| > m$ where m is a non-negative integer. Then the disturbances u_t can be represented by the moving average model

$$u_t = \sum_{\tau=0}^{m} \mu_\tau \varepsilon_{t-\tau}, \mu_0 = 1(t = 1, 2, \ldots, T), \tag{4}$$

where the ε_t are normally and independently distributed with zero means and common variance σ^2. Substituting equations (4) in (3), the complete model may be written as

$$y_t = \sum_{\tau=1}^{c} \gamma_\tau y_{t-\tau} + \sum_{\tau=0}^{a} \alpha_\tau z_{t-\tau} + \sum_{\tau=0}^{m} \mu_\tau \varepsilon_{t-\tau}. \tag{5}$$

We define the polynomials $P_\gamma(S)$, $P_\alpha(S)$ and $P_\mu(S)$ by

$$P_\gamma(S) = 1 - \sum_{\tau=1}^{c} \gamma_\tau S^\tau$$

$$P_\alpha(S) = \sum_{\tau=0}^{a} \alpha_\tau S^\tau \tag{6}$$

$$P_\mu(S) = \sum_{\tau=0}^{m} \mu_\tau S^\tau, \mu_0 = 1.$$

Let L be a lag operator such that $L^h X_t = X_{t-h}$ for any series X_t and any integer h. Then equation (5) may be written as

$$P_\gamma(L)y_t = P_\alpha(L)z_t + P_\mu(L)\varepsilon_t. \tag{7}$$

We specify that the polynomial $P_\mu(S)$ has no zeros inside the unit circle. This specification does not impose restrictions on the process $\{u_t\}$, but ensures that the parameters μ_τ and σ^2 are uniquely determined if the serial covariance function of $\{u_t\}$ is given. We further specify that in at least one of the polynomials $P_\gamma(S)$, $P_\alpha(S)$, and $P_\mu(S)$ the coefficient of the highest power of S is non-zero and that the three polynomials have no common factor. These conditions ensure that the parameters γ_τ, α_τ, μ_τ and σ^2 are uniquely determined if the covariance functions of the processes $\{y_t\}$ and $\{z_t\}$ are given, provided mild conditions on these processes are satisfied.

Mathematical functions such as a constant term, time trends, and seasonal dummy variables can be included in the model without affecting the estimation methods developed below. They have been omitted to avoid unnecessary notational complexity.

The model in matrix notation

It will be convenient to write the model in matrix notation. We define the following vectors and matrices

$$y = \begin{bmatrix} y_1 \\ \cdot \\ \cdot \\ \cdot \\ y_T \end{bmatrix} \quad Y = \begin{bmatrix} y_0 \cdots y_{-c+1} \\ \cdot & \cdot \\ \cdot & \cdot \\ \cdot & \cdot \\ y_{T-1} \cdots y_{T-c} \end{bmatrix} \quad Z = \begin{bmatrix} z_1 \cdots z_{-a+1} \\ \cdot & \cdot \\ \cdot & \cdot \\ \cdot & \cdot \\ z_T \cdots z_{T-a} \end{bmatrix}$$

$$\gamma = \begin{bmatrix} \gamma_1 \\ \cdot \\ \cdot \\ \cdot \\ \gamma_c \end{bmatrix} \quad \alpha = \begin{bmatrix} \alpha_0 \\ \cdot \\ \cdot \\ \cdot \\ \alpha_a \end{bmatrix} \quad u = \begin{bmatrix} u_1 \\ \cdot \\ \cdot \\ \cdot \\ u_T \end{bmatrix}. \tag{8}$$

Using these definitions the set of equations (3) may be written as

$$y = Y\gamma + Z\alpha + u. \tag{9}$$

To write equations (4) in matrix form we define the following vectors and matrices

$$
[\mathbf{M}^*\!:\!\mathbf{M}] =
\begin{bmatrix}
\mu_m & \cdot & \cdot & \cdot & \mu_1 & \vdots & 1 & 0 & \cdot & \cdot & \cdot & \cdot & \cdot & \cdot & 0 \\
 & & & & & \vdots & & & & & & & & & \\
0 & & \cdot & & & \vdots & \mu_1 & & & & & & & & \\
 & & & & & \vdots & & & & & & & & & \\
\cdot & & & & \mu_m & \vdots & & & & & & & & & \\
 & & & & & \vdots & & & & & & & & & \\
\cdot & & & 0 & \vdots & \mu_m & \cdot & & & & & & \cdot & \\
 & & & & \cdot & \vdots & 0 & \cdot & \cdot & & & & & 0 \\
\cdot & & & & \cdot & \vdots & \cdot & \cdot & \cdot & & \cdot & & & \\
0 & \cdot & \cdot & \cdot & 0 & \vdots & 0 & \cdot & 0 & \mu_m & \cdot & \cdot & \cdot & \mu_1 & 1
\end{bmatrix}
\begin{bmatrix}
\varepsilon^* \\
\cdots \\
\varepsilon
\end{bmatrix}
\begin{bmatrix}
\varepsilon_{-m+1} \\
\cdot \\
\cdot \\
\varepsilon_0 \\
\cdots \\
\varepsilon_1 \\
\cdot \\
\cdot \\
\varepsilon_T
\end{bmatrix}
$$

$$
\mathbf{J} = T^{1/2}
\begin{bmatrix}
\mathbf{I}_m \\
\cdots \\
\mathbf{O}
\end{bmatrix}
\qquad
\eta =
\begin{bmatrix}
\eta_1 \\
\cdot \\
\cdot \\
\cdot \\
\eta_m
\end{bmatrix},
\tag{10}
$$

where $\mathbf{M}^*$ is of order $T \times m$, $\mathbf{M}$ is of order $T \times T$, $\mathbf{J}$ is of the order $T \times m$, $\mathbf{I}_m$ is the unit matrix of order m, and the elements η_τ of η are given by

$$
\eta_\tau = T^{-1/2}(\mu_\tau \varepsilon_0 + \mu_{\tau+1}\varepsilon_{-1} + \ldots \mu_m \varepsilon_{\tau-m}) \quad (\tau = 1, \ldots, m). \tag{11}
$$

Using the definitions (10) and (11), the set of equations (4) can be written as

$$
\begin{aligned}
\mathbf{u} &= \mathbf{M}^*\varepsilon^* + \mathbf{M}\varepsilon \\
&= \mathbf{J}\eta + \mathbf{M}\varepsilon.
\end{aligned}
\tag{12}
$$

Substituting equation (12) in (9), the complete model may be written in the form

$$
\mathbf{y} = \mathbf{Y}\gamma + \mathbf{Z}\alpha + \mathbf{J}\eta + \mathbf{M}\varepsilon \tag{13}
$$

or

$$
\mathbf{y} = \mathbf{X}\beta + \mathbf{M}\varepsilon, \tag{14}
$$

where

$$\mathbf{X} = [\mathbf{Y} \vdots \mathbf{Z} \vdots \mathbf{J}] \text{ and } \beta = \begin{bmatrix} \gamma \\ \alpha \\ \eta \end{bmatrix}. \tag{15}$$

The likelihood function

Let $\mathbf{y}$ and $\mathbf{z}$ denote the observations $y_1, \ldots, y_T$ and $z_1, \ldots z_T$ respectively, and let $\mathbf{y}^*$ and $\mathbf{z}^*$ denote the initial values $y_0, y_{-1}, \ldots, y_{-c+1}$ and z_0, $z_{-1}, \ldots, z_{-a+1}$. The method of estimation will be based on maximisation of the joint likelihood of $\mathbf{y}$ and $\mathbf{z}$ with the initial values $\mathbf{y}^*$ and $\mathbf{z}^*$ taken as fixed numbers. For consistency we must also take the initial values of ε_t for $t = 0, -1, \ldots, -m+1$ as fixed numbers. This implies that the elements η_τ of η are fixed numbers. Since these elements enter into the likelihood function but are unknown, we treat them as additional parameters to be estimated from the data. The vector η has therefore been included with γ and α in the vector of unknown parameters β. Let μ and θ be the vectors

$$\mu = \begin{bmatrix} \mu_1 \\ \vdots \\ \mu_m \end{bmatrix} \text{ and } \theta = \begin{bmatrix} \beta \\ \cdots \\ \mu \end{bmatrix}. \tag{16}$$

The complete set of parameters to be estimated is θ and σ^2.

Let $F_1(y, \mathbf{z}|\mathbf{y}^*, \mathbf{z}^*; \theta, \sigma^2)$ be the joint probability density function of $\mathbf{y}$ and $\mathbf{z}$, or likelihood function of θ, σ^2. Then

$$F_1(y, \mathbf{z}|\mathbf{y}^*, \mathbf{z}^*; \theta, \sigma^2) = F(\mathbf{y}|\mathbf{z}, \mathbf{y}^*, \mathbf{z}^*; \theta, \sigma^2)F_2(\mathbf{z}|\mathbf{y}^*, \mathbf{z}^*), \tag{17}$$

where $F(y|\mathbf{z}, \mathbf{y}^*, \mathbf{z}^*; \theta, \sigma^2)$ is the conditional density function of $\mathbf{y}$ given $\mathbf{z}$, and $F_2(\mathbf{z}|\mathbf{y}^*, \mathbf{z}^*)$ is the marginal density function of $\mathbf{z}$ with $\mathbf{y}^*$ and $\mathbf{z}^*$ taken as fixed. We shall specify that the function $F_2(\mathbf{z}|\mathbf{y}^*, \mathbf{z}^*)$ does not involve any of the parameters in θ and σ^2. Then it is clear from equation (17) that the values of θ and σ^2 which maximise $F_1(y, \mathbf{z}|\mathbf{y}^*, \mathbf{z}^*; \theta, \sigma^2)$ are the same as the values which maximise $F(y|\mathbf{z}, \mathbf{y}^*, \mathbf{z}^*; \theta, \sigma^2)$, so we may base the method of estimation on maximisation of the latter function.

It is shown in section 3 below that the specification that $F_2(\mathbf{z}|\mathbf{y}^*, \mathbf{z}^*)$ does not involve any of the parameters in θ and σ^2 is satisfied even if z_t depends on $y_{t-1}, y_{t-2}, \ldots$, through a relation if the general form $z_t = (fy_{t-1}, y_{t-2}, \ldots, z_{t-1}, z_{t-2}, \ldots) + u_t^*$, where the function f does not involve any of the parameters, provided u_t^* is independent of u_{t-r} for all values of t and r, and provided the contemporaneous variable y_t is not included in the function f. It is also shown that the parameters remain identified in this case provided the variance of the process u_t^* is not zero. This result, which holds also when z_t and u_t^* are vector processes, gives the conditions under which it is possible to estimate separately the parameters in a single equation which is part of a system of equations. It is, of course, merely a generalisation to the case of autocorrelated disturbances of the well-known proposition that the equations of a recursive system can be estimated individually.

The joint probability density function of the elements $\varepsilon_1, \ldots, \varepsilon_T$ in ε is $(2\pi)^{-T/2}(\sigma^{-2})^{T/2}\exp\{-\frac{1}{2}\sigma^{-2}\varepsilon'\varepsilon\}$. With $\mathbf{y}^*$, $\mathbf{z}$ and $\mathbf{z}^*$ given and ε^* fixed, equation (5), or equivalently (14), defines a transformation from ε to $\mathbf{y}$, the Jacobian being the determinant of $\mathbf{M}$, which is unity. The joint probability density function of $y_1, \ldots, y_T$ is therefore

$$F(y|z, y^*, z^*; \theta, \sigma^2) = (2\pi)^{-T/2}(\sigma^{-2})^{T/2}\exp\left\{-\frac{1}{2}\sigma^{-2}Q(\theta)\right\}, \quad (18)$$

where

$$Q(\theta) = \varepsilon'\varepsilon$$
$$= (y - X\beta)'\mathbf{M}^{'-1}\mathbf{M}^{-1}(y - X\beta). \quad (19)$$

The maximum likelihood estimate of $\hat{\theta}$ of θ is the value which maximises F in equation (18), that is which minimises Q in equation (19). Differentiating $\log F$ with respect to σ^{-2} we have

$$\frac{\partial F}{\partial \sigma^{-2}} = \frac{T}{2}\sigma^2 - \frac{1}{2}Q(\theta). \quad (20)$$

For a maximum the derivative is zero, so the maximum likelihood estimate $\hat{\sigma}^2$ of σ^2 is given by

$$\hat{\sigma}^2 = \frac{1}{T}Q(\hat{\theta}). \quad (21)$$

The iterative procedure

Minimisation of Q in equation (19) is not straightforward, since it is not quadratic in the parameters. We therefore adopt an iterative procedure. The procedure is equivalent to linearising the term $\mathbf{M}\varepsilon$ in equation (14) by taking a Taylor series expansion around estimates $\mathbf{M}_r$, and ε_r and ignoring the second-order term, and then applying least squares to obtain new estimates of the parameters in the linearised equation.

Let θ_r, be the rth estimate of θ, with corresponding estimates β_r, μ_r and M_r of β, μ and M. Let the corresponding estimate of ε be ε_r defined by the equation

$$y = X\beta_r + M_r\varepsilon_r. \tag{22}$$

Subtracting equation (22) from (14) we have

$$0 = X(\beta - \beta_r) + M\varepsilon - M_r\varepsilon_r. \tag{23}$$

Consider now the identity

$$M\varepsilon - M_r\varepsilon_r \equiv (M - M_r)\varepsilon_r + M_r(\varepsilon - \varepsilon_r) + (M - M_r)(\varepsilon - \varepsilon_r). \tag{24}$$

From the definition of M and ε in (10) and of μ in (16) it can readily be verified that the first term on the right-hand side of identity (24) can be written in the form

$$(M - M_r)\varepsilon_r = E_r(\mu - \mu_r), \tag{25}$$

where E_r is the rth estimate of E, which is defined as

$$E = \begin{bmatrix} 0 & \cdot & \cdot & \cdot & 0 \\ \varepsilon_1 & & & & \cdot \\ \cdot & \varepsilon_1 & & & \cdot \\ \cdot & & \varepsilon_1 & & \cdot \\ \cdot & & & \varepsilon_1 & 0 \\ \cdot & & & & \varepsilon_1 \\ \cdot & & & & \\ \varepsilon_{T-1} & \varepsilon_{T-2} & \cdot & \cdot & \varepsilon_{T-m} \end{bmatrix}. \tag{26}$$

On substituting equation (25) in (24) and the result in (23), pre-multiplying by M_r^{-1}, and rearranging the terms, we obtain

$$\varepsilon_r = M_r^{-1}[X(\beta - \beta_r) + E_r(\mu - \mu_r)] + \varepsilon + M_r^{-1}(M - M_r(\varepsilon - \varepsilon_r). \tag{27}$$

We define W_r by

$$W_r = M_r^{-1}[X \vdots E_r]. \tag{28}$$

Remembering that $\theta' = [\beta' \vdots \mu']$ we see that equation (27) may be written as

$$\varepsilon_r = \mathbf{W}_r(\theta - \theta_r) + \varepsilon + \mathbf{M}_r^{-1}(\mathbf{M} - \mathbf{M}_r)(\varepsilon - \varepsilon_r). \tag{29}$$

Let $\bar{\theta}_{r+1}$ be the value of θ which minimises $\varepsilon'\varepsilon$ in equation (29) ignoring the term $\mathbf{M}_r^{-1}(\mathbf{M} - \mathbf{M}_r)(\varepsilon - \varepsilon_r)$, which is of the second order in the errors of the rth estimates. Thus $\bar{\theta}_{r+1}$ is given by

$$\bar{\theta}_{r+1} - \theta_r = (\mathbf{W}_r'\mathbf{W}_r)^{-1}\mathbf{W}_r'\varepsilon_r. \tag{30}$$

Then we take the $(r + 1)$th estimate θ_{r+1} to be

$$\theta_{r+1} = \theta_r + \lambda_r(\bar{\theta}_{r+1} - \theta_r), \tag{31}$$

where λ_r is a positive scalar so chosen that

$$Q(\theta_{r+1}) \leq Q(\theta_r). \tag{32}$$

If $\theta_r \neq \hat{\theta}$ there will exist values of λ_r such that the inequality sign in (32) holds, provided $\mathbf{W}_r'\mathbf{W}_r$ is non-singular. With a suitable choice of the successive values of λ_r the iterative process will then converge to the maximum likelihood estimate $\hat{\theta}$.

The iterative procedure may be summarised as follows. Given the estimate θ_r we calculate successively

$$\varepsilon_r = \mathbf{M}_r^{-1}(\mathbf{y} - \mathbf{X}\beta_r)$$

$$Q(\theta_r) = \varepsilon_r'\varepsilon_r$$

$$\mathbf{W}_r = \mathbf{M}_r^{-1}[\mathbf{X} \vdots \mathbf{E}_r]$$

$$\bar{\theta}_{r+1} - \theta_r = (\mathbf{W}_r'\mathbf{W}_r)^{-1}\mathbf{W}_r'\varepsilon_r \tag{33}$$

$$\theta_{r+1} = \theta_r + \lambda_r(\bar{\theta}_{r+1} - \theta_r)$$

$$\varepsilon_{r+1} = \mathbf{M}_{r+1}^{-1}(\mathbf{y} - \mathbf{X}\beta_{r+1})$$

$$Q(\theta_{r+1}, \lambda_r) = \varepsilon_{r+1}'\varepsilon_{r+1}.$$

We may take a trial value of λ_r as unity and if $Q(\theta_{r+1}) < Q(\theta_r)$ proceed to the next iteration. If $Q(\theta_{r+1}) \geq Q(\theta_r)$, decrease the value of λ_r towards zero until $Q(\theta_{r+1}) < Q(\theta_r)$ and then proceed to the next iteration. Proceeding in this way, the successive values of $\bar{\theta}_{r+1} - \theta_r$ will converge to zero, and the successive values of θ_r will converge to $\hat{\theta}$. In practice the process will be stopped when $\bar{\theta}_{r+1} - \theta_r$ is sufficiently small. A reasonable procedure would be to stop the iteration when every element of $\bar{\theta}_{r+1} - \theta_r$ becomes less than a specified proportion, say 0.01 or 0.001, of the estimated standard error of the corresponding element of $\bar{\theta}_{r+1}$. As in the Newton–Raphson method, which is similar in some respects to the method described here, it is not necessary to recalculate the matrix

$(\mathbf{W}_r'\mathbf{W}_r)^{-1}$ at every iteration. It may often be computationally more efficient to use the same matrix for a number of successive iterations.

There is no need to invert the $T \times T$ matrix $\mathbf{M}_r$ when computing ε_r and $\mathbf{W}_r$ in equations (33). Owing to the very simple form of the matrix $\mathbf{M}_r$ the calculations can be reduced to a simple recurrence relation. For example, let $\mathbf{h}_r = \mathbf{y} - \mathbf{X}\beta_r$. Given $\mathbf{h}r$ we need to compute $\varepsilon_r = \mathbf{M}_r^{-1}\mathbf{h}_r$. Write this as $\mathbf{M}_r\varepsilon_r = \mathbf{h}_r$. Let $\mathbf{h}_{tr}$ and ε_{tr} be the tth elements of $\mathbf{h}_r$ and ε_r. Then ε_r can be computed using the recurrence relation

$$\varepsilon_{tr} = h_{tr} - \sum_{\tau} \mu_{\tau} h_{t-\tau, r} \quad (t = 1, \ldots, T) \tag{34}$$

where the summation over τ runs from 1 to m or $t - 1$, whichever is the smaller. We note that the successive columns of $\mathbf{M}_r^{-1}\varepsilon_r$ contain only lagged elements of the first column, so that only the first column of $\mathbf{M}_r^{-1}\varepsilon_r$ needs to be calculated.

In the next section we give a method for obtaining first estimates θ_1 which are consistent and of order $T^{-1/2}$ in probability. Let $\mathbf{M}_1$ and ε_1 be the corresponding first estimates of $\mathbf{M}$ and ε, and $P_{\mu 1}(S)$ the corresponding first estimate of the polynomial $P_\mu(S)$. Then the elements of $\mathbf{M} - \mathbf{M}_1$ and $\varepsilon - \varepsilon_1$ are of order $T^{-1/2}$ in probability, and since $\mathbf{M}$ is a bond matrix the elements of the vector $(\mathbf{M} - \mathbf{M}_1)(\varepsilon - \varepsilon_1)$ are of order T^{-1} in probability. $\mathbf{M}_1^{-1}$ is a lower triangular matrix whose elements in each column from the diagonal downwards are the coefficients of successive powers of S in the power series expansion of $[P_{\mu_1}(S)]^{-1}$. If all the zeros of $P_{\mu_1}(S)$ lie outside the unit circle then absolute values of the successive coefficients of the expansion of $[P_{\mu_1}(S)]^{-1}$ are dominated by a decreasing geometric series. The elements of the vector $\mathbf{M}_1^{-1}(\mathbf{M} - \mathbf{M}_1)(\varepsilon - \varepsilon_1)$, which is the last term in equation (29), are then of order T^{-1} in probability, and consequently the second estimate $\bar{\theta}_2$ obtained from equation (30) differs from the maximum likelihood estimate θ by terms of order T^{-1} in probability. It can be shown, though with some difficulty, that if $P_{\mu_1}(S)$ has one or more zeros on the unit circle the estimate $\bar{\theta}_2$ will still differ from $\hat{\theta}$ by terms of order T^{-1} in probability. The method given below for estimating θ_1 ensures that no zeros of $P_{\mu_1}(S)$ lie inside the unit circle. The estimate $\bar{\theta}_2$ using θ_1 will therefore always differ from $\hat{\theta}$ by terms of order T^{-1} in probability. In most cases $\hat{\theta}$ has sampling errors of order $T^{-1/2}$ in probability, and the estimate $\bar{\theta}_2$ is then asymptotically efficient.

In the preceding paragraph, and elsewhere in the paper when considering the asymptotic properties of estimators, we confine our attention to the case in which the processes $\{y_t\}$ and $\{z_t\}$ are stationary. The estimation methods remain valid, however, when $\{y_t\}$ and $\{z_t\}$ are non-stationary.

It may be shown that when θ_1 is consistent and has sampling errors of order $T^{-1/2}$ in probability, the variance matrix of $\bar{\theta}_{r+1}$ for $r \geq 1$ is given by

$$V(\theta_{r+1}) = \sigma_{r+1}^2 (\mathbf{W}_r' \mathbf{W}_r)^{-1} + 0(T^{-1}) \tag{35}$$

where

$$\sigma_{r+1}^2 = \frac{1}{T} Q(\bar{\theta}_{r+1}). \tag{36}$$

First estimates

From equations (3) and (4) we see that plim $(1/T)\Sigma_{t=1}^T y_{t-\tau} u_t = 0$ for $\tau > m$. We have specified that z_t may satisfy an equation of the form $z_t = f(y_{t-b}, y_{t-b-1}, \ldots, z_{t-1}, \ldots) + u_t^*$ where $b \geq 1$ and u_t^* has non-zero variance and is independent of u_{t-r} for all values of t and r. In this case plim $(1/T)\Sigma_{t=1}^T z_{t-\tau} u_t = 0$ for $\tau > m - b$.

To obtain consistent estimates of γ_τ and α_τ in equations (3) we may therefore use the method of instrumental variables, with $y_{t-\tau-m}$ as instrument for $y_{t-\tau}(\tau = 1, 2, \ldots, c)$ and $z_{t-\tau-(m-b+1)}$ as instrument for $z_{t-\tau}$ ($\tau = 0, 1, \ldots, a$) if $m - b + 1 > 0$. If $m - b + 1 \leq 0$, or if z_t is independent of u_{t-r} for all values of t and r, we may use $z_{t-\tau}$ as instrument for itself. The resulting estimates are consistent and having sampling errors of order $T^{-1/2}$ in probability. Let γ_1 and α_1 be the first estimates of γ and α obtained in this way, and let $\mathbf{u}$ be defined as

$$\check{\mathbf{u}} = \mathbf{y} - \mathbf{Y}\gamma_1 - \mathbf{Z}\alpha_1. \tag{37}$$

The $\check{\mathbf{u}}$ is a consistent estimate of $\mathbf{u}$.

To obtain a consistent estimate of μ, we consider the model (4) or (12), but now with the initial values of ε_t for $t \leq 0$ taken as stochastic instead of fixed. The variance matrix $\mathbf{C}$ of the vector $\mathbf{u}$ is then given by

$$\mathbf{C} = E(\mathbf{uu}')$$
$$= \sigma^2 [\mathbf{M}^* \vdots \mathbf{M}][\mathbf{M}^* \vdots \mathbf{M}]'. \tag{38}$$

Methods for estimating μ in this model when $\mathbf{u}$ is known have been given by Durbin (1959, 1960) and Walker (1961). A consistent estimate of μ could be obtained using either of these methods with $\mathbf{u}$ replaced by its estimate $\check{\mathbf{u}}$. We give now another method for estimating μ which is perhaps more convenient for the present purpose. Consider the transformation from $\mathbf{u}$ to a vector $\mathbf{v}$ defined by

$$\mathbf{v} = \mathbf{C}^{-1}\mathbf{u}. \tag{39}$$

The variance matrix of $\mathbf{v}$ is

$$E(\mathbf{vv'}) = E(\mathbf{C}^{-1}\mathbf{uu'}\mathbf{C}^{-1}) = \mathbf{C}^{-1}. \tag{40}$$

The probability density function of $\mathbf{v}$ is therefore $(2\pi)^{-T/2}(\det \mathbf{C})^{1/2}$ $\exp\{-\frac{1}{2}\mathbf{v'Cv}\}$ and the log likelihood is $-(T/2)\log(2\pi) + \frac{1}{2}\log \det \mathbf{C} - \frac{1}{2}\mathbf{v'Cv}$. The term $\log \det \mathbf{C}$ is of low order in T compared with the $\mathbf{v'Cv}$ and may be ignored to the order of approximation required here. If $\mathbf{v}$ were known we could therefore estimate $\boldsymbol{\mu}$ by minimising $\mathbf{v'Cv}$ with respect to $\boldsymbol{\mu}$.

In fact $\mathbf{v}$ is not known. We can, however, obtain an estimate of it which is consistent and has errors of order $T^{-1/2}$ in probability. Let $\breve{u}_t$ be the tth element of $\breve{\mathbf{u}}$ in (37), and define $\breve{c}_\tau$ by

$$\breve{c}_\tau = \frac{1}{T} \sum_{t=\tau+1}^{T} \breve{u}_t \breve{u}_{t-\tau} \quad (\tau = 0, 1, \ldots, m). \tag{41}$$

Then a consistent estimate $\breve{C}$ of $\mathbf{C}$ is given by

$$\breve{C} = \begin{bmatrix} \breve{c}_o & \cdot & \breve{c}_m & 0 & \cdot & 0 \\ \cdot & & & & & \cdot \\ \breve{c}_m & & \cdot & & \cdot & 0 \\ 0 & \cdot & & \cdot & & \breve{c}_m \\ \cdot & & & & & \cdot \\ 0 & \cdot & 0 & \breve{c}_m & \cdot & \breve{c}_o \end{bmatrix} \tag{42}$$

and a consistent estimate $\breve{\mathbf{v}}$ of $\mathbf{v}$ is obtained from

$$\breve{\mathbf{v}} = \breve{C}^{-1}\breve{\mathbf{u}}. \tag{43}$$

We then take $\boldsymbol{\mu}_1$ to be the value of $\boldsymbol{\mu}$ which minimises $\breve{\mathbf{v}}'\mathbf{C}\breve{\mathbf{v}}$. It is easily verified that the elements $\breve{\mu}_\tau$ of $\boldsymbol{\mu}_1$ are given by the solutions of the equations

$$\sum_t \breve{v}_t \breve{v}_{t-\tau} + \breve{\mu}_1 \sum_t \breve{v}_{t-1} \breve{v}_{t-\tau} + \ldots + \breve{\mu}_m \sum_t \breve{v}_{t-m} \breve{v}_{t-\tau}$$
$$= 0(r = 1, 2, \ldots, m), \tag{44}$$

where $\breve{v}_t$ is the tth element of $\breve{\mathbf{v}}$ and each of the summations in (44) is taken over all possible values of t.

There is no need to invert the $T \times T$ matrix $\breve{C}$ in order to calculate $\breve{\mathbf{v}}$. The simplest procedure is to factor $\breve{C}$ in the form

$$\check{C} = KDK', \tag{45}$$

where K is a band matrix with diagonal elements unity and zeros above the diagonal, and D is a diagonal matrix. It can be seen that this factoring reduces to a simple recurrence relation. Then from equations (43) and (45) we have

$$KDK'\check{v} = \check{u}. \tag{46}$$

and the vectors $(DK'\check{v})$, $(K'\check{v})$, and $\check{v}$ can be calculated successively by recurrence relations.

From the definitions (10) and (11) we see that η is of order $T^{-1/2}$. We therefore take $\eta_1 = 0$ as the first estimate of η. We then have first estimates γ_1, α_1, μ_1 and η_1, which give the first estimates β_1, θ_1 and M_1 needed to start the iterative procedure shown in equations (33).

3 A system of difference equations with moving average disturbances

The model

We now consider the system of difference equations

$$\Gamma y_t = \sum_{\tau=1}^{c} \Gamma_\tau y_{t-\tau} + \sum_{\tau=0}^{a} A_\tau z_{t-\tau} + u_t \quad (t = 1, \dots, T), \tag{47}$$

where Γ is a $g \times g$ non-singular matrix with diagonal elements unity, the Γ_τ are $g \times g$ matrices, and the A_τ are $g \times k$ matrices. y_t and z_t vectors of observations at time period t, y_t being of order $g \times 1$ and z_t of order $k \times 1$. u_t is a $g \times 1$ vector of disturbances. We specify that u_t has the moving average representation

$$u_t = \sum_{\tau=0}^{m} M_\tau \varepsilon_{t-\tau}, \qquad M_0 = I, \tag{48}$$

where the M_τ are $g \times g$ matrices, ε_t is a $g \times 1$ vector whose elements are jointly normal with zero means, and

$$E(\varepsilon_\tau \varepsilon'_{t-\tau}) = \begin{cases} \Sigma, & \text{for } \tau = 0 \\ 0, & \text{for } \tau \neq 0 \end{cases}, \tag{49}$$

Σ being a $g \times g$ positive define matrix.

We assume either that z_t is a stochastic process with non-singular variance matrix and is independent of u_{t-r} for all values of t and r, or alternatively that z_t satisfies an equation of the form $z_t = f(y_{t-b}, y_{t-b-1}, \dots, z_{t-1}, z_{t-2}, \dots) + u_t^*$ where $b \geq 1$ and u_t^* is a stochastic process which has a non-singular variance matrix and is independent of u_{t-r} for all values of t and r. We also assume that a number of elements of the matrices in (47) are known to be zero, the number of positions of these zero restrictions being such as to ensure that equation in the system is identified. The conditions for identification are considered in section 3.5 below.

Substituting (48) in (47), the complete model may be written as

$$\Gamma y_t = \sum_{\tau=1}^{c} \Gamma_\tau y_{t-\tau} + \sum_{\tau=0}^{a} A_\tau z_{t-\tau} + \sum_{\tau=0}^{m} M_\tau \varepsilon_{t-\tau}. \tag{50}$$

We define the following polynomials with matrix coefficients

$$P_\Gamma(S) = \Gamma - \sum_{t=1}^{c} \Gamma_\tau S^\tau$$

$$P_A(S) = \sum_{\tau=0}^{a} A_\tau S^\tau \tag{51}$$

$$P_M(S) = \sum_{\tau=0}^{m} M_\tau S^\tau, \, M_0 = I.$$

Then the system (50) may be written as

$$P_\Gamma(L)y_t = P_A(L)z_t + P_M(L)\varepsilon_t. \tag{52}$$

We specify, without loss of generality, that the determinant of $P_M(S)$ has no zeros inside the unit circle. We also specify that after the zero restrictions have been applied the coefficient of the highest remaining power of S is non-zero in at least one of the polynomial elements in each row of the matrix $[P_\Gamma(S):P_A(S):P_M(S)]$, and that the polynomial elements in any row have no common factor. These specifications, together with the assumptions made in the previous paragraph, ensure that all the parameters in the model are uniquely determined if the covariance functions of $\{y_t\}$ and $\{z_t\}$ are given.

We now define the matrix B and vector x_t by

$$B = [\Gamma_1 \ldots \Gamma_c A_0 \ldots A_a]$$

$$x_t' = [y_{t-1}' \ldots y_{t-c}' z_t' \ldots z_{t-a}'] \tag{53}$$

and write the system in the more familiar form

$$\Gamma y_t = Bx_t + u_t. \tag{54}$$

First estimates

In order to obtain consistent estimates of the parameters in (47) we use a
modified form of the method introduced by Zellner and Theil (1962) for
obtaining two-stage least-square estimates of systems in which $m = 0$. We
write the ith equation of (54) in the form

$$y_{it} = Y_{it}\gamma_i + X_{it}\beta_i + u_{it} \quad (i = 1, \ldots, g; \ t = 1, \ldots, T), \tag{55}$$

where y_{it} is the ith element of y_t, γ_i is the $h_i \times 1$ vector whose elements are
the unknown parameters in the ith row of Γ, Y_{it} is the $1 \times h_i$ vector of
corresponding elements in y_t, β_i is the $p_i \times 1$ vector whose elements are
the unknown parameters in the ith row of B, X_{it} is the $1 \times p_i$ vector of
corresponding elements in x_t and u_{it} is the ith element of u_t.

We define the vectors and matrices

$$\mathbf{y}_i = \begin{bmatrix} y_{i\ell} \\ \vdots \\ y_{iT} \end{bmatrix} \quad \mathbf{Y}_i = \begin{bmatrix} Y_{i\ell} \\ \vdots \\ Y_{iT} \end{bmatrix}$$

$$\mathbf{X}_i = \begin{bmatrix} X_{i\ell} \\ \vdots \\ X_{iT} \end{bmatrix} \quad \mathbf{X} = \begin{bmatrix} x_1' \\ \vdots \\ x_T' \end{bmatrix} \quad \mathbf{u}_i = \begin{bmatrix} u_{i1} \\ \vdots \\ u_{iT} \end{bmatrix} \tag{56}$$

$$\mathbf{R}_i = [\mathbf{Y}_i \vdots \mathbf{X}_i] \ \delta_i = \begin{bmatrix} \gamma_i \\ \beta_i \end{bmatrix}.$$

Then the set of equations (55) with $t = 1, \ldots, T$ may be written as

$$y_i = \mathbf{Y}_i\gamma_i + \mathbf{X}_i\beta_i + \mathbf{u}_i = \mathbf{R}_i\delta_i + \mathbf{u}_i. \tag{57}$$

We also define the vector x_{*_t}' and the matrix X_*' by

$$\begin{aligned} x_{*_t}' &= [y_{t-1-m}' \cdots y_{t-c-m}' z_{t-d}' \cdots z_{t-a-d}'] \\ X_*' &= [x_{*_1} \cdots x_{*\rho}], \end{aligned} \tag{58}$$

where $d = 0$ if z_t is independent of u_{t-r} for all values of t and r, and also if
$b > m$, and $d = m - b + 1$ if $b \le m$. If some or all of the initial values of
y_t for $t < -c + 1$ and of z_t for $t < -a + 1$ are unknown, they are set equal
to zero in the matrix X_*'.

Pre-multiplying equation (57) by X_*', we have

$$X_*'y_i = X_*'R_i\delta_i + X_*'u_i. \tag{59}$$

The variables in X'_* have been lagged a sufficient number of time periods to ensure that plim $(1/T)X'_*u_i = 0$. If the variance matrix $E(X'_*u_iu'_iX_*)$ of X'_*u_i were known, we could apply generalised least squares to equation (59) to estimate δ_i. This variance matrix is a function of the unknown matrices M_τ in (48). If all the M_τ were zero we should have $E(X'_*u_iu'_iX_*) = \sigma_{ii}X'_*X_*$, where σ_{ii} is the variance of u_{it}. The generalised least-squares estimate $\breve{\delta}_i$ of δ_i would then be given by the solution of the equation

$$R'_iX_*(X'_*)^{-1}X'_*y_i = R'_iX_*(X'_*X_*)^{-1}X'_*R_i\breve{\delta}_i. \tag{60}$$

We shall take this estimate $\breve{\delta}_i$ as our first estimate of δ_i. Even when the M_τ are not zero, it is consistent and of order $T^{-1/2}$ in probability.

Estimating each equation in (54) in this way we obtain first estimates $\breve{\delta}_i, \ldots, \breve{\delta}_g$, which we write more concisely as δ_1, where

$$\delta_1 = \begin{bmatrix} \breve{\delta}_1 \\ \vdots \\ \breve{\delta}_g \end{bmatrix}. \tag{61}$$

We define $\breve{u}$ by

$$\breve{u}_i = y_i - R_i\breve{\delta}_i \quad (i = 1, \ldots, g) \tag{62}$$

and $\breve{u}_t$, $\breve{u}$ and u by

$$\breve{u}_t = \begin{bmatrix} \breve{u}_{1t} \\ \vdots \\ \breve{u}_{gt} \end{bmatrix} \quad \breve{u} = \begin{bmatrix} \breve{u}_1 \\ \vdots \\ \breve{u}_T \end{bmatrix} \quad u = \begin{bmatrix} u_1 \\ \vdots \\ u_T \end{bmatrix}, \tag{63}$$

where $\breve{u}_{it}$ is the tth element of $\breve{u}_i$. Then $\breve{u}_t$ is a consistent estimate of u_t and $\breve{u}$ is a consistent estimate of $\mathbf{u}$.

As the procedure for obtaining consistent estimates of the M_τ and Σ is analogous to that given in section 2 for the single-equation case, it will be sufficient to show the main steps. An estimate $\mathbf{C}$ of the variance matrix of $\mathbf{u}$ is obtained by calculating

$$\breve{c}_\tau = \frac{1}{T} \sum_{t=\tau+1}^{T} \breve{u}_t\breve{u}'_{t-\tau} \quad (\tau = 0, 1, \ldots, m) \tag{64}$$

and forming the matrix

$$
\check{\mathbf{C}} =
\begin{bmatrix}
\check{c}_0 & \cdots & \check{c}'_m & \cdots & 0 \\
\vdots & \ddots & & \ddots & \vdots \\
\check{c}_m & & \ddots & & \check{c}'_m \\
& \ddots & & \ddots & \vdots \\
0 & & \check{c}_m & \cdots & \check{c}_0
\end{bmatrix}.
$$

We then obtain vector $\check{v}$ using

$$
\check{\mathbf{C}}\check{\mathbf{v}} = \mathbf{KDK}'\check{\mathbf{v}} = \check{\mathbf{u}}. \tag{65}
$$

$\mathbf{C}$ being first factored in $\mathbf{KDK}'$, where $\mathbf{D}$ is a block diagonal matrix with blocks of order $g \times g$ along the diagonal, and K is a band matrix with unit matrix blocks of order $g \times g$ along the diagonal and zeros above the diagonal. Then the vectors $(\mathbf{DK}'\check{\mathbf{v}})$, $(\mathbf{K}'\check{\mathbf{v}})$, and $\check{\mathbf{v}}$ are easily computed.

Initial estimates $\check{M}_\tau$ are then obtained as the solution of the equations

$$
\sum_t \check{v}_{t+\tau}\check{v}'_t + \sum_t \check{v}_{t+\tau}v'_{t+1}\check{M}_1 + \ldots + \sum_t \check{v}_{t+\tau}\check{v}'_{t+m}\check{M}_m
$$
$$
= 0(\tau = 1, \ldots, m) \tag{66}
$$

where each of the summations is taken over all possible values of t. From a consideration of the likelihood of $\mathbf{v}$ we also find that a suitable estimate $\check{\Sigma}^{-1}$ of Σ^{-1} is given by

$$
\check{\Sigma}^{-1} = \frac{1}{T}\left[\sum_t \check{v}_t\check{v}'_t + \left(\sum_t \check{v}_t\check{v}'_{t+1} \right)\check{M}_1 + \ldots \right.
$$
$$
\left. + \left(\sum_t \check{v}_t\check{v}'_{t+m} \right)\check{M}_m \right] \tag{67}
$$

where again the summations are over all possible value of t.

The model in matrix notation

We define

$$
\mathbf{y}_t \begin{bmatrix} \mathbf{Y}_{1t} & 0 & \cdot & \cdot & 0 \\ & \cdot & \cdot & & \cdot \\ \cdot & & & & \cdot \\ \cdot & & & \cdot & 0 \\ 0 & \cdot & \cdot & \cdot & \mathbf{Y}_{gt} \end{bmatrix} \quad \mathbf{X}_t = \begin{bmatrix} \mathbf{X}_{1t} & 0 & \cdot & \cdot & 0 \\ & 0 & \cdot & & \cdot \\ \cdot & & & & \cdot \\ \cdot & & & \cdot & 0 \\ 0 & \cdot & \cdot & 0 & \mathbf{X}_{gt} \end{bmatrix}
$$

$$
\mathbf{y} = \begin{bmatrix} \mathbf{y}_1 \\ \vdots \\ \mathbf{y}_T \end{bmatrix} \quad \mathbf{Y} = \begin{bmatrix} \mathbf{Y}_1 \\ \vdots \\ \mathbf{Y}_T \end{bmatrix} \quad \mathbf{X} = \begin{bmatrix} \mathbf{X}_1 \\ \vdots \\ \mathbf{X}_T \end{bmatrix}. \tag{68}
$$

Using these definitions the complete set of equations (55) for $i = 1, \ldots, g$ and $t = 1, \ldots, T$ may be written as

$$
\mathbf{y} = \mathbf{Y}\gamma + \mathbf{X}\beta + \mathbf{u}. \tag{69}
$$

We define also matrices $\mathbf{M}^*$, $\mathbf{M}$ and $\mathbf{J}$, and vectors ε^*, ε and η as in equations (10) and (11), except that now $\mathbf{M}^*$ and $\mathbf{M}$ are of order $gT \times gm$ and $gT \times gT$ respectively, with the elements u_τ replaced by the sub-matrices M_τ, $\mathbf{J}$ is of order $gT \times gm$ with a unit matrix of order $gm \times gm$, and ε^*, ε and η are of order $gm \times 1$, $gT \times 1$ and $gm \times 1$ respectively. As in the single-equation case, $\mathbf{u}$ can then be written as

$$
\mathbf{u} = \mathbf{J}\eta + \mathbf{M}\varepsilon \tag{70}
$$

and the complete model as

$$
\mathbf{y} = \mathbf{Y}\gamma + \mathbf{X}\beta + \mathbf{J}\eta + \mathbf{M}\varepsilon. \tag{71}
$$

We shall not impose any restrictions on the matrix Σ. We may therefore transform from Σ to a matrix Ω defined by

$$
\Omega = \Gamma^{-1}\Sigma\Gamma^{-1} \tag{72}
$$

and estimate Ω instead of Σ. It turns out to be simpler to do this. For convenience we define $g \times 1$ vector ξ_t by

$$
\xi_t = \Gamma^{-1}\varepsilon_t \tag{73}
$$

so that

$$
E(\xi_t \xi_{t-\tau}) = \begin{cases} \Omega, & \text{for } \tau = 0 \\ 0, & \text{for } \tau \neq 0. \end{cases} \tag{74}
$$

We define the $gT \times gT$ matrices Γ and Ω and the $gT \times 1$ vector ξ by

$$\Gamma = \begin{bmatrix} \Gamma & 0 & \cdot & \cdot & 0 \\ 0 & \cdot & & & \cdot \\ \cdot & & \cdot & & \cdot \\ \cdot & & & \cdot & 0 \\ 0 & \cdot & \cdot & 0 & \Gamma \end{bmatrix} \quad \Omega = \begin{bmatrix} \Omega & 0 & \cdot & \cdot & 0 \\ 0 & \cdot & & & \cdot \\ \cdot & & \cdot & & \cdot \\ \cdot & & & \cdot & 0 \\ 0 & \cdot & \cdot & 0 & \Omega \end{bmatrix} \quad \xi = \begin{bmatrix} \xi_1 \\ \cdot \\ \cdot \\ \cdot \\ \xi_T \end{bmatrix}.$$

$$(75)$$

Then

$$\varepsilon = \Gamma\xi \tag{76}$$

and

$$E(\xi\xi) = \Omega. \tag{77}$$

Substituting equation (76) in (71) we write the complete model in the form

$$y = Y_\gamma + X\beta + J\eta + M\Gamma\xi. \tag{78}$$

The likelihood function

From the probability density function of ξ and a transformation from ξ to y we find that the probability density function of y conditional on $z_1 \ldots, z_t$ taking all initial values for $t \leq 0$ as fixed, is given by

$$F(y) = (2\pi)^{-gT/2}(\det \Omega^{-1})^{1/2} \exp\{-\frac{1}{2}Q(\theta, \Omega)\}, \tag{79}$$

where θ is used to denote collectively the parameters in γ, β, η and in the matrices M_τ, and

$$Q(\theta, \Omega) = \xi'\Omega^{-1}\xi, \tag{80}$$

where

$$\xi = \Gamma^{-1}M^{-1}(y - Y\gamma - X\beta - J\eta). \tag{81}$$

The maximum likelihood estimate $\hat{\theta}$ is therefore the value of θ which minimises $Q(\theta, \Omega)$ when Ω has its maximum likelihood value.

Differentiating $\log F$ with respect to Ω^{-1} and setting the derivative equal to zero for a maximum, we obtain

$$\frac{T}{2}\Omega - \frac{1}{2}\xi'\xi = 0. \tag{82}$$

The maximum likelihood estimate $\hat{\Omega}$ is therefore

$$\hat{\Omega} = \frac{1}{T}\hat{\xi}'\hat{\xi}, \tag{83}$$

where by $\hat{\xi}$ we mean the value given by equation (81) when the parameters on the right-hand side have their maximum likelihood values.

Using equation (79) it may easily be verified that if Σ and the M_τ are block diagonal matrices with corresponding partitioning, and if Γ is a block triangular matrix with the same partitioning, the log likelihood can be expressed as the sum of a number of terms, each of which involves only the parameters occurring in one block of equations. It follows that each block of equations can then be estimated independently of the rest of the system.

The iterative process

Let a quantity written with the subscript r denote the rth estimate of that quantity. We define ε_r by

$$\mathbf{y} = \mathbf{Y}\gamma_r + \mathbf{X}\beta_r + \mathbf{J}\eta_r + \mathbf{M}_r\varepsilon_r. \tag{84}$$

Subtracting equation (84) from (71) gives

$$0 = \mathbf{Y}(\gamma - \gamma_r) + \mathbf{X}(\beta - \beta_r) + \mathbf{J}(\eta - \eta_r) + \mathbf{M}\varepsilon - \mathbf{M}_r\varepsilon_r. \tag{85}$$

Using the identity (24) we write this as

$$\begin{aligned} 0 = \mathbf{Y}(\gamma - \gamma_r) + \mathbf{X}(\beta - \beta_r) + \mathbf{J}(\eta - \eta_r) + (\mathbf{M} - \mathbf{M}_r)\varepsilon_r \\ + \mathbf{M}(\varepsilon - \varepsilon_r) + \zeta_1 \end{aligned} \tag{86}$$

where ζ_1 is used to denote the last term in identity (24) and is of the second order in the errors of the rth estimates.

Let μ_i' be the $1 \times gm$ vector of parameters in the ith row of the matrix $[M_1 \ldots M_m]$ and define the $1 \times gm$ vector ε_{it} by

$$\mathbf{E}_{it} = [\varepsilon_{i,t-1}', \ldots, \varepsilon_{i,t-m}'], \tag{87}$$

the quantities ε_s' being set equal to zero when $s \le 0$. Define also

$$\mathbf{E}_t = \begin{bmatrix} \mathbf{E}_{1t} & 0 & \cdot & \cdot & 0 \\ 0 & \cdot & & & \cdot \\ \cdot & & \cdot & & \cdot \\ \cdot & & & \cdot & 0 \\ 0 & \cdot & \cdot & 0 & \mathbf{E}_{gt} \end{bmatrix} \quad E = \begin{bmatrix} \mathbf{E}_1 \\ \cdot \\ \cdot \\ \cdot \\ \mathbf{E}_T \end{bmatrix} \quad \mu = \begin{bmatrix} \mu_1 \\ \cdot \\ \cdot \\ \cdot \\ \mu_g \end{bmatrix}. \tag{88}$$

With these definitions the term $(\mathbf{M} - \mathbf{M}_r)\varepsilon_r$ can be written as

$$(\mathbf{M} - \mathbf{M}_r)\varepsilon_r = \mathbf{E}_r(\mu - \mu_r). \tag{89}$$

Substituting equation (89) in (86), pre-multiplying by $\mathbf{M}_r^{-1}$, and using equation (76) we obtain

$$
\begin{aligned}
0 = {}& \mathbf{M}_r^{-1}[\mathbf{Y}(\gamma - \gamma_r) + \mathbf{X}(\beta - \beta_r) + \mathbf{J}(\eta - \eta_r) + \mathbf{E}_\gamma(\mu - \mu_r)] \\
& + \Gamma\xi - \Gamma_r\xi_r + \zeta_2,
\end{aligned} \tag{90}
$$

where $\zeta_2 = M_r^{-1}\zeta_1$ and ξ_r is defined by

$$\varepsilon_r = \Gamma_r\xi_r. \tag{91}$$

Let Ξ be the $h_i \times 1$ vector consisting of those elements of ξ_t whose positions correspond with the positions of the unknown parameters in the ith row of Γ, and let Ξ_t and Ξ be defined by

$$
\Xi_t = \begin{bmatrix} \Xi'_{1t} & 0 & \cdot & \cdot & 0 \\ & 0 & & & \cdot \\ \cdot & & \cdot & & \cdot \\ \cdot & & & \cdot & 0 \\ 0 & \cdot & \cdot & \cdot & \Xi'_{gt} \end{bmatrix} \quad \Xi = \begin{bmatrix} \Xi_1 \\ \cdot \\ \cdot \\ \cdot \\ \Xi_T \end{bmatrix}. \tag{92}
$$

Consider now the identity

$$\Gamma\xi - \Gamma_r\xi_r = (\Gamma - \Gamma_r)\xi_r + \Gamma_r(\xi - \xi_r) + (\Gamma - \Gamma_r)(\xi - \xi_r) \tag{93}$$

the last term of which is of the second order in the errors of the rth estimates. Then the first term on the right-hand side of identity (93) may be written as

$$(\Gamma - \Gamma_r)\xi_r = \Xi(\gamma - \gamma_r). \tag{94}$$

Substituting equation (94) in (90), pre-multiplying by Γ_r^{-1}, and rearranging we obtain

$$
\begin{aligned}
\xi_r = {}& \Gamma_r^{-1}[(\mathbf{M}_r^{-1}\mathbf{Y} - \Xi_r)(\gamma - \gamma_r) \\
& + \mathbf{M}_r^{-1}\{\mathbf{X}(\beta - \beta_r) + \mathbf{J}(\eta - \eta_r) + \mathbf{E}_r(\mu - \mu_r)\}] + \xi + \zeta_3,
\end{aligned} \tag{95}
$$

where $\zeta_3 = \Gamma_r^{-1}\{\zeta_2 + (\Gamma - \Gamma_r)(\xi - \xi_r)\}$, and so is of the second order in the errors of the rth estimates.

Defining $\mathbf{W_r}$ and θ by

$$\mathbf{W}_r = \Gamma_r^{-1}[\mathbf{M}_r^{-1}\mathbf{Y} - \Xi_r\vdots\mathbf{M}_r^{-1}\mathbf{X}\vdots\mathbf{M}_r^{-1}\mathbf{J}\vdots\mathbf{M}_r^{-1}\varepsilon_r] \tag{96}$$

$$\theta' = [\gamma'\vdots\beta'\vdots\eta'\vdots\mu'] $$

we write equation (95) as

$$\xi_r = \mathbf{W}_r(\theta - \theta_r) + \xi + \zeta_3. \tag{97}$$

Let $\bar{\theta}_{r+1}$ be the value of θ which minimises $\xi'\Omega_r^{-1}\xi$ in equation (97) ignoring the term ζ_3. Then

$$\bar{\theta}_{r+1} - \theta_r = (\mathbf{W}_r\Omega_r^{-1}\mathbf{W}_r)^{-1}\mathbf{W}_r\Omega_r^{-1}\xi_r. \tag{98}$$

As the single-equation case, we take the $(r+1)$th estimate θ_{r+1} to be

$$\theta_{r+1} = \theta_r + \lambda_r(\bar{\theta}_{r+1} - \theta_r), \tag{99}$$

where λ_r is a positive scalar. The $(r+1)$th estimate of Ω is then given by

$$\Omega_{r+1} = \frac{1}{T}\xi'_{r+1}\xi_{r+1}. \tag{100}$$

We take a trial value of λ_r as unity and test whether

$$Q(\theta_{r+1}, \Omega_{r+1}) < Q(\theta_r, \Omega_r). \tag{101}$$

If the condition (101) is satisfied we proceed to the next iteration. If not, λ_r is reduced until condition (101) is satisfied and we then proceed to the next iteration. Convergence of the process leads to the maximum likelihood estimates $\hat{\theta}$ and $\hat{\Omega}$. There is no need to invert $gT \times gT$ matrixes Γ_r and $\mathbf{M}_r$ when calculating $\mathbf{W}_r$ in one of the equations (96). Γ_r is a block diagonal matrix with blocks Γ_r which can be treated separately, and the simple form of $\mathbf{M}_r$ allows a recurrence relation to be used as described for the single-equation case in section 2.

The iterative process can be started with estimates θ_1 and Ω_1 obtained from the first estimates γ_1, α_1 and $\check{\mathbf{M}}_r$ and $\check{\Sigma}^{-1}$ described in the second part of this section, together with the first estimate of η given by $\eta_1 = 0$. It can be shown that the estimates $\bar{\theta}_2$ and Ω_2 then differ from the maximum likelihood estimates by terms of order T^{-1} in probability. The variance matrix of $\bar{\theta}_r$ for $r \geq 2$ can be shown to be

$$V(\bar{\theta}_r) = (\mathbf{W}'_r\Omega_r^{-1}\mathbf{W}_r)^{-1} + 0(t^{-1}). \tag{102}$$

The likelihood ratio method may be used to test the hypothesis that some of the elements of θ are zero. Alternatively, an F test can be used as in normal regression analyses. The F test is asymptotically equivalent to the likelihood ratio test, and may possibly have some advantage in the finite case. Either of these tests is asymptotically valid if applied to the second or subsequent estimates.

Using tests of hypothesis it is possible to estimate the values of a and b in equations (47) and m in equations (48) (and similarly in equations (3) and (4) in the single-equation case), which so far we have taken as given. The model can be fitted with successively higher values of these integers and we can test the hypothesis that the additional parameters so introduced are zero.

Notes

Phillips described this chapter as a 'Preliminary draft. Paper to be read at a meeting of the Econometric Society in San Francisco on 27 December 1966. Research supported by a grant from the Ford Foundation to the Research Techniques Division of the London School of Economics.' At the end of the original paper, Phillips included a section 3.5 entitled 'Separation, Identification and Uniqueness' plus a section 4 entitled 'Some Applications of the Model with Moving Average Disturbances', with the statement 'Text of sections 3.5 and 4 to follow later'. A later version of this paper with a slightly different title ('Estimation of Stochastic Difference Equations with Moving Average Disturbances') in which these sections appeared, circulated privately in the late 1960s. Unfortunately, a copy of this extended paper has not been found. It appears that Phillips only kept a copy of the earlier version reprinted here.

The Unpublished Papers

46   The Estimation of Continuous Time Models

A.R. Bergstrom

Chapter 47 is a brief outline of a paper presented at a meeting at Nuffield College, Oxford in 1962. It refers to chapter 48 for details of proposed methods of estimating the parameters of continuous time dynamic models from observations of the variables at equispaced points of time. Chapter 48 is a sequel to chapter 42, an important and influential essay which Phillips had published in *Biometrika* in 1959.

Although Koopmans (1950b) was the first econometrician to recognise the potential importance of continuous time models in econometrics and Bartlett (1946) had earlier dealt with estimation problems in some simple special cases, it was Phillips in 1959 (chapter 42) who produced the first detailed algorithm for estimating a continuous time model of sufficient generality to be of use in macroeconometric work. Moreover, chapter 42 provided the initial stimulus for work on continuous time methods by other econometricians. In particular, it was the major stimulus to my own work on this subject, which commenced, at the LSE in 1962–3 and has continued for more than thirty years (Bergstrom 1990).

The main contribution of chapter 42 was to show how to derive the parameters of a stochastic differential equation system from a sequence of values of the correlation function at unit intervals. The route that he followed was to first derive the correlation function from its values at unit intervals, next, by taking the Laplace transform of the correlation function obtain the transfer function of dependence of the variables generated by the differential system on the white noise innovations and, finally, obtain the parameters of the differential system from the transfer function. This procedure will yield asymptotically efficient estimators, however, only if we have asymptotically efficient estimates of the values of the correlation function at unit intervals, taking account of the assumed structure of the model generating the variables. One way of obtaining such estimates would be to obtain asymptotically efficient estimates of the parameters of the VARMA (vector autoregressive moving average) model that must be satisfied by the observations of the variables at equispaced points of time.

The main contribution of chapter 48 is to outline a new method of obtaining asymptotically efficient estimates of the parameters of an auto-regressive moving-average model. This method could be extended to the estimation of the parameters of a VARMA model (that is, the multi-variate case) and hence provide the basis for the estimation of the par-ameters of a system of stochastic differential equations by the route followed in chapter 40.

The method proposed in chapter 48 is to generalise an ingenious method developed by Durbin (1959) for estimating the parameters of a moving-average model. Durbin's method is a two-stage procedure, which has the computational advantage that each stage involves only the sol-ution of a set of linear equations. At the first stage, a high-order auto-regressive equation is fitted to the data, while at the second stage, a function involving the estimated autoregressive coefficients is maximised with respect to the parameters of the moving-average model to obtain estimates of the latter parameters. Durbin shows that the resulting esti-mates are asymptotically efficient, provided that the order of the fitted autoregressive equation tends to infinity as the sample size does, but at a slower rate. The sample size may need to be very large, however, in order for the estimates to be approximately as good as the maximum likelihood estimates. The latter estimates are, of course, more difficult to compute.

The potential usefulness of the methods proposed in chapters 42, 47 and 48 in applied econometric work with continuous time models is limited by the fact that they do not take account of *a priori* restrictions, such as those implied by economic theory. Such restrictions are very important in applied econometric work, because of the smallness of the samples available and the need to take account of *a priori* restrictions in order to increase the efficiency of the estimates. In my own work with continuous time models, I have taken account of these restrictions by deriving the parameters of the VARMA model or VARMAX model (vector autoregressive moving-average model with exogenous variables) as explicit functions of a much smaller number of structural parameters of the continuous time model. For example, in the 14 equation second-order continuous time macroeconometric model of the United Kingdom developed by Bergstrom, Nowman and Wymer (1992), the VARMAX model satisfied by the discrete observations contains 1477 parameters all of which are very complicated (but known) transcendental functions of 168 unknown structural parameters of the continuous time model. It would have been impossible to estimate a VARMAX model of this size from the sample available without taking account of the restrictions implied by this parsimonious parametrisation.

Although Phillips' methods of estimating the parameters of continuous time models have never been fully used (probably, for the reason mentioned in the preceding paragraph), it was his pioneering work that stimulated other econometricians to work in this field. During the last twenty-five years, leading econometricians in both England and America have contributed to the theory of identification and estimation of the parameters of continuous time dynamic models from discrete time data. Moreover, applied econometric work with continuous time models has been undertaken by a much wider group of econometricians, and continuous time macroeconometric models have been developed for many different countries.[1] Much of the latter work was stimulated by the disequilibrium neoclassical growth model of the United Kingdom developed by Bergstrom and Wymer (1976) which was the first economy-wide continuous time macroeconometric model. As I have shown in chapter 20, the model of Bergstrom and Wymer (1976) is descended from the cyclical growth model developed in another of Phillips' pioneering contributions (see chapter 21).

Notes

1 See my surveys, Bergstrom (1988 and 1996) for an account of this work.

47 Estimation in Continuous Time Series Models with Auto-correlated Disturbances

A.W. Phillips

Assume that we observe two stationary time series y_t and x_t with zero means, and that we know that y_t is generated by the lagged dependence

$$y_t = \sum_{\tau=0}^{\infty} v_\tau x_{t-\tau} + \eta_t, \tag{1}$$

where $\{\eta_t\}$ is an unobserved stationary process which is independent of x_{t-h} for all values of h. The processes $\{x_t\}$ and $\{\eta_t\}$ may be autocorrelated. We may suppose η_t to be generated by the lagged dependence

$$\eta_t = \sum_{\tau=0}^{\infty} w_\tau \varepsilon_{t-\tau}, \tag{2}$$

where $\{\varepsilon_t\}$ is a non-autocorrelated process with zero mean and constant variance, and is uncorrelated with x_{t-h} for all h.

Our problem is to estimate from observations y_t and x_t, $(t = 1, 2, \ldots, T)$, the weighting functions v_τ and w_τ which define the distributed lags of the dependencies (1) and (2). Since T is finite we must approximate the weighting functions by functions containing a finite, and usually quite small, number of parameters. We shall assume that the function v_τ and w_τ can be adequately approximated by the sum of m and n geometric series respectively, the geometric series being either real or occurring in conjugate pairs which can be reduced to damped sinusoids. It can easily be shown that (1) and (2) can then be written as

$$y_t = \frac{G(E^{-1})}{H(E^{-1})} x_t + \eta_t \tag{3}$$

and

449

$$\eta_t = \frac{\beta(E^{-1})}{\alpha(E^{-1})}\varepsilon_t, \tag{4}$$

where E^{-h} is the shift operator defined by $E^{-h}y_t = y_{t-h}$ and G, H, β and α are the polynomials

$$G(E^{-1}) = G_0 + G_1 E^{-1} + \ldots + G_{m-1} E^{-m+1}$$

$$H(E^{-1}) = 1 + H_1 E^{-1} + \ldots + H_m E^{-m}, \quad (H_m \neq 0)$$

$$\beta(E^{-1}) = 1 + \beta_1 E^{-1} + \ldots + \beta_{n-1} E^{-n+1}$$

$$\alpha(E^{-1}) = 1 + \alpha_1 E^{-1} + \ldots + \alpha_n E^{-n}, \quad (\alpha_n \neq 0).$$

We may substitute (4) in (3) and write the theoretical model as

$$y_t \frac{G(E^{-1})}{H(E^{-1})} x_t + \frac{\beta(E^{-1})}{\alpha(E^{-1})}\varepsilon_t. \tag{5}$$

An alternative specification of the model, which differs from (5) only in the number of coefficients involved, may be obtained by multiplying (5) through by $H(E^{-1})\alpha(E^{-1})$ to give

$$P(E^{-1})y_t = Q(E^{-1})x_t + R(E^{-1})\varepsilon_t \tag{6}$$

where $P = H\alpha$, $Q = G\alpha$ and $R = H\beta$. $P(E^{-1})$ is then of degree $n + m$, while $Q(E^{-1})$ and $R(E^{-1})$ are of degree $n + m - 1$ at most.

A description will be given at the meeting of methods which have been developed for obtaining asymptotically efficient estimates of the coefficients of the polynomials in (5) or in (6) from a set of observations y_t and x_t, $(t = 1, 2, \ldots, T)$. The methods extend to the case of multiple time series, in which y_t, x_t and ε_t are vectors and G, H, β and α, or P, Q and R, are matrices whose elements are polynomials in E^{-1}, provided the equations in the system are identified.

A wider class of problems, of which that considered above is a special case, arises when the discrete processes $\{y_t\}$ and $\{x_t\}$ are values at equally spaced points of time, or alternatively are averages over equal consecutive intervals of time, of corresponding continuous processes $\{y(t)\}$ and $\{x(t)\}$, and it is desired to estimate the weighting functions of the distributed lags in the continuous system. Methods for solving this wider class of problems are indicated in the attached introduction to a paper on the estimation of rational spectral density functions and transfer functions.

Note

Outline of the subject to be introduced by A.W. Phillips at a meeting at Nuffield College on 14 April 1962 (dated 12 April 1962).

48 Efficient Fitting of Rational Spectral Density Functions and Transfer Functions

A.W. Phillips

1 Introduction and summary

Consider a stationary process $\{x(t)\}$ with continuous time parameter t and having mean μ, autocovariance $\phi(\tau)$ and a rational spectral density function $f(\omega)$. That is

$$E\{x(t)\} = \mu, \tag{1}$$

$$E[\{x(t) - \mu\}\{x(t - \tau) - \mu\}] = \phi(\tau), \tag{2}$$

$$\int_{-\infty}^{\infty} \phi(\tau)e^{-i\omega\tau}\,d\tau = f(\omega)$$

$$= \frac{g(\omega)}{h(\omega)} \tag{3}$$

$$= \frac{g_0 + g_1\omega^2 + \ldots + g_{m-1}\omega^{2m-2}}{1 + h_1\omega^2 + \ldots + h_m\omega^{2m}}.$$

We define also the discrete process $\{x_r\}$ by

$$x_r = x(r\delta), \quad (r = \ldots, -1, 0, 1, \ldots), \tag{4}$$

where δ is a positive constant, so that x_r is the series of values taken by $x(t)$ at equally spaced points of time, with time-interval δ.

We shall be concerned in this paper with the problem of estimating the spectral density function $f(\omega)$ of the continuous process $\{x(t)\}$ from a sample of T observations x_r, $r = 1, 2, \ldots, T$. The approach adopted follows that of Phillips (chapter 42). Considering for simplicity only cases in which the roots of the equation $h(\omega) = 0$ are distinct, it is shown in section 2 below that since $f(\omega)$ is a rational function of degree m in ω^2 the autocovariance function $\phi(\tau)$ is the sum of m exponential functions which are either real or occur in conjugate complex pairs. In the latter

451

case each pair of conjugate complex exponentials can be written as a real damped sinusoid. Defining the discrete function ϕ_q by

$$\phi q = \phi(q\delta), \quad (q = \ldots, -1, 0, 1, \ldots), \tag{5}$$

so that ϕq is the autocovariance function of the discrete process $\{x_r\}$, we find from consideration of the function ϕq that the discrete process $\{x_r\}$ satisfies a stochastic difference equation of the form

$$(x_r) + \alpha_1(x_{r-1} - \mu) + \ldots + \alpha_m(x_{r-m} - \mu)$$

$$= \varepsilon_r + \beta_1 \varepsilon_{r-1} + \ldots + \beta_{m-1} \varepsilon_{r-m+1} \quad (r = \ldots, -1, 0, 1, \ldots), \tag{6}$$

where the process $\{\varepsilon_r\}$ is a series of independently and identically distributed random variables with zero mean and constant variance v, and the α's and β's are constants which, together with v, can be uniquely determined from the g's and h's in (3). Moreover provided the time interval δ between successive observations of $x(t)$ is less than half the period of any real sinusoidal component of $\phi(\tau)$ that g's and h's in (3), and so the spectral density function $f(\omega)$, can be determined uniquely if v and the α's and β's are known. We shall *assume* that δ is in fact less than half the period of any real sinusoidal component of $\phi(\tau)$, and calculate an estimate of $f(\omega)$ from estimates of v and of the α's and β's. Our problem then reduces to that of estimating the parameters of the general linear stochastic difference equation (6).

In the special case in which $\beta_j = 0$, $(j = 1, 2, \ldots, m - 1)$ equation (6) defines an autoregressive process of order m. Least squares estimates of α_j, $(j = 1, 2, \ldots, m)$ are then easily obtained by the solution of a set of linear equations. Another special case is that in which $\alpha_j = 0$, $(j = 1, 2 \ldots, m)$. Equation (6) then defines a moving average process of order $m - 1$. In this case estimation methods based directly on least-squares or maximum likelihood lead to an intractable set of non-linear equations in the estimators of β_j, $(j = 1, 2, \ldots, m - 1)$. However, Durbin (1959) has developed a method of obtaining asymptotically efficient estimates of the β's in a moving average process by a two-stage procedure, each stage of which involves only the solution of a set of linear equations. Durbin obtained his estimators of the β's by maximising the asymptotic likelihood of the set of coefficients obtained by fitting a high order autoregressive model to the moving average process.

In section 3 of the present paper Durbin's estimators of the β's of a moving average process are derived in a different way, which brings out more clearly their relation to the least squares estimators, and which is then generalised to provide asymptotically efficient estimators of the α's and β's in the mixed moving average autoregressive process, or general linear process (6). For ease of exposition the extension to the mixed case is first shown for the first order process $x_r + \alpha x_{r-1} = \varepsilon_r + \beta \varepsilon_{r-1}$, which is treated in section 4. The observed means and variances of estimates of α and β obtained by this method from fifty samples, each of 100 observations, from a process with $\alpha = -0.8$ and $\beta = 0.5$ are also given in this section. The observed sampling variances are in close agreement with the theoretical minimum variances calculated from asymptotic formulae due to Whittle (1951, 1953b).

In section 5 the method is generalised to linear systems of any order. Estimates of the parameters in (6), for example, are obtained from the linear regression

$$w_p = \sum_{j=1}^{A} \hat{\alpha}_j u_{jp} + \sum_{j=1}^{B} \hat{\beta}_j v_{jp} + e_p, \quad (p = 1, 2, \ldots), \tag{7}$$

where the series w_p, u_{jp} and v_{jp} are derived from the coefficients a_i $(i = 1, 2, \ldots, k)$ obtained by fitting an autoregressive model of higher order k to the observations x_r, $(r = 1, 2, \ldots, T)$. Estimates of the sampling variances and covariances of the $\hat{\alpha}_j$ and $\hat{\beta}_j$ are obtained from the regression (7) in the usual way. It is especially simple with this method of estimation to use the tests of hypotheses proposed by Whittle (1951, 1953b) as a criterion for choosing the number of parameters to be fitted on the autoregressive and moving average sides of the linear process (6), i.e., for choosing A and B in (7), since the variance of residuals of (7) is readily compared with the variance of residuals of the fitted autoregressive model of order k, which is taken as the broadest model of the process.

The difference equation (6) may be written, assuming for simplicity that $\mu = 0$, as

$$\begin{aligned} x_r &= \frac{\beta(E^{-1})}{\alpha(E^{-1})} \varepsilon_r, \\ &= F(E^{-1}) \varepsilon_r, \end{aligned} \tag{8}$$

where E^{-1} is the lag operator defined for any series y_r by $E^{-q} y_r = y_{r-q}$, $\alpha(E^{-1})$ is the polynomial $1 + \alpha_1 E^{-1} + \ldots + \alpha_m E^{-m}$, $(\alpha_m \neq 0)$, and $\beta(E^{-1})$ is the polynomial $1 + \beta_1 E^{-1} + \ldots + \beta_{m-1} E^{-m+1}$. We shall call the rational function $F(E^{-1})$ the 'transfer operator' of the dependence of x on ε. This dependence may also be written in the form

$$x_r = \sum_{q=0}^{\infty} w_q \varepsilon_{r-q}, \tag{9}$$

where w_q is the coefficient of E^{-q} in the expansion of $F(E^{-1})$ in a power series in E^{-1}. The function w_q, $(q = 0, 1, \ldots)$ will be called the 'weighting function' of the dependence of x on ε. We denote the generating function of w_q (which we shall also refer to as the z transform of w_q) by $W(z)$, so that

$$W(z) = \sum_{q=0}^{\infty} w_q z^q. \tag{10}$$

The function $W(z)$ will be called the 'transfer function' of the dependence of x on ε. It can be readily verified that $W(z) = F(z)$ and that

$$w_q = \sum_{j=1}^{m} A_j(\mu_j)^q, \tag{11}$$

where A_j and μ_j, $(j = 1, 2, \ldots, m)$ can be found from the partial fraction expansion of $W(z)$,

$$W(z) = \sum_{j=1}^{m} \frac{A_j}{1 - \mu_j z}. \tag{12}$$

Thus if the transfer function of a dependence is a proper rational function whose denominator is of degree m, the weighting function of the dependence is the sum of m geometric series, and the converse is also true. The geometric series may of course occur in conjugate complex pairs which can be written alternatively as real damped sinusoids. It may also be easily verified that the spectral density function of the discrete process x_r is given by $|W(e^{i\omega})|^2$, and that the two-sided z transform of the covariance function of x_r is $W(z)W(z^{-1})$.

Analogous relationships hold for continuous processes. Thus the continuous process $\{x(t)\}$ can be considered as generated by the stochastic differential equation

$$\gamma(D)x(t) = \delta(D)\zeta(t), \tag{13}$$

where D is the differential operator d/dt, $\gamma(D)$ is the polynomial $1 + \gamma_1 D + \ldots + \gamma_m D^m$, $(\gamma_m = 0)$, $\delta(D)$ is the polynomial $1 + \delta_1 D + \ldots + \delta_{m-1}D^{m-1}$ and $\zeta(t)$ is the stochastic process known as 'white noise', whose covariance function may be written

$$E\{\zeta(t)\zeta(t-\tau)\} = K_{\lambda \to 0}^{\lim} \frac{1}{\lambda} e^{-\lambda|\tau|}, \tag{14}$$

K being a constant. The rational function $\delta(D)/\gamma(D)$ is then the 'transfer operator' of the dependence of $x(t)$ on $\zeta(t)$. This dependence can also be written as

$$x(t) = \int_0^\infty u(\tau)\zeta(t - \tau)d\tau, \tag{15}$$

where $u(\tau)$ is the 'weighting function' of the dependence. Let $U(s)$ be the Laplace transform of $u(\tau)$, so that

$$U(s) = \int_0^\infty u(\tau)e^{-s\tau}d\tau. \tag{16}$$

The $U(s)$ is the 'transfer function' of the dependence. It may be verified that $U(s) = \delta(s)/\gamma(s)$ and that

$$u(\tau) = \sum_{j=1}^m H_j e^{\lambda_j \tau}, \tag{17}$$

where H_j and λ_j, $(j = 1, 2, \ldots, m)$ can be found form the partial fraction expansion of $U(s)$

$$U(s) = \sum_{j=1}^m \frac{j}{s - \lambda_j}. \tag{18}$$

Thus if the transfer function of a continuous dependence is a proper rational function whose denominator is of degree m, the weighting function of the dependence is the sum of m exponential functions which may be real or may occur in conjugate complex pairs. Also, the spectral density function of the continuous process $\{x(t)\}$ is given by $|U(i\omega)|^2$ and the two-sided Laplace transform of the covariance function of $x(t)$ is $U(s)U(-s)$.

Using the terminology introduced in the last two paragraphs, the estimation problem considered earlier is that of fitting a rational transfer function $U(s)$ (or equivalently a weighting function $u(\tau)$ which is the sum of real exponential functions and/or damped sinusoids) to describe the dependence of $x(t)$ on an unobserved white noise process $\zeta(t)$. An obvious and important extension of this problem is to fit rational transfer functions $\hat{U}(s)$ and $\hat{V}(s)$ to the dependence

$$y(t) = \int_0^\infty v(\tau)x(t - \tau)d\tau + \int_0^\infty u(\tau)\zeta(t - \tau)d\tau \tag{19}$$

where $\{y(t)\}$ and $\{x(t)\}$ are continuous stochastic processes, with rational spectral density functions, which are observed at equally spaced points of time, $\{\zeta(t)\}$ is an unobserved white noise process which is independent of

$\{x(t)\}$, and $u(\tau)$ and $v(\tau)$ are weighting functions with rational Laplace transforms $U(s)$ and $V(s)$ which we estimate by $\hat{U}(s)$ and $\hat{V}(s)$. This problem is considered in section 6, where it is shown that the discrete variables $y_r = y(r\delta)$ and $x_r = x(r\delta)$ satisfy a difference equation of the form

$$y_r = \frac{G(E^{-1})}{H(E^{-1})} x_r + \frac{B(E^{-1})}{\alpha(E^{-1})} \varepsilon_r, \tag{20}$$

where, G, H, β and α are polynomials of finite degree in E^{-1} and $\{\varepsilon_r\}$ is a non-autocorrelated process with constant variance. Also, provided δ is less than half the period of any sinusoidal component of the covariance function of $\{y_r\}$, the transfer functions $U(s)$ and $V(s)$ of the continuous process (19) can be determined uniquely if the coefficients of G, H, β, and α, the variance of ε_r, and the spectral density function of $\{x_r\}$ are known.

A rational spectral density function can be fitted to observations x_r, $(r = 1, 2, \ldots, T)$ by the method discussed above. To obtain estimates of the coefficients of the polynomials G, H, β and α we first fit the regression

$$y_r + a_1 y_{r-1} + \ldots + a_k y_{r-k} = b_0 x_r + b_1 x_{r-1} + \ldots + b_c x_{r-c} + e_r \tag{21}$$

by least squares, k and c being taken large enough to ensure that there is negligible autocorrelation of the residual e_r though they must be kept fairly small relatively to T. Asymptotically efficient estimates of the coefficients of the polynomials $\alpha(E^{-1})$ and $\beta(E^{-1})$ can then be obtained from the fitted coefficients a_j, $(j = 1, 2, \ldots, k)$ in exactly the same way as these estimates were obtained when fitting a rational spectral density function to the process $\{x_r\}$. A somewhat similar procedure for obtaining asymptotically efficient estimates of $G(E^{-1})$ and $H(E^{-1})$ from the fitted coefficients b_j, $(j = 0, 1, \ldots, c)$, the estimates of $\alpha(E^{-1})$ and $\beta(E^{-1})$, and the spectral density function fitted to the process $\{x_r\}$, are given in section 7.

The methods developed in this paper make it possible to obtain asymptotically efficient estimates of dependencies which involve fairly general forms of distributed time lags and which are subject to disturbances with fairly general autocorrelation properties. Their main advantages lies in the fact that there is no need to solve sets of non-linear estimating equations or to employ any kind of iterative procedures. On the other hand, the series available must be long enough to permit a representation by an autoregressive process or by an equation of the form (21) with k and c sufficiently large to ensure negligible autocorrelation of ε_r, though still small relatively to T.

The methods are readily extended to multiple time series. In the case of estimation of the spectral density functions and cross-spectral density functions of a vector process $x(t)$ no new issues of principle arise. If, however, it is desired to represent the vector process by a set of structural equations, identification conditions must be satisfied, and these conditions are made more severe by relaxation of the usual condition that the disturbances be non-autocorrelated.

Note

Phillips labelled this paper 'preliminary and incomplete'. It introduced an essay which appears not to have survived.

Phillips' Foreshadowing of the Lucas Critique

49 The Lucas Critique: Did Phillips Make a Comparable Contribution?

Robin Court

Econometric models may be used to provide assessment of and feedback to economic theory, and also for the interrelated purposes of policy and forecasting.[1] Chapter 50, first published in 1968, makes a significant contribution to the latter purposes by pursuing a fundamental question about the feasibility of using aggregate econometric models for purposes of policy, forecasting and economic control. Phillips' question seems to have some relationship, indeed it appears in some ways to make a very similar point, to that which has become very well known in more recent years as the Lucas Critique.

Phillips presented his essay on underidentification in models of economic control at a conference on mathematical modelling held in London in early July 1967. It was the last essay published during his lifetime and probably his least well-known contribution to economics. Lucas gave the paper containing his critique at a Carnegie-Rochester conference on public policy in April 1973, as part of a series of papers with the Phillips Curve as a major theme.

Phillips noted that governments carry out a degree of conscious control over their economies for the purposes of overcoming severe fluctuations in general economic activity and employment. He also noted that results of research in model building and econometric estimation were used in this process. His stated purposes in his paper were to 'give an outline of this method and the way it would be used in economic control', to 'indicate an inherent limitation of the method' and to 'state the need for developing improved computational methods in order to facilitate the use of methods of learning or adaptive control'.

Phillips' 'inherent limitation of the method' is of fundamental relevance to the possibilities or otherwise of using econometric models for uses such as forecasting if at the same time they are used for purposes of policy application or control. Basically, his argument was that if the reduced form is used for policy control in conjunction with an optimal decision rule, which consists of a subset of the variables contained in the reduced form, then the reduced form cannot be distinguished from arbitrary combinations of itself with the decision rule, and thus (in Phillips' words) 'may no longer be identified'.[2]

As is well known, and widely discussed in econometrics texts, the identification problem may raise a serious question as to what one is actually finding out from the application of statistical methods to economic models. A Nobel prize-winning early contributor noted that 'Identification is not a statistical concept, and criteria for the existence of identification must be examined before the methods of statistical estimation are applied' (Klein 1974, 18). The form of the econometric models Phillips considered were actually already in their reduced forms, and since econometricians are not normally accustomed to thinking of the reduced form as underidentified,[3] Klein's injunction could easily be overlooked in the type of situation addressed by Phillips.

It is not hard to give examples which may lead to some intuitive feeling for the substance of Phillips' idea. For instance, suppose a central bank uses its econometric model to forecast inflation to be 5 per cent under an interest rate of 5 per cent but, regarding this forecast inflation as too high if it were to eventuate, it adjusts the interest rate[4] to 10 per cent predicting, through its model, that the inflation will thereby turn out to be 2 per cent. The forecast outcome of 5 per cent can scarcely be identified as having the same meaning as the 2 per cent actual outcome, since in the one case it is an endogenous outcome, in the other an exogenous target (determined directly from welfare or other grounds).

The structure of the model has changed because of the application of the policy, variables which were respectively treated as endogenous and exogenous during estimation of the model having switched these positions during application of the policy.[5] Further, it is not reasonable to suppose that the observed values of inflation and interest rate after application of the policy could add any information to that which is already contained within the model, because they did not vary independently of the estimated model. Thus these additional observed outcomes cannot validly be used to provide additional information to re-estimate the model. Also, one may reasonably ask whether the observed divergence between inflation forecast and inflation outcome should be seen as evidence that the model is good (because it allowed an effective application of policy to change a bad outcome to a good one) or that the model is bad (because its forecast of inflation diverged considerably from the actual outcome).[6]

Some years ago, I used Phillips' idea to demonstrate, at least to my own satisfaction, that the widely used 'demand forecasting' approach to energy planning tended to be generally fallacious. It is based on under-identified 'demand' and, consequently, the vast amounts of resources channelled by many countries into satisfying the projected 'demands' were in grave danger of being misdirected (Court 1979).[7] I am not aware of other developments that have followed directly from Phillips' idea.

In 1976, Robert Lucas published his article 'Econometric Policy Evaluation: A Critique' in *The Phillips Curve and Labor Markets*, a volume based on another of Phillips' contributions to economics. Lucas' critique has been widely discussed, his article has become a standard reference and (quoting from the Royal Swedish Academy of Sciences citation when awarding Lucas his 1995 Nobel Prize) he 'has had a profound influence on economic policy recommendations'.

Lucas (1976, 20) states that there is little in his own essay which was not implicit or explicit in work by earlier writers including Friedman, Muth, Knight, Marschak and Tinbergen.[8] Although in his discussion he illustrates some points he raises by specifically referring to the Phillips Curve, he does not refer to other work by Phillips. In particular, he does not refer to work by Phillips which seems most directly related to the topic of his critique, notably that (quoting again from the citation by the Royal Swedish Academy) related to 'providing insights into the difficulties of using economic policy to control the economy and possibilities of reliably evaluating economic policy with statistical methods'.

Lucas' critique has been summarised by a number of writers. Berndt (1991, 536) puts it as

Lucas argued that because government policies are likely to change peoples' expectations, one cannot naively simulate the effects of policy changes and implicitly assume that parameters reflecting expectations will remain unchanged once policy changes are put in place.

Much subsequent discussion of the Lucas critique has involved expectations, more so than Lucas' original exposition seems to have done. This is probably because the close analysis of expectations, their formation and their consequences, seems to have evolved as part of the general approach to attacking the problem highlighted by Lucas.

At the end of his essay, Lucas (1976, 41) summarised his view by stating that

Given that the structure of an econometric model consists of optimal decision rules of economic agents, and that optimal decision rules vary systematically with changes in the structure of series relevant to the decision maker, it follows that any change in policy will systematically alter the structure of econometric models.

Lucas thus relied for his conclusions at least in part on the assumption of optimal decision rules, presumably on the part of agents implementing the policy as well as those affected by it.

In chapter 50, Phillips' summary (p. 472) of his own main point was

When control is being applied in strict accordance with (an optimal decision rule) then the (econometric model) may no longer be identified. By this we mean that new observations generated by the complete system (of model plus decision rule) may give no further information by which to improve the estimates of the parameters of the (econometric model).

Phillips' conclusion of underidentification rested on optimal decision making primarily by those implementing the policy, with any decisions, optimal or otherwise, by those affected being implicitly subsumed into the specification of the econometric model.

Since Phillips' argument does not seem to be well known in either the econometric or general economic literature, a brief semi-technical interpretation now follows.

Consider the very simple model

$$Y_t = \alpha + \beta X_t + \gamma Z_t + \varepsilon_t \tag{1}$$

which is proposed to be estimated from a sample $t = 1, 2, \ldots, T$. Here, Y_t is a dependent variable, X_t is an instrument or decision variable (using the Tinbergen or Phillips terminology respectively) which is initially (that is, over the period $t = 1, 2, \ldots T$) taken as exogenous if no systematic policy actions are undertaken over this period to use it to try to control Y_t. Z_t is a truly exogenous variable determined outside the model and not within the control of policy makers. ε_t is a standard econometric random variable. Such a model is straightforward to estimate.

Suppose now that, after time T, policy is implemented in each period in accordance with a quadratic[9] decision criterion

$$C_t = a(Y_t - Y^0)^2 + 2b(Y_t - Y^0)(X_t - X^0) + c(X_t - X^0)^2 \tag{2}$$

describing the cost of deviations of the variables which are partly or wholly under policy control from their target values Y^0 and X^0. If policy makers attempt to optimise this criterion but are constrained in so doing by their knowledge of the relationship between Y and X, that is, as given by the model, then they need to ensure Y and X move together during the policy periods in the relationship[10]

$$(\alpha\beta + b)Y_t + (b\beta + c)X_t = V_t, \tag{3}$$

where V_t consists of a linear combination of the targets and any random variations from exact implementation of the policy.

Thus, after the implementation of the policy, the structure of the model has changed, from equation (1) which prevailed alone during the initial (that is, the estimation, but non-policy) period, to both (1) and (3) which prevail in the period during which the policy operates. At the very least there has been a change in structure because of the operation of the policy, a similar or identical point to that subsequently made by Lucas (1976, 41).

Phillips further suggested that, unless the variables in V_t contain independent sources of variation which were not part of the initial model[11] then, during the policy period the model equation (1) cannot be statistically distinguished from arbitrary combinations of itself with the decision rule, equation (3), and is thus not identified. In such a case, it follows that during operation of the policy no additional independent information comes to hand for improvement of the initial estimation and thus no additional information for either evaluating or improving the operation of the policy.

Common to both the Phillips and Lucas contributions, and indeed seemingly the central theme of each, is the notion that the application of decision rules in conjunction with econometric models makes it difficult to obtain further reliable information about the econometric models. Phillips basically cast his problem in terms of identification, Lucas expressed his as hard-to-analyse changes in the structure of the model.

Lucas actually did not address the identification question in his entire article. He presents the equations $y_{t+1} = F(y_t, x_t, \theta, \varepsilon_t)$ as describing the economic structure and $x_t = G(y_t, \lambda, \eta_t)$ as representing policies and other disturbances (1976, 39–40).[12] He further states that 'there are compelling empirical and theoretical reasons for believing that (the structure) will not be of use for forecasting'. But he does not seem to explicitly include underidentification (which undoubtedly is a cause of serious problems for forecasting) among these difficulties.

It seems probable that, despite the interesting overlap in topic coverage, Lucas was not aware of Phillips' contribution when he wrote his critique. It is interesting, but probably idle, to speculate whether it would have made any difference to Lucas' exposition, his general approach and, given the enormous influence he and his critique have had on the subsequent development of macroeconomics and policy analysis, whether it would have had any influence on subsequent developments in these areas. As it turned out, declining health and declining interest ensured that Phillips was not in a good position to pursue his own views very much further. I express my own regrets that his significant and potentially very powerful contribution to economic and econometric modelling of policy has remained as a relatively obscure published article.

Phillips' investigations of the relationship between policy control and model identification actually extended over the last few years of his life, so the topic was presumably interesting and important to him. He raised the problem in chapter 51, a previously unpublished essay, in which he considered how a standard econometric simultaneous equations model might be used for policy control and noted:

If it is possible to obtain such estimates we shall be able to design an adaptive control strategy, the (relevant) parameters being estimated from time to time, using observations obtained from the operation of the system while a control policy based on earlier estimates was in operation, and each new set of estimates being used to derive a new control policy. Whether or not such estimation is possible will depend on whether the (relevant) equations are identified.

One gains the impression that his confidence in whether or not identification could be achieved while decision rules were in operation decreased the more he studied the problem.

Phillips was still pursuing this problem near the end of his life. In chapter 52, a previously unpublished handwritten manuscript located amongst his private papers (with the first page missing), he pursues further the relationship between policy control and identification, making extensive use of matrix notation (unlike chapter 50). This handwritten paper must have included some of the last research material he wrote. Its concluding paragraph is given verbatim in the following (in his notation, y_t is national income and x_t is a policy variable):

During the operation of this decision rule, equations (the decision rule) and (national income determination) together form the system

$$\begin{cases} y_t = \alpha y_{t-1} + \gamma + x_t + \varepsilon_t \\ x_t = g y_{t-1} + h \end{cases}$$

Considering now this system as the basis for an econometric model, we immediately see that the first equation for national income is now not identified, for the second equation does not involve any variable ~~or constant~~[13] which is excluded from the first. Thus a linear combination of the second with the first is indistinguishable from the first, meaning that the first is not identified. Thus observations during the period of the control cannot be used to obtain improved estimates of the parameters which is a serious drawback.

If, in this system, one replaces y_t by y_{t+1} (which is an essentially trivial matter of alternative notation) then these two equations seem very similar to those in Lucas (1976), as given above. The extent to which the independently derived Phillips and Lucas conclusions are similar, and which cause the greater problems for economic policy and econometric knowledge, may best be left to the judgement of the reader.

Notes

In writing this chapter I have received helpful advice and encouragement from Conrad Blyth and Robert Leeson

1 Regarding the relative importance of these uses, it is interesting to observe that Goldberger (1964) devotes, in his section on 'Applications of Structural Econometric Models', one short paragraph to testing and assessment of theory using the structural model, and some 14 pages to the estimation and uses of the reduced form, this latter being traditionally the main vehicle for policy and forecasting.

2 He took a stronger position than this in a seminar on this topic given at the University of New South Wales in 1968, considering by then that the reduced form was in fact not identified. At that time he also stated that he did not know whether or not this result was well known in the econometric literature, since he had been reading Chinese novels rather than keeping up to date with econometric reading.

3 For instance, Lucas and Sargent (1981a, 298–9) describe 'the identification problem of econometrics' as 'it is not generally possible to work backwards from estimates of the (reduced form parameters) alone to derive unique estimates of the structural parameters'. A reader might infer from this that they take the reduced form to be identified. In chapter 50, Phillips (p. 473) notes the possibility that the structural equations may be identified even if those of the reduced form are not. Lucas and Sargent then go on to say 'the problem of identifying a structural model from a collection of economic time series is one that might be solved by anyone who claims the ability to give quantitative economic advice'.

4 In this example, the interest rate is what Phillips in chapter 50 calls a 'decision variable', a terminology which Wold (1968) writing in the same set of essays which included Phillips' contribution, considered redundant, since he regarded Tinbergen's 'instruments' as having adequately served the purpose for some years. Otherwise, Wold seemed happy enough with Phillips' idea.

5 In this example, during estimation, inflation is taken to depend on the interest rate, whereas during application of policy the interest rate depends on desired inflation. The latter, if the bank is competent, will be close to actual inflation, if not the bank should not be in this type of business.

6 Noting that there may be a difference between conditional and unconditional forecasts may be valid enough comment but does not directly bear on the question of identification, that is, whether the estimated model in fact represents what it is claimed to represent. From merely comparing forecasts with actual outcomes, it is not possible to determine whether the model is in fact good or bad.

7 In this I agreed fully with Lucas' (1976, 42) conclusion: 'In short, it seems that policy makers, if they wish to forecast the response of citizens, must take the latter into their confidence', although I had not at that time read Lucas' contribution.

8 A re-reading of Tinbergen (1966) did not turn up what seemed to me a particularly strong connection, although some of Marschak's (1953) comments seemed rather relevant. The contribution by Koopmans (1953, 46–7) immediately following that of Marschak, contains a rather intriguing comment which, in the light of the subsequent Phillips, and particularly the highly successful Lucas material, might have been usefully followed up: 'In many practical situations it is required to predict the values of one or more economic variables... under hypothetical changes in structural parameters that can be brought about through policy based in part on the prediction made. Knowledge (in this case) is likely to be available as to the effect of such structural change on the parameters.' Unfortunately, Koopmans was not explicit about the nature and reliability of such knowledge. On the base of Phillips' work one may, in fact, reasonably conjecture that Koopmans was wrong, and that such knowledge, in that case, is unlikely to be available.

9 This is assumed mainly for simplicity since it leads to a linear decision rule. If alternative decision criteria are used, then computation may become more complex (chapter 50, p. 470) and a more explicit consideration may be required as to whether identification can be achieved by variations in function form. This line is not very pertinent for purposes of the present discussion.

10 Or, substituting for Y from the model, the relationship could be expressed as between X and Z, with the consequent presumption that, after the policy comes into operation, X can no longer be treated as exogenous since it now depends on Z and the policy parameters.

11 If there were such information, then it presumably would have, or should have, been used in the process of the initial estimation.

12 I hope I am not misreading Lucas in perceiving a conceptual similarity between these and Phillips' equations (1) and (4) in chapter 50 (pp. 470, 472), or perhaps more obviously, between Lucas' equations and Phillips' equations (19) at the end of chapter 52. On the face of it Lucas' $F(.)$ equation seems as if it may not be identified as different from arbitrary combinations of his $F(.)$ and $G(.)$ without some more explicitly stated prior information.

13 Crossing out as in the handwritten original.

50　Models for the Control of Economic Fluctuations

A. W. Phillips

E32

For the last two decades the governments of most Western countries have been carrying out some degree of conscious control over their economies with the purpose of overcoming the severe fluctuation in the general level of economic activity and employment which plagued all free-enterprise countries for a century or more before the First World War and which reached catastrophic proportions in the inter-war years. A fair degree of success has been achieved. In Britain the range of variation in unemployment since the last war has been about 2 per cent, compared with about 10 per cent in the typical cycles of the century before the First World War and more than 20 per cent in the inter-war period. The range of the percentage variation in total output about its trend has, however, been greater; about 8 per cent, or four times that of unemployment. This degree of success is probably sufficient to permit the survival of free-enterprise economic systems and democratic forms of government, but further improvement is clearly desirable.

The results of research in model building and econometric estimation are being used by government departments, though as yet in a rather rudimentary way, in the practical task of controlling economic fluctuations. Little if any use seems to have been made, however, of systematic methods of decision analysis, although the linear decision rule method of analysis, developed by Theil and others in Holland and independently by Holt and others in the United States (and similar to the method developed independently by Kalman and others for the control of chemical processes) has been available for some years (Van der Bogaard and Theil 1959; Theil 1964; Holt 1962; Holt *et al.* 1960; Kalman *et al.* 1959). My first purpose is to give an outline of this method and the way it would be used in economic control. I then briefly indicate an inherent limitation of the method and state the need for developing improved computational methods in order to facilitate the use of methods of learning or adaptive control.

468

Let the vector x_t be the set of values given in time-period t to the variables over which the government has complete control and which it uses to influence the economy. We will refer to these as decision variables. In practice they may include such quantities as tax rates, hire purchase deposit percentages and repayment times, investment allowances and grants, and a number of monetary and financial quantities. Let the vector y_t be the set of values taken by other variables in which the government has a policy interest, but which it can influence only through its control of the decision variables. We shall call these the policy variables. They will include the percentage unemployment, the price level and its rate of change, the balance of payments on current account, the level of foreign reserves and perhaps other variables. If more disaggregated policy objectives are specified some of these quantities may themselves be vectors, for example the percentage unemployment in different regions or sectors and indices of prices of various broad classes of goods and services.

The values of the policy variables will depend not only on the values of the decision variables, but also on others, which can be classified into three sets; non-policy endogenous variables, which both influence and are influenced by the policy variables, exogenous variables, which influence the policy variables but are not influenced by them, and unobservable 'disturbances', which affect the system but are assumed to be unaffected by it. The number of truly exogenous variables is small; strictly perhaps only physical phenomena such as weather come into this category. However variables such as incomes and price levels for other countries are approximately exogenous and for practical purposes may often be treated as if they were truly exogenous. Some approximate decomposition of this kind is forced upon us if we are to avoid treating the whole world as a single system.

An econometric model is a mathematical representation of the way in which the policy and non-policy endogenous variables depend on one another and on the decision variables, exogenous variables and disturbances. A considerable amount of experience in setting up, estimating and testing such models has now been accumulated, particularly in the United States, Holland and more recently in Japan. The only model so far available for Britain is the one developed at Oxford by Klein, Ball, Hazlewood and Vandome (1961), and recently modified and re-estimated by Professor Ball at the London Graduate School of Business Studies.

For the purpose of decision analysis the non-policy endogenous variables are irrelevant. They can be eliminated from the econometric model by the usual mathematical procedures, giving a reduced system showing the dependence of the policy variables on the decision variables, exogenous variables, and disturbances. The reduced system will be in the form of a system of difference equations. If these are not already linear in the variables and parameters they can, by further approximation, be converted into a linear system, which may be written in the general form

$$\sum_{r=0}^{a} A_r y_{t-r} + \sum_{r=0}^{b} B_r x_{t-r} + \sum_{r=0}^{c} C_r z_{t-r} + d_r + \sum_{r=0}^{m} M_r e_{t-r} = 0, \quad (1)$$

where A_o and M_o are unit matrices, y_t is the vector of policy variables, x_t the vector of decision variables, z_t is the vector of exogenous variables, d_t is a vector of constants or trend terms and e_t is a vector of serially uncorrelated random variables with zero means. Numerical estimates of the matrices A_r, B_r, C_r and M_r, the scalers a, b, c and m, the parameters of the trend terms d_t, and the variance matrix of the random vector e_t can be calculated from estimates of the parameters of the econometric model. Alternatively if certain identification conditions are satisfied these values can be estimated directly from past observations of y_t, x_t and z_t using methods due to Phillips (chapter 45).

The estimated reduced system (1) gives an approximate representation of the effects on the policy variables y_t of alternative choices of the decision variables x_t. To make further progress it is necessary to have a clear quantitative specification of the objectives of policy, or targets, and a criterion function giving the cost or disutility of deviations of the actual values of the variables from their target values. Although these are fundamental requirements of any rational process of decision making, those responsible for the decisions are usually reluctant even to admit the need for them, and still more reluctant to engage in the intellectually difficult and politically hazardous task of actually specifying quantitative objectives and a criterion of performance. In economic control the most immediate gain from analysis of the decision problem will probably come, as they have in other fields of operational research, from inducing policy makers to state these quantities more clearly.

There are immense computational advantages in dealing with a criterion which is quadratic in the variables involved, and we shall assume that the criterion can be adequately approximated by this form of function. Let $\bar{y}_t$ and $\bar{x}_t$ denote target values of the variables, and let q_t $(y_t, \bar{y}_t, x_t, \bar{x}_t)$ be a quadratic function giving the cost, or disutility, in period t of deviations from target values. Let Q_T be the present value of the total cost over periods 1 to T, where the next decision to be made is that for the period $t = 1$, and T, the decision horizon, is fairly large. Then if W_t is the present value of unit cost in a future period t, Q_T is given by

$$Q_T = \sum_{t=1}^{T} W_t q_t. \tag{2}$$

If the future values of the exogenous variables and disturbances were known, an optional sequence of decisions could be calculated by choosing the x_t, $t = 1, 2, \ldots, T$, to minimise Q_T subject to the constraints imposed by (1). Since Q_T is quadratic and the constraints are linear, the solutions can be obtained by straightforward methods of linear algebra.[1]

Since the future of the exogenous variable and disturbances will not be known we cannot in fact choose the x_t to minimise Q_T. The best we can do is to choose the x_t to minimise the mathematical expectation of Q_T conditional upon the information available in period 0. Since differentiation and the taking of mathematical expectations are linear operations the order of carrying out these operations can be reversed, the differentiation being done first. We are thus led to a solution for the optimal decision sequence which is the same as would have been obtained if the future values of the exogenous variables and disturbances had been known, except that these future values are replaced by their conditional expectations, which are the same as their minimum-variance forecasts. This property of linear systems with quadratic criteria is known as the principle of certainty equivalence. The first term in the decision sequence is the optimal decision set for period one, the remaining terms are present best estimates of what the future decisions will be. But before each succeeding decision is taken new information will have become available enabling improved forecasts to be made and used. It turns out, however, that the same equation or decision rule holds for each time period. All that is necessary is to raise the time-subscripts of all variables by unity and insert the most recent forecasts.

There is no difficulty in obtaining forecasts of the disturbances. The random variables e_t in (1) are serially uncorrected with zero means, and it follows that the conditional expectations of all future e_t are zero. Forecasts of the exogenous z_t variables may be obtained in a variety of ways. A purely statistical forecasting procedure is to fit to past observations, say for $t = -N, \ldots, 0$, the mixed autoregressive moving average model

$$\sum_{r=0}^{g} G_r z_{t-r} + k_t = \sum_{r=0}^{h} H_r \varepsilon_{t-r}, \quad G_o = 1, \ H_o = 1, \tag{3}$$

where G_r and H_r, are matrices, k_t is a vector of constants or polynomials of low degree representing trend terms and the ε_t are serially uncorrected random vectors with zero means. The method due to Phillips (chapter 45) can be used to fit the model, giving estimates of the parameters and of past values of the vectors ε_t. Since the conditional expectations of future vectors ε_t are zero, forecasts of z_t are obtained by putting $\varepsilon_t = 0$ for $t > 0$ and using the fitted model to calculate successively the forecast values of $z_1, \ldots, z_T$.

The solution for the optimal decision rule for the system (1) is of the form

$$\sum_{r=1}^{a} A_r^* y_{t-r} + \sum_{r=0}^{b} B_r^* x_{t-r} + V_t = 0, \ B_o^* = 1, \tag{4}$$

where V_t is a linear combination of the targets $\bar{y}_s$ and $\bar{x}_s$, the trend terms d_s and the forecast values of the exogenous variables z_s for $s = t$, $t + 1, \ldots, t + T - 1$ and also of the initial values of z_s for $s = t - c, \ldots$, $t - 1$ and of e_s for $s = t - m, \ldots, t - 1$. If the decision rule is used for determining the values of x_t in successive period, t, equations (4) and (1) become two sub-systems forming a single system, and we immediately note an important possibility, that when control is being applied in strict accordance with (4) the sub-system (1) may no longer be identified. By this we mean that new observations generated by the operation of the complete system may give no further information by which to improve the estimates of the parameters of the sub-system (1).[2]

The possibility of lack of identification can be illustrated by considering the case in which the targets are constants and the exogenous variables are not serially correlated, so that their forecasts are constants. Then the vector V_t involves only a constant vector and the variables $z_{t-c}, \ldots, z_{t-1}; e_{t-m}, \ldots, e_{t-1}$, all of which quantities occur also in the last three terms of (1). Moreover all the variables entering into the first two terms of (4) are also included in the first two terms of (1). Any scaler equation in (1) may therefore be replaced by any linear combination of itself and any scaler equation in (4) without change of form. Such a transformation leaves the statistical properties of the complete system unchanged, and it follows that none of the equations in (1) can be re-estimated directly from observations generated by the operations of the complete system.

In general the possibility of re-estimating the subsystem (1) from observations generated by the complete system will depend on the detailed structure of the model. I shall mention three factors which may lead to identification and so permit re-estimation.

(a) The reduced system (1) is derived from a wider structural model by elimination of non-policy endogenous variables. It is possible that the equations of the structural model may be identified even though those of the reduced system (1) are not.

(b) *A priori* specification may be sufficient to give identification of the equations in the reduced system itself. This will be so, for example, if there is a one-period time lag in the response of the system to the decision variables, so that B_0 in (1) is zero.

(c) In practice the control is not likely to be applied exactly in accordance with the calculated rule (4), so that another disturbance vector will be added to (4), which may be independent of the disturbance vector in (1) and lead to identification of the equations in (1). The disturbances added to (4) may of course be deliberately applied for the purpose of obtaining better estimates of the system, and are then referred to as probes or perturbations.

The possibility that operation of the control may prevent re-estimation of the system should lead us to ask whether the decision analysis we have been considering does not have some fundamental deficiency. And indeed it has. The basic defect is simply that in deriving the decision rules no account was taken of the fact that the parameters of the system are not known exactly, and no consideration was given to ways in which we can improve our knowledge of the system while we are controlling it. In my view it cannot be too strongly stated that in attempting to control economic fluctuations we do not have the two separate problems of estimating the system and of controlling it, we have a single problem of jointly controlling and learning about the system, that is, a problem of learning control or adaptive control.

There is already a fairly extensive literature on methods of adaptive control, some of which are cited in Bellman (1961). The subject is closely related to the Bayesian approach to statistical decision theory as developed by Raiffa and Schlaiffer (1961). There is no major difficulty in principle in deriving an optimal learning or adaptive control for the type of system we have described; the major obstacle is that the function to be minimised is no longer quadratic so that the simple methods of linear algebra cannot be used to solve for the sequence of decision vectors. Numerical solutions have been obtained for extremely simple systems,[3] but for all but the simplest cases the computational difficulties have so far proved insuperable. Further computational advances will be needed before practical procedures of optimal learning control can be devised for a problem as complex as that of the control of economic fluctuations.

Notes

First published in Kendal (1968).

1 See, for example, Theil (1964), especially chapter 4.
2 The concept of identification is treated in texts on econometrics, for example, Malinvaud (1966).
3 See, for example, Florentin (1962).

51 Statistical Estimation for the Purpose of Economic Regulation

A.W. Phillips

C51

Consider the system

$$[\Gamma_1 \vdots \Gamma_2]\begin{bmatrix} y_1 \\ \cdots \\ y_2 \end{bmatrix}_t + BX_t = u_{1,t}. \tag{1}$$

In (1), $y_{2,t}$ is a vector of q variables whose values can be freely chosen by the government in successive time periods t. $y_{1,t}$ is a vector of p variables ($p \geq q$) whose values are determined by non-government economic decision-makers in accordance with (1). X_t is a vector whose elements are exogenous or lagged endogenous time series. $u_{1,t}$ is a vector of p unobservable random disturbances with zero means.

Let Y_t be the vector

$$\begin{bmatrix} y_1 \\ \cdots \\ y_2 \end{bmatrix}_t$$

and suppose the government wishes Y_t to be as close as possible to a given vector Y_t^* for $t = 0, 1, \ldots$, the vector $y_{2,t}$ being chosen in each period on the basis of the observed series X_{t-h} and Y_{t-h} ($h = 1, 2, \ldots$). We shall consider only the simplest case in which Y_t^* is constant. Then the elements of Y_t can be measured as deviations from Y_t^*, so that Y_t can be taken as zero.

The vector $y_{2,t}(t \geq 0)$ may be chosen in a variety of ways. In practice it seems that in each period governments attempt to forecast future values of $y_{1,t}$ given alternative assumptions about $y_{2,t}$, the forecasts being largely projections based on past values of Y_t and X_t, and then choose $y_{2,t}$ on the basis of some preference criterion involving the resulting estimated deviations $\hat{Y}_t - Y_t^*$ for $t \geq 0$. It can readily be shown that if the criterion is quadratic in these deviations and the forecasts are obtained by some form

475

of least squares fitting and extrapolation of past values of Y_t and X_t this procedure is equivalent to using a linear decision rule of the form

$$[0 \vdots 1] \begin{bmatrix} y_1 \\ \cdots \\ y_2 \end{bmatrix}_t + A_2 X_t = v_{2,t}. \tag{2}$$

(We specify that X_t contains an appropriate number of lagged values of the predetermined variables.) This is also the form of the optimum control policy that would be derived by application of the Wiener–Hopf optimisation methods, or equivalently by the methods, due to Holt and others, for obtaining optimum linear decision rules. If the same forecasting procedure and preference criterion was used in successive periods the term $v_{2,t}$ in (2) would be zero.

In order to use any of the decision methods mentioned above it is necessary to have some knowledge of the system (1). Specifically, they amount to choosing the $y_{2,t}$ to minimise the expected value of some scalar function of the deviations $Y_t - Y_t^*$, $t \geq 0$, given Y_t and X_t for $t < 0$, subject to the constraints implied by (1). Since the constraints will not be affected if (1) is pre-multiplied by an arbitrary matrix, a knowledge of the parameters after (1) has been pre-multiplied by, say, Γ_1^{-1}, would give all the information needed for the derivation of an optimum policy of the form (2). The complete system, including the government control policy, would then be

$$\begin{bmatrix} I & C \\ \cdots & \vdots & \cdots \\ 0 & I \end{bmatrix} \begin{bmatrix} y_1 \\ \cdots \\ y_2 \end{bmatrix} + \begin{bmatrix} A_1 \\ \cdots \\ A_2 \end{bmatrix} X_t = \begin{bmatrix} v_1 \\ \cdots \\ v_2 \end{bmatrix}, \tag{3}$$

where $C = \Gamma_1^{-1}$, $A_1 = \Gamma_1^{-1} B$ and $v_{1,t} = \Gamma_1^{-1} u_{1,t}$.

The problem we wish to consider is that of obtaining estimates of C, A and the autocovariance function of $v_{1,t}$ in (3), given observations on $y_{1,t}$, $y_{2,t}$ and X_t for a number of consecutive time periods during which a government control policy described by the lower row of (3) has been in operation. If it is possible to obtain such estimates we shall be able to design an adaptive control strategy, the parameters in the first row of (3) being estimated from time to time, using observations obtained from the operation of the system while a control policy based on earlier estimates was in operation, and each new set of estimates being used to derive a new control policy.

Whether or not such estimation is possible will depend on whether the group of equations in the upper row of (3), (or alternatively the equations in (1)), are identified. In an aggregate economic model it is likely that the predetermined variables X_t will consist mainly or wholly of lagged endogenous variables rather than exogenous ones. Possible specification of zero elements in the matrix B in (1) would therefore depend on the detailed form of the lag structure of the equations, about which we are not likely to have reliable *a priori* knowledge. We shall therefore ignore the possibility of making use of zero elements in B. The identification problem can then be considered in terms of the equations in the upper row of (3). It is clear that these equations are not identified without further restrictions on C or A, or on the covariance matrix of $v_{1,t}$ and $v_{2,t}$. We shall consider three alternative sets of restrictions, each of which would lead to identification and so permit the desired estimation.

1 (a) The control variables $y_{2,t}$ do not affect the system until after a delay of at least one period, so that $C = 0$. (b) The vector X_t contains only a finite number of elements. (c) The vector sequence $v_{1,t}$ is not serially correlated. (d) The vector $v_{2,t}$ has a non singular covariance matrix.

If these conditions are satisfied the upper equations in (3) are identified. However, it is doubtful whether these conditions would all hold in practice. In particular, if the time interval between successive observations (and control decisions) is short enough for the delay condition 1(a) to hold, condition 1(c) about serial correlation may not be satisfied.

2 The matrix

$$\begin{bmatrix} A_1 \\ \cdots \\ A_2 \end{bmatrix}$$

is of the form

$$\begin{bmatrix} 0 & A_{12} \\ \cdots & \vdots & \cdots \\ I & A_{22} \end{bmatrix}$$

with q columns to the left of the partition, and the first q elements of X_t have non-singular covariance matrix. The equations in the upper row of (3) are then identified without restrictions on the serial or cross correlation functions of $v_{1,t}$ and $v_{2,t}$. We note that the first q elements of X_t are then time series which can be chosen by the government and which would have to be made identically zero in order to obtain optimum control if the system was known exactly. They are, in fact, perturbations deliberately applied for the purpose of identification and estimation. Such deliberate perturbations of a system are commonly employed in the estimation, for example, of chemical processes for the purpose of designing satisfactory regulation or control. Whether a government could be persuaded to introduce deliberate perturbations in order to estimate the system and so derive improved control in the future is somewhat doubtful.

3 The vector $v_{2,t}$ has a non-singular auto-covariance function and the expected value of $v_{1,t}\, v'_{2,t-r}$ is zero for all r. It is well known from the properties of recursive systems that if $v_{1,t}$ and $v_{2,t}$ are not serially correlated the equations in (3) are then identified. It is not difficult to show that they remain identified even if $v_{1,t}$ and $v_{2,t}$ are serially correlated provided $E(v_{1,t}v'_{2,t-r}) = 0$ for all r. We note that this condition again implies perturbation of the system by the government, since $v_{2,t}$ would be identically zero if a consistent control policy were being applied. In this case, however, the perturbation need not be deliberate, but may result from basic elements of indeterminancy in government control policies. No doubt such elements of indeterminancy exist, but it is not so certain that they give rise to disturbances which are uncorrelated with the disturbances $v_{2,t}$ resulting from non-government economic decisions.

Note

1 Phillips wrote at the top of this paper 'Preliminary draft'. It was dated 9 September 1964.

52   The Last Paper: A Foreshadowing of the Lucas Critique?

A.W. Phillips

C50

... Moreover, (4) may be written in matrix form as

$$
\begin{bmatrix}
1 & 0 & \cdot & \cdot & \cdot & \cdot & 0 \\
-\alpha & \cdot & & & & & \cdot \\
0 & \cdot & \cdot & & & & \cdot \\
\cdot & & \cdot & \cdot & & & \cdot \\
\cdot & & & \cdot & \cdot & & \cdot \\
\cdot & & & & \cdot & \cdot & \cdot \\
0 & \cdot & \cdot & \cdot & 0 & -\alpha & 1
\end{bmatrix}
\begin{bmatrix}
y_1 \\ y_2 \\ y_3 \\ \cdot \\ \cdot \\ \cdot \\ y_N
\end{bmatrix}
=
\begin{bmatrix}
\alpha y_o \\ 0 \\ 0 \\ \cdot \\ \cdot \\ \cdot \\ 0
\end{bmatrix}
+
\begin{bmatrix}
\gamma \\ \gamma \\ \gamma \\ \cdot \\ \cdot \\ \cdot \\ \gamma
\end{bmatrix}
$$

$$
+
\begin{bmatrix}
x_1 \\ x_2 \\ x_3 \\ \cdot \\ \cdot \\ \cdot \\ x_N
\end{bmatrix}
+
\begin{bmatrix}
\varepsilon_1 \\ \varepsilon_2 \\ \varepsilon_3 \\ \cdot \\ \cdot \\ \cdot \\ \varepsilon_N
\end{bmatrix}
\tag{4a}
$$

or more concisely as

$$\mathbf{A}\mathbf{y} = \mathbf{i} + c + \mathbf{x} + \boldsymbol{\varepsilon}, \tag{4b}$$

where the $N \times N$ matrix $\mathbf{A}$ and the $N \times 1$ vectors $\mathbf{y}$, $\mathbf{i}$, $\mathbf{c}$ and $\boldsymbol{\varepsilon}$ are defined by their expanded forms as given in (4a).

The expression for L_N in (2) may then also be written in the form

$$L_N = \mathbf{y}'\mathbf{y} + k\mathbf{x}'\mathbf{x}. \tag{2a}$$

479

From (4b) we obtain, from multiplying by A^{-1}

$$\mathbf{y} = \mathbf{A}^{-1}(\mathbf{i} + \mathbf{c} + \mathbf{x} + \boldsymbol{\varepsilon}), \tag{4c}$$

and substitution of (4c) in (2a) gives

$$
\begin{aligned}
L_N &= (\mathbf{i} + \mathbf{c} + \mathbf{x} + \boldsymbol{\varepsilon})' \mathbf{A}^{'-1} A^{-1}(\mathbf{i} + \mathbf{c} + \mathbf{x} + \boldsymbol{\varepsilon}) + k\mathbf{x}'\mathbf{x}, \\
&= \mathbf{x}'(\mathbf{A}^{'-1}\mathbf{A}^{-1} + kI)x \\
&\quad + 2\mathbf{x}'\mathbf{A}^{'-1}\mathbf{A}^{-1}(\mathbf{i} + \mathbf{c} + \boldsymbol{\varepsilon}) \\
&\quad + (\mathbf{i} + \mathbf{c} + \boldsymbol{\varepsilon})'\mathbf{A}^{'-1}\mathbf{A}^{-1}(\mathbf{i} + \mathbf{c} + \boldsymbol{\varepsilon}).
\end{aligned}
\tag{2b}
$$

Consider now the problem of deciding on budget policy for the period $t = 1$, that is, of choosing a value for the element $\mathbf{x}_1$ in the vector $\mathbf{x}$, the value of y_o being then known. If the true values of α and β, and therefore also of γ, were known, and if the expression for L_N did not involve the random vector $\boldsymbol{\varepsilon}$, it would be possible to use (2b) to minimise L_N with respect to the elements x_t of the vector x and then, by elimination of the elements x_t for $t \geq 1$, to find the optimum value of x_1 in terms of the known parameters and the already observed value of y_o. To deal with the problem of the random vector $\boldsymbol{\varepsilon}$ it is usually proposed to modify the optimality criterion to minimisation of the expected value of the loss function L_N instead of minimisation of L_N itself. To deal with the problem that the true values of the parameters α and β, and therefore also of γ, are unknown, Theil proposes that econometric estimates be used in place of the true values, and in his example of a policy for the USA he uses estimates from the Klein model as if they were true values.

Let us follow these proposals in the case of our model and then consider the resulting decision rule.

We first need to minimise the expectation of L_N with respect to the policy vector $\mathbf{x}$. Since the expectation of L_N is in fact an integral over the probability function of $\boldsymbol{\varepsilon}$, we may reverse the order of differentiation and integration provided, as we shall assume, the conditions for differentiation under the integral sign are satisfied. That is, we take as the optimum vector $\mathring{\mathbf{x}}$ the solution of the equations

$$E\left[\frac{\delta}{\delta \mathbf{x}} L_N\right] = 0. \tag{3}$$

Carrying out the differentiation of L_N as expressed in (2b), we obtain for (3)

$$E\left[\frac{\delta}{\delta\mathbf{x}}L_N\right] = E2\left[\mathbf{A}^{'-1}\mathbf{A}^{-1} + kI\right]\overset{\circ}{\mathbf{x}} + 2E\left[\mathbf{A}^{'-1}\mathbf{A}^{-1}(\mathbf{i} + \mathbf{c} + \boldsymbol{\varepsilon})\right] = 0.$$

(4)

Pre-multiplying (4) by $\frac{1}{2}(\mathbf{A}^{'-1}\mathbf{A}^{-1})^{-1} = \frac{1}{2}AA'$ we obtain

$$E\left[(I + kAA')\overset{\circ}{\mathbf{x}} + (\mathbf{i} + \mathbf{c} + \boldsymbol{\varepsilon})\right] = 0,$$

(5)

where $\overset{\circ}{\mathbf{x}}$ is the vector which minimises $E[L_N]$, given the information available at the end of period 0. Actually, however, at that point of time we need only find the first element of $\overset{\circ}{\mathbf{x}}$, that is $\overset{\circ}{\mathbf{x}}_1$, since further information about y_t for $t > 0$ will become available before it is necessary to decide the values of $\overset{\circ}{\mathbf{x}}_2, \overset{\circ}{\mathbf{x}}_3, \ldots$ and to minimise the expected loss this later information must be used in deciding on these later values of $\overset{\circ}{\mathbf{x}}_t$. We must therefore eliminate from the set of equations (5) the variables $\overset{\circ}{\mathbf{x}}_2$, $\overset{\circ}{\mathbf{x}}_3, \ldots, \overset{\circ}{\mathbf{x}}_N$ and so obtain an expression for $\overset{\circ}{\mathbf{x}}_1$ alone. Note also that the vector $\boldsymbol{\varepsilon}$ in (5) may be deleted, since its expectation is zero. The expectation sign, E, may then also be dropped from (5), since all the remaining terms after it are constants, not random variables. Carrying out these operations we obtain from (5)

$$(I + k\mathbf{A}\mathbf{A}')\overset{\circ}{\mathbf{x}} = -(\mathbf{i} + \mathbf{c}).$$

(6)

To solve (6) for $\overset{\circ}{\mathbf{x}}_1$ in terms of the elements of $\mathbf{i}$ and $\mathbf{c}$ we first note that

$$\mathbf{AA'} = \begin{bmatrix} 1 & 0 & \cdot & \cdot & \cdot & \cdot & 0 \\ -\alpha & \cdot & & & & & \cdot \\ 0 & \cdot & \cdot & & & & \cdot \\ \cdot & & \cdot & \cdot & & & \cdot \\ \cdot & & & \cdot & \cdot & & \cdot \\ \cdot & & & & \cdot & \cdot & 0 \\ \cdot & & & & \cdot & \cdot & 0 \\ 0 & \cdot & \cdot & \cdot & 0 & -\alpha & 1 \end{bmatrix} \begin{bmatrix} 1 & -\alpha & 0 & \cdot & \cdot & \cdot & 0 \\ 0 & \cdot & \cdot & & & & \cdot \\ \cdot & & \cdot & \cdot & & & \cdot \\ \cdot & & & \cdot & \cdot & & \cdot \\ \cdot & & & & \cdot & \cdot & 0 \\ \cdot & & & & & \cdot & -\alpha \\ 0 & \cdot & \cdot & \cdot & \cdot & 0 & 1 \end{bmatrix}$$

$$
= \begin{bmatrix}
1 & & -\alpha & 0 & \cdot & \cdot & 0 \\
 & 1+\alpha^2 & & & \cdot & & \cdot \\
-\alpha & & \cdot & & \cdot & & \cdot \\
0 & \cdot & & \cdot & & \cdot & 0 \\
\cdot & & & & \cdot & & -\alpha \\
\cdot & & & \cdot & & \cdot & \\
0 & \cdot & & \cdot & 0 & -\alpha & 1+\alpha^2
\end{bmatrix} \tag{7}
$$

so that

$$
I + k\mathbf{A}\mathbf{A} = \begin{bmatrix}
1+k & & -k\alpha & 0 & \cdot & \cdot & 0 \\
 & 1+k(1+\alpha^2) & & & \cdot & & \cdot \\
-k\alpha & & \cdot & & \cdot & & \cdot \\
0 & \cdot & & \cdot & & \cdot & 0 \\
\cdot & & & & \cdot & & -k\alpha \\
\cdot & & & \cdot & & \cdot & \\
0 & \cdot & & \cdot & 0 & -k\alpha & 1+k(1+\alpha^2)
\end{bmatrix} \tag{8}
$$

Writing $\mathbf{M}$ for $I + k\mathbf{A}\mathbf{A}'$, a_1 for $1+k$, a for $1+k(1+\alpha^2)$ and b for $-k\alpha$, we have

$$
\mathbf{M} = \begin{bmatrix}
a_1 & b & 0 & \cdot & \cdot & \cdot & 0 \\
b & a & \cdot & & & & \cdot \\
0 & \cdot & \cdot & \cdot & & & \cdot \\
\cdot & & \cdot & \cdot & \cdot & & \cdot \\
\cdot & & & \cdot & \cdot & \cdot & 0 \\
\cdot & & & & \cdot & \cdot & b \\
0 & \cdot & \cdot & \cdot & 0 & b & a
\end{bmatrix} \tag{9}
$$

It can be verified that $\mathbf{M}$ is positive definite and that it can be factored in the form

$$
\mathbf{M} = \mathbf{H}'\mathbf{D}\mathbf{H}, \tag{10}
$$

where $\mathbf{H}$ and $\mathbf{D}$ are of the form

$$
\mathbf{H} = \begin{bmatrix}
1 & 0 & \cdot & \cdot & \cdot & 0 \\
h_{N-1} & \cdot & & & & \cdot \\
0 & h_{N-2} & \cdot & & & \cdot \\
\cdot & & & \cdot & & \cdot \\
\cdot & & & \cdot & \cdot & 0 \\
0 & \cdot & \cdot & 0 & h_1 & 1
\end{bmatrix},
$$

$$
\mathbf{D} = \begin{bmatrix}
d_N & 0 & \cdot & \cdot & \cdot & 0 \\
0 & d_{N-1} & & & & \cdot \\
\cdot & & \cdot & & & \cdot \\
\cdot & & & \cdot & & \cdot \\
\cdot & & & & d_2 & 0 \\
0 & \cdot & \cdot & \cdot & 0 & d_1
\end{bmatrix}
$$

(11)

and $\mathbf{H}'$ is the transpose of $\mathbf{H}$. Then

$$
\mathbf{DH} = \begin{bmatrix}
d_N & 0 & \cdot & \cdot & \cdot & 0 \\
& d_{N-1} & & & & \cdot \\
d_{N-1}h_{N-1} & & \cdot & & & \cdot \\
0 & \cdot & & \cdot & & \cdot \\
\cdot & & & d_2h_2 & & d_2 & 0 \\
0 & \cdot & & 0 & d_1h_1 & & d_1
\end{bmatrix}
$$

(12)

so that

$$
\begin{bmatrix}
1 & 0 & \cdot & \cdot & \cdot & 0 \\
h_{N-1} & \cdot & & & & \cdot \\
0 & h_{N-2} & \cdot & & & \cdot \\
\cdot & & \cdot & \cdot & & \cdot \\
\cdot & & & \cdot & \cdot & 0 \\
0 & \cdot & & \cdot & 0 & h_1 & 1
\end{bmatrix}
\begin{bmatrix}
d_N & 0 & \cdot & & \cdot & \cdot & 0 \\
 & d_{N-1} & & & & & \cdot \\
d_{N-1}h_{N-1} & & & & & & \\
0 & & \cdot & & & & \\
\cdot & & & & d_2h_2 & & d_2 & 0 \\
0 & & \cdot & & 0 & d_1h_1 & & d_1
\end{bmatrix}
$$

$$
=
\begin{bmatrix}
a_1 & b & 0 & \cdot & \cdot & \cdot & 0 \\
b & a & \cdot & & & & \cdot \\
0 & \cdot & \cdot & \cdot & & & \cdot \\
\cdot & & \cdot & \cdot & \cdot & & \cdot \\
\cdot & & & \cdot & \cdot & \cdot & 0 \\
\cdot & & & & \cdot & \cdot & b \\
0 & \cdot & \cdot & \cdot & 0 & b & a
\end{bmatrix}.
\tag{13}
$$

From the ith row times $(i+1)$th column of (13) we find that $h_j d_j = b_j$, $j = 1, 2, \ldots, N-1$. Therefore, substituting this in (13) we obtain

$$
\begin{bmatrix}
1 & h_{N-1} & 0 & \cdot & 0 \\
0 & \cdot & h_{N-2} & & \cdot \\
\cdot & & \cdot & \cdot & 0 \\
\cdot & & & \cdot & h_1 \\
0 & \cdot & & \cdot & 0 & 1
\end{bmatrix}
\begin{bmatrix}
d_N & 0 & \cdot & \cdot & 0 \\
b & d_{N-1} & & & \cdot \\
0 & \cdot & \cdot & & \cdot \\
\cdot & & \cdot & d_2 & 0 \\
0 & \cdot & 0 & b & d_1
\end{bmatrix}
\tag{14}
$$

$$
=
\begin{bmatrix}
a_1 & b & 0 & \cdot & 0 \\
b & a & \cdot & & \cdot \\
0 & \cdot & \cdot & \cdot & 0 \\
\cdot & & \cdot & \cdot & b \\
0 & \cdot & 0 & b & a
\end{bmatrix}.
$$

From the ith row times ith column of (14) we obtain the set of equations

$$d_1 = a$$
$$d_2 + h_1 b = a$$
$$d_3 + h_2 b = a$$

$$\vdots$$

$$d_{N-1} + h_{N-2} b = a$$
$$d_N + h_{N-1} b = a_1,$$

which may be written as the recurrence relation

$$d_1 = a$$
$$d_{r+1} = a - \frac{b^2}{d_N}, \quad r = 1, 2, \ldots, N-2$$
$$d_N = a_1 - \frac{b^2}{d_{N-1}}.$$

We now write the optimising equations (6) in the form

$$\mathbf{H'DH}\overset{\circ}{\mathbf{x}} = -(\mathbf{i} + \mathbf{c}), \tag{15}$$

and so, on premultiplying by $H'^{-1}D^{-1}$ we obtain

$$\mathbf{H}\overset{\circ}{\mathbf{x}} = -\mathbf{D}^{-1}\mathbf{H'}^{-1}(\mathbf{i} + \mathbf{c}) \tag{16}$$

We easily see that the leading element in $\mathbf{H}$ and in H'^{-1} is unity. On multiplying out the expressions on both sides of (16) and equating the first elements of the resulting vectors we obtain an equation of the form

$$\overset{\circ}{x}_1 = g y_0 + h \tag{17}$$

where

$$g = -\frac{\alpha y_0}{d_N}$$

and

$$h = \frac{\gamma}{d_N}$$

times (sum of 1st row elements of H'^{-1}).

Equation (17) gives the optimal value for x_1. After the end of the first period the value of y_1 will be known and, by a similar calculation to that shown above, the optimal value of x_2 will be found to be

$$\overset{o}{x}_2 = gy_1 + h$$

In the same way at the end of each succeeding period the optimal value of x_t will be found to be

$$\overset{o}{x}_1 = gy_{t-1} + h_1 (t = 3, 4, \ldots, N-1) \tag{18}$$

Equation (18) is therefore the optimal decision rule to be applied in all periods t.

During the operation of this decision rule, equations (18) and (4) together form the system

$$\begin{aligned} y_t &= \alpha y_{t-1} + \gamma + x_t + \varepsilon_t \\ x_t &= gy_{t-1} + h \end{aligned} \tag{19}$$

Considering now the system (19) as the basis for an econometric model, we immediately see that the first equation for national income is now not identified, for the second equation does not involve any variable ~~or con-stant~~[1] which is excluded from the first. Thus a linear combination of the second with the first is indistinguishable from the first, meaning that the first is not identified. Thus observations during the period of the control cannot be used to obtain improved estimates of the parameters, which is a serious drawback.

Note

Phillips signed and dated this handwritten paper on 24 July 1972. The first page, and hence the title (if there was one) appears not to have survived.

1 Crossing out in the original.

References

Aigner, D.J. 1971. A Compendium on Estimation of the Autoregressive Moving Average Model from Time Series Data. *International Economic Review* 12: 348–69.

Ait-Sahalia, Y. 1996. Nonparametric Pricing of Interest Rate Derivative Securities. *Econometrica* 64, 3: 527–60.

Allen, R.G.D. 1955. The Engineers' Approach to Economic Models. *Economica* 22, May: 158–68.

1956. *Mathematical Economics*. London: Macmillan.

1963. *Mathematical Economics*. London: Macmillan. 2nd edition.

Anderson, T.W. 1980. Maximum Likelihood Estimation for Vector Auto-regressive Moving Average Models. In Brillinger and Tiao eds. (45–59).

Arrow, K.J., Karlin, S. and Suppes, P. eds. 1959. *Mathematical Methods in the Social Sciences*. Stanford: Stanford University Press.

Athans, M. and Falb, P. 1966. *Optimal Control*. New York: McGraw-Hill.

Backhouse, R.E. and Salanti, A. eds. 2000. *Macroeconomics and the Real World*. Oxford: Oxford University Press.

Backus, D.K. and Driffill, J. 1985. Inflation and Reputation. *American Economic Review* 75: 530–8.

Banerjee, A., Dolado, J., Galbraith, J.W. and Hendry, D.F. 1993. *Co-integration, Error-Correction, and the Econometric Analysis of Non-Stationary Data*. Oxford: Oxford University Press.

Barnett, W.A., Gandolfo, G. and Hillinger, C. eds. 1996. *Dynamic Disequilibrium Modelling*. Cambridge: Cambridge University Press.

Barr, N.A. 1973. The Phillips Machine Returns to Life. *LSE Magazine* 46, November: 16.

Barro, R.J. ed. 1989. *Modern Business Cycle Theory*. Oxford: Blackwell.

Barro, R.J. and Gordon, D.B. 1983a. A Positive Theory of Monetary Policy in a Natural Rate Model. *Journal of Political Economy* 91: 589–610.

1983b. Rules, Discretion and Reputation in a Model of Monetary Policy. *Journal of Monetary Economics* 112: 101–21.

Bartlett, M.S. 1946. On the Theoretical Specification and Sampling Properties of Autocorrelated Time-Series. *Journal of the Royal Statistical Society* Series B, 8: 27–41.

1955. *Stochastic Processes*. Cambridge: Cambridge University Press.

Bartlett, M.S. and Rajalakshman, D.V. 1953. Goodness of Fit Tests for Simultaneous Autoregressive Series. *Journal of the Royal Statistical Society* Series B, 15: 107–24.

Baumol, W.J. 1961. Pitfalls in Contracyclical Policies: Some Tools and Results. *Review of Economics and Statistics* 43: 21–6.

1978. On the Stochastic Unemployment Distribution Model and the Long-Run Phillips Curve. In Bergstrom *et al.* eds.

Baumol, W.J. and Blinder, A. 1979. *Economics*. New York: Harcourt Brace Jovanovich. 1st edition.

Bean, C.R. 1994. European Unemployment: A Survey. *Journal of Economic Literature* 32: 573–619.

Begg, D., Fischer, S. and Dornbusch, R. 1997. *Economics*. New York: McGraw-Hill. 5th edition.

Bellman, R. 1961. *Adaptive Control Processes: A Guided Tour*. Princeton: Princeton University Press.

Bergstrom, A.R. 1962. A Model of Technical Progress, the Production Function and Cyclical Growth. *Economica* 29: 357–70. Reprinted as chapter 1 (23–37) of Bergstrom 1990.

1966a. Nonrecursive Models as Discrete Approximations to Systems of Stochastic Differential Equations. *Econometrica* 34: 173–82. Reprinted as chapter 3 (51–61) of Bergstrom 1990.

1966b. Monetary Phenomena and Economic Growth: A Synthesis of Neoclassical and Keynesian Theories. *Economic Studies Quarterly* 17: 1–8.

1967. *The Construction and Use of Economic Models*. London: English Universities Press.

1983. Gaussian Estimation of Structural Parameters in Higher Order Continuous Time Dynamic Models. *Econometrica* 51: 117–52.

1984. Continuous Time Stochastic Models and Issues of Aggregation Over Time. In Griliches and Intriligator eds. (chapter 20).

1988. The History of Continuous Time Econometric Models. *Econometric Theory* 4: 365–83.

1990. *Continuous Time Econometric Modelling*. Oxford: Oxford University Press.

1996. A Survey of Continuous Time Econometrics. In Barnett, Gandolfo and Hillinger eds.

Bergstrom, A.R. ed. 1976. *Statistical Inference in Continuous Time Economic Models*. Amsterdam: North-Holland.

Bergstrom, A.R., Catt, A.J.L., Peston, M.H. and Silverstone, B.D.J. eds. 1978. *Stability and Inflation: A Volume of Essays to Honour the Memory of A.W.H. Phillips*. Chichester and New York: Wiley.

Bergstrom, A.R. Nowman, K.B. and Wandasiewicz, S. 1994. Monetary and Fiscal Policy in a Second-Order Continuous Time Macroeconometric

Model of the United Kingdom. *Journal of Economic Dynamics and Control* 18: 731–61.

Bergstrom, A.R., Nowman, K.B. and Wymer, C.R. 1992. Gaussian Estimation of a Second Order Continuous Time Macroeconometric Model of the United Kingdom. *Economic Modelling* 9: 313–52.

Bergstrom, A.R. and Wymer, C.R. 1976. A Model of Disequilibrium Neoclassical Growth and its Application to the United Kingdom. In Bergstrom ed.

Berndt, Ernst R. 1991. *The Practice of Econometrics: Classic and Contemporary.* Reading, Massachusetts: Addison-Wesley.

Beveridge, W.H. 1944. *Full Employment in a Free Society: A Report.* London: Allen and Unwin.

Bhattia, R.J. 1961. Unemployment and the Rate of Change of Money Earnings in the United States 1900–1958. *Economica*, 28 August: 286–96.

Blaug, M. 1980. *The Methodology of Economics or How Economists Explain.* Cambridge: Cambridge University Press.

1985. *Great Economists Since Keynes.* Hemel Hempstead: Wheatsheaf.

Blinder, A. and Solow, R.M. 1973. Does Fiscal Policy Matter? *Journal of Public Economics* 2: 319–37.

Blyth, C.A. 1975. A.W.H. Phillips, M.B.E.: 1914–1975. *Economic Record* 51, 135, September: 303–7.

1978. A.W.H. Phillips M.B.E. In Bergstrom *et al.* eds.

1989. Alban William Housego Phillips. In Eatwell *et al.* eds. (857–8).

Boulding, K. 1948. *Economic Analysis.* London: Hamish Hamilton. 2nd edition.

1955. *Economic Analysis.* London: Hamish Hamilton. 3rd edition.

Bowley, A.L. 1937. *Wages and Income in the United Kingdom since 1860.* Cambridge: Cambridge University Press.

Box, G.E.P. and Jenkins, G.M. 1970. *Times Series Analysis: Forecasting and Control.* San Francisco: Holden-Day.

1976. *Time Series Analysis: Forecasting and Control.* San Francisco: Holden-Day. 2nd edition.

Brillinger, D.R. and Tiao, G.C. eds. 1980. *New Directions in Time Series.* Institute of Mathematical Statistics.

Brown, S. and Campbell, D.P. 1948. *Principles of Servomechanisms.* New York: Wiley.

Brunner, K. and Meltzer, A.H. eds. 1976. *The Phillips Curve and Labor Markets.* Amsterdam: North-Holland.

1987. *Bubbles and Other Essays.* Carnegie-Rochester Conference Series on Public Policy, Vol. 26.

Buiter, W.H. and Marston, R.C. eds. 1985. *International Economic Policy Coordination.* Cambridge: Cambridge University Press.

Cagan, P. 1956. Monetary Dynamics of Hyperinflations. In Friedman ed.

1991. Expectations in the German Hyperinflation Reconsidered. *Journal of International Money and Finance* 10: 552–60.

Campos, J., Ericsson, N.R. and Hendry, D.F. 1990. An Analogue Model of Phase-Averaging Procedures. *Journal of Econometrics* 43: 275–92.

Carey, J. 1995. *The Faber Book of Science*. London: Faber.

Carslaw, H.S. and Jeager, J.C. 1948. *Operations Methods in Applied Mathematics*. Oxford: Oxford University Press.

Caves, R. and Johnson, H. eds. 1968. *Readings in International Economics*. London: George Allen and Unwin.

Cheung, Y-W. and Lai, K.S. 1993. Finite-Sample Sizes of Johansen's Likelihood Ratio Tests for Cointegration. *Oxford Bulletin of Economics and Statistics* 55: 313–28.

Chow, G.C. 1960. Tests of Equality Between Sets of Coefficients in Two Linear Regressions. *Econometrica* 28: 591–605.

Chow, G.C. and Corsi, P. eds. 1982. *Evaluating the Reliability of Macro-Economic Models*. New York: Wiley.

Christ, C.F. 1966. *Econometric Models and Methods*. New York: Wiley.

Christ, C.F. 1975. Judging the Performance of Econometric Models of the US Economy. *International Economic Review* 16: 54–74.

Christiano, L.J. 1984. The Effects of Aggregation over Time on Tests of the Representative Agent Model of Consumption. Mimeo. Federal Reserve Bank of Minneapolis.

Christiano, L.J. and Eichenbaum, M. 1987. Temporal Aggregation and Structural Inference in Macroeconomics. In Brunner and Meltzer eds.

Clements, M.P. and Hendry, D.F. 1995a. Forecasting in Macro-economics. In Cox, Hinkley and Barndorff-Nielsen eds. (99–138).

    1995b. Macroeconomic Forecasting and Modelling. *Economic Journal* 105: 1001–13.

Cochrane, D. and Orcutt, G.H. 1949. Application of Least Squares Regression to Relationships Containing Auto-correlated Error Terms. *Journal of the American Statistical Association* 44: 32–61.

Committee of Economic Inquiry. 1965. *Report of the Committee of Economic Inquiry* (Vernon Committee Report). Commonwealth of Australia: Canberra.

Cooper, J.P. and Fischer, S. 1974. Monetary and Fiscal Policy in the Fully Stochastic St Louis Econometric Model. *Journal of Money Credit and Banking* 6: 1–22.

Corry, B. 1995. Politics and the Natural Rate of Unemployment. In Cross ed.

Court, R.H. 1979. Defective Energy Planning and the Need for More Public Information. *New Zealand Economic Papers* 13: 24–35.

Cox, D., Hinkley, D. and Barndorff-Nielsen, O. eds. 1995. *Time Series Models in Econometrics, Finance and Other Fields*. London: Chapman and Hall.

Crawford, J. 1968. *The Development of Trade Policy*. Eighth Edward Shann Memorial Lecture in Economics. Perth: University of Western Australia Press.

Cross, R. ed. 1995. *The Natural Rate of Unemployment: Reflections on 25 years of the Hypothesis*. Cambridge: Cambridge University Press.

Currie, D. and Levine, P. 1985. Macroeconomic Policy Design in an Interdependent World. In Buiter and Marston eds.

Davidson, J.E.H. 1981. Problems with the Estimation of Moving Average Processes. *Journal of Econometrics* 16: 295–310.

Davidson, J.E.H., Hendry, D.F., Srba, F. and Yeo, S. 1978. Econometric Modelling of the Aggregate Time-series Relationship Between Consumers' Expenditure and Income in the United Kingdom. *Economic Journal* 88: 661–92. Reprinted in Hendry 1993.

Deaton, A.S. ed. 1981. *Essays in the Theory and Measurement of Consumers' Behaviour*. Cambridge: Cambridge University Press.

Desai, M.J. 1975. The Phillips Curve: A Revisionist Interpretation. *Economica* 42: 1–19.

1984. Wages, and Prices and Unemployment a Quarter of a Century after the Phillips Curve. In Hendry and Wallis eds. (251–73).

1995. The Natural Rate of Unemployment: a Fundamentalist View. In Cross ed.

Dicks-Mireaux, L.A. and Dow, J.C.R. 1959. The Determinants of Wage Inflation: United Kingdom, 1946–56. *Journal of the Royal Statistical Society* Series A, 2, 122: 145–74.

Doornik, J.A. and Hendry, D.F. 1994. *PcFiml 8.0: Interactive Econometric Modelling of Dynamic Systems*. Oxford: Institute of Economics and Statistics, University of Oxford.

Dornbusch, R. and Fischer, S. 1987. *Macroeconomics*. New York: McGraw-Hill. 4th edition.

1994. *Macroeconomics*. New York: McGraw-Hill. 6th edition.

Duffie, D. 1988. *Security Markets: Stochastic Models*. Boston: Academic Press.

Duggal, V. 1967. Fiscal Policy and Economic Stabilisation. Ph.D. Thesis, Harvard University.

1975. Fiscal Policy and Economic Stabilisation. In Klein and Fromm eds. (220–52).

Dunlop, E.E. 1990. *The War Diaries of Weary Dunlop*. London: Penguin.

Durbin, J. 1959. Efficient Estimation of Parameters in Moving Average Models. *Biometrika* 46, 3 and 4, December: 306–16.

1960. The Fitting of Time Series Models. *International Statistical Review* 28, 3, December: 233–44.

Eatwell, J., Milgate, M. and Newman, P. eds. 1989. *The New Palgrave Dictionary of Economics*. London: MacMillan. Vol. III.

Ebury, S. 1994. *Weary: The Life of Sir Edward Dunlop*. Australia: Penguin.

Eckstein, O. 1981. *Core Inflation*. Englewood Cliffs: Prentice Hall.

Engle, R.F. 1982. Autoregressive Conditional Heteroscedasticity, with Estimates of the Variance of United Kingdom Inflations. *Econometrica* 50: 987–1007.

Engle, R.F. and Granger, C.W.J. 1987. Cointegration and Error Correction: Representation, Estimation and Testing. *Econometrica* 55: 251–76.

Engle, R.F. and Granger, C.W.J. eds. 1991. *LongRun Economic Relationships*. Oxford: Oxford University Press.

Engle, R.F. and Hendry, D.F. 1993. Testing Super Exogeneity and Invariance in Regression Models. *Journal of Econometrics* 56, 1/2: 119–39.

Engle, R.F., Hendry, D.F. and Richard, J.-F. 1983. Exogeneity. *Econometrica* 51: 277–304. Reprinted in Hendry 1993.

Ericsson, N.R. 1992. Cointegration, Exogeneity, and Policy Analysis: An Overview. *Journal of Policy Modelling* 14, 3: 251–80.

Ezekiel, M. 1941. *Methods of Correlation Analysis.* New York: Wiley. 2nd edition.

Farrington, G.H. 1951. *Fundamentals of Automatic Control.* London: Chapman and Hall.

Feldstein, M. and Stock, J.H. 1993. The Use of Monetary Aggregate to Target Nominal GDP. National Bureau of Economic Research Working Paper No 4303.

Fisher, I. 1926. A Statistical Relationship Between Unemployment and Price Changes. *International Labour Review* 13, 6: 785–92.

Fisher, M. 1978. Some Thoughts on Inflation and Unemployment from a Human Capital Standpoint. In Bergstrom *et al.* eds.

Florence Science Museum. No date. Mathematical Instruments in Florence. Mimeo. Florence.

Florentin, J.J. 1962. *Optimal, Probing, Adaptive Control of a Simple Bayesian System. Control Section.* Institution of Electrical Engineers: London.

Frazer, R.A., Duncan, W.J. and Collar, A.R. 1950. *Elementary Matrices.* Cambridge University Press.

Frenkel, J.A and Johnson, H.G. eds. 1976. *The Monetary Approach to the Balance of Payments.* London: Allen and Unwin.

Friedman, M. 1953a. *Essays in Positive Economics.* Chicago: University of Chicago Press.

   1953b. The Effects of a Full Employment Policy on Economic Stability: A Formal Analysis. In Friedman 1953a (117–32).

   1953c. A Monetary and Fiscal Framework for Economic Stability. In Friedman 1953a (133–56).

   1961. The Lag in the Effect of Monetary Policy. *Journal of Political Economy* 69: 447–66.

   1968. The Role of Monetary Policy. *American Economic Review* 58: 1–17.

   1969. *The Optimum Quantity of Money and Other Essays.* Chicago: Aldine.

   1970. A Theoretical Framework for Monetary Analysis. *Journal of Political Economy* 78: 193–238.

   1977. Nobel Lecture: Inflation and Unemployment. *Journal of Political Economy* 85: 451–72.

Friedman, M. ed. 1956. *Studies in the Quantity Theory of Money.* Chicago: University of Chicago Press.

Gandolfo, G. 1981. *Quantitative Analysis and Econometric Estimation of Continuous Time Dynamic Models.* Amsterdam: North-Holland.

Gardner, M.F. and Barnes, J.L. 1942. *Transients in Linear Systems.* New York: Wiley.

Geweke, J.B. 1978. Temporal Aggregation in the Multivariate Regression Model. *Econometrica* 46: 643–62.

1984. Inference and Causality in Economic Time Series Models. In Griliches and Intriligator eds. (chapter 19).

Gilbert, C.L. 1976. The Original Phillips Curve Estimates. *Economica* 43: 51–7.

1989. LSE and the British Approach to Time-series Econometrics. *Oxford Economic Papers* 41: 108–28.

Godfrey, L.G. and Wickens, M.R. 1982. Tests of Misspecification Using Locally Equivalent Alternative Models. In Chow and Corsi eds. (chapter 6).

Godley, W. and Cripps, F. 1985. *Macroeconomics*. Oxford: Oxford University Press and London: Fontana.

Goldberger, A. S. 1964. *Econometric Theory*. New York: Wiley.

Goodwin, R.M. 1948. Secular and Cyclical Aspects of the Multiplier and the Accelerator. In Metzler ed. 1948a.

1949. The Multiplier as Matrix. *Economic Journal* December: 537–55.

1992. Foreseeing Chaos. *Royal Economic Society Newsletter* 77, April: 13.

Gordon, R.J. 1978. *Macroeconomics*. Boston: Little Brown. 1st edition.

Granger, C.W.J. 1969. Investigating Causal Relations by Econometric Models and Cross-spectral Methods. *Econometrica* 37: 424–38.

1981. Some Properties of Time Series Data and their Use in Econometric Model Specification. *Journal of Econometrics* 16: 121–30.

1983. Co-Integrated Variables and Error-Correcting Models. Unpublished University of California at San Diego Discussion Paper 83–13.

1986. Developments in the Study of Cointegrated Economic Variables. *Oxford Bulletin of Economics and Statistics* 48, 3: 213–28.

Granger, C.W.J. and Lee, T-H. 1991. Multicointegration. In Engle and Granger eds. (179–90).

Grenander, U. 1950. Stochastic Processes and Statistical Inference. *Arkiv För Matematik* 1: 195–275.

Griliches, Z. 1967. Distributed Lags – A Survey. *Econometrica* 35: 16–49.

Griliches, Z. and Intriligator, M.D. eds. 1984. *Handbook of Econometrics*. Amsterdam: North-Holland. Vols. II and III.

Hahn, F. 1995. Theoretical Reflections on the 'Natural Rate of Unemployment'. In Cross ed.

Hahn, F. and Solow, R.M. 1995. *A Critical Essay on Modern Macroeconomic Theory*. Oxford: Blackwell.

Halle, L. 1972. *The Ideological Imagination*. London: Chatto and Windus.

Hammersley, J.M. and Handscomb, D.C. 1964. *Monte Carlo Methods*. London: Chapman and Hall.

Hannan, E.J. 1969. The Identification of Vector, Mixed Autoregressive-Moving Average Systems. *Biometrika* 56: 223–5.

1970. *Multiple Time Series*. New York:Wiley.

1971. The Identification Problem for Multiple Equation Systems with Moving Average Errors. *Econometrica* 39: 751–65.

Hannan, E.J. and Dreistler, M. 1988. *The Statistical Theory of Linear Systems*. New York: Wiley.

Hannan, E.J. and Kavalieris, L. 1984. A Method for Autoregressive-moving Average Estimation. *Biometrika* 72: 273–80.

Hannan, E.J. and Rissanen, J. 1982. Recursive Estimation of ARMA Order. *Biometrika* 69: 273–80 [Corrigenda, *Biometrika* 1983, 70].

Hansen, B. 1951. *A Study in the Theory of Inflation*. London: Allen & Unwin.

Hansen, L.P. and Sargent, T.J. 1983. The Dimensionality of the Aliasing Problem in Models with Rational Spectral Densities. *Econometrica* 51: 377–87.

1991b. Identification of Continuous Time Linear Rational Expectations Models. In Hansen and Sargent eds.

Hansen, L.P. and Sargent, T.J. eds. 1991. *Rational Expectations Econometrics*. Boulder Colorado: Westview Press.

Hansen, L.P. and Scheinkman, J.A. 1995. Back to the Future: Generating Moment Implications for Continuous-Time Markov Processes. *Econometrica* 63: 767–804.

Harrod, R.F. 1939. An Essay in Dynamic Theory. *Economic Journal* 49, March: 14–33.

1948. *Towards a Dynamic Economics*. London: Macmillan.

Hart, P.E., Mills, G. and Whitaker, J.K. eds. 1964. *Econometric Analysis for National Economic Planning*. Vol 16 of Colston Papers. London: Butterworth.

Harvey, A.C. and Phillips, G.D.A. 1979. The Estimation of Regression Models with Autoregressive-moving Average Disturbances. *Biometrika* 66: 49–58.

Heaton, J. 1993. The Interaction Between Time-Nonseparable Preferences and Time Aggregation. *Econometrica* 61: 353–86.

Hendry, D.F. 1977. On the Time Series Approach to Econometric Model Building. In Sims ed. (183–202). Reprinted in Hendry 1993.

1993. *Econometrics: Alchemy or Science?* Oxford: Blackwell.

Hendry, D.F. and Anderson, G.J. 1977. Testing Dynamic Specification in Small Simultaneous systems: An Application to a Model of Building Society Behaviour in the United Kingdom. In Intriligator ed. (361–83). Reprinted in Hendry 1993.

Hendry, D.F. and Doornik, J.A. 1994. Modelling Linear Dynamic Econometric Systems. *Scottish Journal of Political Economy* 41, 1: 1–33.

Hendry, D.F. and Ericsson, N.R. 1991. An Econometric Analysis of UK Money Demand in *Monetary Trends in the United States and the United Kingdom* by Milton Friedman and Anna J. Schwartz. *American Economic Review* 81: 8–38.

Hendry, D.F. and Mizon, G.E. 1978. Serial Correlation as a Convenient Simplification, not a Nuisance: A Comment on a Study of the Demand for Money by the Bank of England. *Economic Journal* 88: 549–63. Reprinted in Hendry 1993.

Hendry, D.F. and Trivedi, P.K. 1972. Maximum Likelihood Estimation of Difference Equations with Moving-average Errors: A Simulation Study. *Review of Economic Studies* 32: 117–45.

Hendry, D.F. and von Ungern-Sternberg, T. 1981. Liquidity and Inflation Effects on Consumers' Expenditure. In Deaton ed. (237–61). Reprinted in Hendry 1993.

Hendry, D.F. and Wallis, K.F. eds. 1984. *Econometrics and Quantitative Economics*. Oxford: Basil Blackwell.

Hicks, J.R. 1937. Mr Keynes and the 'Classics': A Suggested Interpretation. *Econometrica* 5, 2, April: 147–59.

1946. *Value and Capital*. Oxford: Clarendon. 2nd edition.

1950. *A Contribution to the Theory of the Trade Cycle*. Oxford: Oxford University Press.

1967. *Critical Issues in Monetary Theory*. Oxford: Clarendon Press.

Holt, C.C. 1962. Linear Decision Rules for Economic Stabilization and Growth. *Quarterly Journal of Economics* 76, February: 20–45.

1970. How Can the Phillips Curve Be Moved to Reduce Both Inflation and Unemployment? In Phelps ed. (224–56).

Holt, C.C. and David, M. 1966. The Concept of Job Vacancies in a Dynamic Theory of the Labor Market. In *The Measurement and Interpretation of Job Vacancies*. National Bureau of Economic Research. Columbia University Press (73–110).

Holt, C.C. and Hay, G.A. 1975. A General Solution for Linear Decision Rules: An Optimal Dynamic Strategy Applicable Under Uncertainty. *Econometrica* 43, 2, March: 231–59.

Holt, C.C. and Lee, K.S. 1978. Dynamic Economic Structure and the Econometrics of Linear Decision Analysis. In Bergstrom *et al.* eds.

Holt, C.C., Modigliani, F., Muth, J.F. and Simon, H. 1960. *Planning Production, Inventories and Work Force*. Englewood Cliffs: Prentice-Hall.

Holt, C.C., Smith, R.E. and Vanski, J.E. 1974. Recession and Unemployment of Demographic Groups. *Brookings Papers on Economic Activity* 3: 737–60.

Hood, W.C. and Koopmans, T.C. eds. 1953. *Studies in Econometric Method*. New York: Wiley.

Hoover, K.D. ed. 1995. *Macroeconometrics: Developments, Tensions and Prospects*. Dordrecht: Kluwer Academic Press.

Howitt, P. 1990. The Keynesian Recovery and Other Essays. London: Phillip Allen.

Hutchison, T.W. 1977. *Keynes versus the 'Keynesians'...?* London: Institute of Economic Affairs.

Ibbotsen-Somervell, C. 1994. As the Twig is Bent: Personal Thoughts, Memories, and Reported Experiences About the Life of my Brother. Mimeo.

Intriligator, M.D. ed. 1977. *Frontiers in Quantitative Economics*. Amsterdam: North-Holland.

Isaacson, W. 1992. *Kissinger*. London: Faber and Faber.

James, N.M., Nichols, N.B. and Phillips, R.S. 1947. *Theory of Servomechanisms*. New York: McGraw Hill.

Johansen, S. 1988. Statistical Analysis of Cointegration Vectors. *Journal of Economic Dynamics and Control* 12, 2/3: 231–54.

Johansen, S. and Juselius, K. 1990. Maximum Likelihood Estimation and Inference on Cointegration – With Applications to the Demand for Money. *Oxford Bulletin of Economics and Statistics* 52, 2: 169–210.

Johnson, E.S. and Johnson, H.G. 1978. *The Shadow of Keynes.* Oxford: Blackwell.

Johnson, H.G. 1960. Arthur Cecil Pigou, 1877–1959. *Canadian Journal of Economics* 26, February: 150–5.

Johnson, P. 1983. *A History of the Modern World.* London: Weidenfeld and Nicolson.

Jorgenson, D.W. 1966. Rational Distributed Lag Functions. *Econometrica* 34: 135–49.

Kahn, R. 1984. *The Making of Keynes' General Theory.* Cambridge: Cambridge University Press.

Kalman, R.E., Lapidees, L. and Shapiro, E. 1959. *On the Optimal Control of Chemical and Petroleum Processes. Symposium on Instrumentation and Computation.* London: Institution of Chemical Engineers.

Kang, K.M. 1973. *A Comparison of Estimators for Moving Average Processes: Report.* Canberra: Australian National Bureau of Statistics.

Kareken, J.H., Muench, T. and Wallace, N. 1973. Optimal Open Market Strategy: The Use of Information Variables. *American Economic Review* 63: 156–72.

Kendall, M.G. 1945. On the Analysis of Oscillatory Time Series. *Journal of the Royal Statistical Society* 108, 93–141.

1946. *Contributions to the Study of Oscillatory Time Series.* Cambridge: Cambridge University Press.

1949. Tables of Autoregressive Series. *Biometrika* 36: 267–89.

Kendall, M.G. 1968. ed. Mathematical Model Building in Economics and Industry. London: Charles Griffin.

Kerr, A. ed. 1991. *We Flew, We Fell, We Survived, Stories of Survival*, Part II. Western Australia Branch of the Royal Air Force Ex-Prisoners-of-War Association.

Keynes, J.M. 1930. *Treatise on Money.* New York: Harcourt Brace.

1936. *The General Theory of Employment Interest and Money.* London: Macmillan.

1946. The Balance of Payments of the United States. *Economic Journal* June: 172–94.

1963. *Essays in Persuasion.* New York: W.W. Norton.

1971–89. *The Collected Writings of J.M Keynes.* Edited by D. Moggridge. London: Macmillan.

Klein, L.R. 1974. *A Textbook of Econometrics.* Englewood Cliffs, NJ: Prentice Hall. 2nd edition.

Klein, L.R. and Ball, R.J. 1959. Some Econometrics of the Determination of Absolute Prices and Wages. *Economic Journal* 69, September: 465–82.

Klein, L.R., Ball, R.J., Hazlewood, A. and Vandome, P. 1961. *An Econometric Model of the U.K.* Oxford: Blackwell.

Klein, L.R. and Fromm, G. eds. 1975. *The Brookings Model: Perspective and Recent Developments.* Amsterdam: North-Holland.

Koopmans, T.C. 1950b. Models Involving a Continuous Time Variable. In Koopmans, ed.

    1950c. When is an Equation System Complete for Statistical Purposes? In Koopmans ed.

    1953. Identification Problems in Economic Model Construction. In Hood and Koopmans ed.

Koopmans, T.C. ed. 1950a. *Statistical Inference in Dynamic Economic Models.* Cowles Commission Monograph, 17. New York: Wiley.

Koyck, L.M. 1954. *Distributed Lags and Investment Analysis.* Amsterdam: North-Holland.

Krugman, P. 1995. *Development, Geography and Economic Theory.* Cambridge, Massachusetts: MIT Press

Krugman, P. and Miller, M. 1992. *Exchange Rate Targets and Currency Bands.* Cambridge: Cambridge University Press.

Kuhn, T. 1962. *The Structure of Scientific Revolutions.* Chicago: University of Chicago Press.

Kydland, F.E. and Prescott, E.C. 1977. Rules Rather than Discretion: The Inconsistency of Optimal Plans. *Journal of Political Economy* 85: 473–91.

Lancaster, K. 1979. A.W. Phillips. In *International Encyclopedia of the Social Sciences.* Vol. XVIII. New York: Free Press.

Laning, J.H. and Battin, R.H. 1956. *Random Processes in Automatic Control.* New York: McGraw Hill.

Leeson, R. 1995. Phillips' Original Data. Working Paper No.125, Department of Economics, Murdoch University.

    1997. The Trade-off Interpretation of Phillips' Dynamic Stabilisation Exercise. *Economica* 64, February: 155–71.

    1999. *The Political Economy of the Inflation Unemployment Trade-Off.*

Lerner, A.P. 1938. Alternative Formulations of the Theory of Interest. *Economic Journal* 48, June: 211–30.

Lipsey, R.G. 1960. The Relationship Between Unemployment and the Rate of Change of Money Wage Rates in the United Kingdom, 1862–1957: A Further Analysis. *Economica* 27: 1–31.

    1964. Structural and Deficient Demand Unemployment Reconsidered. In Ross ed.

    1974. The Micro Theory of the Phillips Curve Reconsidered: A Reply to Homes and Smyth. *Economica* n.s. 41: 62–70.

    1978. The Place of the Phillips Curve in Macro Economic Models. In Bergstrom *et al.* eds. (49–75).

    1981. The Understanding and Control of Inflation. *Canadian Journal of Economics* November, 14, 4: 545–76.

    1997. *Microeconomics, Growth and Political Economy: The Selected Essays of Richard Lipsey.* Volume I. Cheltenham: Edward Elgar.

498   **References**

2000. IS-LM, Keynesianism and the New Classicalism. In Backhouse and Salanti eds.

Lipsey, R.G. and Chrystal, K.A. 1995. *An Introduction to Positive Economics*. Oxford: Oxford University Press. 8th edition.

Lipsey, R.G. and Steiner, P.O. 1980. *Economics*. New York: Harper and Row. 6th edition.

Lipsey, R.G. and Steuer, M.D. 1961. The Relation Between Profits and Wage Rates. *Economica* 28: 137–55.

Lorenz, E. 1993. *The Essence of Chaos*. Seattle: University of Washington Press.

Lovell, M.C. and Prescott, E. 1968. Money Multiplier Accelerator Interaction. *Southern Economic Journal* 35: 60–72.

Lucas, R.E. 1976. Econometric Policy Evaluation: A Critique. In Brunner and Meltzer eds. (19–46).

Lucas, R.E. and Sargent, T.J. 1981a. After Keynesian Macroeconomics. In Lucas and Sargent eds. 1981b.

Lucas, R.E. and Sargent, T.J. eds. 1981b. *Rational Expectations and Econometric Practice*. London: Allen and Unwin.

Lucas R.E. and Stokey, N. 1987. Money and Interest in a Cash-in-advance Economy. *Econometrica* 55: 491–513.

Machlup, F. 1939. Period Analysis and Multiplier Theory. *Quarterly Journal of Economics* November: 1–27.

Malinvaud, E. 1966. *Statistical Methods of Econometrics*. Amsterdam: North-Holland.

Marcet, A. 1991. Temporal Aggregation of Economic Time Series. In Hansen and Sargent 1991a eds.

Marschak, J. 1953. Economic Measurements for Policy and Prediction. In Hood and Koopmans eds.

McCallum, B.T. 1988. Robustness Properties of a Rule for Monetary Policy. *Carnegie-Rochester Conference Series on Public Policy* 29: 173–204.

1989. Real Business Cycle Models. In Barro ed. (chapter 1).

McCloskey, D.N. 1986. *The Rhetoric of Economics*. Hemel Hempstead: Wheatsheaf.

McKibbin, W.J. and Sachs, J.D. 1991. *Global Linkages*. Washington: Brookings Institution.

McLintock, A.H. ed. 1966. *An Encylopaedia of New Zealand*. Wellington: Government Printer.

Meade, J.E. 1938. *Consumers' Credit and Unemployment*. London: Oxford University Press.

1948. National Income, National Expenditure and the Balance of Payments. *Economic Journal* December: 483–505.

1949. National Income, National Expenditure and the Balance of Payments. *Economic Journal* March: 17–39.

1951a. *The Balance of Payments*. London: Oxford University Press.

1951b. That's the Way the Money Goes. *London School of Economics Society Magazine* January: 10–11.

1961. *A Neo-Classical Theory of Economic Growth.* London: Allen and Unwin.

Meiselman, D. 1968. Comment: Is There a Meaningful Trade-off Between Inflation and Unemployment? *Journal of Political Economy* 76: 743–9.

Merton, R.C. 1990. *Continuous Time Finance.* Oxford: Blackwell.

Metzler, L.A. 1941. The Nature and Stability of Inventory Cycles. *Review of Economic Statistics* 23, August: 113–29.

1948. Three Lags in the Circular Flow of Income. In Metzler ed.

Metzler, L.A. ed. 1948. *Income Employment and Public Policy: Essays in Honor of Alvin H. Hansen.* New York: Norton.

Miller, K.S. 1956. *Engineering Mathematics.* London: Constable.

Mizon, G.E. 1995. Progressive Modelling of Macroeconomic Time Series: the LSE Methodology. In Hoover ed. (107–69).

Mizon, G.E. and Hendry, D.F. 1980. An Empirical Application and Monte Carlo Analysis of Tests of Dynamic Specification. *Review of Economic Studies* 49: 21–45. Reprinted in Hendry 1993.

Moghadam, R. 1988. Technical Description of the Phillips Machine. Mimeo.

Moghadam, R. and Carter, C. 1989. The Restoration of the Phillips Machine: Pumping up the Economy. *Economic Affairs* October/November: 21–7.

Monfort, A. 1996. A Reappraisal of Misspecified Models. *Econometric Theory* 12: 597–619.

Morgan, M.S. and Boumans, M. 1998. The Secret Hidden by Two-dimensionality: Modelling the Economy as a Hydraulic System. *Research Memoranda in the History and Methodology of Economics* 98/2, Faculty of Economics and Econometrics, University of Amsterdam.

Mundell, R.A. 1962. The Appropriate Use of Fiscal and Monetary Policy for Internal and External Stability. *IMF Staff Papers* 9: 70–9.

Muth, J.F. 1960. Optimal Properties of Exponentially Weighted Forecasts. *Journal of the American Statistical Association* 55: 299–306.

1961. Rational Expectations and the Theory of Price Movements. *Econometrica* 29: 315–35.

National Physical Laboratory. 1951. *Report for the Year 1950.* Department of Scientific and Industrial Research: HMSO.

1955. *Report for the Year 1954.* Department of Scientific and Industrial Research: HMSO.

1955. *NPL News* No. 61, 16 May.

Newlyn, W.T. 1950. The Phillips/Newlyn Hydraulic Model. *Yorkshire Bulletin of Economic and Social Research* 2.2, September: 110–27.

1992. A Back of the Garage Job. *Royal Economic Society Newsletter* 77, April: 12.

Nicholls, D.F., Pagan, A.R. and Terrell, R.D. 1975. The Estimation and Use of Models with Moving Average Disturbance Terms: A Survey. *International Economic Review* 16: 113–34.

Nickell, S.J. 1984. The Modelling of Wages and Unemployment. In Hendry and Wallis (13–35).

1985. Error Correction, Partial Adjustment and all that: An Expository Note. *Oxford Bulletin of Economics and Statistics* 47: 119–30.

500   **References**

1990a. Unemployment: A Survey. *Economic Journal* 100: 391–439.

1990b. Inflation and the UK Labour Market. *Oxford Review of Economic Policy* 6: 26–35.

Nove, A. 1992. Kondratiev's Final Work. *Royal Economic Society Newsletter* April, 77: 2–3.

Osborn, D.R. 1976. Maximum Likelihood Estimation of Moving Average Processes. *Annals of Economic and Social Measurement* 5: 75–87.

1977. Exact and Approximate Maximum Likelihood Estimators for Vector Moving Average Processes. *Journal of the Royal Statistical Society* B, 39: 114–18.

Osterwald-Lenum, M. 1992. A Note with Quantiles of the Asymptotic Distribution of the ML Cointegration Rank Test Statistics. *Oxford Bulletin of Economics and Statistics* 54: 461–72.

Pagan, A.R. and Nicholls, D.F. 1976. Exact Maximum Likelihood Estimation of Regression Models with Finite Order Moving Average Errors. *Review of Economic Studies* 43: 383–7.

Paish, F.W. 1962. Output, Inflation and Growth. In Paish, F.W. *Studies in an Inflationary Economy, the United Kingdom 1948–1961*. London: Macmillan.

Patinkin, D. 1965. *Money Interest and Prices*. New York: Harper and Row. 2nd edition.

Phelps, E.S. 1967. Phillips Curves, Expectations of Inflation and Optimal Unemployment Over Time. *Economica* 34, August: 254–81.

1989. The Phillips Curve. In Eatwell *et al*. eds.

Phelps, E.S. ed. 1970. *The Microeconomic Foundations of Employment and Inflation Theory*. New York: Norton.

Phelps Brown, E.H. 1975. Obituary: Prof. A.W.H. Phillips. *The Times* Thursday March 6: 16.

Phelps Brown, E.H. and Hopkins, S. 1950. The Course of Wage Rates in Five Countries 1860–1939. *Oxford Economic Papers*: 226–96.

Phillips, A.W.H. 1953. *Dynamic Models in Economics*. Unpublished Ph.D. thesis, University of London.

1966. Estimation of Stochastic Difference Equations with Moving Average Disturbances. Walras-Bowley lecture, Econometric Society, San Francisco.

1978. Estimation of Systems of Difference Equations with Moving Average Disturbances. In Bergstrom *et al*. eds (181–99).

Phillips, P.C.B. 1972. The Structural Estimation of a Stochastic Differential Equation System. *Econometrica* 40: 1021–41.

1973. The Problem of Identification in Finite Parameter Continuous Time Models. *Journal of Econometrics* 1: 351–62.

1974. The Estimation of Some Continuous Time Models. *Econometrica* 42: 803–23.

Phillips, P.C.B. ed. 1993. *Models, Methods and Applications of Econometrics*. Oxford: Blackwell.

Phillips, P.C.B. and Loretan, M. 1991. Estimating Long-run Economic Equilibria. *Review of Economic Studies* 59: 407–36.

Piaggio, H.T.H. 1949. *Differential Equations.* London: Bell.

Pigou, A.C. 1943. The Classical Stationary State. *Economic Journal* December: 343–51.

—— 1947. Economic Progress in a Stable Environment. *Economica* August: 180–8.

Pitchford, J.D. 1968. An Analysis of Price Movements in Australia 1947–68. *Australian Economic Papers* 7, December: 111–35.

Porter, A. 1950. *An Introduction to Servomechanisms.* London: Metheun.

Powell, A.A. and Murphy, C.W. 1995. *Inside a Modern Macro-Econometric Model*, Lecture Notes in Economics and Mathematical Systems, No. 428. Berlin: Spring-Verlag.

Preston, A.J. 1978. Concepts of Structure and Model Identifiability for Economic Systems. In Bergstrom *et al.* eds.

Quenouille, M.H. 1947. A Large Sample Test for the Goodness-of-fit of Autoregressive Schemes. *Journal of the Royal Statistical Society* A: 110: 123–9.

—— 1957. *The Analysis of Multiple Time Series.* London: Griffin.

Radcliffe, Lord. 1959. Report of the Committee on the Workings of the Monetary System. London: HMSO, Cnd. 827.

Radford, R.A. 1945. The Economic Organisation of a P.O.W. Camp. *Economica* November: 189–201.

Raiffa, H. and Schlaiffer, R. 1961. *Applied Statistical Decision Theory.* Cambridge, Massachusetts: Harvard University Press.

Reimers, H-E. 1992. Comparisons of Tests for Multivariate Cointegration. *Statistical Papers* 33: 335–59.

Reinsel, G. 1979. Maximum Likelihood Estimation of Stochastic Linear Difference Equations with Autoregressive Moving Average Errors. *Econometrica* 47: 129–52.

Robbins, L.C. 1972. Notes by Shirley Chapman [then LSE Information Officer] on a Conversation with Lord Robbins about Bill Phillips and the Machine.

Roberts, B.C. 1958. *The Trade Union Congress, 1868–1921.* Cambridge, Massachusetts: Harvard University Press.

Ross, A.M. ed. 1964. *Employment Policy and the Labor Market.* California: University of California Press.

Routh, G. 1959. The Relation between Unemployment and the Rate of Change of Money Wage Rates: A Comment. *Economica* (n.s) 26 November: 299–315.

Salmon, M. 1982. Error Correction Mechanisms. *Economic Journal* 92: 615–29.

Samuelson, P.A. 1939. Interaction Between the Multiplier Analysis and the Principle of Acceleration. *Review of Economic Statistics* 21: 75–8.

—— 1947. *Foundations of Economic Analysis.* Cambridge, Massachusetts: Harvard University Press.

—— 1961. *Economics: An Introductory Analysis.* New York: McGraw-Hill. 5th edition.

Samuelson, P.A. and Nordhaus, W.D. 1996. *Economics.* New York: McGraw-Hill. 15th edition.

Samuelson, P.A. and Solow, R. 1960. Analytical Aspects of Anti Inflation Policy. *American Economic Review* 50, May: 177–204.

Sargan, J.D. 1964. Wages and Prices in the United Kingdom: A Study in Econometric Methodology. In Hart, Mills, and Whittaker, eds. (25–54). Reprinted in Hendry and Wallis 1984 (275–314).

   1974. Some Discrete Approximations to Continuous Time Stochastic Models. *Journal of the Royal Statistical Society* B, 36: 74–90.

   1980. A Model of Wage-price Inflation. *Review of Economic Studies* 47: 979–1012. Reprinted in Sargan 1988 (170–90).

   1988. *Contributions to Econometrics.* Vol. I. Cambridge: Cambridge University Press.

Sargan, J.D. and Bhargava, A. 1983. Maximum Likelihood Estimation of Regression Models with First Order Moving Average Errors When the Error Lies on the Unit Circle. *Econometrica* 51: 799–820.

Sargan, J.D. and Mikhail, W.M. 1971. A General Approximation to the Distribution of Instrumental Variables Estimators. *Econometrica* 39: 131–69.

Sargent, T.J. 1993. *Bounded Rationality in Macroeconomics.* Oxford: Oxford University Press.

Sargent, T.J. and Wallace, N. 1973. The Stability of Models of Money and Growth with Perfect Foresight. *Econometrica* 41: 1043–8.

   1976. Rational Expectations and the Theory of Economic Policy. *Journal of Monetary Economics* 2: 169–83.

Schlote, W. 1952. *British Overseas Trade from 1700 to the 1930s.* Oxford: Blackwell. Translated from the German by W.O. Henderson and W.H. Chaloner. Issued under the auspices of the Institute for the Study of World Economic Affairs, University of Kiel. First published in Germany in 1938.

Shadman-Mehta, F. 1996. An Empirical Study of the Determinants of Real Wages and Employment: The Phillips Curve Revisited. Unpublished thesis, Universite Catholique de Louvain, CIACO, Louvain-la-Neuve.

Sims, C.A. 1971a. Discrete Approximations to Continuous Time Lag Distributions in Econometrics. *Econometrica* 39: 545–64.

   1971b. Approximate Specification in Distributed Lag Models. *Bulletin of the International Statistical Institute* 48: 285–94.

   1972. Money, Income and Causality. *American Economic Review* 62: 540–52.

   1984. Martingale-like Behavior of Prices and Interest Rates. Mimeo. University of Minnesota working paper, October.

Sims, C.A. ed. 1977. *New Methods in Business Cycle Research.* Minneapolis: Federal Reserve Bank of Minneapolis.

Skidelsky, R. 1983. *John Maynard Keynes: Hopes Betrayed 1883–1920.* London: Macmillan.

Sleeman, A.G. 1981. The Relation Between Unemployment and the Rate of Change of Money Wage Rates in the United Kingdom, 1851–1979. Paper presented to the Atlantic Economic Society, LSE.

Slutsky, E. 1937. The Summation of Random Causes as the Source of Cyclic Processes. *Econometrica* 5: 105–46. (Translation from the Russian version of 1927).

Small, J. 1993. General-purpose Electronic Analog Computing: 1945–1965. *IEEE Annals of the History of Computing* 15, 2: 8–18.

Solow, R.M. 1956. A Contribution to the Theory of Economic Growth. *Quarterly Journal of Economics* 70: 65–94.

1959. Investment and Technical Progress. In Arrow, Karlin and Suppes eds.

1979. Review of *Stability and Inflation* by Bergstrom *et al.* eds. *Economica* 46, August: 310–11.

Stemp, P.J. and Turnovsky, S.J. 1987. Optimal Monetary Policy in an Open Economy. *European Economic Review* 31: 1113–35.

Stern, N. 1992. A Coupling and a Search. *Royal Economic Society Newsletter* 77, April: 12.

STICERD Bulletin. 1995. The Phillips Machine: Coming Events. No. 26, Winter.

Stiglitz, J.E. 1993. *Economics*. New York: Norton. 2nd edition. See also http://www.norton.com/college/econ/stec2.htm.

Swan, T.W. 1956. Economic Growth and Capital Accumulation. *Economic Record* 32: 334–61.

1960. Economic Control in a Dependent Economy. *Economic Record* 36: 51-66.

1968. Longer Run Problems of the Balance of Payments. In Caves and Johnson eds.

Telser, L.G. 1967. Discrete Samples and Moving Sums in Stationary Stochastic Processes. *Journal of the American Statistical Association* 62: 484–99.

Theil, H. 1964. *Optimal Decision Rules for Government and Business*. Amsterdam: North-Holland.

Thomas, J.J. 1984. Wages and Prices in the United Kingdom, 1862–1913: A Re-examination of the Phillips Curve. Paper presented to the ESRC Quantitative Economic History Study, Oxford.

Tinbergen, J. 1939. *Statistical Testing of Business-Cycle Theories II: Business Cycles in the United States of America, 1919–1932*. Geneva: League of Nations.

1952. *On the Theory of Economic Policy*. Amsterdam: North-Holland.

1966. *Economic Policy, Principles and Design*. Amsterdam: North-Holland. 3rd printing.

Tobin, J. 1969. A General Equilibrium Approach to Monetary Theory. *Journal of Money Credit and Banking* 1: 15–29.

1975. Keynesian Models of Recession and Depression. *American Economic Review Papers and Proceedings* 65: 195–202.

1980. *Asset Accumulation and Economic Activity; Reflections on Contemporary Macroeconomic Theory*. Chicago: University of Chicago Press.

1982. Money and Finance in the Macroeconomic Process. *Journal of Money Credit and Banking* 14: 171–204.

Trivedi, P.K. 1970. Inventory Behaviour in UK Manufacturing 1956–67. *Review of Economic Studies* 37: 517–36.

Truxal, J.G. 1955. *Automatic Feedback Control System Synthesis*. New York: McGraw Hill.

Turnovsky, S.J. 1973. Optimal Stabilization Policies for Deterministic and Stochastic Linear Economic Systems. *Review of Economic Studies* 40: 79–96.

1977. *Macroeconomic Analysis and Stabilization Policy*. Cambridge: Cambridge University Press.

1980. The Choice of Monetary Instrument Under Alternative Forms of Price Expectations. *Manchester School* 48: 39–63.

Tustin, A. ed. 1952. *Automatic and Manual Control*. London: Butterworths.

Tustin, A. 1954. *The Mechanisms of Economic Systems – An Approach to the Problems of Economic Stabilisation from the Point of View of Control-System Engineering*. London: Heinemann.

Van den Bogaard, P.J.M. and Theil, H. 1959. Macrodynamic Policy-Making: An Application of Strategy and Certainty Equivalence to the Economy of the United States 1933–36. *Metroeconomica* 11: 149–67.

Van der Post, L. 1985. *The Night of the New Moon*. London: Chatto and Windus.

Vines, D., Maciejowski, J. and Meade, J.E. 1983. *Demand Management*. London: George Allen and Unwin.

Walker, A.M. 1961. Large Sample Estimates of Parameters for Moving Average Models. *Biometrica* 48, Parts 3 and 4, December: 343–57.

Walley, R. 1991. In Kerr ed.

Weale, M., Blake, A., Christodoulakis, N., Meade, J.E. and Vines, D. 1989. *Macroeconomic Policy: Inflation, Wealth and the Exchange Rate*. London: Unwin Hyman.

White, H. 1980. A Heteroskedastic-Consistent Covariance Matrix Estimator and a Direct Test for Heteroskedasticity. *Econometrica* 48: 817–38.

Whittle, P. 1951. *Hypothesis Testing in Time Series*. Uppsala: Almqvist and Wicksell.

1952. Tests of Fit in Time Series. *Biometrika* 39: 309–18.

1953a. The Analysis of Multiple Stationary Time-series. *Journal of the Royal Statistical Society* B, 15: 125–39.

1953b. Some Recent Contributions to the Theory of Stationary Processes. Appendix 2 in Wold.

1963. *Prediction and Regulation by Linear Least-Square Methods*. Princeton: Van Nostrand.

Widder, D.V. 1946. *The Laplace Transform*. Princeton: Princeton University Press.

Wiener, N. 1923. Differential Space. *Journal of Mathematical Physics* 2: 132–74.

1949. *Extrapolation, Interpolation, and Smoothing of Stationary Time Series*. New York: Wiley.

Wilson, G.T. 1973. The Estimation of Parameters in Multivariate Time Series Models. *Journal of the Royal Statistical Society* Series B, 35: 76–85.

Wise, J. 1956. Regression Analysis of Relationships between Autocorrelated Time-Series. *Journal of the Royal Statistical Society* Series B, 18: 240–56.

Wold, H.O.A. 1949a. Statistical Estimation of Economic Relationships. *Econometrica* 17: 1–21. Supplement.

1949b. A Large-sample Test for Moving Averages. *Journal of the Royal Statistical Society* 11: 297–305.

1953. *A Study in the Analysis of Stationary Time Series*. Stockholm: Almqvist and Wicksell. 2nd edition.

1968. Model Building and Scientific Method. In Kendall ed.

Wold, H.O.A. and Jureen, L. 1953. *Demand Analysis*. New York: Wiley.

Wulwick, N. 1989. Phillips' Approximate Regression. *Oxford Economic Papers* 41: 170–88.

Yates, D.M. 1997. *Turing's Legacy: A History of Computing at the National Physical Laboratory, 1945–1995*. London: Science Museum.

Yule, G.U. 1927. On a Method of Investigating Periodicities in Disturbed Series, With Special Reference to Wolfer's Sunspot Numbers. *Philosophical Transactions of the Royal Society* A, 226: 267–98.

Zellner, A. and Theil, H. 1962. Three Stage Least Squares: Simultaneous Estimation of Simultaneous Equations. *Econometrica* 30, 1, January: 54–78.

Index of Names

Index of Subjects

accelerator 80–1
adaptive expectations formula 22
Association of University Teachers of
    Economics 37, 106
Australian National University (ANU)
    7

Carnegie Mellon University 308, 313
closed economy 52–4
continuous time modelling 342–4,
    446–50

Dannevirke High School 3
Department of Applied Economics,
    Cambridge University 23
dynamic stabilisation 130–87

Econometric Society xvi
economic dynamics, mechanical
    models 68–86
economic fluctuations 468–78
economic policy and development
    224–9
ENIAC 10

full employment 54–5

growth 190–223
    constant rate of interest 198–200
    consumption function 197
    employment and growth 220–1
    employment and inflation 207–23

employment, money and prices
    195–205
fluctuations in employment 214–17
fluctuations and stability 209–17
investment function 197–8
lag distributions and stabilisation
    policy 203–4
normal capacity output 196
rate of change in the price level
    200
rate of economic growth 196
rate of exchange 221–3
rate of interest 200–1

hyperinflation 22

Institute of Electrical Engineers 4
internal and external balance 55–6,
    63–5
inventory model with error correction
    177–80

London School of Economics (LSE)
    xvi, 4
Lucas Critique 346–7, 410–17, 460–5,
    479–86

model with error correction 170–7
multiplier 45–7, 77–80

NAIRU 132
national income monetary flow 58–9

511